HUMAN
RIGHTS
WATCH

WORLD REPORT

2015
EVENTS OF 2014

D1115981

ISBN-13: 978-1-60980-581-4

Front cover photo: **Central African Republic** – *Muslims flee Bangui,
capital of the Central African Republic, aided by Chadian special forces.*
© 2014 Marcus Bleasdale/VII for Human Rights Watch

Back cover photo: **United States** – *Alina Diaz, a farmworker advocate,
with Lidia Franco, Gisela Castillo and Marilu Nava-Cervantes, members of the
Alianza Nacional de Campesinas. Alianza is a national organization that works
to mobilize farmworker women around the country to engage with national
policymakers about workplace abuses, including unpaid wages, pesticide
exposure, and sexual harassment.*
© 2013 Platon for Human Rights Watch

www.hrw.org

Human Rights Watch defends the rights of people worldwide.

We scrupulously investigate abuses, expose the facts widely, and pressure those with power to respect rights and secure justice.

Human Rights Watch is an independent, international organization that works as part of a vibrant movement to uphold human dignity and advance the cause of human rights for all.

Human Rights Watch began in 1978 with the founding of its Europe and Central Asia division (then known as Helsinki Watch). Today, it also includes divisions covering Africa; the Americas; Asia; and the Middle East and North Africa; a United States program; thematic divisions or programs on arms; business and human rights; children's rights; disability rights; health and human rights; international justice; lesbian, gay, bisexual, and transgender rights; refugees; women's rights; and an emergencies program. It maintains offices in Amsterdam, Beirut, Berlin, Brussels, Chicago, Geneva, Johannesburg, London, Los Angeles, Moscow, Nairobi, New York, Paris, Oslo, San Francisco, Sao Paulo, Sydney, Tokyo, Toronto, Washington DC, and Zurich, and field presences in 20 other locations globally. Human Rights Watch is an independent, nongovernmental organization, supported by contributions from private individuals and foundations worldwide. It accepts no government funds, directly or indirectly.

Table of Contents

COUNTRIES   **45**

Foreword

World Report 2015 is Human Rights Watch's 25th annual review of human rights practices around the globe. It summarizes key human rights issues in more than 90 countries and territories worldwide, drawing on events from the end of 2013 through November 2014.

The book is divided into two main parts: an essay section, and country-specific chapters.

In his introductory essay, "Tyranny's False Comfort: Why Rights Aren't Wrong in Tough Times," Human Rights Watch Executive Director Kenneth Roth reflects on a year so tumultuous, "it can seem as if the world is unraveling." The rise of Islamic extremists, the retreat of hoped-for gains after the Arab uprisings, and the creeping frost of Cold War-style tensions, he writes, have prompted many governments to view human rights as a "luxury for less trying periods." But, he says, retreating from such ideals and falling back on established relationships with strongmen, as many influential governments and important international actors have done, is both myopic and counterproductive. Surveying several of the year's most daunting security challenges—including the rise of the extremist group Islamic State (also known as ISIS), China's crackdown on Uighurs in Xinjiang, and Mexico's abuse-riddled war on drugs—Roth stresses the important role that human rights violations played in fomenting and aggravating those crises. He argues that ending and redressing those violations is essential if sustainable solutions are to be found and affected societies put on a firmer foundation.

Until the summer of Snowden in 2013—when former National Security Agency contractor Edward Snowden exposed details of the agency's previously secret spying programs—international momentum and commitment to global Internet freedom had been building. That movement has since been derailed by revelations that the United States and United Kingdom have been engaging in mass surveillance—a practice widely condemned, but also increasingly emulated by other countries. The result, warns Cynthia Wong in "Internet at a Crossroads: How Government Surveillance Threatens How We Communicate," could be a "truly Orwellian" scenario in which "every online search, electronic contact, email, or transaction is stored away" in government databases, vulnerable to misuse. With fundamental human rights—including freedom of expression, association, and information—on the line, Wong insists that privacy and surveillance remain on the human rights agenda of the global community, and that various United Nations institutions, as well as Germany, Brazil, and other countries that are taking up the mantle of Internet freedom, continue to pressure the US and UK to implement meaningful reforms.

Most civilians killed or wounded in warfare today are the victims of explosive weapons—a lethal range of munitions that include aircraft bombs, mortars, artillery, rockets, barrel bombs, and ballistic missiles— detonated in populated areas. In "Deadly Cargo: Explosive Weapons in Populated Areas," Steve Goose and Ole Solvang provide a stark picture of the devastating human and physical damage caused by these weapons in such environments, where flying shrapnel finds easy targets. In the past two years alone, explosive weapons have maimed and killed tens of thousands of people—mostly civilians—in attacks that often violate international law. Noting building international momentum to address the issue, Goose and Solvang call on countries to—among other steps—cease using such weapons, especially those with wide area effects, in populated areas, as well as review national policies that outline how and when they are deployed. "Curbing their use," they write, "would have a bigger impact on the protection of civilians during armed conflict than anything else we could do."

Finally, in "Raising the Bar: Mega-Sporting Events and Human Rights," Minky Worden highlights the contradiction between the lofty ideals surrounding the Olympics and other large-scale sporting events, and the often-grim rights-abusing reality on the ground. Russia's 2014 Sochi Olympics, for example, resulted in forced evictions, violations of workers' rights, a crackdown on civil society and journalists, and anti-LGBT discrimination; construction in Qatar related to the 2022 World Cup has resulted in the death of hundreds of South Asians working in a highly abusive construction sector. With just two countries in the running to host the 2022 Winter Olympics—Kazakhstan and China, both flagrant human rights abusers—the International Olympic Committee, Worden says, faces a "crisis of choice" that provides the impetus for the IOC and other international sporting bodies to finally reform a system "that for too-long has rewarded human rights abusers while often creating misery for local populations."

The rest of the volume consists of individual country entries, each of which identifies significant human rights issues, examines the freedom of local human rights defenders to conduct their work, and surveys the response of key international actors, such as the UN, the European Union, the US, and various regional and international organizations and institutions.

The report reflects extensive investigative work that Human Rights Watch staff undertook in 2014, usually in close partnership with human rights activists in the country in question. It also reflects the work of our advocacy team, which monitors policy developments and strives to persuade governments and international institutions to curb abuses and promote human rights. Human Rights Watch publications, issued throughout the year, contain more detailed accounts of many of the issues addressed in the brief summaries in this volume. They can be found on the Human Rights Watch website, www.hrw.org.

As in past years, this report does not include a chapter on every country where Human Rights Watch works, nor does it discuss every issue of importance. The absence of a particular country or issue often simply reflects staffing limitations and should not be taken as commentary on the significance of the problem. There are many serious human rights violations that Human Rights Watch simply lacks the capacity to address.

The factors we considered in determining the focus of our work in 2014 (and hence the content of this volume) include the number of people affected and the severity of abuse, access to the country and the availability of information about it, the susceptibility of abusive forces to influence, and the importance of addressing certain thematic concerns and of reinforcing the work of local rights organizations.

The World Report does not have separate chapters addressing our thematic work but instead incorporates such material directly into the country entries. Please consult the Human Rights Watch website for more detailed treatment of our work on children's rights, women's rights, arms and military issues, business and human rights, health and human rights, disability rights, international justice, terrorism and counterterrorism, refugees and displaced people, and lesbian, gay, bisexual, and transgender people's rights, and for information about our international film festivals.

Tyranny's False Comfort
Why Rights Aren't Wrong in Tough Times
By Kenneth Roth

The world has not seen this much tumult for a generation. The once-heralded Arab Spring has given way almost everywhere to conflict and repression. Islamist extremists commit mass atrocities and threaten civilians throughout the Middle East and parts of Asia and Africa. Cold War-type tensions have revived over Ukraine, with even a civilian jetliner shot out of the sky. Sometimes it can seem as if the world is unraveling.

Many governments have responded to the turmoil by downplaying or abandoning human rights. Governments directly affected by the ferment are often eager for an excuse to suppress popular pressure for democratic change. Other influential governments are frequently more comfortable falling back on familiar relationships with autocrats than contending with the uncertainty of popular rule. Some of these governments continue to raise human rights concerns, but many appear to have concluded that today's serious security threats must take precedence over human rights. In this difficult moment, they seem to argue, human rights must be put on the back burner, a luxury for less trying times.

That subordination of human rights is not only wrong, but also shortsighted and counterproductive. Human rights violations played a major role in spawning or aggravating most of today's crises. Protecting human rights and enabling people to have a say in how their governments address the crises will be key to their resolution. Particularly in periods of challenges and difficult choices, human rights are an essential compass for political action.

The Rise of ISIS

No challenge in the past year has exploded more dramatically than the emergence of the self-proclaimed Islamic State, the extremist group also known as ISIS. One can only be appalled at ISIS's mass execution of captured combatants and disfavored civilians. This Sunni armed group has singled out Yazidis, Turkmen, Kurds, Shia, and even other Sunnis who contest its extreme interpretation of Islamic law. Its militants have enslaved, forcibly married, and raped Yazidi women and girls, and beheaded journalists and aid workers in gruesome videotaped spectacles. Rarely has an armed force engendered such widespread revulsion and opposition.

Yet ISIS did not emerge in a vacuum. In part it is a product of the United States-led war and military occupation of Iraq that began in 2003, which produced, among other things, a security vacuum and the abuses of detainees in Abu Ghraib prison and other US-run detention centers. Funding of extremist groups by Gulf states and their citizens also played a role. More recently, the sectarian policies of the Iraqi and Syrian governments, and international indifference to those governments' serious rights abuses, have been important factors. If the conditions that led to ISIS are left to fester, the group could deepen its hold on the two countries and expand into Lebanon, Jordan, Libya, and beyond.

Iraq

In Iraq, ISIS owes much of its emergence to the abusive sectarian rule of former Prime Minister Nouri al-Maliki and the resulting radicalization of the Sunni community. With Iranian backing, Maliki took personal control of Iraqi security forces and supported the formation of Shia militia, many of which brutally persecuted the minority Sunni population. Sunnis were excluded from select government jobs, rounded up and arbitrarily detained under new overbroad laws, summarily executed, and indiscriminately bombed.

The severity of the persecution can be measured by its effects. ISIS's predecessor, Al-Qaeda in Iraq (AQI), was defeated with the help of a military coalition of Sunni tribes in western Iraq known as the Awakening Councils. But many of the tribes that nearly single-handedly defeated AQI became so fearful of slaughter and persecution by pro-government security forces that when conflict broke out in 2014, they felt safer fighting those forces than ISIS.

Human rights groups persistently called attention to Maliki's abusive rule, but the US, the United Kingdom, and other countries, eager to put their own military involvement in Iraq behind them, largely shut their eyes to this sectarian reign—and even plied it with arms.

Today, there is wider recognition that this indifference to atrocities under Maliki was a mistake. Eventually he was forced from office and replaced by Haider al-Abadi, who has pledged a more inclusive form of governance. But as Western military aid still flows into Iraq, abusive sectarianism has not ended. Maliki continues to serve as one of Iraq's three vice presidents, and the weak government has vastly increased its reliance on Shia militia, allowing the mobilization of almost one million Shia fighters without government oversight or regulation. Indeed, because of the Iraqi army's disarray, the militias are the lead ground forces fighting ISIS, despite their ongoing killing and cleansing of Sunnis as ostensible ISIS sympathizers. Until these atrocities end, the Shia militias are likely to do more to aid ISIS recruitment than to defeat ISIS on the battlefield.

Meanwhile, the Iraqi government has not ended indiscriminate military attacks in civilian areas or released a significant number of detainees held without a warrant or after completion of their sentences. The corrupt and abusive judiciary remains unreformed, and Abadi's calls for an end to abusive, exclusionary rule remain unimplemented. Over the long term, completing these reforms will be at least as important as military action to protect civilians from ISIS atrocities.

Syria

In Syria, ISIS owes its rise to various factors, including porous borders with Turkey that have enabled fighters armed and funded by foreign governments to flow in. Many then joined the extremist group. ISIS has also generated funds through exorbitant ransom demands and "taxes" on people in territory it controls, as well as selling Syrian oil and antiquities.

With these building blocks, ISIS came to portray itself as the force most capable of standing up to the extraordinary brutality of President Bashar al-Assad and his troops. In vicious fashion, Assad's forces have been deliberately attacking civilians who happen to live in opposition-held areas, aiming to depopulate these areas and punish presumed rebel sympathizers.

Since the Syrian government turned over its chemical weapons, its most notorious tool has been the barrel bomb, an oil drum or similar container filled with high explosives and metal fragments. Also used by the Iraqi air force, it has gained notoriety in Syria, where the air force typically drops it from a helicopter hovering at high altitudes to avoid anti-aircraft fire. From that height, the barrel bomb is impossible to target with any precision. It simply tumbles to earth, making its dreaded swishing sound as its contents shift back and forth, until it hits the ground and deto-nates.

Barrel bombs are so inaccurate that the Syrian military does not dare use them near the front lines for fear of hitting its own troops. Rather, it drops them well into territory held by rebel groups, knowing that they will destroy apartment buildings, hospitals, schools, and other institutions of civilian life. These indiscriminate weapons have made life so miserable for many civilians that some who do not flee the country choose to move their families near the front line, preferring to brave snipers and artillery rather than the horror of the barrel bombs.

When the Syrian government attacked civilians with chemical weapons, the United Nations Security Council pressured Assad to stop and to surrender his weapons. But as the Syrian government killed countless more civilians by indiscriminate at-tacks with conventional weapons such as barrel bombs, as well as cluster muni-tions, incendiary weapons, and unguided rockets, the Security Council has largely stood on the sidelines. A number of states have condemned the slaughter, but they have done little more to generate pressure to end it.

Russia has used its Security Council veto power to stop unified efforts to end the carnage. Russia, as well as Iran, has also refused to use their enormous influence in Damascus to press for an end to the indiscriminate attacks, despite demands from the Security Council, including Russia, for such attacks to cease. Referring Syria to the International Criminal Court (ICC) to address serious international crimes by all sides, a step endorsed by more than 65 countries, remains anathema to Moscow.

The US-led coalition has taken on ISIS, but no nation—whether adversaries like the US, or backers like Russia and Iran—have increased pressure on Assad to stop the slaughter of civilians. The two cannot, and should not, be so easily separated

This selective concern has been a gift to ISIS recruiters, who portray themselves as the only ones willing and able to stand up to Assad's atrocities. Simply attacking ISIS is clearly not going to end its appeal. A broader concern with protecting Syrian civilians is required.

Intensified Repression in Egypt

In Egypt, the brutal reign of the general-turned-president, Abdel Fattah al-Sisi, has sought to crush the democratic aspirations of Tahrir Square. The uprising that overthrew President Hosni Mubarak's authoritarian government gave Egypt its first free and fair presidential election, which was won by the Muslim Brotherhood's Mohamed Morsy. The Morsy government ruled in a way that left many Egyptians fearing (whether legitimately or not) the gradual emergence of a strict Islamic regime, but its abuses never came close to those now being visited upon the Egyptian people by the military-dominated government that overthrew Morsy on June 30, 2013.

The military coup led by Sisi devastated the Brotherhood and its supporters. In just 12 hours on August 14, 2013, security forces overseen by Sisi and Interior Minister Mohamed Ibrahim systematically shot dead at least 817 mostly peaceful protesters in Cairo's Rab'a Square, where they had conducted a weeks-long mass sit-in to protest Morsy's removal.

The security forces claimed self-defense, but their handful of casualties paled in comparison to the number of protesters shot by snipers and other gunmen, many as they sought medical aid. Egyptian authorities had planned the violent dispersal of the sit-in weeks in advance, and fully anticipated a massive death toll. It was the largest massacre of protesters in recent history—the most deadly since at least China's repression of the Tiananmen Square democracy movement in 1989.

Since the coup, Sisi's security forces have imprisoned tens of thousands of suspected Muslim Brotherhood members, often without charge or trial, as well as many secular activists. Egyptian courts have handed down death sentences by the hundreds after mass trials that make no pretense of individualizing proof or providing a meaningful opportunity for a defense.

The international community's response to this unprecedented repression has been shamefully inadequate. At the UN Human Rights Council, 27 countries pressed Egypt to investigate the Rab'a Square massacre but did not achieve a majority within the council. There is little appetite among the US, the UK, and other key European governments to look into the military government's abuses. Indeed, while Washington will apply selective sanctions on Venezuelan officials (a move we support) for their security forces' brutal response to protests—which took the lives of no more than a few dozen protesters (though victimized many more)—it has fought sanctions for Egypt, despite the government's murder of close to 1,000 protesters at Rab'a Square.

Congress cut off some military aid even though the Obama administration resisted calling the takeover a "coup" for fear of further ramifications under US law. Secretary of State John Kerry repeatedly spoke of a transition to democracy that was supposedly under way in Egypt despite the lack of supporting evidence. Now that Congress has added a new national security exception to the military aid conditions in place, the US government seems likely to restore most, if not all, of its military support for Cairo without any letup in its repression. This rush to turn the aid spigot back on is driven by a prioritization of enlisting the Egyptian military to curtail an insurgency in the Sinai, back Israel's fight against Hamas in Gaza, and support the anti-ISIS war in Syria and Iraq over supporting the rights of the Egyptian people. The UK, France, and other European governments have also done little to reverse Sisi's unprecedented crackdown.

Saudi Arabia and the United Arab Emirates (UAE) have eagerly helped Egypt to crush the Muslim Brotherhood. As monarchies that invoke Islam for their own legitimacy, they appear terrified of a religious movement that rules in the name of Islam yet embraces democratic elections. They have thrown billions of dollars at Sisi's project of suppression and have labeled the Brotherhood a terrorist organization. The UAE has hunted down those at home deemed to represent Brotherhood views.

International support for the repressive Sisi government is not only a disaster for Egyptian hopes of a democratic future; it sends an appalling message to the region. ISIS can now credibly argue that violence is the only path to power for Islamists because when they sought power through fair elections and won, they were ousted with little international protest. Again, the short-term convenience of some influential powers—suppressing the Muslim Brotherhood—threatens a long-term debacle for the region's political future.

Israeli-Palestinian Conflict

The past year saw more settlement construction by Israel, more tit-for-tat violence in the West Bank, and another round of bloody armed conflict in Gaza. Hamas and other Palestinian armed groups in Gaza fired thousands of indiscriminate rockets and mortars toward Israeli population centers. In some cases, Hamas and its allies unnecessarily endangered Palestinian civilians by fighting from populated areas, and summarily executed alleged Palestinian traitors.

Tens of thousands of Israeli rockets, bombs, and artillery attacks, as well as an expansive definition of legitimate military targets, attacks without any evident military target, and lax concern for civilian casualties, left an estimated 1,500 civilians dead in Gaza and wreaked unprecedented destruction on civilian homes and infrastructure. In the occupied West Bank, beyond the settlement expansion, Israel continued its discriminatory and punitive demolitions of Palestinian homes, and unnecessary use of lethal force against Palestinians, killing dozens, including children.

Israel has a poor record of holding its own forces to account for serious laws-of-war violations; Hamas has not even claimed to investigate violations by Palestinian fighters. The involvement of the ICC could help to deter both sides from committing war crimes, while potentially offering victims a modicum of justice. With its UN observer-state status, Palestine is eligible to join the ICC, and it marked the New Year by finally doing so. The ICC will have jurisdiction over war crimes committed in or from Palestinian territory; that is, its mandate will apply to both sides in the conflict.

However, the US and leading EU countries tried to prevent this development by placing misguided pressure on Palestine not to join the Hague-based court.. But they take the opposite position in virtually every other situation of large-scale war crimes, where they recognize that curbing these crimes is often a prerequisite to building the trust needed for productive peace talks. No one has credibly explained why the Israeli-Palestinian conflict should be an exception to this rule.

The real motive of Western governments is to protect Israelis from possible prosecution. That kind of selective embrace undermines the power and legitimacy of international justice around the world. It emboldens critics who argue that international justice is reserved for weak nations that are not close allies of the powerful.

Boko Haram Atrocities in Nigeria

The problem of turmoil trumping rights is not confined to the Middle East. Human rights concerns are central to the conflict in Nigeria, where the militant Islamist group Boko Haram attacks civilians as well as Nigeria's security forces. The armed group has become notorious for cruelly planting bombs in markets, mosques, and schools, killing thousands of civilians. This past year, Boko Haram abducted hundreds of schoolgirls and young women in the northeast. Some were forced to marry militants and were subjected to sexual violence. One mass abduction in April provoked a worldwide social media campaign, "#BringBackOurGirls," but those victims and many others remain in captivity.

Oil-rich Nigeria should be able to field a professional, rights-respecting army capable of protecting Nigerians from this abusive group. However, the country's leadership has left its military ill-equipped and poorly motivated to defend against Boko Haram attacks.

When the army has acted it has often done so in an abusive manner, rounding up hundreds of men and boys suspected of supporting Boko Haram, detaining them in inhuman conditions, and physically abusing or even killing them. Many other community members have been forcibly disappeared, allegedly by security forces. When Boko Haram suspects escaped in March from a famously abusive detention center, Giwa Barracks, Nigerian security forces reportedly recaptured and summarily executed hundreds of them.

The persistent lack of accountability for these atrocities has made it difficult for Nigeria's allies to provide security assistance for fear of themselves becoming complicit in abuses. The failure of Nigeria's leadership to rein in security forces has also alienated local communities that might otherwise have willingly provided intelligence to the authorities. Winning the "hearts and minds" of the civilian population will require that the government transparently investigate alleged army abuses and punish offenders.

Kenya's Abusive Response to Al-Shabaab

Like Nigeria, Kenya has experienced a major increase in extremist attacks on civilians at least partly fueled by an abusive security force response. Al-Shabaab, the Somali Islamist insurgent group, carried out its highest-profile attacks at a Nairobi shopping mall, in Mpeketoni and nearby villages along Kenya's coast, and in northeastern Mandera.

Kenya's response has been riddled with abuses. Instead of building public confidence in the ability of the security forces to combat such attacks, the security-force operations have generated public anger and mistrust. In April, after a spate of bombing and grenade attacks in Nairobi, the military and police carried out Operation Usalama Watch in the city's Eastleigh neighborhood—a sweeping campaign that entailed rights violations of registered asylum seekers and refugees, undocumented Somalis and other foreign nationals, and ethnic Somali Kenyans. As in previous similar operations, Kenyan police arbitrarily detained several thousand people and used excessive force, raiding homes, extorting residents, and physically abusing ethnic Somalis.

Meanwhile, evidence mounted that Kenyan anti-terrorism units were forcibly disappearing and extrajudicially executing terrorism suspects rather than bringing them to court. Rather than respond to the public outcry, the government has tried to gag the messenger by further empowering security forces and strengthening legislative controls over media, civil society, and other sources of independent criticism. Donor countries, particularly the US and UK, that provide significant counter-terrorism support to the Kenyan security services have been slow to respond to the growing body of evidence of this abusive behavior.

Russia and the Crisis in Ukraine

Russia's occupation of Ukraine's Crimea and its military assistance to rebels in eastern Ukraine have been major political and security challenges for Western governments. The core of the dispute involves issues of sovereignty on which Human Rights Watch takes no position. However, the relatively narrow Western reaction to intensifying human rights violations that had been brewing in Russia during the two preceding years may well have aggravated the Ukrainian crisis.

Western governments imposed intense political pressure on Russia, including targeted sanctions, to encourage it to withdraw from Crimea and stop supporting the rebels. However, these governments for the most part either underestimated growing authoritarian rule in Russia since Putin's return to the Kremlin, or struggled to respond to it.

Fearing a possible "color revolution," the Kremlin in 2012 began what has become the most intense crackdown on dissent since the Soviet era. By targeting human rights groups, dissidents, independent journalists, peaceful protesters, and Internet critics, the Russian government radically reduced the possibility that critical voices would reach large numbers of people. The resulting closed information system enabled the Kremlin to suppress most public criticism of its actions in Ukraine. The health of political rights in Russia should be a central part of any effort to resolve the Ukrainian conflict, but has not been.

By the same token, caught in what at times seems like a new Cold War with Russia over Ukraine, the West also has tended to fall back on a good-versus-bad mentality. The desire to present Ukraine as the innocent victim of Russian aggression has made the West reluctant to challenge troubling aspects of Ukraine's behavior, whether the use of "voluntary battalions" that routinely abuse detainees, or the indiscriminate firing of weapons into populated areas. Meanwhile, pro-Russian forces in eastern Ukraine themselves have seriously abused detainees and have endangered the civilian population by launching rockets from their midst. The Western reluctance to address Ukrainian abuses has politicized what should be a principled appeal to both sides to respect international humanitarian law—an appeal that, if successful, would lower temperatures and increase the possibility of a broader political solution.

China's Crackdown on Uighurs in Xinjiang

The Chinese government's approach to Xinjiang, the northwestern province that is home to the Muslim Uighur minority, is to respond to complaints about human rights abuses with more human rights abuses and restrictions. Beijing claims that its crackdown is necessary to fight separatism and terrorism, but its tactic is to impose some of the most draconian and discriminatory policies against Uighurs, including prohibitions on wearing beards and veils, restrictions on fasting, and overt discrimination with respect to religious education.

The escalating deadly attacks against civilians and security forces in Xinjiang are a grave concern for the government. But the haste with which the government attributes violence to "Uighur terrorists"—while rarely producing evidence and routinely denying suspects the right to a fair trial—creates a vicious cycle in which already-repressed Uighurs feel under constant siege from the state. From the little information made publicly available, it is impossible to assess with any confidence whether those convicted and often sentenced to death are responsible for violence and whether the government's severe counterterrorism measures are aimed at the right people.

As illustrated by the extraordinarily harsh life sentence handed down in September to Ilham Tohti, a moderate Uighur economist, the state remains unwilling to distinguish between peaceful criticism and those who engage in violence. Viciously prosecuting peaceful criticism, leaving virtually no room for religious or cultural freedom, and expanding an economic strategy in which Uighurs cannot compete equally with Han Chinese migrants is a recipe for increased violence.

Mexico's Abuse-Riddled War on Drugs

Beginning in 2007, the government of then-President Felipe Calderón opened a "war on drugs" in Mexico, deploying security forces en masse to fight the country's violent drug cartels. The result was an epidemic of summary executions, enforced disappearances, and torture by the military and police, spiraling violence among competing criminal organizations, and a public security catastrophe that has taken the lives of more than 90,000 Mexicans. In his two years in office, Mexico's current president, Enrique Peña Nieto, has dialed down the rhetoric but has not made significant inroads in curtailing the corruption and impunity that allow these atrocities to flourish.

Washington has supported Mexico's "drug war" policies, providing assistance to the country's security forces, while repeatedly praising their efforts to confront the cartels. What it has not done is speak out about the terrible abuses that these forces commit, or enforce the human rights conditions that the US Congress placed on a portion of the assistance it gives them. Rather than embarrass an important ally and risk bilateral cooperation on counter-narcotics and other policy priorities, the Obama administration has preferred to remain silent, facilitating Mexico's efforts to downplay its serious human rights problems.

Some US states have done more by legalizing marijuana, undermining the illicit market for this drug. The Obama administration has acquiesced in these initiatives but has hardly embraced them. It should. They are not only the right thing to do from the perspective of the right to privacy, but also an important step for under-cutting the profits on which drug traffickers thrive.

United States: CIA Torture with Impunity

The year concluded with the US Senate Select Committee on Intelligence publish-ing a redacted summary of its report on the Central Intelligence Agency's use of torture against terrorist suspects under the administration of former President George W. Bush.

President Obama has taken a firm stand against torture during his tenure, using his second day in office to ban the Bush administration's "enhanced interrogation techniques"—a euphemism for torture—and to close the secret CIA detention facil-ities where much of the torture was carried out. Nonetheless, Obama has stead-fastly refused to investigate, let alone prosecute, the Bush CIA's torture, even though that is required by the Convention against Torture, which the US ratified in 1994.

There are various possible reasons for Obama's refusal to allow prosecutions. He may have feared that they would be politically divisive, undermining the support of Bush backers in the US Congress for his legislative agenda, even though there has been little such cooperation. He may have felt it unfair to prosecute after the Jus-tice Department's Office of Legal Counsel had ruled that the "enhanced interroga-tion techniques" were legal, even though the Senate report shows that the CIA knew these amounted to torture and went shopping for politicized government counsel who would justify the unjustifiable. He may have felt that the serious secu-rity threat faced after the September 11, 2001 attacks made resorting to extreme forms of interrogation understandable, even though the Senate report shows that they produced little if any actionable intelligence while undermining America's standing in the world and impeding counterterrorism efforts.

Obama's refusal to allow prosecutions means the basic criminal prohibition of tor-ture remains unenforced in the United States. That enables future US presidents, who inevitably will face serious security threats, to treat torture as a policy option. It also greatly weakens the US government's ability to press other countries to prosecute their own torturers, weakening an important voice for human rights at a moment when principled support is urgently needed.

The revelations in the Senate report also require action in Europe, particularly in countries that hosted CIA detention sites or were complicit in renditions and resulting torture. To date, Italy is the only European country that has prosecuted people for involvement in CIA abuses. Poland has finally admitted it hosted a black site but a criminal investigation is stalled. Romania and Lithuania are both in denial.

Criminal investigations are ongoing in the UK, but its government has reneged on its promise to conduct a genuinely independent judicial inquiry into Britain's involvement in rendition and torture. Meaningful accountability for Europe's role in these abuses is vital to hold those responsible to account and to prevent them from being repeated in the future.

Conclusion: The Central Role of Human Rights

In all of these cases, policymakers inevitably can cite seemingly good reasons for downplaying human rights. Human rights require restraint that can feel antithetical to a "do what it takes" attitude that often prevails in the face of serious security challenges. But the last year shows how short-sighted that reflex can be. Violations of human rights often sparked these security challenges, and their continued violation frequently aggravates them.

Human rights are not just arbitrary restraints on governments. They reflect fundamental values, widely shared and deeply held, imposing limits on the power of governments and essential safeguards for human dignity and autonomy. Betraying those values rarely turns out well. Meeting security challenges demands not only containing certain dangerous individuals but also rebuilding a moral fabric that underpins the social and political order.

The short-term gains of undermining those core values and the fundamental wisdom that they reflect are rarely worth the long-term price that must inevitably be paid. Rather than treating human rights as a chafing restraint on their latitude for action, policymakers would do better to recognize them as moral guides as well as legal obligations. The results are likely to be both the right, and the most effective, thing to do.

Kenneth Roth is the executive director of Human Rights Watch.

Internet at a Crossroads:
How Government Surveillance Threatens How We Communicate

By Cynthia M. Wong

We have reached an inflection point for the future of the Internet. To preserve the Internet as an open, global platform for rights, development, and commerce, we need principled rules to govern digital surveillance and protect privacy that apply to every government.

Until the summer of 2013, the global movement for Internet freedom had been gaining momentum. A diverse range of governments had formed the Freedom Online Coalition and publicly committed to promoting a free, open, and global Internet through coordinated diplomatic efforts, led by the United States, United Kingdom, and their allies. There was broad recognition at the United Nations Human Rights Council that the same rights we enjoy offline must also apply online.

However, global trust in US and UK leadership on Internet freedom has evaporated ever since former National Security Agency (NSA) contractor Edward Snowden began releasing evidence of mass surveillance by the NSA and its British counterpart, the Government Communications Headquarters (GCHQ). In a blistering critique at the UN in September 2013, Brazilian President Dilma Rousseff condemned these practices: "In the absence of the right to privacy, there can be no true freedom of expression and opinion, and therefore no effective democracy," Rouseff declared. "The right to safety of citizens of one country can never be guaranteed by violating the rights of citizens of another country."

Snowden's revelations laid bare the rift between the stated values of the US and UK and their behavior. Even while championing an open and free Internet, these governments were collecting data on hundreds of million people worldwide every day, including, in the case of the US, Dilma Rousseff herself. To make it easier to spy on people online and identify security threats, they have also surreptitiously weakened Internet security, paradoxically making all Internet users less safe and more vulnerable to hackers and identity thieves.

While many governments expressed outrage over snooping by the NSA and GCHQ, many may have also responded privately with envy. Though few can match the resources of the NSA or GCHQ, governments everywhere are expanding their own mass surveillance capacity, and are likely emulating the US and UK.

Left unchecked, this dynamic could soon produce a world in which every online search, electronic contact, email, or transaction is stored away in one or more government databases. With no government able to ensure the privacy of its own citizens from foreign snooping and intelligence agencies teaming up to share data about the citizens of other countries, a truly Orwellian scenario could unfold. While the US asserts it will not use intelligence gathering to quash dissent or discriminate, governments have repeatedly used surveillance to these ends.

President Obama has welcomed a debate about modern surveillance, but talk of safeguards and reform in the US has led to little or no discernible change for global Internet users. The Obama administration has committed to additional protections for personal information it has collected but has done little to rein in the sheer scale of surveillance the NSA conducts, especially abroad. The UK, for its part, has refused to answer even the most basic questions about its intelligence gathering practices and, in an astounding act of hubris and blatant disregard for rights, rushed through a law in July 2014 that extends its surveillance powers. In defending its program, neither government has been fully willing to recognize the privacy interests of people outside its borders.

The picture is not entirely bleak, however. In 2014, several important actors stepped into the leadership void left by the US and UK. Major UN human rights institutions have begun to articulate what it means to protect privacy when technology makes surveillance potentially ubiquitous. And a new coalition of states, led by Germany and Brazil, has taken up the mantle of Internet freedom to press these efforts, while the Freedom Online Coalition strives to restore its credibility.

It is critical to continue pushing the US and UK for real reform, but the rest of the world should not wait for them to act. Fears of terrorism, and the comparative advantage that the US and UK have in surveillance are blinding them to the harms their practices pose, not only to their alliances but also to their own democratic institutions. Those harms include chilling basic freedoms of expression and association, weakening the press and freedom of information, and degrading access to legal advice and defense. Indeed, these countries might not change course until their own citizens face comparable levels of surveillance by foreign powers.

In the meantime, other countries should keep surveillance and privacy on the human rights agenda at the UN and elsewhere. These issues should be consistently raised in bilateral meetings as well so the US and the UK are not let off the hook. Experience has shown that the US and UK, though often unwilling to be at the vanguard in developing international norms, eventually conform their practices to principled rules to which other countries agree to be bound.

"Collect it All"

We now live in an age of "big data," when our communications and activities routinely leave rich digital traces that can be collected, analyzed, and stored at low cost. In parallel, commercial imperatives drive a range of companies to amass vast stores of information about our social networks, health, finances, and shopping habits. The plummeting cost of storage and computing means that such data can be retained for longer and mined for future, unforeseen purposes.

These digital dossiers appeal to governments for a range of purposes, both legitimate and illegitimate. By accessing data held by the private sector, governments can easily uncover patterns of behavior and associations, both offline and online—whether to thwart security threats or to identify a particularly vocal online critic of government policy.

Security agencies in the US and UK have responded by building enormous storage facilities and voraciously collecting as much data as they can. In a 2008 visit to the United Kingdom, US General Keith Alexander, then-director of the NSA, asked, "Why can't we collect all the signals, all the time?" The UK set out to meet that challenge with its Tempora program, which involves mass interception of data flowing over 200 undersea cables connecting Europe to the Americas, Africa, and beyond. Media reports from the past year also indicate that the GCHQ may be secretly capturing and storing webcam images of millions of Internet users.

In the US, the NSA has wholeheartedly embraced bulk collection of metadata from private telecom operators (and perhaps other unknown entities), as well as mass fiber optic cable tapping. In 2014, reports based on the Snowden documents showed that the US may be collecting millions of text messages worldwide each day, gathering all mobile phone metadata in five countries, and intercepting all phone calls in two of these countries.

In the name of security, the US and UK have thrown away any notion of proportionality, where surveillance is targeted only at individuals they have reason to believe present a genuine threat. Only a tiny fraction of Internet or mobile phone users being surveilled today will ever be suspected of wrongdoing, let alone ties to terrorist activity.

Most of this has happened largely in secret, punctuated with brief windows of insight provided by national security whistleblowers over the years and the much larger window opened by Snowden's disclosures.

Failure of Leadership

What have the US and UK done to rein in mass surveillance in response to public outrage? For the billions of global Internet users outside these countries, the answer is: almost nothing.

On January 17, 2014, President Obama announced measures to restrict the use, retention, and dissemination of personal data gathered by intelligence agencies in Presidential Policy Directive 28. These new measures purport to bring rules for data collected on non-US persons (foreigners abroad) closer to those governing data collected on US persons. While the directive represents a greater level of disclosure (especially compared to most governments), the rules themselves are vague, do not go far enough to prevent abuse, and do not create rights that non-US persons can assert in court. They are also not entrenched, given that they are not embodied in legislation and can therefore be changed by any subsequent US administration. Most critically, the new measures do not prevent large-scale gathering of data and communications of individuals not linked to any wrongdoing, leaving the vast databanks of intercepted information growing larger for future administrations to exploit.

The USA Freedom Act, the main legislative vehicle for reform in the US, intended to end bulk collection of metadata and other records in the US. The bill failed to move forward in Congress in November 2014. However, even if the USA Freedom Act had passed, important as its passage would have been, it would have addressed only one of the programs revealed by the Snowden documents and would have done almost nothing to address the privacy concerns of billions of global Internet users outside the US whose personal information may be sitting in NSA databases. At time of writing, it appears that a Republican-led Congress may be even less receptive to efforts to rein in bulk collection.

In the UK, authorities continue to "neither confirm nor deny" that GCHQ intercepts the communications of millions of individuals. The government has refused to answer the most basic questions about its practices, so it is exceedingly difficult to assess its claims that these programs are lawful and necessary for protecting security. However, in a response to a court challenge, the UK government acknowledged that it interprets the law to allow agencies to gather potentially millions of communications via popular services like Twitter, Gmail, and Facebook without a warrant, merely because the servers of these companies are often located abroad. This disclosure raises serious questions about the GCHQ's claims that these powers are necessary to protect public safety.

Most troubling, the US and UK continue to argue that they have no legal obligation to safeguard the privacy of anyone outside their respective territories. In other areas of human rights law, the US has argued that it has no obligations to individuals outside its territory and has only admitted this year that it may have some duties under the Convention against Torture towards foreigners it physically captures, but only in territories where it exercises "governmental authority." In contrast to its resistance to assuming extraterritorial obligations with respect to surveillance, the US asserts authority to compel US-based companies to hand over information about any user around the world, regardless of where that data is stored, with almost no protections for the privacy of non-Americans abroad. The UK has also conceded extraterritorial human rights obligations in circumstances such as detention of foreigners abroad. But in the area of privacy and surveillance, the UK labels communications that travel outside the British Isles as "external," and UK law provides scant safeguards for the privacy of "external" communications.

The shortsighted approaches of the US and UK will almost certainly come back to harm their own citizens as other governments follow their lead. As Internet networks continue to globalize, an increasing amount of data about American and British residents will travel outside US and UK territory, and other countries will feel free to gather and store that data without limit.

The US and UK have provided a roadmap for governments of all political persua-
sions to build their own systems of mass surveillance. Though few can match the
NSA's and GCHQ's resources or capabilities today, many other governments take
an equally opaque and rapacious approach to digital data gathering.

Vilifying Encryption

The Snowden documents reveal that the NSA has also weakened encryption standards and withheld information about security holes in commercial products so
that it can exploit them before companies can fix them. In addition, media reports
suggest the GCHQ is developing ways to defeat encryption, especially for Internet
traffic that it intercepts. These tactics can facilitate surreptitious monitoring and
data collection from devices and networks, not just by the US and UK but potentially by other actors as well. While code breaking has always been at the heart of
the NSA's mission, any techniques that undermine the broader security of Internet
applications and networks put all Internet users at risk.

In 2014, major US technology companies redoubled efforts to harden the security
of their devices and services against spying. These measures have become a commercial imperative as loss of trust drives users to non-American companies. In
September 2014, Google and Apple announced that data stored on their mobile
devices would be encrypted by default, and neither company would be able to de-
crypt stored data in response to government requests. Google, Microsoft, Yahoo,
Facebook, and other services have taken additional steps to secure emails and
messages as they transit the Internet changes that security experts and rights activists have pushed for years. As journalists and rights groups increasingly rely on
global online tools for their work, many view these security improvements as a crucial post-Snowden outcome. For vulnerable groups or those living under authoritarian regimes, shielding communications and associations from abusive spying can
be a matter of life and death.

Yet government officials in the US and UK have responded to these new security
measures by accusing technology firms of facilitating murder, terrorism, and child
abuse. In his first week in office in November 2014, Robert Hannigan, head of
GCHQ, penned an op-ed calling US technology companies the "command-and-con-
trol network of choice for terrorists and criminals," citing increased encryption as
especially useful for the extremist group Islamic State, also known as ISIS, and

other terrorist organizations. Similarly, in a September 2014 speech, James Comey, head of the FBI, argued that "encryption threatens to lead all of us to a very dark place" and puts criminals beyond the law. Officials seek even greater cooperation from major technology firms, including through "back doors" built into devices and services that will allow them greater access to user communication.

Law enforcement and security officials argue that encryption back doors are necessary to protect public security. Yet these actions ironically leave Internet and mobile phone users—all of us—less secure. Security experts affirm that such back doors, once in place, create new vulnerabilities since they can be misused by hackers, identity thieves, and other malicious actors. From a technical standpoint, it is almost impossible to create a back door that can only be exploited by designated "good" actors.

Opponents of encryption in the US and UK governments also forget that they are not the only ones who will demand access to back doors. If Google, Apple, and other firms capitulate to their demands, it will be difficult to refuse the same access by other governments. Baking privacy and security into technology by design is the most effective way to protect the security of users from a range of bad actors. If GCHQ cannot force Apple to unlock an iPhone because Apple does not hold the key, then neither can intelligence agencies in China or Russia.

True Costs of Surveillance

As a global community, we have not even begun to grapple with the true costs of surveillance, not only to privacy but also to other rights and closely held values.

A joint report published by Human Rights Watch and the American Civil Liberties Union in July 2014 documented the insidious effects of large-scale surveillance on the practice of journalism and law in the US. Interviews with dozens of journalists showed that increased surveillance, combined with tightened measures to prevent leaks and government contact with media, are intimidating sources, keeping them from talking to journalists (even about unclassified topics of public concern) out of fear that they could face retaliation, lose their security clearances or jobs, or even face prosecution. Ultimately, this is having a detrimental impact on the amount and quality of news coverage, particularly on matters related to national security,

intelligence, and law enforcement. This effect undermines the role of the fourth es-
tate in holding government to account.

Steve Coll, staff writer for the New Yorker and dean of the Graduate School of Journalism at Columbia University, explained: "Every national security reporter I know
would say that the atmosphere in which professional reporters seek insight into
policy failures [and] bad military decisions is just much tougher and much chillier."
Public understanding of national security policies that are carried out in our name
is essential to the functioning of healthy democracies and open societies.

Another national security reporter described the impact of the Snowden revelations on the ability of journalists to protect their sources: "I used to think that the
most careful people were not at risk, [that they] could protect sources and kept
them from being known. Now we know that isn't the case. That's what Snowden
meant for me. There's a record of everywhere I've walked, everywhere I've been."

Many journalists are taking extraordinary measures to protect their sources and
shield them from retribution, including by using disposable burner phones or
strong encryption, or avoiding phones and the Internet altogether. As one journalist put it, they are being forced to adopt the tactics of drug dealers and criminals
just to do their job. Lawyers—and particularly defense attorneys—who spoke to
Human Rights Watch described adopting similar tactics to protect the confidentiality of their communications with clients, which is essential to the right to counsel.

In the UK, documents released in November 2014 as a result of a legal challenge
show that UK security and intelligence services have policies permitting the interception of privileged lawyer-client communications on national security grounds,
including potentially in cases in which the agencies were defendants. The human
rights group Reprieve brought the case on behalf of Libyan families who allege that
they were subjected to extraordinary rendition and torture. Reprieve's legal director, Cori Crider, stated that these policies raise "troubling implications for the
whole British justice system" and questioned how often the government has
"rigged the game in their favor in the ongoing court case over torture."

This initial research only scratches the surface. For example, an April 2014 poll of
2,000 Americans on the impact of NSA revelations found that almost half—47 percent—had changed their approach to online activity in response to reports of NSA
surveillance. Survey participants reported thinking more carefully about where

they go, what they say, and what they do online, and about a quarter are less inclined to use email. Other studies have documented the real and projected economic costs of NSA surveillance to the US Internet industry (as high as US$180 million in lost sales for the cloud computing industry) as loss of trust in US-origin technologies and services drives business overseas. A report from Open Technology Institute released in July 2014 begins to catalogue some of these costs, as well as harm to Internet openness, US foreign policy interests, and cyber security.

Perhaps one of the biggest casualties of the Snowden revelations has been the US and UK's moral authority to criticize the surveillance abuses of other governments and lead by example.

A March 2014 Human Rights Watch report documented how the Ethiopian government uses surveillance to monitor opposition groups and journalists and silence dissenting voices. With unfettered access to mobile networks, security agencies regularly intercept calls and access phone records, which are then played during abusive interrogations, without any process or oversight.

A former Ethiopian opposition party member told Human Rights Watch: "One day they arrested me and they showed me everything. They showed me a list of all my phone calls and they played a conversation I had with my brother. They arrested me because we talked about politics on the phone. It was the first phone I ever owned, and I thought I could finally talk freely."

Earlier in 2014, the Ethiopian government arrested a group of bloggers who wrote on current events under a collective known as Zone 9. The Zone 9 bloggers now face politically motivated charges under Ethiopia's deeply flawed anti-terrorism law. The charges cite as evidence the fact that the bloggers traveled out of the country to receive training in encrypting their communications.

The Ethiopian state is not the US or the UK, but the US and UK statements and actions set a troubling precedent that undermine their credibility on rights and will be cited by many other governments. If the US, the UK, and their allies continue to argue, for example, that metadata deserves little privacy protection, then how can they effectively challenge Ethiopia when the government adopts the same legal argument? And if US and UK authorities continue to vilify and weaken broad use of encryption to protect ordinary Internet users, how can their governments credibly condemn other governments that outlaw and punish use of encryption in the name of security?

International Standards for the Digital Age

The Snowden revelations have launched a global debate about modern surveillance, national security, and human rights. Privacy is now on the agenda of a range of states and international institutions for the first time.

Several major UN human rights institutions have begun to examine modern surveillance practices. In March 2014, the Human Rights Committee, an international expert body and authoritative interpreter of the International Covenant on Civil and Political Rights (ICCPR)—a global treaty to which the US is party—called on the US to ensure all surveillance is necessary and proportionate to achieving legitimate objectives regardless of the nationality or location of individuals who are affected.

In July 2014, the UN's top human rights official, then-High Commissioner for Human Rights Navi Pillay, issued a groundbreaking report on privacy in the digital age that directly challenges US and UK arguments for secret mass surveillance.

Pillay notably concluded that mass surveillance was "emerging as a dangerous habit rather than an exceptional measure." She said unchecked snooping could harm a range of human rights, including freedom of expression and association. The onus was on governments, she said, to demonstrate that their practices were necessary and proportionate to their security aims. In other words, spying on everyone because you can does not mean you should.

The high commissioner's report followed sustained action from privacy advocates and a group of countries, led by Germany and Brazil, to press the US and UK to stop mass surveillance and safeguard the privacy of people around the world. Stepping into the leadership vacuum, Germany and Brazil, along with Austria, Liechtenstein, Mexico, Norway, and Switzerland, led the passage of the December 2013 UN General Assembly resolution calling for the high commissioner's report.

In the face of inaction by the US, the UK, and their closest allies, these UN institutions have begun to lay out a principled approach to surveillance and human rights in the digital age, grounded in widely accepted standards of international human rights law.

Several critical themes emerging from this work directly challenge the defenses of mass surveillance:

- **Surveillance harms a range of rights beyond privacy, including freedom of expression, association, and movement, as well as the right to counsel.** If individuals cannot go online without fear of undue monitoring, the power of digital technologies to enable rights will be deeply undermined. Journalists cannot protect their sources, lawyers cannot ensure the confidentiality of their communications with clients, and human rights defenders cannot do their work safely.

- **States have obligations to safeguard the privacy rights of users outside their borders.** In our globally networked age, it is untenable to argue that the right to privacy stops at the border while surveillance is borderless.

- **Mass surveillance is by nature indiscriminate and it is presumptively illegal.** Article 17 of the ICCPR requires that any interference with privacy be proportionate and narrowly tailored. Just because mass surveillance and bulk data collection might yield some information that may one day be useful, it cannot justify the invasion of everyone's privacy.

- **States should recognize that privacy and other rights are harmed when they collect private data, regardless of whether that data is used.** Knowing that the government can acquire data about your communications and online activities can chill freedom of expression and association, even if the data collected is never misused. States should impose meaningful limits on when data can be collected, as well as on how data may be used and how long it is retained.

- **States should increase transparency and oversight over surveillance and intelligence gathering powers.** There are legitimate reasons for secrecy when addressing national security threats. But such powers must be subject to oversight to prevent overreach and abuse, including through judicial and parliamentary bodies.

- **The private sector has a responsibility to respect rights when asked to facilitate surveillance or data collection.** Where Internet or telecommunications companies turn over user data or assist with surveillance without adequate safeguards, they risk complicity in resulting violations.

The Way Ahead

While the Snowden controversy has focused on the US and UK, as noted above, there is no reason to assume that other governments' laws or practices are better. Most privacy regimes were put in place during the Internet's infancy, before social media or smart phones existed, and they are now falling short in providing meaningful protection for rights. And, of course, there are those governments like Ethiopia, China, and Russia who routinely engage in abusive surveillance as a matter of policy and design.

Thanks to Brazil and Germany, there is international momentum to develop norms and guidance and establish institutions to ensure that privacy still has meaning in the digital age. As part of this effort in the coming months, Human Rights Watch will support the creation of a new special rapporteur on the right to privacy at the UN Human Rights Council—an independent expert tasked with scrutinizing state surveillance practices in a sustained and systematic way.

At time of writing, however, there is still a desire to secure buy-in from the US and UK as mass surveillance debates play out at these international venues. The instinct to treat the US and UK with diplomatic kid gloves is not surprising, given their technological capacity and political power. But ultimately, this approach may be counterproductive. In the short term, they are more likely to play the role of spoilers rather than promoters of principled standards. This was certainly true during the debate that led to the December 2013 UN General Assembly resolution on privacy in the digital age, when the US and UK pushed, somewhat successfully, to water down the text behind the scenes, and again in November 2014, with respect to the follow-on resolution on the same topic.

Of course, we must continue to press for reforms in the US and UK and urge these governments to extend privacy protections to those outside their borders. But we should not allow political paralysis in the US and UK to hamper development of international privacy norms. A process of broad international engagement, including with strategic allies, can facilitate the US and UK's eventual acceptance and internalization of strong international standards over time. When other nations and international institutions lead by example and establish strong human rights standards, they will bring the US and UK along.

Global norm development is just a first step, however. The Snowden revelations have shown how far security agencies are liable to go when they are allowed to operate with inadequate oversight and accountability. As new surveillance capabilities develop and states grapple with renewed security threats—whether terrorism and violent extremism or cyber attacks—sustained public scrutiny and national implementation of global norms are needed. The Pillay report has provided much-needed guidance. The onus is now on parliaments and legislatures around the world to examine surveillance practices and assess their costs and tangible benefits more closely and publicly within a human rights frame.

Surveillance must remain on the human rights agenda, nationally and globally. Otherwise, we risk transforming the Internet into every government's all-seeing panopticon.

Cynthia Wong is senior researcher on the Internet and human rights at Human Rights Watch.

Deadly Cargo:
Explosive Weapons in Populated Areas

By Steve Goose and Ole Solvang

Late in the evening of September 1, 2014, an Iraqi air force plane dropped a bomb on a school in Al-Alam near Tikrit in northern Iraq, which had recently fallen under the control of the extremist group Islamic State (also known as ISIS). Dozens of displaced families were sheltering in the building at the time. The immense explosion and flying shrapnel killed at least 31 civilians, including 24 children, and wounded 41 others. One survivor who spoke to Human Rights Watch lost his wife, two sons, a daughter, a sister, and a nephew in the blast. Five members of his family were also wounded, including his son Yazin, just six months old.

Modern and not-so-modern armies rely on explosive weapons—including aircraft bombs, mortars, artillery, rockets, and even ballistic missiles—to conduct military operations, not ubiquitous assault rifles and machine guns. As a result, when civilians are killed or wounded in fighting in populated areas, it is usually these weapons that inflict the harm.

In 2014 alone, Human Rights Watch documented the use of explosive weapons in populated areas in violation of international humanitarian law (the laws of war) in at least 12 countries, including Syria, Iraq, Israel/Gaza, Ukraine, Libya, Pakistan, Afghanistan, Sudan, Nigeria, Somalia, Thailand, and Colombia. Such unlawful attacks were typically indiscriminate because they did not distinguish between the military target and civilians, or were disproportionate because the anticipated civilian loss from the attack exceeded the expected military gain.

Ranging from cheap and easy to produce to complex and expensive, explosive weapons are often deadly to anyone nearby. According to Action on Armed Violence, a United Kingdom-based nongovernmental organization, explosive weapons maimed and killed almost 38,000 people in 2013—82 percent of them civilians. Not surprisingly, when more civilians are present, the percentage of civilian casualties jumps; explosive weapon use in populated areas resulted in civilian dead and injured reaching 93 percent in the same period. In Syria, explosive weapons have been responsible for more than 50 percent of the civilian deaths (about 40,000 of more than 75,000) documented by the Violations Documentation Center, a Syrian-based monitoring group, since conflict erupted there in 2011.

Not all uses of explosive weapons in populated areas violate international humanitarian law. But the increase in urban warfare and rapidly mounting civilian casualties around the world scream for urgent action. For several years, international momentum has been building to curtail the use of explosive weapons in populated areas, including halting the use of those with wide area effects. Doing so would help save lives, alleviate civilian suffering, and reduce destruction of civilian infrastructure, which would facilitate post-conflict recovery. It could be the single most crucial step that nations take to protect civilians from the horrors of war.

***

When explosive weapons detonate, they send a powerful and destructive blast wave that travels faster than the speed of sound. Often, however, the most lethal effects are caused by flying fragments of casing—shrapnel—which can have a long reach. The Syrian government's OFAB 250-270 aircraft bomb, for example, can inflict damage and injuries within a 155-meter radius from where it strikes. The casing can also be designed to shatter into sharp pieces of metal that can penetrate the body and rip internal organs, causing life-threatening injuries.

The wide area effect of some explosive weapons is a key reason why they kill and injure so many civilians. A weapon that can injure people within a radius of dozens or hundreds of meters of its strike will almost certainly kill or wound civilians when used in populated areas. Many explosive weapons are also unguided or are used without spotters, which means that they cannot be targeted precisely, posing additional risk to civilians. A doctor at a morgue in eastern Ukraine told Human Rights Watch that 99 percent of the civilian war victims it had received had died of fragmentation injuries caused by explosive weapons.

In Syria, where the use of explosive weapons in populated areas has been particularly extensive, the government has used a broad range of such weapons since 2011, including mortars, artillery, rockets, fuel-air explosives, and ballistic missiles. Since late 2013, the government has also increasingly used "barrel bombs." Built locally from oil drums, gas cylinders, and water tanks, they are packed with a deadly cargo of high explosives, oil, chemicals, and scrap metal to enhance fragmentation on impact.

In 2014, Human Rights Watch documented hundreds of irregularly shaped blast craters in Aleppo caused by such bombs, and recorded dozens of injuries and fatalities, including that of Noura al-Abdu, 13, who was decapitated in Hraytan, northwest of Aleppo, in a December 2013 barrel bomb attack that also severed the leg of a 9-year-old girl as she sought shelter from a helicopter overhead.

Armed groups opposed to the Syrian government have also fired mortar and artillery shells and launched rockets into populated government-controlled areas, and their powerful car bombs have killed hundreds of civilians. A twin bomb attack targeting a school in Homs, Syria on October 1 reportedly killed dozens of children and several adults. On April 29, two mortar shells also struck the Badr el-Din Hussaini educational complex in the al-Shaghour neighborhood of Damascus, a pro-government area, killing 17 children and at least two parents and injuring 50 others.

In Iraq, ISIS has earned a reputation for limitless cruelty by shooting and beheading hundreds of non-combatants in cold blood. But they have also fired mortar shells into populated areas, killing and maiming civilians, and used car bomb attacks across the country that have killed hundreds of people and likely amount to crimes against humanity. The government's response to ISIS has included the use of barrel bombs and a string of indiscriminate attacks.

In Gaza, Israeli forces fired tens of thousands of explosive weapons into populated areas where Hamas was deployed during a seven-week-long war in July and August. Hamas itself fired thousands of rockets and mortars toward Israeli population centers. Israeli attacks killed more than 2,100 Palestinians, including at least 1,486 civilians, according to the United Nations. Daily casualty reports from local human rights organizations in Gaza show that nearly all the deaths were due to explosive weapons.

In Ukraine, government forces have fired artillery, multiple-launch Grad rockets, and other explosive weapons into populated areas where pro-Russia rebel forces were deployed, killing dozens and injuring many more. The pro-Russia forces have used the same kind of explosive weapons against government forces, also killing and injuring civilians.

In Sudan, persistent government bombing of populated areas in the Nuba Mountains (Southern Kordofan) and Blue Nile has killed and maimed hundreds of civilians and damaged humanitarian aid structures since the conflict started in 2011. A surge in bombing in May and June of 2014 damaged humanitarian aid facilities and forced the humanitarian organization Médecins Sans Frontières (Doctors Without Borders) to withdraw.

Using explosive weapons in populated areas not only causes civilian casualties, but also destroys civilian infrastructure such as schools, hospitals, water pipes, and electrical power grids, prolonging the impact of armed conflict for civilians.

For example, when government and rebel forces were firing unguided rockets, artillery and other explosive weapons at each other in Luhansk, eastern Ukraine, tens of thousands of people trapped in the city were left without running water and electricity for weeks. When a Human Rights Watch researcher visited in late August, hundreds of people were braving regular bombardment to line up for hours at dawn for water and food at distribution points across the city, carrying empty bottles and containers.

Israeli explosive weapons destroyed or damaged more than 15,000 buildings in Gaza during the summer's conflict, according to satellite imagery analysis conducted by the United Nations Institute for Training and Research. Schools were particularly affected; 228 were damaged, according to a UN special rapporteur, severely impacting children's education. When the school year began in September, around 90 percent of Gaza's schools were running on a double shift, with students attending for just four hours each day.

In northern Syria, government air strikes, some seemingly deliberate, have damaged and destroyed hospitals, leaving the medical system in shambles. Physicians for Human Rights, a group that documents the plight of medical personnel, has recorded nearly 200 attacks on hospitals in Syria since the start of the conflict. The few medical resources that are available are insufficient to cope with war-related injuries; maternal health, vaccinations, burns, and chronic diseases are neglected. In northern and eastern Syria, the collapse of the medical system contributed to the outbreak of polio, a disease not seen in the country since 1999.

The use of explosive weapons in populated areas is also one of the main reasons for displacement of civilians. Most people we interviewed in refugee camps in Turkey, Jordan, and Lebanon said they had fled Syria because of the government's constant bombardment of areas held by non-state armed groups. People fleeing Luhansk in Ukraine said the same.

International law prohibits the use of certain explosive weapons, most notably antipersonnel landmines and cluster munitions. But for the most part, the legality of explosive weapon use is decided on a case-by-case basis by general provisions in international humanitarian law—such as the obligation to conduct attacks using weapons in a matter that can distinguish between civilians and combatants or other military objectives.

This piecemeal analysis does not lend itself to a categorical finding regarding a broad category of weapons (e.g. explosive weapons) in a general type of setting (e.g. populated areas). As a result, it cannot set a clear boundary on this issue.

So what can be done?

A legally binding ban on the use of all explosive weapons in populated areas would not be politically feasible, but it *is* possible to set standards that would significantly raise the bar. Human Rights Watch is a founding member of the International Network on Explosive Weapons (INEW), a global coalition of NGOs established in 2011 to work to prevent harm from the use of explosive weapons in populated areas. INEW calls on governments to "develop stronger international standards, including certain prohibitions and restrictions on the use of explosive weapons in populated areas."

Building these standards takes time. But states and other actors should now acknowledge the problem in international discussions and review national policies that outline what weapons are appropriate for use in populated areas and under what circumstances. They should seek to develop a common position that aims to further limit the use of explosive weapons in populated areas. In particular, they should agree to halt altogether the use of explosive weapons with wide area effects in populated areas. As a matter of policy, military commanders should not order the use of explosive weapons with wide area effects in populated areas due to the foreseeable harm to civilians.

Emphasizing explosive weapons with wide area effects is crucial because they have caused the most civilian harm. The concept of wide area effect will need to be more precisely defined, but it should include heavy weapons that produce a wide blast and/or fragmentation radius (like large aircraft bombs); weapons with multiple munitions or explosive warheads that cover a large area (like Grads and other multiple launch rocket systems); and weapons that are so inaccurate that they cannot be effectively targeted (like barrel bombs).

Other measures could be considered that could go beyond the minimum requirements of international humanitarian law, apart from halting the use of explosive weapons with wide area effects in populated areas. Possibilities that have been discussed include restricting the use of indirect fire weapons or unguided weapons in populated areas and committing to using the least destructive force to achieve a military advantage. States could articulate best practices related to doctrine, operational policies, planning directives, rules of engagement, and other such guidance.

Despite the increasing use of explosive weapons in populated areas in 2014, the year also saw significant international efforts to address this issue—and momentum is likely to grow. The UN secretary-general, several UN agencies (notably the Office for the Coordination of Humanitarian Affairs, or OCHA), and the International Committee of the Red Cross (ICRC) have all called on states to refrain from using explosive weapons with wide area effect in populated areas. In March, the ICRC held a meeting to consider how to strengthen the protection of civilians from explosive weapons used in populated areas. In June, Norway hosted an informal experts meeting with OCHA with the same purpose. Austria has announced that it will host a follow-up meeting in 2015.

A sustained international process to address the use of explosive weapons in populated areas is getting underway. Views appear to be coalescing around two notions: that the most feasible outcome of international discussions is likely to be a politically binding commitment—such as a joint declaration of guidelines—rather than a new legal instrument; and that there should be a focus on explosive weapons with wide area effects.

Some government and military experts have expressed concern about the growing effort to curb explosive weapon use in populated areas based on two arguments: first, that many governments already significantly do this through domestic policies and regulations, and second, that the most serious violators will not comply with international guidelines on the issue since they already violate other laws with impunity.

It is true that non-binding guidelines might not have an immediate effect on the Assads of the world. But the power of international norm setting should not be underestimated. Today, few countries, even those that have not signed the relevant treaties, are comfortable admitting that they use landmines or cluster bombs. And the fact that many countries already restrict the use of explosive weapons in populated areas is actually an argument for, not against, developing international guidelines, which would help to spread the practice to other countries.

Other critics have speculated that limiting the use of explosive weapons in populated areas would encourage opposition forces to move into cities and towns and prevent civilians from leaving—all to deter belligerent forces from attacking with explosive weapons. But such actions, which would amount to using human shields or otherwise deliberately putting civilians at risk, are already prohibited under international humanitarian law and could alienate the civilian population.

A future political declaration regarding the use of explosive weapons in populated areas should affirm the obligation to avoid co-location of military objectives and civilians. But it should not be aimed at preventing the use of appropriate means and methods of warfare to address such a situation, and could help to better elaborate what those means and methods might be.

Explosive weapons kill and injure thousands of civilians every year and seriously damage civilian infrastructure. Clear international guidelines on the use of explosive weapons in populated areas could have prevented the 31 deaths of civilians at the Tikrit school, as well as countless deaths, injuries, and suffering in other places. Curbing their use would have a bigger impact on the protection of civilians during armed conflict than anything else we could do.

Steve Goose is director of the Arms Division at Human Rights Watch.

Ole Solvang is a senior emergencies researcher at Human Rights Watch.

Raising the Bar:
Mega-Sporting Events and Human Rights

By Minky Worden

As fireworks cascaded over Sochi's February 2014 Winter Olympics opening cere-mony, Anastasia Smirnova sat miles away in St. Petersburg police custody. A top Russian advocate for lesbian, gay, bisexual, and transgender (LGBT) rights, Smirnova had recently met with International Olympic Committee (IOC) President Thomas Bach to explain how the country's anti-gay laws were creating a climate of violence and discrimination ahead of the Sochi Olympics. Russian authorities, keen to ensure that the Games' luster not be sullied by exposure of human rights abuses, detained Smirnova as she held aloft a banner emblazoned with Principle 6 of the Olympic Charter: "Discrimination is incompatible with belonging to the Olympic Movement."

Human rights were broadly trampled upon before and during the Sochi Olympics, amid forced evictions, violations of workers' rights, a worsening crackdown on civil society and journalists, and anti-LGBT discrimination that caused worldwide revul-sion. Looking ahead to future games, the human rights situation does not look much better.

Since South Korea and Tokyo have established domestic human rights monitors, their selection as hosts for the 2018 Winter Games and the 2020 Summer Games is not cause for alarm. But the outlook for the 2022 Winter Olympics—with Kaza-khstan and China as the only contenders—should be keeping the IOC up at night.

Both countries have abysmal press freedom records and journalists languishing in jail. Beijing has launched its harshest crackdown since the 1989 protests in Tiananmen Square that ended in bloodshed, is jailing journalists, and is breaking an international agreement to allow free elections in Hong Kong. In Almaty, where peaceful dissenters are routinely imprisoned and labor rights often flouted, the IOC could experience a disastrous déjà vu of the Sochi clampdown and abuses.

This crisis of choice for 2022 should, finally, provide the impetus for the IOC and other international sporting bodies to reform a system that for too long has re-warded human rights abusers while often creating misery for local populations.

In October 2014, Norway—which had made respect for human rights part of its Olympic bid—pulled out of the contest to host the 2022 Winter Games, leaving Kazakhstan and China as the only contenders.

Oil-rich Kazakhstan craves the global prestige that hosting the Games would bring, while China is seeking to burnish its reputation on the world stage, as it did during the 2008 Beijing Games. Meanwhile, Azerbaijan is set to host the first European Games in 2015—launched and administered by the European Olympic Committees—against the backdrop of an escalating crackdown on critics in the country.

For too long, governments have said whatever it took to win the right to host the Olympics, only to be unreliable partners later on who flouted key promises as the IOC declared itself powerless to act. With Nobel Peace Prize-hosting Norway out, the IOC is well and truly stuck with the choice of two competitors for the 2022 Games with terrible human rights records.

In both China and Kazakhstan, peaceful critics languish in jail; each country has a recent history of censoring the Internet and crushing press freedom. Migrant workers in China who would build new stadiums face exploitation and dangerous conditions, while Kazakhstan's abusive handling in 2011 of extended labor strikes and its recent adoption of a law on trade unions have seriously curtailed freedom of association. Lawsuits against an advertising agency for a poster showing a same-sex kiss and renewed calls for a ban on "homosexual propaganda" in September expose Kazakhstan's problematic record on LGBT rights.

To host the Olympics, governments pledge not only to build sparkling new stadiums but also to uphold the "Fundamental Principles of Olympism"—human dignity, press freedom, and a complete rejection of "any form of discrimination." These principles are enshrined in the Olympic Charter, a lofty document that supposedly guides the Games' preparation and advances "human dignity."

Human rights crises around so-called "mega-sporting events" are not limited to the Olympics. The scale of abuse in Qatar as it builds a dozen 2022 World Cup stadiums and US$200 billion worth of infrastructure is immense: already, hundreds of South Asian migrant workers who toiled in the heat and dust of a highly abusive construction sector have been sent home in body bags, with authorities ignoring calls for investigations into their deaths. Russia has a grim record of failing migrant workers who were exploited and cheated as they built infrastructure for the $53 billion Sochi Olympics, and is set to host the 2018 World Cup.

The prospects for change now are greater than before: sports fans, corporate sponsors, and the general public are increasingly turned off by reports of human rights violations when sporting extravaganzas are staged.

With this perfect storm of abuses tied to, and often caused by preparation for, mega-sporting events, it is time for practical reform to encourage governments to clean up their human rights acts before hosting. International sporting bodies need to accept that awarding contracts for massive infrastructure to governments that violate human rights will only compound existing violations; while governing bodies for global sports need to reform from within, with the mantra that there is no successful sporting event where there are major human rights violations.

Mega-Sporting Events: Five Main Abuses

When athletes break the rules in Olympic competitions, they are harshly sanctioned. When host countries flout the rules, they have largely got away with it. Former IOC President Jacques Rogge often insisted that the Olympics are a "force for good" but refused to criticize blatant violations of the Olympic Charter by Olympic hosts.

Human Rights Watch has extensively documented how mega-sporting events can bring mega-violations when Games are awarded to governments who fail to respect human rights. No country has a perfect human rights record, but increasingly it is the more abusive states that most want to burnish their international reputation and need the patriotic boost gained by hosting world media and leaders for a global sport extravaganza.

Over a decade of research, Human Rights Watch has documented five signature types of serious human rights violations that are typically tied to mega-sporting events.

The first is **forced evictions without due process or compensation** due to massive new infrastructure construction. Before 2008, thousands of citizens in Beijing were forcibly evicted from their homes with little due process in terms of consultation or adequate compensation. Residents who protested the demolition of their homes were arrested. Fair compensation and due process were serious problems in Sochi as well.

As massive stadiums are constructed for opening ceremonies, soccer games, or swimming and other events, the bulk of the work is often done by **abused and exploited migrant workers,** who face hazardous working conditions, long hours, and being cheated of pay.

Major infrastructure construction often also leads to environmental and other complaints. **The silencing of civil society and rights activists** has been a signature abuse ahead of both the Beijing and Russian Olympics. Instead of the promised human rights improvements, the period leading up to the Beijing Games was marred by jailings and house arrests of activists who criticized the Olympics (including Sakharov Prize winner Hu Jia), and a three-year jail sentence for an environmental activist in Russia. In Beijing, citizens like 59-year-old Ji Sizun—who attempted to use the "Olympic protest zones" officially set up by the Chinese government to supposedly allow peaceful protest—were arrested. In Sochi, members of the feminist punk group Pussy Riot who staged a small protest during the Winter Games in February 2014 were visibly tackled and beaten by Cossacks while the police did nothing.

The Olympic Charter expressly guarantees press freedom—the sale of media rights is a major source of revenue for the International Olympic Committee. But both the Beijing and Sochi Olympics were marred by **threats, intimidation, and arrests of journalists**. When 25,000 journalists arrived in China to cover the Beijing Olympics, they were surprised to find Internet news blocked—until the IOC forced China to cease web censorship for the duration of the Games. News that China's milk supply was poisoned nationwide with melamine was censored until after the Games closed, and at least six babies died as a result of this tragic poisoning (and the media blackout about it). In the lead-up to the Sochi Games, Russian police harassed, detained, and threatened to imprison two journalists from a Norwegian television station, before sarcastically saying, "Welcome to Sochi" when the journalists' ordeal was over. So egregious was their treatment that Russian authorities issued a rare apology.

Mega-sporting events are supposed to be moments to celebrate diversity and human achievement. But too often they are settings that expose **ugly discrimina-**

tion. Until just days before the launch of the London 2012 Olympics, Saudi Arabia was still planning to send a male-only national team, as in all past Olympics, and also to the 2014 Asian Games. Extreme pressure—brought about in part by Human Rights Watch's "Let Them Play" campaign—finally led to two Saudi women being allowed to compete in 2012. But back in Saudi Arabia, as documented by Human Rights Watch's 2012 report "Steps of the Devil," the country still bans sport for all girls in state schools and has no women's sports federations, a clear violation of the Olympic Charter's non-discrimination clause.

In June 2013, Russian President Vladimir Putin signed into law an anti-LGBT "propaganda" bill. The law uses the pretext of protecting children to ban spreading information about equality, tolerance, and other issues affecting the LGBT community and demonized LGBT people and activists in the public eye. This has helped spark a surge in harassment and violent attacks against LGBT people, and the IOC raised no concerns about how this could be compatible with a commitment to non-discrimination.

In some parts of the world, women cannot even attend a sporting event as a spectator. Equal access to sporting events for women has become a serious concern, with the Fédération Internationale de Football Association, the international governing body for soccer known as FIFA, allowing a ban on women spectators for football matches since the 1980s in Iran. In 2012, Iranian officials extended the ban to volleyball matches.

Law student Ghoncheh Ghavami was arrested in June 2014 and jailed for months in Iran's notorious Evin prison after she and others protested a ban on women entering a stadium to watch a World League match. In November, the International Federation for Volleyball (known as FIVB) called on the Iranian government to release Ghavami, and affirmed its commitment to "inclusivity and the right of women to participate in sport on an equal basis" at the organization's World Congress. The FIVB flagged that Iran's policy could limit its ability to host international tournaments in the future. Ghavami was released on bail in late November, but not before a revolutionary court convicted her of "propaganda against the state" and sentenced her to one year in prison. She was appealing the decision at time of writing.

In November 2014, the Asian Volleyball Confederation announced that it had selected Iran to co-host the 2015 Asian Men's Volleyball Championships. Ghavami's conviction and Iran's continuing ban on women spectators attending men's sporting events should prompt international sporting groups to pull all major tournaments from offending countries until women are guaranteed the right to attend matches as spectators without the prospect of arrest and jailing.

Taking a Stand, Making Reforms

It has often taken getting a major black eye in the press for the IOC to finally react to egregious abuses extensively documented by Human Rights Watch and other organizations. The IOC has responded to earlier scandals including doping, environmental degradation, illegal betting, and corruption with concrete reforms that included setting up an anti-doping agency, environmental impact statements, and term limits for the IOC leadership.

In the last century, the IOC helped combat discrimination in sport by banning Apartheid-era South Africa for sending whites-only teams, and Taliban-run Afghanistan for discrimination against women and girls. Facing public demonstrations that could have ended in a bloodbath, the IOC told South Korea's military dictatorship to hold elections or it would jeopardize Seoul's hosting of the 1988 Olympics (South Korea has since been a durable democracy and is due to host the 2018 Winter Olympics.

The International Olympic Committee and FIFA are the two largest players on the field of mega-sporting events. They need to use this crisis to act on reforms before the next Olympics and the next World Cup.

In autumn 2014, IOC President Thomas Bach put in place a series of reforms that Human Rights Watch has long sought that could curb abuses—a sign the body may no longer want to play ball with rights-violating host countries. Starting with the 2022 Olympics, the International Olympic Committee Host City contracts will include human rights and labor rights protections, including non-discrimination. Olympic Host City contracts have generally been secret and have never before expressly included rights protections.

The success of contract reforms will depend on how serious the IOC is about implementation. By picking up the reform baton dropped by his predecessors, the IOC and Thomas Bach could launch a new era of zero tolerance for serious abuses around mega-sporting events.

Russia's Olympics, marred by entirely predictable rights abuses, may have been a turning point. As Human Rights Watch documented in a book-length 2013 report, Race to the Bottom, many migrant workers who built the Games' infrastructure were abused and cheated of their wages. In some cases, those who complained were beaten and deported. The IOC ultimately took up those cases with Russia, which admitted that workers were still owed $8 million in unpaid wages and pledged to ensure that employers make these payments. Russia's anti-LGBT law led to global protests by leading athletes and extensive negative press coverage. In September 2014, the IOC belatedly rebuked Russia by adding an anti-discrimination clause in future host city contracts and in December, in a unanimous vote, the IOC added "sexual orientation" as an explicit protected ground against discrimination in Principle 6 of the Olympic Charter.

Future Risky Hosts

FIFA has deservedly faced a firestorm of criticism for awarding the 2022 World Cup to **Qatar** without making labor reforms a prerequisite for them hosting the tournament. The result is that the migrant workers building football stadiums and billions of dollars of new infrastructure are highly vulnerable to trafficking and forced labor.

The "Supreme Committee for Qatar 2022"—the tournament's quasi-governmental delivery committee—has pledged to improve conditions for workers on projects directly related to the World Cup.

But Qatar is not pledging to seriously reform exploitative laws such as the kafala system that ties workers to employers; it has refused to abolish a pointless and entirely illegitimate exit visa system that traps workers in the country; and it has not outlined how it plans to stop the systematic confiscation of passports and the imposition of illegal recruitment fees on workers.

Oil-rich **Azerbaijan**, where the government has recently jailed the country's top human rights defenders, will host the inaugural European Games, which will take place in Baku in 2015 (the Organizing Committee is chaired by the first lady, Mehriban Aliyeva).

The European Games are organized by the European National Olympic Committees, which means that Olympic Charter human rights principles should apply. Despite the stated goal of "spreading throughout Europe of the Olympic ideals as defined by the IOC Charter," the Azerbaijan authorities have instead been crushing critics, cutting foreign funding, and freezing bank accounts of independent groups, and threatening or jailing journalists and social media activists.

The European Games organizers should urgently study the ugly history of the 2012 Eurovision Song Contest hosted by Azerbaijan: the atmosphere for political activists and independent and pro-opposition journalists grew acutely hostile; critics were jailed, demonstrations dispersed, and activists were arrested.The December 2014 arrest of Khadija Ismayilova, Azerbaijan's leading investigative journalist and ardent government critic, is a devastating blow to critical voices in Azerbaijan, and a clear violation of the Olympic Charter's press freedom protections.

Bridging Words and Reality

The Olympic Charter states that "sport is a human right." It elevates the principle of human dignity and proclaims, "The goal of Olympism is to place sport at the service of the harmonious development of humankind, with a view to promoting a peaceful society concerned with the preservation of human dignity." Similarly, the FIFA statutes stress the importance of "humanitarian values" and state: "Discrimination of any kind against a country, private person or group of people on account of ethnic origin, gender, language, religion, politics or any other reason is strictly prohibited ..."

For now, the IOC and FIFA have a serious problem: how to bridge the gap between these lofty words and the ugly reality on the ground.

One answer to this is to **build human rights monitoring into the hosting process**— assessing progress towards press freedom and international human rights standards, just as they now do to build ski jumps, swimming pools, and equestrian facilities on time. Similar changes are needed in the FIFA Statutes to ensure that dazzling soccer stadiums are not built on the backs of migrant workers toiling for low wages in hazardous conditions.

The IOC has a massive structure in place to evaluate host cities, and that same flyspecking care should be brought to bear on publicly available information on human rights abuses, in particular as they relate to the hosting of the Olympics. Spectators do not want to cheer in a stadium that costs not just millions of dollars—but dozens of human lives—to build. Social media can send news of a gold medal around the world in seconds, but it can also send images of water cannons and bloodied peaceful protesters.

Selecting future host countries should involve a **complete and meaningful evaluation of governments' commitment** to respect human rights in compliance with international human rights norms, as well as the "Fundamental Principles" of the Olympic Charter. These standards can easily be included in the IOC Model Candidature for Olympic host countries, and compliance should be facilitated by making host city contracts public in the interest of greater transparency.

For all future mega-sporting events, evaluations of candidates should include **human rights benchmarks,** including those related to media and Internet freedom; fair compensation for forced evictions; labor rights for workers building venues; protections for activists and peaceful protests; and protection against discrimination, including based on race, religion, politics, gender, nationality, disability, or sexual orientation and gender identity.

Sports associations should **not bring events to countries where women will not be welcome as spectators**, or where they could get attacked or arrested for cheering a team. Sporting federations can and should play a positive role in quashing discrimination by insisting women have equal access to mega-sporting events and tournaments, which should not go forward with a male-only spectator policy, as in Iran. Sports leaders need to state in public that they will not back mega-sporting event hosts who violate the foundations of sport.

It is time to level the playing field and put an end to the high human cost of awarding mega-sporting events to repressive governments. In launching "Agenda 2020" reforms that include human rights protections for the first time, IOC President Bach has begun to take overdue steps in this direction. Now is the moment for FIFA and other international sports bodies to reform as well. There cannot be a truly successful global sporting event in countries where there are major human rights abuses.

Minky Worden is director of global initiatives at Human Rights Watch.

HUMAN
RIGHTS
WATCH

EXPLOITATION IN THE NAME
OF EDUCATION
Uneven Progress in Ending Forced Child Begging in Senegal

HUMAN
RIGHTS
WATCH

WORLD REPORT
2015

COUNTRIES

Afghanistan

Afghanistan entered a new period of instability in 2014, with important implications for human rights. The June 2014 final round of the presidential election resulted in political impasse as both candidates, Ashraf Ghani and Abdullah Abdullah, claimed victory after accusing each other's teams of engaging in fraud. On September 21, the two candidates signed a deal making Ghani the president, and Abdullah the chief executive. The bitterly fought campaign and months-long standoff raised fears of continuing instability, and lingering disagreements over the terms of the deal delayed the formation of a cabinet.

Uncertainty surrounding the political transition, along with growing pressure from Taliban insurgents, contributed to a decline in respect for human rights throughout the country, including impunity for abuses by security forces, threats to women's rights and freedom of expression, and indiscriminate attacks that killed civilians.

Preparations for the withdrawal of international combat troops by the end of 2014 continued, with foreign troops largely departed or sequestered in their bases. As insurgent forces launched sustained attacks on a number of vital districts, Afghan security forces suffered increasingly higher casualties on the battlefield. However, civilians still bore the brunt of the violence. The United Nations recorded a 24 percent rise in civilian casualties in the first six months of 2014 compared to 2013, most due to insurgent attacks.

Election Violence and Attacks on Civilians

Early in the year, the Taliban stepped up attacks on officials and workers associated with the presidential elections, and targeted other civilians and foreigners. On January 17, a suicide attack on a Kabul restaurant, La Taverna, resulted in the deaths of 20 people, including 13 foreign nationals and 7 Afghans. The Taliban claimed responsibility, apparently targeting the restaurant because of its popularity with foreigners. On March 21, gunmen attacked the dining room of the high-security Serena Hotel in central Kabul, killing nine people, including Agence France Presse journalist Sardar Ahmad, his wife, and two of their children. A third child was wounded.

In a March 11 statement, the Taliban vowed to "use all force" to disrupt the vote, and to "target all workers, activists, callers, security apparatus, and offices." Violent incidents in the period included kidnappings of election workers, and targeted attacks on campaign rallies, and candidates' staff and offices. Taliban forces killed some 40 civilians in attacks during the election, injured at least 100, and severed fingers of 11 men in Herat who voted in the run-off poll on June 14.

Torture, Extrajudicial Executions, and Enforced Disappearances

Impunity for abuses by government security forces remained the norm. The police in Kandahar, in particular, were cited by the United Nations, human rights groups, and journalists in numerous reports of torture, summary executions, and forcible disappearances through 2014. The torture and death in custody of Hazrat Ali, a 23-year-old plumber, as reported in the *New York Times*, prompted Minister of Interior Umer Daudzai to promise an inquiry, but no results had been made public at time of writing.

Despite a 2013 government investigation into allegations of ill-treatment and torture, not a single member of the Afghan security forces was prosecuted during the year for such abuses. Kandahar police reportedly maintained at least four secret detention centers, to which the UN Assistance Mission to Afghanistan (UNAMA) and the International Committee of the Red Cross (ICRC), had no access.

A number of high-level police and army officials made statements that appeared to endorse a "take no prisoners" policy toward captured Taliban fighters, blaming government policy and corruption for the fact that released detainees were returning to the fight. In June, Kandahar police chief, Brigadier General Raziq, stated that his police had orders to kill all Taliban on the battlefield. Raziq later retracted that statement. Just before leaving office, President Karzai promoted Raziq to a three-star rank. Kunduz Police Chief Mustafa Mohseni echoed Raziq's sentiment, stating that police had no option but to kill captured insurgents because they could not be effectively prosecuted in a corrupt judicial system. On August 23, Gen. Murad Ali Murad, commander of the Afghanistan National Army's infantry also called for "giving no quarter" to captured insurgents in clear violation of international humanitarian law.

Since 2013, Afghan authorities released hundreds of detainees from the Bagram Detention Facility, including 65 who were freed in February over the objections of the United States military, which argued that the men continued to pose a threat. In August and September, the US released and repatriated 2 Yemenis and 14 Pakistanis from Bagram.

Police impunity in 2014 extended to other crimes against civilians: in April, Meena Intizar, a poet, claimed that she had fled Kandahar city after one of Raziq's deputies, Abdul Wadood Sarhadi Jajo, threatened to rape and kill her and family members after she filed a complaint that Jajo's forces raided her home and stole electronics, jewelry, and money. Jajo had been accused previously of sexual assault, but was never prosecuted. In May, he was killed in a suicide attack.

The Afghan Local Police (ALP)—a network of local defense forces established largely by the US military in cooperation with the Afghan government—continued to be responsible for serious human rights violations, including extrajudicial executions. During an offensive against the Taliban in August in Zhare district, Kandahar, an ALP unit under Brigadier General Raziq's command reportedly captured and executed six Kuchi nomads it accused of working with the Taliban. In June, ALP members under Commander Abdullah summarily executed three villagers in Andar district following a clash with Taliban forces in the area. According to UNAMA, at time of writing there had been no accountability for the killings.

Women's Rights

Women's rights remained under threat in 2014. In January, a provision in Afghanistan's draft criminal procedure code became the latest in a series of attempts to roll back the already fragile legal protections for women and girls. As passed by parliament, article 26 of the draft code included "relatives of the accused," among a list of people who "cannot be questioned as witnesses" in criminal proceedings, thereby making successful prosecutions of those committing domestic violence extremely unlikely. In late February, President Hamid Karzai signed the law but amended article 26 by decree to state that relatives of the accused are permitted to testify voluntarily. It also allows compelled testimony from any "complainant or informant regarding the crime" and slightly narrows the definition of "relatives." However, the amended article still exempts many family members from being called as witnesses.

In June, the government rejected recommendations from UN member countries to abolish prosecution of women for so-called moral crimes. Other setbacks for women's rights in 2014 included a continuing series of attacks on, threats toward, and assassinations of, high-profile women, including police women and activists, to which the government failed to respond with meaningful measures to protect women at risk. The implementation by law enforcement officials of Afghanistan's landmark 2009 Law on the Elimination of Violence Against Women remained poor, with many cases of violence against women ignored or resolved through "mediation" that denied victims their day in court.

More positively, women's rights activists through hard work and constant advocacy were able to inject some discussion of women's rights into the election process. This included a successful effort by the Afghan Women's Network (AWN) to obtain signatures from Ashraf Ghani and Abdullah Abdullah, after both survived the first election round, to commit to following 30 recommendations that support women's rights. AWN and its member organizations planned to follow up with the new president to ensure his compliance.

Transitional Justice

Early in the year, the Afghanistan Independent Human Rights Commission presented President Karzai with a copy of its 800-page report mapping war crimes and crimes against humanity in Afghanistan since the Communist era. Completed in December 2011, the report would provide a foundation for future steps to prosecute those implicated in past abuses. President Karzai had rejected calls to release the report publicly. Although Ashraf Ghani had vowed before the election to release the report, at time of writing there was no planned release date.

Freedom of Expression and Association

The rights to freedom of expression and association of media and political parties, hailed as one of Afghanistan's clear human rights successes since 2001, increasingly came under threat in 2014.

Two credible Afghan media organizations, *Nai* Supporting Open Media, and the Afghanistan Journalists' Safety Committee, documented some 68 attacks on journalists in the first six months of 2014, compared to around 41 attacks in the same period in 2013. The groups attributed 63 percent of the attacks and threats to government officials and Afghan security forces, almost 12 percent to insurgent forces, and the remainder to other powerful figures or unidentified sources. The attacks included the killing of *New York Times* reporter Noor Ahmad Noori on January 23, 2014, by unidentified assailants in Helmand province. Foreign journalists were also victims of violence; on March 11, an unidentified guman shot dead Swedish journalist Nils Horner in Kabul, and on April 4, a policeman in Khost shot dead photojournalist Anja Niedringhaus and wounded Associated Press reporter Kathy Gannon while they were covering preparations for the country's April 5 presidential election.

On May 23, WikiLeaks revealed that the US National Security Agency (NSA) conducted mass phone surveillance in Afghanistan on a scale far greater than the NSA's controversial metadata collection program in the United States. According to WikiLeaks, since 2013, the NSA has been recording and storing almost all phone calls, including those made by Afghan journalists.

Internally Displaced Persons and Refugees

The intensified fighting displaced thousands of people throughout Afghanistan, particularly in Helmand and Kunduz provinces. The UN High Commissioner for Refugees (UNHCR) documented an increase of over 38,340 in the number of internally displaced people from January through September 2014, bringing the total to over 755,011. The main causes of displacement were armed conflict and diminished security.

Deteriorating security and growing fears for the future contributed to an increasing number of Afghans fleeing their homes for other countries, or choosing not to return home from overseas. The number of Afghans seeking safety outside the country also grew, with some making dangerous journeys from Afghanistan through the mountains into Iran toward Europe or by boat to Australia. The number of refugees returning to Afghanistan from neighboring countries has fallen in recent years, according to UNHCR.

Afghans arriving in other countries faced increasing hostility, including draconian policies in Australia diverting asylum seekers to third countries, and governmental proposals in European countries, including the United Kingdom and Norway, to deport unaccompanied Afghan children back to Afghanistan. The several million Afghans in Iran continued to face discrimination and abuses.

Key International Actors

International fatigue with Afghanistan among countries that have contributed troops or significant amounts of aid post-2001—particularly the US, which has had the largest military and aid involvement—reduced political pressure on the Afghan government to respect human rights, particularly in the areas of security force abuses and women's rights.

While many countries pledged to continue aid to Afghanistan, political engagement waned and donors scaled back most forms of assistance. In October, President Ghani signed the Bilateral Security Agreement (BSA) with the US, a key step in determining the scope of NATO's military presence in Afghanistan post-2014.

The International Criminal Court, which since 2007 has been looking into allegations of serious international crimes in Afghanistan, expanded its preliminary analysis to include admissibility issues, including the efficacy of relevant national proceedings to address accountability.

HUMAN
RIGHTS
WATCH

OFF THE RADAR
Human Rights in the Tindouf Refugee Camps

Algeria

2014 saw no overall improvement in human rights conditions in Algeria despite promises tha the government has made since 2011 to introduce reforms. Authorities curtailed free speech and the rights to freedom of association, assembly, and peaceful protest, and arrested and prosecuted political and trade union activists.

Abdelaziz Bouteflika, president since 1999, was re-elected for the fourth time on April 17, 2014, despite his reported ill-health. Several opposition parties boycotted the election and called instead for democratic reforms and genuinely pluralistic elections.

The government authorized Human Rights Watch to make an official visit, in October 2014, to the country for the first time since 2005 and to hold a press conference on the human rights situation in the Tindouf Refugee camps. However, it continued to block the legal registration of Algerian human rights nongovernmental organizations (NGOs) and maintained its non-cooperation with United Nations human rights experts and mechanisms.

Freedom of Assembly

Authorities continued their policy of pre-emptively suppressing peaceful protests by rounding up and arresting protest organizers in advance and then using the police to block access to demonstration venues. Those arrested and prosecuted on charges of gathering illegally included human rights activists and trade union leaders.

In April, authorities forcibly dispersed protesters opposed to President Abdelaziz Bouteflika's re-election, and arrested and detained hundreds, including many supporters of the Barakat ("Enough") movement. Police held those they arrested for hours in police stations before releasing some and prosecuting others. Those charged included Mohand Kadi, a youth activist, and Moez Bennecir, a Tunisian resident in Algeria. On May 18, a court convicted both men of participating in an "unlawful non-armed gathering harming public order," under articles 97 and 98 of the penal code, and handed down suspended six month prison sentences.

In another case, on June 18, the First Instance Court in Laghouat imposed prison sentences ranging from six months to two years on 26 defendants after convicting them on charges that included "armed gathering" and violence against the police based on police testimonies that did not incriminate the defendants individually. The 26 included 17 local human rights activists whom the court convicted in absentia. They surrendered to the authorities and received a new trial, at which they were acquitted.

Freedom of Association

Authorities continued to frustrate efforts by human rights and other organizations to obtain official registration in compliance with Law 12-06 of 2012. This requires all associations, including those previously registered, to obtain a registration receipt from the Ministry of Interior before they can operate legally. The law also empowers the ministry to refuse to register an association whose activities it deems are contrary to Algeria's "fundamental principles (*constantes nationales*) and values, public order, public morals and the applicable laws and regulations."

These vague criteria give the authorities broad leeway to deny registration, without which organizations cannot lawfully hold public meetings or accept funds from abroad. Authorities also curtailed activities of some organizations that had obtained registration prior to the 2012 law by administrative means, such as by withholding official receipts for which they had applied and declining to make public venues available for them to hold annual general meetings that they are required by law to hold.

Law 12-06 also empowers the Interior Ministry to suspend or dissolve any organization it considers "interferes with the internal affairs of the state or violates national sovereignty," and makes any "cooperation agreement" between an Algerian and an international organization conditional on prior government approval. This latter requirement tightened the previous restriction whereby Algerian organizations had to obtain prior government approval for their "membership" in an international organization.

The 2012 law maintains the previous requirement that Algerian organizations obtain government approval before they can receive foreign funding but added the additional requirement that they must first have a "cooperation agreement."

These requirements afford the government excessive powers over the legal establishment and functioning of independent organizations, rendering their members liable to prosecution on illegal gathering charges, and makes such organizations vulnerable to excessive government interference. The rules governing foreign funding, a lifeline for some independent human rights organizations, are particularly problematic.

Labor Rights

The government continued to prevent or disrupt efforts by workers to form independent unions, and to clamp down on peaceful protests and strikes. Authorities used administrative chicanery to withhold legal status from independent unions that seek to operate outside the General Union of Algerian Workers (Union générale des travailleurs algériens, UGTA), the national trade union federation that many consider too close to the government.

Under the law, workers are entitled to form trade unions simply by providing authorities with written notification, after which the Ministry of Interior should issue them with a receipt confirming the union's registration. In many cases, however, the ministry either failed to issue a receipt, leaving the union unable to prove its registration, or requested additional information from applicants or instructed unions to modify their statutes before it would issue them a registration receipt. In some cases, the ministry failed to issue a receipt even after unions complied with its instructions. Without a receipt, a union cannot legally represent workers.

Organizers and workers in autonomous unions face arbitrary arrest and prosecution and other forms of harassment, such as dismissal from public service employment, for peacefully pursuing their trade union activities and demonstrating in support of better labor rights. On April 16, 2014, for example, the Appeals Court of Ouargla, imposed a suspended prison sentence of one year on union activist Houari Djelouli and fined him for distributing "leaflets likely to undermine the national interest." Police arrested Djelouli on April 8, 2013, in Ouargla city center as he prepared to distribute leaflets for the CNDDC union calling for a peaceful sit-in protest outside the *wilaya* (provincial headquarters) of Ouargla in support of the right to work.

Freedom of Speech

Despite the adoption in 2012 of a new law on information that removed imprisonment as a penalty for speech offences, such as defaming or showing "contempt" to the president, state institutions, or the courts, authorities continued to prosecute and imprison peaceful critics using provisions of the Code of Criminal Procedures.

On September 1, the Court of Appeal of Ghardaïa in southern Algeria confirmed a two-year prison sentence and fine that a First Instance Tribunal had imposed in June on Youssef Ouled Dada after convicting him on charges of "insulting state institutions" and "publishing material that threatens public interest," under articles 146 and 96 of the criminal code. The charges arose after Dada posted a video on his Facebook page that allegedly showed police officers robbing a store in El Guerrara, 115 kilometers northeast of Ghardaïa, during violent unrest in the town in November 2013.

Accountability for Past Crimes

The Law on Peace and National Reconciliation, adopted in 2006, continued to afford legal immunity to perpetrators of torture, enforced disappearances, unlawful killings, and other serious rights abuses during the internal armed conflict of the 1990s. The law also criminalizes any expression that authorities believe denigrates state institutions or security forces for their conduct during that conflict. However, to Human Rights Watch's knowledge, there have been no prosecutions based on this law to date. Despite this and continued official harassment, associations representing the rights of the disappeared continued to call for truth and justice.

Counterterrorism

Algeria increased its security cooperation and joint military operations with Tunisia, following several attacks by armed militants on the Tunisian army and National Guard along the border with Algeria. Several high level representatives of western countries who visited Algeria, such as the French defense minister and US secretary of state, said their governments wished to strengthen security cooperation with Algeria to fight terrorism in the region.

On September 24, fighters who, according to news reports, claimed allegiance to the extremist group Islamic State, also known as ISIS, beheaded a French citizen in Algeria and released a video showing the killing. They kidnapped him after ISIS called on its supporters around the world to retaliate against the participation of French armed forces in military airstrikes in Iraq.

Polisario-Run Sahrawi Refugee Camps

The Polisario Front has governed camps in southwest Algeria since the late 1970s for refugees who fled Western Sahara after Morocco invaded it. Critics of the Polisario were able to hold small, sporadic public demonstrations in 2014. None were imprisoned for their political views, to Human Rights Watch's knowledge, but at least a few faced harassment for openly criticizing the Polisario.

Refugees were largely free to leave the camps for Mauritania or to return permanently or temporarily to Moroccan-controlled Western Sahara. A Sahrawi woman, Mahdjouba Mohamed Hamdidaf, who had emigrated to Spain and was visiting her family in the refugee camps was forcibly confined by her family for more than two months after she sought to depart as planned in August. The Polisario Front did little to end herconfinement and protect her freedom of movement until it came under strong international pressure. At time of writing, there were reportedly other cases of Sahrawi women with legal residency in Europe whose families have forcibly confined them while visiting the camps.

The government of Algeria did not, to Human Rights Watch's knowledge, explicitly recognize its responsibility for safeguarding the human rights of Sahrawis living in Polisario-run camps on Algerian soil.

Key International Actors

In the framework of its European Neighborhood Policy (ENP), the European Union engaged in negotiations with Algeria on an action plan. ENP action plans are supposed to demonstrate partner countries' commitment to, among other things, democracy, human rights, rule of law, and good governance.

The government of Algeria has not granted access to United Nations human rights mechanisms since 2011. Pending requests for access include the special rapporteurs on torture and on freedom of peaceful assembly and of association, and the UN Working Groups on Enforced or Involuntary Disappearances and on Arbitrary Detention.

Angola

President José Eduardo dos Santos, in power for 35 years, has faced increasing criticism in Angola for rampant corruption, bad governance, and government repression. Although the 2012 elections ended in another victory for his ruling Popular Movement for the Liberation of Angola (MPLA), the authorities intensified repressive measures, restricting freedom of expression, association, and assembly. In 2014, the government once again delayed long-overdue local elections.

The government continues targeting outspoken journalists and activists with criminal defamation lawsuits, arbitrary arrests, unfair trials, intimidation, harassment, and surveillance. The police use excessive force and engage in arbitrary arrests to stop peaceful anti-government protests and other gatherings. In 2014, authorities conducted the first post-colonial population and housing census, and in late 2013 launched a civil registration campaign that promotes free access to birth certificates and identity documents. However, the government also stepped up mass forced evictions in Luanda, the capital, and continued there and in other cities to violently remove street traders, including pregnant women and women with children. Outspoken human rights activists, journalists, human rights lawyers, and youth protest activists reported repeated harassment, intimidation, and pervasive surveillance by police and intelligence agents.

Freedom of Expression

Freedom of expression is severely restricted in Angola due to censorship and self-censorship in state media and ruling party-controlled private media and other forms of government repression. In such a climate, Internet blogs and social media have become the main channels for open debate.

The government has regularly used criminal defamation laws and other abusive legal provisions to silence journalists.

In July, the prominent investigative journalist Rafael Marques was formally notified of criminal libel charges filed by seven high-ranking Angolan army generals and the diamond mining company Sociedade Mineira do Cuango. The plaintiffs are jointly demanding US$1.2 million in damages from Marques. The lawsuits have been pending since 2013, and the legal time limit to present the formal charges expired in June. At time of writing he was awaiting trial. A further criminal lawsuit filed by another diamond company, ITM Mining, is pending. Marques had accused the plaintiffs of involvement in torture, rape, and killings in a book he published in Portugal in 2011. Angola's Attorney General's Office shelved a complaint filed by Marques against the generals and business associates in 2012, and has failed to investigate the allegations.

The same generals are also demanding $376,000 in damages in a civil lawsuit against Marques and his editor in Portugal on the same matter. In February, Angola security agents harassed and threatened two Angolan defense witnesses, brought to a court hearing in Portugal by Marques, before their travel to Portugal and upon their return to Angola. A previous criminal lawsuit against Marques by the same plaintiffs in Portugal had been dismissed by the Portuguese prosecutor.

On February 2, police in the police headquarters of Cacuaco, Luanda, arrested Queirós Anastácio Chilúvia, editor of Rádio Despertar, which is owned by the opposition party, National Union for the Total Liberation of Angola (UNITA). He was there to seek an official explanation from the police after trasmitting, live on Rádio Despertar, cries for help from jailed detainees. Chilúvia was held in custody for five days without charge. On February 7, a court sentenced him to 180 days in prison, suspended for two years, and a fine of $600 on the charges of defamation and slander, disobedience against a corporate public authority, and "abuse of press freedom"—a vaguely defined crime under the 2006 Press Law.

On May 28, police briefly arrested Rádio Despertar journalist Adérito Pascual at a police station in Viana when he asked for an official statement for a live broadcast on a violent operation to remove street traders. Police seized his phone, recorder, and identification, and government agents forced him to delete videos he had taken. He was released after two hours and his equipment returned. In a similar incident on September 24, police briefly arrested Álvaro Victoria, a journalist with the privately owned weekly newspaper *Novo Jornal*, at the S. Paulo market in Luanda, where he was taking videos of police beating street traders. Police roughed him up, threatened him, and held him for two hours. He was then released without charge.

Right to Peaceful Assembly

Since 2011, the government has responded to any kind of peaceful anti-government protest with excessive force, arbitrary arrests, unfair trials, harassment and intimidation of protest activists, and attacks against reporters and passers-by. In 2014, violent crackdowns against youth and other peaceful protesters continued.

In incidents on May 27, July 26, August 16 and 21, September 5 and 7, and October 3 and 11, police used excessive force to disperse youth demonstrations in Luanda, and arbitrarily arrested dozens of people. Many of the demonstrators were protesting silently and only displaying handwritten messages.

On November 23, a group of police commanders and state security agents cuffed and brutally beat the 26-year-old youth activist Laurinda Gouveia during two hours in a school, and filmed the beatings. Police arrested her when she took pictures of police mistreating two youth demonstrators at Independence Square in Luanda. The incident followed an intense campaign of intimidation by the authorities against the youth movement, which since October had been planning a peaceful anti-dos Santos rally on November 22 and 23.

On October 11, police arrested at least 12 youth protesters in Luanda and injured several with metal bars and batons. Most protesters were released that day without charge. One protester received a 30-day sentence for allegedly having torn the uniform of a police agent, and five more were held for nearly two weeks before being released, pending their trial on disobedience charges. They were denied medical care and access to lawyers until five days after their arrest.

On June 21, in Lubango, Huila province, police used teargas to disperse a peaceful rally of the teacher's union; teachers were then on strike. Police arrested 20 teachers and held them for four days without charges.

On May 27, rapid intervention police beat and arrested 17 protesters at Luanda's Independence Square, and threw teargas into the police vans where they were held. Police also arrested two opposition politicians who happened to be sitting in a nearby coffee shop. They were brutally beaten, photographed, and later released. The youth protest had called for justice for Isaías Cassule and António Alves Kamulingue, both protest activists who were abducted and executed by security agents in May 2012, and Manuel de Carvalho Ganga, an opposition activist who was killed by a presidential guard in November 2013.

Impunity for violent abuses by security agents against protest activists, opposition politicians, and journalists has been common. For example, the presidential guard who killed Manuel Ganga was charged, but at time of writing had not been arrested. On September 1, however, a Luanda court opened a trial against seven suspects—all police and intelligence officials in pretrial detention—for the killing of Cassule and Kamulingue. On September 7, the court suspended the trial alleging incompetence to judge over one of the main suspects, the former head of Luanda's domestic intelligence services. The suspect was promoted by President dos Santos to the rank of general in May. After criticism, the president later withdrew his promotion, and trial sessions resumed on November 18.

On August 14, a Luanda court acquitted the activist Manuel Nito Alves, who had been charged with "outrage" against the president.

Forced Evictions

Angola's laws neither adequately protect people from forced eviction nor enshrine the right to adequate housing. The majority of Angola's urban population lives in informal settlements without legal protection. In 2014, the authorities forcibly evicted an estimated 17,500 people from their homes in Luanda. Most evictions were carried out without prior notice or adequate compensation, and many with excessive use of force by police, armed forces, and government agents.

In January, the authorities demolished 2,000 houses in Luanda's central Chicala-Quilombo neighborhood. The government provided alternative housing to 700 families, and moved 1,200 families—an estimated 6,000 people—to land plots without any infrastructure in Quissama, 80 kilometers away. At time of writing, most were still living in improvised shelters with limited access to social services and drinking water. In two further large-scale, forced evictions in Luanda in April and September—both without prior notice or compensation—authorities left an estimated 7,500 residents homeless.

The authorities also used excessive force in small-scale forced evictions. For example, on June 3, military and police destroyed 57 houses without prior notice in Luanda's Viana municipality, mistreated four residents, and temporarily arrested two men, including Rafael Morais, the coordinator of the housing rights organization SOS Habitat, who lives in the same neighborhood.

More positively, in August the government provided housing to 166 families in Luanda's outskirts—10 years after their forced eviction from the center.

Key International Actors

Angola's oil wealth and military power have made the country an influential power in Africa, attracting business interests from all over the world with very little consideration for the country's poor governance and human rights record.

In 2014, for the second time, Angola won a non-permanent seat on the United Nations Security Council and underwent its second Universal Periodic Review at the UN Human Rights Council in October. In apparent anticipation of such high-level reviews of its human rights performance, in September 2013 Angola signed—but has yet to ratify—four human rights treaties, including the Convention against Torture and its Optional Protocol.

Similarly, in April and May 2014, Angola, for the first time, hosted a session of the African Commission on Human and Peoples' Rights and a civil society forum. However, while the government signalled willingness to engage more constructively with African civil society, Angolan civil society complained about excessive government control of the participants and claimed that the government appeared more interested in using the gathering to promote its image by organizing guided tours in the capital.

Argentina

Argentina's human rights record remains mixed. While many basic freedoms are protected, there still ongoing concerns, including threats to freedom of expression, lack of comprehensive freedom of information legislation, police abuse, poor prison conditions, barriers to accessing reproductive health products and services, and failure to protect indigenous rights.

Argentina continues to make significant progress regarding LGBT rights and prosecuting officials for abuses committed during the country's "Dirty War" (1976-1983), although trials have been subject to delays.

Freedom of Expression

High fines and criminal prosecutions in specific cases have undermined the right to freely publish information of public interest. In 2011, the Ministry of Commerce imposed a fine of 500,000 pesos (approximately US$ 125,000) on 11 economists and consulting firms for publishing unofficial inflation statistics challenging the accuracy of official ones. One of the economists, Graciela Bevacqua, was subject to two fines, and was also criminally investigated at the request of the former secretary of commerce for allegedly "defrauding commerce and industry." As of November 2014, the criminal case along with one of the fines against Bevacqua remained pending.

In May, journalist Juan Pablo Suárez was charged with "incitement of collective violence" with the intention of "terrorizing the population,"the first time prosecutors had invoked a 2011 law allowing enhanced penalties for certain "terrorism" crimes. Suárez, who works for an online news outlet, had published information on police strikes in Santiago del Estero province. The aggravated penalty was dropped following strong public backlash, but the case against Suárez continued at time of writing.

In 2011, journalist Juan Alberto Gaspari was fined 50,000 pesos (approximately $12,500) for criticizing a public official in Mendoza. According to Gaspari, the public official's father, who was "disappeared" during Argentina's military dictatorship, had not been the legitimate owner of land. As of November 2014, an appeal remained pending before the Supreme Court.

The absence of transparent criteria for using government funds at the federal level, and in some provinces to purchase media advertisements, creates a risk of discrimination against media outlets that criticize government officials. In two 2007 and 2011 rulings, the Supreme Court found that while media companies have no right to receive public advertising contracts, government officials may not apply discriminatory criteria when deciding where to place advertisements.

Argentina does not have a national law ensuring public access to information held by government bodies. An existing presidential decree on the matter only applies to the federal executive branch, and some provincial governments have adopted regulations for their jurisdictions.

In 2009, Congress approved a law to regulate the broadcast media that includes provisions to increase plurality in the media. In 2013, the Supreme Court established clear parameters regarding how the law should be implemented to protect free expression. However, the federal authority in charge of implementing the law has failed to ensure a diverse range of perspectives in state-run media programming. In 2014, it unilaterally adopted a plan to force Argentina's largest media conglomerate, the Clarin Group, to comply with the law's limits on broadcasting outlets ownership, after rejecting the company's proposal on how to do so.

Transnational Justice

At time of writing, no one has been convicted for the 1994 bombing of the Argentine Israelite Mutual Association (AMIA) in Buenos Aires that killed 85 people and injured over 300. From the investigation's outset, judicial corruption and political obstruction hindered criminal investigations and prosecutions.

In January 2013, Argentina and Iran, which was suspected of ordering the attack, signed a memorandum of understanding (MOU) to create an international commission of jurists to review evidence and question Iranian suspects identified by Argentina. In May 2014, an Argentine federal court ruled the MOU unconstitutional. At time of writing, the ruling was on appeal and the MOU has not been implemented.

Confronting Past Abuses

Several cases of human rights violations committed during Argentina's military dictatorship (1976-1983) were reopened in 2003 after Congress annulled existing amnesty laws. Subsequently, the Supreme Court ruled that the amnesty laws were unconstitutional, and federal judges struck down pardons favoring former officials convicted of, or facing trial for, human rights violations.

As of August 2014, 121 trials had been conducted for crimes against humanity originating from the dictatorship, resulting in 503 convictions. The Center of Legal and Social Studies (CELS) has reported that 42 people have been acquitted during the trials, and another 1,611 suspects are under investigation.

Given the large number of victims, suspects, and cases, prosecutors and judges face challenges in bringing those responsible to justice while also respecting due process rights of the accused. Other concerns include significant trial delays, the failure to capture two convicted military officers who escaped in July 2013, and the unresolved fate of Jorge Julio López, a former torture victim who disappeared in 2006 a day before he was due to attend the trial of one of his torturers.

Argentina has made significant progress in identifying children of the disappeared who were illegally appropriated during the dictatorship, and connecting them to their biological families. In July 2014, the National Bank of Genetic Data identified the grandson of Estela de Carlotto, the founder of Grandmothers of Plaza de Mayo. As of August, 115 grandchildren had been found. At time of writing, a legal challenge to a 2009 law that would limit collection of DNA samples to cases of the dictatorship was pending before the Supreme Court.

In December 2013, César Milani, head of the armed forces, was promoted to army chief of staff, despite being under criminal investigation for the 1976 disappearance of a soldier in Tucumán province, and the torture of a civilian in La Rioja province in 1977.

Police Abuse

Police abuse remains a serious problem, despite a 2011 commitment by authorities in at least 19 provinces not to resort to excessive use of force when dealing with public protests. In May 2014, 22 people were injured after local police forces dispersed a workers' demonstration in the province of Tucumán, using rubber bullets and police batons with excessive force, according to CELS. In June, police in the province of Chaco fired rubber bullets at demonstrators and beat and detained protesters, leaving more than 100 people injured.

Prison Conditions

Overcrowding, ill-treatment by prison guards, inadequate facilities, and inmate violence continue to be serious problems in prisons. According to the National Penitentiary Office (Procuración Penitenciaria de la Nación), an official body created by Congress, there were 88 deaths, including 41 violent ones, in federal prisons between January 2013 and October 2014. The office also documented 724 cases of torture or ill-treatment in federal prisons in 2013, and 520 in the first 10 months of 2014.

Indigenous Rights

Indigenous people in Argentina face obstacles in accessing justice, land, education, healthcare, and other basic services.

Existing laws require the government to perform a survey of land occupied by indigenous communities by November 2017, before which date authorities cannot lawfully evict communities. In June 2014, eight human rights organizations filed an amicus brief before the Supreme Court, arguing that a land survey in Formosa province had failed to guarantee the rights of members of the Potae Napocna Navogoh indigenous community.

Reproductive Rights

Abortion is illegal in Argentina, with limited exceptions, and women and girls face numerous obstacles accessing reproductive health products and services, such as contraception, voluntary sterilization procedures, and abortion after rape or if the health or life of the woman is at risk (the few circumstances in which abortion is not punished). These barriers mean that women and girls may face unwanted or health or life-threatening pregnancies, and are subject to criminal prosecution for seeking abortions.

In June 2014, after seeking medical attention for abdominal pain, a woman in the province of Jujuy was arrested and charged with homicide based on suspicion that she had had an abortion. The woman, who later confessed under coercion that she had an abortion after being raped, remained incarcerated at time of writing, along with two co-workers who were also charged with homicide for their alleged participation in the procedure.

In a landmark ruling in March 2012, the Supreme Court determined that prior judicial authorization was unnecessary for abortion after rape and urged provincial governments to ensure access to legal abortions. As of March 2014, more than half of Argentina's 23 provinces still had not adopted protocols that met the court's requirements, according to local groups.

Sexual Orientation and Gender Identity

In 2010, Argentina became the first Latin American country to legalize same-sex marriage. The Civil Marriage Law allows same-sex couples to enter into civil marriages and provides for equal rights and the legal protections of marriage afforded to opposite-sex couples including, among others, adoption rights and pension benefits. Since then, nearly 10,000 same-sex couples have married nationwide.

In 2012, the landmark Gender Identity Law established the right of individuals over the age of 18 to choose their gender identity, undergo gender reassignment, and revise official documents without any prior judicial or medical approval. Surgical and hormonal reassignment procedures are covered as part of public and private health insurance.

Key International Actors

A December 2013 report of the Committee on Enforced Disappearances, the body that oversees the enforcement of the Convention on the Protection of All Persons From Enforced Disappearances, recognized that Argentina's enforced disappearances legislation is largely in line with its international obligations, but noted with concern that insufficient statistical data is available to assess its compliance with international norms.

In April, the United Nations Committee on the Rights of Persons with Disabilities found that Argentine authorities had failed to ensure that a prisoner with disabilities had equal access to prison facilities and services, and underscored the state's obligation to take steps to rectify this situation and prevent similar violations in other cases.

Prompted by its debt crisis, Argentina pushed for an international resolution on sovereign debt restructuring, arguing that it was necessary for governments to fulfill certain rights obligations. In September, the UN General Assembly adopted one, establishing a multilateral framework to assist countries facing such restructuring. As a member of the UN Human Rights Council, Argentina supported UN action to put human rights violations in North Korea, Sri Lanka, Belarus, Iran, the Occupied Palestinian Territories, and Syria under close scrutiny. Argentina has been a leading supporter of international efforts to better protect schools through the process to develop and implement the *Lucens Guidelines to Protect Schools and Universities from Military Use during Armed Conflict.*

In September 2014, Argentina was one of the co-sponsors of an important UN Human Rights Council resolution on combating violence and discrimination based on sexual orientation and gender identity. The resolution called on the high commissioner for human rights to update a 2012 report on violence and discrimination, with a view to sharing best practices to overcome these abuses.

Armenia

Armenia's human rights record remained uneven in 2014. Authorities continued to interfere with peaceful protests. Torture and ill-treatment in custody remained a problem, and investigations are ineffective, even when opened. Journalists continued to face pressure and violence. Although changes to alternative service to compulsory military service garnered praise, serious abuses in the army persist. Local groups documented forced psychiatric hospitalization. Violence and discrimination based on sexual orientation and gender identity are serious problems. The government has yet to lift unnecessary restrictions on access to pain medications for people with terminal illnesses.

Freedom of Assembly

Authorities interfered with free assembly throughout the year. According to human rights groups, police in the capital, Yerevan, detained at least 70 activists in the first half of 2014 during peaceful protests on pension reform, environmental concerns, utility prices, and other issues. Most people detained were released within a day; some faced administrative fines.

Three Yerevan metro employees alleged they were fired after participating in a February protest about controversial pension reforms and, at time of writing, were suing for reinstatement and lost wages. During a series of protests in June, Yerevan police detained activists protesting the demolition of the Afrikyan House, a historical monument. On June 23, Yerevan police detained 27 people protesting increased electricity tariffs. The Armenian ombudsperson found the police actions disproportionate. Authorities opened an investigation into police conduct and suspended several policemen pending inquiry.

Local human rights activists consider the prosecution and conviction of controversial political opposition leader Shant Harutyunyan and 13 of his supporters to be politically motivated. Authorities arrested the activists in November 2013 after clashes with police during an attempted march to the presidential administration building in Yerevan. In October, a Yerevan court convicted them of violence against the authorities and sentenced them to prison terms, ranging from one to seven years. Harutyunyan and activist Vardan Vardanyan allege police beat them immediately following their detention; the authorities refused to investigate.

In April, authorities charged Harutyunyan's 15-year-old son with disorderly conduct for attempting to interfere with the arrest of his father; he was given a suspended four-year jail term in October.

During the first hearing of the activists' trial in June, authorities denied journalists and family members access to the courtroom, falsely claiming overcrowding.

Torture and Ill-Treatment in Custody

Local human rights activists report the continued use of torture and ill-treatment in custody, including in police stations and pretrial detention to coerce confessions, as well as in prisons and other facilities. Some victims file complaints; many decline, fearing retaliation and further ill-treatment. The authorities do not always conduct thorough and impartial investigations.

According to the Armenian Helsinki Association, authorities have refused to investigate credible allegations that Yerevan police beat, pulled the hair of, and threatened to harm relatives of Aik Agamalyan, 16, to coerce a confession to an April 2013 murder. Agamalyan's trial was ongoing at time of writing. Similarly, authorities and a Vanadzor court have refused to act on complaints by Karen Kurngurtsev that police ill-treated him after detaining him in October 2013 on murder charges. Kurngurtsev denies the charges; his trial was ongoing at time of writing.

After an April 4 visit, a public prison monitoring group reported that two inmates at the Artik Penitentiary alleged Gyumri police had ill-treated them in separate incidents to force confessions, including with beatings, kicking, and threats of rape. The investigation was ongoing at time of writing.

On June 12, police detained and beat Hayk Kyureghyan, who demonstrated outside a Yerevan court to support Harutyunyan and other activists on trial. After extensive media coverage of Kyureghyan's allegations of ill-treatment, authorities opened an investigation, which was pending at time of writing.

Freedom of Expression

Media pluralism remains limited. Media nongovernmental organizations (NGOs) condemned a draft law that would hold media outlets responsible for libelous or insulting comments made in public forums, including social media, by anonymous or unidentified users.

The Committee to Protect Freedom of Expression reported that in the first half of 2014 journalists and media outlets continued to face threats and spurious law suits, and documented at least five incidents of physical violence against journalists.

For example, during the detentions of opposition activists on February 12, police seized video cameras from, and briefly detained, Ani and Sarkis Gevorgyan, siblings and journalists with the *Chorrord Ishkhanutyun* newspaper and *iLur.am* news site, respectively. While in custody, police erased their cameras, slapped Ani Gevorgyan, and seized her phone. Following a complaint by Gevorgyan, authorities opened a criminal investigation but concluded it in June, citing absence of a crime. Gevorgyan appealed. Organization for Security and Co-operation in Europe (OSCE) Representative on Freedom of the Media Dunja Mijatović expressed concern about the incident.

On June 24, journalists and others waited outside a Yerevan police department for the release of activists detained earlier that day. As police dispersed the crowd they also attacked several journalists. Police hit Ani Gevorgyan and Arpi Makhsudian of CivilNet.TV and smashed GALA TV cameraman Paylak Fahradian's laptop. Police detained Sarkis Gevorgyan. Ani and Sarkis Gevorgyan filed a complaint; the investigation was ongoing at time of writing.

On June 26, a Yerevan court ordered *Hraparak* newspaper and Ilur.am news portal to disclose their sources as part of a criminal investigation involving a high-level police official. The OSCE representative on freedom of the media expressed concern about the ruling's possible "chilling effect" and emphasized journalists' right to protect sources as a key principle of investigative journalism and freedom of expression.

Alternative Military Service Reform and Army Abuses

According to the religious freedom monitoring group Forum 18, for the first time since 1993 there are no Jehovah's Witnesses imprisoned for conscientious objection to military service. A June fact-finding mission report by the Parliamentary Assembly of the Council of Europe (PACE) found that 2013 changes to the alternative service law corrected long-standing problems and that most religious and social groups now accept the terms of alternative service.

However, other concerns related to the army persist. The Helsinki Citizens' Assembly-Vanadzor received 42 complaints following the 2013 winter and 2014 summer call-ups about inadequate medical examinations and medical care for new conscripts, resulting in some conscripts with serious health problems being drafted. In some cases, conscripts with health problems were not referred to additional testing, or additional tests were only undertaken as a formality. Activists remain concerned about the thoroughness, transparency, and impartiality of investigations into non-combat deaths that are officially ruled accidents or suicides but where there may be evidence of violence.

Disability Rights

A Helsinki Citizen's Assembly-Vanadzor office study of five state-run psychiatric hospitals based on over 300 interviews with medical staff and patients found that some people with actual or perceived psychosocial disabilities are confined in institutions without their informed consent. Under the civil code, a court can declare an individual as "mentally incompetent" without the person in question appearing. No independent mechanism exists to ensure that persons with psychosocial disabilities are not arbitrarily detained in psychiatric institutions.

A deputy ombudsman from the ombudsman's office stated that the office frequently receives complaints about forced institutionalization in psychiatric hospitals and violence by staff, including beatings, use of restraints, and sedation.

Palliative Care

Armenia continues to discuss reforming its complicated and time-consuming prescription and procurement procedures for opioid medications. However, these shortcomings continue to obstruct the delivery of adequate palliative care, condemning most terminally ill patients to unnecessary suffering. Although morphine is a safe, effective, and inexpensive way to improve the lives of terminally ill people, oral morphine is unavailable in Armenia, and tight police controls on injectable opioids and restrictive policies on procurement, prescription, and disbursement violate many of the World Health Organization's recommendations on palliative care.

Minority Rights

Local lesbian, gay, bisexual, and transgender (LGBT) activists reported that LGBT people continue to face discrimination, harassment, and physical violence. Hate speech against LGBT people, including by public officials, remains a serious issue. Gender identity and sexual orientation are not included in anti-discrimination or hate speech laws, limiting legal recourse for many crimes against LGBT people.

Iravunq newspaper published several online articles calling for LGBT people and organizations working to protect them to be excluded from public life and for their families to shun them. A May 17 article included a "blacklist" of 60 people with links to their social media pages. Several people named in the article requested a retraction, but the paper refused. Sixteen people filed lawsuits for damage to honor and dignity, but a court rejected their claims in October.

In December 2013, a court upheld the Education Ministry's refusal, on privacy grounds, to respond to an information request filed by a nongovernmental organization regarding 20 teachers allegedly fired from public schools for holding minority religious views. Media had reported on the dismissals in 2012, citing the ministry's claim that the teachers had been proselytizing in schools.

Key International Actors

Following its review of Armenia in May, the United Nations Committee on Economic, Social, and Cultural Rights underscored concerns about corruption, the lack of judicial independence, and need for a comprehensive anti-discrimination framework.

The PACE fact-finding mission report noted the improved political climate and progress toward Armenia's fulfilment of its Council of Europe (CoE) membership obligations but also highlighted serious shortcomings, including the lack of judicial independence, abuses in the military, domestic violence, and hostility toward religious minorities and LGBT people.

In its March 'European Neighborhood' progress report on Armenia, the European Union noted concerns with implementation of legislation, poor prison conditions, and the "alarming" prevalence of domestic and gender-based violence. The report also found that the definition of torture does not comply with international standards.

A July joint statement by the UN, EU, OSCE, and CoE commended Armenia for adopting a Human Rights Action Plan as an opportunity for meaningful accountability and human rights progress.

Australia

Australia has a solid record of protecting civil and political rights, with robust institutions and a vibrant press and civil society that act as a check on government power. The government's failure to respect international standards protecting asylum seekers and refugees, however, continues to take a heavy human toll and undermines Australia's ability to call for stronger human rights protections abroad. In 2014, Australia introduced new overbroad counterterrorism measures that would infringe on freedoms of expression and movement. The government has also done too little to address indigenous rights and disability rights.

Asylum Seekers and Refugees

To deter boat arrivals of unauthorized migrants, the government has continued its harsh policy of transferring all asylum seekers who arrive by boat to other countries for processing and resettlement. In 2014, the government concluded negotiations with Cambodia to accept refugees from Nauru for resettlement, ignoring concerns about safety and the lack of capacity of the Cambodian government.

As of October 31, 2014, 1,056 men were detained on Manus Island, Papua New Guinea, and 1,095 men, women, and children were detained on Nauru. At time of writing, only 10 of the Manus Island detainees had received final refugee status determinations. As of October 31, 2014, 261 of the Nauru detainees had been determined to be refugees and released into the community; 72 were denied refugee status.

The United Nations Refugee Agency (UNHCR) has criticized Australia's offshore detention policy as "return-oriented." The detention centers are overcrowded and dirty. Asylum claims are not processed in a fair, transparent, or expedient manner, with significant cost to detainees' physical and mental health.

According to media reports, gay asylum seekers detained on Manus Island fear persecution and sexual assault. They also fear resettlement in Papua New Guinea, where consensual adult same-sex relations are criminalized.

The government has offered cash payments of thousands of dollars to entice asylum seekers to return home.

In February 2014, the Australian Human Rights Commission launched a national inquiry into the approximately 1,000 children in immigration detention. Staff working at detention centers gave evidence that conditions were substandard, unsafe, and inappropriate.

As of October 31, 2014, 2,693 people were in immigration detention on Australian territory. About 50 refugees are being detained indefinitely based on adverse security assessments and many have been in detention for over four years. In May, the government passed the Migration Amendment Bill, further strengthening Australian Secret Intelligence Organization's (ASIO) power to administer adverse security assessments through a secretive process that is not subject to judicial review.

Immigration authorities use "enhanced screening" techniques whereby immigration officials conduct cursory interviews to determine asylum claims. More than 3,500 asylum seekers, over 99 percent of whom are from Sri Lanka, have been screened under this procedure, with no access to legal representation or right to appeal. Of the Sri Lankan asylum seekers, 42 percent were screened out and 32 percent were screened in, but no outcome was given in the remainder of the cases.

In June 2014, Australian custom officials separately intercepted two vessels in the Indian Ocean carrying Sri Lankans bound for Australia. After cursory screening interviews at sea, customs officials handed over all 41 asylum seekers aboard the first vessel to the Sri Lankan navy who returned them to Sri Lanka.

The High Court issued an interim injunction to prevent the return of the second vessel. After almost a month of detention at sea and failed attempts to send the asylum seekers to India, the Immigration department eventually sent all 157 Sri Lankan Tamil asylum seekers to Nauru for processing.

In September 2014, incoming UN High Commissioner for Human Rights Zeid Ra'ad Al-Hussein stated that Australia's policies are "leading to a chain of human rights violations, including arbitrary detention and possible torture following return to home countries."

Indigenous People's Rights

The government controversially established an indigenous advisory council while defunding the Congress of Australia's First Peoples. The government has taken some steps towards a possible referendum on changing the constitution to recognize indigenous Australians.

While indigenous Australians account for only 3 percent of Australia's population, they account for 27 percent of Australia's prison population. In part because they are disproportionately represented in the criminal justice system, indigenous Australians are more likely to face stigma and discrimination in employment.

While some health and socioeconomic indicators are improving for indigenous Australians, they still on average live 10-12 years less than non-indigenous Australians, have an infant mortality rate almost two times higher, and continue to die at alarmingly high rates from treatable and preventable conditions such as diabetes and respiratory illnesses.

Disability Rights

In April, the Australian Human Rights Commission found that inadequate safeguards and poor access to support services leave many people with disabilities without adequate legal or social protection when they come into contact with the criminal justice system.

Forty-five percent of people with disabilities live near or below the poverty line. People with disabilities are also disproportionately at risk of violence in the community and in institutional settings, and are more likely to be jailed. Some are deemed unfit to stand trial based on prejudicial assessments of their competency to give evidence and then indefinitely detained in prisons, psychiatric facilities, or other highly restrictive places of detention without appropriate review mechanisms.

In its 2014 Federal Budget, the government committed to fully funding the rollout of the new National Disability Insurance Scheme but announced changes to the Disability Support Pension which will likely result in many people with disabilities being moved to significantly lower welfare payments. The government also effectively abolished the disability discrimination commissioner position at the Human Rights Commission, leaving people with disabilities without a full-time advocate.

Sexual Orientation and Gender Identity

Despite increasing public support for same-sex marriage in Australia, marriage remains restricted to heterosexual relationships in accordance with the federal Marriage Act. Some states or territories have moved to develop laws recognizing same-sex marriage, but only one territory actually enacted laws. In December 2013 the High Court ruled that the laws recognizing same-sex marriage were inconsistent with federal legislation and were therefore invalid.

Freedom of Expression

In July 2014, the government revised its agreements with community legal centers to prohibit such centers from using federal funds for law reform or advocacy efforts.

In August, bowing to pressure from ethnic and community groups, the government dropped its proposed repeal of section 18C of the Racial Discrimination Act, which makes it unlawful for a person to commit an act that is likely to offend, insult, humiliate, or intimidate someone on the basis of race, color, or national or ethnic origin.

Also in August, the government announced the introduction of a range of new counterterrorism provisions in response to the threat of "home-grown terrorism." The law introduces an overly broad new offense of "advocating terrorism" and extends use of control orders and preventative detention. It also makes it a criminal offense to travel to "declared areas" abroad unless the travel is for a legitimate reason, which overly restricts freedom of movement.

The government has also proposed additional measures that would force telecommunications companies to retain metadata for a period of two years so Australian intelligence organizations can access the data.

The National Security Legislation Amendment Act, passed in October 2014, grants Australian Security Intelligence Organization officials immunity from civil and criminal prosecution for acts committed in the course of security operations. The legislation also makes it an offense for intelligence staff or contractors to disclose information relating to "special intelligence operations." Journalists who disclose information relating to a "special intelligence operation" face penalties of up to 10 years prison. The legislation does not provide any "public interest" exception to this offense.

Foreign Policy

Australia held a two-year rotating seat on the UN Security Council starting in 2013. In 2014, it used its seat to press for resolutions on Syria, call for the provision of humanitarian aid, and call for unfettered access to the MH17 Malaysian Air crash site in Ukraine.

In January 2014, the government announced that it was cutting its foreign aid budget by more than $A600 million (US$526 million). Its foreign aid priorities are the Asia-Pacific Region, economic empowerment, and private sector partnerships. Indonesia and Papua New Guinea remain the top two aid recipients.

The government held closed-door human rights dialogues with China and Vietnam in 2014 but failed to back up these dialogues with public statements on rights in high-level visits.

Besides trade and security, a large driver of the Australian government's foreign policy is its single-minded focus on ensuring that all asylum seekers or refugees are processed at offshore facilities. The government has muted its criticism of authoritarian governments in Sri Lanka and Cambodia in recent years, apparently in hopes of winning the support of such governments for its refugee policies.

In March 2014, the UN Human Rights Council in Geneva voted overwhelmingly in favor of a resolution establishing an international inquiry into human rights abuses in Sri Lanka. Australia did not co-sponsor the resolution as it had done in previous years. Instead, Foreign Minister Julie Bishop said that she was not convinced that a resolution calling for "a separate, internationally-led investigation without the cooperation of the Sri Lankan government is the best way forward" and that the resolution did not adequately recognize the "significant progress taken by the Sri Lankan government to promote economic growth." Australia is bidding for a seat on the Human Rights Council in 2018.

Azerbaijan

The Azerbaijani government escalated repression against its critics, marking a dramatic deterioration in its already poor rights record. The authorities convicted or imprisoned at least 33 human rights defenders, political and civil activists, journalists, and bloggers on politically motivated charges, prompting others to flee the country or go into hiding. Authorities froze the bank accounts of independent civic groups and their leaders, impeded their work by refusing to register foreign grants, and imposed foreign travel bans on some. Many of those detained complained of ill-treatment in police custody. Many organizations, including several leading rights groups, were forced to cease activities.

The crackdown continued even as Azerbaijan in May took over the six-month rotating chairmanship of the Committee of Ministers of the Council of Europe, Europe's foremost human rights body.

While criticizing the increasing crackdown on civil society groups, Azerbaijan's international partners failed to make full use of their relationships with the government to secure rights improvements.

Prosecuting Government Critics

Authorities used a range of spurious charges—including narcotics and weapons possession, hooliganism, incitement, and even treason—to imprison critics. These included several leading human rights defenders such as Leyla Yunus, director of the Institute for Peace and Democracy, and her husband, Arif Yunus, arrested in July and August, and charged with treason, tax evasion, and illegal entrepreneurship. They also included Rasul Jafarov, Human Rights Club director, and Intigam Aliyev, head of the Legal Education Society—both of whom were arrested in August and charged with tax evasion, illegal entrepreneurship, and abuse of authority. All were in pretrial custody at time of writing.

In May, a court convicted eight youth opposition movement activists who were arrested in 2013 on drug and other charges related to an alleged plan to instigate violence at a peaceful protest, and sentenced them to prison terms ranging from six to eight years; the president pardoned two of them in October after they wrote letters of repentence. At trial, at least three said they were beaten in police custody, but the authorities failed to effectively investigate.

In March, a court sentenced Ilgar Mammadov, a prominent political analyst and chairman of the opposition group REAL, and Tofig Yagublu, deputy chair of the opposition Musavat party and a columnist with the opposition daily *Yeni Musavat,* to seven and five years in prison, respectively. Both were found guilty of inciting violence. In May, the European Court of Human Rights found that the authorities had arrested Mammadov "to silence or punish [him] for criticizing the Government."

In January, a court sentenced Yadigar Sadigov, a Musavat advisor, to six years in prison on spurious hooliganism charges. An appeals court reduced the sentence to four years. In August, authorities arrested Murad Adilov, an opposition Popular Front Party activist, on spurious drug charges. Adilov's lawyer claimed that his client had been beaten in police custody. Authorities failed to effectively investigate. Also in August, police arrested Khagani Mammad, a Musavat activist, on criminal hooliganism charges after he complained of being attacked by two unknown women in a street. Both were in pretrial custody at time of writing.

Freedom of Media

At least 10 journalists, bloggers, and social media activists were arrested or convicted in 2014 on spurious charges in apparent retaliation for critical and investigative journalism.

In April, authorities arrested Rauf Mirgadirov, an outspoken Ankara-based correspondent for two independent Azerbaijani newspapers, after he was unlawfully deported from Turkey. At time of writing, Mirgadirov was in pretrial custody on espionage charges stemming from his participation in people-to-people diplomacy between Armenia and Azerbaijan.

In May, a court convicted Parviz Hashimli, editor of a news website and a reporter for the opposition daily *Bizim Yol*, on smuggling and illegal weapons possession and sentenced him to eight years in prison.

In August, police arrested Seymur Hazi, a columnist with the opposition daily *Azadlig*, on spurious hooliganism charges after an unidentified man assaulted him near his house. A court remanded him to pretrial custody.

In 2014, authorities arrested or convicted at least six Facebook and other social media activists on bogus drug possession charges. They were: Abdul Abilov, Omar Mammadov, Elsever Murselli, Ilham Muradov, and Faraj and Siraj Karimli. All had large social media followers and administered Facebook pages that criticized the government.

Courts sentenced Abilov, Mammadov, and Murselli to between five and five-and-a-half years in prison, while the others remained in pretrial custody at time of writing. None had access to a lawyer of his choosing during initial interrogations or remand hearings, and at least three complained of ill-treatment in police custody, which authorities failed to effectively investigate. An appeals court reduced Murselli's sentence to two years after he wrote a letter of apology, and was released in October following a presidential pardon.

Authorities repeatedly interrogated Khadija Ismayilova, an outspoken investigative journalist reporting on government corruption, including the businesses of the ruling family, as a witness to an investigation into leaking state secrets. In October, authorities imposed a foreign travel ban on Ismayilova without providing any legal grounds for it. Pro-government media continued the public smear campaign against her that they had begun in 2012.

The opposition paper *Azadlig* continued to face financial constraints due to mounting defamation claims brought by officials, frozen bank accounts, and government-imposed restrictions on distribution.

Freedom of Association

In February, President Ilham Aliyev signed into law amendments imposing additional restrictions and requirements on nongovernmental groups (NGOs). Most are minor but can serve as grounds for penalties, official warnings, and eventually temporary or permanent closure. The amendments also introduced new administrative offenses, higher financial and criminal penalties for other minor infractions, and new grounds for authorities to deny registration and to temporarily or permanently close local and international groups.

In November, Aliyev signed into law further restrictive amendments requiring government licensing of all foreign donors and approval of each funded project by the relevant authorities.

Following prosecutors' requests, courts have frozen bank accounts of at least 50 organizations and in some cases accounts of staff, as part of ongoing criminal investigations against several foreign donors and organizations. Tax offices audited many of those groups, and the prosecutor's office repeatedly interrogated their staff. At least three groups closed, and numerous others had to halt operations as they could no longer make bank transactions. These problems forced dozens of groups involved in an international natural resource transparency initiative to suspend operations.

In August, police searched the office of the Institute for Reporters Freedom and Safety (IRFS), a leading media monitoring group, confiscated computers and reports, and sealed the office. Authorities repeatedly questioned IRFS employees and prevented its director, Emin Huseynov, from leaving the country. He remained in hiding at time of writing.

Also in August, authorities confiscated computers and documents of the Legal Education Society and sealed the office. Headed by Intigam Aliyev, the group had brought hundreds of cases against Azerbaijan to the European Court of Human Rights. The Prosecutor's Office also sealed the office of Leyla Yunus's organization.

Torture and Ill-Treatment

Torture and ill-treatment continue with impunity. In September, the United Nations Subcommitee on Torture suspended its visit to Azerbaijan, citing official obstruction in visiting places of detention. In May, police arrested opposition activist Kemale Benenyarli at a protest rally following the conviction of activists from "NIDA," a youth organization. She alleged that police struck her several times on the head while questioning her. According to her lawyer, Benenyarli sustained several bruises on her head and experienced headaches and vomiting as a result. Interior Ministry denied the allegations and failed to investigate.

Several youth activists arrested in 2014 claimed they were beaten, harassed, and forced to sign incriminating confessions while in police custody. They also complained of undue restrictions in accessing their lawyers. For example, blogger Abdul Abilov was able to meet his lawyer only six days after his November 2013 arrest and alleged that he had been punched, insulted, and threatened with further violence until he agreed to sign incriminating testimony. Authorities failed to conclusively investigate.

Human Rights Defenders

In addition to the cases described above, in March, police in Ganja arrested Hasan Huseynli, a social rights campaigner and head of an independent group, on hooliganism charges after an unknown person attacked him. In July, a court convicted him and sentenced him to six years in prison. Months before his arrest, police and local authorities had warned Huseynli to stop co-operating with foreign donors. Huseynli was released in October, following a presidential pardon.

In May, a court convicted Anar Mammadli, chair of an independent election monitoring group in Azerbaijan, of tax evasion, illegal entrepreneurship, and abuse of office, and sentenced him to five-and-a-half years in prison. Together with Mammadli, the court convicted Bashir Suleymanli, the group's executive director, and Elnur Mammadov, head of one of the group's partner organizations, and sentenced them to three years and six months and two years on probation, respectively.

In April and May, police arrested Emil Mammadli, and Tofig Gasimov, head and member, respectively, of an independent group in southeastern Azerbaijan that exposed allegations of local corruption. Both were accused of extortion. In September, a court handed them a two-year suspended sentence.

In August, unidentified assailants attacked Ilgar Nasibov, a journalist and human rights defender with the Nakhchivan Resource Center, the only independent rights group in the region. The attackers beat Nasibov unconscious and ransacked the group's office. He sustained a concussion, multiple broken bones, and temporary loss of vision in one eye. Police claimed that Nasibov was injured after brawling with his friend, Farid Asgarov, which Nasibov denied. Police arrested Asgarov, who pleaded guilty at a trial. Although Nasibov insisted there was more than one assailant, he agreed to reconcile with Asgarov and did not pursue the case further. The court dismissed the cases against both men in November.

Isa Shahmarly, former chair of the Free (Azad) LGBT group, hanged himself with a rainbow flag in his Baku apartment in late January 2014, writing in a note that Azerbaijan society was "not for him."

Key International Actors

The European Union, United States, and other international and regional actors and institutions expressed concern about politically motivated prosecutions, but did not impose concrete consequences for Azerbaijan's rapidly deteriorating human rights record.

Following the arrests of prominent rights defenders, three United Nations human rights experts in August issued a joint statement condemning the prosecutions and urged the government "to show leadership and reverse the trend of repression." Responding to the same, EU High Representative Catherine Ashton and Commissioner Stefan Fule jointly criticized Baku for "systematically restricting the space for public discourse and civil society in Azerbaijan." In September, the European Parliament adopted a resolution stressing that the EU's closer ties with Azerbaijan should be conditioned on the release of imprisoned human rights defenders and calling for an "end to repression and intimidation of NGOs."

The Organization for Security and Co-operation in Europe's special representative on media freedom, and the Council of Europe's (CoE) secretary general and human rights commissioner also spoke out about the arrests, with the latter calling on the authorities to release "all those who are detained because of the views they expressed." In June, the CoE's Parliamentary Assembly appointed a rapporteur on the issue of political prisoners in Azerbaijan.

The Extractive Industries Transparency Initiative (EITI)—which brings together governments, companies, and NGOs to foster open public debate in resource-rich countries about how oil, gas, and mining revenues are used—decided to require Azerbaijan to undergo an early review, by January 2015, of its compliance with the group's membership rules.

The US State Department and the embassy in Baku issued several statements on related issues during 2014, flagging concerns about restrictions on freedom of expression and assembly and politically motivated imprisonment.

Bahrain

In 2014, the main opposition party continued to refuse to participate in the national dialogue process to protest authorities prosecuting some of its senior members and, with other opposition parties, boycotted November's elections in protest at an unfair electoral system.

Bahrain's courts convicted and imprisoned peaceful dissenters and failed to hold officials accountable for torture and other serious rights violations. The high rate of successful prosecutions on vague terrorism charges, imposition of long prison sentences, and failure to address the security forces' use of lethal and apparently disproportionate force all reflected the weakness of the justice system and its lack of independence.

Human rights activists and members of the political opposition continued to face arrest and prosecution, and the government invested itself with further powers to arbitrarily strip critics of their citizenship and the rights that attach to it.

Judicial System

Bahraini courts sentenced more than 200 defendants to long prison sentences, including at least 70 for life, on terrorism or national security charges.

The number of prosecutions, the often vague nature of the charges, the high rate of convictions, and the length of the sentences imposed raised serious due process concerns. Bahrain's civilian criminal courts failed to provide impartial justice and frequently convicted defendants on terrorism charges for acts that amount to legitimate exercise of their rights to freedom of expression and association.

In 2013, for example, an appeals court concluded that a lower court had been right to convict Abdul Wahab Hussain, an opposition leader, on terrorism charges and sentence him to life imprisonment because he had founded a group dedicated to establishing a republic in Bahrain. The same appeals court also upheld the terrorism convictions and life sentences for Hassan Mushaima and Abdul Jalil al-Singace, members of the unlicensed opposition group Al Haq, because they had participated in meetings of the group that Hussain founded and possessed "publications advocating for the group." The court declared that while unlawful means, such as the use of force, are required for an act to qualify as terrorism, such force "need not necessarily be military [askari]," because "moral pressure" could result in terrorism.

Fifty individuals were convicted on charges of establishing and joining a group known as the February 14 Coalition with the aim of "sowing chaos in the country, committing crimes of violence and sedition, attacking public and private property, intimidating citizens and harming national unity." The court found that only one of the 50 defendants had committed an identifiable act of violence—assaulting a policeman during his arrest at his home, causing "cut and scratch injuries" to the officer. The defendants received sentences ranging from 5 to 15 years in prison.

Excessive Use of Force and Lack of Accountability

Security forces fatally shot at least three people in circumstances indicating that they used excessive force. Bahraini authorities and courts have rarely held members of the security forces accountable for unlawfully using force against protestors and detainees.

In January, security forces shot and killed Fadhel Abbas Muslim Marhoon. Authorities said police officers shot him in self-defense as he drove an "oncoming car" towards them, but photographs of his body appeared to contradict this version and show that he had sustained a gunshot wound to the back of his head. In February, security forces shot Abdulaziz al-Abar at a funeral procession; surgeons removed shotgun pellets from his brain, but he died on May 18.

In May, security forces shot and killed Sayed Mahmood, 14, after police dispersed a funeral protest. A hospital death certificate, three witness accounts, images of the wound, and a forensic pathologist's opinion indicated that his death had resulted from unlawful use of lethal force by security forces, to whom he had posed no threat when he was shot.

In 2011, the Bahrain Independent Commission of Inquiry (BICI), appointed to investigate official conduct during anti-government protests that year, concluded that "police units used force against civilians in a manner that was both unnecessary and disproportionate."

In response to one of the BICI's recommendations, the government established the Office of the Ombudsman within the Interior Ministry "to ensure compliance with professional standards of policing set forth in the Code of Conduct for the Police" and to report misconduct to the ministry and any criminal acts to the public prosecutor. The government created a Special Investigations Unit within the Public Prosecution Office as well.

The Office of the Ombudsman issued its first annual report in May, which listed 11 deaths under investigation, including that of Fadhel Marhoon, whom police shot and fatally wounded on January 8. The Ombudsman's Office told Human Rights Watch that it had forwarded details of the deaths of al-Abar and Mahmood to the Special Investigations Unit for investigation.

The BICI also found that Bahrain's security forces had killed at least 18 demonstrators and detainees without justification and recommended that the authorities investigate the deaths "with a view to bringing legal and disciplinary action against such individuals, including those in the chain of command, military and civilian, who are found to be responsible under international standards of 'superior responsibility.'"

An analysis of court documents conducted by Human Rights Watch showed that the justice system has failed to hold members of the security forces accountable for serious rights violations, including in cases where their use of excessive and unlawful force proved fatal. The authorities have prosecuted only a few of the security personnel implicated in the serious and widespread abuses that the BICI documented, focusing almost exclusively on low-ranking officers who, in most cases, have been acquitted or punished with disproportionately lenient sentences.

For example, a court convicted a police officer only of assault, although it accepted that he had shot and fatally wounded a man from a distance of one meter because it concluded that the officer did not open fire with an intent to kill. The court imposed a seven-year prison term in this case, which an appellate court later reduced to six months. In another case, an appeals court slashed to two years the ten-year prison terms that a lower court imposed on two police officers convicted of beating a detainee to death. The appeals court said that the two defendants deserved "clemency" on the absurd grounds that they had been "preserving the life of detainees, among them the victim." These and similar decisions by courts threaten to undermine the ability of the Ombudsman's Office to carry out its responsibility to ensure that police and other security forces comply with the law.

Human Rights Defenders

On August 30, Bahrain's public prosecutor charged human rights activist Maryam al-Khawaja with assaulting a police officer at Manama airport when she arrived from abroad to visit her father, Abdulhadi al-Khawaja, who is serving a sentence of life imprisonment for his political activities. Authorities released her on bail on September 18.

Bahrain authorities arrested a prominent rights activist, Nabeel Rajab, on October 1. At time of writing he faced a three-year prison sentence on charges that he "offended national institutions" due to comments he made on social media. Rajab, who was released from prison on May 24 after serving two years for organizing and participating in demonstrations, criticized the government for using counterterrorism laws to prosecute human rights defenders and accused Bahraini security forces of fostering violent beliefs akin to those of the extremist group Islamic State, also known as ISIS.

Rights activist Zainab al-Khawaja spent five weeks in prison after her arrest on October 15 on charges that she insulted the king after she ripped up a photo of King Hamad during a court hearing. At time of writing, she faced six outstanding charges, five of which, according to information provided by her lawyer, clearly violate her right to free expression. She had been released in February 2014 after serving a one-year prison term for illegal assembly and insulting the police.

German authorities granted political asylum to a senior staff member of the Bahrain Center for Human Rights (BCHR), Sayed Yousif Almuhafdah, in March. Almuhafdah had been the subject of death threats on social media after the BCHR launched a campaign that accused senior members of the ruling Al-Khalifa family of responsibility for serious rights abuses and called for their criminal prosecution. Almuhafdah sought asylum after he and his wife received summonses to appear before Bahrain's public prosecutor.

Freedom of Expression and Association

In April, King Hamad ratified Law 1/2014, which amends article 214 of the penal code to provide for a maximum jail term of seven years and a fine of up to 10,000 Bahraini dinars (US$26,500) for offending the king, Bahrain's flag, or the national emblem.

On July 10, the public prosecutor charged Sheikh Ali Salman and Khalil al-Marzooq, respectively leader and deputy leader of Al Wifaq, Bahrain's main Shia opposition party, with violating the law on political associations. This occurred after they met the visiting United States assistant secretary of state for democracy, human rights and labor, Tom Malinowski, without the government's permission. On July 7, the authorities declared Malinowski *persona non grata* and ordered him to leave Bahrain.

The year 2014 saw four award-winning Bahraini photographers either in jail or facing criminal charges, some or all of whom were apparently targeted by the authorities on account of their peaceful exercise of their profession. They included Hussain Hubail, sentenced by a court to a five-year prison term on April 28 on charges that included using social media networks to "incite hatred of the regime," calling on people to ignore the law, and calling for illegal demonstrations. His family and that of Ahmed Humaidan, another photographer whose 10-year sentence was confirmed by the Supreme Court in August, alleged that authorities mistreated the men in pretrial detention.

Citizenship

The government published amendments to the 1963 Citizenship Law in the Official Gazette on July 24. Article 10 now permits the Interior Ministry, with cabinet approval, to revoke the citizenship of any Bahraini who "aids or is involved in the service of a hostile state" or who "causes harm to the interests of the Kingdom or acts in a way that contravenes his duty of loyalty to it."

Authorities either obstructed the right of appeal or refused to justify their 2012 decision to arbitrarily revoke the citizenship of 31 Bahrainis, including 9 men and 1 woman who remain in Bahrain, for allegedly "damaging the security of the state." Only 1 of the 31 was able to appeal against the Ministry of Interior decision to revoke his citizenship, but a court upheld the minister's decision on April

29 and asserted, without citing evidence, that it was "intimately related to national security." The court noted that the Interior Ministry was not obliged to justify its decision and that the ministry's actions were "not subject to judicial oversight as long as its decisions are free from abuse of authority."

Women's Rights

Law no. 19 of 2009 on the Promulgation of the Law of Family Rulings regulates matters of personal status in Bahrain's Sunni courts. It does not apply in the country's Shia courts, with the consequence that Shia women, who comprise the majority of women in Bahrain, are not covered by a codified personal status law. Domestic violence is not specifically addressed in the penal code and marital rape is not considered a crime.

Migrant Workers

Approximately 460,000 migrant workers, mostly from Asia, make up 77 percent of Bahrain's private workforce. Due to shortcomings in Bahrain's legal and regulatory framework and the authorities' failure to enforce relevant labor laws, they endure serious abuses, such as unpaid wages, passport confiscation, unsafe housing, excessive work hours, physical abuse, and forced labor. Conditions for female domestic workers are of particular concern. A regional Gulf Cooperation Council unified contract for domestic workers has yet to be approved, but early drafts fall short of the minimum standards outlined in the Domestic Workers Convention that the International Labour Organization adopted in 2011.

Key International Actors

Forty-seven states, including the US and the United Kingdom, signed a joint statement criticizing Bahrain and calling for the release of political prisoners at the United Nations Human Rights Council in Geneva in June. However, despite ongoing rights abuses and the expulsion of a senior US diplomat in July, Bahrain's key allies—the UK, the US, and the European Union—failed to make explicit calls for the immediate and unconditional release of 13 high-profile activists serving long-term sentences in Bahrain.

In February, the European Parliament did, however, adopt a strong resolution condemning human rights violations in Bahrain and calling on the EU high representative and EU member states to develop a clear strategy setting out how the EU will, both publicly and privately, actively push for the release of imprisoned activists. No such strategy emerged.

Bahrain, along with its closest regional ally and benefactor, Saudi Arabia, and other Gulf states, participated in US-led air strikes against Islamic militant groups in Iraq and Syria.

Bangladesh

Prime Minister Sheikh Hasina's Awami League party and its allies swept to power in the January national elections after key opposition parties refused to participate. The opposition demanded polls under a neutral caretaker government and all attempts at negotiations, including by the United Nations, failed to resolve the stalemate. Hundreds were killed and injured in violent attacks surrounding the elections.

The trend toward increasing restrictions on civil society continued, with the government introducing a draft bill that imposes restrictions on already beleaguered nongovernmental organizations (NGOs) and their access to foreign funding. The government also introduced a new media policy that imposes unacceptable limits on free expression and speech.

Security forces carried out abductions, killings, and arbitrary arrests, particularly targeting opposition leaders and supporters. In a positive development, after years of impunity for the security forces, several members of the notorious Rapid Action Battalion (RAB) were arrested following the abduction and apparent contract killings of seven people in May.

Compensation and relief for victims and survivors of the April 2013 collapse of the Rana Plaza in Dhaka was slow because international companies that sourced garments from the five factories operating in the building failed to contribute enough to the financial trust fund set up to support survivors and the families of those who died. After the accident, the government amended its labor laws to make it easier for workers to form unions. However, workers reported tremendous pressure from owners and managers not to do so.

Electoral Violence

Hundreds were killed and injured in violent attacks surrounding the controversial January elections. Both Bangladesh's ruling party, as well as opposition parties, were responsible for the violence.

Supporters of the opposition Bangladesh Nationalist Party and the Jamaat-e-Islami party threw petrol bombs to enforce strikes and economic blockades. Be-

HUMAN RIGHTS WATCH

DEMOCRACY IN THE CROSSFIRE
Opposition Violence and Government Abuses
in the 2014 Pre- and Post- Election Period in Bangladesh

fore and after the election, attackers also vandalized homes and shops owned by members of Bangladesh's Hindu and Christian communities.

In response, the government cracked down on opposition members, naming hundreds of them as suspects in violent attacks. Members of law enforcement agencies carried out extrajudicial executions, enforced disappearances, arbitrary arrests, and unlawful destruction of private property.

Civil Society and Media

The government introduced several measures aimed at cracking down on critics, continuing a trend from the previous year.

In July, the government proposed the draft Foreign Donations (Voluntary Activities) Regulation Act, designed to regulate operations and funding for any group receiving foreign grants, including Bangladesh offices of foreign and international organizations. The draft law contains unnecessary, onerous, and intrusive provisions, with vague and overly broad language to control NGOs.

In August, the government published a new media policy for all audio, video, and audio-visual content transmitted through any means which contains overly broad language aimed at significantly curtailing critical reporting. Several television and news outlets that were shut down in 2013 for critical reporting remained closed through 2014.

Accountability for Security Forces

Authorities arrested several members of the notorious Rapid Action Battalion (RAB) following intense public outrage over the abduction and apparent contract killings of seven men in Narayangunj in April.

Although the government claims that almost 2,000 RAB members have been punished for various misdemeanors since the group's inception, there was not a single prosecution for extrajudicial executions, torture, or arbitrary arrests before the Narayanganj incident. Independent organizations estimate that the RAB has been responsible for approximately 800 unlawful killings over the past 10 years. Allegations of violations by members of the police and other law enforcement agencies, including the Border Guard Bangladesh, were not independently investigated or prosecuted.

Labor Rights

April marked one year since the collapse of the Rana Plaza building, in which over 1,100 garment workers died and an estimated 2,500 were injured. Six months prior, a deadly factory fire at Tazreen Fashions killed at least 112 people. Survivors and relatives reported that they continue to suffer from life-changing injuries, psychological trauma, and lost income.

After the Rana Plaza accident, a compensation fund set up through the International Labour Organization (ILO) was designed to raise US$40 million. But one year later, only $15 million had been raised, with most funds coming from just one company.

After the Rana Plaza tragedy, the Bangladesh government and Western retailers set up an inspection regime for more than 3,500 garment factories to ensure structural integrity and fire and electrical safety. A group of North American retailers inspected about 587 factories. A second body, formed by mainly European retailers, inspected 1,545 factories.

While they published details of their inspections, at time of writing, the government had not published information on the remaining inspections it had conducted. The government amended its labor laws to make it easier for workers to form and join unions. However, workers said they continued to face tremendous pressure—including intimidation, mistreatment, and even death threats from managers—not to do so.

Workers in the tanneries of Hazaribagh, a residential area in Dhaka, continue to suffer from highly toxic and dangerous working conditions. Although some tanneries have begun to build new premises at a dedicated industrial zone in Savar, their planned relocation continued to be delayed. Residents of nearby slums complain of illnesses caused by the extreme tannery pollution of air, water, and soil. The government continues its de facto policy of not enforcing labor and environmental laws with respect to the Hazaribagh tanneries.

Bangladeshi migrant workers, especially in the construction and domestic service sectors in the Gulf, are often deceived by recruiters about their contracts and charged excessive fees that leave them deeply in debt and vulnerable to abuse abroad, including passport confiscation, unpaid wages, hazardous work, and forced labor. Migrants rarely receive effective assistance from their embassies.

War Crimes Tribunal

Trials against those accused of genocide, crimes against humanity, and war crimes committed during the country's 1971 war of independence continued in spite of serious ongoing concerns about deep flaws in the trials. The prosecution in the trials urged the law minister to amend the tribunal's statute to allow it to prosecute the entire Jamaat-e-Islaami party, which had opposed the movement for secession from Pakistan, and the issue is still pending before the judges.

In November, the appellate division of the Supreme Court confirmed the death penalty in the war crimes case against Muhamed Kamaruzzaman, despite serious fair trial concerns.

Women

Child marriage in Bangladesh remains extremely prevalent. In July 2014, Prime Minister Sheik Hasina pledged at the London Girl Summit to reform the law on child marriage, end child marriage under age 15 by 2021, and end child marriage completely by 2041. However, proposals from her cabinet in October to lower the age of marriage for girls from 18 to 16 undermined her call.

Bangladesh's personal status laws governing marriage, separation, and divorce overtly discriminate against women, and the government showed no sign of willingness to undertake a comprehensive review to ensure equality and protection for women and girls.

Children's Rights

Several children were injured during election violence due to indiscriminate petrol bombings and other attacks by opposition supporters. In some cases, opposition groups also recruited children to carry out the attacks. Although members of opposition parties were arrested and charged with violence, the government continued to fail to take action against them for deliberately putting children in harm's way as part of their campaign of protests.

Death Penalty

Bangladesh continues to implement the death penalty. Abdul Qader Mollah, a leader of the Jamaat-e-Islami party, was hanged in December 2013 after a final verdict found him guilty of war crimes and crimes against humanity during the 1971 war for independence.

Key International Actors

Several countries condemned the attacks surrounding the polls, which were the most violent since the country's independence. The international community attempted to facilitate a negotiated settlement to prevent the one-sided national elections in January. However, countries including the United States and India, that have some influence in Bangladesh, were unable to press for an agreement. Efforts by the UN to mediate also failed.

Several countries including the US and United Kingdom expressed concern about violations by security forces. However, they failed to call for the RAB to be disbanded. The US continued to engage with the RAB on establishing internal discipline mechanisms.

There was intense international scrutiny on international brands sourcing from Bangladesh after the collapse of Rana Plaza.

Both the US and the European Union, Bangladesh's two largest overseas markets for garments, called on the government and garments industry to implement global labor standards. The US continued to suspend Bangladesh's trade benefits under the Generalized System of Preferences (GSP). In July 2013, the EU warned that Bangladesh might lose its duty-free and quota-free access if it did not improve its record on labor rights and workplace safety, but did not take any further steps.

The United Nations High Commissioner for Refugees (UNHCR) and other humanitarian organizations working with the Rohingya refugees at the Burmese border continued to face pressure from the government and limited access to the camps.

Belarus

Belarusian authorities made no meaningful improvements in the country's poor human rights record in 2014. President Aliaxander Lukashenka's government continues to severely restrict freedom of expression and association, including by harassing journalists and imposing restrictive legislation on nongovernmental organizations_(NGOs). Legislative amendments during the year simplified the reporting requirements for NGOs, but introduced new pretexts for liquidating them.

Authorities arbitrarily detained activists to prevent them from participating in public events, including before the May International Ice Hockey Federation World Championship. Belarus courts sentenced four people to death and executed two of the men, one of whom had a case challenging the legality of the sentence pending decision before the United Nations Human Rights Committee. The authorities released human rights defender Ales Bialiatski who had spent almost three years in prison on politically motivated charges. Members of the lesbian, gay, bisexual, and transgender (LGBT) community face deep-rooted homophobia and discrimination.

Death Penalty

Belarus remains the only European country to have the death penalty. In April, authorities executed by firing squad Pavel Sialiun, whom a regional court sentenced to death in June 2013 for murder and theft, among other charges. The Supreme Court upheld the sentence. Sialiun was executed despite a pending case before the UN Human Rights Committee challenging his conviction and sentence. The exact date of Sialiun's execution is not known. Sialiun's mother learned of her son's death from his lawyer.

In May, authorities executed Ryhor Yuzepchuk, sentenced to death in April for murder. At time of writing, two other men remained on death row after the Supreme Court upheld their death sentences.

In April, the UN special rapporteur on Belarus expressed concern at the lack of transparency surrounding Belarus' death penalty system, and in October 2013, stated that "the way the death penalty is carried out in Belarus amounts to inhuman treatment."

Arrests and Harassment of Human Rights Defenders and Critics

In June, a court found Andrei Bandarenka, who leads the human rights group Platform Innovation, guilty on spurious criminal hooliganism charges and sentenced him to three years' imprisonment. Bandarenka previously headed a prison monitoring group that authorities dissolved in October 2012 for alleged tax violations. Rights groups believe that Bandarenka's prosecution was in retaliation for his human rights work.

According to rights groups, seven people remain in detention following politically motivated prosecutions. These prisoners are regularly subjected to undue restrictions on correspondence and meetings with families, psychological pressure, and other forms of ill-treatment as punishments.

At least 33 former political prisoners, who were pardoned by the government, still face restrictions and harassment by authorities. The criminal records have not been expunged, preventing them from occupying governmental jobs or standing in elections. Some have been forbidden from leaving Belarus. Those pardoned or released before serving their full sentences remain on law enforcement agencies' "preventative watch lists," which authorize police to question them frequently.

In November, authorities annulled the residence permit of Elena Tonkacheva, a top Belarusian human rights lawyer and Russian national who had lived in Belarus for over 30 years, for speed limit violations.

In a positive development in June, authorities released leading human rights defender Ales Bialiatski, head of a human rights group assisting political prisoners and their families. Bialiatski served almost 3 years of a 4.5-year prison sentence on politically motivated charges of tax evasion.

Freedom of Assembly

The authorities continue to arbitrarily detain civil and political activists to prevent them from attending peaceful rallies, and ahead of important public events.

Between April 22 and May 25, police detained at least 43 civil society and human rights activists on misdemeanor charges, detaining some as they walked on the street or drove to events. Administrative courts ordered up to 25 days of detention for all activists, some of whom were denied access to a lawyer. Most court rulings contained identical language alleging hooliganism, disobeying police orders, or both. The "preventative" arrests coincided with the annual Minsk march commemorating the 1986 Chernobyl nuclear disaster and the International Ice Hockey Federation World Championship.

Freedom of Expression, Attacks on Journalists

Authorities routinely harass and interfere with the work of independent and opposition journalists and bloggers. According to the Belarusian Association of Journalists, since the beginning of 2014, authorities arbitrarily detained 15 journalists. For example, in March, Minsk police detained seven journalists covering a protest near the Russian embassy against Russia's annexation of Crimea. Courts charged at least three of them with misdemeanor "hooliganism" and imposed fines and up to 10 days' detention.

Law enforcement officials initiated misdemeanor proceedings against three independent journalists because of their cooperation with foreign media outlets not registered in Belarus, and threatened six others with similar charges. In April, a court fined a reporter for *Belsat*, a Poland-based satellite television station known for its critical reporting of Belarus, approximately US$428.

In February, prosecutors initiated a criminal investigation on charges of "defamation of government officials" against Aleh Zhalnou, an independent blogger who published audio and video material allegedly showing unlawful police actions. The authorities initiated fourteen cases against Zhalnou including four criminal cases, nine administrative proceedings, and one civil suit. Since February, police have questioned Zhalnou 40 times.

In June, authorities initiated a criminal investigation on libel charges against human rights activist Yekaterina Sadovskaya after she criticized, in a Minsk court visitors' comments book, the authorities' harassment and detention of activists ahead of the International Ice Hockey Federation World Championship. Authorities alleged the comment was "degrading" to President Lukashenka. If convicted, Sadovskaya faces a fine or up to three years in prison.

Freedom of Association

Authorities continued to enforce repressive legislation that criminalizes involvement in an unregistered organization, and at the same time arbitrarily refused to register opposition political groups, human rights, and other groups critical of the government.

In January, the prosecutor's office issued a warning to the Belarusian Christian Democratic party's organizing committee chairman for acting on behalf of an unregistered group and reminded him of criminal liability. The party has attempted to register at least four times since it was established in 2009, but authorities repeatedly denied registration requests on arbitrary pretexts.

In August, the Ministry of Justice refused to register the Movement for the Implementation of the International Covenant on Civil and Political Rights, *Pakt* (Covenant), citing minor spelling errors in the group's application.

Amendments to the legislation governing NGOs adopted in November 2013 decreased the number of documents required for NGO registration and simplified the process for registering international organizations, but introduced the failure to submit an annual report within three years as additional grounds for authorities to liquidate organizations.

Authorities continued to harass LGBT persons, and in 2013, banned the main gathering of the December Gay Pride festival. Also in December 2013, police raided the Minsk Pride organizing committee's office, alleging noise, and briefly detained one organiser.

Key International Actors

Key international actors, including the European Union, the Organization for Security and Co-operation in Europe (OSCE), the United Kingdom, and United States welcomed the release of Ales Bialiatski. The chair of the OSCE Parliamentary Assembly's Ad Hoc Working Group on Belarus called Bialiatski's release "hopefully a sign of more to come" and urged Belarus to immediately release all those imprisoned on politically motivated charges and to demonstrate "genuine commitment to upholding OSCE commitments, particularly in the spheres of democracy and human rights." The US State Department spokesperson, welcoming Bialiatski's release, stated that such actions would "pave the way for normalization of relations between the United States and Belarus."

Overall, however, Belarus authorities' remained closed to human rights scrutiny.

The government continued to actively oppose the mandate of UN Special Rapporteur on Belarus Miklos Haraszti, insisting that it is political. Ever since the UN Human Rights Council appointed a special rapporteur for the country in 2012, Belarus authorities have refused to cooperate with him and have repeatedly denied him a visa. During its June session, the council extended the rapporteur's mandate for one year.

In February, the government announced that it would grant access to a number of UN special procedures mandate holders, including the special rapporteurs on freedom of expression, freedom of religion, and the independence of judges and lawyers. At time of writing, the invitations had not been issued.

In its concluding observations from its November 2013 review, the UN Committee on Economic, Social and Cultural Rights urged Belarus to abolish compulsory labor for persons deprived of their liberty, persons affected by alcoholism, or drug dependent persons who are interned in so-called medical labor centers, and parents who have had their parental rights removed.

The committee expressed concern at the lack of adequate social housing for disadvantaged groups, including persons with disabilities and refugees, and at the insufficient level of education of Roma children. It also encouraged the government to adopt domestic violence legislation.

In April, the president of the Parliamentary Assembly of the Council of Europe called the recent death penalty execution in Belarus "barbaric" and expressed regret that little progress has been made to abolish the death penalty.

The EU reaffirmed that developing bilateral relations was conditional on Belarus' progress towards respect for democracy, the rule of law, and human rights. In January 2013, the EU and Belarus launched negotiations on a visa facilitation and a readmission agreement.

The EU also extended existing sanctions for another year and expanded the list of persons subject to travel bans and asset freezes to 232 persons and 25 entities.

Bolivia

In October 2014, Evo Morales was reelected as president of Bolivia with 61 percent of the vote, and the ruling party won two-thirds of the seats in the Plurinational Assembly.

Threats to judicial independence and impunity for violent crime and human rights violations remain serious problems in Bolivia. Extensive and arbitrary use of pretrial detention and trial delays undermine defendants' rights and contribute to prison overcrowding.

The administration of President Morales continued to target human rights defenders and critical journalists in 2014, and failed to fully respect the right to free, prior, and informed consent of indigenous groups. Violence against women, and child labor, are major concerns.

Judicial Independence and Access to Justice

The Bolivian justice system has been plagued by corruption, delays, and political interference for years. The 2009 constitution provided for judicial elections to overhaul Bolivia's highest courts, but the Plurinational Assembly selected candidates through a process that lacked transparency and did not adequately consider their qualifications.

In July 2014, the Plurinational Assembly had initiated an impeachment process, targeting three Constitutional Court magistrates under a 2010 law that allows the legislature to remove judges and impose criminal penalties on them, undermining judicial independence. As of November, the three magistrates had been suspended from office and at least one more was being investigated.

Impunity for Abuses and Violent Crime

Bolivia has made little progress prosecuting human rights violations committed under authoritarian governments between 1964 and 1982, and has not adequately compensated victims of political violence. A contributing factor has been the unwillingness of the armed forces to provide information on the fate of people killed or disappeared during this period. A proposal to create a truth commission to investigate these crimes—made up of seven members, including four appointed by the government—was pending before the Plurinational Assembly at time of writing.

Efforts to bring to justice those allegedly responsible for killings during violent clashes in 2008 between supporters and opponents of President Morales have made little progress. As of September 2014, a La Paz court was still hearing evidence in a case involving Leopoldo Fernández, former prefect of Pando Department, and five local officials charged in 2008 for their roles in the killing of 13 people. Prosecutorial inefficiency has undermined victims' right to justice and suspects' due process rights.

The government has not reopened an investigation into the April 2009 killing of two Hungarians (one of Bolivian birth) and an Irishman, who the government alleged were mercenaries involved in a separatist plot. Police shot them dead after storming into their hotel rooms in Santa Cruz. Credible reports suggest that at least two of the three may have been extrajudicially executed. In October, the United Nations Working Group on Arbitrary Detention ruled that a Croatian-Bolivian citizen implicated in the case had been arbitrarly detained, and called on Bolivia to release him.

The government has yet to fully investigate the use of excessive force by police in 2011 to disperse a largely peaceful demonstration against a proposed highway in the Isiboro Secure National Park and Indigenous Territory (known as "TIPNIS"). The police gagged, stripped, and beat demonstrators, according to the Ombudsman's Office.

The lack of access to justice has led to mob attacks (or "lynchings") against citizens or police officers believed responsible for crimes. Ten people were reportedly killed in lynchings in 2013, and at least another eleven in 2014. Impunity for lynchings remains the norm.

Military Abuses and Jurisdiction

Human rights violations against soldiers remain a problem. In May, a soldier who led a demonstration protesting for better working conditions for low ranking officials was charged with sedition and rebellion. In July, five soldiers were allegedly stripped, beaten, and subject to electric shocks by their superiors in response to the loss of a rifle.

The Constitutional Court ruled in 2012 that a civilian court should have jurisdiction in the case of a conscript who died in 2011 following a combat training exercise after instructors allegedly beat him on the head and chest. The court urged lawmakers to reform Bolivia's military justice code to ensure that human rights violations are heard in civilian courts. As of November, the code had not been reformed.

Due Process and Prison Conditions

Judges' broad discretion to order pretrial detention and lack of access to public defenders have undermined defendants' due process rights, particularly among Bolivia's poor.

Bolivia has one of the highest rates of unconvicted prisoners in the region (more than 80 percent, as of December 2013). Extended pretrial detention and trial delays have led to increased overcrowding and poor conditions in prisons, where food and medical attention are inadequate and internal control is often left to prisoners. As of February 2014, there were 14,700 inmates in prisons with a maximum capacity of 4,884, according to the Ombudsman's Office.

In September, four people died and 11 were wounded during clashes amongst detainees in a maximum security prision in Cochabamba. According to the Ombudsman's Office, penitentiary guards failed to oversee a party organized by inmates, and to assist victims after the violence.

Decrees adopted since 2012 allow the president to lower the sentences of detainees sentenced to less than eight years in prison, and to pardon those in pretrial detention for crimes with penalties of up to four years in prison. In August 2014, the director of the penitentiary system reportedly stated that 957 prisoners had been released.

Human Rights Defenders

Human rights defenders continue to operate in a hostile environment that undermines their ability to work independently.

In 2013, President Morales adopted a decree granting the government broad powers to dissolve civil society organizations. Under the decree, any government office may request the Ministry of Autonomy to revoke an organization's permit to operate if it performs activities different from those listed in its statute, or if the organization's representative is criminally sanctioned for carrying out activities that "undermine security or public order." The Plurinational Assembly may also request that the permit be revoked in cases of "necessity or public interest."

In December 2013, the government expelled the Danish nongovernmental organization IBIS, which had worked with and funded indigenous groups in Bolivia since 1984. The minister of the presidency stated that the government would not tolerate IBIS's "political interference" in Bolivia, and threatened that "all nongovernmental organizations involved in political interference will be expelled."

Freedom of Expression

While public debate is robust, the Morales administration has repeatedly accused journalists of lies and politically motivated distortions. In April, the solicitor general brought a criminal case against two journalists from *La Razón* newspaper, accusing them of "espionage" and "revealing state secrets" for publishing an article on the government's strategy in an international dispute regarding maritime borders with Chile. In August, the case was transferred to a specialized "press court" with powers to impose fines instead of criminal penalties.

A government-sponsored bill on access to information remained pending before the Plurinational Assembly at time of writing.

Indigenous Rights

The 2009 Bolivian Constitution includes comprehensive guarantees to protect the rights of indigenous groups, including collective land titling, intercultural education, prior consultation on development projects, and protection of indigenous justice systems. A 2011 law establishing jurisdictional boundaries between indigenous and ordinary justice systems has yet to be fully put into practice.

The implementation of the right to prior, free, and informed consent, particularly with respect to extractive industry projects, remains pending. According to the UN Human Rights Committee, the development of a draft law on this topic has been accompanied by consultation but not adequate consent of indigenous communities.

Gender-Based Violence and Reproductive Rights

Women and girls in Bolivia remain at high risk for gender-based violence, despite a 2013 law that provides for comprehensive measures to prevent and sanction violence against women. Implementation of the law, which created the crime of "femicide" and called for special prosecutors and courts for gender-based crimes and shelters for women, has moved very slowly.

In March, the UN Office in Bolivia stated that 154 cases of political violence against women in 2013 had not been brought to justice. The law defines "political violence" as actions or "physical, psychological, or sexual aggressions" against women who are candidates or hold public office, or against their families, undermining their work.

In November, the Bolivian police reported there had been 95 "femicides" in the country in 2014, opened a toll-free number to report such cases, and created a "group of immediate reaction" to address incoming reports of violence.

Women and girls face numerous obstacles to accessing reproductive health products and services, such as contraception and abortion after rape (one of the few circumstances when abortion is not penalized). According to Ipas, between 2008 and 2013, 775 women were criminally prosecuted for having an abortion, and thousands sought medical care for incomplete abortions. In February, the Constitutional Court ruled that obtaining prior judicial authorization and initiating a formal criminal investigation was not required to obtain access to legal abortion after rape.

Child Labor

In July 2014, the Plurinational Assembly adopted legislation, which the vice president signed into law, allowing children as young as 10 to work, violating international standards and making Bolivia the first country in the world to legalize employment at such a low age. According to the latest available official statistics from 2008, at least 746,000 children work in Bolivia.

Sexual Orientation and Gender Identity

Impunity for acts of violence and discrimination on grounds of sexual orientation or gender identity persists. In 2014, the Ombudsman's Office reported that those responsible for the deaths of 55 LGBT persons since 2004 had not been brought to justice.

The 2009 constitution defines marriage as the union of a man and a woman. Several proposals to amend the constitution or legalize same-sex marriage or civil unions remained pending at time of writing.

Key International Actors

Bolivia has supported a campaign by Ecuador to undermine the independence of the Inter-American Commission on Human Rights and limit the funding and effectiveness of its special rapporteurship on freedom of expression. President Morales announced in 2013 that he was "seriously considering withdrawing" from the commission, but Bolivia participated in hearings there in October 2014.

The International Labour Organization, which is reviewing Bolivia's new legislation on child labor, stated in July 2014 that the law could violate several international treaties that Bolivia has ratified.

Bosnia and Herzegovina

Political deadlock in Bosnia and Herzegovina (BiH) continued to impede needed reforms in 2014 despite widespread protests in February expressing broad economic and political dissatisfaction. The protests were marked by incidents of police brutality. Journalists remained vulnerable to intimidation and threats. A fresh ruling from the European Court of Human Rights (ECtHR) underscored the government's ongoing failure to end restrictions on Jews, Roma, and other minorities running for political office. Roma remain the most vulnerable group, subject to widespread discrimination.

Ethnic and Religious Discrimination

The government made no progress towards amending the country's constitution to eliminate ethnic and religious discrimination in the national tri-partite presidency and House of Peoples, despite a July ruling by the ECtHR affirming its 2009 judgment that the constitution violates the European Convention on Human Rights. Both institutions currently permit candidates only from the three main ethnic groups (Bosniaks, Serbs, and Croats). European Union high level dialogues with the main political parties to facilitate an agreement collapsed in February.

General elections were held in October without the constitutional amendments required by the European Court. A new government had yet to be formed at time of writing.

Authorities in Mostar missed an August deadline to make changes to its voting system ordered by the Bosnian Constitutional Court, resulting in Mostar's exclusion from general elections and the disenfranchisement of its voters.

Roma remain the most vulnerable group in the country, facing widespread discrimination in employment, education, and political representation. Lack of a free and universal birth registration system means that many Roma are not on the national public registry that records births, deaths, and marriage. This impedes their access to public services, including health care.

Refugees and Internally Displaced Persons

According to the United Nations High Commissioner for Refugees (UNHCR) only 29 refugees and 66 internally displaced persons (IDPs) returned to their areas of origin in the first half of 2014, a significant decrease compared to the same period in 2013. As of July 2014, there were still 84,500 registered IDPs in BiH. Severe flooding in BiH in May and August disproportionally affected IDPs and returnees, forcing many families to relocate and further delayed the implementation of a 2010 strategy aimed at supporting the return of refugees and IDPs to their pre-war homes or finding them other durable solutions that would allow the remaining collective centers occupied by IDPs to be closed.

War Crimes Accountability

Implementation by the Bosnian government of the national war crimes strategy, adopted in 2008 to improve domestic war crimes prosecution, remains slow. There continues to be insufficient capacity and funding for prosecutors, particularly at the district and cantonal level. By November 2014, the war crimes chamber of the State Court of BiH had reached verdicts in 33 cases, increasing the total number of completed cases to 250 since the court became fully operational in 2005. During the year, the Republika Srpska entity prime minister repeatedly challenged the legitimacy of State Court and Prosecutor's Office claiming they are unconstitutional and called for their abolition.

In July, the State Court began the first retrial of a war crimes suspect among the dozens whose convictions were quashed following a 2013 ECtHR ruling that stated that Bosnian courts had wrongly applied law not in force at the time of the offences committed during the 1992 to 1995 Bosnian war.

The decision in November by the State Court to quash under the ECtHR ruling the genocide conviction of Milorad Trbic, a former commander with Bosnian Serb forces, and the prospect of his release from custody pending retrial, prompted concern from UN experts, who called on the BiH government to ensure victim protection, the right to truth and justice, and the adoption of a comprehensive transitional justice strategy. The case had been transferred to the Bosnian court from the International Cirminal Tribunal for the Former Yugoslavia (ICTY) in 2007.

In April, the State Prosecutor's Office signed a cooperation agreement with its counterpart in Montenegro on prosecuting war crimes, crimes against humanity, and genocide, following similar agreements with Croatia and Serbia from 2013.

The trial of Bosnian Serb wartime General Radtko Mladic continued at the ICTY with the opening of the defense on May 19. A request to dismiss the case by Maldic—charged with genocide, war crimes, and crimes against humanity, including in Srebrenica in July 1995—on the grounds the prosecution had failed to provide sufficient evidence of genocidal intent was rejected in April. Mladic's ill-health repeatedly interrupted the trial that began in 2011.

In July, Bosnian Serb wartime President Radovan Karadzic, also on trial at the ICTY under many of the same charges as Mladic, demanded a new trial citing unfair treatment and prosecution errors. His claim was rejected and his trial continued. Closing arguments were heard in late September, and at time of writing a verdict was expected in the second half of 2015.

National Security and Human Rights

At time of writing, two foreign nationals remained in indefinite detention on national security grounds in BiH. Imad Al Husin, a naturalized Bosnian from Syria detained in 2008, remained in indefinite detention, despite a 2012 ECtHR ruling that required BiH to charge him, find a safe third country to resettle him, or release him.

Zeyad Khalaf Al Gertani, another foreign national security suspect from Iraq, remained in detention despite United Nations Human Rights Committee findings from November 2013 that BiH was in breach of article 9 of the International Covenant on Civil and Political Rights, which prohibits arbitrary arrest or detention and requires that anyone who is arrested be informed, at the time of arrest, of the reasons for the arrest.

Freedom of Media

Threats and acts of intimidation against journalists by political and religious authorities continued in 2014. As of November, the national journalists' association recorded 27 violations of freedom of expression, including 5 physical and 14 verbal assaults, and 1 death threat.

In February, the United States, European Union, and Organization for Security and Co-operation in Europe (OSCE) condemned accusations by authorities in the Republika Srpska entity that certain media outlets are "foreign agents."

During the February protests, police intimidated and beat journalists and confiscated raw footage, violating the right to freedom of expression.

Freedom of Assembly and Expression

Police in Sarajevo and Tuzla used excessive force during the February protests, as well as during the subsequent detention of protesters. Internal investigations into the events were ongoing at time of writing.

Political leaders from among each of three main ethnic groups sought to dismiss the protests as staged efforts to provoke inter-ethnic violence or attempts by one entity to destabilize the other, rather than engaging with the concerns voiced by protesters.

In February, 10 assailants attacked a group of people attending the Merlinka Film festival, organized by the lesbian, gay, bisexual, and transgender (LGBT) rights organization Sarajevo Open Centre, leaving 2 injured. No police were present at the time, despite a prior agreement between organizers and police to provide security during the event. At time of writing, no one had been charged in connection with the attacks. The center documented 15 cases of hate speech and 14 cases of hate crime in the first 10 months of 2014.

Key International Actors

When protests emerged in February, the United States, EU, the Office of the High Representative (OHR), and OSCE voiced support for the right to peaceful protest and called on Bosnian authorities to use the opportunity to implement necessary reforms.

In March, amid preparations for the October general elections, the then-head of the OSCE Mission to BiH called for increased efforts to strengthen gender equality and women's representation in political office. The number of women in political office at different levels of government continued to fall short of quota provisions in the election law requiring that at least 40 percent of candidates on party lists are women.

Also in March, the UN secretary-general published a report on conflict-related sexual violence, including a section on BiH, following a June 2013 country visit by the Special Representative on Sexual Violence in Conflict Zainab Hawa Bangura. The report cited a continued need for increased capacity to prosecute perpetrators, improve comprehensive support for survivors, and end stigmatization. An April OSCE report on the same issue highlighted the need to increase capacity to prioritize, investigate, and prosecute conflict-related sexual violence and improve public awareness, while commending the BiH Prosecutor's Office on efforts made so far to address concerns.

In April, on the occasion of the International Roma Day, the OSCE, EU, and an international nongovernmental organization coalition called in a joint statement for greater efforts to end Roma exclusion in BiH.

After a May visit, the OSCE high representative for national minorities, Astrid Thors, stressed the need to improve equal rights and effective political participation of national minorities, including the need to implement the 2009 ECtHR ruling.

In July, a Dutch district court in The Hague found the Netherlands liable for 300 deaths during the 1995 Srebrenica genocide and ordered compensation payments to hundreds of victims because its peacekeeping troops had failed to protect people seeking refuge in a UN compound in the town.

In September, the Parliamentary Assembly of the Council of Europe deliberated suspending BiH from the organization unless there is "substantial progress" in the implementation of the 2009 ECtHR ruling.

In its annual progress report published in October, the European Commission identified the continued need for constitutional reform and rising political and financial pressure on media, as well as violence and discrimination against vulnerable minorities, particularly LGBT people, among the main outstanding concerns.

During the second Universal Periodic Review of BiH at the Human Rights Council in November, member states cited the need for constitutional reform, increased efforts to combat human trafficking and violence against women, improving rights of people with disabilities, and further promoting integration of Roma in all levels of society as important issues to be addressed.

Brazil

Brazil is among the most influential democracies in regional and global affairs, and in recent years has emerged as an increasingly important voice in debates over international responses to human rights problems. At home, the country continues to confront serious human rights challenges, including the use of torture and ill-treatment, unlawful police killings, prison overcrowding, and ongoing impunity for abuses committed during the country's military rule (1964-1985).

Violent criminal gangs and abusive policing are significant problems in many Brazilian cities. In recent years, the São Paulo and Rio de Janeiro state governments have implemented measures aimed at improving police performance and curbing abuses, yet police misreporting and other forms of cover-up persist.

During the year leading up to the 2014 World Cup, there were major protests throughout the country. Dozens of people were injured in confrontations between protesters and police, including journalists. In several incidents, police used excessive force, including beating people who had not resisted arrest, and firing teargas canisters at protesters from short range.

Public Security and Police Conduct

Police were responsible for 436 killings in the state of Rio de Janeiro and 505 killings in the state of São Paulo in the first nine months of 2014. In the state of São Paulo, this represents an increase of 93 percent over the same period in 2013. According to the most recent available information compiled by the Brazilian Forum on Public Security, a nongovernmental organization (NGO), more than 2,200 people died during police operations throughout Brazil in 2013, averaging 6 people a day.

Police routinely report these deaths as the result of shoot-outs with criminals. While some police killings result from legitimate use of force, others do not, a fact documented by Human Rights Watch and other groups, and recognized by Brazilian criminal justice officials.

In an effort to prevent cover-ups of unlawful police killings, the São Paulo state government issued a resolution in January 2013 prohibiting police from removing victims' corpses from the scenes of shootings. Yet significant obstacles to accountability for unlawful killings in São Paulo persist, including the failure of police to preserve crucial evidence, and the failure of authorities to allocate sufficient staff and resources to prosecutors responsible for investigating these cases.

In the state of Rio de Janeiro, nearly 2,900 police officers and other public servants received financial compensation in May 2014 for meeting crime reduction targets, including reductions in police homicides.

Prison Conditions, Torture, and Ill-Treatment of Detainees

Many Brazilian prisons and jails are severely overcrowded and plagued by violence. The country's incarceration rate increased by 45 percent between 2006 and 2013, according to data from the Ministry of Justice's Integrated System of Penitentiary Information (InfoPen). The adult prison population exceeds half a million people—37 percent more than the prisons were built for, according to the National Council of Justice in June 2014.

In addition, more than 20,000 children are currently serving prison sentences. Delays within the justice system contribute to the overcrowding. Over 230,000 individuals are being held in pretrial detention in prisons. In Piauí state, 68 percent of detainees are in pretrial detention, the highest rate in the country. Overcrowding and poor sanitation facilitate the spread of disease, and prisoners' access to medical care remains inadequate.

Torture is a chronic problem in police stations and detention centers. Between January 2012 and June 2014, the national Human Rights Ombudsman's Office received 5,431 complaints of torture and cruel, inhuman, or degrading treatment (about 181 complaints per month) from all over the country through a telephone hotline service. Of these, 84 percent referred to incidents at police stations, jails, prisons, and juvenile detention centers.

Video footage posted online by the *Folha de São Paulo* newspaper on January 7, 2014, shows the remains of the decapitated corpses of three of the four inmates who were killed by fellow prisoners at the Pedrinhas Prison Complex in Maranhão state on December 17, 2013. A total of 60 inmates were killed in the state in 2013, according to the National Council of Justice (NCJ), which conducted an investigation in five Maranhão prisons and found what it called an "utter lack of security" for inmates. In April 2014, the NCJ issued a recommendation to courts setting out basic steps that judges should take to investigate credible allegations of torture and ill-treatment.

Law enforcement agents who commit abuses against inmates and detainees are rarely brought to justice. In a notable exception, a total of 73 police officers were convicted of homicide in 2013 and 2014 for their participation in the 1992 killing of 111 detainees in the Carandiru prison in São Paulo state.

In July 2014, President Dilma Rousseff appointed the 23 members of the National Committee for the Prevention and Combatting of Torture, which is part of the National System to Prevent and Combat Torture, created by law in August 2013. In November, the committee appointed a panel of 11 experts that will have the authority to conduct unannounced visits to detention centers, open investigations into possible cases of torture, and make recommendations to public and private institutions.

Freedom of Expression, Internet Freedom, and Privacy

According to the Brazilian Association of Investigative Journalism, state security forces injured or detained 178 journalists who covered demonstrations in various parts of the country in the year leading up to the 2014 World Cup.

A federal access to information law went into effect in 2012; a majority of states have since passed implementing legislation. The law establishes that the public should have unfettered access to information regarding violations of fundamental rights.

Brazil took an important step by enacting the Brazilian Digital Bill of Rights in April 2014. The Bill of Rights includes protection for the right to privacy and free expression online, and serves to reinforce application of the rule of law in the digital sphere. The law establishes Brazilian support for net neutrality as a guiding principle for future Internet developments. It has yet to be implemented.

Reproductive Rights

Brazil's criminal code prohibits abortion except in cases of rape or when necessary to save a woman's life. In 2012, the Supreme Court expanded the exceptions to include cases of anencephaly, in which the fetus has a fatal congenital brain disorder. Women and girls who obtain an abortion outside of these exceptions may face sentences of up to three years in prison, while people who perform abortions face up to four years' imprisonment.

Abortions performed in clandestine clinics put women at high risk, as exemplified in the high profile case of Jandira dos Santos Cruz, who police suspect died from a botched illegal abortion in late August 2014, and whose body was later mutilated to obscure her identity.

In August 2013, President Rousseff signed into law a bill that requires public hospitals to provide comprehensive care for victims of sexual violence, including "pregnancy prophylaxis" for rape victims and information on the right to access abortion in cases where it is legal. In 2014, the Ministry of Health issued a resolution extending national health insurance to cover legal abortion, but revoked the resolution a week later in response to political pressure.

Sexual Orientation and Gender Identity

The national Human Rights Ombudsman's Office received more than 1,500 complaints of violence and discrimination against lesbian, gay, bisexual, and transgender (LGBT) persons in 2013. In the first six months of 2014, the Ombudsman's Office reported over 500 such complaints. The office also reported a spike in complaints after a presidential candidate called for LGBT people to get psychological treatment during a televised debate.

Labor Rights

Federal government efforts to eradicate forced labor have resulted in more than 46,000 workers being freed from slave-like conditions since 1995, according to official data. However, the Pastoral Land Commission, a Catholic NGO, received complaints that approximately 3,000 individuals were victims of forced labor in 2013. Criminal accountability for offending employers remains relatively rare.

In June 2014, the Congress adopted a constitutional amendment that allows the government to confiscate property, without providing compensation to the property owner, where forced labor is found to have been used. Lawmakers have yet to approve a law defining the meaning of forced labor and explaining how property expropriation will be carried out in such cases.

Brazil adopted a constitutional amendment in March 2013 that entitles the country's estimated 6.5 million domestic workers to overtime pay, unemployment insurance, pensions, a maximum 8-hour workday, and a 44-hour work week. Proposed legislation implementing the constitutional amendment is still pending in the Brazilian Senate.

Rural Violence

Rural activists and indigenous leaders involved in conflicts over land continue to face threats and violence. According to the most recent numbers of the Pastoral Land Commission, 34 people involved in land conflicts were killed and 15 were victims of attempted murder throughout the country in 2013. As of August, the commission had already reported 23 people killed in land conflicts in 2014. Nearly 2,500 rural activists have received death threats over the past decade.

According to the Indigenous Missionary Council of the Catholic Church (Cimi), 53 indigenous people were killed in Brazil in 2013, 33 of them in Mato Grosso do Sul, the state with the highest homicide rate of indigenous people in Brazil. Thirty-three of the victims were members of the Guarani-Kaiowá indigenous group and two were members of the Terena indigenous group.

Confronting Military-Era Abuses

In May 2012, a national truth commission began investigating the systematic human rights violations that occurred during military rule from 1964 to 1985, including extrajudicial killings, forced disappearances, torture, arbitrary detention, and the curtailment of free expression. In February, the truth commission presented a preliminary report that identified seven armed forces installations where political prisoners were tortured and died during the dictatorship period. At time of writing, the truth commission's final report was due to be released in December 2014.

The perpetrators of these crimes have been shielded from justice by a 1979 amnesty law. In April 2010, the Brazilian Supreme Court reaffirmed lower court rulings that the amnesty barred most prosecutions of state agents for the crimes. However, six months later, the Inter-American Court of Human Rights ruled that this interpretation violated Brazil's obligations under international law, and that the amnesty should not be an obstacle to prosecuting serious human rights violations committed under military rule.

In April 2013, São Paulo prosecutors filed criminal charges against a retired army colonel and police investigator for concealing the body of a medical student killed during military rule. The case is still being litigated in Brazilian courts. In June 2013, however, a judge in Rio de Janeiro refused to try state agents for their alleged involvement in the enforced disappearance of a journalist in 1970.

Key International Actors

Following a petition presented by the Inter-American Commission on Human Rights, which pointed out ongoing human rights abuses in the Pedrinhas Prison Complex in Maranhão state, the Inter-American Court of Human Rights called upon Brazil in November 2014 to immediately adopt measures to protect the life and personal integrity of all prisoners in the prison complex.

Foreign Policy

As a returning member of the UN Human Rights Council (HRC), Brazil maintained a positive voting record in 2014, supporting the adoption of resolutions on a number of critical human rights situations. In June, Brazil voted in favor of a resolution condemning military operations conducted by Israeli forces in Gaza, condemning abuses against civilians by both sides, and dispatching an international commission of inquiry to investigate violations of humanitarian law and human rights law. In September 2014, Brazil was one of the sponsors of an HRC resolution on combating violence and discrimination based on sexual orientation and gender identity. The resolution called on the UN high commissioner for human rights to update a 2012 report on violence and discrimination, with a view to share best practices to overcome these abuses. Brazil abstained, however, from a contentious HRC resolution that did not recognize the many different forms families can take.

At the UN General Assembly, Brazil has played a leading role in promoting privacy in the digital era. In December 2013, the General Assembly adopted a resolution proposed by Brazil and Germany calling on all states to protect and respect the right to privacy and tasking the high commissioner for human rights to report on the issue. That report, issued in July 2014, concluded that mass surveillance had become "a dangerous habit" in some countries and that many states were falling short on privacy protections. Brazil was continuing to press for further action by the General Assembly on these issues at time of writing.

In November 2014, Brazil voted in favor of a landmark resolution adopted by the General Assembly calling for the Security Council to refer North Korea to the International Criminal Court for crimes against humanity.

At the Organization of American States, Brazil presented a resolution prohibiting all types of discrimination against LGBT people, including discrimination that limits their political participation and involvement in other aspects of public life. The resolution was approved in June 2014.

In April 2014, Brazil organized and hosted NetMundial, a global gathering of governments, nongovernmental groups, technologists, and private sector actors concerned with the future of the Internet. NetMundial participants produced an outcome statement that prioritized human rights principles and provided a roadmap for future multi-stakeholder Internet governance conversations.

Burma

The reform process in Burma experienced significant slowdowns and in some cases reversals of basic freedoms and democratic progress in 2014. The government continued to pass laws with significant human rights limitations, failed to address calls for constitutional reform ahead of the 2015 elections, and increased arrests of peaceful critics, including land protesters and journalists.

Slowing Political Reforms

The government's commitment to staging free and fair elections in 2015 came under question in 2014 as it cancelled planned bi-elections and made no commitment to amend the deeply flawed 2008 constitution. The opposition National League for Democracy party and donor governments pressed for constitutional reform, particularly article 59(f), which effectively disqualifies opposition leader Aung San Suu Kyi from the presidency, and article 436, which provides the military 25 percent of seats in parliament, granting it an effective veto over constitutional amendments. The government resisted demands for substantive discussions of federalism.

The Burmese Defense Services, or Tatmadaw, rejected constitutional amendments, and senior military leaders in numerous speeches vowed to safeguard the existing constitution as one of the military's core duties. Military leaders also maintained that they should retain their quota of reserved seats in parliament, control of key ministries, and emergency powers.

Freedom of Association and Assembly

There were at least 27 political prisoners in Burma at time of writing, according to former prisoner groups. Some 200 other people face charges for what appears to be efforts to exercise their rights to freedom of assembly and expression. The joint government and civil society political prisoner review committee, formed in early 2013 to resolve remaining cases, broke down in 2014 due to disputes between the committee chair, President's Office Minister Soe Thane, and former prisoners. Soe Thane reportedly threatened members of the committee with loss of citizenship if they continued their criticism of the government. A presidential amnesty in October released 3,000 prisoners, only about a dozen of whom were political prisoners, including a number of ethnic Rohingya prisoners.

Protests over land rights intensified in 2014 as farmers faced evictions, at times receiving inadequate compensation or relocation terms. Soldiers committed violence against farmers who had returned to symbolically work their land and call for its return. Military members of the national parliament shut down parliamentary debates on the extent of land-taking over previous decades by the armed forces.

In June, the parliament bowed to popular pressure and amended the Peaceful Procession and Assembly Law, but maintained controversial section 18, which grants broad latitude to local officials to deny permission for gatherings. The draft Association Law, which has attracted widespread civil society criticisms, was still being discussed at time of writing, with the military controlled Ministry of Home Affairs unwilling to remove provisions granting the authorities wide powers to restrict registration of national and international nongovernmental organizations.

Freedom of Media

Media freedoms, viewed by some donor countries as a key indicator of human rights progress, took a sharp downturn in 2014 as the government increased its intimidation of media.

In January, the Ministry of Information exerted pressure on publishers to change editorial content and bring publications in line with official spellings, and began imposing visa restrictions on exiled Burmese and foreign journalists entering the country by reducing their permission to stay from 3-6 months to only 28 days.

In July, a court sentenced four journalists and the editor of the weekly journal *Unity* to 10 years in prison, later reduced to 7 years, for breaches of the Official Secrets Act over a story alleging a suspected Burmese military chemical weapons plant had been built on seized land. The case alarmed many journalists who saw it as a return to past draconian punishments of media.

In October, the army detained freelance reporter Aung Kyaw Naing (also known as Par Gyi) while he was reporting on fighting between the army and ethnic rebels in Mon State. The army claimed that Par Gyi was shot and killed while attempting to escape; his body was buried near the army camp. The government called on the National Human Rights Commission (NHRC) to investigate, and Par Gyi's body was exhumed and examined, which proved he had been severely torured and shot to death. On December 2, the NHRC determined the case should be referred to, and heard in, a civil court.

Proposed media laws making their way through parliament will further constrain journalists from reporting openly. One, the Public Service Media Bill, will foster the development of a publicly funded media conglomerate that can be expected to serve as a powerful pro-government voice.

Sectarian Tensions and Violence

Tensions between Burma's Buddhist and Muslim communities continued through 2014. Ultra-nationalist Buddhist monks in the "969 Movement" used inflammatory rhetoric that at times incited violence against Muslims. In July, attacks against Muslim-owned property in central Mandalay resulted in the killing of two men, one Buddhist and one Muslim, until security forces acted to end the violence and impose a curfew.

The authorities investigated and prosecuted some people involved in violence against Muslims, including suspects in the Mandalay violence. In October, seven men were sentenced to seven years in prison for killing ten Muslim pilgrims on a bus in Thandwe township in Arakan State in 2012. The attack increased tensions in the region that led to major violence, including a campaign of "ethnic cleansing" against Rohingya Muslims, in June and October 2012.

The nationwide League to Protect Race and Religion (widely known by its Burmese acronym, Ma Ba Tha) has continued to urge the government to enact four laws designed to protect Buddhism, although the laws appear to be thinly veiled measures to further marginalize Muslim communities. The measures include draft laws on interfaith marriage, religious conversion, family planning and polygamy. One draft law on religious conversion was released to the public for feedback in May, but was criticized as an intrusion into personal matters of faith. Nearly 100 Burmese civil society groups wrote to protest the law. The 969 leadership, including ultra-nationalist monk U Wirathu, denounced the groups, calling them "traitors."

Abuses against Rohingya

Systematic repression of ethnic Rohingya Muslims in Burma's western Arakan State continued in 2014, especially against 140,000 internally displaced Rohingya forced out of their homes during the violence in 2012. An estimated one million Rohingya in Maungdaw and Buthidaung townships along the Bangladesh border continue to face restrictions on movement, employment, and religious freedom.

All Rohingya in Burma are effectively denied citizenship on the basis of the 1982 Citizenship Law, rendering many of them, including children, stateless. The nationwide census conducted in March-April 2014 did not permit Rohingya to self-identify as such, and according to results released in September, 1.2 million people in Arakan State were not included in the census. The number of Rohingya fleeing Arakan State by boat rose dramatically in 2014, with estimates suggesting that 50-100,000 have fled since the start of 2013, mostly for Malaysia.

A January 2014 incident in a Rohingya village called Du Chee Yar Tan in Maungdaw township reportedly resulted in the killing of between 40 and 60 Rohingya villagers by security forces and Arakanese residents. One policeman was also reportedly killed. The United Nations Office of the High Commissioner for Human Rights conducted a short investigation under restrictive government conditions and confirmed that a violent incident had taken place, and estimated that dozens of killings had occurred.

Two government investigations and one by the Myanmar National Human Rights Commission, which were below international standards and did not include impartial investigators, dismissed the incident as exaggerated. Journalists and independent human rights monitors have not been given adequate access to the area to investigate.

Partly as fallout over this incident, the government suspended on a technicality the work of the humanitarian organization Médecins Sans Frontières (MSF) in Arakan State. This left tens of thousands of Rohingya without badly needed primary health care until MSF was permitted to resume activities in September.

In late March, Arakanese ultra-nationalists conducted coordinated attacks on offices and warehouses of UN and international organizations in in Sittwe, forcing the evacuation of over 200 foreign and Burmese aid workers. Continuing restrictions by security forces and threats by local militants have inhibited aid operations.

In October, the secretive government Rakhine [Arakan] State Action Plan for long-term development was leaked. It included provisions for the forced relocation of all Rohingya camps, housing an estimated 130,000 people, to unspecified sites, and a nationality verification process to determine eligibility for citizenship under the discriminatory 1982 Citizenship Law. Those deemed ineligible would be sent to detention camps and face possible deportation. At time of writing the plan had still not been finalized or publicly released.

Ethnic Conflict and Forced Displacement

Amid nationwide ceasefire talks, fighting between the Burmese government and ethnic armed groups intensified in 2014, particularly between the Tatmadaw and Shan, Ta-aung, and Kachin rebels in Kachin and Shan States. Several thousand civilians have fled military abuses, including reported shelling of populated areas.

More than 100,000 civilians in Kachin State have yet to return home following fighting from 2011 to 2013. The security situation remains tense with a large Burmese army troop presence, landmines, and continued abuses by government forces, making the situation not conducive to returns of displaced persons and refugees in safety and dignity. Displaced persons in government-controlled areas face arbitrary arrest and torture from security forces, including for allegedly supporting Kachin insurgents in violation of the Unlawful Associations Act.

An estimated 350,000 people remain internally displaced in eastern Burma, and more than 110,000 refugees live in nine camps across the border in Thailand. Discussions between the Burmese military leadership and Thailand's new military junta in 2014 led to an agreement to repatriate these refugees. Under current conditions—lack of security in the area, extensive landmine infestation, poor rule of law, and an absence of even basic infrastructure and services—any returns would not be sustainable and in line with international standards.

Key International Actors

All major aid donors—including those from the European Union, Australia, the United Kingdom, and Japan—increased aid and development support to Burma in 2014. The World Bank and Asian Development Bank also increased grants to Burma in 2014.

Yanghee Lee, the new UN special rapporteur for human rights in Burma, visited the country in July and reported that despite some progress, the human rights landscape remained serious, particularly in regards to the Rohingya. President Thein Sein did not follow-up on his pledge to US President Barack Obama to permit the formal establishment of an office of the UN High Commissioner for Human Rights (OHCHR).

The government had objected to the inclusion of human rights monitoring and reporting in addition to capacity-building in the office's mandate. Four OHCHR staff members operate in the country on short-term visas and restricted travel, but they are able to interact with government officials.

In speeches at the UN General Assembly and at the annual Asia-Europe meeting in Italy, the Burmese president and foreign minister claimed the government had made sufficient progress to warrant a downgrading of scrutiny of the country's human rights record. Even formerly reluctant critics such as Germany's Chancellor Angela Merkel voiced concern over continuing religious intolerance and ethnic violence during Thein Sein's bilateral visit in September.

The UK, United States, and Australia continued preliminary non-lethal military engagement with the Burmese armed forces said to be designed to foster respect for the rule of law and military transformation.

Burma's armed forces continue to illegally recruit and deploy child soldiers despite cooperation with the UN on a joint action plan to end child recruitment. In 2014 the government staged four child soldier release ceremonies, discharging a total of 378 underage soldiers. Non-state armed groups, particularly in Burma's northern states where fighting has increased, also recruit and use child soldiers, according to widespread reports.

Burundi

State repression against opponents and critics increased ahead of elections scheduled for 2015. The government repeatedly harassed opposition parties, civil society activists, and journalists, and blocked their activities. Members of the youth league of the ruling National Council for the Defense of Democracy-Forces for the Defense of Democracy (CNDD-FDD) used violence, and carried out abuses, against perceived opponents. Leading human rights activist Pierre Claver Mbonimpa was arrested and charged for remarks he made on the radio. On September 29, judges provisionally released him on grounds of ill-health.

The split of the opposition party UPRONA into two factions, in part due to alleged government interference in the choice of party leaders, triggered a political crisis and led to all three UPRONA ministers resigning. Draft constitutional amendments, which might have allowed President Pierre Nkurunziza to stand for a third term and altered the voting system in parliament, were defeated by just one vote in March.

Impunity for human rights abuses, particularly by state agents and youth of the ruling party, remains a concern. There was very little progress in investigating scores of extrajudicial killings between 2010 and 2012. The justice system suffers from a lack of independence and allegations of corruption.

Civil Society

The government persistently harassed civil society activists and blocked their activities, accusing them of being political opponents and interfering with the course of justice.

Pierre Claver Mbonimpa, president of the Association for the Protection of Human Rights and Detained Persons (APRODH), was arrested in the capital, Bujumbura, on May 15. He was charged with endangering internal and external state security and using false documents, in connection with allegations he made on Radio Publique Africaine (RPA) on May 6 that young Burundians were being given weapons and military uniforms and sent for military training in the Democratic Republic of Congo. The court in Bujumbura turned down his lawyers' request for his provisional release three times, even after he became seriously ill and was hospitalized. On September 29, following the report of a court-ordered medical commission that listed several serious medical conditions, judges ordered Mbonimpa's provisional release on grounds of ill-health. His case triggered widespread public reaction and numerous calls for his release inside and outside Burundi.

Following the adoption of a new law on public gatherings and demonstrations in December 2013, government officials repeatedly prohibited demonstrations and other activities by civil society organizations. The mayor of Bujumbura prohibited a peaceful march in support of Mbonimpa in June, claiming it had "an insurrectional character." The minister of interior upheld his decision, telling the organizers they should let justice do its work instead of "distracting the public."

Bujumbura's mayor also prohibited a civil society demonstration planned for August 1 to call for an independent justice system. In July and September, police stopped Gabriel Rufyiri, president of the anti-corruption organization OLUCOME, from holding a one-person protest against illicit enrichment. Authorities also stopped civil society organizations from holding a march in April to mark the fifth anniversary of the murder of anti-corruption activist Ernest Manirumva.

Journalists

As with civil society organizations, government officials threatened and harassed independent journalists, claiming they were mouthpieces of the political opposition. In July, the National Communications Council (CNC) banned radio stations from playing a song about Mbonimpa. In August, the CNC warned RPA to stop broadcasting interviews with people who claimed to have information backing up Mbonimpa's allegations about military training of Burundians in Congo.

Following a legal challenge by the Union of Burundian Journalists (UBJ) regarding a restrictive press law adopted in 2013, the Constitutional Court ruled on January 7, 2014, that several articles of the press law did not comply with Burundi's Constitution. A parallel case by the UBJ challenging the law at the East African Court of Justice was pending at time of writing.

Opposition Parties

Restrictions on opposition parties increased as the CNDD-FDD tried to position itself for another victory in the 2015 elections. Government and ruling party officials blocked and interfered with the activities of opposition parties. Longstanding divisions in the opposition party UPRONA came to a head in early 2014, when the party broke into two factions, following alleged interference by government officials in the choice of party leaders. The government only recognized the faction headed by the new, CNDD-FDD-compliant leaders, leaving the other faction unable to operate legally.

Members of the youth league of the ruling party, known as *Imbonerakure*, carried out abuses against real or perceived opponents, including beatings, disruption of party meetings, and other acts of violence and intimidation. Youths of other parties sometimes retaliated, leading to violent clashes.

On March 8 and 9, 70 people, mostly members of the Movement for Solidarity and Democracy (MSD) opposition party, were arrested, many of them arbitrarily. Some were arrested in connection with alleged plans to hold an authorized demonstration, others following a clash between MSD members and the police, during which some MSD members took two policemen hostage.

All were tried together, on March 18, charged with rebellion, insults and acts of violence against law enforcement agents, grievous bodily harm and participation in an insurrectional movement. During the trial, which lasted just one day, neither the defendants nor their lawyers were able to prepare their defense properly, and little attempt was made to establish individual culpability. On March 21, a court in Bujumbura sentenced 21 defendants to life imprisonment, 10 defendants to 10 years in prison, and 14 defendants to five years in prison. It acquitted 22 defendants. A separate chamber for minors tried three defendants aged about 17 and sentenced them to two years in prison. Appeal hearings were delayed until the end of December. The government suspended the MSD for four months following its clash with police.

Prisoner Releases

On June 27, a presidential decree ordered the release of several categories of prisoners, including those sentenced to five years' imprisonment or less, pregnant women, prisoners suffering from incurable illnesses, those aged over 60, and those under 18. However, progress in releasing prisoners has been slow.

Impunity

Most of the perpetrators of scores of extrajudicial killings and other acts of political violence between 2010 and 2012 continue to evade justice. An appeal hearing in the case of Deputy Police Commissioner Michel Nurweze, alias Rwembe ("razor blade" in Kirundi), was held on November 6 after being repeatedly delayed for more than a year. In a rare prosecution of an official for human rights abuses, a court in Gitega had tried Nurweze in 2013 on charges of murder, torture, and attempted murder. However, after at least two prosecution witnesses refused to testify due to a lack of adequate protection, he was acquitted for murder and torture but found guilty of grievous bodily harm and sentenced to three months' imprisonment. He was released as he had already served a year in prison.

Three police officers accused of involvement in the killing of nine religious worshippers at Businde in March 2013 had not been tried at time of writing. They were arrested in 2013 and provisionally released after three months. There were further arrests of worshippers from the same informal spiritual movement who make monthly pilgrimages to Businde.

In May, Burundi adopted a law establishing a Truth and Reconciliation Commission to cover grave violations of human rights and international humanitarian law committed between 1962 and 2008. The commission had not been set up at time of writing. The law did not include any reference to the creation of a special tribunal or other judicial mechanism to try these crimes.

Key International Actors

Mbonimpa's arrest triggered widespread international reactions. Several governments and embassies, including those of the United States, the European Union, France, the United Kingdom, and Belgium, expressed concern, particularly after Mbonimpa's hospitalization. In September, the European Parliament passed a resolution calling for his immediate and unconditional release and expressing concern about other human rights abuses in Burundi. On September 23, US

President Barack Obama said he stood in solidarity with Mbonimpa and called for his release.

The mandate of the United Nations Office in Burundi, BNUB, was due to end on December 31, 2014, despite the worsening human rights situation ahead of the 2015 elections. At time of writing, plans were underway to set up by January 2015 a human rights presence in Burundi under the Office of the UN High Commissioner for Human Rights, as recommended by the UN Joint Transition Plan, presented to the government on May 16.

The UN Security Council also requested that the secretary-general establish an electoral observer mission to monitor and report before, during, and after the elections in response to a request from Burundi's government. In April, the government expelled BNUB's security advisor to protest a leaked UN confidential cable containing allegations that military officers had distributed weapons and military and police uniforms to the *Imbonerakure*.

The African Commission on Human and Peoples' Rights agreed to consider four complaints on extrajudicial killings in Burundi submitted in June by four Burundian civil society organizations and the Swiss-based organization Track Impunity Always (TRIAL).

On November 25, following a visit to the country, the UN special rapporteur on the situation of human rights defenders, Michael Forst, condemned as unacceptable the "escalation of the harassment of defenders" and criticized attempts to restrict the work of civil society actors by equating them with political opponents.

Cambodia

The past year saw determined and often-violent efforts by the government of Prime Minister Hun Sen and his Cambodian People's Party (CPP) to suppress mass protests against the deeply flawed July 2013 parliamentary elections, and force the opposition Cambodia National Rescue Party (CNRP), to accept the election results, and end its boycott of the National Assembly. The government imposed bans on peaceful protests, including strikes by trade unions campaigning for increased wages. In some cases, protesters engaged in attacks in response to security force repression.

A July 2014, CPP-CNRP agreement ended the opposition's boycott of the National Assembly. The agreement, which followed the arrest of prominent CNRP leader Mu Sochua, and six other CNRP assembly members on trumped-up charges, failed to commit the CPP to implement institutional and legal reforms to ensure that future elections will be free and fair, or to guarantee freedom of expression and opinion, peaceful assembly and association, or fair trials.

Poverty remained particularly severe in the countryside, while urban workers also suffered from wages so low they contribute to widespread malnutrition. Victims of land concessions to agro-industrial business interests—the major cause of dispossession of land from farmers, and resulting land disputes—made little progress in receiving adequate compensation and resettlement packages. Government officials and judges remained mired in corruption, but almost all were immune from action by courts and the government's Anti-Corruption Unit, which only targeted petty cases involving those without CPP political protection.

Excessive Use of Lethal and Other Force

In early January, authorities banned all protests, in part to try to force organized labor in the garment industry to lower their demands for a minimum wage increase. Gendarme, police, and para-police personnel killed at least seven people and injured dozens of others mostly during the first seven months of the year, before the ban was partly lifted. Protesters also injured several members of the security forces.

Impunity and Politically Motivated Prosecutions

Since the CPP has been in power, members and commanders of government se-curity forces have enjoyed impunity from investigation, let alone prosecution, for serious human rights abuses, including political assassinations, other extrajudi-cial killings, and torture. Instead, politically partisan police, prosecutors, and judges pursued at least 87 trumped-up cases against CNRP leaders and activists, members of other opposition political groups, prominent trade union figures, urban civil society organizers, and ordinary workers from factories around Phnom Penh.

The Phnom Penh Municipal Court sentenced 55 people to prison after unfair tri-als, on charges such as "treacherously plotting" to stage an armed insurrection, or instigating, inciting, or perpetrating violence, obstructing traffic, or "violent resistance against a public official." In these proceedings, no credible evidence was presented to support a guilty verdict, while evidence of security force vio-lence was systematically disallowed. Although 30 of the 55 received suspended sentences, 23 had already spent many months of pretrial detention in an over-crowded, substandard, and isolated prison.

Criminal cases pending included, alleged incitement to violence by CNRP Presi-dent Sam Rainsy, Vice President Kem Sokha, and union leader Rong Chhun for opposing the government's blanket ban on protests; charges against seven other CNRP assembly members and nine CNRP activists for leading, or participat-ing in a violent "insurrection" and other crimes related to a security force-pro-voked melee at a CNRP-sponsored protest in July 2014; charges of incitement to violence and other crimes against six union leaders in connection with worker unrest during a general strike in December 2013-January 2014; charges of "treacherous plotting" and other crimes against a political activist for distribut-ing a banned book in 2014; and charges against a Buddhist monk and three youths in connection with protests against election unfairness and other alleged government abuses dating back to 2011.

Land Confiscation and Forced Evictions

The ill-effects of often illegal land acquisitions, by politically powerful individu-als and their business partners, and forced evictions, continued to mount. The number of people affected by state-involved land conflicts since 2000 passed the half-million mark in March 2014, according to calculations by the local non-governmental organization LICADHO. The rate of new disputes was higher than in 2013. Many of the new disputes ensued from the failure of the authorities to distribute land titles awarded to rural residents as part of a 2012-2013 scheme, personally conceived and overseen by Hun Sen.

In August 2014, Hun Sen blamed his government subordinates for failing to re-solve disputes, repeating many previous pledges to end unlawful land takings. At least four people remain imprisoned after convictions in previous years for op-posing land takings, while charges against at least 19 others were pending in various provincial courts.

Arbitrary Detention, Torture, and Other Ill-Treatment

The authorities detained hundreds of people they deemed to be "undesirable," without judicial recourse in so-called drug treatment centers, where they face torture, sexual violence, and—in at least two centers—forced labor. Authorities locked up alleged drug users, homeless people, beggars, street children, sex workers, and people with disabilities in these centers for arbitrary periods.

People held during investigation, or prosecution for common criminal offenses, or convicted in court, were still routinely tortured, or otherwise ill-treated. The police and prison authorities, beat, pistol-whipped, used electro-shock, kicked, slapped, and punched inmates, often until they become unconscious. Much of the torture was aimed at extracting confessions or extorting money.

New Laws Strengthening Government Control of the Judiciary

Amid politically motivated prosecutions and unfair trials, the CPP further tight-ened its control over the judiciary by rushing passage of three laws through the National Assembly during the opposition boycott.

Laws on the Organization of the Courts, the Statute of Judges and Prosecutors, and the Organization and Functioning of the Supreme Council of the Magistracy, promulgated on July 13, 2014, increased government control over a politically subservient Supreme Council of the Magistracy, and weakened provisions for ju-dicial independence.

Together, the laws facilitated further encroachment by the government on areas properly reserved for the judiciary under the principle of separation of powers including, government control over the judiciary's budgetary finance and administrative matters, restrictions on the rights of judges and prosecutors to freedom of expression, and fewer safeguards for judicial independence in selection, promotion, removal, and disciplinary procedures for judges.

The legislation put the minister of justice at the center of all key decision-making by the judiciary and the Supreme Council of the Magistracy, the body charged with appointing, disciplining, and overseeing the country's judicial system.

Khmer Rouge Tribunal

On August 7, 2014, eight years after the creation of the United Nations-assisted Extraordinary Chambers in the Courts of Cambodia, former Khmer Rouge leaders Nuon Chea and Khieu Samphan were convicted of crimes against humanity, including extermination and political persecution. These were committed as part of the Khmer Rouge's forced relocations of Cambodians from urban areas to the countryside and around the countryside in 1975, during which many were executed.

The two continued to face trial on other charges, including genocide, in connection with Khmer Rouge policies and practices from 1975 to 1979. However, given their advanced age, it was far from certain that a second trial would ever be completed. Hun Sen's public opposition to trials of other Khmer Rouge suspects made it unlikely that others responsible for the deaths of as many as 2 million people, would be held accountable. While the trial had initially generated considerable interest, the drawn-out proceedings over many years resulted in the Cambodian public showing little interest by the trial's end.

Labor Rights

The brutal suppression of garment and textile worker protests in January, and the subsequent prosecution of labor leaders and workers on trumped-up charges, did not deter some trade unions from continuing to protest for an increased minimum wage, demanding US$177 monthly, as suggested in a government task force report. Instead, the government on November 12 declared a minimum wage of $128.

The authorities introduced more burdensome procedures for union registration, and independent unions complained that their union registration was intentionally being delayed. The government also moved toward passage of a revised law on trade unions that fell far short of international standards guaranteeing freedom of association.

Ongoing reports of employees fainting en masse in factories, prompted authorities to create a committee to investigate the causes. However, the general state of labor inspection and remedial action remained poor, although officials from the Ministry of Labor and Vocational Training began conducting joint inspections of "low compliance" factories named in the Transparency Database launched by the International Labour Organization's Better Factories Cambodia program.

Key International Actors

China, Vietnam, Japan, and South Korea were Cambodia's major foreign investors during the year, while Japan, the European Union and United States were the major foreign donors. China, Vietnam, and the US provided material military assistance and training to the Cambodian security forces, including units known to have recently been involved in serious human rights violations.

Positively, the US conspicuously refrained from endorsing the 2013 elections as free and fair, and repeatedly and publicly called on the authorities to respect human rights, especially to restore the rights to freedom of association and peaceful assembly. However, the US was virtually alone among foreign countries in seriously addressing Cambodia's human rights crises, whether in public or private.

The World Bank, which suspended new lending to Cambodia in 2011 because the government had forcibly evicted people in a manner violating bank policy, began to consider resuming funding for government land projects, even though the government had not fully resolved the problem that had led to the suspension, or ceased and remedied reprisals against those who have advocated on these issues, among them activists sentenced to prison in November

In September, Cambodia agreed with Australia to accept an unknown number of refugees transferred from the island nation of Nauru. The Australian government will pay costs towards "resettling" the refugees, and also agreed to pay $35million in developmental assistance over four years towards electoral reform, demining, and rice-milling as part of the bilateral refugee agreement.

Canada

Canada enjoys a global reputation as a defender of human rights, aided by a solid record on core civil and political rights protections that are guaranteed by the Canadian Charter of Rights and Freedoms. Nonetheless, in 2014, the sitting majority in parliament refused to take essential steps to remedy serious human rights concerns, particularly with regard to violence against indigenous women, the legal status of sex work, and the impact of Canada's extractive industries abroad.

Violence against Indigenous Women and Girls

A 2014 data collection effort by the Royal Canadian Mounted Police (RCMP) identified 1,181 cases of murders and disappearances of indigenous women and girls between 1980 and 2012, double previous estimates. The study found that indigenous women and girls are overrepresented among homicide victims, constituting 16 percent of female homicide victims, despite making up only 4.3 percent of Canada's female population. A 2013 Human Rights Watch report documented the RCMP's failure in British Columbia to protect indigenous women and girls from violence, as well as from abusive police behavior, including excessive use of force and physical and sexual assault.

Despite growing public concern over the murders and disappearances, the government of Prime Minister Stephen Harper continued to resist calls from provincial leaders, opposition political parties, and civil society for a national inquiry into the violence.

A special parliamentary committee convened to address the issue broke along party lines, and the Conservative majority failed to recommend an inquiry or any steps to address police accountability for misconduct. Recent signs that the government may agree to a ministerial roundtable on violence offer some promise for an inquiry but would not be an adequate substitute. In Canada, public national inquiries allow for impartial investigation into issues of national importance.

Sex Work

In 2014, parliament began debating new provisions criminalizing aspects of sex work following the Supreme Court of Canada's 2013 ruling striking down previous restrictions that the court deemed violated the rights and security of sex workers.

Justice Minister Peter MacKay tabled Bill C-36, which would criminalize communicating for the purposes of selling sexual services in public, or buying, advertising or benefitting from the sale of sexual services. The bill would severely limit sex workers' abilities to take life-saving measures, such as screening clients. Criminalizing communication disproportionately impacts street-based sex workers, many of whom are indigenous, poor, or transgender, forcing them to work in more dangerous and isolated locations.

Surveillance and Privacy

In January 2014, media reported that the Communications Security Establishment of Canada (CSEC) was conducting indiscriminate collection and analysis of communications data. This information was based on documents widely released by former US National Security Agency contractor Edward Snowden. The documents revealed that the intelligence agency was provided with metadata captured from travelers' wireless devices in a major Canadian airport over a two-week period.

The agency then tracked travelers' subsequent movements as their mobile phones or laptops connected to other wi-fi access points in airports, hotels, and restaurants. Reports suggest that this initiative was a 2012 trial run for a program that may now be operational. Additional media stories revealed that CSEC may be operating several Internet and phone metadata collection programs. Details remain secret.

The programs described to date only involve collection of metadata, not the content of communications. However, metadata, or data about a communication, can be highly revealing of movements, associations, and activity. The government insists on the legality of metadata collection programs, raising concerns that legal reforms are necessary to ensure meaningful protections for the right to privacy in intelligence gathering programs.

Counterterrorism

Canada has continued to deny Omar Khadr—a Canadian citizen who was detained from the age of 15 in Guantanamo for 10 years and pleaded guilty to terrorism-related charges in the fundamentally flawed military commissions system—access to rehabilitation and reintegration services as required for former child soldiers.

Khadr remains incarcerated. In July, an appeals court ruled that Khadr would have been considered a youth offender if sentenced in Canada and should serve out the remainder of his 8-year sentence in a provincial facility, where he would have access to educational and rehabilitative programming, in accordance with Canadian law for youth offenders. A federal government appeal is pending.

Mining Industry Abuses

Canada is the mining industry's most important global financing hub, home to a majority of the world's mining and exploration companies. These firms have an enormous collective impact on the human rights of vulnerable communities worldwide.

In 2013, Human Rights Watch documented allegations that Vancouver-based Nevsun Resources' flagship Bisha gold mine in Eritrea was partly built using forced labor deployed by local state-owned contractor, Segen Construction. In a statement, Nevsun expressed "regret if certain employees of Segen were conscripts" during the mine's construction and insisted there were no ongoing abuses. The company subsequently carried out a human rights impact assessment and promised to integrate human rights considerations into its policies. However, it has refused to sever ties with Segen.

In 2011, Human Rights Watch documented allegations that security guards employed by Canadian mining giant Barrick Gold had gang-raped women at a Papua New Guinea mine site and engaged in other violent abuses. The company has since taken steps to prevent further abuses. In 2014, it paid out claims consisting of cash and other forms of assistance to over 100 women who suffered sexual violence at the hands of company employees. This unprecedented remediation scheme has struggled with design and implementation issues and has attracted considerable criticism. In spite of its flaws, this initiative could emerge as a path-breaking example of how companies can move proactively to respond to serious abuses linked to their global operations. It is too early to judge whether it will result in lasting, positive outcomes for the women involved.

The Canadian government neither regulates nor monitors the human rights practices of Canadian mining companies when they go abroad. Its sole action on this front was to establish in 2009 a corporate social responsibility counselor whose office is without oversight or investigatory powers.

Cluster Munitions

In 2014, the Canadian Parliament continued to debate contentious Bill C-6 to implement the Convention on Cluster Munitions. The convention bans the use, production, transfer, and stockpiling of these weapons, as well as assisting anyone with these activities. The convention further requires states to destroy stockpiles, clear cluster munition remnants, and assist victims. Canada, a signatory to the convention, requires the adoption of implementation legislation before ratification.

Certain provisions of Bill C-6 run counter to the treaty's spirit and letter. It would allow Canadian armed forces to assist with use and other prohibited activities during joint military operations with a state not party. For example, Canadian commanders could direct or authorize an ally's armed forces to use cluster munitions. The bill would also allow cluster munitions to be stockpiled and transported through Canadian territory.

The Senate Standing Committee on Foreign Affairs and International Trade planned to review the bill in October 2014. The House of Commons had made one change to the original bill, and Human Rights Watch urged the Senate committee to revise it further to bring Canada in line with its international commitments. It is hoped that Canada will be a state party by the convention's First Review Conference in September 2015.

Despite this, Canada should be commended for completing destruction of its cluster munition stockpiles in 2014, in accordance with the convention.

Central African Republic

Attacks on civilians remained alarming and widespread in the Central African Republic, despite a decrease of violent attacks from the previous year. The sectarian violence between the predominately Muslim Seleka rebels and the "anti-balaka," a group harboring hatred towards Muslims, spread from western parts of the country toward central and eastern areas. Witnesses on both sides frequently described the attacks as retaliatory in nature, indicating a growing cycle of revenge killings. By the end of 2014, thousands of civilians had been killed by both sides and over 800,000 people displaced from their homes, of which an estimated 415,000 people, many of them Muslim, took refuge across the borders in neighboring countries. A transitional government, led by the interim president, Catherine Samba-Panza, appointed in January, struggled to establish security. A ceasefire agreement signed by the warring factions in July was widely ignored.

In April, the United Nations Security Council authorized a new peacekeeping mission for the Central African Republic, known as MINUSCA, to protect civilians, facilitate humanitarian access, and monitor, investigate, and report on human rights abuses. It took over from the African Union (AU) on September 15, integrating 4,800 AU troops into MINUSCA, and began deploying additional troops. At time of writing, 8,500 of the force's potential 11,800 had been deployed. Approximately 2,000 French peacekeepers, authorized by the Security Council in late 2013, remained in the country.

Some AU peacekeepers, while providing important civilian protection during their deployment, also committed serious human rights abuses, although according to the UN Department of Peacekeeping Operations, those facing allegations were not integrated into MINUSCA.

Tackling impunity and re-establishing the rule of law remain a serious challenge. In September, the International Criminal Court (ICC) announced it would begin an investigation into war crimes and crimes against humanity committed in the country since 2012, following a referral from interim President Samba-Panza.

Attacks by Seleka Rebels

The Seleka ("alliance" in Sango, the country's principal language), a predominantly Muslim rebel group that launched a coup d'etat in March 2013, were forced out of power in December 2013 following the deployment of French peacekeeping forces. The Seleka re-established their military base in Bambari, a city in the center of the country, from where they sought to control eastern and northern areas.

The Seleka continued to carry out brutal attacks against civilians often under the pretext of seeking out their enemies, the anti-balaka fighters. The Seleka destroyed villages, engaged in wide spread looting, and raped women and girls. For example, on February 26, Seleka fighters, aided by ethnic Peuhl cattle herders, killed eight people and wounded at least 10 others—mostly young children—in the village of Bowai, northeast of Bossangoa. In a similar attack in June in Liwa, near Bambari, Seleka rebels together with ethnic Peuhl killed at least 10 people and then burned down the entire village. Civilians were also attacked in or near their villages along roads that Seleka rebels considered to be strategic. In June, scores of civilians were killed in and around Bakala, just to the north of Bambari and near several gold mining sites. A number of the victims were tied up before the Seleka slit their throats.

Rival factions within the Seleka vied for control of the group, sometimes through armed attacks against each other, leading to the death of scores of Seleka fighters in Bambari in September. Several civilians were also killed in the attacks.

Anti-Balaka Attacks

The anti-balaka, a collection of local armed groups that emerged in mid-2013 to fight against the Seleka, continued to commit large-scale reprisal attacks against Muslim civilians and later against non-Muslim civilians. The majority of Muslims fled from the capital and the west of the country. Thousands were trapped in enclaves, such as in Carnot and Boda, where they lived in precarious conditions with peacekeepers attempting to provide some protection. In February, at least 72 Muslim civilians were killed by anti-balaka forces in the southwest of the country. In one incident on February 5 in Guen, the anti-balaka attacked a property where hundreds of Muslims had sought refuge. The attackers divided some

45 men into two groups, led them out of the compound, forced them to lie on the ground, and executed them. The attackers pursued the fleeing Muslims to the nearby town of Djomo, where many Muslims sought shelter in a Catholic parish. The anti-balaka continued to attack them there.

The anti-balaka also attacked Muslims in central and eastern areas. In June, anti-balaka forces attacked an ethnic Peuhl community at Ardondjobdi, near Bambari, as the men were finishing their morning prayers. At least 20 people, including women and children, were killed, the majority from machete blows to the head and neck. Three victims' throats were cut while they were still inside the local mosque.

Refugees and Internally Displaced Persons

The situation for the estimated 800,000 refugees and internally displaced persons remained serious, with only a small number feeling secure enough to come home. In western areas, roughly 12,000 Muslim civilians lived in isolated enclaves protected by AU, and later UN peacekeepers, too frightened to return. In Bangui, civilians living in one of the city's largest Muslim neighborhoods, called "5 Kilo," remained isolated from the rest of the city, fearing attack if they left the area.

Displacement camps and other locations where civilians sought safety were frequently attacked by armed fighters from both sides. On May 28, a displacement camp in Bangui's Fatima neighborhood was attacked by armed Muslim men from 5 Kilo after anti-balaka fighters attacked the Muslim enclave. In Bambari at least 27 civilians were killed by Seleka fighters and their allies in July while taking shelter in a displacement camp at the Saint Joseph Parish and the adjacent bishop's residence. In both attacks, AU and French peacekeepers were stationed within a few kilometers but were unable to respond quickly enough to protect civilians.

Lack of humanitarian assistance remained a major problem for the displaced. The UN Office for the Coordination of Humanitarian Affairs and other humanitarian organizations cited insecurity as a major obstacle in delivering much needed life-saving assistance.

African Union Forces

AU peacekeepers were implicated in human rights abuses, including enforced disappearances, and extrajudicial executions.

Republic of Congo soldiers operating as AU peacekeepers were responsible for at least two serious incidents of abuse. On December 22, 2013, Republic of Congo soldiers tortured to death two anti-balaka fighters held in detention in revenge for the death of a soldier from within their own ranks. On March 24, Republic of Congo soldiers summarily executed between 11 and 18 people, a mix of both anti-balaka fighters and civilians, in Boali after they were attacked by the anti-balaka and lost one of their men. The AU suspended the two commanders responsible for the soldiers in each location, rotated the troops out of the areas, and publicly declared it would launch an investigation. At time of writing, there had been little progress in identifying those responsible for the killings.

In March, Chadian peacekeepers with the AU mission were accused by the transitional government of firing indiscriminately at civilians in Bangui's PK 12 neighborhood, killing dozens of people. Following a public outcry, the Chadian government withdrew its 850 troops from the AU peacekeeping mission.

National Judicial Efforts

On April 9, interim President Samba-Panza issued a decree establishing a special investigative cell to investigate and prosecute serious crimes committed in the country since 2004. The UN peacekeeping mission also consulted with the transitional government on the establishment of a judicial mechanism to enable the country's judiciary to work alongside international actors to tackle impunity.

In August, the peacekeeping mission and the government signed a Memorandum of Understanding to create a Special Criminal Court to try grave human rights violations and violations of international humanitarian law. In the memorandum, the government commits to take the necessary legislative steps as soon as possible to create the special court.

On September 24, the ICC prosecutor announced that her office would open a second investigation in the country for crimes committed since 2012, following an earlier request from interim President Samba-Panza. In 2007, the ICC opened its first investigation in the country for crimes committed during the 2002-2003 civil war. The investigation led to the arrest of Jean-Pierre Bemba Gombo, a Congolese national and former vice president of the Democratic Republic of Congo. His trial was ongoing at the ICC at time of writing.

Key International Actors

Regional African actors and France took a lead in responding to the crisis. Chad and the Republic of Congo each hosted conferences aimed at establishing frameworks for peace. France increased its peacekeeping troops to an estimated 2,000 soldiers.

In April, the Security Council authorized the deployment of a new peacekeeping mission and in May imposed sanctions on former President Francois Bozize and two other rebel leaders for their role in the violence. The United States and the European Union provided important financial support to peacekeeping efforts in the country. In addition the US has provided more than US$145 million in humanitarian aid to help those affected by the conflict in CAR, including for refugees outside the country.

In August, the secretary-general reported to the Security Council that civilians were the targets of sectarian violence and reprisal killings every day and serious violations of human rights and international humanitarian law were committed with total impunity.

Chile

In March 2014, President Michelle Bachelet began her second term in office with a committment to tackle social and economic inequality, focusing initially on overhauling the education and taxation systems. Her campaign platform included a pledge to bring Chile's counterterrorism law into conformity with international standards, and to present a law to end the prohibition of abortion when a pregnancy endangers the life of the woman or girl, is unviable, or results from rape. Her administration also undertook to end the jurisdiction of military courts over alleged human rights abuses committed by Carabineros (police responsible for public order and crime prevention).

While courts continue to prosecute individuals for abuses committed during the Augusto Pinochet dictatorship (1973-1990), the Supreme Court has used its discretionary powers in many cases to reduce sentences against human rights violators, resulting in sentences that are incommensurate with the gravity of the crimes.

Counterterrorism Laws

Following repeated recommendations by United Nations human rights bodies, officials announced in 2014 that the Bachelet administration would not use the 1984 counterterrorism law to address violence arising from indigenous protests over land.

The law's overly broad definition of terrorism continues to allow for the prosecution on terrorism charges of activists allegedly responsible for acts such as arson and the destruction of private property, although in most recent cases judges have rejected the terrorism charges as unfounded. Another concern is a provision in the legislation allowing prosecutors to withhold the identity of certain witnesses, which has led to the detention of some suspects for over a year on the basis of evidence they cannot effectively challenge.

In September 2014, 14 people were injured by a bomb placed in a refuse bin in a crowded shopping center at a Santiago subway station. A string of such attacks attributed to anarchist groups had been reported over several years, but until the September incident, explosive devices had never been left in daytime in crowded places, and no bystanders had been seriously injured. Although several of the past incidents led to prosecutions under the counterterrorism law, in each case courts rejected terrorism charges for lack of evidence.

In November, the government presented to the Senate a bill to replace the present counterterrorism law. The bill strengthens due process guarantees by giving defense attorneys the right to be informed of the identity of protected witnesses as well as to question the witnesses about their evidence and probe their credibility. It also allows police to use undercover agents to gather evidence about terrorist groups, giving them immunity from prosecution for actions committed in pursuit of their judicial mandate.

Military Jurisdiction

Legislation approved by Congress in September 2010 under the administration of Sebastian Piñera finally ended the jurisdiction of military courts over civilians, a reform urged by the Inter-American Court of Human Rights in its 2005 ruling in the *Palamara Iribarne* case. However, the reform left untouched the jurisdiction of military courts over abuses committed by the uniformed police, Carabineros.

Military courts are composed of military officers on active service, and lack the independence and due process guarantees of ordinary criminal proceedings. Investigations are secret, criminal proceedings are conducted mainly in writing, and lawyers have limited opportunities to cross-examine witnesses.

Most complaints filed with military courts for human rights abuses in which civilians are alleged victims are dismissed. According to data published in 2014 by the National Institute for Human Rights (INDH—Chile's human rights ombudsman), the number of convictions for police abuses in Chile's central regions between 2005 and 2011 fell to 0.48 percent of the complaints filed, compared to 3.2 percent for the period from 1990-2004, even though the number of complaints increased significantly.

Chile's top courts have increasingly opposed military jurisdiction in such cases. In May, the Constitutional Court ruled that the decision of a civilian judge to decline jurisdiction over police accused of blinding a demonstrator by firing a paintball into his eye during a 2013 street protest was unconstitutional, and issued a similar decision in a separate case the following month. The Supreme

Court's criminal chamber has ruled in favor of civilian court jurisdiction in several cases, including one involving the death of a detainee who suffocated after being abandoned in a police vehicle in hot temperatures.

In May 2014, the minister of defense promised to present draft legislation before the end of June 2015 that would overhaul the military criminal code and end military jurisdiction over crimes committed by the armed forces (including Carabineros) against civilians.

Police Conduct

Information published by the INDH in 2014 revealed that police handling of public protests fell short of international human rights standards. The institute concluded that use of anti-riot equipment such as water cannons and tear gas by Carabineros in response to violence by protesters in 2013 was indiscriminate in 70 percent of the demonstrations it observed. More often than not, Carabineros used these methods disproportionately to the threat faced, and also used disproportionate force in making arrests.

Public protests and the number of abuses by Carabineros reported in this context declined significantly in 2014. In August, at the insistence of the INDH, Carabineros for the first time authorized the publication of its operational protocols when dealing with public protests.

Prison Conditions

Many of Chile's prisons are grossly overcrowded and conditions remain poor despite government reform efforts. A study of 44 prisons published in March 2014 by the INDH reported beatings by prison guards, and high levels of inmate violence in some prisons that resulted in 35 deaths from January to October 2012.

Prisoners are often arbitrarily confined in punishment cells without adequate light, ventilation, basic access to water, sanitation, and hygiene, or medical attention. On her retirement in 2014, a Supreme Court official responsible for monitoring prison conditions described this practice as "flagrant cruel and inhuman treatment."

Torture

Cases of torture continue to be reported and impunity is common. Between 2011 and August 2014, the INDH filed 33 complaints of torture with the courts—16 for acts allegedly committed by Carabineros, 10 by prison guards, and 7 by the Investigations Police (PDI).

Confronting Past Abuses

The chief justice stated in March 2014 that 1,022 cases of human rights violations committed during the Pinochet dictatorship (1973-1990) were under adjudication by the courts, 72 of which were cases of torture. According to the human rights unit within the Ministry of Interior (a party to about 800 of the cases under court investigation), as of October, 1,086 individuals had been charged with or convicted of human rights violations including killings and enforced disappearances, 279 had final judgments rendered against them, and 75 were serving prison sentences.

The Supreme Court's criminal chamber has been inconsistent in reviewing sentences in important human rights cases. The Observatory of Transitional Justice at Diego Portales University, which monitors human rights trials, has found that in enforced disappearance cases the court often confirms prison sentences that comply with Chile's obligation to hold perpetrators accountable through appropriate punishments. In extrajudicial execution cases, however, the court has often reduced prison terms and allowed alternatives to prison if significant time has elapsed since the criminal act.

Reproductive Rights

Chile is one of four countries in Latin America (the other three being El Salvador, Honduras, and Nicaragua) with an absolute prohibition on abortion, even in the event of medical necessity or rape. In her annual address to the nation in May 2014, President Bachelet announced that her government would present legislation to decriminalize abortion in cases where there was a risk to the life of the woman or girl, fetal unviability, or rape. As of November 2014, the government had not presented its bill to Congress. Two bills presented by members of the chamber of deputies and senators in May and July 2013 were still under discussion in committee at time of writing.

Sexual Orientation and Gender Identity

A bill tabled by five senators in May 2013 to achieve legal recognition of the gender identity of transgender people was still under discussion in the Senate in November 2014. The bill would allow individuals to change their name and legal gender on birth certificates and identity cards so that official documents match their gender identity. Another bill presented by former president Sebastián Piñera in 2011 that would provide legal recognition and protection for same sex couples was approved by the Senate in October 2014 and at time of writing was awaiting a vote in the Chamber of Deputies.

Key International Actors

As a member of the United Nations Human Rights Council (HRC), Chile supported UN efforts to put human rights violations in North Korea, Sri Lanka, Belarus, Iran, the Occupied Palestinian Territories, Ukraine, and Syria under scrutiny. Chile was also one of four countries that presented a landmark HRC resolution on combating violence and discrimination based on sexual orientation and gender identity in September 2014, and was the only Latin American member of the HRC opposing a contentious resolution in June 2014 that did not recognize the many different forms families can take.

In January 2014, Chile's human rights performance was assessed as part of the HRC's "periodic review" process. Several countries praised Chile's establishment of the INDH as an independent human rights monitoring body and Chile's anti-discrimination legislation passed in 2012.

Many also called for a debate to end the criminalization of abortion. Chile accepted this recommendation (which it had rejected at the 2009 UPR) while pointing out that proposed legislation would be limited to pregnancies that endangered the life of the mother, were unviable, or resulted from rape.

In July 2014, in its concluding observations on Chile's sixth periodic report, the Human Rights Committee, the international expert body tasked with interpreting the International Covenant on Civil and Political Rights, recommended that Chile reform its counterterrorism legislation to ensure that terrorism crimes are clearly defined in the law, and urged Chile not to apply the law in a discriminatory manner to Mapuches. The committee also expressed concern about the Supreme Court practice of lowering sentences for grave human rights violations committed in the 1970s and 1980s.

In Norín Catrimán and others v. Chile, the Inter-American Court of Human Rights ruled in May 2014 that Chile was responsible for violating the rights to due process, freedom of thought and expression, and personal liberty of seven Mapuche leaders and an activist convicted on terrorism charges in 2003 and 2004.

China

China remains an authoritarian state, one that systematically curbs fundamental rights, including freedom of expression, association, assembly, and religion, when their exercise is perceived to threaten one-party rule. Since a new leadership assumed power in March 2013, authorities have undertaken positive steps in certain areas, including abolishing the arbitrary detention system known as Re-education through Labor (RTL), announcing limited reforms of the hukou system of household registration that has denied social services to China's internal migrants, and giving slightly greater access for persons with disabilities to the all-important university entrance exam.

But during the same period, authorities have also unleashed an extraordinary assault on basic human rights and their defenders with a ferocity unseen in recent years—an alarming sign given that the current leadership will likely remain in power through 2023. From mid-2013, the Chinese government and the ruling Chinese Communist Party (CCP) have issued directives insisting on "correct" ideology among party members, university lecturers, students, researchers, and journalists. These documents warn against the perils of "universal values" and human rights, and assert the importance of a pro-government and pro-CCP stance.

Rather than embrace lawyers, writers, and whistleblowers as allies in an effort to deal effectively with rising social unrest, the government remains hostile to criticism. The government targets activists and their family members for harassment, arbitrary detention, legally baseless imprisonment, torture, and denial of access to adequate medical treatment. It has also significantly narrowed space for the press and the Internet, further limiting opportunities for citizens to press for much-needed reforms.

The Chinese government's open hostility towards human rights activists was tragically illustrated by the death of grassroots activist Cao Shunli in March. Cao was detained for trying to participate in the 2013 Universal Periodic Review of China's human rights record at the United Nations Human Rights Council (HRC) in Geneva. For several months, authorities denied her access to adequate health care even though she was seriously ill, and she died in March 2014, just days after authorities finally transferred her from detention to a hospital.

The government continued its anti-corruption campaign, taking aim at senior officials, including former security czar Zhou Yongkang, as well as lower-level officials. But the campaign has been conducted in ways that further undermine the rule of law, with accused officials held in an unlawful detention system, deprived of basic legal protections, and often coerced to confess. The civic group known as the New Citizens Movement, best known for its campaign to combat corruption through public disclosure of officials' assets, has endured especially harsh reprisals.

In response to the Chinese government's decision on August 31 denying genuine democracy in Hong Kong, students boycotted classes and launched demonstrations. Police initially tried to clear some demonstrators with pepper spray and tear gas, which prompted hundreds of thousands to join the protests and block major roads in several locations.

While senior Hong Kong government officials reluctantly met once with student leaders, they proposed no changes to the electoral process. Hundreds remained in three "Occupy Central" zones through November, when courts ruled some areas could be cleared and the government responded, using excessive force in arresting protest leaders and aggressively using pepper spray once again.

Protests continued in other areas, some student leaders embarked on a hunger strike with the aim of re-engaging the government in dialogue, while other protest leaders turned themselves in to the police as a gesture underscoring their civil disobedience. Despite the waning of street protests, the underlying political issues remained unresolved and combustible at time of writing.

Human Rights Defenders

Activists increasingly face arbitrary detention, imprisonment, commitment to psychiatric facilities, or house arrest. Physical abuse, harassment, and intimidation are routine.

The government has convicted and imprisoned nine people for their involvement in the New Citizens Movement—including its founder, prominent legal scholar Xu Zhiyong—mostly on vaguely worded public order charges. Well-known lawyer Pu Zhiqiang and journalist Gao Yu, among others, were arrested around the 25th anniversary of the Tiananmen Massacre in June 2014. Many activists continue to be detained pending trial, and some, including lawyers Chang Boyang and Guo Feixiong, have been repeatedly denied access to lawyers. Virtually all face sentences heavier than activists received for similar activities in past years. The increased use of criminal detention may stem from the abolition of the RTL administrative detention system in late 2013.

China has 500,000 registered nongovernmental organizations (NGOs), though many are effectively government-run. An estimated 1.5 million more NGOs operate without proper registration because the criteria for doing so remain stringent despite gradual relaxation in recent years. The government remains suspicious of NGOs, and there are signs that authorities stepped up surveillance of some groups in 2014.

In June, a Chinese website posted an internal National Security Commission document that announced a nationwide investigation of foreign-based groups operating in China and Chinese groups that work with them. Subsequently, a number of groups reportedly were made to answer detailed questionnaires about their operations and funding, and were visited by the police. In June and July, Yirenping, an anti-discrimination organization, had its bank account frozen and its office searched by the police in connection with the activism of one of its legal representatives.

Xinjiang

Pervasive ethnic discrimination, severe religious repression, and increasing cultural suppression justified by the government in the name of the "fight against separatism, religious extremism, and terrorism" continue to fuel rising tensions in the Xinjiang Uighur Autonomous Region (XUAR).

In March, at least 30 people were killed when Uighur assailants attacked people with knives at the train station in Kunming, Yunnan Province. In May, 31 people died when a busy market in Urumqi was bombed. In August, official press reports stated than approximately 100 people died in Yarkand (or Shache) County in XUAR when assailants attacked police stations, government offices, and vehicles on a road. The Chinese government has blamed "terrorist" groups for these attacks.

Following the Urumqi attack, the Chinese government announced a year-long anti-terrorism crackdown in Xinjiang. Within the first month, police arrested 380 suspects and tried more than 300 for terror-related offenses. Authorities also convened thousands of people for the public sentencing of dozens of those tried. In August, authorities executed three Uighurs who were convicted of orchestrating an attack in Beijing's Tiananmen Square in October 2013. Fair trial rights remain a grave concern given the lack of independent information about the cases, the government's insistence on expedited procedures, the fact that terror suspects can be held without legal counsel for months under Chinese law, and China's record of police torture.

While there is reason for the government's concern with violence, discriminatory and repressive minority policies only exacerbate the problem. In January, police took into custody Ilham Tohti, a Uyghur professor at Beijing's Minzu University critical of the Chinese government's Xinjiang policy. Tohti remains detained and is charged with "separatism," which can result in life imprisonment. In August, Uighur linguist Abduweli Ayup was given an 18-month sentence for "illegal fundraising" after trying to raise money for Uighur-language schools.

Tibet

A series of self-immolations by Tibetans protesting Chinese government repression appeared to have abated by early 2014. The authorities punished families and communities for allegedly inciting or being involved in these protests; punishment of individuals included imprisonment, hefty fines, and restrictions of movement.

Authorities were intolerant of peaceful protests by Tibetans, harshly responding with beatings and arrests to protests against mines on land considered sacred and against detention of local Tibetan leaders. According to press reports, in June, police beat and detained Tibetans for protesting against copper mining in southwestern Yunnan province. In August, police in the Ganzi prefecture of Sichuan province fired into a crowd of unarmed protesters demonstrating against the detention of a village leader. Also in June, Dhondup Wangchen, who had been imprisoned for his role in filming a clandestine documentary in Tibetan areas, was released after six years in prison.

China's mass rehousing and relocation policy has radically changed Tibetans' way of life and livelihoods, in some cases impoverishing them or making them dependent on state subsidies. Since 2006, over 2 million Tibetans, both farmers and herders, have been involuntarily "rehoused"—through government-ordered renovation or construction of new houses—in the TAR; hundreds of thousands of nomadic herders in the eastern part of the Tibetan plateau have been relocated or settled in "New Socialist Villages."

Hong Kong

In January 2013, Hong Kong professor Benny Tai first proposed the "Occupy Central with Love and Peace" movement, designed to pressure Beijing to grant genuine democracy to Hong Kong in accordance with the Basic Law, Hong Kong's quasi-constitution, which applies the International Covenant on Civil and Political Rights (ICCPR) to the territory. The ICCPR requires that people should have equal rights to vote and to stand for election. In June 2014, nearly 800,000 voted in favor of democracy in an unofficial "referendum" organized by Occupy Central; in July, at least 510,000 people marched for democracy.

On August 31, China's top legislature announced it would impose a stringent screening mechanism that effectively bars candidates the central government dislikes from nomination for chief executive. In response, students boycotted classes in late September and held a small peaceful protest outside government headquarters. The police responded by dispersing the students with pepper spray and arrests.

These tactics prompted hundreds of thousands to join the students. Organizers of the Occupy Central movement announced that they were officially launching their planned demonstrations and joined the student protest. On September 28, Hong Kong police declared the protest illegal and cordoned off the government headquarters grounds. This decision prompted more protesters to gather in the areas near government headquarters, demanding that police reopen the area. The two groups of protesters—those corralled in the government headquarters and their supporters on the other side—eventually walked out onto the major thoroughfares between them and effectively blocked the roads.

The protests eventually occupied several large key areas in Hong Kong's business and government centers. After several incidents of excessive force on the part of police against the overwhelmingly peaceful protests, including continued aggressive use of pepper spray and several beatings recorded on video, the government adopted a passive stance, waiting for private groups to win injunctions before moving to clear out protest sites in a strategy of waiting for public opinion to turn against the demonstrators.

When courts handed down the injunctions, police cleared two areas and later thwarted an effort to block access to government offices, but two other smaller sites in the city remained occupied at time of writing with students considering whether to abandon "occupation" as a tactic.

The underlying political issues, however, remained unresolved, with both Chinese and Hong Kong authorities standing firm on Beijing's August 31 decision. Benny Tai and other Occupy Central leaders tried to turn themselves in to police to underscore both respect for rule of law and their stance of civil disobedience, while student leaders held peaceful hunger strikes in an effort to persuade the government to reengage in dialogue.

Although media has greater freedom in Hong Kong than elsewhere in China, journalists and media owners, particularly those critical of Beijing, came under increasing pressure in 2014. In February, a prominent editor, Kevin Lau, was stabbed by unidentified thugs; in July, HouseNews, a popular independent news website known for supporting democracy in Hong Kong, was shuttered by its founder, who cited fear of political retaliation from China; throughout 2014, Jimmy Lai and his media businesses, known for critical reporting on China, were repeatedly threatened.

Freedom of Expression

The Chinese government targeted the Internet and the press with further restrictions in 2014. All media are already subject to pervasive control and censorship. The government maintains a nationwide Internet firewall exclude politically unacceptable information.

Since August 2013, the government has targeted WeChat—an instant messaging app that has gained increasing popularity—by closing popular "public accounts" that report and comment on current affairs. Another 20 million accounts were shuttered for allegedly soliciting "prostitutes." Authorities also issued new rules requiring new WeChat users to register with real names. In July and August 2014 , it suspended popular foreign instant messaging services including Kakao Talk, saying the service was being used for "distributing terrorism-related information."

Authorities also tightened press restrictions. The State Administration of Press Publication, Radio, Film, and Television issued a directive in July requiring that Chinese journalists sign an agreement stating that they will not release unpublished information without prior approval from their employers and requiring that they pass political ideology exams before they can be issued official press cards.

In July, the CCP's disciplinary commission announced that researchers at the central Chinese Academic of Social Sciences had been "infiltrated by foreign forces" and participated in "illegal collusion" during politically sensitive periods. The party subsequently issued a rule that would make ideological evaluation a top requirement for assessing CASS researchers; those who fail are to be expelled.

Freedom of Religion

Although the constitution guarantees freedom of religion, the government restricts religious practices to officially approved mosques, churches, temples, and monasteries organized by five officially recognized religious organizations; any religious activity not considered by the state to be "normal" is prohibited. It audits the activities, employee details, and financial records of religious bodies, and retains control over religious personnel appointments, publications, and seminary applications. In 2014, the government stepped up its control over religion, with particular focus on Christian churches.

Between late 2013 and early July, the government removed 150 crosses from churches in Zhejiang Province, which is considered to be a center of Christianity. In July, the government handed down a particularly harsh 12-year sentence to Christian pastor Zhang Shaojie. Also in July, Zhuhai authorities raided the compound of Buddhist leader Wu Zeheng and detained him and at least a dozen followers, although no legal reason was given for doing so. The Chinese government also expelled hundreds of foreign missionaries from China, according to press reports, and it failed to publicly respond to Pope Francis's mid-August statement that the Vatican wishes to "establish full relations with China."

The government classifies many religious groups outside of its control as "evil cults." Falun Gong, a meditation-focused spiritual group banned since July 1999, continues to suffer state persecution. In June, authorities in Inner Mongolia detained 15 members of what it called another "evil cult" called the "Apostles' Congregation" for dancing publicly and "tempting" people to become new members.

Women's Rights

Women's reproductive rights and access to reproductive health remain severely curtailed under China's population planning regulations. That policy includes the use of legal and other coercive measures, such as administrative sanctions, fines, and coercive measures, including forced insertion of intrauterine devices and forced abortion, to control reproductive choices.

In September and October, female protestors in Hong Kong alleged that assailants sexually assaulted them, and that police at those locations did little to intervene.

China was reviewed under the Convention on the Elimination of All Forms of Discrimination against Women (CEDAW) in October. The committee expressed concerns over the lack of judicial independence and access to justice for women and retaliation against women rights activists. Chinese authorities prevented two activists from participating in the review: Ye Haiyan, China's most prominent sex worker rights activist, was placed under administrative detention, while HIV-AIDS activist Wang Quinan's passport was confiscated.

In November, the government released for comment the long-awaited law against domestic violence. While a step in the right direction, it falls short of international standards and good practices. The definition of domestic violence is overly narrow, and the protection orders that women can seek are poor and are tied to victims subsequently filing a court case against the abuser.

Disability Rights

Although China ratified the Convention on the Rights of Persons with Disabilities (CRPD) in June 2008, persons with disabilities face a range of barriers, including lack of access to education and forced institutionalization (including as a form of punishment).

In China, one in four children with disabilities is not in school because of discrimination and exclusion. Official guidelines even allow universities to deny enrollment in certain subjects if the applicants have certain disabilities. In April, the Chinese Education Ministry announced that it would allow Braille or electronic exams for national university entrance, but in a landmark case to test this initiative, blind activist Li Jincheng was not provided with the electronic exams he had requested, but a Braille version which he did not know how to read. Li's case highlights the difficulties people with disabilities have in being provided with reasonable accommodation, a right that is still not recognized under Chinese law. New regulations on access to education for people with disabilities drafted in 2013 were not adopted in 2014.

The Mental Health Law, which came into effect in 2013, stipulates that treatment and hospitalization should be voluntary except in cases where individuals with severe mental illnesses pose a danger to, or have harmed, themselves or others. In an important step in November, a patient currently held in a psychiatric hospital invoked the law in a lawsuit brought in Shanghai challenging his confinement. According to Chinese Human Rights Defenders (CHRD), central government rules require local officials to meet a quota of institutionalizing two out of every 1,000 people who allegedly have "serious mental illnesses."

Sexual Orientation and Gender Identity

Homosexuality was decriminalized in 1997, but was remained classified as a mental illness until 2001. To date there is no law protecting people from discrimination on the basis of sexual orientation or gender identity. There is no legal recognition of same-sex partnership.

Despite this lack of legal protection, individuals and organizations brought cases to court to try to better protect their rights. In February, an activist sued the government after the Hunan Province Civil Affairs Department refused to register his organization focused on lesbian, gay, bisexual, and transgender (LGBT) issues, stating that homosexuality had no place in Chinese traditional culture and "the building of spiritual civilization." The court dismissed the case in March on the ground that the government had not defamed homosexuals.

LGBT groups continue to document the phenomenon of "conversion therapy," in which clinics offer to "cure" homosexuality. In March 2014, a man who calls himself Xiao Zhen filed a lawsuit against a clinic in Chongqing, which he said had administered electroshock therapy to him. It was the first time a court in China heard a case involving "conversion therapy."

In November, a man filed a lawsuit in Shenzhen alleging discrimination on the grounds of sexual orientation; if the court accepts the case it will be the first such case heard in China.

During China's October CEDAW review, a state representative noted that: "the rights of all Chinese citizens [are] protected by Chinese law, regardless of their sexual orientation."

Key International Actors

Even as China has taken major steps backwards on human rights under Xi Jinping, most foreign governments have muted their criticisms of its record, opting to prioritize economic and security issues or trying to win Chinese co-operation on issues like climate change. Few bilateral human rights dialogues were held in 2014, and few governments that had pointed to such dialogues as centerpieces of their human rights strategy developed effective, alternative long-term strategies, such as elevating their engagement with Chinese civil society.

Foreign governments also largely failed to mark the 25th anniversary of the Tiananmen massacre, or to speak up for Hong Kong when China ruled out true universal suffrage for the territory, though several noted the harsh sentences handed down to high-profile human rights defenders and the release of Gao Zhisheng, who, however, remains under heavy surveillance. For the third time in recent years, South African authorities indicated they would not grant a visa to the Dalai Lama.

United Nations Secretary-General Ban Ki-moon similarly failed to criticize the Chinese government's deteriorating rights records during his August visit, instead praising the government for "its contributions to the promotion of ... human rights."

Foreign Policy

China's 2013 leadership change has not yielded fundamental changes in its foreign policy, though it has more aggressively advanced its territorial claims in parts of Asia.

While China engages with various UN mechanisms, it has not significantly improved its compliance with international human rights standards nor pushed for improved human rights protections in other countries, such as North Korea. There are eight outstanding requests by UN special rapporteurs to visit China, and UN agencies operating inside China remain tightly restricted, their activities closely monitored by authorities.

As a member of the UN Human Rights Council, China regularly votes to prevent scrutiny of serious human rights situations around the world. In 2014, China voted down resolutions spotlighting abuses in North Korea, Iran, Sri Lanka, Belarus, Ukraine, as well as Syria.

China repeated its calls for "political solutions" in Syria, Sudan, and South Sudan in 2014, but took steps that prolonged human rights crises in all three. Particularly noteworthy was its veto of a Security Council resolution referring the situation in Syria to the International Criminal Court. The latter was its fourth veto, alongside Russia, of Security Council action to address human rights violations in Syria since 2011.

In September 2014, however, a Chinese embassy official in Juba claimed that Chinese weapons sales to South Sudan had been halted; the change in policy had not been independently verified at time of writing. China also continued to pressure governments to forcibly return Chinese asylum seekers and to deny visas to individuals it dislikes, such as the Dalai Lama.

HUMAN
RIGHTS
WATCH

THE CRISIS IN BUENAVENTURA

Disappearances, Dismemberment, and Displacement
in Colombia's Main Pacific Port

Colombia

Civilians in Colombia continue to suffer serious abuses perpetrated by guerrillas, as well as by paramilitary successor groups that emerged after an official paramilitary demobilization process a decade ago. Violence associated with Colombia's internal armed conflict have forcibly displaced more than 5.7 million Colombians, and upward of 200,000 continue to flee their homes each year, generating the world's second largest population of internally displaced persons (IDPs). Human rights defenders, trade unionists, journalists, indigenous and Afro-Colombian leaders, and other community activists face death threats and violence. The administration of President Juan Manuel Santos consistently condemns these attacks, but lack of effective investigations means perpetrators are rarely arrested.

The Santos administration continues to promote several bills that would undercut accountability for unlawful killings of civilians by the military, including so-called false positive killings. The proposed legislation creates a serious risk that such cases will be transferred from the civilian to the military justice system, which lacks independence and has a very poor record investigating human rights violations.

The Colombian government and Revolutionary Armed Forces of Colombia (FARC) guerrillas have been engaged in peace talks in Cuba since 2012; at time of writing they had reached an agreement on three of the six items on the negotiating agenda. On June 10, the government and National Liberation Army (ELN), Colombia's second largest guerrilla group, announced they had begun exploratory peace talks.

In March, the government removed the mayor of Bogotá from office despite a legally binding precautionary measure issued by the Inter-American Commission on Human Rights calling for it not to do so. President Santos subsequently implemented a court order to reinstate the mayor.

Guerrilla Abuses

FARC guerrillas routinely attack civilians. For example, in Tumaco municipality in southwest Colombia, the FARC was responsible for widespread abuses in 2013 and 2014, including killings, disappearances, torture, sexual violence, forced displacement, recruitment of children, extortion, and death threats against community leaders. In one case from June, there is compelling evidence that FARC members abducted, tortured, and killed Mónica Julieth Pernia, a 25-year-old Tumaco resident.

The ELN also continues to commit serious abuses against civilians, such as killings, abductions, and child recruitment. On September 15, 2014, the ELN shot dead two oil workers who were inspecting a pipeline in the northeastern municipality of Teorama.

The FARC and ELN continue to use antipersonnel landmines. The government reported that landmines and unexploded ordnances killed 6 civilians and injured 65 between January and August 2014.

Paramilitaries and Their Successors

Between 2003 and 2006, right-wing paramilitary organizations with close ties to security forces and politicians underwent a deeply flawed government demobilization process in which many members remained active and reorganized into new groups. Successor groups to paramilitaries, often led by members of demobilized paramilitary organizations, commit widespread abuses, such as killings, disappearances, and sexual violence.

In Buenaventura, a largely Afro-Colombian port on the Pacific coast, paramilitary successor groups such as the Urabeños continue to commit atrocities, including abducting and dismembering people. The groups have caused Buenaventura to have the highest rate of forced displacement in Colombia, with more than 33,000 residents fleeing their homes in 2013, and 22,383 between January and November 1, 2014, according to government data released in November.

The groups have at times benefited from the tolerance and collusion of state agents. In March, prosecutors ordered the arrest of retired army Col. Robinson González del Río for allegedly leading a network of active and retired security force members that sold weapons to the Urabeños.

Implementation of the Justice and Peace law, which offers dramatically reduced sentences to demobilized paramilitaries who confess their crimes, has been very slow. As of September 2014, only 37 of the more than 30,000 paramilitaries who officially demobilized had been convicted of crimes under the Justice and Peace law—9 years after it was approved. The convictions cover a small portion of the nearly 70,000 crimes confessed by defendants seeking the law's benefits.

"Parapolitics" investigations into current and former members of Congress accused of conspiring with paramilitaries continued: more than 55 legislators have been convicted since 2006.

On September 17, 2014, the Colombian Senate held a debate about alleged links between paramilitaries and former President Álvaro Uribe (2002-2010), who became a senator in 2014.

Abuses by Public Security Forces

During the Uribe administration, Colombian military personnel executed large numbers of civilians, particularly between 2002 and 2008. In many cases—commonly referred to as "false positives"—soldiers and officers under pressure from superiors to boost body counts killed civilians and reported them as enemy combat casualites. There has been a dramatic reduction in cases of alleged unlawful killings attributed to security forces since 2009; nevertheless, there were credible reports of some new cases in 2013 and 2014.

The government does not keep statistics for "false positives" as a category of crime distinct from other types of unlawful killings. However, as of July 2014, the Human Rights Unit of the Attorney General's Office was investigating more than 3,500 unlawful killings allegedly committed by state agents between 2002 and 2008, and had obtained convictions for 402 of them. The vast majority of the 785 army members convicted are low-ranking soldiers and non-commissioned officers. Some military personnel convicted of the crimes have enjoyed extravagant privileges in military detention centers.

The defense minister and senior military officials have taken actions to discredit false positive investigations. In September, after the media reported that prosecutors had requested that investigations be opened into nine current and former army generals for their possible role in false positives, the defense minister said "excessive attention" was being given to the testimony on which the prosecutors based their requests. In February, President Santos fired the head of the armed forces after *Semana* magazine published an audio recording from 2012 in which the general told an army colonel under prosecution for false positives to "create a mafia" to smear prosecutors.

In February, the head of army intelligence was removed from his post after *Semana* revealed that justice authorities had raided a location in Bogotá where military intelligence personnel were alleged to be illegally intercepting the communications of the government's peace negotiators and others.

Reforms Promoting Impunity

In 2013 and 2014, the defense minister submitted three different bills to Congress that would open the door to false positives being transferred from civilian prosecutors to the military justice system, which has long failed to hold perpetrators accountable. Under the bills, the military justice system would also handle other past and possible future human rights abuses by military personnel, as well as other serious crimes such as conspiring with paramilitaries or gangs to traffic drugs. One of the bills would authorize the security forces to use lethal force against civilians in a dangerously broad range of situations.

The bills are similar to a constitutional change to the military justice system that the Santos administration pushed through Congress in December 2012, which the Constitutional Court subsequently struck down on procedural grounds in October 2013.

In June 2012, the government secured Congressional approval of the Legal Framework for Peace constitutional amendment, which paves the way for widespread impunity for atrocities by guerrillas, paramilitaries, and the military if a peace agreement is reached with the FARC. The amendment empowers Congress to limit the scope of prosecutions of atrocities to individuals found "most responsible"—a category the amendment does not define—and provide statutory immunity to everyone else.

While the amendment also enabled Congress to fully suspend prison sentences for all guerrillas, paramilitaries, and military personnel convicted of atrocities, the Constitutional Court ruled in August 2013 that those "most responsible" for crimes against humanity could not have their penalties fully suspended. However, the amendment still allows for "alternative penalties," and in April, Colombia's attorney general proposed that top FARC commanders could receive an alternative penalty of community service instead of going to prison.

Internal Displacement and Land Restitution

More than 5.7 million Colombians have been internally displaced since 1985, according to government figures. The government registered more than 220,000 newly displaced people in 2013.

The government's implementation of land restitution under the Victims Law continues to be slow. The law was enacted in 2011 to restore millions of hectares of stolen and abandoned land to internally displace persons (IDPs). The government initially estimated that by the end of 2015 there would be judicial rulings in more than 150,000 land restitution cases under the Victims Law.

However, as of September 2014, the government had obtained land restitution rulings for just 1,546 of the nearly 68,000 claims it had received. As of September 2013, the government could only confirm three cases of families who had returned to live on their land due to rulings under the law. At time of writing, the land restitution office had not provided updated data on the number families who have returned to live on their land as result of the law.

IDPs face threats and violence for attempting to reclaim their land. No one has been held accountable for the majority of killings of land restitution claimants and leaders.

Gender-Based Violence

Gender-based violence (GBV) is widespread in Colombia. Lack of training and poor implementation of protocols create obstacles for women and girls seeking post-violence care, with the result that victims may face delays in accessing essential medical services. Perpetrators of GBV crimes are rarely brought to justice.

In June, the government enacted a law to improve access to justice and protection for sexual violence survivors, especially those who are raped or assaulted in the context of the internal armed conflict.

Violence against Human Rights Defenders, Journalists, and Trade Unionists

Rights advocates and journalists continue to be targeted for threats and attacks. The FLIP, a respected Colombian nongovernmental organization (NGO) that monitors press freedoms, reported 2 journalists killed and 75 threatened in 2013, and 58 victims of such threats between January and September 2014.

The National Labor School (ENS), Colombia's leading labor rights NGO, continues to report killings of trade unionists. As of September 2014, the special prosecutorial unit dedicated to anti-union violence had opened investigations into more than 110 cases of trade unionist killings committed since 2009, but obtained convictions in just 9 of them.

The Inspector-General's Office continued its disciplinary investigation against Congressman Iván Cepeda, a prominent victim's rights advocate, for collecting information about possible paramilitary abuses and submitting it to justice authorities. The investigation, which relates to Congressman Cepeda's interviews of ex-paramilitaries about former President Uribe's alleged ties to paramilitaries, appears to be entirely unfounded and could have a chilling effect on others who seek accountability for human rights abuses.

The Interior Ministry runs a protection program that covers thousands of at-risk members of vulnerable groups, including human rights defenders, trade unionists, and journalists.

Key International Actors

The United States remains the most influential foreign actor in Colombia. In 2014, it provided approximately US$225 million in military and police aid, and $165 million in humanitarian and development aid. A portion of US military aid is subject to human rights conditions, including a requirement that civilian authorities investigate and try all alleged human rights violations. In September 2014, the State Department certified that Colombia met these conditions, despite the government's continued promotion of legislation that would place human rights crimes in military courts, and the recent transfer of some such cases to the military justice system. The State Department justified its decision by saying that human rights cases are "generally" prosecuted in civilian courts, even though the condition requires that such crimes be subject "only" to civilian jurisdiction.

In August, the Inter-American Commission on Human Rights published an extensive report on Colombia, which raised serious concerns over the Legal Framework for Peace and military justice system reforms, among other issues.

The office of the prosecutor (OTP) of the International Criminal Court (ICC) continues to monitor local investigations into crimes that may fall within the ICC's jurisdiction. In November 2013, the OTP reported that there is reason to believe that false positives were committed "pursuant to a policy adopted at least at the level of certain brigades within the armed forces," and that it was continuing to analyze whether the policy extended to higher-level state officials.

Côte d'Ivoire

Ahead of the 2015 general election, the government of President Alassane Ouattara made some progress in security sector reform and improving discipline within the security forces. However, there was insufficient progress in strengthening the judiciary, tackling corruption, or pursuing impartial justice for the serious crimes committed during the 2010-2011 post-election period. The Ivorian government has failed to arrest any member of the pro-Ouattara Republican Forces implicated in the post-election violence, undermining hopes for meaningful reconciliation.

The 2010-2011 crisis capped a decade of conflict and unrest rooted in ethno-communal tensions and land disputes during which armed groups and security forces from all sides perpetrated serious human rights abuses with complete impunity. International and Ivorian commissions of inquiry found that both sides committed war crimes and possible crimes against humanity during the 2010-2011 crisis.

There were several cross border attacks from Liberia though fewer episodes of intercommunal violence than in past years. Criminality and banditry by often-violent armed gangs continued to be a serious problem. Progress on disarmament was slow and largely benefited pro-Ouattara forces, spurring some protests.

Members of the security forces continued to be implicated in serious violations, though the number of incidents decreased compared to past years. Widespread corruption and plunder, especially by members of the security forces, remain a serious concern. However, there was some progress in reducing security force extortion and dismantling illegal checkpoints.

Côte d'Ivoire's key partners—the European Union, the United Nations, France, and the United States—were reluctant to publicly criticize the lack of accountability for past crimes. The International Criminal Court (ICC) made progress by way of the investigation of former President Laurent Gbagbo and one of his ministers. However, their lack of progress in the investigation of crimes by pro-Ouattara forces drew criticism.

National Justice for Post-Election Violence

Since the end of the crisis, progress toward justice has been largely one-sided. While Ivorian authorities have charged more than 150 pro-Gbagbo civilian and military leaders for abuses committed during the 2010-2011 crisis, and convicted nine in a military court, not one member of Ouattara's Republican Forces has been brought to account.

At the start of the year, the work of the Special Investigative Cell (*cellule spéciale d'enquête*, or CSE) was stymied by staff cuts and inadequate logistical support. Although additional staff was provided in May, the CSE's work continued to be hampered by its lack of independence from the government. It has focused primarily on crimes by pro-Gbagbo forces. The civilian courts have yet to hold a trial for those from any side indicted for crimes related to the post-election period, in violation of the right to a trial within a reasonable time.

In 2014, the judiciary provisionally released some 200 pro-Gbagbo defendants, raising concerns of a de facto amnesty for perpetrators from all sides. In August, the president pardoned 3,000 prisoners convicted of minor crimes, raising concerns about government interference with the judiciary.

In February, the president extended the mandate of the Dialogue, Truth and Reconciliation Commission. In September, it held three weeks of public hearings. The commission has been widely criticized for doing little to fulfill its mandate.

International Criminal Court

In June, the ICC confirmed charges against Laurent Gbagbo, rejecting an appeal and ordering him to remain in detention until his trial that was scheduled at time of writing to begin on July 7, 2015.

In March, Charles Blé Goudé, a former youth minister and leader of a pro-Gbagbo militia, was surrendered to the ICC by Ivorian authorities after being transferred to Côte d'Ivoire from Ghana, where he had fled in 2011. At year's end, ICC judges were deliberating as to whether there was enough evidence to send his case to trial; if so, prosecutors have asked to combine Blé Goudé's and Laurent Gbagbo's cases into one trial.

Simone Gbagbo, charged by the ICC with four counts of crimes against humanity, remained in detention in Côte d'Ivoire. In October 2013, the Ivorian government challenged the admissibility of the ICC's case on the grounds that she is being tried on the same charges in domestic courts. On October 22, 2014 Simone Gbagbo and 82 other pro-Gbagbo defendants were brought before an Ivorian court on charges pertaining to threats against state security, but the trial was indefinitely postponed because the defense needed more time to prepare, among other reasons.

Security Force Abuses

Members of the security forces including soldiers, gendarmes, and police perpetrated numerous serious human rights abuses, including mistreatment and torture of detainees, sometimes to extract confessions; extrajudicial killings; rape; and extortion. Several commanders implicated in serious human rights abuses remain in key positions in the security forces.

Many abuses were perpetrated in response to security threats. The UN independent expert on the situation of human rights in Côte d'Ivoire reported that soldiers tortured numerous people they had detained in connection with raids near the Liberian border, while other abuses were perpetrated as they responded to the threat of armed criminal gangs in Abidjan.

In recent years, some soldiers were prosecuted for murder and theft in less politically sensitive cases. However, impunity for other crimes persisted, including for the July 2012 attack on the Nahibly internally displaced persons camp, which left at least 12 dead, and for arbitrary detention and torture committed in 2012 following attacks on military installations.

Investigations into numerous other crimes by soldiers were blocked largely due to a legal requirement that the Ministry of Defense sign the prosecutorial order before an investigation can begin, resulting in soldiers credibly implicated in crimes being protected from inquiries.

The government took steps to combat widespread extortion and racketeering at checkpoints manned by the security forces and other armed groups. Some unauthorized checkpoints were dismantled and the military courts prosecuted several members of the security forces and pro-government militia for extortion and racketeering. Progress was also made in removing soldiers from properties they had illegally seized during the crisis. But the security forces' ability to protect the population from armed bandits, particularly in the morth, was hampered by inadequate personnel and resources.

Land Rights

Land disputes, particularly in western Côte d'Ivoire, have underscored over a decade of instability and conflict. They remain largely unresolved.

Extreme violence during the post-election crisis forced hundreds of thousands of people to seek refuge in neighboring countries or elsewhere in Côte d'Ivoire. Many displaced returned home to find their land illegally occupied or sold, violating their property rights and rights as returning refugees. By mid-2014, over half of returning refugees were homeless according to the UN High Commissioner for Refugees (UNHCR).

In 2013, the Ivorian government passed several reforms to land tenure and nationality laws, but the government's failure to fund or staff local administrative and judiciary structures to implement the reforms undermined their ability to resolve land disputes.

Disarmament and Security Sector Reform

Spurred on by concerns related to potential violence during the 2015 presidential polls, the government made some progress in security sector reform by disarming tens of thousands of former combatants who fought during the crisis.

As of October, the UN reported over 21,000 former combatants had been disarmed, more than 30,000 had benefitted from reinsertion support, and 7,429 weapons had been collected. However, disarmament has been one-sided, mostly benefitting forces loyal to President Ouattara. Only 13 percent of those disarmed were combatants affiliated with Gbagbo and large numbers of beneficiaries were not listed in the national Disarmament, Demobilisation and Reintegration database. Demonstrations by former combatants in western Côte d'Ivoire in February and March turned violent.

The government made some progress in returning basic security functions from the military to the police and gendarmerie, though the military continue to man checkpoints and at times act as first responders to security threats. In November, thousands of soldiers at several military bases, including Abdijan, Daloa, Bouaké, and Korhogo demonstrated over claims of unpaid wages.

Sexual Violence

High levels of gender-based violence continue. Many of these assaults targeted children and elderly women. In the first five months of 2014, the UN secretary-general's report on the UN Operations in Cote d'Ivoire (UNOCI) reported at least 170 cases of rape, including many gang rapes.

The government has taken some steps to address the widespread sexual violence. In September, with UN support, the government launched a national strategy against sexual violence with a strong commitment to prosecute perpetrators. But the *cour d'assises* mandated to try such cases rarely functioned. Many serious cases are downgraded to indecent assault in order to be heard in regular courts, which carry a more lenient penalty, furthering impunity. Social stigma, lack of access to justice and the cost of a medical certificate are significant barriers to ensuring accountability for violent sexual crimes.

Trafficking of women and girls, often from Nigeria, into Côte d'Ivoire for sex work, continues to be a problem.

Corruption

The Ivorian government has been slow to combat allegations of corruption, which continues to be a major problem, undermining the fulfillment of key social and economic rights such as basic healthcare and education. An anti-corruption law drafted in 2012 has not been adopted and there is no independent anti-corruption commission with the power to investigate and prosecute. However, in April, the Defense Ministry pledged to eliminate thousands of "ghost" soldiers in the army.

Since Ouattara assumed power, security forces loyal to him have plundered revenues through smuggling and parallel tax systems on cocoa, timber, diamonds and other natural resources. The UN Group of Experts, appointed by the UN Security Council to monitor the sanctions regime in Cote d'Ivoire, reported in 2014

curity Council to monitor the sanctions regime in Cote d'Ivoire, reported in 2014 that commanders are using income from illicit sources for personal enrichment and as a tool for retaining ex-combatant loyalty.

LGBTI Rights

Côte d'Ivoire does not criminalize homosexuality and has traditionally been relatively tolerant, though lesbian, gay, bisexual, transexual, and intersex (LGBTI) people are not protected under the law and can be prosecuted for public acts of indecency. There were a few violent attacks on LGBTI activists in Abidjan in 2014, with little accountability for those responsible.

In January, a series of attacks by mobs on Alternative-CI, a local non-profit working on LGBTI rights and HIV prevention, culminated in an attack on their Abidjan office. Police intervened and escorted the activists to safety, but failed to launch an investigation into the incident. Alternative-CI's director had been targeted a few days earlier at his home.

In April, Cote d'Ivoire's Universal Periodic Review raised some key human rights recommendations. Cote d'Ivoire rejected all those relating to the prevention of discrimination on the basis of sexual orientation and gender identity.

Key International Actors

Côte d'Ivoire's partners largely failed to prioritize the importance of impartial justice. The UN's independent expert on human rights published two reports highlighting continued security force abuses, the prevalence of sexual violence, and the need for reparations. He also raised concern that provisional releases of perpetrators of crimes committed during the crisis amounted to a de facto amnesty, saying that reconciliation and justice cannot be separated.

In June, the Human Rights Council passed a resolution maintaining the mandate of an independent expert on Cote d'Ivoire, but, at the request of the Ivorian government, imposed changes both of the expert in charge, and of the mandate, which now prioritizes technical cooperation. On April 29, the UN lifted an embargo on the sale and export of diamonds, in place since 2005, and relaxed its arms embargo, reflecting improvements in security. The UNOCI began scaling down its mission, including the planned elimination of the rule of law component.

The EU, France, and the US continued to take the lead on justice and security sector reform, along with UNOCI.

Cuba

In 2010 and 2011, Cuba's government released dozens of political prisoners on condition that they accept exile in exchange for freedom. Since then, the Cuban government has relied less on long-term prison sentences to punish dissent and has relaxed draconian travel restrictions that divided families and prevented its critics from leaving and returning to the island.

Nevertheless, the Cuban government continues to repress individuals and groups who criticize the government or call for basic human rights. Officials employ a range of tactics to punish dissent and instill fear in the public, including beatings, public acts of shaming, termination of employment, and threats of long-term imprisonment.

Short-term arbitrary arrests have increased dramatically in recent years and routinely prevent human rights defenders, independent journalists, and others from gathering or moving about freely.

Arbitrary Detentions and Short-Term Imprisonment

The government continues to rely on arbitrary detention to harass and intimidate individuals who exercise their fundamental rights. The Cuban Commission for Human Rights and National Reconciliation (CCDHRN)—an independent human rights group the government views as illegal—received over 7,188 reports of arbitrary detentions from January through August 2014, a sharp increase from approximately 2,900 in 2013 and 1,100 in 2010 during the same time period.

Security officers virtually never present arrest orders to justify the detention of critics and threaten them with criminal sentences if they continue to participate in "counterrevolutionary" activities. In some cases, detainees are released after receiving official warnings, which prosecutors can then use in subsequent criminal trials to show a pattern of delinquent behavior. Dissidents said these warnings aim to discourage them from participating in activities seen as critical of the government.

Detention is often used preemptively to prevent individuals from participating in peaceful marches or meetings to discuss politics. In the days leading up to the summit meeting of the Community of Latin American and Caribbean States

(CELAC), for example, which took place in Havana on January 28 and 29, 2014, at least 40 people were arbitrarily detained, and 5 held under house arrest until the conference had ended, according to the CCDHRN.

Members of the Damas de Blanco (Ladies in White)—a group founded by the wives, mothers, and daughters of political prisoners and which the government considers illegal—are routinely detained before or after they attend Sunday mass. On May 4, for example, more than 80 women were detained before attending mass throughout the island. On July 13, 129 members of the group were detained as they prepared to attend commemorative ceremonies honoring Cubans who died attempting to leave the island in 1994.

Detainees are often beaten, threatened, and held incommunicado for hours and even days. The former political prisoner Guillermo Fariñas, who was placed under house arrest for the duration of the CELAC conference and then arrested when he attempted to leave home, reported suffering two broken ribs and other injuries as a result of a beating he received while in detention. Yilenni Aguilera Santos, a member of the Damas de Blanco movement in Holguín, reported suffering a miscarriage when security agents subjected her to a severe beating after arresting her on her way to mass on June 22.

Political Prisoners

Cubans who criticize the government may face criminal prosecution. They do not benefit from due process guarantees, such as the right to fair and public hearings by a competent and impartial tribunal. In practice, courts are "subordinated" to the executive and legislative branches, denying meaningful judicial independence. Political prisoners are routinely denied parole after completing the minimum required sentence as punishment for refusing to participate in mandatory ideological activities, such as "reeducation" classes.

Scores of political prisoners remain in Cuban prisons according to local human rights groups. These groups estimate that there are more political prisoners whose cases they cannot document because the government prevents independent national or international human rights groups from accessing its prisons. Iván Fernández Depestre, a member of the Frente Nacional de Resistencia Cívica Orlando Zapata Tamayo, was detained in July 2013 while participating in a public protest. Three days later, he was convicted of "dangerousness" in a closed, summary trial, and given a three-year prison sentence.

Freedom of Expression

The government controls all media outlets in Cuba and tightly restricts access to outside information, severely limiting the right to freedom of expression. Only a very small fraction of Cubans are able to read independent websites and blogs because of the high cost of, and limited access to, the Internet. While people in cities like Havana, Santiago de Cuba, or Santa Clara have access to the Internet, people in more rural areas are not able to go online.

A May 2013 government decree directed at expanding Internet access stipulates that the Internet cannot be used for activities that undermine "public security, the integrity, the economy, independence, and national security" of Cuba— broadly worded conditions that could be used against government critics.

A small number of independent journalists and bloggers manage to write articles for websites or blogs, or publish tweets. Yet those who publish information considered critical of the government are sometimes subject to smear campaigns, attacks, and arbitrary arrests, as are artists and academics who demand greater freedoms.

In May 2014, blogger Yoani Sanchez launched the website 14ymedio, Cuba's first independent online newspaper. Within hours, the site was hacked, and visitors were directed to a page dedicated to scathing criticisms of Sanchez. The site was restored the following day, but blocked again several days later, and has remained inaccessible to Internet users within Cuba ever since.

In May 2013, the director of the government-run Casa de las Americas cultural institute, Roberto Zurbano, published an article in the *New York Times* highlighting persistent inequality and prejudice affecting Afro-Cubans. He was subsequently attacked in the government-controlled press and demoted to a lesser job at the institute.

Travel Restrictions and Family Separation

Reforms to travel regulations that went into effect in January 2013 eliminate the need for an exit visa to leave the island, which had previously been used to deny the right to travel to people critical of the government and their families. Since then, many people who had been previously denied permission to travel have been able to do so, including human rights defenders and independent bloggers.

Nonetheless, the reform included very broad discretionary powers that allow the government to restrict the right to travel on the grounds of "defense and national security" or "other reasons of public interest," allowing the authorities to deny exit to people who express dissent. For example, authorities have repeatedly denied Manuel Cuesta Morúa the right to travel abroad since he attempted to organize a parallel summit to the CELAC conference in January 2014.

The government also continues to arbitrarily deny Cubans living abroad the right to visit the island. In August 2013, the Cuban government denied Blanca Reyes, a Damas de Blanco member living in exile in Spain, permission to travel to Cuba to visit her ailing 93-year-old father, who died in October before she could visit him.

The government restricts the movement of citizens within Cuba through a 1997 law known as Decree 217. Designed to limit migration to Havana, the decree requires that Cubans obtain government permission before moving to the country's capital. It is often used to prevent dissidents from traveling there to attend meetings and to harass dissidents from other parts of Cuba who live in the capital.

Prison Conditions

Prisons are overcrowded, and unhygienic and unhealthy conditions lead to extensive malnutrition and illness. Prisoners are forced to work 12-hour days and punished if they do not meet production quotas, according to former political prisoners. Inmates have no effective complaint mechanism to seek redress, and those who criticize the government, or engage in hunger strikes and other forms of protest, are subjected to extended solitary confinement, beatings, restrictions on family visits, and denial of medical care.

While the government allowed select members of the foreign press to conduct controlled visits to a handful of prisons in April 2013, it continues to deny international human rights groups and independent Cuban organizations access to its prisons.

Human Rights Defenders

The Cuban government still refuses to recognize human rights monitoring as a legitimate activity and denies legal status to local human rights groups. Meanwhile, government authorities harass, assault, and imprison human rights defenders who attempt to document abuses.

Key International Actors

The United States' economic embargo of Cuba, in place for more than half a century, continues to impose indiscriminate hardship on the Cuban people and has done nothing to improve the country's human rights record. The UN General Assembly has repeatedly called for an end to the US embargo on Cuba. In October 2014, 188 of the 192 member countries voted for a resolution condemning the embargo.

In 2009, US President Barack Obama enacted reforms to eliminate restrictions on travel and remittances by Cuban Americans to Cuba, restrictions put in place during the administration of President George W. Bush in 2004. In 2011, President Obama used his executive powers to ease "people-to-people" travel restrictions, allowing religious, educational, and cultural groups from the US to travel to Cuba. However, in 2012 the Obama administration established additional requirements for "people-to-people" licenses, which has reduced the frequency of such trips.

The European Union (EU) continues to retain its "Common Position" on Cuba, adopted in 1996, which conditions full EU economic cooperation with Cuba on the country's transition to a pluralist democracy and respect for human rights. However, after a meeting in April 2014 in Havana, European Union and Cuban delegates agreed on establishing a road map for "normalizing" relations. EU officials indicated that concerns about civil liberties and democratic participation would continue to influence EU policy towards Cuba.

At the Organization of American States General Assembly in June, governments throughout the region called for the attendance of Cuba at the next Summit of the Americas in Panama in 2015.

Former US Agency for International Development contractor Alan Gross remains in prison despite a UN Working Group on Arbitrary Detention report in November

2012 that called for his immediate release. Gross was detained in Cuba in December 2009 and later sentenced to 15 years in prison for distributing telecommunications equipment to religious groups. The working group said Gross's detention was arbitrary and that Cuba's government had failed to provide sufficient evidence to support the charges against him.

In November 2013, Cuba was re-elected to a seat on the United Nations Human Rights Council (UNHRC), defeating Uruguay for a regional position despite its poor human rights record and its consistent efforts to undermine important council work. As a UNHRC member, Cuba regularly voted to prevent scrutiny of serious human rights situations around the world, opposing resolutions spotlighting abuses in North Korea, Syria, Iran, Sri Lanka, Belarus, and Ukraine. Cuba, however, supported the landmark resolution on sexual orientation and gender identity adopted by the council in September 2014.

Democratic Republic Of Congo

In late 2013, there was a period of optimism that armed violence and attacks on civilians might decrease in eastern Democratic Republic of Congo, following the defeat of the abusive M23 armed group, and the subsequent surrender of combatants from other armed groups. But in 2014, the government made little progress in capitalizing on these opportunities to improve security for civilians in the east.

The M23, whose fighters carried out widespread war crimes during its 19-month rebellion, was defeated in November 2013 after international pressure on the group's Rwandan backers and the deployment of a United Nations "intervention brigade" to conduct offensive operations against armed groups and strengthen the MONUSCO peacekeeping mission. Several thousand fighters from other armed groups surrendered in the weeks that followed. But the government stalled in implementing a new Disarmament, Demobilization, and Reintegration (DDR) program for former combatants, and there were few efforts made to bring to justice M23 and other armed group leaders implicated in abuses. Numerous armed groups remain active and their fighters continue to carry out brutal attacks on civilians. Government security forces also committed serious abuses against civilians.

Abuses by Security Forces

In the capital, Kinshasa, the Congolese police launched "Operation Likofi" in November 2013 to remove gang members known as "kuluna" from the streets. During the operation, the police extrajudicially executed at least 51 young men and boys and forcibly disappeared 33 others. Police dragged some of victims out of their houses at night and shot them dead before taking their bodies away.

In October and November 2013, as the army moved into territories previously controlled by the M23 in eastern Congo, soldiers raped at least 41 women and girls. Soldiers and intelligence officers in Rutshuru arbitrarily arrested several people, accused them of supporting the M23, and forced them to pay money for their release.

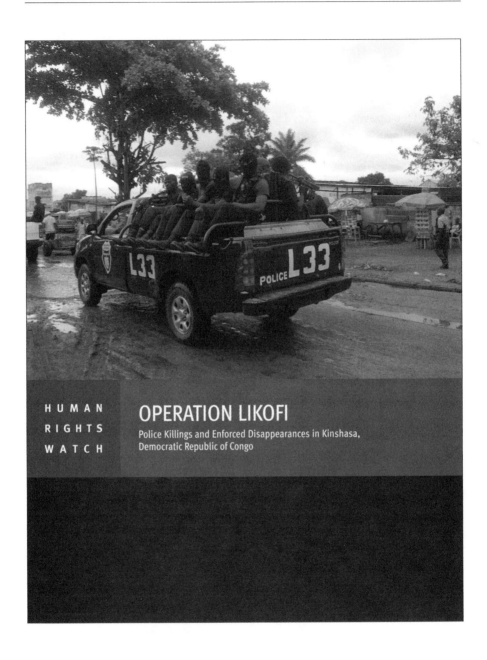

HUMAN
RIGHTS
WATCH

OPERATION LIKOFI
Police Killings and Enforced Disappearances in Kinshasa,
Democratic Republic of Congo

State Neglect of Former Combatants

Over 100 former combatants from various armed groups in eastern Congo, their wives and children died from starvation and disease in Kotakoli, a remote military camp in Congo's Equateur province, after government officials failed to provide them with adequate food and health care. The victims were part of a group of 941 former combatants and their dependents sent to Kotakoli in September 2013 after they had voluntarily surrendered.

Conditions were also difficult for former combatants in the east. After the M23's defeat, several thousand fighters from more than 20 armed groups surrendered. But the surrender rate quickly slowed as former fighters languished in squalid conditions at a regroupment site in Bweremana, North Kivu. Tired of waiting and receiving mixed messages from the government, many fighters and their leaders left.

Plans for the government's new "DDR III" program were finalized in June, but implementation was delayed as wrangling continued among the government, donors, and MONUSCO about the program's funding.

Attacks on Civilians by Armed Groups

Numerous armed groups carried out brutal attacks on civilians in eastern Congo, including in North and South Kivu, Katanga, and Orientale provinces. Mai Mai Sheka fighters—led by Ntabo Ntaberi Sheka, sought on a Congolese arrest warrant for crimes against humanity—killed, mutilated, and raped civilians in North Kivu. In September and October 2013, Sheka fighters abducted at least 20 schoolchildren, marched them through the forest, and killed those who were too tired or weak. In late 2013, Raia Mutomboki combatants hacked to death by machete or shot dead at least 21 Hutu civilians in Masisi, North Kivu. In June, armed assailants killed at least 30 people in Mutarule, South Kivu, including many who were attending an outdoor church service. Congolese soldiers and MONUSCO peacekeepers stationed nearby were aware of the attack but failed to intervene.

In January, the army began operations in Beni territory, North Kivu, against the Allied Democratic Forces (ADF), an armed group made up of Congolese and Ugandan fighters who have killed and kidnapped numerous civilians. During a spate of attacks in October and November, over 100 civilians were killed in Beni.

Many were hacked to death by machetes and axes. At time of writing, it remained unclear who was responsible for the attacks.

In September, the Democratic Forces for the Liberation of Rwanda (FDLR) attacked Buruko, North Kivu, killing three adults and two children. The FDLR is a largely Rwandan Hutu armed group, some of whose members participated in the 1994 genocide in Rwanda. FDLR combatants have been responsible for widespread war crimes in eastern Congo, including ethnic massacres and mass rapes. Soon after the M23's defeat, and following indications that military operations might be launched against them, the FDLR leadership announced they were going to lay down their weapons. In May and June, nearly 200 FDLR combatants surrendered. The International Conference on the Great Lakes Region (ICGLR), a regional grouping of 12 countries, gave the FDLR a six-month deadline to disarm before the Congolese army and MONUSCO would launch military operations.

Freedom of Expression and Peaceful Assembly

State agents arbitrarily detained and threatened Virunga National Park rangers and activists after they criticized plans for oil exploration by SOCO International, a British oil company. On April 15, unidentified armed men shot and seriously wounded the park's director, Emmanuel de Mérode. In April and May, two fishermen were found dead hours after they had criticized SOCO's activities in the park and argued with soldiers who work alongside SOCO.

Political tensions increased with protests across the country against proposals to change Congo's constitution and allow President Joseph Kabila to run for a third term. On several occasions, authorities blocked the activities of Vital Kamerhe, president of one of Congo's main opposition parties, the Union for the Congolese Nation (UNC). During an opposition rally in Bukavu in February, at least 25 civilians were injured when police beat protesters and fired teargas and live bullets at the crowd. In September, six demonstrators and several student bystanders were injured when police fired teargas and beat opposition supporters during a march in Goma.

On August 5, UNC Secretary-General Bertrand Ewanga was arrested after giving a speech at an opposition rally. Following an apparently politically motivated trial with numerous irregularities, Ewanga was convicted by Congo's Supreme Court and sentenced to one year in prison for insulting the president, the prime minister, and both presidents of parliament.

Justice and Accountability

A draft Congolese law to establish specialized mixed chambers to try war crimes and crimes against humanity committed in Congo since the 1990s was adopted by the Council of Ministers on April 22 and presented to the National Assembly on May 2. The proposed chambers would benefit initially from the presence of non-Congolese staff. Citing technical concerns, members of parliament rejected the admissibility of the text on May 8. Government officials have said they will correct the technical errors and resubmit the draft law to parliament.

A year after the mass rape of at least 76 women and girls by soldiers in and around Minova, Congo's Military Operational Court opened a trial on November 20, 2013, for 39 soldiers, including five high-ranking officers, on charges of war crimes and other offenses. On May 5, the verdict was announced, with only two low-ranking soldiers convicted of rape.

On March 7, the International Criminal Court (ICC) found Germain Katanga guilty of war crimes and crimes against humanity for being an accomplice in murders and an attack on civilians in Bogoro, Ituri, on February 24, 2003. On May 23, he was sentenced to 12 years in prison. Katanga is the former chief of staff of the Patriotic Resistance Front in Ituri (FRPI). Katanga decided not to appeal the decision and issued an apology to the victims.

On June 9, the ICC confirmed 18 charges of war crimes and crimes against humanity committed in northeastern Congo in 2002 and 2003 against Bosco Ntaganda, a former Congolese military commander and leader of various Rwandan-backed armed groups in Congo since the late 1990s. Ntaganda had surrendered to the United States embassy in Rwanda in March 2013 and was transferred to The Hague.

The ICC arrest warrant for war crimes against Gen. Sylvestre Mudacumura, the FDLR's military leader, has been pending since 2012.

HUMAN
RIGHTS
WATCH

**ENDING IMPUNITY
FOR SEXUAL VIOLENCE**
New Judicial Mechanism Needed to Bring Perpetrators to Justice

Key International Actors

Since the M23's defeat, there has been minimal progress in implementing the "Peace, Security and Cooperation Framework for the Democratic Republic of Congo and the Region" (also known as the "Framework Agreement"), signed by 11 African countries in February 2013, under the auspices of the UN secretary-general.

The Congolese government passed an amnesty law in February for insurrectional acts, acts of war, and political infractions committed between 2006 and 2013. The amnesty does not apply to grave international and human rights crimes.

Many of the M23 leaders responsible for serious human rights abuses remain in Rwanda and Uganda, including over a dozen who are sought on Congolese arrest warrants. They are effectively shielded from justice, despite commitments made by the Rwandan and Ugandan governments to support regional justice efforts and to neither harbor nor protect people accused of war crimes or crimes against humanity.

In July, UN Secretary-General Ban Ki-moon appointed Algerian diplomat Said Djinnit as UN special envoy for the Great Lakes region, succeeding former President of Ireland Mary Robinson. US Special Envoy Russ Feingold continues to play an important role in pressing regional countries to respect their commitments in the Framework Agreement.

Following a high-level Global Summit to End Sexual Violence in Conflict in London in June, President Kabila appointed Jeanine Mabunda as presidential adviser on sexual violence and child recruitment in Congo. In August, the Congolese government launched a comprehensive action plan to tackle sexual violence by soldiers.

Ecuador

The administration of President Rafael Correa has expanded state control over media and civil society. In 2014, tactics included criminal defamation prosecutions and administrative sanctions against critical journalists and media outlets, and aggressive efforts to discredit human rights advocates within the country.

In September, security forces used excessive force to disperse largely peaceful demonstrations in Quito, subjecting demonstrators and bystanders to serious physical abuse. The government has also used broad counterterrorism legislation to prosecute protesters and indigenous leaders who have challenged extractive industry projects. In December 2013, it arbitrarily shut down a prominent nongovernmental organization (NGO) dedicated to promoting indigenous and environmental rights.

A judicial council made up almost entirely of former members of the Correa administration has appointed and removed hundreds of judges through highly questionable methods, posing a serious threat to judicial independence.

In October, the Constitutional Court ruled that Congress could initiate a process to amend 16 articles of the constitution, including reforms that would grant the armed forces powers to participate in public security operations, grant the government broad regulatory powers over "communications" by calling them a "public service," and allow for unlimited re-election of the president.

Other ongoing problems include poor prison conditions and women's and girls' limited access to reproductive health care.

Excessive Use of Force Against Protesters

In September, security force response to largely peaceful demonstrations in Quito included many instances of excessive force and arbitrary detention of protesters and bystanders. Dozens of detainees suffered serious physical abuse, including severe beatings, kicks, and electric shocks, during arrest and detention. A minority of protesters engaged in violence, clashing with police and leaving more than 30 officers injured.

Within 24 hours of being detained, more than 100 detainees were brought before judges and charged with offenses such as attacking or resisting authority and damaging public or private property. Detainees were not informed of the charges against them before the hearings and had no contact with family members or lawyers until immediately before the hearings.

The government responded to reports and allegations of abuse by publicly congratulating the National Police on their role during the protests, threatening to prosecute lawyers who reported human rights violations, and challenging media outlets that published information on the abuses.

Freedom of Expression

A 2013 Communications Law gives the government broad powers to limit free speech. The law requires that all information disseminated by media be "verified" and "precise," opening the door to censorship by allowing the government to decide what information meets these vague criteria. It also prohibits "media lynching," defined as "repeatedly disseminating information with the purpose of discrediting or harming the reputation of a person or entity." And it prohibits censorship, which it defines to include the failure of private media outlets to cover issues that the government considers to be of "public interest." In September 2014, the Constitutional Court rejected key challenges to the constitutionality of the law.

The Superintendency of Information and Communication, a government regulatory body created by the Communications Law, has repeatedly ordered media outlets and journalists to rectify or publicly apologize for publishing information and opinions it considers to be untruthful. For example, in January, it ordered a cartoonist known as Bonil to "amend" a cartoon that depicted police searching the house of a journalist who had been convicted of defaming Correa. The Superintendency also ordered the newspaper that had published the cartoon, El Universo, to pay a fine of approximately US$140,000.

A new criminal code that entered into force in August 2014 eliminates several defamation provisions, but retains slander, a criminal charge used repeatedly by Correa to target his critics. In January, the National Court of Justice upheld the conviction for slander of Cléver Jiménez, an opposition legislator; Carlos Figueroa, a union leader; and Fernando Villavicencio, a journalist and union leader.

The three had asked the attorney general to investigate Correa for allegedly ordering an armed assault on a hospital during a September 2010 police mutiny that the government considered an attempted coup. The court sentenced Jiménez and Villavicencio to 18 months in prison, and Figueroa to 6 months. It ordered them to publicly apologize to the president and pay him approximately $145,000. Figueroa was arrested in July, while Jiménez and Villavicencio remained at large at time of writing.

The Correa government frequently requires private media outlets to transmit official broadcasts responding to unfavorable news coverage or opinions. For example, in December 2013, it required radio stations to interrupt their morning news programs to air an official broadcast responding to critical statements by Sister Elsie Monge of the Ecumenical Commission of Human Rights. The broadcast said that in "no cases" had Ecuador violated human rights.

Online service providers have blocked videos, photos, and accounts criticizing the Correa administration after a firm in Spain claimed they violated US copyright laws. Even though Ecuadorian authorities have denied involvement, the notices sent to request the takedowns state that the firm represented Ecuadorian state actors. In October 2013, YouTube blocked access for several weeks to a documentary purporting to show harassment of the Íntag community for its opposition to mining activities in the area. The firm in Spain argued that using images from Ecuador's public TV violated copyright law.

Judicial Independence

Corruption, inefficiency, and political influence have plagued Ecuador's judiciary for years. With a popular mandate following a 2011 referendum, the Correa administration initiated a sweeping judicial reform process to address these chronic problems. As a part of this process, however, the Council of the Judiciary appointed and removed hundreds of judges, including all magistrates of the National Court of Justice, through highly questionable mechanisms that undermine judicial independence.

A report published in July by three international NGOs—the Due Process of Law Foundation, Dejusticia, and the Institute for Legal Defense—documented routine executive interference with judicial decisions, misuse of the penal system to target individuals who question the government's policies, and misuse of the judiciary's internal disciplinary system to sanction judges whose rulings were inconsistent with the Correa administration's policies.

Disproportionate Criminal Charges against Protesters

Sweeping provisions of the "sabotage and terrorism" chapter in the criminal code have been repeatedly applied by prosecutors against protesters. The provisions have been used to convict more than 100 people for participating in allegedly violent protest activity during the police mutiny in September 2010.

In March 2014, María Alejandra Cevallos, a university student, was sentenced to four years in prison. Cevallos was one of several protesters who was accused of forcibly entering the offices of the public television channel during the mutiny—after the government had ordered all the other stations to transmit its programming—to demand an opportunity to speak to the public. Another student was sentenced to two years in prison as an accomplice because "with his applause he externalized his general agreement with the [group's] actions."

In April, three women protesting with other mostly female demonstrators outside a prison in Quito against a prisoner's transfer were detained and charged under the sabotage and terrorism provisions. According to a police report, the protesters had "shouted 'torturer' at [the interior minister] and for this reason the minister ordered the immediate detention of three citizens." The three women spent 18 days in prison before a prosecutor dropped the charges.

Human Rights Defenders and Civil Society Organizations

In 2013, President Correa issued a sweeping executive decree that grants the government broad powers to intervene in NGO operations, including dissolving groups on the grounds that they have "compromise[d] public peace" or have engaged in activities that are different from the activities they identified when registering with the government.

In December 2013, the government dissolved the Pachamama Foundation, an NGO that had engaged in environmental and human rights advocacy for more than 16 years, on the grounds that several of its members had allegedly participated in a violent demonstration against oil drilling in the Amazon region.

Pachamama was not given advanced notice of the dissolution, and its legal challenges to the order were all rejected.

The government has routinely sought to discredit civil society groups by accusing them of seeking to destabilize the government. In April, Correa accused members of Yasunidos, a grassroots environmental group, of being liars, incoherent, and "rock throwers." Yasunidos had collected more than 700,000 signatures for a referendum on whether the Yasuni National Park in the Amazon should be opened to further oil exploration.

Accountability for Past Abuses

Efforts to hold Ecuadoran officials to account for human rights violations committed from 1984 to 2008 continued to make slow progress. In 2014, a court ruled that statutes of limitations do not apply to gross human rights violations, and Edgar Vaca, a key former police commander accused of committing crimes against humanity during León Febres Cordero's presidency (1984-1988), was detained in the United States. His extradition was pending at time of writing.

In 2010, a special prosecutorial unit was formed to investigate 118 cases involving 456 victims (including 68 victims of extrajudicial execution and 17 of enforced disappearance) documented by a truth commission created by the Correa administration. At time of writing, prosecutors had brought charges in seven cases, including two in which suspects were convicted and one in which they were acquitted.

Reproductive Rights

The right to seek an abortion is limited to instances in which the woman's health or life is at risk or when pregnancies result from the rape of a "woman with a mental disability." Fear of prosecution drives some women and girls to have illegal and unsafe abortions, and impedes health care and post-rape services for victims of sexual violence. Fear of prosecution also hinders detection and prevention of sexual and gender-based violence. One in four women over 15 years old in Ecuador has been a victim of sexual violence, according to official statistics.

Refugees

According to the latest available official statistics, from 2013, Ecuador has nearly 55,000 registered refugees, the largest number of any Latin American country. Most are Colombians fleeing armed conflict.

In September, the Constitutional Court ruled that several provisions of a 2012 presidential decree regulating asylum procedures were unconstitutional. The court ruled that the decree's definition of "refugee" was too narrow and was inconsistent with the definition set forth in the 1984 Cartagena Declaration on Refugees. It also extended the deadline to file an asylum request to three months after the petitioner's entry, and provided additional protections for appeal of asylum decisions, stating that refugees cannot be returned until a judge has made a final decision on the case.

The ruling, however, upheld other problematic provisions of the decree, including unfair procedures for determining which asylum claims should be deemed "manifestly unfounded," and overly broad powers to revoke refugee status.

Prison Conditions

Two long-standing problems in Ecuador are prison overcrowding and poor prison conditions. Since 2012, the government has invested millions of dollars to construct new detention centers. Yet the distant location of these centers and their strict and limited visitation rules impede prisoners' contact with family members. Visitors reportedly have been subjected to vaginal and anal inspections.

Key International Actors

Ecuador, with the support of members of the Bolivarian Alliance for the Americas (ALBA), continued to engage in an international campaign to undermine the independence of the Inter-American Commission on Human Rights, especially the office of its special rapporteur on freedom of expression. The government failed to participate in public hearings on Ecuador convened by the commission, and announced it would not comply with precautionary measures ordered by it. In January, Correa suggested again that Ecuador might leave the Inter-American Human Rights system.

The United States Agency for International Development (USAID) and the Konrad Adenauer Stiftung (KAS), a German political party foundation, shut their offices in Ecuador in September. USAID stated that this was a "result of the Government of Ecuador's decision to prohibit approval of new USAID assistance programs," while KAS cited the "increasing control and influence of the government in the political work of foundations and NGOs."

Egypt

Egypt's human rights crisis, the most serious in the country's modern history, continued unabated throughout 2014. The government consolidated control through constriction of basic freedoms and a stifling campaign of arrests targeting political opponents. Former Defense Minister Abdel Fattah al-Sisi, who took office in June, has overseen a reversal of the human rights gains that followed the 2011 uprising. Security forces and an increasingly politicized judiciary—apparently unnerved by rising armed group attacks—invoked national security to muzzle nearly all dissent.

Judges routinely ordered detainees held for months based on little, if any, evidence. Thousands arrested after mass protests in 2013 remained in pretrial detention. Pervasive impunity characterized the government's response to security force abuses. Only four officers have faced charges for human rights violations since July 3, 2013, when the military overthrew President Mohamed Morsy. All the charges stemmed from one incident in August 2013 in which police tear gassed a packed prison van, killing 37 detainees. There has been no accountability for the deaths of more than 1,000 protesters in a series of mostly peaceful demonstrations in July and August 2013.

Protester Killings and Impunity

Security forces used excessive force to disperse protests early in the year. Nearly 20 people, most of them Morsy supporters, died in clashes with police in the first three days of January. On January 25, the third anniversary of the 2011 uprising, at least 64 demonstrators died in clashes with police in protests throughout the country.

Outgoing interim president, Adly Mansour, who handed over power to al-Sisi on June 8, established a presidential fact-finding committee in December 2013 "to gather information and evidence for the violent events" that accompanied the June 30 mass protests and July 3 coup that brought down Morsy, Egypt's first freely elected president. An executive summary of the commission's report, released on November 26, did not recommend that charges be brought against any member of the security forces or government for the mass killing. Its man-

HUMAN
RIGHTS
WATCH

ALL ACCORDING TO PLAN
The Rab'a Massacre and Mass Killings of Protesters in Egypt

date did not authorize it to subpoena witnesses or documents, establish individual criminal liability, or make its findings public.

In March, Mansour asked the Justice Ministry to open a judicial investigation into the August 14, 2013, dispersals of pro-Morsy sit-ins at Rab'a and Nahda squares in Cairo in which more than 800 protesters died. The ministry announced it would not assign a judge to investigate these events because this was the prerogative of the prosecutor general, whose office claimed it was already investigating.

A March 18 court ruling sentenced a police captain to 10 years in prison and three lower-ranking officers to one-year suspended sentences for their role in the tear gas suffocation of 37 protesters in a police van outside Abu Zaabel Prison on August 18, 2013. An appeals court overturned the convictions on June 7 and referred the case to the prosecutor general for further investigation. A retrial is scheduled to begin on January 22, 2015.

Mass Arrests

An Interior Ministry official acknowledged in July 2014 that since Morsy's ouster a year earlier authorities had arrested 22,000 people, most if not all suspected supporters of the Muslim Brotherhood. According to the Egyptian Center for Economic and Social Rights, more than 41,000 people were arrested or faced criminal charges between July 2013 and May 2014.

Judges routinely renewed detention orders of many of those arrested for months without charge or trial and convicted many others in mass trials without establishing individual guilt for criminal offenses. As of July 2014, according to Interior Ministry data provided to the presidential fact-finding committee, more than 7,000 people arrested in the fallout from Morsy's removal remained in pretrial detention.

Those detained include around 29,000 Brotherhood members, including its high and mid-level leadership, according to the Brotherhood. The arrest campaign expanded in 2014 to include secular and leftist activists on charges that include protesting without authorization, incitement, "thuggery," vandalism, blocking roads, and belonging to banned or "terrorist" groups.

Due Process Violations and Mass Death Sentences

Egypt's judiciary exhibited serious procedural deficiencies that deprived detainees of basic due process rights. Though authorities in November 2013 lifted the state of emergency imposed at the time of Morsy's removal, judges often renewed pretrial detention orders despite a lack of evidence that would warrant prosecution.

Many trials violated Egyptian law as well as international standards. In March and April, a criminal court judge in the governorate of Minya handed down the death penalty to more than 1,200 people allegedly involved in two attacks on police that resulted in the death of one officer. The judge did not allow the defendants the right to mount a meaningful defense or ensure that all had access to counsel.

The first trial, which resulted in 529 death sentences, lasted less than an hour, and only 74 defendants were present. The court also barred some defense lawyers from attending. In the second trial, which yielded 683 death sentences, none of the defendants attended.

Following legally mandated advice from the grand mufti, Egypt's top religious authority, the judge confirmed 220 of the death sentences, which the prosecutor general automatically appealed as required by law. In December, a separate judge in the governorate of Giza issued preliminary death sentences to 188 people accused of attacking a police station in August 2013 and killing 14 policemen. According to the Brotherhood, 259 of its members, including Supreme Guide Mohamed Badie, have been sentenced to death since Morsy's ouster.

Egypt's 2014 constitution permits military trials for civilians, and on October 27, 2014, al-Sisi issued a decree expanding military court jurisdiction to cover crimes that occur on any public, state-owned, or "vital" property. Since the decree, prosecutors have referred at least 455 people—the vast majority of them Brotherhood members—to military court. In April, a military court sentenced a social media manager for the online news website Rassd to one year in prison for helping to leak a tape of remarks by al-Sisi during his time as defense minister. The court acquitted one Rassd employee and handed down three-year sentences to an army conscript and two other men who remain at large. In May and September, military courts handed down one-year sentences to 10 people—most of them Brotherhood members or allied politicians—for attempting to cross into Sudan illegally. In November, a military court in Suez sentenced 17 people to between 5 and 10 years in prison for throwing rocks and incendiary devices at soldiers during the violence following Morsy's removal.

Torture and Ill-Treatment

At least 90 people died in local police stations and security directorates in the governorates of Cairo and Giza alone in 2014, according to an investigation by the Egyptian newspaper *Al Watan*, which cited statistics from the Justice Ministry's Forensic Medical Authority. That number represented a 38 percent increase from the year before.

A spokesman for the authority told the newspaper that prison overcrowding had forced authorities to hold detainees in police stations and other places of temporary detention which were not well ventilated or otherwise properly equipped. Witnesses told Human Rights Watch that police and prison authorities often failed to provide proper medical care to prisoners, leading to death. In some cases of deaths in detention, lawyers and relatives alleged that authorities had tortured the victim.

Detainees also described severe beatings during arrest, arrival at police stations, and transfer between prisons. Scores detained in January protests complained of torture, including electric shocks, to coerce confessions. The Egyptian Initiative for Personal Rights documented the enforced disappearance and torture of dozens of civilians in military detention.

Attacks by Armed Groups

The security situation deteriorated, particularly in the Sinai, as armed groups targeted security forces, buildings, checkpoints, and vehicles. An Egyptian insurgent group, Ansar Beit al-Maqdis, announced that it has joined the extremist group Islamic State (also known as ISIS). Some attacks targeted tourists or indiscriminately harmed ordinary citizens. At least 892 people—including militants, civilians and security forces—died in the governorate of North Sinai in 2014, according to press reports.

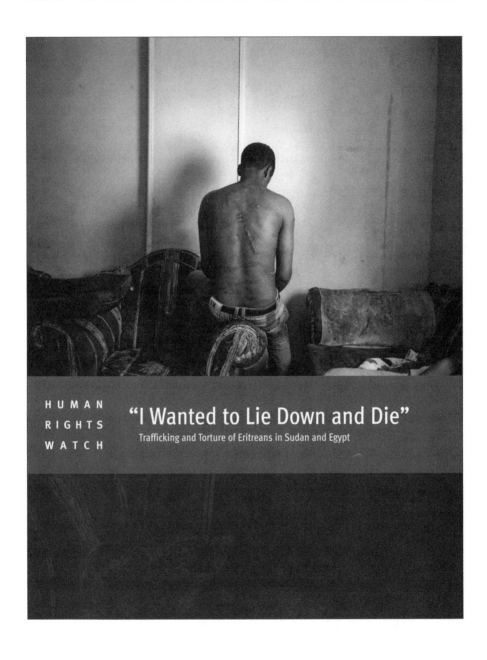

Freedom of Association, Expression, and Assembly

Egypt's new constitution contains language that appears to protect free expression, peaceful assembly, and association, but authorities detained thousands solely for their peaceful exercise of these rights.

Free Expression

Authorities detained dozens of people for such offences as possessing flyers with anti-military slogans, rapping in public against the police, or displaying signs commemorating victims of the Rab'a dispersal. Journalists, academics, former lawmakers and human rights defenders were among those charged with crimes or banned from travel outside Egypt. Police arrested three Al Jazeera English journalists, Mohamed Fahmy, Peter Greste, and Baher Mohamed, in late December 2013, and a court handed down multi-year prison sentences in June 2014 after a trial in which prosecutors failed to present any credible evidence of criminal wrongdoing.

Free Assembly

A November 2013 law on public assembly allowed the Interior Ministry to ban and forcefully disperse protests and arrest participants on vague grounds such as "imped[ing] citizens' interests." On April 7, 2014, a court rejected appeals from April 6 Youth Movement co-founders Ahmed Maher and Mohamed Adel and activist Ahmed Douma against their three-year sentences for breaking the law. Authorities also used the law to detain prominent activist Alaa Abdel Fattah and human rights defenders Mahienour al-Masry and Yara Sallam.

Free Association

In September 2014, al-Sisi signed an amendment to the penal code that mandates a life sentence and a fine of 500,000 Egyptian pounds (US$69,900) for anyone who takes foreign funding to harm the national "interest" or "unity," a provision Egyptian rights activists fear will be used against them and other nongovernmental organizations (NGOs).

Authorities banned the Muslim Brotherhood and declared it a terrorist organization in December 2013, following a bomb attack on a Nile Delta police station claimed by Ansar Beit al-Maqdis. Authorities put forward no evidence to support the designation, but in a television statement Deputy Prime Minister Hossam Eisa cited as justification the 1948 assassination of Egypt's prime minister and the alleged torture of Brotherhood opponents during the pro-Morsy sit-ins in July and August 2013. Authorities froze the assets of more than 1,000 associations allegedly tied to the Brotherhood, such as the Islamic Medical Association, which served residents of poor neighborhoods, in addition to dozens of Brother-hood-affiliated schools.

On April 28, the Court of Urgent Matters banned activities of the April 6 Youth Movement and authorized the authorities to shut its headquarters on grounds that it engaged in espionage and harmed Egypt's image abroad, based on a complaint from lawyer Ashraf Said, who said recorded phone calls among April 6 members aired on television "proved" the activists had "conspired against state institutions."

Authorities raided the Alexandria office of the Egyptian Center for Economic and Social Rights on May 22, briefly arresting at least 15 activists and lawyers and subjecting them to sexual harassment and beatings. Riot police and military troops also broke up labor protests and strikes.

The Social Solidarity Ministry in June 2014 presented a draft law on associations that would give the government security agencies veto power over NGO activities as well as their registration and funding. The law would also cripple their capac-ity to communicate or co-operate with groups abroad.

The Social Solidarity Ministry did not enforce a November 10 deadline for all NGOs to register under the current Law of Civic Associations and Foundations (Law 84 of 2002), which would give the government tight control over their activ-ities. Many Egyptian human rights organizations are currently registered as civil companies or law firms due to the highly restrictive law. However, several high-profile human rights defenders left the country fearing arrest and prosecution, and some groups suspended their activities. The government has pledged to make the NGOs register.

Freedom of Religion and Sectarian Violence

Egypt's 2014 constitution guarantees freedom of religion and the rights of minorities, but authorities continued to prosecute writers and activists on charges of "contempt of religion" and "blasphemy," including religious minorities and proclaimed atheists. In June, an appeals court in the governorate of Beni Suef upheld a five-year sentence in absentia for author Karam Saber, a Muslim convicted for contempt of religion in 2013 for his short story collection *Where Is God?* Attacks on churches and properties of Christians continued in 2014, and in many cases authorities failed to intervene.

Violence and Discrimination against Women

Sexual harassment and assault of women and girls in public spaces continued in spite of recent government efforts to combat the practice, including arresting and prosecuting some men for such crimes, which have long been committed with impunity.

Egyptian rights groups documented at least nine incidents of mob sexual assault and harassment in Cairo's Tahrir Square between June 3 and June 8, 2014, as demonstrators celebrated al-Sisi's election. Seven men were eventually handed sentences ranging to life for the attacks, and interim President Mansour issued a law on June 5 that for the first time defined and outlawed sexual harassment and set escalating penalties for different offenses.

Al-Sisi ordered the formation of a ministerial committee to determine a national strategy to address harassment. On June 12, the committee met and proposed plans that included increasing security for women in public squares and gatherings, as well as raising awareness about harassment against women through media campaigns and schools. The committee has not proposed a comprehensive law on violence against women nor a national strategy to implement such a law.

No law criminalizes domestic violence. Other forms of violence against women, including child marriage and female genital mutilation (FGM), continued in some areas, despite laws prohibiting them. On November 20, the country's first trial for FGM, which began after a 13-year-old girl died from an allergic reaction to penicillin, ended in an acquittal for the girl's father and the doctor who performed the procedure. The prosecutor appealed the acquittal. Personal status laws in Egypt continue to discriminate against women in relation to marriage, divorce, child custody, and inheritance.

LGBT Rights

Authorities arrested more than 95 lesbian, gay, bisexual, and transgender (LGBT) people between July 2013 and December 2014. On December 7, police raided a Cairo bathhouse and arrested at least 25 men whom they accused of "practicing debauchery." Activists said police used fake online dating profiles to target gay men and others, including sex workers.

On September 25, a court sentenced six men to two years in jail with labor for "committing debauchery." Earlier in September, prosecutors filed charges of "inciting debauchery" against eight men who allegedly participated in a videotaped same-sex wedding which later circulated on social media. In April, a court sentenced four men to eight years in prison for "debauchery" after finding makeup and women's clothing in an apartment where they allegedly held parties.

Refugees, Asylum Seekers, and Migrants

Egypt violated the rights of refugees, asylum seekers, and migrants within its borders. Syrians represent one of the largest refugee populations, with nearly 140,000 registered with the United Nations High Commissioner for Refugees (UNHCR). Egypt prevented the UNHCR from registering Palestinians from Syria, and security officials maintained a restrictive visa and security clearance requirement enacted following the ouster of Morsy. In some instances authorities coerced refugees from Syria to leave to Lebanon, without assurances they would be protected there, and to Syria, where they face persecution, detention, and violence.

Key International Actors

The United States welcomed al-Sisi's election despite the climate of political intimidation. Israel, Saudi Arabia, and the United Arab Emirates (UAE) strongly urged the US to normalize relations with al-Sisi's government despite ongoing human rights abuses. Washington announced in September 2014 that it would deliver 10 Apache attack helicopters earlier placed on hold by Congress to support counterterrorism efforts in the Sinai.

According to the White House, US President Barack Obama raised human rights concerns when he met with al-Sisi during the United Nations General Assembly in September. Secretary of State John Kerry in April said he was unable to certify that Egypt was engaged in a "democratic transition" in order to release additional military aid unrelated to counterterrorism. In December, the US Congress included new language in the law governing military aid to Egypt that would allow Kerry to waive the required democracy certification if it is in the interest of national security.

The report of the European Union mission to monitor the May presidential election noted that "respect for the freedoms of association, assembly and expression remained areas of concern" and that police used "disproportional force against peaceful protesters," resulting in a "chilling impact on the expression of political dissent."

The EU suspended military exports to Egypt in August 2013. In September, French Foreign Minister Laurent Fabius said he was "confident" that co-operation between the countries would increase "in areas that affect security."

Saudi Arabia, Kuwait and the UAE pledged more than $18 billion in loans, fuel subsidies, and grants, in addition to investments in residential and commercial property.

The African Union suspended Egypt following the July 2013 coup but reinstated Egypt's membership in June, after the constitution had been approved by referendum and al-Sisi took office.

On May 1, International Criminal Court (ICC) prosecutors dismissed a communication filed by lawyers representing Morsy and his defunct Freedom and Justice Party seeking ICC jurisdiction in Egypt. The ICC dismissed the declaration on the grounds that the statement purporting to grant the ICC jurisdiction was not filed by the recognized government of Egypt itself.

Equatorial Guinea

Corruption, poverty, and repression continue to plague Equatorial Guinea under President Teodoro Obiang Nguema Mbasogo, who has been in power since 1979. Vast oil revenues fund lavish lifestyles for the small elite surrounding the president, while a large proportion of the population continues to live in poverty. Mismanagement of public funds and credible allegations of high-level corruption persist, as do other serious abuses, including torture, arbitrary detention, secret detention, and unfair trials.

Throughout the year, President Obiang made sizable donations to international organizations, hired public relations firms, traveled widely to visit leaders in other countries, and hosted international events in order to improve his image. His efforts bore some results: the United Nations secretary-general and other dignitaries made official visits during the African Union Summit held in June, and an association of Portuguese-speaking countries in July accepted Equatorial Guinea's bid for membership, which the country had pursued for a decade.

Obiang's eldest son and possible successor, Teodorin, was indicted in France in March on money-laundering charges stemming from a long-running investigation, while the United States agreed to settle its forfeiture claim against Teodorin in October in a separate case that produced thousands of pages of evidence of alleged corruption, extortion, and money laundering. To pay the US$30 million settlement, Teodorin had to sell his Malibu mansion and other US holdings. The US Justice Department said the seized assets would be used to benefit Equatorial Guinea's people.

Economic and Social Rights

Equatorial Guinea is among the top five oil producers in sub-Saharan Africa and has a population of approximately 700,000 people. It is classified as a high-income country by the World Bank. According to the UN 2014 Human Development Report, the country has a per capita gross domestic product of $37,478.85, which is the highest wealth ranking of any African country and one of the highest in the world, yet it ranks 144 out of 187 countries in the Human Development Index that measures social and economic development. As a result, Equatorial

Guinea has by far the world's largest gap of all countries between its per capita wealth and its human development score.

Despite the country's abundant natural resource wealth and government's obligations to advance the economic and social rights of its citizens, it has directed little of this wealth to meet their needs. About half of the population lacks access to clean water and basic sanitation facilities, according to official 2012 statistics. Childhood malnutrition, as seen in the percentage of children whose growth is stunted, stands at 35 percent, according to the United Nations Children's Fund, UNICEF. A large portion of the population also lacks access to quality healthcare, decent schools, or reliable electricity. Net enrollment in primary education was only 61 percent in 2012. Despite tremendous resources, Equatorial Guinea has very low vaccination rates, including the worst polio vaccination rate in the world, 39 percent, according to the World Health Organization. As of mid-2014, five cases of polio were confirmed there, prompting a belated vaccination campaign.

The government's statistics are unreliable and it makes few efforts to reliably track basic indicators. International organizations frequently have to make their estimates based on computer models because they only have limited information. According to such models, Equatorial Guinea has reduced maternal mortality rates by 81 percent since 1990 and has met a Millenium Development Goal target ahead of schedule.

The government does not publish basic information on budgets and spending, and citizens and journalists are unable to effectively monitor the use of the country's natural resource wealth. In August, the government confirmed that it would seek to reapply to an international transparency initiative on oil, gas, and mining payments from which it was expelled in 2010. A key requirement of the Extractive Industries Transparency Initiative is that governments openly engage with activists about the management of the country's natural resources, without intimidation or reprisal, and guarantee an "enabling environment" for their full participation.

Freedom of Expression and Association

Equatorial Guinea has long had a poor record on press freedom. In January, security officials detained two *Financial Times* journalists for several hours and confiscated their computers, notebooks, and recording equipment, which were not returned. The journalists were able to recover their passports and mobile phones, then left the country earlier than planned.

Local journalists are unable to criticize the government or address issues the authorities disapprove of without risk of censorship or reprisal. Only a few private media outlets exist in the country, and they are generally owned by persons close to President Obiang; self-censorship is common. Foreign news is available to the small minority with access to satellite broadcasts and the Internet; others have access only to limited foreign radio programming.

Freedom of association and assembly are severely curtailed in Equatorial Guinea, greatly limiting space for independent groups. The government imposes restrictive conditions on the registration and operation of nongovernmental groups. The country has no legally registered independent human rights groups. The few local activists who seek to address human rights-related issues face intimidation, harassment, and reprisals.

Political Parties and Opposition

The ruling Democratic Party (PDGE) maintains a monopoly over political life. All but two officially recognized political parties are aligned with the ruling party. Equatorial Guinea's two-chamber parliament with a total of 175 seats has only one opposition representative in each chamber. President Obiang appointed 20 senators, five more than allowed under the 2011 constitution.

Members of the political opposition face arbitrary arrest, intimidation, and harassment. In July, Santiago Martín Engono Esono, the leader of the youth wing of the Convergence for Social Democracy (CPDS), was arbitrarily arrested and jailed for five days in Bata, the country's second largest city.

In August, President Obiang announced that a national political dialogue scheduled for November would for the first time include opposition leaders in exile. In preparation for this dialogue, President Obiang declared general political amnesty for exiled opposition figures in October but did not extend it to jailed political prisoners convicted for alleged security offenses. In part for this reason, three political parties, including the only opposition party with representation in parliament, withdrew from the dialogue and declared it a failure.

Presidential elections are scheduled for 2016 but there is speculation they may be brought forward in 2015. National legislative elections in 2013 were marred by serious human rights violations and a denial of fundamental freedoms, including arbitrary arrests and restrictions on freedom of assembly.

Torture, Arbitrary Detention, and Unfair Trials

Due process rights are routinely flouted in Equatorial Guinea and prisoner mistreatment remains common. Torture continues to take place, despite government denials. Many detainees are held indefinitely without knowing the charges against them. Some are held in secret detention. Poor conditions in prisons and jails can be life-threatening.

President Obiang exercises inordinate control over the judiciary, which lacks independence. The president is designated as the country's "chief magistrate." Among other powers, he chairs the body that oversees judges and appoints the body's remaining members.

In February 2014, the Obiang government announced a temporary moratorium on the death penalty. The Community of Portuguese-Speaking Countries (CPLP) admitted Equatorial Guinea on that basis, believing it was a first step toward eliminating the death penalty. Only two weeks before announcing the moratorium, the government executed up to nine people who had been sentenced to death. In July, President Obiang stated in an interview that he continued to support the death penalty.

Agustín Esono Nsogo, a teacher held without charge for over a year, was released in February 2014. According to his lawyer, Esono was tortured on three occasions in an effort to get him to confess to an alleged plot to destabilize the country. He was denied medical attention for his injuries.

Cipriano Nguema Mba, a former military officer who was granted refugee status in Belgium in 2013, was abducted while visiting Nigeria in late 2013 and illegally returned to Equatorial Guinea, where he was secretly held by government authorities and tortured.

This is the second time Nguema was kidnapped from exile abroad. On both ocassions, authorities belatedly acknowledged holding him and claimed he was discovered inside the country and imprisoned to serve an earlier sentence. Following a new trial, in September 2014 Nguema was convicted for an alleged coup attempt and and sentenced to 27 years in prison. His lawyers were not able to visit him and were unable to represent him at trial. Five other people allegedly connected to Nguema were also tried without legal representation, convicted, and handed harsh sentences.

During the year Roberto Berardi, an Italian national, was tortured, held for months in solitary confinement in inhumane conditions, and repeatedly denied medical treatment and access to his lawyer or diplomatic representatives. His family said he was denied food and water for several days in September after a visit to the prison by the ambassador of Equatorial Guinea to Italy, in which she reportedly rebuked Berardi for an open letter he published from jail. Berardi is imprisoned in an apparent attempt to protect his business partner, Teodorín, from disclosures about corruption allegations. President Obiang did not release Berardi on humanitarian grounds, as promised in April under international pressure. He remained in prison at time of writing.

Key International Actors

The United States is Equatorial Guinea's main trading partner and source of investment in the oil sector. It raised human rights concerns throughout the year. In August, Obiang participated alongside dozens of other leaders in the US-Africa Summit hosted by US President Barack Obama, sparking media controversy that he was permitted to attend despite Equatorial Guinea's poor record on human rights and corruption. While in Washington, Obiang was also the guest of honor at a dinner and conference organized by the Corporate Council on Africa.

Spain, the former colonial power, eased pressure on Equatorial Guinea to improve its human rights record. In June, Prime Minister Mariano Rajoy attended the African Union Summit outside Malabo, marking the first visit by a Spanish prime minister since 1991. Early in the year, Rajoy had declined to meet bilaterally with Obiang.

Irina Bokova, director-general of the *United Nations Educational, Scientific and Cultural Organization* (UNESCO) traveled twice to Equatorial Guinea, including to attend a September prize ceremony hosted by President Obiang for an award he funded and sought to have named after himself. She had previously tried to block UNESCO's approval of the controversial award.

Equatorial Guinea underwent a second cycle of the Universal Periodic Review at the UN in Geneva and received many recommendations on torture, arbitrary detention, rule of law, freedom of association, press freedom, anti-corruption, and social and economic rights. The government accepted most recommendations and rejected very few. Expectations that this would lead to positive change on the ground are low, however, as the government did not implement changes promised following an earlier UN peer review.

Eritrea

Eritrea's dismal human rights situation, exacerbated by indefinite military conscription, is causing thousands of Eritreans to flee their country every month. In early 2014, President Isaias Afewerki confirmed his lack of interest in an open society, stating: "[I]f there is anyone who thinks there will be democracy or [a] multiparty system in this country . . . then that person can think of such things in another world."

The United Nations High Commissioner for Refugees (UNHCR) estimates that about 4,000 Eritreans flee the country each month and that as of mid-2014, more than 313,000 Eritrean –over 5 percent of the population–have fled. More than 5,000 crossed into Ethiopia in October alone. Many have experienced further abuses or death at the hands of traffickers en route to Israel and Europe, while thousands of others have been detained in Libya and Israel in deplorable conditions.

In June, the Human Rights Council condemned Eritrea's "continued widespread and systematic violations of human rights and fundamental freedoms," and adopted a resolution establishing a commission of inquiry to investigate abuses in the country. The most common patterns of abuse include open-ended military conscription; forced labor during conscription; arbitrary arrests, detentions, and disappearances; torture and other degrading treatment in detention; restrictions on freedoms of expression, conscience, and movement; and repression of religious freedom. Members of the Afar and Kunama ethnic groups flee because of land expropriations and discrimination by the government.

In September, Eritrea acceded to the United Nations Convention against Torture.

Indefinite Conscription and Forced Labor

The threat of indefinite military conscription compels thousands of young Eritreans to flee their country. Among recent defections were 11 members of the national football team, including the coach, who fled while in Kenya in December 2013. The national football squad has lost almost 50 members in such defections over the past five years.

By law, each Eritrean is compelled to serve 18 months in national service starting at age 18 but in practice conscripts serve indefinitely, many for over a decade. One 14-year-old refugee said, "The military does not have an end, it is for life." While most young Eritreans begin military training for the last year of high school, children as young as 15 are sometimes conscripted. Desertions and refusals to report became more common in 2014.

Conscripts receive inadequate pay to support family members, a financial plight exacerbated by food-price inflation in 2014. Conscripts are also subject to military discipline and are harshly treated throughout their long service. Perceived infractions result in incarceration and in physical abuse often amounting to torture. The length of incarceration and type of physical abuse inflicted is at the whim of military commanders and jailers. Female conscripts are frequently sexually abused by commanders.

While some conscripts work in civil service jobs at conscript pay, others are used as forced labor on construction sites and government-owned farms. The Eritrean construction industry is a government monopoly that uses forced conscript labor. In 2013, Human Rights Watch found that several hundred conscripts had been used by state-owned Segen Construction Co. to build infrastructure at the Bisha mine, Eritrea's only operating mineral mine. Bisha is majority-owned by Nevsun Resources, a Canadian mining company. Nevsun has expressed "regret if certain employees of Segen were conscripts" during the mine's construction, but insists there are no ongoing abuses. Segen remains a contractor at Bisha. Able-bodied men older than 50 have been forced to perform militia duty several times a week without pay since 2012. They are used as armed guards and as labor on public workprojects, prompting some to flee.

Arbitrary Arrest, Prolonged Detention, and Inhumane Conditions

Arbitrary arrests are the norm. A prisoner may or may not be told the reason for the arrest; even prison authorities may not be informed. Detainees are held indefinitely; releases are as arbitrary as arrest, and few, if any, detainees are brought to trial. The most prominent political prisoners are 21 senior government officials and journalists arrested in September 2001 and held in solitary confinement ever since; defecting jailers claim that half have died in captivity. The then-

15-year-old daughter of a government minister arrested immediately after her father defected in 2012 remains incarcerated.

Prisoners are held in vastly overcrowded underground cells or shipping containers, with no space to lie down, little or no light, oppressive heat or cold, and vermin. Food, water, and sanitation are inadequate, beatings and other physical abuse are common, deaths not unusual. Some of the leaders of an attempted 2013 takeover of the Ministry of Information died in prison in 2014, according to unconfirmed reports.

Freedom of Expression and Association

In May, the country's Roman Catholic bishops released an unprecedented letter underlining their concern at "the prospect of a drastic depopulation of the country." The letter highlighted forced "military service unlimited in terms of time and monetary reward" and "the imprisonment of many young people in actual prison or in punishment camps." The bishops called on the government to "initiat[e] a political system that is clear, transparent and lawful," to liberate "those who have been detained illegally, those forgotten in prison," and to allow "open discussion of the problems of the country . . . [and] access to objective verifiable information."

The bishops' letter is a rare public criticism of the government from within the country. Since 2001, the government has tightly controlled access to information, permitting no independent media, labor unions, or nongovernmental associations to operate.

At least six government journalists arrested in 2009 and 2011 remain in solitary confinement without trial. Foreign broadcasts are sometimes jammed.

Internet access is available but few can afford private access, and Internet cafés are monitored, as are telephone calls.

Freedom of Religion

The government severely harasses citizens who practice religions other than the four it recognizes—Sunni Islam and the Eritrean Orthodox, Roman Catholic, and Lutheran churches. Prayer meetings of unrecognized religions are disrupted and participants arrested. A condition for release is often a signed statement by the prisoner recanting their religious affiliation.

Jehovah's Witnesses are especially persecuted. Three who were arrested in 1994 for refusing to serve in the military remain imprisoned 20 years later. They are among 73 jailed Jehovah's Witnesses. The latest group of 19 was arrested in April 2014 during Bible study.

The government interferes with the practices even of the four religions it recognizes. The government appointed the Sunni imam in 1996, deposed the patriarch of the Eritrean Orthodox Church in 2005, and appointed his successor. The deposed patriarch remains under house arrest nine years later. In October, several monasteries denounced the government-appointed administrators of the church.

Migration and Asylum

Eritreans fleeing their country have experienced horrific abuses. Since 2004, over 200,000 Eritreans have fled to remote border camps in eastern Sudan and Ethiopia, evading Eritrean border guards with shoot to kill orders against people leaving without permission. The lack of work prospects in or near the camps caused tens of thousands to pay smugglers to take them through Sinai to Israel. Egyptian traffickers have tortured scores of Eritreans for ransom in the Sinai Peninsula, including through rape, burning, and mutilation. Some victims said the Egyptian traffickers had tortured them to extort up to US$40,000 from their relatives.

Despite these atrocities, about 37,000 Eritreans had entered Israel by the time Israel all but sealed off its border with Egypt in December 2012. Since June 2012, Israeli authorities have indefinitely detained thousands of Eritreans for entering Israel irregularly and have applied coercive measures to "make their lives miserable" and "encourage the illegals to leave," in the words of Israeli officials. Measures include indefinite detention, obstacles to accessing Israel's asylum system, the rejection of 99.9 percent of Eritrean claims, ambiguous policies on being allowed to work, and severely restricted access to healthcare. In September 2014, the Israeli Supreme Court held the detention law to be unconstitutional and later ordered the release of some detainees.

Key International Actors

President Isaias uses the lingering tension from the 1998-2000 border war with Ethiopia as an excuse for keeping the country on a permanent emergency military footing. Eritrea's foreign policy of supporting Ethiopian, Somali, and other rebel groups has also led to its political isolation in the region. Eritrea fought a brief border skirmish with Djibouti in 2008, and Qatar has been trying to mediate this border dispute since 2011 without progress. Eritrea denies it holds 18 Djibouti prisoners of war even though three escaped in 2011.

The United Nations Security Council voted to retain an arms embargo on Eritrea and to renew the mandate of its Monitoring Group on Somalia and Eritrea for another year.

Foreign mining company projects in which the Eritrean government has 40-50 percent stakes provide it with significant foreign exchange. Nevsun, the Canadian owner of Bisha, estimates it will pay $14 billion to Eritrea over the next 10 years, according to the UN Monitoring Group. Another Canadian company, Sunridge Gold Corporation, announced it will begin gold and copper production in 2015. The largest extraction projectof potash salts in the Danakil Depression, by South Boulder Mines of Australia, remains in the pre-feasibility study stage.

Economic relations with China remain important. One Chinese firm, SFECO Group, reportedly received orders worth $340 million in 2014 for agricultural and industrial construction projects. The Chinese government in July agreed to fund part of a $33 million first-phase project to construct a college of science southwest of Asmara.

Canada threatened in 2014 to close the Eritrean consulate in Toronto unless it stopped collecting taxes from Eritrean-Canadians. A 2 percent tax on the income of émigrés remains an important but diminishing source of revenue for the government.

Ethiopia

Hopes that Ethiopia's government would ease its crackdown on dissent ahead of the May 2015 elections were dashed in 2014.

Instead the government continued to use arbitrary arrests and prosecutions to silence journalists, bloggers, protesters, and supporters of opposition political parties; police responded to peaceful protests with excessive force; and there was no indication of any government willingness to amend repressive legislation that was increasingly condemned for violating international standards, including at Ethiopia's Universal Periodic Review at the United Nations Human Rights Council.

Freedom of Peaceful Assembly

Security forces have harassed and detained leaders and supporters of Ethiopian opposition parties. In July, leaders of the Semawayi ("Blue") Party, the Unity for Democracy and Justice (UDJ), and the Arena Tigray Party were arrested. At time of writing, they had not been charged but remained in detention.

The Semawayi Party's attempts to hold protests were regularly blocked in 2014. Its applications to hold demonstrations were denied at least three times and organizers were arrested. Over the course of the year, authorities repeatedly harassed, threatened, and detained party leaders.

In June, Andargachew Tsige, a British citizen and secretary general of the Ginbot 7 organization, a group banned for advocating armed overthrow of the government, was deported to Ethiopia from Yemen while in transit. The transfer violated international law prohibitions against sending someone to a country where they are likely to face torture or other mistreatment. Tsige had twice been sentenced to death in absentia for his involvement with Ginbot 7. He was detained incommunicado in Ethiopia without access to family members, legal counsel, or United Kingdom consular officials for more than six weeks. He remains in detention in an unknown location.

Protests by members of some Muslim communities against perceived government interference in their religious affairs continued in 2014, albeit with less frequency. As in 2013, these protests were met by excessive force and arbitrary

arrests from security forces. The trials continue of the 29 protest leaders who were arrested and charged under the Anti-Terrorism Proclamation in July 2012.

In April and May, protests erupted in towns throughout the region of Oromia against the planned expansion of Addis Ababa's municipal boundary into Oromia. Security personnel used excessive force, including live ammunition, against protesters in several cities. At least several dozen people were confirmed dead and hundreds were arrested. Many of them remain in custody without charge.

Restrictions on human rights monitoring and on independent media make it difficult to ascertain the precise extent of casualties and arrests. Foreign journalists who attempted to reach the demonstrations were turned away or detained by security personnel. Ethnic Oromos make up approximately 45 percent of Ethiopia's population and are often arbitrarily arrested and accused of belonging to the banned Oromo Liberation Front (OLF).

Freedom of Association

The Charities and Societies Proclamation (CSO law), enacted in 2009, has severely curtailed the ability of independent nongovernmental organizations to work on human rights. The law bars work on human rights, good governance, conflict resolution, and advocacy on the rights of women, children and people with disabilities if organizations receive more than 10 percent of their funds from foreign sources. The law was more rigorously enforced in 2014.

In March, Ethiopia was approved for membership in the Extractive Industries Transparency Initiative (EITI), which promotes transparency on oil, gas, and mining revenues, despite the requirement for candidate countries to make a commitment to meaningful participation of independent groups in public debate on natural resource management. Ethiopia's previous application was denied in 2010 based on concerns over the CSO law.

Freedom of Expression

Media remain under a government stranglehold, with many journalists having to choose between self-censorship, harassment and arrest, or exile. In 2014, dozens of journalists and bloggers fled the country following threats. In August 2014, the owners of six private newspapers were charged following a lengthy campaign of threats and harassment against their publications. According to the Committee to Protect Journalists, Ethiopia is one of three countries in the world with the highest number of journalists in exile.

Since 2009, the Anti-Terrorism Proclamation has been used to target political opponents, stifle dissent, and silence journalists. In July, Ethiopia charged 10 bloggers and journalists known as the Zone 9 Collective under the Anti-Terrorism Proclamation after they spent over 80 days in pre-charge detention. The charges included having links to banned opposition groups and trying to violently overthrow the government. The bloggers regularly wrote about current events in Ethiopia. Among the evidence cited was attending a digital security training course in Kenya and the use of "security in-a-box"-a publicly available training tool used by advocates and human rights defenders. Due process concerns have marred the court proceedings.

Other journalists convicted under the Anti-Terrorism Proclamation-including Eskinder Nega, Reeyot Alemu, and Woubshet Taye-remain in prison.

The government continues to block even mildly critical web pages and blogs. The majority of opposition media websites are blocked and media outlets regularly limit their criticism of government in order to be able to work in the country.

The government regularly monitors and records telephone calls, particularly international calls, among family members and friends. Such recordings are often played during interrogations in which detainees are accused of belonging to banned organizations. Mobile networks have been shut down during peaceful protests and protesters' locations identified using information from their mobile phones. The government has monitored digital communications using highly intrusive spyware that monitors all activity on an individual's computer, including logging of keystrokes and recording of skype calls. The government's monopoly over all mobile and Internet services through its sole, state-owned telecom operator, Ethio Telecom, facilitates abuse of surveillance powers.

Abuses of Migrant Workers

Hundreds of thousands of Ethiopians continue to pursue economic opportunities in Saudi Arabia, Yemen, Bahrain, and other Gulf countries, risking mistreatment from human traffickers along the migration routes. In Yemen, migrants have been taken captive by traffickers in order to extort large sums of money from their family members. In late 2013 and early 2014, hundreds of thousands of migrant workers, mainly Ethiopians, were detained and deported from Saudi Arabia to Ethiopia. Saudi security forces and civilians attacked Ethiopians, prompting restrictions on migration to certain countries.

Forced Displacement

Both the government of Ethiopia and the donor community failed to adequately investigate allegations of abuses associated with Ethiopia's "villagization program." Under this program, 1.5 million rural people were planned to be relocated, ostensibly to improve their access to basic services. Some relocations during the program's first year in Gambella region were accompanied by violence, including beatings, arbitrary arrests, and insufficient consultation and compensation.

A 2013 complaint to the World Bank's Inspection Panel from Ethiopian refugees, the institution's independent accountability mechanism, continues to be investigated. Ethiopian refugees alleged that the bank violated its own policies on indigenous people and involuntary resettlement in the manner a national program was implemented in Gambella. In July, a UK court ruled that allegations that the UK Department for International Development (DFID) did not adequately assess evidence of human rights violations in the villagization program deserved a full judicial review. The judicial review had yet to be heard at time of writing.

Ethiopia is continuing to develop sugar plantations in the Lower Omo Valley, clearing 245,000 hectares of land that is home to 200,000 indigenous people. Indigenous people continue to be displaced without appropriate consultation or compensation. Households have found their grazing land cleared to make way for state-run sugar plantations, and access to the Omo River, used for growing food, restricted. Individuals who have questioned the development plans face arrest and harassment. Local and foreign journalists have been restricted from accessing the Omo Valley to cover these issues.

LGBT Rights

Ethiopia's criminal code punishes consensual adult same-sex relations with up to 15 years in prison. In March, Ethiopia's lawmakers proposed legislation that would make same-sex conduct a non-pardonable offense, thereby ensuring that LGBT people convicted under the law could not be granted early leave from prison. However, in April the government dropped the proposed legislation.

Ethiopia came for Universal Periodic Review in May 2014, and they rejected all recommendations to decriminalize same-sex conduct and to take measures to combat discrimination based on sexual orientation.

Key International Actors

Ethiopia continues to enjoy unquestioned support from foreign donors and most of its regional neighbors, based on its role as host of the African Union (AU); its contribution to UN peacekeeping, security and aid partnerships with Western countries; and its stated progress on development indicators.

Its relations with Egypt are strained due to Ethiopia's construction of the Grand Renaissance Dam, which will divert water from the Nile and is due to be completed in 2018. In 2014, Ethiopia negotiated between warring parties in South Sudan, and its troops maintained calm in the disputed Abyei Region. Ethiopia continues to deploy its troops inside Somalia; they were included in the AU mission as of January.

Ethiopia is one of the largest recipients of donor aid in Africa, receiving almost US$4 billion in 2014, which amounted to approximately 45 percent of its budget. Donors remain muted in their criticism of Ethiopia's human rights record and took little meaningful action to investigate allegations of abuses. Donors, including the World Bank, have yet to take the necessary measures to ensure that their development aid does not contribute to or exacerbate human rights problems in Ethiopia.

Ethiopia rejected recommendations to amend the CSO law and the Anti-Terrorism Proclamation that several countries made during the examination of its rights record under the Universal Periodic Review in May.

European Union

The success in May of populist and Eurosceptic parties in European Parliament elections amid continued economic and political fragility underscored the need for a stronger European Union commitment to human rights protection inside its own borders. In March, the European Commission agreed a rule of law mechanism for crisis situations, and in June, the Council of the European Union endorsed the idea of an EU internal human rights strategy. But the EU, particularly the council, remained reluctant to press member states on abusive practices.

EU Migration and Asylum Policy

Strategic guidelines that the European Council adopted in June on migration and asylum, while affirming respect for human rights and the need for a comprehensive EU migration policy, largely emphasized enhanced border control without envisioning new measures to facilitate legal migration or safe access to asylum in the EU.

By mid-November, over 155,000 people had reached EU shores—primarily those of Italy, but also Malta, Greece, Spain, and Cyprus. Italy's Mare Nostrum operation rescued tens of thousands of people from boats in distress, but over 3,000 died at sea since January according to a September International Organization for Migration estimate, including in some cases as a result of deliberate actions by smugglers. In November, the EU border agency Frontex launched a more limited operation in the Mediterranean as Italy wound down Mare Nostrum.

New Frontex regulations clarifying search and rescue obligations, as well as procedures to ensure speedy disembarkation, entered into force in July.

There were reports throughout the year of summary returns, including of Syrians, by Bulgaria, Greece, and Spain, and of excessive use of force by border guards of those three countries. There were almost 122,030 asylum applicants in EU member states in the first half of 2014, according to Eurostat, up 22 percent from the same period in 2013.

People fleeing Syria enjoyed high protection rates, but also faced returns to the first EU country of entry under the EU's Dublin regulation and under bilateral readmission agreements, without due regard to individual circumstances, in-

HUMAN
RIGHTS
WATCH

CONTAINMENT PLAN
Bulgaria's Pushbacks and Detention of Syrian and Other
Asylum Seekers and Migrants

cluding family reunification. Fourteen EU countries offered to resettle 31,817 vulnerable Syrian refugees, with Germany's quota of 25,500 far outstripping all others, although the numbers actually resettled at time of writing was far smaller.

Asylum seekers were held in substandard reception conditions in several countries, including Italy, Bulgaria, Greece, and Cyprus. Abysmal conditions in Bulgaria improved significantly early in the year as the number of asylum seekers, primarily from Syria, fell, although numbers were again rising at time of writing.

In June, the Court of Justice of the European Union (CJEU) said lack of identity papers cannot justify extending immigration detention.

The UN Human Rights Committee expressed concern in October over automatic, lengthy detention of migrants in Malta. Malta continued to detain migrant children whose age is disputed, despite a pledge in March to end immigration detention of children.

In January, the European Committee of Social Rights expressed concern about access to health care for undocumented migrants in several EU countries, including Spain, Belgium, Bulgaria, and France. In March, the EU Fundamental Rights Agency (FRA) expressed concern about criminalization of irregular immigration, and recommended improving access to justice for undocumented migrants.

A June European Commission proposal to clarify responsibility for processing asylum claims from unaccompanied children was pending examination by the European Parliament and Council at time of writing.

Discrimination and Intolerance

Roma continue to experience discrimination, social exclusion, and deprivation across the EU, with an October EU FRA survey finding that Roma women are disproportionately affected. In December 2013, the Council of the EU made recommendations to guide implementation of national Roma integration strategies. In September, the European Commission announced enforcement action against the Czech Republic over the long-standing failure to desegregate Roma children in school.

In January, Council of Europe (CoE) Human Rights Commissioner Nils Muižnieks warned of growing anti-Semitism in Europe. There was repeated evidence to justify his warning during the year, including a gun attack at a Jewish museum in Brussels that left four dead, and rising reports of anti-Semitic violence and incidents including in France, Germany, and the United Kingdom. Authorities generally responded strongly. The alleged museum attacker was on trial at time of writing.

The Council of the EU adopted conclusions in December 2013 calling for adequate recording, investigation, and prosecution of hate crimes, as well as assistance, support, and protection for victims.

The CoE Convention on preventing and combating violence against women and domestic violence (known as the Istanbul Convention) came into force in August. At time of writing, eight EU countries had ratified. In March, the FRA published results of the first ever EU-wide survey on violence against women, with one in three women reporting they had experienced physical and/or sexual violence since the age of 15.

A FRA report in March noted that fear of deportation deters irregular migrants from reporting crimes to the police, either as a victim or as a witness.

The European Court of Human Rights (ECtHR) in July approved France's 2010 law banning the full face-veil, despite its negative impact on women's right to personal autonomy and religious freedom. Similar laws exist in Belgium and several towns in Spain.

The Parliamentary Assembly of the Council of Europe (PACE) called on European governments in June to tackle racism in the police, including by prohibiting racial profiling, and providing training on identity checks. A December report by FRA made similar recommendations.

In October, the results of a FRA survey of lesbian, gay, bisexual, and transgender (LGBT) people across the EU found high rates of bullying in schools and harassment and discrimination against transgender people and lesbian women. Respondents said they rarely report such incidents to the authorities.

A May survey by the FRA concluded that persons with disabilities face considerable obstacles to political participation, while in 15 EU countries, people with intellectual or psychosocial disabilities under legal guardianship are stripped of their voting rights.

Counterterrorism

In a March resolution on communications surveillance, the EP called on EU member states, particularly the UK, France, Germany, Sweden, the Netherlands, and Poland, to review laws governing their intelligence agencies to ensure they are in line with the ECHR and subject to effective oversight.

In a report on the right to privacy in the digital age published in July, the UN high commissioner for human rights urged states to conduct surveillance only if necessary and proportionate.

The CJEU struck down the EU Data Retention Directive in April, finding that requiring telecom providers to engage in blanket data retention violated privacy rights.

The ECtHR ruled in July that Poland was complicit in the rendition, secret detention, and torture of two terrorism suspects by the CIA in 2002 and 2003 and had made no real progress in investigating the abuses. Despite credible evidence that many other EU countries—including Denmark, Germany, Lithuania, Macedonia, Romania, Spain, Sweden, and the UK—were involved in the CIA renditions program, only Italy has prosecuted anyone.

Croatia

Despite limited reforms in June, the guardianship system continues to deny roughly 18,000 persons with disabilities the right to make decisions about their lives. Implementation of a 2011 deinstitutionalization plan progressed slowly, with 554 people transitioned to community living, while more than 8,200 remained institutionalized as of September.

Croatia's constitution was amended in December 2013 to ban same-sex marriage following a referendum. In July, Croatia's parliament passed a law allowing civil partnership for same-sex couples.

In June, the ECtHR ruled that Croatia failed to investigate adequately the death of a Serb civilian killed by the Croatian police during the 1991-1995 war. National courts have yet to address more than 200 war crimes cases.

Serbs continued to face discrimination, with those stripped of tenancy rights during the war facing ongoing difficulties benefitting from the 2010 government program that permits the purchase of property at below market rates.

Harassment and discrimination against Roma continue, with stateless Roma facing particular difficulties accessing basic state services such as health care, social assistance, or education.

The asylum and migration system remains inadequate. In the first half of 2014, there were 271 new applications, and 19 people granted protection. Asylum seekers continue to be detained. Unaccompanied children are placed in a residential home for children with behavior problems in Zagreb without adequate guardianship.

France

The government failed to enact in-depth reforms to address abusive police identity checks, including ethnic profiling. A new code of police ethics entered into force in January requiring the use of the polite form of address but with minimal guidance on the use of pat-downs.

Evictions of Roma living in informal settlements continued, with rights groups reporting that 10,355 people had been evicted between January and September 2014, most of whom did not have adequate alternative housing. In September, the CoE human rights commissioner called on France to end such forced evictions. An internal police instruction to police to systematically evict Roma living in the streets of Paris' 6th arrondissement was leaked to the press in April. The government subsequently announced that it had been rectified.

In June, a 16-year-old Roma boy was badly beaten and left unconscious in a shopping cart in a Paris suburb. A criminal investigation into attempted homicide, abduction, and detention by an organized group was ongoing at time of writing, but no arrests had been made.

Hundreds of migrants and asylum seekers were evicted from makeshift camps around Calais area in May and July. In most cases, authorities did not provide adequate alternative accommodation.

Parliament passed a new gender equality law in July with measures to encourage paternity leave, protect victims of domestic violence, and ensure equal pay between men and women. The new law also removes a requirement that women who seek an abortion are "in distress."

In July, the government banned several pro-Palestinian demonstrations and a pro-Israeli demonstration on public order grounds, in breach of the rights to freedom of expression and assembly. In July, a kosher restaurant in Paris was attacked. In nearby Sarcelles, a kosher store and a Jewish-owned chemist were burned, amid riots that erupted after a pro-Palestinian demonstration was banned. A dozen people had been convicted or were under investigation for the violence in Sarcelles at time of writing, including a man sentenced to four years' imprisonment in October for burning the kosher store, looting, and attacking police officers. Also in July, police arrested a man for an attempted arson attack against a Jewish cultural center in Toulouse.

In July, the government proposed a new asylum bill to increase accommodation for asylum-seekers, give suspensive effect to all appeals against negative asylum decisions, and speed-up the asylum process. It also proposed a new immigration bill allowing French authorities to ban citizens from other EU countries from traveling inside France for up to three years if they are deemed a threat to a "fundamental interest of society" or "abuse the law"—a move that appears to target Roma. Both bills were before parliament at time of writing.

In November, parliament approved a counterterrorism law prohibiting people from going abroad if it is suspected they would participate in terrorist activities, or would pose a threat to public safety on return; creates a criminal offense of "individual terrorist enterprise;" and allows the authorities to require Internet service providers to block websites that incite or promote terrorism.

In October, a man died during a demonstration against the construction of a dam in the Tarn area. His death appeared to have been caused by a stun grenade fired by gendarmes. An investigation was underway at time of writing.

In its annual report published in April, the National Consultative Human Rights Commission found widespread and increasing prejudice against Roma, and, for the third year in a row, an increase in attacks and threats against Muslims.

A December 2013 law allowing for far-reaching government surveillance of communications in breach of the right to privacy prompted little public debate.

HUMAN RIGHTS WATCH

THE LONG ARM OF JUSTICE
Lessons from Specialized War Crimes Units in France, Germany, and the Netherlands

Germany

In February, the European Commission against Racism and Intolerance (ECRI) highlighted the practice of ethnic profiling by police in Germany, inadequate state response to crimes with a racist motivation, and discrimination against LGBT people.

Demonstrations against the conflict in Gaza in July were overshadowed by anti-Semitic assaults in several German cities. In August, the federal government tabled a new hate crimes law to include racist motivation as an aggravating circumstance in criminal prosecution, pending in parliament at time of writing.

Asylum seekers and refugees protested conditions in reception centres and restrictions of freedom of movement throughout 2014, including with hunger strikes. Police launched an investigation in September into allegations that private security guards repeatedly abused asylum seekers at a reception center in North Rhine-Westphalia state. At time if writing, there were 34 open criminal investigations involving similar allegations against security guards in 7 out of 20 facilities in the state since January 2013.

The German Institute for Human Rights raised concerns about a draft law on asylum policy adopted in September that designates Bosnia and Herzegovina, Serbia, and Macedonia as safe countries of origin subject to accelerated asylum procedures. At least three federal states continued to return Roma, Ashkali, and Egyptians to Kosovo despite concerns about discrimination and inadequate integration measures on return.

The trial continued of an alleged member of a neo-Nazi cell and four alleged accomplices accused of murdering nine immigrants and a policewoman between 2000 and 2007.

Media reports indicated that there was cooperation between German and US agencies in mass surveillance activities. A commission of inquiry formed in March is investigating mass surveillance in Germany.

Greece

In a report released in March, the UN independent expert on foreign debt and human rights warned that the impact of the austerity measures in Greece had been particularly severe on the most vulnerable. Golden Dawn established itself as the third most popular party in the country with 9.4 percent of the vote in May's European Parliament elections.

Attacks on migrants and asylum seekers, and LGBT people continued, with a network of nongovernmental organizations (NGOs) recording more than 400 incidents over the last three years.

A ministerial decree adopted in June introduced residence permits on humanitarian grounds for undocumented victims and witnesses of hate crimes. In September, an Egyptian migrant seriously injured in an attack in 2012 became the first person to receive such a permit.

In September, an anti-racism law improving state response to hate crimes and lifting barriers to justice for victims of racist attacks entered into force, but measures criminalizing speech falling short of incitement raised free expression concerns.

In April, two men were sentenced to life imprisonment for the January 2013 murder in Athens of a Pakistani worker. The court failed to classify the act as racially motivated.

The trial over the September 2013 murder of anti-fascist rapper Pavlos Fyssas by an alleged member of Golden Dawn was expected to start before the end of the year.

At time of writing, criminal charges had been brought against 70 suspects, including all Golden Dawn members of parliament and several high-ranking party officials, for creation and participation in a criminal organization.

In July, two of the four men charged for the 2013 shooting of 28 migrant strawberry pickers were acquitted, including the farm's owner. In October, the Supreme Court decided that the case should not be retried. The victims' lawyers said they would appeal to the ECtHR.

Increased security along the land border with Turkey coincided with increasing numbers of migrants and asylum seekers, including Syrians, seeking access through Aegean Sea islands. In October, the United Nations High Commissioner for Refugees (UNHCR) warned that the situation on the islands was becoming a crisis. Sea crossings were marked by at least 40 deaths. There were continuing allegations that Greek border guards engaged in collective expulsions and push-backs of migrants and asylum seekers at the borders with Turkey.

The CoE human rights commissioner raised concerns in August over the shelving of an incident in January 2013 in which 12 women and children died off the Greek island of Farmakonisi, in what survivors allege was a pushback operation in poor weather.

The UN Working Group on Arbitrary Detention in June and FRA in December 2013 criticized abusive stops during police operation Xenios Zeus against irregular migrants. In July, the government launched police operation Theseus against drug users, sex workers, and irregular migrants in the center of Athens.

The ECtHR held Greece responsible for inhuman and degrading treatment in immigration detention in eight separate cases since December 2013. In May, an Athens court ruled that the government's February decision to permit detention of migrants beyond the 18 months permitted by EU law violated national and international law.

In an October report, the European Committee for the Prevention of Torture (CPT) described as "totally unacceptable" the conditions in which irregular migrants are held in police stations for prolonged periods.

Despite improvements in the asylum system and significant increase in Greece's protection rates, asylum seekers under the old system still face a backlog of an estimated 45,000 cases. Access to asylum outside Athens and in detention remained difficult.

In January, a man was sentenced to 10 months in jail, suspended for three years, for running a satirical Facebook profile making fun of a deceased Greek Orthodox monk.

Hungary

Rule of law and human rights further deteriorated in 2014. The ruling party won another term in April with a two-thirds majority in Hungary's single chamber parliament. In a speech to ethnic Hungarians in Romania in late July, Prime Minister Viktor Orban declared his desire to end liberal democracy in Hungary. There was fresh pressure on media and civil society.

The Constitutional Court ruled in May that website operators are responsible for any comments to blog posts or news commentary that violate the media law, hamper free speech, public debate, or Internet freedom.

In a June judgment, the Supreme Court held that ATV, a TV station critical of the government, had violated the media law's restrictions on commentary by describing the Jobbik party as "far-right" in a newscast. The same month, the editor-in-chief of Origo, an independent news website, was dismissed after publishing a story on alleged misuse of public funds by the prime minister's cabinet chief.

Neelie Kroes, then-European Commission vice president, stated in July that an advertising tax adopted in June shows that free and plural media remains under threat in Hungary. The tax primarily affects RTL Klub, one of few remaining independent TV channels.

Civil society came under pressure in June when the state audit office conducted surprise inspections of three NGOs that administer foreign donor money, and the government published a list smearing 13 other recipient NGOs, including leading rights groups, as "left-leaning" and "problematic."

In September, police raided two NGOs that disburse grants, seizing laptops, documents, and servers. In October, the state audit office published a report of its audit of the four grant administering NGOs and 55 others that receive grants, alleging fraud, misappropriation of assets, and other financial irregularities. At time of writing, there were at least two criminal investigations into the alleged financial irregularities.

US President Barack Obama identified Hungary in a September speech about pressure on civil society. In contrast, EU institutions were reluctant to speak out on the issue.

By November 2014, 234 homeless people were charged with misdemeanors under a local decree banning homeless people from residing habitually in public spaces. At time of writing, there were no reports of homeless people being jailed.

Roma continue to face discrimination and harassment. In May, a Roma house in northeast Hungary was attacked with two petrol bombs. No one was hurt, and police were investigating at time of writing. Two Roma families were evicted in a larger eviction campaign by local government in the city of Miskolc that targeted some 923 Roma.

Hungary signed the Istanbul Convention in May but had yet to ratify it at time of writing. In September, the ECtHR upheld its April ruling finding Hungary in violation of freedom of religion and association for stripping religious groups of their status as churches in 2010.

Italy

Between January and November, over 155,000 people reached Italy by sea, many of them rescued in the Mediterranean by the Italian navy. While many traveled onward to other EU countries, over 44,000 people applied for asylum in Italy by October, amid concerns about substandard reception conditions, including in roughly 200 emergency shelters.

The government increased to 13,000 spaces in specialized reception centers. Tensions flared in some communities hosting reception centers, including in Rome in November when authorities removed 45 migrant children from a center after neighborhood residents protested violently. The ECtHR ruled in November that Switzerland could not return an Afghan asylum-seeking family to Italy due to the risk of inadequate reception arrangements, particularly for children.

In October, parliament reduced maximum immigration detention from 18 to 3 months. Throughout the year, detainees in such centers had protested conditions and length of stay.

Undocumented entry and stay was decriminalized in April, though it remains an administrative offense.

In October, the ECtHR ruled against Italy over its practice of summarily returning migrants to Greece without individual screening for protection needs and despite risk of inhuman and degrading treatment upon return.

Episodes of xenophobic violence occurred throughout the year. In March, police intervened but made no arrests during attacks over two days on an informal Roma settlement in Naples, leading to its evacuation. Eight men went on trial in September for the racially motivated firebomb attack on a Roma camp in Turin in December 2011. A 17 year old who beat a homeless Pakistani man to death in

Rome in September was charged with the killing but police discounted racist motivation.

The European Commission initiated enforcement action against Italy during 2014 over its discriminatory segregation of Roma in substandard, official camps. Roma living in informal settlements were subject to serial evictions.

In July, the UN Working Group on Arbitrary Detention urged measures to end over-incarceration and disproportionate use of pretrial detention against foreigners and Roma. Prison overcrowding remained a problem despite measures, including reforms adopted in June, to reduce sentences and increase recourse to alternatives to detention.

The fatal shooting by a Carabiniere of 17-year-old Davide Bifolco in Naples in September reignited concerns about excessive use of force. In October, an appeals court acquitted six doctors, three nurses, and three prison officers over the 2009 death of Stefano Cucchi. Prosecutors alleged medical staff failed to treat injuries he suffered while beaten in custody. A lower court had convicted five of the doctors of manslaughter in 2013 and acquitted the others.

The Netherlands

Following criticism from political parties and rights groups, the Dutch government in April abandoned plans to criminalize irregular stay.

Dozens of rejected asylum-seekers continued to live in degrading conditions in squats in Amsterdam. Many were from countries to which they could not be safely returned, such as Somalia and Eritrea. The government did not provide them with any support.

In July, the European Committee of Social Rights found that the European Social Charter required the Dutch government to provide shelter, clothes, and food to irregular migrants at risk of destitution. At time of writing, the government had yet to implement the decision.

In April, the UN Committee against Enforced Disappearances urged the Dutch government to ensure that the appeals procedure for rejected asylum applications include substantive review, including of any risk of enforced disappearance upon return.

A law allowing transgender people from the age of 16 to change their gender on their identity papers without having to undergo sex reassignment surgery entered into force in July. Applicants must provide a statement from a medical expert affirming their permanent conviction to belong to another gender.

In a report published in October, the CoE human rights commissioner criticized the extensive use of detention for migrants and asylum seekers.

In November, the Council of State, the highest administrative court, ruled that Somalis cannot be deported to Somalia on the ground that such removals could not be carried out within a reasonable amount of time.

In July, the UN Working Group of Experts on People of African Descent expressed concerns about racial profiling by Dutch police. The experts welcomed the debate on the traditional "Black Piet" (Zwarte Piet) figure of the Sinterklaas festival and called for a respectful tone by media during the discussions.

In August and September, the government proposed revoking the Dutch citizenship of dual nationals enlisted in a terrorist group but not convicted of a criminal offense and of those convicted of various terrorism-related offences. Neither proposal had been adopted at time of writing.

Poland

The six-year investigation into secret CIA detention in Poland continued amid criticism and lack of transparency. In September, the Krakow Prosecutor's Office requested a four-month extension. In October, the government lodged an appeal against the ECtHR ruling on the issue. In March, Polish prosecutors refused to recognize a Saudi national detained at Guantanamo Bay as a victim in the pending investigation.

In a June report, the CPT warned about a significant number of allegations of ill-treatment in police custody, and called upon the government to strengthen safeguards against such abuse.

In March, the UN Committee on the Elimination of Racial Discrimination expressed concern over the small number of hate crime cases referred to the courts, despite rising incidents.

HUMAN
RIGHTS
WATCH

SHATTERED DREAMS
Impact of Spain's Housing Crisis on Vulnerable Groups

A January change to the criminal code permitted prison governors to apply for detention orders for long-term prisoners deemed to pose a threat to the life, health, or sexual freedom of others. There are concerns among civil society that the law creates a form of preventive detention and will allow for the long-term detention of people after they complete their sentences.

There was pressure in May to narrow Poland's already restrictive abortion law when over 3,000 people, mostly medical professionals, signed a "declaration of faith" against abortion and other reproductive services.

A so-called conscience clause in Poland permits medical professionals to refuse to carry out an abortion if it conflicts with their faith. In June, then-Prime Minister Donald Tusk stated that medical personnel must put legal obligations to the patient above personal beliefs.

Following its October review of Poland, the UN Committee on the Elimination of Discrimination against Women recommended the establishment of less restrictive conditions and clear standards for legal abortion and effective remedies to contest refusals of abortion.

Spain

The government responded to increased attempts by migrants and asylum seekers to enter Spanish enclaves in Morocco, Ceuta, and Melilla (in the latter, up 234 percent compared to 2013), with enhanced border control. Fifteen people died in February as they attempted to reach Ceuta by sea; the Spanish Guardia Civil fired rubber bullets and tear gas in their direction. The judicial investigation into the deaths was ongoing.

In September, a judge in Melilla charged the head of the local Guardia Civil over summary returns to Morocco. NGOs documented pushbacks and excessive use of force. Several investigations and trials were ongoing in Spain against a handful of officials for violence against detainees in immigration detention facilities.

The European Commission, the Council of Europe, and the UN expressed concern about proposed legal changes to formalize summary returns from the enclaves to Morocco. The government announced in November it would create border posts where asylum seekers could register.

Widespread opposition forced the government to abandon, in September, a bill that would have restricted access to safe and legal abortion. The government indicated it would pursue changes to require parental consent for 16 and 17 year olds.

Government bills to modify the criminal code and create a new public security law, under examination in parliament at time of writing, raised concerns about interference with fair trial rights and the rights to peaceful assembly and freedom of expression. In October, the ECtHR ruled twice against Spain for failing to investigate effectively allegations of ill-treatment during incommunicado detention and endorsed the CPT's recommendations to Spain to allow access to a lawyer from the outset of detention and medical examination by a doctor of choice.

In September, data showed mortgage evictions remain a serious problem, exposing vulnerable persons to insecure housing and significant debt, and the government announced an extension of the moratorium on evictions without broadening narrow criteria. The CJEU ruled in July, for the second time in two years, that Spain's inadequate safeguards against unfair mortgage terms violate EU law.

In separate July reports, the UN Working Group on Enforced Disappearances and UN special rapporteur on truth and justice criticized March reforms limiting the ability of courts to prosecute suspects of grave international crimes committed outside Spain. Both made recommendations to ensure accountability for Franco era crimes, including by making enforced disappearance a domestic crime. In October, a military court indicted five servicemen for the 2004 torture of two Iraqi prisoners in Iraq.

Spain ratified the Istanbul Convention in April, and at time of writing continued a review of existing national law on domestic violence. By the end of August, 28 women had been killed by their intimate partner since the start of the year.

According to the Spanish General Council of the Judiciary, the number of people with disabilities stripped of their legal capacity increased 172 percent between 2005 and 2013.

United Kingdom

The government failed to honor its promise of a new independent judge-led inquiry into the UK's involvement in renditions and complicity in overseas torture. In December 2013, the government announced the inquiry would be conducted by the Intelligence and Security Committee (ISC), a parliamentary body that lacks full independence from government and has repeatedly failed to exercise effective oversight of the security services.

The law enabling same sex marriage in England and Wales came into effect in March. In Scotland, the law was passed in March and is expected to go into force in December.

A government-sponsored bill to combat modern slavery, before parliament at time of writing, included inadequate safeguards against employer abuse of migrant domestic workers. In April, a parliamentary committee urged the government to restore the ability of migrant domestic workers in the UK to change employer, having found that a visa tying them to one employer "institutionalizes their abuse."

During a visit in April, the UN Special Rapporteur on Violence against Women Rashida Manjoo was barred from entering Yarl's Wood immigration removal center, where migrant and asylum-seekers, most of them women, are detained. In her initial report, Manjoo noted the impact of legal aid cuts on access to justice for women victims of violence.

The International Criminal Court (ICC) prosecutor announced in May a preliminary examination into allegations of systematic abuse of detainees by UK armed forces in Iraq between 2003 and 2008.

In July, the High Court ruled that the accelerated "detained fast track" procedure denies asylum applicants the legal representation needed to prepare their case effectively. Rights group charge the system puts people at risk of being removed to countries where they risk persecution, torture, or other ill-treatment.

In July, parliament passed emergency legislation renewing the government's powers to collect data on the communications of millions of people, contradicting the April ruling by the CJEU on blanket data retention. The law also extended UK surveillance powers extraterritorially. In November, the government disclosed

the existence of policies allowing UK intelligence agencies to intercept confidential lawyer-client communications on national security grounds.

A law passed in July allows the government to revoke the citizenship of naturalized UK citizens if they engage in terrorism or other actions "seriously prejudicial to the vital interests" of the UK, even if it renders them stateless. In November, the government published draft legislation to ban people suspected of involvement in terrorism abroad from returning to the UK for two years and allow police to confiscate the passports of those suspected of travelling overseas to join armed groups.

An NGO,recorded an increase in anti-Semitic incidents from January to June compared to the same period in 2013, including violent assaults, damage, and desecration of property and threats. In London, the Metropolitan police recorded a 92.8 percent increase in anti-Semitic crime in the 12 months leading to October 2014.

According to official statistics, there were 88 suicides in prison between April 2013 and March 2014, a 69 percent rise compared to the previous 12 month period and the highest figure in a decade.

Foreign Policy

The EU remained among the largest humanitarian donors to the Syrian crisis. In March, EU foreign ministers finally expressed clear EU support for referring the situation in Syria to the ICC. However, the EU high representative missed the opportunity to engage the entire EU framework with a strategy on how best to advance strong global support for a UN Security Council referral.

In March, Xi Jinping paid his first visit to Brussels as China's president. During this visit, EU leaders, including European Parliament President Martin Schulz, ducked their obligation to publicly raise concerns about the shrinking space for rights advocates in China.

In May, EU foreign ministers adopted EU Guidelines on Freedom of Expression online and offline, adding to the EU's Human Rights Guidelines. The guidelines, which include specific commitments and objectives, were designed to enable the EU to better promote and protect freedom of expression worldwide.

The EU's 28 member states rallied behind a Swiss-led joint statement on the human rights situation in Bahrain delivered at the UN Human Rights Council in June. The statement called on Bahraini authorities *to release all individuals "imprisoned solely for exercising human rights" in the country*. In response to EU support for the statement, the Gulf Cooperation Council (GCC) cancelled the EU-GCC Ministerial meeting that had been scheduled to take place in late June.

Marking the 10th anniversary of the adoption of the EU Guidelines on Human Rights Defenders, EU foreign ministers adopted conclusions reiterating their strong support to human rights defenders. However, throughout 2014, the EU's response to the crackdown on human rights defenders and activists worldwide was inconsistent. Strong responses, such as EU condemnation of the life sentence handed to Uighur scholar Ilham Tohti in China, tended to be the exception rather than the norm.

Numerous weak statements were issued in response to the arrest of leading rights defenders in countries such as Azerbaijan and Burundi. While the EU supported the above-mentioned Joint Statement on Bahrain, the EU high representative and EU member states failed to pursue any meaningful strategy, as called for by the European Parliament, to secure the release of imprisoned Bahraini activists, two of whom hold EU citizenship.

The EU continued to be one of the most outspoken international actors criticizing Israel for its illegal settlement activities. The EU's guidelines excluding West Bank Jewish settlements from EU-funded projects came into effect on January 1. Under the guidelines, the EU will only give "grants, prizes and other financial instruments [loans]" to Israeli entities that do not operate in the occupied Palestinian territories and promise not to spend the money there.

Despite the EU being a staunch supporter of the ICC and of accountability for war crimes and crimes against humanity, some EU member states continued to press Palestine not to seek access to the ICC. On July 22, EU foreign ministers seemingly warned Palestinians against the ICC, asking the Palestinian leadership "to use constructively its UN status and not to undertake steps which would lead further away from a negotiated solution." The same statement recognized that Israel's continued settlement expansion, settler violence, evictions, forced transfer of Palestinians, and demolitions (including of EU-funded projects) risked the irreversible "loss of the two state solution." Near total impunity for serious international crimes in the Palestine-Israel conflict continued to fuel abuses by all sides.

The EU imposed restrictive measures against Russia in response to its occupation of Crimea in March, support for abusive separatists and interference in Eastern Ukraine. The sanctions target individuals and Russia's state finances, energy, and arms sectors. In September, the European Parliament gave its consent to an EU-Ukraine Association agreement.

The EU continued to play a leadership role on certain country resolutions at the UN Human Rights Council and UN General Assembly, including on Belarus, North Korea, and Burma, securing continuation of important UN reporting mechanisms for all three countries. But the EU failed to play a leading role in bringing new human rights crisis, such as the recent crackdown in Egypt or the situation in Uzbekistan, to the agenda of multilateral forums.

The European Parliament awarded the 2014 Sakharov Prize for Freedom of Thought to Dr. Denis Mukwege from the Democratic Republic of Congo for his fight for survivors of sexual violence.

In August, Italy's Foreign Minister Federica Mogherini was appointed as the next EU high representative for security and foreign policy at an EU leaders meeting in Brussels. Mogherini, who is also vice president of the European Commission, took up office in November.

Georgia

Georgia's ruling coalition swept to an overwhelming victory in municipal elections in 2014 amid some concerns of pre-election pressure on opposition candidates and violence. Investigations into past abuses continued to raise some questions regarding selective justice and politically motivated prosecutions. Lack of accountability for abuses committed by law enforcement remained a problem. Other areas of concern include minority and women rights.

Georgia deepened its ties with the European Union by signing and ratifying the Association Agreement that is closely tied to progress in governance and human rights.

Municipal Elections

The ruling Georgian Dream party won an overwhelming victory in local municipal elections in June and July, giving it full control of all the executive branches of local self-governing bodies across the country, as well as a majority of seats in local councils. Domestic election observers noted some technical flaws and procedural irregularities during the vote, but claimed these had no effect on the overall outcome.

During the pre-election period, however, media and nongovernmental groups (NGOs) reported multiple allegations of pressure on opposition candidates to withdraw their candidacies, including actual withdrawals in more than a dozen municipalities, disruption of opposition gatherings, and several episodes of violence against candidates' campaigners. In June, the Chief Prosecutor's Office said that it had launched criminal investigations into four cases out of 80 complaints they received related to alleged pressure on opposition candidates.

Violent incidents included mobs disrupting the opposition United National Movement's (UNM) campaign events in four cities and towns in April, and an attack by unidentified assailants in March on Nugzar Tsiklauri, an outspoken UNM MP who was briefly hospitalized for minor injuries. In May, several men attacked Zurab Chiaberashvili, a former health minister and leading UNM member; Chiaberashvili was briefly hospitalized for head injuries. The authorities failed to prosecute his assailants despite the fact that they were publicly identified.

Shortly after the elections, a number of employees of Tbilisi municipality reported pressure on them to "voluntarily" resign from their jobs or face criminal prosecutions. According to ISFED, a local election monitoring group, between August 1 and September 7, Tbilisi City Hall dismissed 155 employees including 115 based on "voluntary" resignation letters, allegedly written under pressure, raising concerns that they had been targeted for their political affiliations.

Investigations into Past Abuses

The Prosecutor's Office studied thousands of complaints received after the government change in 2012, categorizing them into property rights violations, torture and ill-treatment, and misuse of the plea bargaining system. In response to those complaints, it initiated dozens of criminal cases, mostly against former officials. The absence of clear criteria to determine which cases to prosecute, as well as the impression that such investigations were overwhelmingly targeting UNM officials, led the opposition to allege that its activists were targeted for political reasons. Transparency International's trial monitoring report of high-profile criminal cases, published in July, did not reveal any significant violations of due process and fair trial norms.

In July, authorities charged ex-President Mikheil Saakashvili with a number of offenses, including embezzlement and exceeding his authority in several separate cases. In August, a court impounded Saakashvili's property, along with that of his spouse, sons, parents, and grandmother. Charges against Saakashvil, who left the country soon after leaving office in November 2013, include an episode related to the November 7, 2007 crackdown on opposition protests and ordering a police raid and seizure of a private TV channel. The court ordered Saakashvili be subject to pretrial detention in absentia.

In July, authorities detained Gigi Ugulava, UNM campaign head and a former mayor of Tbilisi, and a court sent him to pretrial detention on alleged embezzlement of GEL 48.2 million (US$30 million) prior to the 2012 parliamentary election. The opposition claimed that Ugulava's arrest violated a moratorium on criminal prosecutions of people involved in the municipal election campaign announced by Prime Minister Garibashvili in April.

In February and August, courts convicted Vano Merabishvili, the UNM's secretary general and former interior minister, on three separate sets of criminal charges of misspending and bribery, infringement on property rights, and exceeding his authority, sentencing him to various prison terms.

In August, the authorities questioned Davit Bakradze, UNM's parliamentary minority leader, and his wife, over undeclared bank accounts.

Concerns about politicized justice intensified in October, when one former and four serving Ministry of Defense officials were arrested on charges of misspending GEL 4.1 million (roughly US$2.31 million) arising from an allegedely sham tender. The authorities denied defense lawyers full access to evidence, claiming it consisted of classified documents. This undermined the right to an effective defense. The Tbilisi City Court sent the detainees to pretrial custody. At time of writing the lawyers were still unable to study the evidence. Garibashvili sacked Defense Minister Irakli Alasania shortly after the latter stated that the charges were politically motivated.

Torture, Ill-Treatment, and Prison Conditions

Lack of accountability for law enforcement officials remained a problem, as Georgia does not have an independent effective mechanism for investigating crimes committed by law enforcements officials.

In August, the Human Rights Center, a local NGO, reported that police in a Tbilisi district physically assaulted Giorgi Tsomaia, a man who had entered a police station at night inebriated and demanded that police return a cellphone they had confiscated in 2013 as evidence in a criminal investigation. Tsomaia claimed that about 11 officers physically assaulted him, and he sustained injuries to his face and head. He was then detained for violence against police and a court sent him to pretrial custody. An investigation into his claims was pending at time of writing.

Georgian Young Lawyers' Association (GYLA), a leading domestic human rights group, received at least 50 complaints in 10 months in 2014; 31 of them about physical and verbal abuse by police, and 19 by penitentiary staff. According to GYLA, the authorities failed to effectively investigate those allegations.

In his annual report released in May, the public defender noted positive changes in the penitentiary system, particularly in healthcare, but also highlighted several cases of alleged ill-treatment of inmates which had not been effectively investigated, and "alarming circumstances surrounding death of several inmates in prisons."

Georgia overhauled its flawed system of administrative detention, reducing the maximum custodial sentence possible for misdeamanor offences from 90 to 15 days ,and introducing due process rights.

Anti-Discrimination and Minority Rights

In May, parliament adopted an anti-discrimination bill that provides for protection against discrimination on the grounds of race, gender, age, sexual orientation, and gender identity. Some criticized the bill for lacking efficient implementation mechanisms, including means for imposing financial penalties for perpetrators. The bill put the Ombudsman's Office in charge of overseeing anti-discrimination measures.

In February, the constitutional court in Georgia struck down a 13-year-old ban on homosexual men being blood donors.

In October, police used disproportionate force to break up a protest in a small village and detain 14 participants demonstrating against the government's plans to rebuild a former mosque as a library. Courts fined 11 of them GEL 250 (roughly $140) each for petty hoolganism and disobeying police orders. Authorities did not effectively investigate police conduct.

Women's Rights

According to media reports, at least 23 women died in the first 10 months of 2014 due to domestic violence.

The ombudsman reported that early marriage of girls was a persistent problem, which took place either with an agreement between parents or through kidnapping. The public defender highlighted a case in eastern Georgia where a father sold his minor daughter for 10 cows to a 45-year-old man. The ombudsman documented three cases of kidnapping girls for marriage in January-February 2014, and more than 20 cases of early marriage.

According to data from the Education Ministry, 7,367 girls stopped going to school from 2011 to 2013 because of early marriage.

Key International Actors

Georgia deepened its political and economic ties with the European Union by signing and ratifying the Association Agreement with the EU, which requires Georgia to fulfill strong human rights commitments as part of the approximation process of aligning national laws and procedures with that of the EU.

Georgia's international partners, including the EU and the United States, expressed concerns about the criminal charges filed against former President Saakashvili, urging authorities to adhere strictly to due process, and ensure that the prosecution is free from political motivations.

In its March European Neighborhood Policy (ENP) progress report, the EU noted that Georgia "continued to deliver on a busy reform and approximation agenda," but also highlighted the need to ensure judicial independence, avoid a perception of selective justice, and increase accountability and democratic oversight of law enforcement agencies.

In an October resolution, the Council of Europe Parliamentary Assembly welcomed Georgia's comprehensive reform plans and called on authorities to ensure that prosecutions of former officials are impartial and fully respect fair trial norms.

Following its July review of Georgia, the United Nations Human Rights Committee welcomed the adoption of the anti-discrimination law, while calling on Georgia to combat existing patriarchal attitudes and stereotypes regarding gender roles in the family and society.

Also in July, the UN Committee on the Elimination of Discrimination against Women (CEDAW) issued an assessment of Georgia, voicing concerns about the continuously decreasing number of women in local legislative bodies, and calling on Georgia to introduce mandatory quotas for political parties to swiftly and significantly increase the number of women in both national and local legislative bodies.

The US-Georgia bilateral working group on democracy and governance under the strategic partnership charter met in April in Tbilisi to discuss Georgia's efforts to strengthen democratic institutions, checks and balances, political pluralism, and electoral processes.

Guatemala

Former Guatemalan leader Efraín Ríos Montt was found guilty in May 2013 of genocide and crimes against humanity, the first time that any head of state has been convicted of genocide in a national court. The ruling was overturned on procedural grounds days later, however, and a new trial is scheduled for early 2015.

The Attorney General's Office has also made progress on other prominent human rights cases, but impunity remains pervasive. In May, then-Attorney General Claudia Paz y Paz, recognized for her advances in reforming the country's prosecutorial system, was removed from office by the Constitutional Court seven months before her term was due to end.

The mandate of the United Nations-backed International Commission Against Impunity in Guatemala (CICIG), which since 2007 has supported efforts to investigate and prosecute organized crime, will end in September 2015. President Otto Pérez Molina has said that this will be the commission's final term.

Accountability for Past Atrocities

In a landmark ruling, former head of state Efraín Ríos Montt was found guilty in May 2013 of genocide and crimes against humanity and sentenced to 80 years in prison. The retired general led a military regime from 1982 to 1983 that carried out hundreds of massacres of unarmed civilians. The ruling was overturned several days later by the Constitutional Court. A retrial is scheduled to commence in early 2015.

In April 2014, the judge who initially convicted Ríos Montt of genocide was suspended and fined by an ethics tribunal for unprofessional conduct, an event described by the Office of the UN High Commissioner for Human Rights in Guatemala as a serious assault on judicial independence. She has since been reinstated.

In May, Guatemala's Congress passed a resolution denying that acts of genocide were committed during the country's civil war, despite findings to the contrary by a UN-sponsored Truth Commission in 1999. President Otto Pérez Molina had previously expressed his support for a public letter signed by a group of politicians calling genocide charges against former military officers a "fabrication."

Ríos Montt has also been charged in a separate case involving the massacre of 300 men, women, and children in the town of Dos Erres in 1982. The trial is stalled pending the resolution of an appeal by defense attorneys who have called into question the independence of the presiding judge.

In July, Felipe Solano Barillas became the first ex-guerrilla to be convicted in connection with atrocities committed during the country's civil war. Found guilty of ordering the massacre of 22 residents of the town of El Aguacate in 1988, he has been ordered to serve 90 years in jail.

In June, Colonel Esteelmer Reyes and Military Commissioner Heriberto Valdez were arrested in connection with sexual violence perpetrated against 15 Q'eqchi' women in the community of Sepur Zarco in 1982.

In June, three former members of the National Police were arrested in connection with the murder of prominent human rights activist Myrna Mack. Mack was killed in 1990 for her role in documenting abuses committed during the country's civil war.

Public Security and the Criminal Justice System

Powerful criminal organizations engage in widespread acts of violence and extortion. Rampant corruption within the justice system, combined with intimidation and inefficient procedures, contribute to high levels of impunity. Frustrated with the lack of criminal enforcement, some communities have resorted to vigilantism. According to the human rights ombudsman, 49 people were killed by lynching in 2013, more than twice the number in 2012.

Despite these problems, prosecutors have made progress in cases of violent crime, as well as torture, extrajudicial killings, and corruption—due in large part to the work of former Attorney General Claudia Paz y Paz, as well as the support of CICIG.

In February, nine members of the Zetas Cartel were convicted for the massacre of 27 farmhands during a dispute over drug trafficking routes in the Petén region. The gang members were sentenced to a total of over 100 years in jail.

In September, former army officer Byron Lima Oliva, imprisoned since 2006 for his role in the 1998 murder of Bishop Juan José Gerardi, was charged with running a criminal network in the prison. At least seven other people were implicated in the case, including the national prison director, Sergio Camargo. The investigation was initiated in 2013 by CICIG, in collaboration with the Attorney General's Office.

Progress in holding perpetrators of serious abuses to account has been undercut by the dilatory strategy of defense lawyers, including the abuse of *amparo* protection appeals, leading to the postponement of trials by months or even years.

Use of Military in Public Security Operations

The government continues to use the military to address public security challenges, despite the latter's long history of human rights abuse. More than 20,000 soldiers are currently deployed throughout the country.

In May, the government announced the creation of a new inter-agency task force to provide security against drug trafficking and related crimes throughout Guatemalan territory. The force is known by the acronym FIAAT, and includes military personnel.

Attacks on Human Rights Defenders, Journalists, and Trade Unionists

Attacks and threats against human rights defenders are common, significantly hampering human rights work in the country. Acts of violence and intimidation against trade unionists endanger freedom of assembly and association and the right to organize and bargain collectively. Fifty-three trade unionists were killed between 2007 and 2013, according to the International Trade Union Conference.

Journalists, especially those covering corruption and drug trafficking, also face threats, attacks, and legal intimidation. In November 2013, President Otto Pérez Molina and Vice President Roxanna Baldetti filed charges against José Rubén Zamora, editor of *El Periodico*, after the newspaper published articles referring to alleged links between the administration and organized crime. In February, a judge barred Zamora from leaving the country pending investigation of the allegations. The president subsequently dropped the charges; the vice president said she would as well, but at time of writing had not done so.

In April, the Guatemalan opposition party LIDER brought charges against the magazine *ContraPoder* after the latter incorrectly claimed that letters of support to the leader of the opposition had been fabricated. Criminal charges have been filed against the organization, despite a public retraction of statements and an apology by the magazine.

Key International Actors

The UN-backed CICIG, established in 2007, plays a key role in assisting Guatemala's justice system in prosecuting violent crime, working with the Attorney General's Office, the police, and other government agencies to investigate, prosecute, and dismantle criminal organizations operating in the country. The CICIG can participate in criminal proceedings as a complementary prosecutor, provide technical assistance, and promote legislative reforms.

Iván Velásquez Gómez, a prominent Colombian jurist, was appointed to lead the CICIG following the resignation of the previous head. Formerly an auxiliary magistrate on Colombia's supreme court, Velásquez played a leading role in investigating ties between politicians and paramilitaries in that country.

The CICIG's mandate will terminate in September 2015, however, and President Pérez Molina has stated that it will not be renewed for an additional term.

The Office of the UN High Commissioner for Human Rights has maintained an office in Guatemala since 2005. The office monitors the human rights situation in the country and provides policy support to the government and civil society.

In June, a Swiss court convicted the former director of the National Police for his role in planning the extrajudicial killings of prisoners in the El Pavón and El Infiernito Prisons in 2005 and 2006. He was sentenced to life in prison.

Despite a recent ban on universal jurisdiction cases in Spanish courts, Judge Santiago Pedraz has stated that he will continue investigations into eight Guatemalan officers implicated in human rights abuses during the country's civil war.

The United States continues to restrict military aid to Guatemala on human rights grounds. The US Consolidated Appropriations Act 2014, requires the Guatemalan government to take "credible steps" to implement the reparations plan for communities affected by construction of the Chixoy Dam, ensure that the army's role is limited to combating external threats, and support the investigation and prosecution of military officers implicated in past atrocities before full aid is restored.

Guinea

The government of President Alpha Condé made progress in addressing the serious governance and human rights problems that characterized Guinea for more than five decades. However, gains in promoting the rule of law and development could be reversed by the 2015 presidential elections, a major trigger for unrest and state-sponsored abuse; lingering ethnic tension; and the Ebola crisis, which appears to have originated in the country's forest region.

The successful completion in 2013 of parliamentary elections advanced Guinea's transition from authoritarian to democratic rule, mitigated the concentration of power in the executive branch, and led to a drastic reduction in violent political unrest and state-sponsored abuses. However, local elections scheduled for 2014 failed to take place, which periodically stoked political tensions. There were also regular protests over electricity cuts, as well as several lethal incidents of communal violence.

Reports of human rights violations by security forces declined significantly. However, security forces were implicated in numerous incidents of excessive use of force and unprofessional conduct as they responded to criminal acts and protests, resulting in several deaths.

Fear of Ebola led to unrest and attacks on health workers and treatment centers in southeastern Guinea, where the outbreak emerged in early 2014: in one such attack, a mob murdered eight health workers and journalists. At years end, the outbreak had killed more than 1,000 Guineans. The Ebola crisis led to deterioration in the right to basic healthcare and a significant economic downturn.

The government made some progress in ensuring accountability for past atrocities, including the 2009 massacre of unarmed demonstrators by security forces. Inadequate progress on strengthening the judiciary and endemic corruption continued to undermine respect for the rule of law and directly led to violations.

There was little progress in establishing a reconciliation commission and independent human rights body. However, the Ministry of Human Rights and Civil Liberties consistently advocated for respect for human rights.

International actors—notably the European Union, United Nations, France, and the United States—rarely spoke out on the need for justice for past and recent crimes by state actors, but worked to strengthen weak rule of law institutions.

Impunity and Accountability for Crimes

Since 2010, the judiciary has opened several investigations into serious violations by the security forces, including the 2007 killing of some 130 unarmed demonstrators, the 2009 massacre and rapes of opposition supporters in a Conakry stadium; the 2010 torture of members of the political opposition; the 2012 killing of six men in the southeastern village of Zoghota; and the 2013 killing of demonstrators protesting the delay in holding parliamentary elections.

In 2014, investigative judges took steps to move most of these investigations forward, but their efforts were severely hampered by the failure of members of the army, gendarmerie, and police to respond to judicial summons.

Justice for the 2009 Stadium Massacre

More than five years on, the domestic investigation continues into the September 2009 massacre of opposition supporters at a rally in Conakry, largely by members of the elite Presidential Guard. Security force members are implicated in the killing of some 150 people and rape of over 100 women during military rule under Moussa Dadis Camara.

Since legal proceedings began in 2010, the panel of judges appointed to investigate the massacre has made important strides, having interviewed more than 400 victims and indicted at least eight suspects, including high-level members of the security forces. Meaningful steps taken in 2014 include the questioning of several key witnesses and accused and of Dadis Camara himself, who has taken refuge in Burkina Faso.

Inconsistent financial and political support from the government, including the failure to suspend high-level suspects from their government posts, undermined the panel's work, as did inadequate security for the judges. Some suspects have been in pre-trial detention for longer than the two years permitted by Guinean law. However, the new minister of justice showed increased commitment to ensuring the panel is able to complete its work.

Judiciary and Detention Conditions

Decades of neglect of the judiciary has led to striking deficiencies in this sector, allowing perpetrators of abuse to enjoy impunity for crimes. The operational budget for the judiciary remained at around 0.5 percent of the national budget, resulting in severe shortages of judicial personnel and insufficient infrastructure and resources. Unprofessional conduct in this sector, including absenteeism and corrupt practices, contributed to widespread detention-related abuses.

Progress in 2014 was evident in improved conditions for judges; the establishment of the Superior Council of Judges (*Conseil supérieur de la magistrature*) tasked with discipline, selection, and promotion of judges; and the revision of key legal texts to bring them in line with international standards, including the Penal Code, the Code of Criminal Procedure, and the Military Code of Justice.

Prison and detention centers in Guinea are severely overcrowded and operate far below international standards. However, the Ministry of Justice took steps to improve prison administration, leading to a sharp reduction in recorded malnutrition rates among inmates and some improvements in healthcare.

Malnutrition rates dropped from 21 percent in 2013 to 13 percent in 2014. The largest detention facility—designed for 300 detainees—accommodates some 1,200. An estimated 65 percent of prisoners in Conakry are held in prolonged pretrial detention. The failure of the *Cour d'assises*—which hears matters involving the most serious crimes—to meet regularly greatly contributes to the problem.

Women's and Children's Rights

Despite a lack of data, sexual and gender-based violence against women and girls remains of grave concern. In 2013, the UN documented 72 cases of rape and sexual assault, 55 of which involved girls. Forced and child marriage is common, and according to government statistics, some 95 per cent of girls and women undergo female genital mutilation, although the government is making efforts to address the problem.

Legislative and Institutional Framework

In 2014, the Reflection Commission, created by presidential decree in June 2011 to promote reconciliation, made little progress in fulfilling its mandate. There was likewise no progress in setting up the independent human rights institution, as mandated by Guinea's 2010 constitution. The institution can be established only by a law approved by the national assembly.

However, the Ministry for Human Rights and Civil Liberties, created in 2012, actively promoted respect for human rights, despite budgetary constraints. Minister Gassama Kalifa Diaby visited prisons, liaised with civil society, and advocated for strengthening the judiciary and respect for freedom of the press.

Guinea has still not ratified the Optional Protocol to the Convention against Torture and other Cruel, Inhuman or Degrading Treatment or Punishment, or the Optional Protocol to the Convention on the Elimination of All Forms of Discrimination against Women. Furthermore, Guinea has yet to codify the crime of torture into its penal code. Guinean law permits the death penalty; however, a moratorium is in effect and the minister of human rights pledged to initiate a national dialogue to build support for abolition.

Security Forces

Discipline within, and civilian control over, the security forces continues to improve, and authorities showed somewhat more willingness to sanction those implicated in violations. The military hierarchy largely ensured that the army and presidential guard—responsible for the most serious abuses during past periods of political unrest—remain in barracks and those mandated to respond to civil unrest, the police and gendarmerie, did so proportionally.

However, members of the security forces were in 2014 implicated in numerous incidents of excessive use of force or the mistreatment of detainees as they responded to protests and criminality. Torture of detainees declined somewhat, but incidents in 2014 resulted in a few deaths. The security forces have also been implicated in numerous acts of extortion, bribe-taking, outright theft and banditry, and, to a lesser extent, rape.

Security forces have long demonstrated a lack of political neutrality evident in the use of racial slurs and failure to provide equal protection to citizens of all ethnic and religious groups, notably those supporting the political opposition. The government's failure to acknowledge this problem raises concern in advance of the 2015 elections.

Key International Actors

Guinea's key international partners, notably the UN, the European Union, France, and the United States, focused on the need to strengthen the rule of law with more limited attention on combatting impunity for past violations of human rights.

In January, the EU, Guinea's biggest donor, released €140 million (USD$192 million) in aid, which had been suspended by delays in parliamentary elections. The funds will be used to finance projects in justice, security sector reform, and the transport sector. In April, the EU lifted the arms embargo in place since 2009. The EU and the UN Development Programme (UNDP) took the lead in strengthening Guinea's judicial system.

The country Office of the UN High Commissioner for Human Rights (OHCHR) actively engaged in human rights education and documentation, though largely failed to publicly denounce human rights concerns. In September, on the fifth anniversary of the Guinea stadium killings, the High Commissioner for Human Rights urged the government to take immediate and concrete steps to advance the investigation and ensure accountability for those responsible. The Office of the Special Representative of the Secretary-General on Sexual Violence in Conflict continued to support accountability for crimes committed during the 2009 stadium massacre and rapes.

The UN Peace Building Commission (PBC) continued to fund programs supporting security sector reform and reconciliation. In July, the board of the Extractives Industry Transparency Initiative deemed Guinea fully "EITI compliant."

The International Criminal Court, which in October 2009 confirmed that the situation in Guinea was under preliminary examination, maintained its pressure on the national authorities to conduct proceedings within a reasonable time frame. Court officials visited the country in February to assess progress.

Haiti

The Haitian government and international community made limited progress in 2014 to address the devastating impact of recent natural disasters and a deadly cholera epidemic. Political stalemates, resource constraints, and weak government institutions continued to hinder the Haitian government's efforts to meet the basic needs of its people and address long-standing human rights problems, such as violence against women and inhumane prison conditions.

For the fourth consecutive year, Haiti failed to hold constitutionally mandated elections, leading to a deteriorating political environment. The terms of another one third of the Senate and a number of deputies were due to end in early 2015, leaving almost all elected national and local positions in Haiti (with the exception of a remaining one third of senators and the president) open or filled by appointees.

As of June, 103,565 internally displaced persons (IDPs) were living in camps established in the aftermath of the 2010 earthquake, according the International Organization for Migration, down more than 90 percent since 2010. The United Nations estimates that some 70,000 of the remaining IDPs have no prospect of a durable solution.

The cholera epidemic has claimed more than 8,500 lives and infected over 700,000 people in four years. Nevertheless, 2014 marked a significant decrease in the number of suspected cases and a dramatic reduction in deaths, down to 51 deaths for the year as of September, compared to over 4,100 deaths in the first three months of 2010.

Criminal Justice System and Detention Conditions

Haiti's prison system remains severely overcrowded, in large part due to high numbers of arbitrary arrests and prolonged pretrial detentions.

The weak capacity of the Haitian National Police (HNP) contributes to overall insecurity in the country. While the government and the United Nations Stablization Mission in Haiti (MINUSTAH), the UN peacekeeping operation in the country, have made police reform a priority, there have been difficulties training sufficient numbers of entry-level cadets. The latest report of the UN secretary-general on MINUSTAH estimated the police-to-population ratio by the end of 2014 would likely be half the minimum recommended number.

Accountability for Past Abuses

Former President Jean-Claude Duvalier returned to Haiti in January 2011 after nearly 25 years in exile. He was charged with financial and human rights crimes allegedly committed during his 15-year tenure as president. From 1971 to 1986, Duvalier commanded a network of security forces that committed serious human rights violations, including arbitrary detentions, torture, disappearances, summary executions, and forced exile.

In 2012, the investigating judge in the case found, contrary to international standards, that the statute of limitations prevented prosecuting Duvalier for his human rights crimes. An appellate court heard testimony in a challenge to the ruling in 2013, with Duvalier appearing in court and answering questions posed by the court and victims' attorneys. In a historic ruling on February 20, the Port-of-Prince Court of Appeal found that the statute of limitations cannot be applied to crimes against humanity and ordered additional investigation into charges against Duvalier. However, Duvalier died on October 4 without having been brought to trial for his crimes. At time of writing, a reopened investigation into crimes committed by Duvalier's collaborators was still pending.

Violence against Women

Gender-based violence is a widespread problem. A draft law on combatting violence against women that would bring Haiti's criminal code in line with international standards has been discussed among members of parliament, but not officially introduced for debate.

A council of advisers to the president was reviewing two pending draft revisions to Haiti's criminal code that include acts of gender-based violence, such as rape and sexual assault, not currently in the code, with the expectation that a conciliated version would be presented to parliament in early 2015.

Children's Domestic Labor

Use of child domestic workers—known as restavèks—continues. Restavèks, the majority of whom are girls, are sent from low-income households to live with wealthier families in the hope that they will be schooled and cared for in exchange for performing light chores.

Though difficult to calculate, some estimates suggest that 225,000 children work as restavèks.These children are often unpaid, denied education, and physically or sexually abused. Haiti's labor code does not set a minimum age for work in domestic services, though the minimum age for work in industrial, agricultural, and commercial enterprises is 15. Most of Haiti's trafficking cases are restavèks. In May, Haiti passed legislation outlawing many forms of trafficking, including hosting a child for the purpose of exploitation.

Human Rights Defenders

Human rights defenders continue to face threats of violence. Malya Vilard Apolon, co-founder of Komisyon Fanm Viktim Pou Viktim (KOFAVIV), a women's rights organization, left Haiti in March after repeated death threats, harassment, and the poisoning of her family dogs. Marie Eramithe Delva, KOFAVIV's other co-founder, reported to police in May that she received death threats by text message from a woman in police custody, and provided screenshots of the threats and phone number. To her knowledge, there was no further investigation into her claims and she received no protection from police, prompting her also to leave Haiti in June.

In February, Daniel Dorsinvil, the general coordinator for the Platform of Haitian Human Rights Organizations (POHDH), and his wife Girldy Lareche were killed while walking in a Port-au-Prince neighborhood near the POHDH offices. In the days after the murders, government officials claimed that the crime occurred during an armed robbery and was unrelated to Dorsinvil's human rights activities or criticism of the government. This claim was not substantiated by a thorough investigation, according to local civil society representatives.

Pierre Espérance, executive director of the Réseau National de Défense des Droits Humains (RNDDH), received a death threat in April accusing him of reporting false human rights claims in an effort to destabilize the government. The handwritten threat also included a bullet and stated "this time you won't escape," referring to an incident in 1999 when Espérance was shot but survived.

Key International Actors

The UN mission, MINUSTAH, has been in Haiti since 2004 and has contributed to efforts to improve public security, protect vulnerable groups, and strengthen the country's democratic institutions. The UN Security Council extended MINUSTAH's mandate through October 15, 2015.

There is mounting evidence that the cholera epidemic that began in October 2010 is likely to have been introduced by UN peacekeepers. A member of the UN's Panel of Experts on the outbreak, stated that "the most likely source of the introduction of cholera into Haiti was someone infected with the Nepal strain of cholera and associated with the United Nations Mirebalais camp."

Responding to the UN's dismissal of claims for compensation from 5,000 victims of the epidemic, the victims' representative, the Institute for Justice and Democracy in Haiti and the Bureau des Avocats Internationaux filed a lawsuit before a US court. At time of writing, a motion to dismiss was pending. To date, there has been no independent adjudication of the facts surrounding the introduction of cholera and the UN's involvement.

According to figures from the UN Office of Internal Oversight Services, at least 93 allegations of sexual abuse or exploitation have been made against MINUSTAH personnel in the last eight years, including 11 in 2014, as of September 30.

In February, the UN independent expert on Haiti, Gustavo Gallón, called for "shock treatment" to significantly reduce the number of persons in pretrial detention.

In May, the Inter-American Commission on Human Rights called on all Organization of American States (OAS) member states to make their archives and official files on the human rights abuses committed under Duvalier open for use as evidence in the investigation. It was unknown whether OAS member states had complied with the commission's request.

Honduras

Honduras suffers from rampant crime and impunity for human rights abuses. The murder rate was again the highest in the world in 2014. The institutions responsible for providing public security continue to prove largely ineffective and remain marred by corruption and abuse, while efforts to reform them have made little progress.

Journalists and peasant activists are particularly vulnerable to violence, yet the government routinely fails to prosecute those responsible and provide protection for those at risk.

After it arbitrarily dismissed four Supreme Court judges in December 2012, Congress passed legislation empowering itself to remove justices and the attorney general, further undermining judicial and prosecutorial independence.

Police Abuses and Corruption

The unlawful use of force by police is a chronic problem. According to a report by the Observatory on Violence at the National Autonomous University of Honduras, police killed 149 people between 2011 and 2012. Then-Commissioner of the Preventative Police Alex Villanueva affirmed the report's findings and said there were likely many more killings by police that were never reported. The government did not respond to calls by the National Autonomous University rector asking it to provide information on how many of those killings had been subject to investigations or resulted in criminal convictions.

Efforts to address endemic corruption within the police force have made little progress. While tests designed to identify corruption have been administered to more than 4,500 police officers, only a fraction of those who have failed the test have been removed from their posts. According to the Public Security Reform Commission, the institution formerly responsible for designing reforms to justice and public security organs, just 3 percent of the 230 officers recommended for dismissal in 2012 were ultimately removed from their posts.

Use of Military in Public Security Operations

In November 2011, Congress passed an emergency decree allowing military personnel to carry out public security duties, which has been extended periodically. In August 2013, a law was passed authorizing the creation of a military police force with powers to impose control over violent neighborhoods and carry out arrests, among other duties, despite a history of abuses by the military against civilians. The military police force was deployed in January 2014.

In August, soldiers detained Marco Medrano Lemus close to his home in La Lima, Cortés. According to local press accounts, he was found dead shortly thereafter and an autopsy showed signs he had been tortured. Eight soldiers were arrested in relation to the incident, and investigations were continuing at time of writing.

Accountability for Post-Coup Abuses

Following a military coup in June 2009, the de facto government suspended key civil liberties, including freedom of the press and assembly. In the ensuing days, security forces responded to generally peaceful demonstrations with excessive force and shut down opposition media outlets, causing several deaths, scores of injuries, and thousands of arbitrary detentions. A truth commission established by former President Porfirio Lobo published a report in July 2011 that documented 20 cases of excessive use of force and killings by security forces.

In August 2014, José Arnulfo Jiménez, a former military officer, was sentenced to five years in jail for the arbitrary closure of Channel 36 in June 2009. Jiménez had led a contingent that occupied the premises of the media outlet, preventing broadcasting for several days. At time of writing, there has been little progress in prosecuting other abuses committed during the post-coup period.

Judicial Independence

Judges face acts of intimidation and political interference. In December 2012, Congress voted to remove four of the five justices in the Supreme Court's Constitutional Chamber after they ruled that a law aimed at addressing police corruption was unconstitutional. Replacements were appointed in January 2013, and the new court rejected a legal challenge by the dismissed justices the following month. Since their removal, the former justices have reported being subject to repeated acts of intimidation, including death threats and police harassment.

A 2011 constitutional reform established a Council of the Judiciary with the authority to appoint and dismiss judges. According to the International Commission of Jurists, the selection process for the council's members lacked safeguards to protect against political interference and was marred by irregularities, including the exclusion of representatives from one of Honduras's two judicial associations. More than 40 judges have been suspended since the council began its work.

Attacks on Journalists

Journalists in Honduras continue to suffer threats, attacks, and killings. Authorities consistently fail to investigate and prosecute these crimes. More than 30 journalists have been murdered since 2009, according to the National Human Rights Commission (CONADEH), though the motive in many of the cases has not been determined.

In December 2013, Juan Carlos Argeñal Medina, a reporter for Globo TV, was shot dead in the city of Danlí, El Progreso, after receiving death threats in connection with his work on corruption in a local hospital. In the past, Globo TV was subject to a series of violent attacks following its critical reporting on the 2009 coup.

Rural Violence

More than 90 people have been killed in recent years in land disputes in the Bajo Aguán Valley, most of them since 2009, according to a March 2013 report by CONADEH. Scores more have been victims of attacks and threats. The disputes often pit international agro-industrial firms against peasant organizations over the rightful ownership of lands transferred following a reform to the country's agrarian law. While most victims have been peasants, private security guards have also been killed and wounded.

Honduran authorities have failed to effectively investigate abuses or provide protection for those at risk. A Human Rights Watch investigation into 29 cases of homicides and 2 abductions in Bajo Aguán found that none of the cases had been successfully prosecuted.

HUMAN
RIGHTS
WATCH

"There Are No Investigations Here"
Impunity for Killings and Other Abuses in Bajo Aguán, Honduras

Prison Conditions

Inhumane conditions, including overcrowding, inadequate nutrition, and poor sanitation, are systemic in Honduran prisons. The country's jails, which can hold a maximum of approximately 8,600 inmates, were holding more than 13,000 in August 2013, according to the Inter-American Commission on Human Rights. Corruption among prison officials is widespread.

Human Rights Defenders

Human rights defenders continue to be subject to violence, threats, and killings. In May, José Guadalupe Ruelas, director of international children's charity, Casa Alianza, which has criticized authorities for failing to protect children from organized crime, was arbitrarily detained and violently beaten by military police. He was released the next day after local human rights organizations intervened on his behalf.

The Lobo administration submitted draft legislation to Congress in August 2013 to protect human rights defenders, journalists, and legal practitioners, but the law had not been passed at time of writing.

Violence against Children

Children experience high levels of violence, largely perpetrated by gangs and other forms of organized crime. In May, five adolescents believed to be associated with the Mara Salvatrucha gang were killed in the El Carmen Pedagogical Center for Rehabilitation, reportedly by members of rival gangs. According to CONADEH, 458 children were murdered between 2010 and 2013. Casa Alianza reports that in the first 4 months of 2014, 270 people under the age of 23 were killed.

It is likely that gang violence has contributed to a surge in youth migration to the United States in recent years. A 2014 report by the United Nations High Commissioner for Refugees found that 34 percent of child migrants from Honduras identified this violence as a motive for leaving their home country.

Key International Actors

The United States allocated more than US$50 million in security aid to Honduras from 2010 to 2014 and continues to provide assistance through the Central American Regional Security Initiative (CARSI). US legislation granting military and police aid to Honduras stipulates that 35 percent of the funds will be available only if the Honduran government meets several important human rights requirements. As of February 2013, the US Congress was reportedly withholding approximately $30 million of aid over human rights concerns.

In February 2013, the United Nations Working Group on the use of mercenaries stated that the government had failed to properly regulate private security firms and expressed concern regarding their "alleged involvement ... in widespread human rights violations including killings, disappearances, forced evictions, and sexual violence."

In January 2014, the ombudsman for the International Finance Corporation (IFC), the private-sector lending arm of the World Bank, found that the IFC had failed to conduct adequate due diligence and to assess and respond to known risks of violence and forced evictions associated with its investment in Dinant, a palm oil and food company that was at the center of a spate of violence and killings in Honduras.

In August, the ombudsman similarly found that the IFC had fallen short in identifying and addressing risks in its investment in Banco Ficohsa, the largest bank in Honduras. Dinant was one of Banco Ficohsa's largest borrowers.

India

India elected a new government in May 2014 led by Narendra Modi of the Bharatiya Janata Party (BJP) as prime minister. After 10 years in opposition, the BJP won a decisive mandate with a significant majority in parliament. The BJP promised to revive growth, end corruption, and pursue development projects.

Modi has stressed protection of women from violence and other abuses, and access to healthcare and sanitation. He has urged members of parliament to establish model villages with better infrastructure and modern sanitation facilities in rural areas, and, in his first public speech, called for a decade-long moratorium on communal divisions and discrimination.

The new government has expressed a commitment to freedom of speech but has not ended state censorship or taken decisive action against ultranationalist and other religious militant groups that respond to views they do not like with threats of violence. In 2014, authorities tightened restrictions on nongovernmental organizations (NGOs). One reason for this has been that civil society groups have been highly critical of big development projects that they say will have a negative impact on the environment, and on the health and livelihoods of affected populations.

While Modi took office with a reputation for having overseen economic growth and improved governance as chief minister of Gujarat, his inability to protect Gujarati Muslims during religious riots in 2002 and promptly prosecute perpetrators continues to cause concern. Some inflammatory remarks by BJP politicians have added to a sense of insecurity among religious minorities.

Caste-based discrimination and neglect of tribal communities is also a continuing problem in India, as is sexual abuse and other violence against women and children. The awarding of the 2014 Nobel Peace Prize to activist Kailash Satyarthi spotlighted the fact that millions of children in India are still engaged in the worst forms of labor. Lack of accountability for security forces and public officials responsible for abuses perpetuates impunity and leads to further abuses. Police reforms are urgently needed to make the force rights-respecting and accountable.

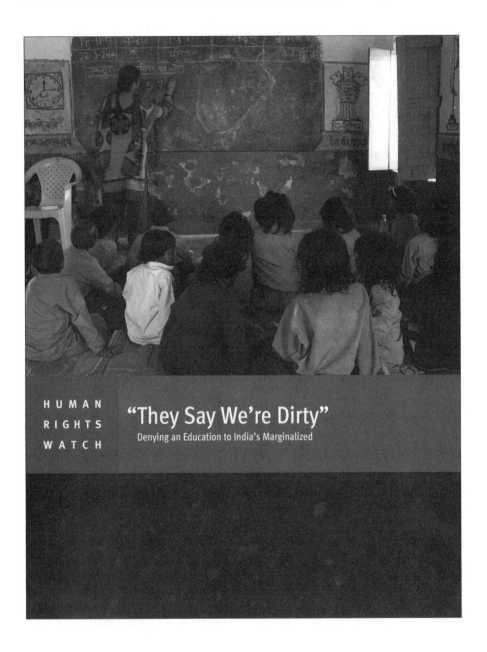

HUMAN RIGHTS WATCH

"They Say We're Dirty"
Denying an Education to India's Marginalized

Treatment of Minorities

Incidents of violence against religious minorities spiked in 2013 in the run-up to national elections; according to government sources 133 people were killed and 2,269 injured in 823 incidents.

More than a year after communal violence killed over 60 people, mostly Muslims, and displaced tens of thousands in Muzaffarnagar and Shamli districts of Uttar Pradesh state, both the central and the state governments had not provided proper relief or justice. The BJP even chose Sanjeev Balyan, charged with inciting violence during the riots, as their candidate in parliamentary elections and appointed him as a minister, intensifying Muslim insecurities. The state government forcibly closed down relief camps and failed to act on allegations that lack of adequate relief services caused the death of over 30 children in the camps.

In June 2014, an ultranationalist Hindu group organized violent protests in the western city of Pune against a social media post derogatory to some Hindu historical and political figures. Some members of the group, assuming that the anonymous post was the work of Muslims, arbitrarily beat and killed Mohsin Shaikh—who had no links to post—but was easily identified as Muslim because of his prayer cap.

Dalits (so-called Untouchables) and tribal groups continued to face discrimination and violence. The difficulties the Dalit community has in obtaining justice were highlighted by recent court verdicts in four cases in Bihar and one in Andhra Pradesh states. In each of the cases, the courts overturned convictions in high-profile incidents that took place between 1991 and 2000 involving killings of Dalits due to lack of evidence, highlighting the failure of prosecutorial authorities.

 Despite numerous initiatives and laws prohibiting "manual scavenging"—the cleaning by hand of human waste by members of communities considered low-caste—the practice persists. Those who try to leave such work face retribution, including threats of violence or displacement. In March 2014, the Supreme Court held that India's constitution requires state intervention to end the practice.

Impunity

Members of India's security forces continue to enjoy impunity for serious human rights violations.

In a rare case in November 2014, the army reported that a military court had sentenced five soldiers, including two officers, to life in prison for a 2010 extrajudicial execution of three innocent villagers. The army ordered a military trial after using the draconian Armed Forces Special Powers Act (AFSPA) to block prosecution by civilian courts.

The army also chose a military trial for the alleged March 2000 extrajudicial killing of five civilians in Pathribal in northern Jammu and Kashmir state. However, in January, the army court of inquiry dismissed charges against five officers. AFSPA, which has been in force for decades in Jammu and Kashmir and India's northeastern states, has provided effective immunity to members of the armed forces for killings of civilians and other serious human rights violations. Numerous independent commissions in India have recommended repealing or amending the law but the government has failed to do so in the face of stiff opposition from the army.

Proposed police reforms have also languished even as police continue to commit human rights violations with impunity. These include arbitrary arrest and detention, torture, and extrajudicial killings. In several states, police are poorly trained and face huge caseloads.

Two separate reports—one by a think tank and another by three senior police officials—found a deficit of trust between Muslim communities and the police. Muslims perceive the police to be communal, biased, and insensitive in part because of the misconduct of some police personnel, especially during communal tensions.

Women's Rights

In November 2014, more than a dozen women died and many others were critically ill after undergoing sterilization procedures in the central Indian state of Chhattisgarh. This led to an outcry against target-driven approaches to family planning programs.

Legal reforms were introduced in response to the 2012 Delhi gang-rape and murder, but at time of writing the Indian government had yet to introduce monitoring and reporting mechanisms to track their implementation. Reports of rape—including of Dalit women, individuals with disabilities, and children—continued to make national news in 2014, leading to protests.

In early 2014, the government introduced guidelines for the medical treatment and examination of women and children who report rape, but failed to allocate resources necessary for their implementation. At time of writing only two states had adopted the guidelines.

Maternal mortality rates have declined in India but remain a concern because of weak referral systems and poor access to medical assistance in many parts of the country.

Children's Rights

By awarding its peace prize to Kailash Satyarthi, the Nobel committee drew attention to the continuing employment of children in the worst of labor. The Right to Education Act and government schemes have resulted in near-universal enrollment of children in early grades. But millions of children, particularly from vulnerable Dalit, tribal, and Muslim communities, facing discrimination, inadequate support in government schools, and pressures to earn money, soon drop out and start working.

In August 2014, the government introduced amendments to the Juvenile Justice Act that, if adopted, would subject 16-18 year olds to prosecution in adult courts when charged with serious crimes such as rape and murder. Child rights activists and the National Commission for Protection of Child Rights strongly opposed the amendments.

In June 2014, the United Nations Committee on the Rights of the Child identified several areas in which the Indian government had failed to ensure protection of children from discrimination, harmful practices, sexual abuse, and child labor. It also raised concerns about Maoist militants recruiting children and attacking schools, and about government armed forces occupying schools in Maoist-affected areas despite Supreme Court rulings prohibiting the practice.

HUMAN RIGHTS WATCH

"Treated Worse than Animals"

Abuses against Women and Girls with Psychosocial or Intellectual Disabilities in Institutions in India

Protection of LGBT Rights

The rights of Lesbian, Gay, Bisexual, and Transgender (LGBT) people suffered a setback in December 2013 when the Supreme Court reversed a landmark 2009 Delhi High Court decision striking down a colonial-era law criminalizing adult consensual same-sex relations. At time of writing, a petition to review the decision was pending before the Supreme Court.

In April 2014, the Supreme Court recognized transgender individuals as a third gender and asked the government to treat them as a minority eligible for quotas in jobs and education.

Palliative Care

In February 2014, India's parliament amended the country's drug laws to allow for better access to pain medicines including morphine. The crucial amendments to the Narcotic Drugs and Psychotropic Substances Act eliminated archaic rules that obligated hospitals and pharmacies to obtain four or five licenses, each from a different government agency, every time they wanted to purchase strong pain medicines. More than 7 million people in India require palliative care every year and the new revisions to the law will help spare them the indignity of suffering needlessly from severe pain.

Rights of Persons with Disabilities

Mental health and support services are severely lacking in India. Fewer than 20 percent of the people who need mental health care have access to treatment. Due to stigma and the shortage of government community-based services, families find it difficult to cope and often end up abandoning or forcibly institutionalizing relatives with intellectual or psychosocial disabilities.

Restrictions on Free Speech

Vaguely worded laws that criminalize free speech continue to be misused. Police in various states have filed charges under the Indian Penal Code or the Information Technology Act for online comments critical of important political figures, including the prime minister. In one instance, five young men were questioned by the police for sharing anti-Modi comments over the phone. The police also tar-

HUMAN
RIGHTS
WATCH

CLEANING HUMAN WASTE
"Manual Scavenging," Caste, and Discrimination in India

geted student magazines in two instances for critical comments on some political figures, including Modi.

Despite commitments to protect freedom of speech, the government has not taken decisive action against militant groups that threaten and attack people over views they do not like. In the face of weak government responses and threats of lawsuits from Hindu ultranationalist groups, a few publishers withdrew or cancelled books being prepared for publication.

Civil Society and Freedom of Association

Authorities have tightened restrictions on civil society organizations. Officials use the Foreign Contribution Regulation Act (FCRA), which tracks grants from foreign donors, to harass organizations that question or criticize government policies, to stymie their activities, and to cut off funds from abroad.

The impact on Indian civil society has been severe. When the Indian Home Ministry conducts an investigation pursuant to the FCRA, it often freezes the accounts of the NGO being investigated, cutting its source of funding, and forcing it to stop its activities. Such tactics have a wider chilling effect on the work of other groups.

In 2014, the Modi government asked the country's central bank to seek prior permission before moving foreign funds into Greenpeace India's accounts, intensifying concerns that the government would be less tolerant of organizations that questioned the government's development and infrastructure projects.

Death Penalty

While there were no executions in 2014, death sentences continued to be handed down. This was despite a Supreme Court decision in November 2012 stating that the "rarest of rare" case standard had not been applied uniformly over the years and needed review.

In a landmark judgment in January 2014, India's Supreme Court commuted the death sentences of 15 prisoners. It ruled that death penalty can be commuted where the defendants are mentally ill or where there are inexplicable government delays in deciding mercy pleas. It also set forth guidelines to safeguard the rights of prisoners on death row and their families.

Foreign Policy

The new government intensified engagement with world leaders to promote trade and investment and revive the Indian economy. Modi invited to his inauguration all neighboring heads of state, including Pakistan's, signifying his commitment to build stronger ties in the region.

Despite repeated militant attacks on Indian assets, including a May 2014 attack on the consulate in Herat, India continued to provide significant assistance to reconstruction efforts in Afghanistan and some training for Afghan security personnel. It has also provided assistance for reconstruction efforts in Sri Lanka.

Both the prior prime minister, Manmohan Singh, and now Modi's government have been reticent on many regional and global human rights issues where their voice could make a difference. The Modi government has focused on foreign policy to revive trade and investment, and called for international cooperation to counter terrorism threats and money laundering. However, it has not made any significant announcements suggesting greater commitment to protecting human rights even in countries like Bangladesh, Nepal, Sri Lanka, or Burma where it has considerable influence. It has abstained on key UN resolutions, including on North Korea in November 2014.

After supporting two resolutions at the UN Human Rights Council on Sri Lanka in 2012 and 2013, in March 2014 India abstained on a resolution requesting the Office of the High Commissioner for Human Rights to investigate serious violations during the conflict between the Sri Lankan government and the Liberation Tigers of Tamil Eelam that ended in May 2009. India said that Sri Lanka should instead be supported in addressing these concerns through wholly domestic efforts.

Human rights did not feature very strongly in public statements when Indian leaders met with counterparts from the United States, Australia, China, and Japan, although they agreed to cooperate on regional issues.

Although it has not ratified the UN refugee conventions, India continued to accept refugees from Tibet, Burma, and, in recent years, Afghanistan.

However, India failed to publicly condemn efforts by Australia to return Sri Lanka refugees without properly evaluating the risk of torture. Nor did India speak up to call for the protection of ethnic Rohingya Muslims in Burma.

Key International Actors

The US, United Kingdom, Japan, China, and Australia, among others, saw the election of Modi as an opportunity to strengthen trade ties with India. With the focus on investment and trade, and given longstanding Indian sensitivity to perceived intervention in its domestic affairs, these countries maintained a low-key approach to human rights, choosing to ignore concerns about protection of religious minorities.

India's record on children's rights and women's rights were reviewed in 2014 by the UN Committee on the Rights of the Child and the UN Committee on the Elimination of Discrimination against Women. Both committees raised concerns about India's failure to implement relevant laws and policies and ensure non-discrimination.

Indonesia

Joko Widodo, popularly known as "Jokowi," took office on October 20, 2014, after winning a tightly contested presidential election on July 9. The election was a watershed; Widodo is the first Indonesian president who has neither a military background nor an elite family pedigree.

Widodo's campaign focused primarily on economic issues, but he made commitments on several of the pressing human rights issues he inherited, including pledges to investigate the enforced disappearance of 13 pro-democracy activists in 1998 in the dying days of the Suharto dictatorship and to lift restrictions on foreign journalists from traveling to and reporting from Papua and West Papua provinces. Those commitments are vague, however, and had yet to be backed by specific directives or policy measures at time of writing.

The human rights record of Jokowi's predecessor, Susilo Bambang Yudhoyono, in office for 10 years, was characterized more by failures and missed opportunities than by successes. Yudhoyono's government made little progress in ending impunity for past serious human rights abuses by security forces; failed to protect the rights of Indonesia's religious minorities from increasing harassment, intimidation, and violence by Islamist militants; allowed the enforcement of local Islamic bylaws that violate rights of women, LGBT people, and religious minorities; and failed to address continuing abuses in Papua.

Freedom of Religion

According to the Jakarta-based Setara Institute, which monitors religious freedom, there were 230 attacks on religious minorities in Indonesia in 2013 and 107 cases in 2014 through November. The alleged perpetrators were almost all Sunni Islamist militants; the targets included Christians, Ahmadiyah, Shia, Sufi Muslims, and native faith believers.

Throughout 2014, two Christian congregations in the Jakarta suburbs—GKI Yasmin and HKBP Filadelfia—continued to worship in private houses due to the government's failure to enforce Supreme Court decisions ordering local officials to issue building permits for the congregations. National regulations, including ministerial decrees on constructing houses of worship and a decree against religious practice by the Ahmadiyah community, discriminate against religious minorities and foster intolerance.

On May 29, Islamist militants carrying wooden bats and iron sticks attacked the home of book publisher Julius Felicianus in Yogyakarta while his family conducted an evening Christian prayer meeting. The attack resulted in injuries to seven participants, including fractures and head wounds. Police arrested the leader of the attack but later released him after local authorities pressured Felicianus to drop charges on the basis of "religious harmony."

On June 1, Islamist militants attacked a building in Pangukan village in Sleman, Central Java, in which residents had been conducting Pentacostal services. Police arrested the leader of the attack, but also filed criminal charges against pastor Nico Lomboan, the owner of the property, for violating a 2012 government ban against using private residences for religious services.

While Yudhoyono condemned sectarian violence by the extremist Islamic State group in Iraq and Syria, he downplayed the harassment, intimidation, and violence committed by Islamist militants against Indonesia's religious minorities, claiming it is "understandable that sometimes there will be conflict between different groups."

In July, Minister of Religious Affairs Lukman Saifuddin publicly expressed support for allowing followers of the Bahai faith to receive national identification cards, marriage certificates, and other official documents that identify them as Bahai. But Home Affairs Minister Gamawan Fauzi rejected Saifuddin's proposal, arguing that he could only legally issue documents listing one of Indonesia's six officially recognized religions: Islam, Protestanism, Catholism, Hinduism, Buddhism, and Confucianism. Fauzi suggested Bahai members choose one of these instead.

On September 4, five law students from the University of Indonesia in Jakarta filed a petition at the Constitutional Court, demanding revocation of an article of the 1974 Marriage Law that bans inter-religious marriage. The petition argues that the law discriminates against mixed-faith couples.

Papua

Papua (used here to refer to the provinces of Papua and West Papua) remained tense in 2014 as security forces continued to confront a low-level pro-independence insurgency movement led by the Free Papua Movement (Organisasi Papua Merdeka, OPM). On July 28, Indonesian media reported that suspected OPM guerrillas killed two police officers and wounded two others in Indawa village, Lanny Jaya regency.

As of October, according to the "Papuans Behind Bars" website, 68 Papuans were imprisoned or awaiting trial for peaceful advocacy of independence.

Indonesian police arrested French journalists Valentine Bourrat and Thomas Dandois on August 6 in Wamena on charges of "working illegally" without a journalist visa while filming a documentary for Franco-German Arte TV. Areki Wanimbo, the Lanny Jaya tribal chief, whom the journalists had interviewed, was also arrested. A police spokesman initially said that the journalists would be charged with subversion for allegedly filming OPM members, but the two ultimately were charged with and convicted of "abusive use of entry visas" on October 24. They left Papua three days later, having served the requisite time in custody. Wanimbo, however, was still being held at time of writing, charged with subversion without a clear factual basis, and facing trial.

On August 26, Martinus Yohame, leader of the West Papua National Committee in Sorong, was found dead inside a sack in the sea, a week after he went missing in the lead-up to President Yudhoyono's visit to Sorong. Yohame had also talked to the French journalists.

Although Jokowi pledged to open Papua to foreign journalists, as noted above, his cabinet also proposed subdividing Papua from two provinces into four smaller provinces and encouraging greater migration to Papua, proposals likely to exacerbate tensions there.

Land Rights

The Ministry of Forestry continued in 2014 to include forest lands claimed by indigenous communities within state forest concessions awarded to timber and plantation companies. In May 2013, the Constitutional Court rebuked the ministry for the practice and declared unconstitutional a provision of the 1999 Forestry Law that had enabled it.

In October 2014, President Widodo merged the Agriculture Ministry and the National Land Authority into a single ministry and did the same with the Ministry of Forestry and the Ministry of Environment. Activists hope the consolidation will improve efficiency, reduce corruption, and allow for more effective government oversight of land issues.

Freedom of Expression

The Indonesian government continues to arrest peaceful protesters who raise separatist flags. On April 25, police in Ambon arrested nine people who led a prayer to commemorate the 1950 declaration of an independent "South Moluccas Republic." The nine were charged with treason and in November were still on trial.

On August 30, Florence Sihombing, a graduate student at Gadjah Mada University in Yogyakarta, was arrested on criminal defamation charges after she called the city "poor, stupid and uncultured" on a social media network. Police dropped all charges and released Sihombing on September 1 on condition that the university impose academic sanctions against her. The university responded on September 9 by suspending Sihombing for one semester.

On August 30, Adrianus Meliala, a member of the official National Police Commission, apologized for calling the force corrupt in a television interview. Meliala's apology followed a threat of criminal defamation charges by National Police Chief General Sutarman.

On August 15, police detained journalist Aprila Wayar of *Jubi*, a Papuan news service, for photographing police beating nine student protesters with rifle butts at Cenderawasih University in Jayapura, Papua. Police released Wayar, along with the photos she had taken, after several hours.

Military Reform and Impunity

Security forces responsible for serious violations of human rights continue to enjoy impunity. September 2014 marked the 10th anniversary of the murder of the prominent human rights defender Munir Said Thalib. Munir was poisoned on a Garuda Indonesia flight on September 7, 2004. Despite strong evidence that the conspiracy to kill Munir went beyond the three individuals convicted in connection with the crime and involved high levels of the National Intelligence Agency, Yudhoyono failed to deliver on promises to bring all perpetrators to justice.

Parliament failed to amend the 1997 Law on Military Tribunals even though the Yudhoyono administration submitted a new draft law in February. The 1997 law is widely seen as providing impunity to members of the military involved in human rights abuses and other crimes. If approved, the amendment would pave the way for soldiers to be tried in civilian courts for human rights violations.

No progress was made on accountability for serious security force abuses during the 32-year rule of President Suharto, including the mass killings of 1965-66, atrocities in counterinsurgency operations in Aceh, East Timor, and Papua, killings in Kalimantan, Lampung, Tanjung priok, and other prominent cases.

Women's and Girls' Rights

Discriminatory regulations against women and girls continued to proliferate in 2014. Indonesia's official Commission on Violence against Women reported that, as of August, national and local governments had passed 23 new discriminatory regulations in 2014.

Indonesia has a total of 279 discriminatory local regulations targeting women. A total of 90 of those rules require girls and women, mostly students and civil servants, to wear the hijab. The mandatory hijab is also imposed on Christian girls in some areas.

On September 27, the Aceh parliament passed two Islamic bylaws which create new discriminatory offenses that do not exist in the Indonesian criminal code. The bylaws extend Islamic law to non-Muslims, criminalizing alcohol drinking, consensual same-sex sexual acts, homosexuality, as well as all sexual relations outside of marriage. The bylaws permit as punishment up to 100 lashes and up to 100 months in prison.

In October, Human Rights Watch released a short report documenting the National Police requirement that female police applicants take an abusive "virginity test."

Refugees and Asylum Seekers

Indonesia remains a transit point to Australia for refugees and asylum seekers fleeing persecution and violence in countries including Somalia, Afghanistan, Pakistan, and Burma.

As of May 2014, there were approximately 10,509 refugees and asylum seekers in Indonesia, all living in legal limbo because Indonesia lacks an asylum law. This number includes 331 migrant children detained in immigration centers, of which 110 were unaccompanied minors.

While Indonesia delegates responsibility for processing refugees and asylum seekers to the office of the United Nations High Commissioner for Refugees (UNHCR), it often refuses to release even UNHCR-recognized refugees from detention centers, where conditions are poor and mistreatment is common. Those who are released face the constant threat of re-arrest and further detention.

Disability Rights

On July 8, the parliament passed a new mental health act to address Indonesia's dire mental healthcare situation. Conditions are particularly horrific for the tens of thousands of Indonesians with psychosocial disabilities who spend their lives shackled (*pasung*) instead of receiving community-based mental health care. When implemented, the new law will address the treatment gap by integrating mental health into general health services, making affordable drug treatments available for people with psychosocial disabilities, and facilitating the training of more mental health professionals.

The law seeks to reduce stigma and discrimination against people with psychosocial disabilities and guarantees the right to protection from neglect, violence, and exploitation. The law also provides accountability for abuses, including *pasung*, and promises access to services in the community. However, the law also contains problematic provisions that allow for treatment without informed consent of persons with psychosocial disabilities if they are deemed "incompetent."

Key International Actors

On August 29, United Nations Secretary-General Ban Ki-moon spoke in Bali and described the country as "living wisely, harmoniously, side-by-side resolving all differences of opinion through dialogue," failing to mention religious intolerance and related violence.

On September 6, US Secretary of State John Kerry issued a statement on the 10th anniversary of rights activist Munir's assasination: "Still today, justice has not been served. Full accountability for all those allegedly involved remains elusive."

In August, Australia and Indonesia signed a vaguely worded agreement on surveillance and intelligence gathering. In October, the Australian senate passed a motion calling for the release of the two French journalists imprisoned in Papua and noting that press freedom in Papua is "tightly restricted" by the Indonesian government.

Iran

2014 saw no significant improvements in human rights in the first full year in office of President Hassan Rouhani. Repressive elements within the security and intelligence forces and the judiciary retained wide powers and continued to be the main perpetrators of rights abuses. Executions, especially for drug-related offenses, continued at a high rate. Security and intelligence forces arrested journalists, bloggers, and social media activists, and revolutionary courts handed down heavy sentences against them.

Death Penalty

According to Iranian media sources, authorities executed at least 200 prisoners as of October 2014, but opposition sources said they carried out another 400 unannounced executions. Some executions were public.

Under Iranian law, many crimes are punishable by death, including some that do not involve violence such as "insulting the Prophet," apostasy, same-sex relations, adultery, and drug-related offenses. Convicted drug offenders sentenced after flawed trials in revolutionary courts formed the majority of prisoners executed in 2014. On November 24, the Supreme Court upheld a criminal court ruling sentencing Soheil Arabi to death for Facebook posts he had written that were interpreted as "insulting the Prophet."

According to unofficial sources, at least eight executed prisoners may have been child offenders aged under eighteen at the time of the murder and rape crimes for which they received death sentences. Dozens of child offenders reportedly remained on death row and at risk of execution. Iranian law allows capital punishment for persons who have reached the official age of puberty: nine for girls, fifteen for boys.

Authorities executed at least nine people in 2014 whom revolutionary courts had sentenced for *moharebeh* ("enmity against God") on account of their alleged ties to armed opposition groups. In January, authorities executed two Iranian Arab activists, Hadi Rashedi and Hashem Shaabaninejad, for *moharebah* according to rights groups. On May 31, authorities executed Gholamreza Khosravi Savadjani, sentenced for his alleged ties to the outlawed Mojahedin-e Khalq opposition group. Dozens of others sentenced on terrorism-related charges, including many Iranian Kurds and Baluch, were on death row following trials rife with due process violations. On June 12, authorities informed the families of Ali Chabishat and Seyed Khaled Mousavi, Iranian-Arabs from Ahvaz in Khuzestan, that they had secretly executed and buried them, despite appeals by the United Nations.

The judiciary continued to allow the execution of prisoners convicted of *moharebeh* despite penal code changes requiring that it review and vacate death sentences unless there is proof that the alleged perpetrator resorted to the use of arms.

Freedom of Expression and Information

Security authorities continued to clamp down on free speech and dissent. In October, according to Reporters Without Borders, Iran held at least 48 journalists, bloggers, and social media activists in detention.

In May 2014, police arrested four young men and three women after a video showing them dancing to the popular song "Happy," went viral on YouTube. Authorities released them to face trial on charges that included engaging in "illicit relations." In May, a Tehran revolutionary court sentenced eight Facebook users to a total of 127 years in prison for allegedly posting messages deemed to insult government officials and "religious sanctities," among other crimes.

Security officials arrested Saba Azarpeik, a journalist for the *Etemad* and *Tejarat-e Farda* media outlets, on May 28 and held her incommunicado for almost three months, then released her on bail, reportedly to face trial on vague charges of "propaganda against the state" and "dissemination of falsehoods." On June 19, a judiciary official announced that 11 people convicted of "designing sites, websites, and creating content for media hostile to the regime" had received prison sentences up to 11 years. They appeared to be people associated with *Narenji*, a popular website, whom Revolutionary Guards had detained on December 3, 2013.

On July 22, unidentified agents arrested *Washington Post* correspondent, Jason Rezaian, his wife Yeganeh Salehi, also a journalist, and two unnamed people—a photojournalist and her spouse. At time of writing, authorities continued to detain Rezaian without charge and without allowing him access to a lawyer, but had released Salehi and the two others.

On August 7, 2014, an appeals court confirmed the manslaughter conviction of a police officer accused in connection with the November 6, 2012 death in custody of blogger Sattar Beheshti. The court imposed a three-year prison term, followed by two years of internal exile, and a flogging of 74 lashes.

Judiciary officials also shut down at least four newspapers apparently for breaching content-based restrictions. They ordered the closure of *Aseman* in February and the arrest of its managing editor for an article that described the Islamic *qesas* retribution laws as "inhumane." Authorities allowed some newspapers to resume publication after bans, but they continued to block websites and jam foreign satellite broadcasts.

Freedom of Assembly and Association

Scores of people held for their affiliation with banned opposition parties, labor unions, and student groups were in prison. The judiciary continued to target independent and unregistered trade unions. On May 1, police attacked and arrested at least 25 workers who were protesting poor wages and labor conditions outside the Labor Ministry and a Tehran bus terminal. Police took the workers to Evin Prison before releasing them. Several of them face charges related to illegal gathering.

Rouhani's interim minister of science, Reza Faraji Dana, responsible for most of Iran's universities, led efforts to reinstate professors and students barred between 2005 and 2012 for their peaceful activities. Dozens remained unable to continue their studies or teach, however, and in August the parliament voted to impeach the minister and refused to confirm several other Rouhani nominations for the post.

Political Prisoners and Human Rights Defenders

The authorities continued to imprison dozens of activists and human rights defenders, such as lawyers Mohammad Seifzadeh and Abdolfattah Soltani, on account of their peaceful or professional activities. In September, a court

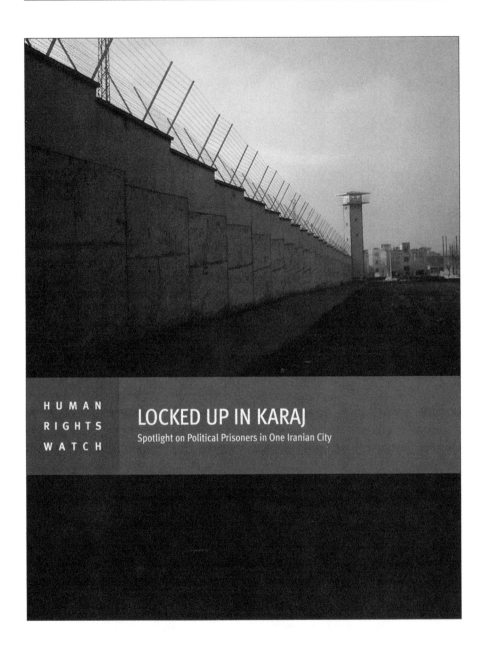

HUMAN
RIGHTS
WATCH

LOCKED UP IN KARAJ
Spotlight on Political Prisoners in One Iranian City

overturned an order that had banned Nasrin Sotoudeh from practicing law for 10 years following her release from prison in 2013, but on October 18 the Iranian Bar Association's disciplinary committee told Sotoudeh that it had revoked her law license for 3 years because of her revolutionary court conviction on vague national security charges in 2011. On November 9, security officials summoned Narges Mohammadi, a rights defender, for questioning after she gave a speech criticizing government policies.

Prominent opposition figures Mir Hossein Mousavi, Zahra Rahnavard, and Mehdi Karroubi, held without charge or trial since February 2011, remained under house arrest. Prisoners, especially those sentenced on politically motivated charges, faced regular abuse by guards and were denied necessary medical treatment. In April, guards severely beat several dozen political prisoners in Ward 350 of Evin Prison and forced around 30 to pass between two rows of guards, who punched, kicked, and beat them with batons, causing some to sustain serious injuries, according to relatives of the victims. Officials later subjected at least 31 prisoners to prolonged solitary confinement and degrading treatment.

Women's Rights

In 2014, authorities announced or implemented discriminatory policies, including restricting the employment of women in coffee shops, certain restaurants, and other public spaces and limiting access to family planning as part of official measures to boost Iran's population.

On June 30, authorities arrested Ghoncheh Ghavami, 25, a dual Iranian-British national, and others who had participated in a peaceful protest against an official ban on women attending men's volleyball matches in Tehran's Azadi Stadium. Ghavami, who was initially detained at Evin prison, where authorities denied her access to a lawyer, was later tried and convicted on the charge of "propaganda against the state" in a closed trial. In September, authorities announced that Shahla Sherkat, editor of a new women's magazine, was to appear before the press court for promoting un-Islamic ideas.

Iranian women face discrimination in many aspects of their lives, including personal status matters related to marriage, divorce, inheritance, and child custody. Regardless of her age, a woman cannot marry without the approval of her male guardian, and women generally cannot pass on their Iranian nationality to a foreign-born spouse or to their children. Child marriage, though not the norm, continues, as the law allows girls to marry at 13 and boys at age 15, and at younger ages if authorized by a judge.

Treatment of Minorities

The government denies freedom of religion to Baha'is, Iran's largest non-Muslim religious minority, and discriminates against them. At least 136 Baha'is were held in Iran's prisons as of May 2014. State authorities also desecrated Baha'i cemeteries, including one in Shiraz which the authorities began excavating in April. Security and intelligence forces also continued to target Christian converts from Islam, Persian-speaking Protestant and evangelical congregations, and members of the home church movement. Many faced charges such as "acting against the national security" and "propaganda against the state."

Authorities restrict political participation and public sector employment of non-Shia Muslim minorities, including Sunnis, who account for about 10 percent of the population. They also prevent Sunnis from constructing their own mosques in Tehran and conducting separate Eid prayers. Government targeting of members of Sufi mystical orders, particularly members of the Nematollahi Gonabadi order, continued. In March, police beat and arrested several demonstrators who gathered outside a judiciary building in Tehran to seek the release of several detained Sufis.

The government restricted cultural as well as political activities among the country's Azeri, Kurdish, Arab, and Baluch minorities. Afghan refugees and migrant workers, estimated at between 2.5 and 3 million, continued to face serious abuses.

Key International Actors

The government continued to block access to Iran by the United Nations special rapporteur on the human rights situation in Iran, Ahmed Shaheed, and other UN rights bodies, but announced in November that they would allow two UN experts to visit the country in 2015. The special rapporteur and other UN officials criticized the "ongoing spike in executions" in Iran and urged the government to impose a moratorium.

Iraq

Human rights conditions in Iraq deteriorated in 2014. Suicide attacks, car bombs, and assassinations became more frequent and lethal, killing more than 12,000 people and injuring more than 22,000 between January and December. Government forces' attacks on largely peaceful demonstrations on December 20, 2013, helped trigger a renewal of armed conflict in Anbar province between local residents, Iraqi security forces, and multiple armed groups. The fighting, which has included indiscriminate attacks by government forces on civilian areas, displaced close to 500,000 people from and within Anbar province between January and September and killed an unknown number of civilians.

The conflict spread north after the extremist group Islamic State, also known as ISIS, took over Mosul, Iraq's second largest city, on June 10. The group has committed numerous atrocities in Iraq, including ongoing car bombings and suicide attacks in civilian areas; summary executions; torture in detention; discrimination against women; forced marriage; sexual assault and slavery of some Yezidi women and girls; destruction of religious property; and killings and kidnappings of members of religious and ethnic minorities –Shia and Yezidis—in Nineveh province.

Government security forces and pro-government militias carried out attacks on civilians in Sunni and mixed Sunni-Shia areas, including kidnapping and summary executions, and were responsible for arbitrary arrests, disappearances, and torture.

In April, in the lead up to parliamentary elections, authorities closed media stations critical of the government and issued mandatory "guidelines" for journalists prohibiting unfavorable coverage of government military and security operations.

Elections on April 30 were largely peaceful but marred by irregularities, including harassment and bribing of voters. Prime Minister Nuri al-Maliki's State of Law coalition won a plurality but Hayder al-Abadi, from the prime minister's party, replaced Maliki as prime minister on September 9 as a result of waning support for Maliki in the aftermath of the loss of Mosul to ISIS. Abadi formed a government on the same day, but was unable to bring parties to agree on the appointment of interior and defense ministers.

On September 14, Abadi order the air force to cease strikes on civilian areas even where ISIS was present, but airstrikes continued in Fallujah and northern Iraq to the end of the year. On September 7, US President Barack Obama authorized US air strikes against ISIS at the request of the Iraqi government. As of December, the US had carried out over 160 air strikes throughout the country.

According to the UN High Commissioner for Refugees, as of September 2014, more than 900,000 Iraqis were internally displaced due to conflict.

Attacks on Civilians

Both government forces and armed groups were responsible for attacks that targeted or indiscriminately harmed civilians.

Indiscriminate air and artillery shelling by government forces killed numerous civilians between February and December. Government forces battling armed groups in Anbar repeatedly struck Fallujah General Hospital with mortar and artillery shells.

Since early May, government forces dropped barrel bombs on residential neighborhoods of Fallujah and surrounding areas, causing civilian casualties and forcing thousands of residents to flee.

Seventeen airstrikes, six of them involving barrel bombs, killed at least 75 people in the first half of July.

Abuses by Security Forces and Government-Backed Militias

In March, former Prime Minister al-Maliki told senior security advisers that he would form a new security force consisting of three militias: Asa'ib, Kita'ib Hezbollah, and the Badr Brigades. These militias kidnapped and murdered Sunni civilians throughout Baghdad, Diyala, and Hilla provinces, at a time when the armed conflict between government forces and Sunni insurgents was intensifying.

According to witnesses and medical and government sources, pro-government militias were responsible for the killing of 61 Sunni men between June 1 and July 9, 2014, and the killing of at least 48 Sunni men in March and April in villages and towns in an area known as the "Baghdad Belt." Dozens of residents of five towns in the Baghdad Belt said that security forces, alongside government-backed militias, attacked their towns, kidnapping and killing residents and setting fire to their homes, livestock, and crops.

A survivor of an attack on a Sunni mosque in eastern Diyala province in August said that members of Asa'ib Ahl al-Haqq entered the mosque during the Friday prayer, shot and killed the imam, and then opened fire on the other men in the mosque, killing at least 70 people. Three other Diyala residents reported that Asa'ib Ahl al-Haqq had kidnapped and killed their relatives.

Iraqi security forces and militias affiliated with the government were responsible for the unlawful execution of at least 255 prisoners in six Iraqi cities and towns in June. The vast majority of security forces and militias are Shia, while the murdered prisoners were Sunni. At least eight of those killed were boys under age 18.

Abuses by Armed Groups

ISIS took over the northern Iraqi city of Mosul on June 10, killing, kidnapping, and threatening civilians, particularly religious and ethnic minorities. It reportedly killed at least 40 Shia Turkmen, including children, and issued orders barring Kurdish, Yazidi and Christian employees from returning to their government jobs. According to Shabak and Shia Turkmen leaders, ISIS killed seven Shabak and at least four of the Turkmen it had taken prisoner.

ISIS summarily executed large numbers of captured Shia security officers. In the largest reported incident, ISIS captured more than a thousand soldiers fleeing Camp Speicher, near Tikrit, then summarily executed at least 800 of them.

Other anti-government Sunni armed groups fighting against the government, including Ba'athists, the Naqshabandi Army, the Islamic Army, Jeish al-Mujahideen, and groups of community-based fighters have also committed abuses against civilians, sometimes fighting alongside ISIS and sometimes against ISIS. In February, fighters from the Military Council, a group of local military leaders, captured and summarily executed 17 SWAT members in Ramadi.

Freedom of Assembly

On December 30, 2013, security forces attacked demonstrators in a public square in Ramadi where Sunnis had gathered every Friday for a year to protest perceived government abuses of the Sunni population. The attack left 17 people dead and helped to trigger renewed conflict in Anbar province that continued throughout the year. The army closed the main eastern, northern, and southern checkpoints to Fallujah, and elsewhere in Anbar, refusing to allow people, medicine, or food to enter or leave the city.

The government failed to investigate the April 23, 2013 attack on a demonstration camp in Hawija in which soldiers, federal police, and SWAT forces fired on a crowd of about 1,000 demonstrators, killing more than 50.

Freedom of Expression

The Committee to Protect Journalists named Iraq the "worst nation" on its 2014 Impunity Index of unsolved journalist murders, noting that a resurgence of armed groups "propelled a spike" in journalist killings.

The government-run Communications and Media Commission issued "mandatory" guidelines on June 18 to regulate media "during the war on terror." Article 1 forbids media from broadcasting or publishing material that "may be interpreted as being against the security forces" and instead requires that they "focus on the security achievements of the armed forces, by repetition throughout the day." This includes "praising the heroic acts of security personnel."

On June 21, the commission wrote to a media outlet that reported critically about the government, warning that "if this kind of broadcasting is repeated" the commission would revoke their license. On June 24, Egypt's broadcast regulator barred two privately owned Iraqi television stations based in Cairo from access to Egypt's main satellite system, after Egyptian officials received complaints from Baghdad about the stations' content. According to a staff member of one of the channels, Al-Baghdadiyya, 16 police officers came to the station's Baghdad office around June 20, beat two guards so badly that they required hospitalization, and confiscated some of the station's equipment.

On June 13, the central and Kurdish regional governments separately blocked social media platforms including Facebook, Twitter, Skype, and YouTube, and in some places tried to block the Internet completely. The government lifted the ban intermittently throughout the rest of the year.

Women's and Girls' Rights

On February 6, Human Rights Watch issued a report documenting how authorities illegally detained women and subjected many to torture and ill-treatment, including sexual abuse. Iraq's judiciary frequently based convictions on coerced confessions and trial proceedings fell far short of international standards, including in cases against women.

Authorities detained many women for months and even years before seeing a judge. Women were frequently detained with their young children, who were deprived of access to education and adequate health care. The government has not investigated these documented allegations of abuse.

On February 25, Iraq's Council of Ministers passed a draft Jaafari Personal Status Law. As of December, parliament had not voted on the discriminatory legislation, which would restrict women's rights in matters of inheritance and parental and other rights after divorce, make it easier for men to take multiple wives, and allow girls to be married from age nine.

Many Iraqi women, having lost their husbands as a result of armed conflict, generalized violence, and displacement, are vulnerable to trafficking for sexual exploitation and prostitution. The parliament passed a counter-trafficking law in April 2012, but authorities have done little to enforce it.

After it took over Mosul, ISIS kidnapped hundreds of Yezidi women and children, and forced some young women and girls to marry its members. The group systematically separated unmarried women and girls as young as 12 from adult relatives. Some women and girls were also subject to sexual assault and slavery. In October, ISIS confirmed that they were enslaving women and attempted to provide religious justification for their actions.

Refugees and Displacement

According to the United Nations High Commissioner for Refugees, Iraq continues to receive large numbers of Syrian refugees, 500,000 since 2011, as well as the return of many Iraqi refugees from Syria. The conflict in Anbar displaced some 500,000 Iraqis. The Iraqi government prevented residents in many parts of Anbar province from leaving areas where fighting is taking place and obstructed humanitarian aid from getting in.

Displaced persons within Iraq in December topped 1.9 million and many reside in squatter settlements without access to necessities such as clean water, electricity, and sanitation, and the government has announced no plan for their return to their homes.

Key International Actors

Despite plentiful evidence that Iraqi security forces systematically abused detainees and indiscriminately attacked civilian areas—abuses that increased in the escalating conflict with ISIS and other armed groups—the US delivered two shipments of weapons, including Hellfire missiles, after Prime Minister al-Maliki visited Washington in December 2013.

On August 7, President Obama authorized military strikes on ISIS forces in Iraq. According to the US Department of Defense, as of September 20 the US had conducted more than 160 strikes near Erbil, Amerli, Sinjar, the Mosul Dam, and Haditha. France, Jordan and the United Arab Emirates all also carried out air strikes, ostensibly against ISIS targets, in September.

US officials have not publicly called on the Iraqi government to investigate abuses committed by security forces and pro-government militia, and has not conditioned military support to Iraq on human rights reforms as required by US law.

On September 1, the UN Human Rights Council requested that the Office of the High Commissioner for Human Rights dispatch a fact-finding committee to investigate violations committed by ISIS and its associates. The council's request failed to include abuses by government forces or its allied militas.

Israel/Palestine

Israel and Hamas committed serious violations of the laws of war during fighting in the Gaza Strip in July and August 2014. At least 2,100 Palestinians were killed, of whom the United Nations identified more than 1,500 as civilians, and approximately 11,000 people, mostly civilians, were injured. The tens of thousands of Israeli attacks caused the vast majority of destruction during the fighting, which left uninhabitable 22,000 homes, displacing 108,000 people, and left hundreds of thousands without adequate water or electricity.

Hamas and Palestinian armed groups in Gaza carried out about 1,700 mortar attacks and 4,800 indiscriminate rocket attacks on Israeli population centers during the fighting. The attacks killed five civilians in Israel, wounded thirty-six, and caused thousands of civilians in communities near Gaza to temporarily leave their homes. Israel's Iron Dome missile defense undoubtedly reduced the possible civilian toll. Sixty-six Israeli soldiers died during the fighting.

Israel and Egypt continued their seven-year blockade of Gaza, which has had a devastating impact on Gaza's economy, infrastructure, and the free flow of people and goods, particularly exports. In September, Israel agreed to allow more imports to Gaza of goods needed for reconstruction, but severe restrictions on exports and travel remain.

Armed groups in Gaza in August summarily executed at least 25 Palestinians whom they accused of collaborating with Israel. Hamas authorities in Gaza conducted arbitrary arrests and tortured detainees. The authorities permitted some local human rights organizations to operate, but suppressed political dissent, freedom of association, and peaceful assembly.

In 2014, Israeli forces killed 43 Palestinians in the West Bank, including East Jerusalem, as of October 31, including unlawful killings of protesters and others who posed no imminent threat to life. Following the June abduction and killing by Palestinian suspects of three Israeli teenagers, Israeli authorities conducted hundreds of apparently arbitrary arrests and punitively destroyed three family homes.

Israeli authorities demolished hundreds of homes under discriminatory policies and practices, forcibly displacing hundreds of Palestinian residents in the West

Bank, including East Jerusalem, as well as Bedouin citizens of Israel. Israeli authorities took inadequate action against Israeli settlers who attacked Palestinians and damaged their property in 307 incidents in 2014 as of December 1, the UN reported. Israel continued to expand unlawful settlements in the occupied West Bank and unlawfully appropriated 400 hectares of land. It also imposed severe restrictions on Palestinians' right to freedom of movement and arbitrarily detained hundreds of Palestinians, including children and peaceful protesters.

In the West Bank, Palestinian Authority (PA) security services beat peaceful demonstrators, detained and harassed journalists, and arbitrarily detained hundreds. Credible allegations of torture of Palestinians by the PA's security services persisted.

Gaza Strip

Israel

The Israel Defense Forces (IDF) launched an aerial offensive in Gaza on July 8, followed by a ground offensive on July 17. A ceasefire agreement was reached on August 26. The UN has identified 538 children among the 1,563 Palestinian civilians it counted as killed.

Among other unlawful attacks, an Israeli attack on July 9 killed nine civilians, including two boys, who had gathered to watch a televised World Cup game in a beach café. An attack on July 16 killed four boys as they played on Gaza City beach. Attacks striking UN schools serving as shelters for displaced people on July 24 and 30 killed 32 people, including 9 children. An August 3 attacker apparently targeting three Palestinian fighters on a motorbike chose to strike as they were just outside a school housing displaced people killed 9 civilians, including 8 children.

Israeli aerial attacks killed two municipal workers cleaning up war damage in the Bureij refugee camp on July 11. In late July, Israeli ground forces in Khuza`a used civilians as human shields, fired at ambulances, and prevented them from reaching the wounded, and shot and killed fleeing civilians.

Israeli military operations severely damaged or destroyed 28 schools, dozens of wells, two major sewage plants, and electricity and other civil infrastructure, according to the UN. Almost all Gaza residents lost access to running water and electricity for days or weeks.

There has been no real accountability for laws of war violations by either side. The Israeli military opened about 100 probes into attacks by its forces in the 2014 fighting and referred 13 cases for criminal investigations, but the nearly complete absence of criminal prosecutions resulting from self-investigations of alleged war crimes committed in Gaza during the fighting in 2008-2009 and 2012 leaves little reason for expecting a different outcome. Hamas took no steps to prosecute Palestinian combatants for indiscriminate and unlawful rocket and mortar attacks at Israeli population centers in 2014 or for prior similar attacks.

In July, the UN Human Rights Council established a Commission of Inquiry to examine alleged laws-of-war violations by all parties to the July-August fighting. In November, Israel stated it would not cooperate with the Commission, alleging it was biased.

Blockade

Israel's continuing blockade of the Gaza Strip amounted to collective punishment of the civilian population. Egypt also blocked all regular movement of goods at the Rafah crossing, and severely restricted the movement of people through the border. More than 80 percent of Gaza's 1.8 million people receive humanitarian assistance, and unemployment had reached 45 percent even before the July-August hostilities in which 128 workshops and businesses were destroyed and another 291 damaged.

Even before the 2014 fighting, Israeli imports to Gaza amounted to a mere 15 percent of 2006 levels (before the blockade). Again, even before the fighting, the blockade had caused a shortage of 71,000 homes and 200 schools in Gaza, according to the UN.

Palestinian armed groups used construction materials, almost certainly imported from Egypt, to build tunnels they used to launch attacks in Israel. To prevent military use of concrete and steel bars, Israel and the Palestinian Authority agreed to a monitoring mechanism for imports of the materials. By December, imported materials fell drastically below the levels needed to rebuild civilian homes and infrastructure destroyed during the summer fighting. Israel maintained restrictions on commercial exports from Gaza without a similar security rationale with severe economic consequences.

After taking power in July 2013, Egypt's military-backed government tightened restrictions on the movement of Palestinians between Gaza and Sinai, cutting the number of Gaza residents passing through the crossing by two-thirds, to an average of 6,444 per month in the first half of 2014. Egypt did not permit regular imports or exports of goods through Rafah. After an October attack by an armed group killed 30 security forces north of the Sinai town of al-Arish, Egypt further restricted border-crossings.

"No-Go" Zones

Before the July-August fighting, Israeli forces continued to shoot at Palestinian civilians in the Israeli-declared "no-go" zone inside Gaza's northern and eastern borders and more than six nautical miles from Gaza's shore. In the first half of 2014, Israeli forces killed four Palestinian civilians and wounded 87 at distances up to 500 meters inside Gaza, the UN reported.

Following the August 26 ceasefire, Israel eased its restrictions on Palestinian fishermen, allowing them to fish up to six, rather than three, nautical miles from shore. The closures still prohibited access to 70 percent of Gaza's maritime area as recognized under international law. In the first six months of 2014, Israeli naval forces shot at or otherwise used force against fishermen 181 times, and wounded eight, according to the UN.

Hamas and Palestinian Armed Groups

Palestinian armed groups launched more than 5,000 rockets and mortars into Israel, killing 5 civilians, including 370 rockets before the escalation of fighting on July 8, repeatedly forcing civilians in cities throughout Israel to seek protection in shelters. The rockets launched by armed groups in Gaza cannot be accurately aimed at military objectives and amount to indiscriminate or deliberate attacks on civilians when directed at Israeli population centers, in violation of the laws of war.

During the July-August fighting, the UN Relief and Works Agency for Palestine Refugees (UNRWA) discovered that Palestinian armed groups had stored rockets in three vacant schools run by UNWRA. Palestinian fighters endangered civilians by launching rockets from populated areas.

On August 21-23, Palestinian armed groups, most likely acting with Hamas's approval, summarily executed 25 men in public who were accused of collaborating with Israel. Armed groups took at least 16 of the men from Hamas-controlled prisons.

Hamas took no apparent steps to arrest or prosecute those responsible.

The Internal Security Agency and Hamas police in Gaza tortured or ill-treated 338 people as of October 31, according to complaints received by the Independent Commission for Human Rights (ICHR), a Palestinian rights body.

Hamas security forces arbitrarily detained civil society activists, university professors, and members of the rival Fatah political faction.

West Bank

Israel

Israeli security forces fatally shot at least 43 Palestinian civilians, including 11 children, in the West Bank as of October 31, many in circumstances that suggest the killings were unlawful. In May, Israeli forces killed Nadim Nuwarah, 17, and Muhammad Abu Thahr, 16, during a Palestinian protest near Ofer, an Israeli military base and prison in the West Bank. Videos showed that at the time he was killed neither of the boys was throwing stones or posed any imminent threat to life. In November, Israeli police arrested a Border Police official suspected of killing Nuwarah unlawfully.

Most of the killings occurred after June 11, when the Israeli military undertook operations in response to the abduction and killing of three Israeli teenagers by Palestinian suspects in the West Bank. Israeli forces conducted more than 1,200 raids on homes, offices, and businesses, often destroying personal property, and arrested more than 500 people, many allegedly Hamas supporters. The men were allegedly Hamas members, though there was no public evidence that Hamas ordered the killings; the group praised the abduction but denied responsibility for the teenagers' murders.

Israeli forces used excessive force responding to protests by Palestinian residents of East Jerusalem after a group of Israelis abducted and burned alive a Palestinian teenager in reprisal for the killing of the three Israeli teens. Undercover Israeli forces arrested and beat unconscious the murdered Palestinian's cousin, a United States citizen, and later raided his uncle's home and arrested him and other relatives, without apparent justification. In August, Israeli forces punitively demolished the Hebron-area family homes of three men suspected in the Israeli teens' killing. In November, Israel punitively demolished the family home of an East Jerusalem man who in October drove his car into a crowded light rail station, killing an infant girl and a 22-year-old woman.

In August, Israeli forces killed three men, including Hashem Abu Maria, who worked with Defense for Children International–Palestine, after a protest in Beit Ummar. None of the men posed an imminent threat to life at the time of their killing.

Israeli authorities failed to take adequate action against Israeli settlers who injured Palestinians and destroyed or damaged Palestinian mosques, homes, schools, cars, and other property. As of October 31, the UN reported 296 such attacks in 2014, including 117 in which Palestinians were injured.

Settlement Building and Discriminatory Home Demolitions

In September, Israel declared 400 hectares of the West Bank "state land," a move settler leaders praised as paving the way for the construction of a large new settlement in the area. Construction work began on 507 settlement housing units during the first half of 2014, a decrease from the 1,807 begun during the same period in 2013, according to Israel's Central Bureau of Statistics.

As of December 1, Israeli authorities demolished 552 Palestinian homes and other buildings in the West Bank (including East Jerusalem), displacing 1,170 people. Building permits are difficult or impossible for Palestinians to obtain in East Jerusalem or in the 61 percent of the West Bank under exclusive Israeli control (Area C), whereas a separate planning process readily grants settlers new construction permits in those areas.

Freedom of Movement

Israel maintained onerous restrictions on the movement of Palestinians in the West Bank, including checkpoints and the separation barrier. Settlement-related movement restrictions forced Palestinians to take time-consuming detours and restricted their access to agricultural land.

In one week in May, Israeli forces twice evicted all 62 residents of a Bedouin community, Humsaal-Buqai'a, from their homes to allow "military training" exercises lasting several hours, the UN reported. Israeli forces had displaced residents 14 times since 2012.

Israel continued construction of the separation barrier around East Jerusalem. Some 85 percent of the barrier's route falls within the West Bank rather than along the Green Line marking the pre-1967 border. The barrier separates Palestinian farmers in 150 communities on the eastern side of the barrier from their lands on the western side, the UN reported.

Arbitrary Detention and Detention of Children

Israeli security forces continued to arrest children suspected of criminal offenses, usually stone-throwing, in their homes at night, at gunpoint; question them without a family member or lawyer present; and coerce them to sign confessions in Hebrew, which they do not understand. As of October 31, 163 Palestinian children were in Israeli detention.

As of October 31, Israel held 457 Palestinian administrative detainees without charge or trial, based on secret evidence. Israeli prison authorities shackled hospitalized Palestinians to their hospital beds after they went on long-term hunger strikes to protest their administrative detention.

Palestinian Authority (PA)

Complaints of torture and ill-treatment by West Bank PA security services persisted. The ICHR reported 108 complaints as of October 31.

In April, PA security forces violently dispersed and arbitrarily detained peaceful protesters in Ramallah. The PA continued to ban the distribution of two pro-Hamas weekly newspapers in the West Bank.

Palestinian courts did not find any West Bank security officers responsible for torture, arbitrary detention, or prior cases of unlawful deaths in custody.

Attacks by Palestinian civilians injured 61 Israeli settlers in the West Bank as of October 31, the UN reported. In addition to the three Israeli teenagers who were killed in June, nine Israeli civilians were killed by Palestinians from August to December, including four men and a police officer killed during an attack in a Jerusalem synagogue for which the Abu Ali Mustafa Brigades, a Palestinian armed group, claimed responsibility.

Palestinian governing authorities in the West Bank, as well as in Gaza, delegated jurisdiction over personal status matters such as marriage and divorce to religious courts. In practice, women seeking marriage and divorce suffered discrimination. Courts required Muslim women to obtain a male relative's consent to marry and to obtain the husband's consent to divorce except in limited cases.

Israel

Bedouin citizens of Israel who live in "unrecognized" villages suffered discriminatory home demolitions on grounds that their homes were built illegally. Israeli authorities refused to prepare plans for the communities or approve construction permits, and rejected plans submitted by the communities themselves, but retroactively legalized Jewish-owned private farms and planned new Jewish communities in the same areas. The Supreme Court rejected a petition for the state to provide "unrecognized" villages with greater security, such as bomb shelters or coverage by Israel's "Iron Dome" anti-rocket system, after rockets from Gaza killed a man and severely wounded three children in Bedouin villages in July.

As of June 1, according to the Israeli Bedouin rights group Dukium, Israeli authorities carried out 52 demolitions of Bedouin homes and property, including ploughing up crops and demolishing protest tents in the village of al-Arakib, where residential structures had been destroyed 64 times, as well as the village's cemetery.

Many of the estimated 200,000 migrant workers in Israel continued to be excluded in practice from rights afforded to other workers, such as paid overtime, under Israel's Work Hours and Rest Law. From 2008 to 2013, 122 Thai migrant workers in the agricultural sector died in Israel, including 43 from "sudden noc-

turnal death syndrome," which affects young and healthy Asian men, and 22 for unknown reasons because police did not request a post-mortem, according to government figures.

Government policies restrict migrant workers from forming families by deporting migrants who marry other migrants while in Israel, or who have children there.

Around 60,000 African migrants and asylum seekers entered Israel irregularly from Egypt since 2005, before Israel completed construction of a fence along its border with Egypt, which prevented any new arrivals in 2014. Israel continued to deny asylum seekers who entered the country irregularly the right to a fair asylum process and detained around 2,500 people, primarily Eritrean and Sudanese nationals. From 2013 through August 2014, some 8,000 Eritreans and Sudanese under indefinite detention or the threat of indefinite detention "chose" to leave Israel.

Israel continued to delegate jurisdiction over marriage, divorce, and some other aspects of personal status to Jewish, Muslim, Christian, and Druze religious courts. In practice, women seeking divorces suffered discrimination, such as refusal of divorce by state-funded Jewish religious courts without the husband's consent in up to 3,400 cases per year, according to women's rights groups. The government did not publish data on spouses denied divorce, but women were reportedly the vast majority.

Key International Actors

Palestine ratified core international human rights treaties, the Geneva Conventions, and other treaties in April, following the collapse of US-sponsored peace talks with Israel in the same month. Palestinian President Mahmoud Abbas took no serious steps to obtain the jurisdiction of the International Criminal Court for grave crimes in the West Bank and Gaza. Israel, the US, and European states pressured Abbas not to take such steps. Sweden recognized Palestine as a state in its bilateral relations.

In October, international donors allocated about half of pledges totaling $5.4 billion to humanitarian assistance to Gaza. Economists estimated the damage from the fighting at more than $5 billion.

The US allocated a total of $4.1 billion in military aid to Israel in 2014, including $1 billion in funding for anti-rocket and missile-defense systems, and $440 million in assistance to Palestinian security forces and economic support to the PA.

The EU allocated €130 million ($160 million) in direct financial support to the PA and €450 million ($555 million) in development and security sector support to the Palestinian territory for 2014.

The EU in 2013 signed a memorandum of understanding with Israel that ensured that no EU research and development funding would support Israeli settlement businesses or activities. In 2014, it indicated it would ban some Israeli agricultural imports unless Israel distinguished them from settlement products. Several European government-run pension funds divested from Israeli businesses they deemed to contribute to or benefit from unlawful Israeli practices in occupied Palestinian territory.

Jordan

Jordan hosted over 618,000 Syrian refugees in 2014, although the authorities tightened entry restrictions and limited new refugee arrivals. The authorities refused entry to all Palestinian refugees escaping Syria and detained and forcibly deported dozens of those who entered the country irregularly. The government amended the State Security Court law to restrict the court's jurisdiction to five crimes, and broadened the anti-terrorism law to include provisions that threaten freedom of expression.

Freedom of Expression and Belief

Jordanian law criminalizes speech deemed critical of the king, government officials, and institutions, as well as Islam and speech considered defamatory of others. In 2014, the authorities failed to amend the penal code to bring it into compliance with constitutional free speech guarantees strengthened in 2011, and continued to prosecute individuals on charges such as "insulting an official body," using vaguely worded penal code articles that place impermissible restrictions on free expression.

In June, Jordan issued amendments to its 2006 Anti-Terrorism Law that broaden the definition of terrorism and include acts such as "disturbing [Jordan's] relations with a foreign state," a charge already criminalized in the penal code that is regularly used to punish peaceful criticism of foreign countries or their rulers. The amendments remove the requirement of a connection to an act of violence, instead including a vague definition that references acts that "sow discord" or "disturb public order."

Pursuant to 2012 amendments to the Press and Publications Law, Jordan's Media Commission continued to censor independent news websites that failed to obtain registration from the commission. On June 30, the Media Commission blocked nine news websites, including an alternate domain name set up by citizen journalism website *7iber*, whose website authorities first blocked in June 2013. Some news websites such as *7iber* refused to register in protest against the onerous press law requirements and to preserve their independence.

On June 6, police raided the headquarters of al-Abbasiya TV, an Amman-based Iraqi opposition television channel, arresting 13 staff members, but later released them without charge.

On August 17, police arrested Abd al-Hadi al-Majali, a columnist for the government-owned *Al-Ra'i* newspaper, after a he wrote a Facebook post that criticized security officials and cursed the country. An Amman court released him on bail August 24, but he faces trial on the charge of "disclosing state secrets" (penal code article 355).

In January, a court convicted four students from Al al-Bayt University in Mafraq on the charge of "insulting a religious symbol" and sentenced them to one month in prison. Prosecutors alleged that their style of dress and musical tastes indicated that they were "devil worshippers."

Freedom of Association and Assembly

Since the amended Public Gatherings Law took effect in March 2011, Jordanians no longer require government permission to hold public meetings or demonstrations. However, Amman hotels and other venues continued to seek the General Intelligence Directorate's permission to host public meetings and events.

The State Security Court delivered judgments in cases against political activists and demonstrators arising from protests in 2011 and 2012. In most cases, the court threw out the charge "undermining the political regime," a terrorism charge under the penal code, and issued convictions on lesser charges carrying three-month jail sentences, which can be substituted with a fine under Jordanian law.

In January, the government amended the State Security Court law to restrict the court's jurisdiction to terrorism, espionage, treason, money counterfeiting, and drugs offences. This would bring the court into compliance with article 101 of the constitution, which allows military judges to try civilians only for these five groups of crimes; however, as the penal code classifies vaguely worded offenses such as "undermining the political regime" as terrorism, the court will still be able to try peaceful protesters and others on such charges.

Refugees and Migrants

By November, over 618,000 persons from Syria had sought refuge in Jordan since 2011, according to the United Nations High Commissioner for Refugees (UNHCR). Of these, approximately 81,000 were housed at the Zaatari Refugee Camp in northern Jordan, down from over 200,000 in 2013, and 3,900 others were at the Emirates-Jordan camp in Zarqa Governorate. The remaining refugees were living outside the camps. In April, Jordan opened a new camp for Syrian refugees near al-Azraq, around 100 kilometers east of Amman, where authorities began placing newly arrived Syrian refugees. When completed, the camp will have the capacity to host 130,000 refugees, though by November only 11,700 were residing in the camp.

In 2014, Jordanian security forces continued to turn away Palestinian refugees seeking to enter Jordan from Syria at the country's borders. Security forces also detained and deported Palestinians who entered at unofficial border crossings using forged Syrian identity documents, or who entered illegally via smuggling networks. Officially, Jordan allowed Palestinians from Syria who hold Jordanian citizenship to enter, but in practice Jordan denied entry to such Palestinians whose Jordanian documents had expired, in some cases arbitrarily stripping them of their Jordanian citizenship and forcibly returning them to Syria.

In 2014, the International Labour Organization (ILO) issued two reports highlighting the prevalence of child labor in Jordan, and Jordan's Ministry of Labor reported that the number of Syrian refugee child laborers had doubled over the previous year, up to 60,000.

Jordan hosted over 70,000 migrant domestic workers in 2014, mostly from the Philippines, Sri Lanka, and Indonesia. Nongovernmental organizations repeatedly referred domestic workers who had suffered multiple abuses to labor ministry investigators who, however, rarely classified them as victims of the crime of trafficking. Instead, they treated each aspect of abuse such as non-payment of salaries separately, sometimes even detaining workers for "escaping" employers.

Women's and Girls' Rights

Jordan's personal status code remains discriminatory despite a 2010 amendment, which included widening women's access to divorce and child custody. Marriages between Muslim women and non-Muslims, for instance, are not recognized.

Article 9 of Jordan's nationality law does not allow Jordanian women married to foreign-born spouses to pass on their nationality to their spouse and children. In November, the cabinet said it would direct government ministries to grant special privileges to non-citizen children of Jordanian women, including free education and access to health services in government institutions. The privileges, however, do not apply to children whose mothers have not resided in Jordan for a minimum of five years, and do not guarantee residency permits.

Despite a minimum age of marriage set at 18, child marriage continued in Jordan, including in the Syrian refugee community.

Penal code articles 98 and 340, which allow reduced sentences for perpetrators of "honor crimes," remained in force. News reports indicated that at least 10 women and girls were killed by male family members in 2014, including Batool Haddad, a Christian-born woman whose father and brother killed her after she converted to Islam.

Torture, Police Violence, and Administrative Detention

Perpetrators of torture or other ill-treatment continued to enjoy near-total impunity due to the authorities' reliance on special police prosecutors and judges to investigate allegations against, prosecute, and try fellow officers. At the Police Court, where many such cases are heard, two out of three sitting judges are serving police officers appointed by the police. To date, no police or intelligence officer has ever been convicted of torture under article 208 of the penal code.

In June, the State Security court exonerated prominent Salafi cleric Omar Uthman, known as Abu Qatada, of terrorism charges stemming from a 1998 plot to bomb several targets in Amman, including an American school. During the proceedings the court admitted into evidence a confession allegedly obtained through torture in contravention of a treaty it signed with the United Kingdom stating that such confessions could not be admitted into the record without prior justification. In September, the court exonerated Abu Qatada on all charges stemming from a second separate terrorism plot and released him.

The authorities failed to investigate credible allegations of excessive use of force by police while dispersing protests. Eight journalists reported that riot police beat them as they covered the dispersal of a July 9 protest near the Israeli embassy in Amman calling for the expulsion of the Israeli ambassador over Israeli airstrikes on Gaza. The Public Security Directorate announced an independent investigation, bypassing the normal complaint procedure, but its outcome was unknown at time of writing.

Local governors continued to use provisions of the Crime Prevention Law of 1954 to place individuals in administrative detention for up to one year in circumvention of the Criminal Procedure Law.

Key International Actors

In February, the United States announced the renewal of a five-year aid package to Jordan through 2019, which provides a minimum of US$360 million in economic assistance, and $300 million in foreign military financing annually. The US granted an additional $340 million in 2014 for "costs related to instability in the region, including for security requirements along the border with Iraq." The US did not publicly criticize human rights violations in Jordan in 2014 except in annual reports.

The European Union continued to disperse funds from a 2012 pledge of 230.9 million Euros ($298 million) to Jordan for refugee support.

In May, Saudi Arabia announced three memorandums of understanding with Jordan to finance development projects worth $232 million.

Kazakhstan

Kazakhstan heavily restricts freedom of assembly, speech, and religion. In 2014, authorities closed newspapers, jailed or fined dozens of people after peaceful but unsanctioned protests, and fined or detained worshipers for practicing religion outside state controls. Government critics, including opposition leader Vladimir Kozlov, remained in detention after unfair trials.

In mid-2014, Kazakhstan adopted new criminal, criminal executive, criminal procedural, and administrative codes, and a new law on trade unions, which contain articles restricting fundamental freedoms and are incompatible with international standards. Torture remains common in places of detention.

Legal Reforms

Rights groups, diplomats, and international bodies raised concerns that the criminal and administrative codes that Kazakhstan adopted contain key articles that would restrict fundamental speech, assembly, association, and religious freedoms.

In July, the European Union, United States, and United Kingdom issued statements of concern, saying the codes could "negatively affect" or "limit" fundamental freedoms. Human rights groups called President Nursultan Nazarbaev to veto the bills.

Civil Society

Civil society activist Vadim Kuramshin continues to serve a 12-year prison sentence, despite procedural violations during his trial and concerns that his sentencing in December 2012 was retribution for public criticism of the government. Kuramshin staged a short hunger strike in June to demand medical attention and transfer to a different colony, alleging other inmates beat and harassed him.

On November 19, labor activist Rosa Tuletaeva was released on parole from the penal colony where she had been serving her five-year prison sentence. In March, labor activist Maksat Dosmagambetov, who is serving a six-year sentence, was transferred to a penal colony, affording him more freedoms than a prison. Dosmagambetov underwent an operation in 2014 to remove a tumor in his cheekbone that developed after he was imprisoned.

In March, political opposition leader Vladimir Kozlov was transferred from a prison in north Kazakhstan to one outside Almaty, close to his residence. In May, an Almaty court upheld orders to confiscate Kozlov's apartment, where his wife and infant son were living, despite legislation preventing the confiscation of a person's sole property.

On July 2, authorities detained Zinaida Mukhortova, a lawyer, after Kazakhstan's Supreme Court upheld a ruling to put her in involuntary psychiatric detention. Mukhortova has been repeatedly subject to forced psychiatric detention since 2009, when she alleged a member of parliament from the ruling party interfered in a civil case in which she was involved. On September 18, the United States called on Kazakhstan to immediately release Mukhortova.

After a January court ruling to extradite Mukhtar Ablyazov to Russia and Ukraine was annulled, another French court in September again ruled to extradite Mukhtar Ablyazov to both countries. His lawyers have challenged the decision, but at time of writing, his case had not been reviewed. In December 2013, six months after they were forcibly taken to Kazakhstan, Ablyazov's wife and daughter were permitted to return to Italy, where they were granted asylum.

On March 11, financial police searched the office of Aman Saulyk, a health and human rights group, and confiscated equipment in connection with a criminal investigation into allegations of "use of funds obtained through illegal means."

Freedom of Expression

Despite widespread calls to decriminalize libel and amend the overbroad criminal offense of "inciting social, national, clan, racial, or religious discord," authorities increased sanctions for these offenses in the new criminal code. The government also adopted implementing legislation in January that excessively restricts freedom of expression during states of emergency. In April, the government also introduced criminal charges for "spreading false information."

Independent and opposition media continued to face harassment and interference in their work. In April, police tried to block journalists from covering a protest outside the Prosecutor General's office in Astana. A Radio Free

Liberty/Radio Europe journalist was jailed for four days on hooliganism charges after covering an anti-Eurasian Economic Union meeting in May.

Media watchdog AdilSoz reported an increase in civil and criminal defamation cases in the first half of 2014, including cases against Internet project *Insiderman* Editor-in-Chief Valeriy Surganov, and former *Assandi Times* journalist Natalya Sadykova.

Courts closed the newspaper *Pravdivaya Gazeta* in February and the *Assandi Times* in April. The Organization for Security and Cooperation in Europe (OSCE) Media Freedom Representative Dunja Mijatovi described the closure of *Pravdivaya Gazeta* as "curb[ing] media pluralism."

Websites, including LiveJournal.com, were blocked at times in 2014. At time of writing, the criminal case against Aleksandr Kharlamov, a journalist, for "inciting religious discord" remained open, although he was released from pretrial detention in 2013.

In a ruling that chills freedom of expression and condones homophobia, an Almaty court in late October awarded 34 million tenge (US$187,000) in damages against Havas Worldwide Kazakhstan, an advertising agency, for a poster featuring Kazakh composer Sagyrbauly Kurmangazy kissing Russian poet Aleksander Pushkin. In September, the agency had been separatelyfined 314 thousand tenge ($1,730) after a court found the same poster "unethnical."

Torture

National Preventative Mechanism Coordination Council monitors began detention visits in 2014. Some police officers faced charges of torture, but impunity remains the norm. According to media reports, on several occasions in 2014, detainees' relatives publicly raised concerns about mass beatings and ill-treatment in detention. At its November review of Kazakhstan,the United Nations Committee Against Torture (CAT) expressed concern about the gap between law and practice and continued impunity for torture.

The committee found Kazakhstan responsible for torture and failure to investigate in the cases of Oleg Evloev in November 2013 and Rasim Bairamov in May 2014. In both cases, the committee urged Kazakhstan to investigate the complainant's allegations, provide redress, and ensure full and adequate reparation.

On July 30, the Prosecutor's Office opened a criminal case into Bairamov's torture allegations.

Mukhtar Dzhakishev, the former president of the state-owned nuclear company imprisoned on embezzlement and fraud charges, alleged that prison officials beat him after his transfer to a penal colony in February. Authorities denied the allegations. In March, the UN Human Rights Committee requested that Kazakhstan "take all necessary measures to protect Mr. Dzhakishev's health."

Freedom of Religion

Minority religious groups continued to be subjected to fines and short-term detention in 2014 for violating a restrictive religion law. According to Forum18, a religious freedom watchdog, as of July, 12 people had been jailed and over 45 people fined. In July, an Almaty court imprisoned five men for up to seven-and-a-half years in connection with their membership in the banned religious organization Hizb ut-Tahrir.

In February, an Astana court released Protestant pastor Bakhytzhan Kashkumbaev after handing him a four-year suspended sentence for "intentionally inflicting grievous bodily harm" on a congregation member.

On April 4, after his mission to Kazakhstan, the UN special rapporteur on freedom of religion recommended "far-reaching reforms" to the 2011 religion law, finding, for example, that "non-registered religious communities ... suffer from serious infringements of their freedom of religion."

Freedom of Assembly

Authorities took no steps to amend a restrictive law on public assemblies and throughout 2014 detained and fined people for organizing or participating in peaceful protests. In February, for example, police in Almaty broke up small-scale protests, including a one-person protest by an Almaty-based blogger.On September 26, police broke up a four-person protest against a Baikonur rocket launch outside the Russian embassy in Astana. The participants were later fined.

In 2014, the rights group Ar.Rukh.Khak filed 32 individual complaints with the UN Human Rights Committee concerning violations of the right to peaceful assembly in Kazakhstan. At time of writing, 11 of the complaints had been regis-tered for consideration by the Human Rights Committee.

Labor Rights

In June, Kazakhstan adopted a new restrictive law on trade unions despite re-peated calls by independent unions to amend the draft to bring it in line with in-ternational human and labor rights standards. In addition, provisions in the new criminal code further limit workers' right to strike. One such provision is the in-troduction of criminal sanctions for calling on workers to continue a strike de-clared illegal by courts.

Other legislation governing the organization, financing, and collective bargain-ing rights of trade unions remain restrictive. In some instances, authorities inter-fered in independent trade union activity. For example, the Almaty-based independent union of journalists has repeatedly been denied registration on technical grounds, most recently in November 2014.

Sexual Orientation and Gender Identity

In late 2013 and again in early 2014, several parliamentarians called for the adoption of legislation banning propaganda of homosexuality. At time of writing, no bill had been proposed for consideration.

Key International Actors

In March 2014, a European Parliament resolution noted that "the human rights situation in [Kazakhstan] has deteriorated" since the violent end to extended labor strikes in Zhanaozen in December 2011. In October, the leaders of the EU and Kazakhstan announced the completion of the negotiations for an Enhanced Partnership and Cooperation Agreement. The EU failed to use the negotiations to secure human rights reforms despite pledges to that effect made previously by then-foreign affairs chief Catherine Ashton, and as called for in EP resolutions.

The United States remains largely muted on human rights concerns in Kaza-khstan. Public comments by Assistant Secretary of State Nisha Biswal in April and Deputy Secretary of State William J. Burns in May focused on security, commercial, and energy aspects of the bilateral relationship and its role in support of the US mission in Afghanistan.

In October, Kazakhstan underwent its second Universal Periodic Review at the UN Human Rights Council. Kazakhstan accepted a number of recommendations, including to abolish the death penalty, but rejected others, including to review the religion law, amend the trade union law, release Zinaida Mukhortova, decriminalize defamation, and remove restrictions on freedom of assembly.

In its March concluding observations, the UN Committee on Elimination of All Forms of Discrimination Against Women called on Kazakhstan to ensure effective investigations into complaints of violence against women and appropriate sanctions for perpetrators.

In March, the UN Committee on the Elimination of Racial Discrimination urged Kazakhstan to continue efforts to adopt a comprehensive anti-discrimination law; expressed concern about "the overly broad" charge of "inciting social, national, clan, racial, or religious discord," saying it could "lead to unnecessary or disproportionate interference with freedom of expression"; and called on Kazakhstan to "clearly define" the offense.

Kenya

Kenya's efforts to tackle a wide array of security threats have been marred by on-going patterns of serious human rights violations by Kenyan security forces, including extrajudicial killings, arbitrary detentions, and torture. Despite evidence of these abuses, the government rarely investigates or prosecutes abusive security officers.

The government has been slow in implementing key reforms that were identified in 2008 as crucial to addressing Kenya's political crisis , including land and accountability, and security sector reforms. There has been no tangible progress on accountability for crimes committed during the post-elections violence of 2007-8, which left at least 1,100 dead and 650,000 displaced. President Uhuru Kenyatta, his deputy William Ruto, and journalist Joshua arap Sang faced charges at the International Criminal Court (ICC) for their role in the violence; in early December, the charges against President Uhuru Kenyatta were dropped, amid concerns over widespread intimidation of witnesses.

The government signaled its intention to introduce new restrictions on non-governmental organizations (NGOs) and passed a law that increases the executive branch's control over the police service. Human rights activists and civil society groups reported harassment and threats for their work on justice and accountability.

Abuses by Government Security Forces

Kenyan security forces conducted several abusive counterterrorism operations in Nairobi, on the coast, and in North Eastern region in 2014 following attacks and intercommunal clashes. The operations largely targeted ethnic Somali and Muslim communities.

During the Usalama Watch operation in Nairobi and Mombasa in April, security officers from multiple agencies raided homes, buildings, and shops, carting away money, cell phones, and other goods. They harassed and detained thousands—including journalists, refugees, Kenyan citizens, and international aid workers—without charge, and in appalling conditions for periods well beyond the 24-hour legal limit.

Various police units have also been implicated in the torture, disappearance, and unlawful killing of alleged terrorism suspects and individuals of Somali origin, Somali refugees, and Muslims in Mombasa, Nairobi, North Eastern region, and other parts of the country.

In August, Human Rights Watch found evidence of at least 10 cases of extrajudicial killings of terrorism suspects by the Anti Terrorism Police Unit (ATPU). Some of the victims who were last seen in ATPU custody, had been threatened by the unit's officers after being released by courts, or had received death threats from ATPU officers they recognized.

Suspects were shot dead in public places, abducted from vehicles and courtrooms, severely beaten during arrest, detained in isolated blocks, and denied contact with their families or access to lawyers. In some cases, members of the anti-riot forces known as the General Service Unit (GSU), military intelligence, and National Intelligence Service (NIS) were also implicated in abuses alongside the ATPU.

Kenyan police have been implicated in hundreds of extrajudicial killings over the past six years, but police have frequently failed to make a report to the Independent Police Oversight Authority (IPOA), a civilian oversight authority, a legal requirement that facilitates investigations.

IPOA has made some progress since it was founded three years ago: it charged a police officer in Nairobi in September for the extrajudicial killing of two brothers who allegedly engaged in criminal activities, and, in August 2014, successfully went to court to nullify a nationwide police recruitment exercise over widespread and systematic corruption.

Lack of Accountability

Accountability mechanisms introduced under the 2010 constitution remain weak and have not been adequately supported by the executive arm of government. For example, although the IPOA issued a public report about the Usalama Watch operation describing 29 complaints of police abuses, those responsible have not been disciplined or prosecuted.

Authorities have rarely investigated or prosecuted police officers, including members of the APTU, alleged to be responsible for killings. A spate of brutal gang attacks on villages in Bungoma and Busia counties in March 2013 left 10 people dead and over 100 seriously wounded. The violence, which marred the national elections and pointed to the government's failure to dismantle criminal gangs often linked to political actors, has gone unpunished.

The response to major incidents such as the September 2013 attack on Nairobi's upscale Westgate mall, which left 67 people dead, has been poor, with authorities failing to follow up on the promise to investigate security lapses and the botched security force response that saw officers from different agencies shooting at each other during the terrorist attack.

The government has made no progress regarding accountability for the post-election violence of 2007-2008. At time of writing, President Kenyatta, his deputy William Ruto, and former radio journalist Joshua arap Sang faced charges of crimes against humanity at the ICC for their alleged roles in the violence.

While Ruto and Sang's trial began in September 2013, Kenyatta's trial has been postponed several times and had yet to start at time of writing, due to witness withdrawals and lack of cooperation from the Kenya government.

Treatment of Refugees

Following a series of grenade and gun attacks in Nairobi's Eastleigh neighborhood and Mombasa in March that killed 12 people and injured 8 others, Kenyan police responded in April and May with widespread abuses, including round ups, torture, detentions of at least 4,000 people, extortion, deportations, and beatings of mainly ethnic Somali Kenyans and Somali refugees.

Kenyan authorities deported 359 Somali and other nationals, including at least three registered refugees, in April and May. The authorities did not allow United Nations or other independent organizations to monitor the screening process, carried out at Nairobi's Kasarani stadium, or challenge deportations to conflict-ridden Somalia.

Detainees were beaten and held in appalling conditions. In Eastleigh's Pangani station, hundreds of detainees were packed into cells designed for just 20 people. Detainees had no room to sit; cells were filthy with urine and excrement. Police also held detainees beyond the 24-hour limit proscribed under Kenyan law, without taking them to court.

The operation followed a March 2014 government directive ordering urban refugees to relocate to the overcrowded refugee camps. In July 2013, the High Court had ruled that an almost identical encampment order violated refugees' freedom of movement and right to dignity as enshrined in the Kenyan constitution. But in June, the High Court upheld the reissued directive, and expressed no concern that it would violate these same fundamental rights and freedoms, although the factual situation remained the same.

Civil Society and Human Rights Defenders

Since early 2013, civil society groups advocating for justice for the victims of 2007-2008 post-election violence and victims of police extrajudicial killings have faced increasing pressure from government and security officials.

During their 2013 election campaign on the Jubilee party ticket, Kenyatta and Ruto accused civil society actors and human rights defenders of serving foreign interests by supporting the ICC. The Jubilee manifesto proposed restricting NGO funding from foreign sources, and the government has since introduced amendments to the Public Benefits Organizations (PBO) Act, 2013, seeking to increase government control over the public benefits authority.

Incidents of intimidation and harassment of NGOs, activists, and perceived witnesses for the ICC increased in 2014. In March, police stopped a meeting of a media NGO with Nakuru residents, arrested and detained the NGO officials and participants briefly, and questioned them on whether the meeting was about the ICC.

On November 24, 2013, the Uasin Gishu county deputy governor stopped a meeting in Eldoret convened by a peace and security NGO. In December 2013, one former and one current official of Muslims for Human Rights (MUHURI) received death threats following the release of the organization's joint report with Open Society Justice Initiative on extrajudicial killing and disappearance of terrorism suspects by Kenyan security forces.

Sexual Orientation and Gender Identity

Existing Kenyan law criminalizes same-sex conduct with up to 14 years' imprisonment. In the coastal county of Mombasa, the municipal by-laws provide further criminal sanctions against "homosexuality." These criminal sanctions against same-sex conduct exacerbate abuses by police and other state agents, who subject LGBTI persons to harassment, extortion, arbitrary arrest and detention without charge or on trumped up charges, denial of services, sexual assault, and rape.

Although these laws are rarely enforced, Kenya's LGBT community continue to experience intolerance and discrimination from members of the community, religious leaders, and politicians. In August, the Republican Liberty Party sought to introduce a law banning all forms of same-sex conduct with maximum sentences of life imprisonment and death by stoning for "homosexuality" and "aggravated homosexuality" respectively. The bill was before the Parliamentary Committee on Justice and Legal affairs for review pending tabling before the house for debate.

Key International Actors

Kenya's relations with some European nations deteriorated in 2014, but Western governments have refrained from clear, public backing for accountability. In 2013, Kenyatta responded to Western criticism of Kenya's lack of accountability by warming up to Russia and China. The Kenyatta administration improved trade ties with these two nations, and in late 2013, Kenya signed a loan agreement worth US$5 billion with China.

Kenyatta visited the United Kingdom in 2013 and the United States in August and September 2014 during the US-Africa Summit and the UN General Assembly. During the US-Africa Summit, the US government announced a Security Governance Initiative (SGI) of up to $65 million that would benefit six African countries, including Kenya.

The Kenyatta adminsitration said Kenya would prioritize relations with African nations, following attempts to seek African Union's (AU) backing for Kenya's anti-ICC campaigns. In 2013, the AU passed a resolution calling for sitting heads of state to have immunity from prosecution before international courts, urging the Kenyan president not to appear before the ICC. In July 2014, the AU approved immunity for some senior officials in a newly adopted protocol to extend the jurisdiction of the African Court of Justice and Human Rights to trials of international crimes.

Kuwait

The government aggressively cracked down on free speech throughout 2014, using provisions in the constitution, the national security law, and other legislation to stifle political dissent. The authorities stripped 33 Kuwaitis of their nationality, including three who appeared to have been targeted because they represented opposition voices.

Freedom of Expression

The authorities used several laws to prosecute at least 13 people in 2014 for criticizing the government or institutions in blogs or on Twitter, Facebook, or other social media. These included the constitution and penal code, laws on printing and publishing, public gatherings, and misuse of telephone communications, and the National Unity Law of 2013. Those accused faced charges such as harming the honor of another person; insulting the emir or other public figures or the judiciary; insulting religion; planning or participating in illegal gatherings; and misusing telephone communications. Other charges included harming state security, inciting the government's overthrow, and harming Kuwait's relations with other states. In 2014, courts convicted at least five of those charged, imposing prison sentences of up to five years and fines.

The government took sweeping new powers to block content, deny access to the Internet, and revoke service providers' licenses without giving reasons under a new telecommunications law adopted in May. The law imposes severe penalties on people who create or send "immoral" messages, and gives unspecified authorities the power to suspend communication services on national security grounds. Any communication service provider that "contributes" to the dissemination of messages that violate these vague standards can be punished. The law provides no opportunity for judicial review.

The government adopted a new method to penalize some critics. Between July and September, it revoked the citizenship of 33 individuals, three apparently for political reasons. The revocation process allows no room for appeal or review.

On July 21, a week after it demanded that authorities take action against people engaged in "acts aiming to undermine the country's security and stability, bringing harm to its institutions," the cabinet stripped five Kuwaitis of their citizenship. One of the five, Ahmed Jabr al-Shammari, owned media outlets that had defied a government ban. He tried to appeal the decision but the Kuwaiti court ruled that it had no jurisdiction over citizenship revocations. On August 11, the government said it had revoked the citizenship of 10 more Kuwaitis, including Nabil al-Awadhi, a conservative cleric widely known for his TV talk shows. On September 29, a new round of revocations included Saad al-Ajmi, the spokesman for Musalam al-Barrak, a leading opposition politician.

The Law of Nationality, 15/1959, allows the authorities to revoke the citizenship of any Kuwaiti, and their dependants, and deport them under certain circumstances. For example the authorities can revoke a person's citizenship if they consider it in the "best interest" of the state or its external security, or if they have evidence that the person concerned has promoted principles that undermine the country's wellbeing. Citizenship can also be revoked if it was obtained fraudulently or if a court convicts a naturalized citizen of a crime related to honor or dishonesty within 15 years of becoming a Kuwaiti.

The government resorted to deportations to remove non-citizens of whom it disapproved. In June, authorities deported an Egyptian imam and his wife and children after he denounced the 2014 Egyptian presidential election in a sermon that he delivered in a Kuwait mosque. The authorities deported him and his family after the Religious Endowments Ministry issued regulations banning "interference in the domestic affairs of other countries" in sermons.

Treatment of Minorities

At least 105,702 Bidun residents of Kuwait remained stateless.

After an initial registration period for citizenship ended in 1960, authorities shifted Bidun citizenship claims to administrative committees that for decades have avoided resolving the claims. Authorities claim that many Bidun are "illegal residents" who deliberately destroyed evidence of another nationality in order to get the generous benefits that Kuwait provides to its citizens.

Members of the Bidun community frequently take to the streets to protest the government's failure to address their citizenship claims, despite government warnings that Bidun should not gather in public. Article 12 of the 1979 Public

Gatherings Law bars non-Kuwaitis from participating in public gatherings. At least seven were arrested for taking part in protests in 2014.

Women's Rights

In March and April 2014, the Justice Ministry prohibited women, but not men, from applying for legal researcher posts until the two-year evaluation of the first group of women admitted in 2013 is completed. A legal researcher post allows women for the first time to become eligible, pending evaluation, for posts as prosecutors, enabling them thereafter to pursue careers as judges. In April 2014, a court struck down the Justice Ministry's order and 21 women have now been admitted.

Women continue to face discrimination in many aspects of their lives, and large legal gaps remain in protections for women. Kuwait has no laws prohibiting domestic violence, sexual harassment, or marital rape. Legislation proposed in April to penalize sexual harassment had still to be debated by November 2014. Kuwaiti women married to non-Kuwaitis, unlike Kuwaiti men, cannot pass on their citizenship to their children or spouses. Kuwaiti law also prevents a woman marrying a partner of her choice without her father's permission.

Migrant Workers

Recognizing the vulnerabilities of foreign migrant workers, particularly domestic workers who are excluded from the Labour Law or any other legal regime, in 2013 the authorities opened a shelter for domestic workers who flee abusive employers. Inadequate staffing prevented the shelter from becoming fully operational and providing in-house services. Designed to accommodate up to 700 people, the shelter had 210 women residing there in September 2014. The shelter accepts victims on referral from a foreign embassy or international organization. Victims are not able to leave the shelter unescorted if they want to return to the shelter.

Terrorism

Extremist militant groups Jabhat al-Nusra and the Islamic State, also known as ISIS, are responsible for systematic rights abuses, including the intentional targeting and abduction of civilians during military operations in Syria and Iraq in 2014. Media reports indicate that ISIS members have included Kuwaiti nationals, and that individual Kuwaitis have financed and supported ISIS and Jabhat al-Nusra military operations.

In August, Kuwait announced new measures to curb funding for extremists. These included banning all fundraising in mosques, requiring greater transparency from charities regarding the sources and destinations of their donations, and obtaining receipts.

On August 6, the US Treasury department sanctioned three Kuwaitis for funding extremist militant groups in Syria and Iraq, by freezing any US-based assets and banning US citizens from doing business with them.

Key International Actors

The parliament debated whether Kuwait should become party to the 2012 Gulf Cooperation Council (GCC) joint security agreement in response to government pressure to ratify it. On April 3, the parliament's foreign affairs committee rejected the agreement, with a majority asserting that it violates Kuwait's constitution. The 20 provisions of GCC agreement could be used to suppress free expression and undermine privacy rights of citizens and residents.

The United States, in its 2014 US State Department annual Trafficking in Persons report, classified Kuwait as Tier 3—among the most problematic countries—for the eighth consecutive year. The report cited Kuwait's failure to prosecute trafficking offenders using the 2013 anti-trafficking law or other laws that address trafficking crimes. It found that efforts to help abused workers were not accompanied by any enforcement activities against the employers from whom the workers had fled. It found also that Kuwaiti authorities failed to protect victims of trafficking.

Kyrgyzstan

Discriminatory legislative proposals, including related to "foreign agents" and "homosexual propaganda," persistent impunity for ill-treatment and torture, and shortcomings in law enforcement and the judiciary undermine and erode democratic progress that Kyrgyzstan has made in recent years. Impunity for violence and discrimination against women and lesbian, gay, bisexual, and transgender (LGBT) people remains pervasive. Freedom of expression and assembly also suffered setbacks in 2014.

Attacks on defendants and lawyers in courts continued in 2014. Rights defender Azimjon Askarov remained wrongfully imprisoned at time of writing, despite his renewed attempts during the year to have a court review his case.

Access to Justice

Since the outbreak of ethnic violence in June 2010, Kyrgyzstan's flawed justice process has produced long prison sentences for mostly ethnic Uzbeks after convictions marred by torture-tainted confessions and other due process violations. Seven further cases related to crimes committed during the violence are pending, including that of a man detained in July 2014. All defendants are ethnic Uzbeks, reinforcing concerns of judicial bias.

Impunity for violent physical and verbal attacks at some hearings continued in 2014, undermining defendants' fair trial rights. After a January hearing in the case of Mahamad Bizurukov, an ethnic Uzbek defendant standing trial for June 2010-related crimes, the United States embassy issued a statement expressing deep concern.

On August 11, Kyrgyzstan's Supreme Court declined to grant Turkish national Ahmet Gunan a retrial despite a United Nations Human Rights Committee 2011 decision finding violations of the International Covenant on Civil and Political Rights. The committee noted that Kyrgyzstan is obligated to remedy the violations, including by releasing Gunan or granting him a retrial, and by providing full reparation, including appropriate compensation.

Torture

Although the government acknowledges that torture occurs in Kyrgyzstan, impunity for torture remains the norm. Criminal cases into allegations of ill-treatment or torture are rare, and investigations and trials are delayed or ineffective.

In its June concluding observations, the UN Committee on the Rights of the Child (CRC) expressed concern about "widespread torture and ill-treatment of children" in detention and closed institutions and called for prompt and effective independent investigations.

According to statistics provided by the Prosecutor General's Office to Golos Svobody, a local anti-torture group, authorities declined to open criminal investigations into 100 of 109 registered complaints of torture in the first half of 2014.

Monitors from the National Center for the Prevention of Torture encountered some problems accessing places of detention. After one incident in March, the center filed a complaint against the director of the Issyk Kul region temporary detention facility for refusing the monitors entry, but at time of writing the director had not been held accountable.

Civil Society

In May, two draft laws were registered in parliament that would restrict the work of nongovernmental organizations (NGOs) and endanger freedom of association in Kyrgyzstan. On May 19, the Justice Ministry proposed "banning" unregistered NGOs, but in November it withdrew the proposed provision. On May 26, parliament deputies registered a bill that would require foreign-funded domestic NGOs engaging in "political activities" to register as "foreign agents" and would create criminal liability for leaders of organizations "whose work incites citizens to refuse to fulfill their civic duties or commit other unlawful acts." At time of writing, parliament had not yet considered the bill.

Civil society activists were harassed via media and physically attacked in 2014. In February, threats were made against an LGBT activist over social media networks after he participated in a Human Rights Watch report release. On March 5, two feminist activists handing out equal rights flyers near a central bazaar were attacked people in a crowd who confused the female gender symbol for a cross and accused the activists of proselytizing. The activists filed a complaint, but authorities twice declined to open a case.

On September 4, Makhamajan Abdujaparov, a senior lawyer at Spravedlivost, a Jalalabad-based rights NGO, was attacked in his office by an unidentified assailant who accused Abdujaparov of cutting him off on the road. Abdujaparov filed a complaint, but was pressured to withdraw it. The man was identified as a National Security Agency (GKNB) officer.

In late September, the GKNB opened a criminal investigation into allegations that a survey on the rights of ethnic minorities in southern Kyrgyzstan conducted by a local group with the support of US-based rights organization Freedom House would incite inter-ethnic discord. The groups challenged the legality of the investigation, but an Osh court rejected their suit. The investigation remained ongoing at time of writing.

Azimjon Askarov, a human rights defender, continues to serve a life sentence after being wrongfully convicted on charges related to the June 2010 violence. His prosecution was marred by serious violations of fair trial standards and allegations of torture. In February, the Prosecutor General's Office declined to reopen his case following a nine-month-long review. After multiple appeals, on September 3 the Supreme Court upheld the decision. Askarov's November 2012 complaint to the UN Human Rights Committee was under review at time of writing.

Freedom of Expression

Kyrgyzstan backtracked on freedom of speech by adopting a new law in May effectively reintroducing criminal libel. Organization for Security and Co-operation in Europe (OSCE) Media Freedom Representative Dunja Mijatovic had called on the president to veto the bill. The US embassy said the law "tarnished Kyrgyzstan's image as an emerging democracy."

On August 17, several assailants attacked Davron Nasipkhanov, a journalist in Osh, outside his home. They called him "sart," a derogatory term for Uzbek, and said that "sarts" should be killed. Authorities opened an investigation but had not pressed charges at time of writing.

Sexual Orientation and Gender-Based Violence

Authorities have not effectively addressed longstanding problems of gender-based violence. Violence and abduction for forced marriage (bride-kidnapping) remain pervasive forms of violence against women and girls in Kyrgyzstan. Impunity remains the norm. Work on a new domestic violence law was ongoing at time of writing.

In June, the CRC noted 2013 Criminal Code amendments increasing sanctions for kidnapping child "brides" younger than 17, and fewer such incidents, but called on Kyrgyzstan to ensure effective investigations, accountability for abuses, and redress for victims.

LGBT people in Kyrgyzstan experience abuse and discrimination from both state and non-state actors. Police violence and harassment against LGBT people includes extortion, ill-treatment, and sexual violence such as rape, including with external objects. Due to widespread homophobia in Kyrgyzstan and fear that personal information will be disclosed, most LGBT victims of police abuse do not file reports.

On October 15, parliament passed in its first reading a homophobic and blatantly discriminatory bill that would impose criminal and administrative sanctions for "creat[ing] a positive attitude toward nontraditional sexual relations" in media or public assemblies. The Anti-Discrimination Coalition, a network of LGBT and other rights groups, collected nearly 800 signatures for an open appeal urging legislators to reject the bill. The US embassy, the OSCE media freedom representative and the Office of the High Commissioner for Human Rights spoke out against the adoption of the bill.

Freedom of Assembly

A court banned all public assemblies in Ala Too Square and other central locations in Bishkek from March 31 to May 1 to prevent "destabilization of the sociopolitical situation by destructive forces." Local rights groups urged authorities to reverse the ban on violating Kyrgyzstan's law on peaceful assemblies. The ban was lifted in April after an appeal by the prosecutor general.

While Kyrgyzstan's constitution guarantees freedom of assembly, on three separate occasions in June and July, police detained activists staging peaceful protests in central Bishkek. In each case the participants received official warnings for allegedly disobeying the police.

Freedom of Religion

According to Forum 18, a religious freedom watchdog, harassment continued in 2014 of minority religious communities, including Jehovah's Witnesses and Ahmadi Muslims, who in 2013 were refused registration by the State Commission for Religious Affairs (GKDR). In July, the GKDR withdrew work permission from the bishop of the Russian Orthodox Church on the grounds that he "threatens the public security of Kyrgyzstan and sows religious discord."

Lawyers told Human Right Watch that authorities in the south continue to arbitrarily detain individuals on extremism-related charges and that they are particularly vulnerable to ill-treatment and torture in custody.

At a roundtable in October, rights activists in Bishkek raised concern that a draft religion law, if adopted, would restrict the right to freedom of religion and belief, for example, by requiring additional licensing and re-registration requirements of religious workers.

Key International Actors

In April, the Parliamentary Assembly of the Council of Europe granted Kyrgyzstan partnership for democracy status, despite a pending propaganda bill that contravenes Council of Europe norms. The accompanying resolution highlighted key areas of concern that Kyrgyzstan was expected to address to strengthen respect for human rights, including rejecting the propaganda law and other laws aimed at limiting civil society.

In its April concluding observations, the UN Human Rights Committee noted serious concerns about violence against LGBT persons and the need for a comprehensive approach to prevent and address violence against women, strengthen efforts to tackle torture and ill-treatment, and ensure the right to freedom of expression and association.

During its annual human rights dialogue with Kyrgyzstan in April, the European Union expressed "serious concerns" about reports of ill-treatment and torture, fair trial shortcomings, discrimination against minority groups, mistreatment of LGBT people, and draft legislation that would restrict civil society.

At the EU-Kyrgyzstan Cooperation Council meeting in November, the EU called on Kyrgyzstan "to pursue reforms leading to transparency, independency of the judiciary, inter-ethnic reconciliation and respect for human rights."

In June, the CRC issued a comprehensive list of recommendations. It called on Kyrgyzstan to take urgent measures to prevent discrimination against marginalized and disadvantaged children, including in minority groups, and to ensure that children from minority communities, especially Uzbeks, have unrestricted access to education in their native language.

Lebanon

The security situation in Lebanon deteriorated in 2014. Violence spilled over from the conflict in Syria and democratic institutions faltered as the parliament failed to elect a president. Parliamentary elections, planned initially for June 2013 and then November 2014, were postponed again until 2017.

Syrian refugees in Lebanon topped 1,143,000 in November and suffered from increasing abuses including locally-imposed curfews, evictions, and violence by non-state actors with little reaction from Lebanese authorities. With limited international support, the government struggled to meet the refugees' needs. Draft laws to stop torture and improve the treatment of migrant domestic workers stalled, but in a breakthrough for women's rights, a law to protect women from domestic violence passed in April.

Spillover Violence from Syria

In 2014, there were multiple shelling attacks from Syria into north Lebanon and the Bekaa Valley, which killed at least 10 civilians and injured at least 19.

There were 14 car bombings or suicide bomb attacks, at least five targeting civilians. Of the 12 attacks, three took place in the Shia Beirut suburbs and three in the Shia town of Hermel in the Bekaa Valley killing 32 people and injuring at least 332. The extremist group Islamic State, also known as ISIS, claimed responsibility for one of these attacks, Jabhat al-Nusra for four, and the Abdullah Azzam Brigade, an Al-Qaeda-affiliate, one. In five other bombings security personnel or Hezbollah officials appeared to be the targets of bombings. These attacks killed 11 people, including five soldiers and a Hezbollah official, and injured 50.

Clashes between militants based in Syria, including from ISIS and Jabhat al-Nusra, and the Lebanese army occurred between August 2 and 5 in Arsal and ended when the Lebanese army pushed the militants outside of the town. During the clashes some Lebanese security personnel were taken as hostages by the militants and at time of writing three of the hostages had been executed.

Lebanese residents of Arsal and Syrians residing there reported that Lebanese soldiers refused to allow Syrians to flee from the town during the fighting and that refugee settlements and other civilian targets were subject to indiscriminate fire including by the Lebanese army. A field hospital in Arsal reported that 489 people were wounded and at least 59 civilians—44 Syrians and 15 Arsal natives— were killed in the fighting.

The hostage taking of Lebanese soldiers and Internal Security Force members led to a string of retaliatory measures against Syrians in the weeks that followed, including the imposition of blanket curfews by municipalities across the country, forced evictions, and violence by non-state actors. By September, at least 40 municipalities had imposed curfews affecting Syrians. Lebanese security forces also conducted arrest operations, sometimes targeting refugee settlements, and in some cases reportedly abused or arbitrarily detained Syrians.

Refugees

By November, over 1,143,000 Syrian refugees in Lebanon had approached United Nations High Commissioner for Refugees (UNHCR) for registration. Registration does not grant legal status, but enables Syrians in some cases to receive assistance. Syrians who enter at official border crossings are granted a six-month residency permit with a one-time possibility of renewal, after which extension requires a US$200 renewal fee. Absent legal status, refugees face the risk of detention for illegal presence in the country.

The Lebanese government began implementing measures in 2014 to reduce the number of Syrians in the country. On October 23, the Lebanese cabinet decided to prevent Syrian refugees from entering Lebanon except in "extreme humanitarian cases," but did not define what constitutes such a case. According to refugees and aid workers, General Security officers at the border seemed to be implementing their own interpretation of the government's recent announcement and making arbitrary and discriminatory entry determinations.

There are approximately 45,000 Palestinians from Syria seeking refuge in Lebanon, joining the estimated 300,000 Palestinian refugees already living in Lebanon. In May, new regulations by the minister of interior limited Palestinians ability to enter the country or renew their residencies. These restrictions followed the forcible deportation of about three dozen Palestinians to Syria on May 4. Authorities began arbitrarily barring Palestinians from Syria from entering the country in August 2013.

Clashes in Tripoli

In the northern city of Tripoli, there were two weeks of deadly violence between armed groups in March in which at least 30 people were killed and 175 wounded, including 33 soldiers. The fighting was most concentrated in the mainly Alawite neighborhood of Jabal Mohsen and the adjacent Sunni neighborhood of Bab al-Tabbaneh.

On April 1, the army implemented a security plan to arrest militants and seize weapons in Jabal Mohsen and Bab al-Tabbaneh. Some local militia leaders and fighters were detained, some of whom are still in detention, but many militia members and leaders remained at large and on August 5-6 clashes resumed as the army withdrew its forces from Bab al-Tabbaneh. An 8-year-old girl was killed in these clashes.

In September, clashes resumed between the army and gunmen and continued into October resulting in casualties on both side and from the residential population.

Lengthy Pretrial Detention, Ill-Treatment

In 2014, Lebanese security forces arrested and pursued investigations in relation to car bombings and other attacks on civilians in Lebanon. Some of these suspects, like those detained in relation to clashes that took place in Saida in June 2013 between the army and supporters of pro-Syrian opposition Imam Sheikh Ahmed al-Assir, have suffered from lengthy pretrial detention and have reported being beaten and tortured by security forces.

Lebanon has not yet established a national preventive mechanism to visit and monitor places of detention, as required under the Optional Protocol to the Convention against Torture, which it ratified in 2008. In its annual report, released in October, the United Nations Committee Against Torture found that "torture in Lebanon is a pervasive practice that is routinely used by the armed forces and law enforcement agencies..."

Freedom of Expression

In 2014, charges and prosecutions against news outlets, journalists, and bloggers threatened freedom of expression. Defaming or criticizing the Lebanese president or army is considered a criminal offense in Lebanon, which can carry a jail sentence. The publications court on February 12 sentenced Jean Assy, a blogger, to two months in jail for defaming and insulting President Michel Sleiman on Twitter.

Ambiguous definitions of defamation and slander open the door for silencing legitimate criticism of public officials. The Internal Security Forces Cybercrimes Bureau brought blogger Imad Bazzi in for questioning on defamation charges on March 13 over his criticism of former State Minister Panos Mangyan for abuse of power.

On February 26, the publications court fined Mohammed Nazzal, an *Al Akhbar* journalist, 27 million LBP (US$18,000) for an article on judicial corruption. Rasha Abou Zaki, an *Al Akhbar* contributor, was fined 4 million LBP ($2,667) by the publications court in February for defaming former Prime Minister Fouad Siniora, after she alleged corruption and embezzlement in the Finance Ministry.

Migrant Workers' Rights

Migrant domestic workers are excluded from the labor law and subject to restrictive immigration rules based on the *kafala* system, the visa sponsorship system that ties workers to their employers and puts workers at risk of exploitation and abuse. In June, a judge ruled in favor of a female migrant domestic worker who was suing her employer for withholding her passport, finding that the practice was discriminatory and an unlawful infringement on her freedom of movement.

Migrant domestic workers suing their employers for abuse continue, however, to face legal obstacles and risk imprisonment and deportation due to the restrictive visa system. From May 2014, and perhaps earlier, Lebanon began denying residency permit renewals for a number of Lebanon-born children of low-wage migrants and their parents and expelling them.

Women's Rights

On April 1, parliament passed the Law on the Protection of Women and Family from Domestic Violence. The new law establishes important protection measures and related policing and court reforms, but leaves women at risk of marital rape and other abuse. One month after the law's implementation, four protection orders were issued based on the law.

In September, a landmark verdict was issued by a judge who ordered the permanent eviction of a woman's husband, son, and daughter-in-law from their house after it was established they had abused her. Under the 15 various Lebanese personal status laws, which are determined by an individual's religious affiliation, women continue to suffer from discrimination including unequal access to divorce and child custody. Lebanese women, unlike Lebanese men, cannot pass on their nationality to foreign husbands and children, and continue to be subject to discriminatory inheritance laws.

Legacy of Past Conflicts and Wars

In October 2012, Justice Minister Shakib Qortbawi put forward a draft decree to the cabinet to establish a national commission to investigate the fate of Lebanese and other nationals who "disappeared" during and after the 1975-1990 Lebanese civil war. The cabinet formed a ministerial committee to examine the draft, but no further action was taken in 2014.

On March 4, Lebanon's State Council ruled that relatives of people who have disappeared in Lebanon have the right to know what happened to their missing family members. On September 20, the families of the disappeared were provided with a copy of the government's investigation file after the judiciary requested in May to postpone the delivery of the file on the grounds that it might endanger civil peace.

In January, the UN's Special Tribunal for Lebanon inabsentia trial began against four indicted members of Hezbollah for the killing of former Prime Minister Rafik Hariri in 2005. A fifth suspect, indicted in 2013, was added to the trial in February.

Key International Actors

Syria, Iran, and Saudi Arabia maintain a strong influence on Lebanese politics through local allies, and increasingly so as Lebanon becomes more involved in the conflict in Syria.

Many countries have given extensive, albeit insufficient, support to help Lebanon cope with the Syrian refugee crisis and to bolster security amidst spillover violence.

The Lebanese armed forces and Internal Security Forces also receive assistance from a range of international donors including the United States, the United Kingdom, and the European Union, all of which have taken some steps to improve the compliance of these forces with international human rights law.

HUMAN
RIGHTS
WATCH

PRIORITIES FOR
LEGISLATIVE REFORM
A Human Rights Roadmap for a New Libya

Libya

Political infighting and clashes between rival militias escalated, triggering armed conflicts in Benghazi and other parts of the east in May, and in Tripoli and its environs in July.

The fighting caused widespread destruction of property, and civilian injuries and deaths. Around 400,000 were internally displaced in Libya, including about 100,000 residents of Tripoli. Another 150,000 people, including foreigners, fled Libya. Most foreign embassies, the United Nations, the International Committee of the Red Cross (ICRC), and international agencies withdrew their staff and closed their missions in July.

Militias attacked, threatened, assaulted, or arbitrarily detained journalists, judges, activists, politicians, and ordinary citizens with impunity. Lack of protection for the judiciary resulted in a near breakdown of the justice sector in cities such as Tripoli, Benghazi, Sirte, Sebha, and Derna.

Political Transition and Constitution

Following an election marred by boycotts and violence, Libyans voted in a 60-member Constitution Drafting Assembly on February 20 to draw up a new constitution. The assembly was expected to produce a new draft constitution by December 2014.

Boycotts, violence, and low voter turnout also marred the June 25 elections for the House of Representatives, a new 200-seat parliament that replaced the interim General National Congress (GNC). Due to boycotts and insecurity, only 188 seats were filled. Following their election, around 158 of the new members of parliament convened in Tobruk, in the east, citing security fears in Tripoli. Around 30 members of parliament boycotted the move. On September 1, the parliament confirmed caretaker Prime Minister Abdullah al-Thinni as Libya's prime minister.

After the Misrata-led Libya Dawn alliance took control of Tripoli in August, some members of the former GNC declared Omar al-Hassi prime minister, in opposition to the Tobruk-based parliament.

The Libyan Supreme Court issued a ruling on November 6, declaring unconstitutional an amendment to the Constitutional Declaration, which paved the way for the House of Representative's election law. The elected parliament rejected the Supreme Court decision, and some members of the former legislature, the GNC, reconvened claiming to be the legitimate legislature and demanded the dissolution of the House of Representatives. At time of writing, both entities remained embroiled in armed conflicts.

Security and Armed Militias

Scores of armed groups remained on the government's payroll and controlled key locations and resources. Some pro-federalism militias, in a dispute over their pay, maintained a blockade of major oil export terminals for a year until July. They had been contracted by the government to guard petroleum facilities after the 2011 revolution as Petroleum Facilities Guards (PFG), operating under the Defense Ministry.

Armed groups and individuals continued to commit unlawful killings, mostly in Benghazi and Derna in the east. At least 250 people died in apparently targeted assassinations in the first nine months of 2014, including security officials, judges and prosecutors, journalists, activists, and Imams. Victims included some women. At time of writing, the authorities conducted no investigations into these attacks and killings, and had not arrested or prosecuted any suspects.

Armed groups continued to target foreigners and diplomats. Unknown armed groups abducted two Tunisian embassy employees in March and April, releasing them on June 25, and unidentified armed men abducted Jordan's ambassador to Libya on April 15, releasing him on May 13 in exchange for the release of a Libyan imprisoned in Jordan since 2007 on terrorism charges. On June 4 in Sirte, unknown assailants gunned down Michael Greub, an ICRC delegate, as he visited the Libyan Red Crescent.

Lack of border controls and tribal infighting aggravated the security situation, allowing continued trafficking of humans, drugs, and weapons across Libya's borders with Chad, Sudan, Egypt, and Algeria.

Credible evidence emerged showing that one or more militia groups used antipersonnel landmines during the armed conflict at Tripoli Airport in July and August 2014. The unit in charge of clearing the airport area, operating under Libya Dawn, said in November it had found and cleared at least 600 landmines.

In October, armed groups in eastern Libya affiliated with the extremist group Islamic State (also known as ISIS), announced the establishment of an autonomous province divided into the Derna and Benghazi sectors. The Islamic Shura Youth Council in Derna, which affiliated itself with ISIS, established an Islamic Court, Islamic Police, and carried out public executions and floggings.

Armed Conflict and War Crimes

In May, former army Gen. Khalifa Hifter launched a military operation against Islamist factions in eastern Libya, ostensibly to "eradicate terrorism." His Libya Dignity Alliance, based in eastern Libya, included army, air force, and special forces personnel, and targeted Islamist factions such as Ansar al-Sharia and the Islamic Shura Youth Council in Derna. In July, the conflict spread to Tripoli where Libya Dawn, a Misrata-led militia alliance that includes Islamist factions, wrested control of the capital from a Zintan-led militia alliance aligned to Libya Dignity. In November, the House of Representatives reinstated General Hiftar and 16 other officers into active duty.

Warring factions indiscriminately shelled civilian areas in both Benghazi and Tripoli, seized people, and looted, burned, and otherwise destroyed civilian property in attacks that in some cases amounted to war crimes. Those seized and still held by militias at time of writing included Suliman Zubi, a former GNC member held since July 21 by the Katibat Barq al-Nasr militia from Zintan, and a Tripoli based activist, Abdelmoez Banoon.

Judicial System and Transitional Justice

Libya's justice system suffered serious setbacks. Militias attacked judges, prosecutors, lawyers, and witnesses, causing the closure of courts and prosecutors' offices in Benghazi, Derna, Sirte, and Sebha, and a near breakdown of the justice system. The Justice Ministry in Tripoli shut down in July due to the fighting there.

The government failed to secure control over detainees held in militia-run facilities, including Saif al-Islam Gaddafi, and retained only nominal control of facilities formally under its authority. Authorities failed to grant detainees basic due process rights, including access to lawyers, judicial reviews of their cases, and access to key evidence.

On March 24, the trial commenced in Tripoli of 37 Gaddafi-era officials and employees accused for their alleged roles during the 2011 revolution. They included Saif al-Islam Gaddafi and Abdullah Sanussi, Muammar Gaddafi's former intelligence chief. On March 6, Niger extradited another Gaddafi son, al-Saadi Gaddafi, to Libya. At time of writing, the court trying the 37 accused had adjourned hearings and al-Saadi Gaddafi remained in pre-charge detention.

On September 14, the House of Representatives passed a counterterrorism law which could undermine freedom of speech, assembly, and association due to overbroad and sweeping definitions of terrorism and harsh prescribed punishments.

Arbitrary Detention, Torture, and Deaths in Custody

The Justice Ministry held approximately 6,100 detainees in 26 prisons, mostly under the nominal authority of the Judicial Police. Only 10 percent of those held had been sentenced, and the rest remained held in pre-charge detention. In addition, the Interior and Defense Ministries continued to hold undisclosed numbers of detainees, while many militias also continued to hold unknown numbers of detainees in informal facilities. Militias remained responsible for widespread abuses, including torture and deaths in custody.

Death Penalty

The former GNC and the newly elected House of Representatives both failed to amend any of over 30 articles in the penal code that provide for the death penalty, including as punishment for exercising rights to freedom of expression and association. Since the overthrow of the Gaddafi regime, civil and military courts have imposed at least 29 death sentences. The authorities had not carried out any executions at time of writing.

The Islamic Shura Youth Council armed group carried out at least three public extra- judicial executions in July and August in Derna of people accused of murder.

International Justice and the International Criminal Court

The government failed to uphold its legal obligation to surrender Saif al-Islam Gaddafi to the International Criminal Court (ICC), where he is wanted on charges of crimes against humanity for his alleged role in trying to suppress the country's 2011 uprising . The ICC has had jurisdiction over the situation in Libya since February 15, 2011, under UN Security Council resolution 1970. On May 21, the ICC issued a final decision rejecting Libya's request to try Gaddafi domestically. On December 10, the ICC issued a finding of non-compliance by Libya after two requests for cooperation to surrender Saif al-Islam Gaddafi to The Hague and referred the issue to the Security Council.

In the case of Abdullah Sanussi, ICC judges approved Libya's bid to prosecute the former intelligence chief at home for his alleged role during the 2011 uprising.

In response to ongoing grave violations, on June 24, the ICC prosecutor issued a statement warning that she would not hesitate to investigate and prosecute perpetrators of crimes within the court's jurisdiction, but at time of writing she had yet to open a new investigation.

Forced Displacement

Miltias mostly from Misrata continued to prevent about 40,000 residents of Tawergha, Tomina, and Karareem from returning to their homes as a form of collective punishment for crimes allegedly committed by some Tawergha residents during the 2011 revolution. Those displaced continued to seek safety and shelter in makeshift camps and private housing in many areas, but they remained subject to attack, harassment, and arbitrary detention by the militias . Libyan authorities and militia commanders failed to end the attacks or hold those responsible to account. The forced displacement of residents of Tawergha amounts to a crime against humanity.

Freedom of Speech and Expression

Armed factions threatened and assaulted dozens of journalists and attacked several media outlets, including private television stations Alassema, Libya Al-Ahrar, and Barqa TV. Several journalists and an activist were abducted or seized.

Abdelmoez Banoon was kidnapped by unknown assailants in July and was still missing at time of writing.

Six journalists were assassinated. Miftah Bouzeid, editor-in-chief of *Burniq* newspaper, was killed on May 26 by unknown assailants in Benghazi. On June 25, unidentified assailants killed activist Salwa Bughaighis at her home in Benghazi. Dozens of journalists fled the country due to attacks, threats, and intimidation. Authorities failed to conduct investigations, or arrest and prosecute perpetrators.

Prosecutors brought criminal defamation charges against several journalists, political analysts, lawmakers, and politicians. Amara al-Khatabi, editor of *Al-Ummah* newspaper, was sentenced in absentia to five years in prison on charges of defaming members of the judiciary; radio presenter Sami al-Sharif faced charges for allegedly defaming a local council official on one of his shows; and political analyst Jamal al-Hajji appealed against a 2013 criminal court sentence of eight months in prison for allegedly libeling businessmen and politicians.

The former GNC failed to amend penal code provisions that breach international law, and instead adopted new repressive measures. On January 22, it passed resolution 5(2014) to ban and prevent the transmission of satellite television stations that criticize the government and the 2011 revolution, and on February 5, the GNC promulgated Law 5(2014) to make any act "harming" the "February 17 revolution" of 2011 a criminal offense.

Women's Rights

Amid the breakdown of law and order and in the prevailing climate of impunity, women continued to suffer from discrimination. Some armed groups imposed restrictions on women based on their ideological beliefs. Guards harassed university students in Tripoli for refusing to wear the hijab. Some women faced harassment while attempting to travel out of Libya without a male guardian. In April, a militia group responsible for security at a university in Derna insisted that a wall be constructed to segregate the sexes, limiting women students' access to education.

Guards at the court trying former Gaddafi officials denied female Libyan journalists access to the court because of their gender and, in April, denied access to foreign female journalists unless they wore head scarves.

In February, the prime minister issued a decree promising compensation for victims of sexual violence but the government had not allocated funds for this purpose at time of writing.

Migrants, Refugees, and Asylum Seekers

Record numbers of migrants and asylum seekers embarked on the perilous sea journey from Libya to Europe with 60,000 reaching Italy alone in 2014. The Italian navy's large- scale rescue operation, Mare Nostrum, rescued around 100,000 from unseaworthy boats, but at least 3,000 still perished at sea.

At time of writing, Libyan authorities held 5,000-10,000 migrants and asylum seekers in detention facilities where they face torture and other abuses, including overcrowding, dire sanitation, lack of access to adequate medical care, and inhuman or degrading treatment. Guards subjected migrants and asylum seekers to beatings, whippings, cigarette burns, and electric shocks. The authorities failed to address these abuses and hold perpetrators accountable.

Key International Actors

Long awaited military training for a Libyan General Purpose Force commenced in Italy, Turkey, and the United Kingdom.

A United States Navy Seals team forcibly took control of an oil tanker on March 16 as it sailed near Cyprus, and returned it to Libya and placed it under the government's control. Pro-federalist militias had intended to sell fuel on their own behalf in response to a long dispute with the government over pay.

On June 15, a US special unit apprehended a Libyan suspect, Ahmed Abu Khatallah, near his Benghazi home. The unit transferred him to the US, where he faces charges for his alleged role in the September 11, 2012 attack on the US consulate in Benghazi that killed four US citizens, including Ambassador Chris Stevens.

The United Nations Security Council passed resolution 2174 (2014) on August 27. This extended sanctions against Libya to target those who engage in or support acts that "threaten the peace, stability or security of Libya" or individuals responsible for human rights abuses. At time of writing, no new names had been added to the existing sanctions list.

In August, the US said the United Arab Emirates and Egypt had conducted air strikes in Tripoli on August 18 and 23, against military positions of the Misrata-led militia alliance, Libya Dawn. On September 15, unidentified warplanes conducted further air strikes against military positions of Libya Dawn-aligned militias in Gharyan. In September, Libya's government accused Sudan of funneling weapons to militias aligned with Libya Dawn, despite the active UN arms embargo. In the same month, the government also accused Qatar of several weapons shipments to forces aligned with Libya Dawn.

On November 19, the Security Council added two entities—Ansar Sharia in Benghazi and in Derna—to the Al-Qaeda Sanctions Regime. Members of these entities are subject to targeted financial sanctions, travel bans, and an arms embargo.

Malaysia

Following 2013 parliamentary elections that returned the ruling party to power, even though the political opposition won a majority of the popular vote, the Malaysian government launched a crackdown on freedom of expression and other civil and political rights that continues to the present. Human rights defenders, activists, and political figures, including opposition leader Anwar Ibrahim, face continuing harassment and persecution.

Freedom of Expression

Article 10 of Malaysia's Constitution guarantees that every citizen has the right to freedom of expression, but the Malaysian government violates that right on a regular basis.

The biggest threat to free speech comes from the government's redoubled use of the Sedition Act to prosecute activists and political opponents for making statements critical of the government, its political leaders, or the prime minister's party, United Malays National Organisation (UMNO), or for remarks the government considers to be derogatory toward Malaysia's sultans or disrespectful of religion.

From January 2013 to November 2014, the government charged at least 20 people with sedition, including four opposition members of parliament. Charges were also brought against state assemblymen, community and NGO activists, Internet bloggers, an academic, and others. Four people, including the late jurist Karpal Singh, were convicted of sedition for remarks and several were sentenced to prison or fined.

Widespread use of the act has marked serious backtracking by Prime Minister Najib Razak on multiple prior pledges to revoke the Sedition Act and replace it with a so-called Harmony Act. Under fire from political conservatives in UMNO, Najib effectively abandoned the National Unity Consultative Council (NUCC) that he had established to make legislative proposals and conduct consultations on the Harmony Act. On October 16, in only the fourth public march in its history, the Malaysia Bar Council demanded repeal of the act. On November 27, Najib told the annual UMNO convention that the Sedition Act would be retained, and amendments made to strengthen it.

On October 1, Professor Azmi Sharom filed a constitutional challenge to the act, claiming that it violates free speech guarantees in article 10 of the constitution. In early November, the High Court transferred the case to the Federal Court, Malaysia's apex court, for consideration.

During the year, the government also charged and sentenced activists for expressing views in ways the government claimed violated penal code provisions criminalizing defamation and "insult with intent to provoke a breach of the peace." It also made use of article 233 of the Communications and Multimedia Act outlawing any communication the government considers "obscene, indecent, false, menacing or offensive."

The government continues to use the Printing Presses and Publication Act (PPPA), which requires that all publishers obtain a license, to limit the content of publications. The home minister may suspend or revoke a license at any time on grounds of security, public order, or morality.

Malaysiakini, an outspoken online daily, has been a frequent government target. Despite an October 2013 Court of Appeal decision holding that a license to publish is a constitutional right, the Ministry of Home Affairs has refused to issue a license to Malaysiakini on grounds that its articles cause "controversy," "lack neutrality," and could cause its readers to "hate national leaders." On May 15, Prime Minister Najib sued Malaysiakini for defamation based on reader comments on two Malaysiakini columns, one focused on government corruption, and the other on Najib's leadership capabilities. In August 2013, *FZ Daily* newspaper received a license to publish, which was suspended a week later and revoked in January 2014. Another newsweekly, *The Heat*, had its license suspended without explanation on December 21, 2013; it was only permitted to start publishing again in February 2014.

The government also continued the prosecution of NGO activist Lena Hendry in 2014 for allegedly violating the Film Censorship Act for her involvement in screening the documentary film "No Fire Zone: The Killing Fields of Sri Lanka" in Kuala Lumpur in July 2013.

Freedom of Assembly and Association

Organizers of assemblies, marches, and demonstrations had more space in 2014 to spontaneously protest government policies due to an appeals court ruling in May that struck down a provision of the Peaceful Assembly Act (PAA) requiring that organizers give police 10-day advance notice. However, the government has appealed the decision and government prosecutors have continued to press charges against at least 20 political activists for allegedly violating the notice requirement when they held so-called Black 505 protests after the May 2013 elections.

The government permitted a May 1 rally protesting price and tax hikes to proceed without interference. But on June 22, police badly beat members of Himpunan Hijau protesting the government's licensing of the Lynas rare earth plant in Pahang. Later, after 15 protesters were arrested and taken to Kuantan police headquarters, thugs roughed up those waiting outside without police intervening.

The government restricts the right to freedom of association by requiring that organizations with seven or more members register with the Registrar of Societies (ROS). The ROS is answerable only to the minister of home affairs who has "absolute discretion" to declare a society illegal. In November, the minister declared the Sarawak Association for Peoples' Aspiration (Sapa) an illegal organization. The ROS remained locked in an almost two-year dispute with the opposition Democratic Action Party (DAP), refusing to recognize the party's central executive committee or its 120 branch offices. The Ministry of Home Affairs stated the Negara-Ku human rights movement would be considered "illegal" if it did not register with the ROS.

Political Prosecution of Anwar Ibrahim and Karpal Singh

The government continued its politically motivated persecution of opposition leader Anwar Ibrahim. Prosecutors appealed his 2012 acquittal on sodomy charges and in a rushed appeals court process, on March 7, 2014, the court overturned the verdict and sentenced him to a five-year prison term. The appeal to the Federal Court was heard in late October and early November, but the verdict had not been announced at time of writing.

Similarly, in February 2014, the High Court overturned DAP chairman Karpal Singh's acquittal on a politically motivated sedition charge and issued a fine that would have disqualified him from serving as a legislator. Karpal appealed but died in a car crash in April before the appeal could be heard.

Police Abuse and Impunity

New cases of police torture of suspects in custody, in some cases resulting in their deaths, and excessive use of force in apprehending suspects continued to be reported in 2014. At least 10 suspicious deaths in police custody were recorded in the first nine months of the year.

Human Rights Watch's report *No Answers, No Apology: Police Abuses and Accountability in Malaysia* released in March found a pattern of police impunity and a lack of effective external oversight. Rather than following up on the findings, police officials dismissed them and would not consider the report's substantive recommendations for improving rights performance and accountability.

On April 15, the government announced the creation and operation of a "coroner's court" with a sessions court judge in each state assigned the duty of examining wrongful deaths and deaths in custody. While this is a small improvement over the previous system in which inexperienced magistrate court judges oversaw inquests, the new approach still is wholly dependent on the police investigating their fellow officers, a situation that has consistently led to cover-ups and impunity.

The government continues to ignore calls from the Malaysia Bar Council and civil society groups to establish an Independent Police Complaints and Misconduct Commission (IPCMC) with the power to receive complaints focused on the police, independently investigate abuses, and sanction those found to have engaged in misconduct. On November 5, the Yang di-Pertuan Agong consented to the appointment of a new chairman and several commissioners for the Enforcement Agencies Integrity Commission (EAIC), the government's preferred yet ineffectual alternative that to date has lacked necessary resources or effective leadership to ensure oversight and accountability of the police and other enforcement agencies under its mandate.

Criminal Justice System

The government undermined positive steps it had taken in prior years, including its repeal of the Internal Security Act (ISA) and the Emergency (Public Order and Prevention of Crime) Ordinance, when it adopted amendments to the Prevention of Crime Act (PCA) that allow for administrative detention of suspects without judicial review. Under the act, a five-member board has the authority to impose a two-year detention, renewable indefinitely, or order the attachment of electronic monitoring devices to suspected offenders.

The similarly restrictive 2012 Security Offenses Special Measures Act (SOSMA), that replaced the ISA, still permits initial, albeit shortened, police detention without judiciary input. It also broadened the definition of a security offense, ceded to the police rather than the judiciary the power to intercept communications, and even in cases where the suspect is acquitted, permits indefinite appeals during which time the person may be held in custody or tethered to a monitoring device.

Malaysia's inspector-general of police dismissed civil society calls for the abolishment of the Dangerous Drugs Act (DDA), which permits detention of suspects without trial or warrant. The National Anti-Drug Agency continues to operate around 20 drug detention centers (recently rebranded as Cure & Care Rehabilitation Centers) where people who use drugs are held for between six months to two years.

Malaysia retains the death penalty for various crimes, including drug trafficking, and is not transparent about when and how decisions are made to carry out executions. More than 1,000 persons are estimated to be on death row. Malaysia undertook a review of sentencing guidelines for drug trafficking in line with its pledge at the United Nations Human Rights Council in October 2013 but the results of that review, conducted by the Attorney General's Office, had not been publicly released at time of writing.

Refugees, Asylum Seekers, and Trafficking Victims

Malaysia's immigration law does not recognize asylum seekers or refugees. The government is not a party to the Refugee Convention. It takes no responsibility

for the education of refugee or migrant children, and does not give refugees legal permission to work.

The Anti-Trafficking in Persons and Anti-Smuggling of Migrants law conflates trafficking and people smuggling and fails to meaningfully protect victims of trafficking. In 2014, the United States government demoted Malaysia to tier 3 in its "Trafficking in Persons" report.

Sexual Orientation and Gender Identity

Discrimination against lesbian, gay, bisexual, and transgender (LGBT) people is pervasive in Malaysia. In September, Human Rights Watch issued a report *"I'm Scared to be a Woman": Human Rights Abuses against Transgender People in Malaysia* that focused on the impact of state-level Sharia (Islamic) laws that prohibit cross-dressing. The report revealed that transgender persons face arbitrary arrest, physical and sexual assault, imprisonment, discriminatory denial of health care and employment, and other abuses. Three transgender women challenged the Sharia ordinance on constitutional grounds in the state of Negeri Sembilan and on November 7, won their appeal in a major victory for rights in the country. However, government prosecutors are expected to appeal the decision.

Key International Actors

Malaysia seeks to position itself in the UN and the international community as a moderate Muslim state prepared to stand up to Islamist extremism, a position for which it gains support from the US and its NATO allies. In October, Malaysia was elected to a seat on the UN Security Council for the 2015-2016 term.

In April, Malaysia hosted US President Barack Obama, and the two countries agreed to upgrade their ties to a "comprehensive partnership." Obama raised human rights prominently during the visit.

Malaysia also has continued its close engagement with China, its largest trading partner, despite frictions caused by the disappearance on March 8 of Malaysia Airlines flight MH370 en route from Beijing to Kuala Lumpur with 239 people on board.

Mali

While the political situation in Mali stabilized in 2014, persistent attacks by numerous pro and anti-government armed groups in the north led to a marked deterioration in security in Gao, Kidal, and Timbuktu regions, where the 2013 French-led intervention sought to restore state control.

Throughout 2014, armed groups linked to Al-Qaeda, along with ethnic Tuareg and Arab movements, some seeking autonomy, dramatically increased attacks on Malian soldiers and neutral peacekeepers, and to a lesser extent, on aid workers and other civilians. Little progress was made in reaching a negotiated settlement, advancing justice for abuses, or addressing development challenges.

The withdrawal in May of Malian civil servants and soldiers from key towns in the north, following a brief resumption of hostilities, resulted in a rise in ethnic tension, left large swaths of territory devoid of state authority, and led to a significant rise in banditry by unidentified gunmen. Meanwhile, there was little progress on security sector reform or the disarmament of fighters in the north.

Malian authorities made little effort to investigate and hold accountable those implicated in serious abuses committed during the 2012-2013 armed conflict. However, there was a decrease in abuses by state security forces and progress in the investigation into the 2012 torture and killing of 21 elite soldiers. Rule of law institutions countrywide were weak, in part due to unprofessional practices and inadequate budgetary allocations for the criminal justice system. Corruption, endemic at all levels of government, further impeded Malians' access to basic health care and education.

Concerns about the deteriorating security situation and re-entrenchment of Al-Qaeda-linked groups in the north sustained diplomatic interest in Mali. The French government played a key role in military matters, the European Union on training and security sector reform, and the United Nations, through the Multidimensional Integrated Stabilization Mission in Mali (MINUSMA), on rule of law and political stability. These actors were largely reluctant to publicly call for investigations into past and ongoing crimes. The International Monetary Fund and World Bank pressed the government over bad economic governance.

**COLLAPSE, CONFLICT
AND ATROCITY IN MALI**
Human Rights Watch Reporting on the 2012-13 Armed Conflict
and Its Aftermath

Abuses by Armed Groups in the North

Since late September 2013, opposition armed groups carried out several dozen ambushes and suicide bombings, and deployed improvised explosive devices and landmines. Most attacks targeted Malian and French troops, though others targeted civilians and peacekeepers in violation of the laws of war. Landmines on key roads and rocket attacks in major towns generated a climate of fear for civilians, and killed and wounded several. Over 30 UN peacekeepers died in attacks.

In February, the Movement for Unity and Jihad in West Africa (MUJAO) kidnapped five aid workers from the International Committee of the Red Cross; they were freed in April during a French military operation. In May, two aid workers with the Norwegian Refugee Council were killed when their vehicle struck an improvised explosive device near Timbuktu.

A visit by the prime minister to the National Movement for the Liberation of Azawad (MNLA) stronghold of Kidal in May led to brief resumption of hostilities. During the clashes, eight civilians, including six civil servants, were allegedly summarily executed by the armed groups occupying Kidal.

Security in the north was further undermined by persistent inter-communal clashes, particularly involving people from the Peuhl, Tuareg, and Arab ethnic groups, which left dozens dead. Al-Qaeda in the Islamic Maghreb (AQIM) continued at time of writing to hold four hostages; one from France, one from the Netherlands, one from Sweden, and a dual British and South African national. During 2014, one French and one Algerian hostage reportedly died in captivity, while two Algerians captured in Gao in 2012 were released.

Abuses by State Security Forces

In 2014, the number of violations committed by the Malian army decreased, but soldiers were implicated in several cases of arbitrary detention, one instance of excessive use of force in responding to a demonstration in Kidal, and several summary executions, largely targeting Tuareg men. The military hierarchy made some effort to investigate and hold to account soldiers implicated in several of these incidents. Members of the security forces were also implicated in acts of extortion, bribe taking, and to a lesser extent rape.

Accountability for Abuses during the 2012-2013 Armed Conflict

The government made little progress in holding to account those from all warring factions responsible for laws of war violations committed during the 2012-2013 armed conflict. The government's provisional release in 2014 of over 40 men associated with the conflict, including several commanders credibly implicated in abuses, raised concern of a de facto amnesty for these crimes. The government characterized the releases, which began in late 2013, as "confidence building measures" in advance of negotiations. They were carried out without regard as to whether the men might have been responsible for serious crimes in violation of international law.

Supreme Court orders passed in 2013 permitted a Bamako court to hear criminal cases from the three northern provinces, and during 2014, dozens of families filed complaints to judicial authorities. With few exceptions, these authorities failed to investigate any of these cases or others that human rights groups and journalists brought to their attention.

There was, however, meaningful progress in the investigation into the torture and enforced disappearance of 21 elite "Red Berets" in 2012. In late 2013 and early 2014, some 25 soldiers, including former coup leader Gen. Amadou Haya Sanogo, were charged in connection with the crimes.

In July 2012, Mali, a state party to the International Criminal Court (ICC), referred "the situation in Mali since January 2012" to the ICC prosecutor for investigation. On January 16, 2013, the ICC prosecutor formally opened an investigation into grave crimes allegedly committed in the northern three regions of Mali, and during 2014, ICC investigators conducted several missions to the country.

Truth and Reconciliation Mechanism

After assuming office in September 2013, President Ibrahim Boubacar Keita dissolved a pre-existing truth commission and, by two executive orders, established the Truth, Justice and Reconciliation Commission; on March 20, the National Assembly ratified the orders. The commission has a three-year mandate, will cover the period from 1960 to 2013, and will consist of 15 members and

7 working groups. It will function under the Ministry of National Reconciliation and Development of the North.

By late 2014, the commissioners had yet to be appointed and the body's credibility was limited because of the failure to consult sufficiently with a wide variety of stakeholders on its members, mandate powers, and degree of independence.

Judiciary

During 2014, there was progress in re-establishing the judiciary in Timbuktu and Gao regions, evident in the rehabilitation of local courthouses and jails and re-deployment of prosecutors, judges, and judicial police who had fled during the armed conflict. However, their ability to conduct investigations outside major towns was limited by the precarious security situation.

Neglect and mismanagement within the Malian judiciary countrywide led to striking deficiencies, including insufficient staffing and logistical constraints. These shortfalls hindered efforts to address impunity for perpetrators of all crimes and contributed to violations of the right to due process.

Because of the courts' inability to adequately process cases, hundreds of detainees are held in extended pretrial detention in overcrowded jails and detention centers. Judges in Bamako mandated to investigate several hundred suspects detained during the offensive to retake the north made some progress, resulting in the release of scores of men who appeared to have been arbitrarily detained, largely as a result of their ethnicity.

Recruitment of Children and Child Labor

Armed groups in the north continued to recruit and use child soldiers, some as young as 12. During 2014, some 20 schools in the north were at various times occupied by members of the armed groups, pro-government militias, the Malian army and, in one case, MINUSMA. Several children suspected of supporting the armed groups were detained in both the Bamako Central Prison and a gendarme camp in Bamako, in contravention of a 2013 protocol signed by the government stipulating that children were to be placed in a care center managed by the UN Children's Rights Emergency and Relief Organization.

Child labor in agriculture, domestic service, mining, and other sectors was common, and often included dangerous work that Malian law prohibits for anyone under the age of 18. Child laborers in artisanal gold mining were exposed to health risks from accidents and exposure to toxic mercury.

Key International Actors

In June, the UN Security Council renewed the mandate of MINUSMA, the peacekeeping mission with a troop ceiling of 11,200 military personnel, some 70 percent of whom are currently deployed. The UN independent expert on the situation of human rights in Mali, Suliman Baldo, conducted two missions and pressed for progress in the fight against impunity. In March, the UN Human Rights Council passed a resolution that welcomed progress, expressed concerns on continued violations and abuses, and renewed the mandate of the independent expert. The UN Peacebuilding fund supported demobilization, reconciliation, and justice projects.

The African Union (AU) brokered a ceasefire in May that paved the way for Algerian and AU-led negotiations between the Malian government and several armed groups; the talks took place in the Algerian capital, Algiers.

The 1,700 strong French military operation known as Operation Serval was in August transformed into a 3,000-strong regional operation—known as Operation Barkhane—to address the threat of instability in Mauritania, Burkina Faso, Niger, and Chad.

The European Union Training Mission in Mali trained eight battalions of Malian soldiers, while the EU Capacity Building Mission, EUCAP Sahel Mali, was established to train the police, gendarmerie, and National Guard.

The EU and Dutch took the lead on justice sector reform and support. The UN Development Programme supported the rehabilitation of courthouses, while the United States provided forensic support to the Ministry of Justice.

In May and June 2014, the International Monetary Fund and the World Bank collectively delayed almost US$70 million in payments to the Malian government following questions surrounding the extra-budgetary purchase of a presidential plane and inflated military contracts. An audit revealed overbilling of over $56 million in the military budget.

Mexico

Upon taking office in December 2012, President Enrique Peña Nieto acknowledged that the "war on drugs" launched by his predecessor Felipe Calderón had led to serious abuses by the security forces. In 2014, the administration adopted a National Human Rights Program outlining its policies for the next 4 years, and recognized that the whereabouts of more than 22,000 people who had been reported missing since 2006 remained unknown.

The forced disappearance of 43 students in September in Iguala, Guerrero, led to widespread protests calling on the government to determine the whereabouts of the missing students, and address the broader problem of corruption and abuse that the case exposed.

Yet the government has made little progress in prosecuting widespread killings, enforced disappearances, and torture committed by soldiers and police in the course of efforts to combat organized crime, including during Peña Nieto's tenure.

Other ongoing problems include restrictions to press freedoms, abuses against migrants, and limits on access to reproductive rights and health care.

Enforced Disappearances

Mexico's security forces have participated in widespread enforced disappearances since former President Calderón (2006-2012) launched a "war on drugs." Members of all security forces continue to carry out disappearances during the Peña Nieto administration, in some cases, collaborating directly with criminal groups.

In September, approximately 30 municipal police officers in Iguala, Guerrero, opened fire without warning on three buses carrying about 90 students from a rural school that trains teachers. During that incident and two subsequent ones in which unidentified people opened fire on the students and others, more than 15 people were injured and 6 were killed. The policemen ordered students in the third bus to leave the vehicle, beat them, and forced them at gunpoint to lie down on the roadside before driving away with them in at least three police cars.

At time of writing, the whereabouts of 42 students remained unknown. The Attorney General's Office claimed that, based on the confession of three alleged perpetrators, the students were handed over to members of a criminal group, who killed them, burnt their bodies, and threw them in a municipal dump. The DNA of a forty-third student was identified among the remains that the Attorney General's Office reports having found in the area. More than 80 people were detained and charged for their alleged involvement in these incidents.

In August 2014, the government acknowledged that the whereabouts of over 22,000 people who had gone missing since 2006 remained unknown, but failed to disclose corroborating evidence, or information on how many of these cases are alleged enforced disappearances. Mexico's National Human Rights Commission (CNDH) has issued 12 reports documenting the enforced disappearance of 30 victims during this time, and found evidence of probable participation of state agents in approximately 600 other disappearances cases.

As of April, according to official information, no one had been convicted for an enforced disappearance committed after 2006. Prosecutors and police routinely fail to carry out basic investigative steps to identify those responsible for disappearances, often blaming victims, and telling their families to investigate. Families of the disappeared may lose access to basic social services that are tied to the victim's employment, such as child care.

The government has pursued potentially promising initiatives to find people who have gone missing, but they have produced limited results. In 2013, it created a unit in the Federal Prosecutor's Office to investigate disappearances, and locate people who had gone missing. As of August 2014, the unit had found 87 people. The implementation of a comprehensive database donated by the International Committee of the Red Cross to cross-reference information on missing people and unidentified bodies, remained pending at time of writing.

Military Abuses and Impunity

Mexico has relied heavily on the military to fight drug-related violence and organized crime, leading to widespread human rights violations. Since 2006, the CNDH received approximately 9,000 complaints of abuse by the army, and issued reports in over 100 cases in which it found that army personnel had committed serious human rights violations.

In April, Congress reformed the Code of Military Justice, stating that abuses committed by members of the military against civilians should be handled by the ordinary criminal justice system. Previously, these cases had been handled by the military justice system, which had routinely failed to hold members of the military accountable for abuses. Under the reform, abuses against soldiers remain subject to the military justice system, which lacks independence and transparency.

In June, military personnel opened fire on a group of 22 civilians who were inside an empty warehouse in Tlatlaya, state of Mexico, killing all of them. One soldier was injured during the incident.

Accounts from witnesses and a report by the CNDH said that at least 12 civilians were extrajudicially executed. State prosecutors detained two of the three surviving witnesses, beat them, repeatedly asphyxiated them with a bag, and threatened them with sexual abuse to force them to confess to having links to people killed in the incidents, and to say that the military was not responsible for the killings, according to the CNDH. They also threatened and mistreated a third witness, and forced the three witnesses to sign documents they were not allowed to read.

In September, the military justice system detained 24 soldiers and one lieutenant who allegedly participated in the incidents, and accused 8 of them of breaches of military discipline. Subsequently, the Attorney General's Office charged seven soldiers and the lieutenant with"undue exercise of public service. Three of the soldiers were also charged with "abuse of authority, aggravated homicide of eight people, and altering the crime scene." The lieutenant was also charged with cover-up.

Torture

Torture is widely practiced in Mexico to obtain forced confessions and extract information. It is most frequently applied in the period between when victims are arbitrarily detained and when they are handed to prosecutors, when they are often held incommunicado at military bases or other illegal detention sites. Common tactics include beatings, waterboarding, electric shocks, and sexual torture. Many judges continue to accept confessions obtained through torture, despite the constitutional prohibition of such evidence.

Criminal Justice System

The criminal justice system routinely fails to provide justice to victims of violent crimes and human rights violations. Causes of this failure include corruption, inadequate training and resources, and the complicity of prosecutors and public defenders.

In 2013, Mexico enacted a federal Victims Law intended to ensure justice, protection, and reparations for victims of crime. At time of writing, the executive had yet to adopt implementing regulations that are necessary to provide reparations to victims. As of March 2014, only six states had enacted legislation in compliance with the Victims Law.

In 2008, Mexico passed a constitutional reform to transform its inquisitorial, written justice system to an adversarial, oral one by 2016. As of November, only 3 states had fully implemented the reform, while 13 had partially transitioned to the new system.

The reform also introduced the provision of *arraigo*, which allows prosecutors, with judicial authorization, to hold organized crime suspects for up to 80 days before they are charged with a crime. In February, the Supreme Court ruled the provision should only be applied in cases of organized crime. A proposal to reduce the maximum time that such individuals can be held without charge to 35 days was pending before the Senate at time of writing.

Self-Defense Groups

The failure of law enforcement has contributed to the emergence of armed citizen self-defense groups in many parts of the country.

Following concerns about some groups' unregulated security actions, self-defense groups in Michoacán state signed an agreement with the government in April stipulating that their members would register their weapons and incorporate into local security forces. At time of writing, there had been no independent assessment of the agreement's implementation, nor its compliance with the vetting procedures for security forces that are required by Mexican law.

Prison Conditions

Prisons are overpopulated, unhygienic, and fail to provide basic security for most inmates. Prisoners who accuse guards or inmates of attacks or other abuses, have no effective system to seek redress. In the majority of prisons, the inmate population is controlled by organized crime, and corruption and violence are rampant.

Freedom of Media

Journalists, particularly those who report on crime or criticize officials, face harassment and attacks. According to the Special Prosecutor's Office for Crimes against Freedom of Expression, between 2000 and May 2014, 102 journalists were killed, and 24 were disappeared—including 2 who were killed in 2014.

Authorities routinely fail to adequately investigate crimes against journalists, often preemptively ruling out their profession as a motive. As of May, the Special Prosecutor's Office was conducting 555 investigations of crimes against journalists or media outlets, and had presented charges in 61 cases.

Journalists are often driven to self-censorship by attacks carried out both by government officials and by criminal groups, while the under-regulation of state advertising can also limit media freedom by giving the government disproportionate financial influence over media outlets.

Women's and Girls' Rights

Mexican laws do not adequately protect women and girls against domestic and sexual violence. Some provisions, including those that make the severity of punishments for some sexual offenses contingent upon the "chastity" of the victim, contradict international standards. Women and girls who have suffered these types of human rights violations generally do not report them to authorities, while those who do generally face suspicion, apathy, and disrespect.

In 2008, the Supreme Court affirmed the constitutionality of a Mexico City law that legalized abortion in the first 12 weeks of pregnancy. Since then, 17 states have legislated to recognize the right to life from the moment of conception.

HUMAN
RIGHTS
WATCH

CARE WHEN THERE IS NO CURE
Ensuring the Right to Palliative Care in Mexico

"[With the pain] I didn't have the desire to do anything. I wasn't hungry and didn't want to walk...nothing. It would anger me when people spoke to me... [With palliative care] I have come back to life."
– REMEDIOS RAMÍREZ FACIO, A 73-YEAR-OLD WOMAN WITH PANCREATIC CANCER
WHO RECEIVES PALLIATIVE CARE AT MEXICO'S NATIONAL CANCER INSTITUTE.

In 2010, the Supreme Court ruled that all states must provide emergency contraception and access to abortion for rape victims. However, in practice many women and girls face serious barriers to accessing abortions after sexual violence, including inaccurate information and intimidation by officials.

Sexual Orientation and Gender Identity

In 2010, the Supreme Court recognized the right of same-sex couples in Mexico City to adopt children and to marry. It ruled that all 31 Mexican states must recognize same-sex marriages that take place in Mexico City, but did not require states to perform same-sex marriages in their respective jurisdictions. In January 2014, the Supreme Court also ruled that same-sex couples can claim the same social security and health insurance benefits that heterosexual couples receive from government entities. In September, Coahuila became the first state to legalize same-sex marriage.

Palliative Care

The Mexican government took a number of important steps to implement legal provisions granting people who are terminally ill access to palliative care. It enacted a new regulation in November 2013, announced an overhaul of drug control regulations to facilitate access to morphine and other opioid analgesics, added partial coverage of palliative care to a government insurance scheme for the poor, and announced an effort to develop a national palliative care strategy. Tens of thousands of patients require end-of-life care in Mexico every year but only a small minority can access it in practice.

Migrants

Hundreds of thousands of undocumented migrants, including unaccompanied children and families, pass through Mexico each year and many are subjected to grave abuses en route at the hands of organized crime, migration authorities, and security forces. A 2013 report by the Inter-American Commission of Human Rights (IACHR) found that "robberies, extortion, kidnappings and physical and psychological assaults, sexual abuse, murders and disappearances to which [migrants] fall victim ... have taken a dramatic turn for the worse" in recent years.

In April, approximately 300 Central American migrants and 3 rights defenders accompanying them were allegedly attacked and forcibly detained by immigration and police officials in Tabasco, according to the IACHR.

Authorities have not taken adequate steps to protect migrants, or to investigate and prosecute those who abuse them. The government has also failed to implement protective measures granted by national and international human rights bodies in favor of migrant shelters' staff, who face threats and harassment from criminal groups and officials.

Labor Rights

The dominance of pro-management unions continues to obstruct legitimate labor-organizing activity. Independent unions are often blocked from entering negotiations with management, while workers who seek to form independent unions risk losing their jobs. A 2012 labor law failed to address the lack of transparency and democracy in the powerful pro-management unions, and failed to protect workers' right to form independent unions and carry out collective bargaining.

Human Rights Defenders

Human rights defenders and activists continue to suffer harassment and attacks, often in the context of opposition to infrastructure, or resource extraction "megaprojects." In many cases, there is evidence that state agents are involved in aggressions against them.

In 2012, Mexico enacted a law to protect human rights defenders and journalists. The protection mechanism created by the law, however, has not been effectively implemented, with protective measures slow to arrive, insufficient, or incomplete in some cases.

Key International Actors

The United States has allocated over US$2 billion in aid to Mexico through the Merida Initiative, an aid package agreed upon in 2007 without a year cap, to help Mexico combat organized crime. Fifteen percent of select portions of the assistance can be disbursed only after the US secretary of state reports that the

Mexican government is meeting human rights requirements. However, the impact of these requirements has been undermined by the fact that the US State Department has repeatedly reported to the US Congress that they are being met, despite overwhelming evidence to the contrary, often citing vague and incomplete progress towards meeting the requirements, leading Congress to release the funds.

In April-May, the UN special rapporteur on torture visited Mexico and found that torture is "generalized." In August, the UN special rapporteur on extrajudicial, summary or arbitrary executions reported that widespread abuses committed with impunity by security forces during the "war on drugs" seriously threatened the right to life. In September, the UN high commissioner for human rights expressed "very serious concern" over attacks against journalists, and urged the government to adopt measures to protect them.

In Mexico, most people with disabilities live in poverty, leading to increased barriers to education, employment, and health care. In its October 2014 review of Mexico's compliance with the UN Convention on the Rights of Persons with Disabilities, the treaty's monitoring body raised concerns about restrictions on the legal capacity of persons with disabilities, violence faced by women and children with disabilities (including involuntary sterilization), institutionalization of children with disabilities and physical coercion, and isolation of people with disabilities in psychiatric hospitals.

Morocco

Morocco's 2011 constitution incorporated strong human rights provisions, but these reforms have not led to improved practices, the passage of significant implementing legislation, or the revision of repressive laws. In 2014, Moroccans exercised their right to peaceful protest in the streets, but police continued to violently disperse them on occasion. Laws that criminalize acts deemed harmful to the king, the monarchy, Islam, or Morocco's claim over Western Sahara limited the rights to peaceful expression, assembly, and association. Courts continued to convict and imprison street protesters and dissidents in unfair trials. On a more positive note, Morocco implemented reforms announced in 2013 to its policies on migrants, granting temporary legal status to hundreds of refugees and to thousands of other foreigners, most of them sub-Saharan.

Freedom of Expression

Independent print and online media continue to investigate and criticize government officials and policies, but face prosecution and harassment if they step too far. The press law mandates prison terms for "maliciously" spreading "false information" that authorities consider likely to disturb the public order, or for speech that is ruled defamatory.

Moroccan state television allows some space for debate and investigative reporting but little for direct criticism of the government or dissent on key issues. Authorities pursued their investigation on terrorism charges of Ali Anouzla, director of the independent news site Lakome.com, because of an article describing, and providing an indirect link to, a jihadist recruitment video. In 2013, Anouzla spent five weeks in detention after publishing the article.

Rapper Mouad Belghouat ("El-Haqed"), whose songs denounce corruption and police abuse, spent four months in prison after being convicted on charges of assaulting police officers, in a trial where the judge refused to summon any defense witnesses or purported victims. Authorities in February prevented a Casablanca bookstore from hosting an event for El-Haqed's new song album. Seventeen-year-old rapper Othmane Atiq ("Mr. Crazy") served a three-month prison term for insulting the police and inciting drug use for his music videos depicting the lives of disaffected urban youth.

Abdessamad Haydour, a student, continued to serve a three -year prison term for insulting the king by calling him a "dog," "a murderer," and "a dictator" in a YouTube video. A court sentenced him in February 2012 under a penal code provision criminalizing "insults to the king."

Freedom of Assembly

Authorities tolerated numerous marches and rallies to demand political reform and protest government actions, but they forcibly dispersed some gatherings, assaulting protesters. In Western Sahara, authorities prohibited all public gatherings deemed hostile to Morocco's contested rule over that territory, dispatching large numbers of police who blocked access to demonstration venues and often forcibly dispersed Sahrawis seeking to assemble.

On April 6, police arrested 11 young men at a pro-reform march in Casablanca and accused them of hitting and insulting the police. A court of first instance on May 22 sentenced nine of them to prison terms of up to one year and two to suspended sentences using similarly worded "confessions" police said they had made in pretrial detention, although the defendants repudiated them in court. On June 17, the court provisionally freed the nine pending the outcome of their appeals trial, which was continuing at time of writing.

Freedom of Association

Officials continue to arbitrarily prevent or impede many associations from obtaining legal registration although the 2011 constitution guarantees the right to form an association. In May, authorities refused to register Freedom Now, a new free speech group and prohibited it from holding a conference at the bar association in Rabat. Other associations denied legal registration included charitable, cultural, and educational associations whose leadership includes members of al-Adl wal-Ihsan (Justice and Spirituality), a nationwide movement that advocates for an Islamic state and questions the king's spiritual authority.

In Western Sahara, authorities withheld recognition for all local human rights organizations whose leaders support independence for that territory, even those that won administrative court rulings that they had wrongfully been denied recognition.

Authorities also prohibited tens of public and non-public activities prepared by legally recognized human rights associations, such as an international youth camp that the national chapter of Amnesty International had organized every summer; and numerous conferences, training sessions, and youth activities organized by the Moroccan Association for Human Rights (AMDH) and its branches.

Between April and October, Morocco expelled at least 40 foreign visitors from Western Sahara. Most of those affected were either European supporters of Sahrawi self-determination or freelance journalists or researchers who had not coordinated their visit with authorities. These expulsions, along with heavy Moroccan police surveillance of foreigners who did visit and met Sahrawi rights activists, undermined Morocco's efforts to showcase the Western Sahara as a place open to international scrutiny.

Police Conduct, Torture, and the Criminal Justice System

Legal reforms advanced slowly. A law promulgated in September empowers the newly created Constitutional Court to block proposed legislation if it contravenes the new constitution, including its human rights provisions. A proposed law that would deny military courts jurisdiction over civilians was awaiting parliamentary approval.

Meanwhile, military courts continued to try civilians, including Mbarek Daoudi, a Sahrawi activist held since September 2013, on weapons charges. Twenty-one other Sahrawis remained in prison serving long sentences imposed by a military court in 2013. The men had been charged in connection with violence that erupted on November 8, 2010, when authorities dismantled the Gdeim Izik protest camp in Western Sahara. Eleven members of the security forces were killed in the violence. The military court failed to investigate defendants' allegations that police officers had tortured or coerced them into signing false statements, and relied heavily on the statements to return its guilty verdict.

Courts failed to uphold the right of defendants to receive fair trials in political and security-related cases. Authorities continued to imprison hundreds of suspected Islamist militants they arrested in the wake of the Casablanca bombings of May 2003. Many were serving sentences imposed after unfair trials following months of secret detention, ill-treatment and, in some cases, torture. Police have arrested hundreds more suspected militants since further terrorist attacks in 2007 and 2011. Courts have convicted and imprisoned many of them on charges of belonging to a "terrorist network" or preparing to join Islamist militants fighting in Iraq or elsewhere. Morocco's 2003 counterterrorism law contains a broad definition of "terrorism" and allows for up to 12 days of *garde à vue* (pre-charge) detention.

After visiting Morocco and Western Sahara in December 2013, the United Nations Working Group on Arbitrary Detention (WGAD) concluded, "The Moroccan criminal judicial system relies heavily on confessions as the main evidence to support conviction. Complaints received by the Working Group indicate the use of torture by State officials to obtain evidence or confessions during initial questioning ... .Courts and prosecutors do not comply with their obligation to initiate an ex officio investigation whenever there are reasonable grounds to believe that a confession has been obtained through the use of torture and ill-treatment." The WGAD said authorities had allowed it to visit the places of detention it had requested, and to interview detainees of its choice in private.

Moroccan courts continue to impose the death penalty, but authorities have not carried out executions since the early 1990s.

Prison conditions are reportedly harsh, largely due to overcrowding, exacerbated by the proclivity of investigating judges to order the pretrial detention of suspects. The National Human Rights Council (CNDH), which urged the government to expand alternative punishments, reported that the prison population had reached 72,000 in 2013, 42 percent of them pretrial, with an average of 2 square meters of space per inmate. The CNDH is a state-funded body that reports to the king.

A court on August 12 sentenced left-wing activist Wafae Charaf to serve one year in prison and pay a fine, and damages for slander and "falsely" reporting an offense, after she filed a complaint after unknown men abducted and tortured her following a workers' protest in April in Tangiers. An appeals court in that city on October 20 doubled her prison term to two years. A Casablanca court sentenced one local activist to three years in prison, a fine, and damages, on the same charges, after he reported having been abducted and tortured by unknown men. The sentences in these two cases could have a chilling effect on people wishing to file complaints of abuse by the security forces.

Sexual Orientation and Gender Identity

Moroccan courts continued to jail persons for homosexual behavior under article 489 of the penal code, which prohibits "lewd or unnatural acts with an individual of the same sex." Two of six men arrested in Beni Mellal in April and charged under this provision received prison terms for this and other offenses.

On October 2, a court sentenced a British tourist and a Moroccan acquaintance to four months in prison for homosexuality. After spending about three weeks in jail, the two men were released pending appeal.

Migrants and Refugees

Implementation continued of a 2013 plan to overhaul national policies toward migrants. Morocco's refugee agency granted one-year renewable residency permits to more than 500 UNHCR-recognized refugees. At time of writing, Morocco had not determined the status it would grant to more than 1,300 Syrians, whom UNHCR recognizes as refugees. Morocco also granted one-year renewable residency permits to thousands of sub-Saharan migrants who were not asylum-seekers but who met certain criteria. However, security forces continued to use excessive force on migrants, especially the mostly sub-Saharan migrants who were camping near, or attempting to scale, the fences separating Morocco from the Spanish enclave of Melilla (see also Spain chapter).

Women's and Girls' Rights

The 2011 constitution guarantees equality for women, "while respecting the provisions of the Constitution, and the laws and permanent characteristics of the Kingdom." In January, Parliament removed from article 475 of the penal code a clause that had, in effect, allowed some men to escape prosecution for raping a minor if they agreed to marry her. The code retains other discriminatory provisions, including article 490, which criminalizes consensual sex between unmarried people and so places rape victims at risk of prosecution if the accused rapist is acquitted.

The Family Code discriminates against women with regard to inheritance and the right of husbands to unilaterally divorce their wives. Reforms to the code in 2004 improved women's rights in divorce and child custody, and raised the age of

HUMAN
RIGHTS
WATCH

ABUSED AND EXPELLED
Ill-Treatment of Sub-Saharan African Migrants in Morocco

marriage from 15 to 18. However, judges routinely allow girls to marry below this age. In September 2014, the Committee on the Rights of the Child expressed concern that Morocco had not adopted a legislation criminalizing all forms of domestic violence, including marital rape, although violence against women and girls in the home is reported to be pervasive.

Domestic Workers

Despite laws prohibiting the employment of children under the age of 15, thousands of children under that age—predominantly girls—are believed to work as domestic workers. According to the UN, nongovernmental organizations, and government sources, the number of child domestic workers has declined in recent years, but girls as young as 8 years old continue to work in private homes for up to 12 hours a day for as little as US$11 per month. In some cases, employers beat and verbally abused the girls, denied them an education, and refused them adequate food. In January 2014, an Agadir court sentenced an employer to 20 years in prison for violence leading to the death of a child domestic worker in her employ. In September 2014, the Committee on the Rights of the Child expressed concern that the government had not taken effective measures to remove children from hazardous domestic labor.

Morocco's labor law excludes domestic workers from its protections, which include a minimum wage, limits to work hours, and a weekly rest day. In 2006, authorities presented a draft law to regulate domestic work and reinforce existing prohibitions on domestic workers under 15 years old. The draft had been modified but not adopted at time of writing.

Key International Actors

France, a close ally and Morocco's leading trading partner, refrained from publicly criticizing human rights violations in the kingdom. Morocco suspended its bilateral judicial cooperation agreements with France in February after a French investigating judge served subpoenas on a visiting Moroccan police commander based on a complaint of complicity in torture. The United States is also a close ally of Morocco. Secretary of State John Kerry, in Rabat in April for the bilateral "Strategic Dialogue," avoided any public mention of human rights concerns.

The government in recent years has granted access to several UN human rights mechanisms seeking to visit Morocco and Western Sahara, including the Working Group on Arbitrary Detention in December 2013 (see above). Then-UN High Commissioner for Human Rights Navi Pillay, on an official visit on May 29, noted Morocco's "great strides towards the better promotion and protection of human rights," but cited several areas of concern, including torture, restraints on freedom of expression, and the need to implement laws guaranteeing rights set out in the 2011 constitution.

As in past years, the UN Security Council in April renewed the mandate of UN peacekeeping forces in Western Sahara (MINURSO) without broadening it to include human rights monitoring, something Morocco strongly opposes.

HUMAN
RIGHTS
WATCH

SILENCED AND FORGOTTEN
Survivors of Nepal's Conflict-Era Sexual Violence

Nepal

A coalition government led by Nepali Congress leader Sushil Koirala took power in February 2014 after months of political stalemate but did not make much progress on human rights. Pressing concerns include lack of accountability for serious human rights violations and war crimes committed during the 1996-2006 civil war, migrant and refugee rights, and women's and girls' rights.

In May, the assembly enacted a law establishing the Commission on Investigation of Disappeared Persons, Truth and Reconciliation to investigate serious rights violations and abuses committed during the civil war, but the law largely replicates a previous version that the Supreme Court struck down as unconstitutional.

Pressure from China has contributed to continuing restrictions on Tibetans in Nepal, including those living in the country and those transiting to India.

The government tried but was unable to press for greater protection of its migrant workers despite reported deaths and injuries, particularly in Qatar.

Accountability and Transitional Justice

Nepal has made little progress on justice for serious abuses committed by both sides during its decade-long civil war, in which an estimated 13,000 people died. Efforts to ensure prosecutions in civilian courts for serious human rights and humanitarian law violations during the conflict remain stalled.

In 2014, authorities in the United Kingdom continued to proceed with the prosecution of Nepali army Col. Kumar Lama, charged with committing torture during the civil war, under English laws of universal jurisdiction for that crime. While Nepal has delivered interim monetary and in-kind compensation to the families of those who were "disappeared" or killed during the conflict, other victims, such as victims of sexual violence or torture, have received no compensation from the state.

Truth and Reconciliation

In January 2014, Nepal's Supreme Court rejected the Truth and Reconciliation (TRC) Ordinance, ruling that any mechanism for transitional justice must conform

HUMAN
RIGHTS
WATCH

UNDER CHINA'S SHADOW
Mistreatment of Tibetans in Nepal

to international legal standards. In May 2014, Nepal's Constituent Assembly passed a new TRC Act, but the law did not address the Supreme Court's concerns. A public interest litigation challenge to the new law has been filed with the Supreme Court.

In July, the United Nations Office of the High Commissioner on Human Rights issued a technical note pointing out that the TRC Act does not conform to Nepal's international legal obligations, including because it allows amnesties for serious international crimes. Five experts at the UN Human Rights Council have voiced similar concerns.

Tibetan Refugees

Nepal imposes strict restrictions on peaceful protests by Tibetan refugees. Since the 2008 uprising in Tibet, Chinese authorities have pressured Nepal to restrict basic rights. Tibetans in Nepal are forbidden from participating in public celebrations of the Dalai Lama's birthday or the Tibetan new year. Buddhist religious sites and monasteries are openly under government surveillance.

A 2014 Human Rights Watch report documented limitations on the fundamental freedoms of Tibetans in Nepal. Nepal's Ministry of Foreign Affairs dismissed the findings, claiming that the report drew on unsubstantiated claims. The ministry did not address Nepal's de facto ban on political protests by Tibetans, its failure to provide them with official identification documents, sharp restrictions on public activities promoting Tibetan culture and religion, and routine abuses by Nepali security forces including excessive use of force, arbitrary detention, and ill-treatment.

Migrant Workers

The Nepali economy depends heavily on remittances from Nepali migrant workers abroad, but the government has done little to support and protect such workers.

In 2014, there were reports that hundreds of Nepali and other migrant workers in Qatar had died due to poor working conditions. Migrant workers often live in cramped, unsanitary conditions, and many workers complain of excessive working hours and unpaid wages. The Nepal government took some steps by suspending some unregulated recruiting agencies and calling upon the Qatar government to provide redress and end practices that facilitate trafficking and forced labor, but was unable to ensure effective protection.

Statelessness

Despite promises of reform, Nepal's citizenship laws leave an estimated 2.1 million people without official status and at risk of statelessness. As a result, many people, particularly women, children born out of wedlock, or children of refugee fathers, are unable to secure drivers' licenses, passports, bank accounts, or voting rights. The flawed citizenship law makes it particularly difficult for women to secure legal proof of citizenship, especially when male family members refuse to assist them or are unavailable to do so, and it effectively denies citizenship to children of non-Nepali fathers.

Women's and Girls' Rights

Victims of rape and other sexual violence committed by both sides during Nepal's civil war are excluded from any compensation under the Interim Relief Program. They also have been denied access to justice through regular courts for a variety of reasons, including that Nepali criminal law has an inflexible 35-day statute of limitations on reporting rape. Despite promises by the previous government, Nepal is yet to amend its laws against sexual assault.

Protecting Disabled Children

In line with its international obligations under the Convention on the Rights of Persons with Disabilities (CRPD), the government has made a commitment to inclusive education, but has failed to effectively implement the policy due to lack of funding, inadequate teacher training, and competing priorities. The enrollment of children with disabilities in primary and secondary education continued to decline in 2014 and an estimated 85 percent of all out-of-school children in Nepal have disabilities.

The government, however, has increased school scholarships for children with disabilities, developed a special curriculum for children with intellectual disabilities, and established a team tasked with developing a new national inclusive education policy.

Key International Actors

The international community was less vocal on human rights in Nepal in 2014. In 2013, European Union missions—including those of Denmark, Finland, France, Germany, and the United Kingdom—and the EU delegation, joined by Norway and Switzerland, had issued a statement calling for credible and independent mechanisms to address war-era violations, emphasizing that there should be no amnesty for serious human rights abuses.

However, in 2014 there were no public statements from the EU despite Nepal's announcement of a flawed commission. Instead, some countries suggested they might fund some part of the commission, although they retreated from this position after the OHCHR issued a technical note pointing out the shortcomings. Donors have yet to publicly state that they will refrain from supporting any process that violates Nepal's international legal obligations.

China has significant influence in Nepal. The two countries have several security and intelligence sharing agreements and exchanged several official high-level visits in 2014. Nepal pledged cooperation with China's People's Armed Police and closely monitored the Tibetan community. China's financial assistance to Nepal has increased, with several proposed hydropower and transit agreements.

The US continued to play the primary role in Tibetan refugee protection issues. The US and other countries have also provided third country settlement to tens of thousands of Bhutanese refugees from Nepal.

During an official state visit, the newly elected prime minister of India, Narendra Modi, committed to providing assistance for development projects and pressed the government to complete drafting a new constitution, but made no mention of conflict-era accountability.

HUMAN
RIGHTS
WATCH

"Those Terrible Weeks
in their Camp"
Boko Haram Violence against Women and Girls in Northeast Nigeria

Nigeria

Intensified violence and atrocities by Boko Haram, Nigeria's home-grown militant insurgent group, dominated the country's human rights landscape in 2014. The group indiscriminately killed civilians, abducted women and girls, forcefully conscripted young men and boys, and destroyed villages, towns, and schools. In April 2014, Boko Haram's abduction of nearly 300 schoolgirls in the town of Chibok focused unprecedented global attention on the group.

In a shocking display of its military power, Boko Haram seized and controlled territory in the beleaguered northeastern states of Borno, Yobe, and Adamawa. In responding to the Islamist group, government security forces were also implicated in grave violations of human rights and international humanitarian law in the treatment of Boko Haram suspects. Violence persisted, despite the imposition of a state of emergency in 2013 that was renewed in May. The conflict resulted in the death of over 2,500 civilians between January and August 2014, and the displacement of over 650,000 residents within Nigeria as well as more than 80,000 as refugees in neighboring countries.

Elsewhere in Nigeria, communal violence, fueled by competition for power and access to land between nomadic pastoralists and farming communities, killed more than 1,200 people in the north-central states in 2014. Security forces, including the police, engaged in human rights abuses including torture throughout the country.

Nigerian authorities made scant effort to investigate or prosecute those responsible for the violence. International actors, notably the United Kingdom, United States, and United Nations, frequently condemned the actions of Boko Haram, but their criticism of the abusive conduct of the Nigerian security forces has not resulted in meaningful change.

Abuses by Boko Haram

Boko Haram attacked and in some cases held more than 130 villages and towns, where it imposed its interpretation of Sharia law. Boko Haram combatants perpetrated killings, and razed and looted homes, businesses, schools, churches, markets, and health facilities in Borno, Yobe, and Adamawa states.

The violence extended to the cities of Kano, Jos, Kaduna, Gombe, Bauchi, Lagos, and Abuja, the federal capital territory, where multiple bombings—for which the insurgents claimed responsibility—killed over 410 people. Out of about 6,000 civilian deaths in Boko Haram attacks since 2009, more than 2,563 people were killed in 2014 alone.

Since 2009, Boko Haram has destroyed at least 211 schools in Borno alone, and abducted more than 500 women and girls from the northeast, of which at least over 100 either escaped, were rescued by security forces, or were released by insurgents. Some abductees suffered other abuses including sexual violence, forced marriage, and forced conversion.

In the largest abduction to date, the group captured 276 female students from a government-run secondary school in Chibok, Borno State; 219 of the schoolgirls remain in captivity. Male students were also targeted in Boko Haram's attacks on schools: insurgents killed over 100 male students at government-owned schools in Buni Yadi and Potiskum, Yobe State, during attacks in February and November. Insurgents have also abducted and forcibly conscripted hundreds of young men and boys; those who resist conscription are executed.

Conduct of Security Forces

Government security forces continued to respond to the Boko Haram violence in a heavy-handed manner, leading to serious human rights violations. Suspects are routinely abused, tortured, and held incommunicado in abusive detention conditions without charge or trial. The Joint Investigation Team, which military authorities commissioned in 2013, has recommended for trial 500 suspects out of 1,400 detainees in the northeast. Fewer than 50 suspects have faced trial.

During a Boko Haram attack in March on the Giwa military barrack and detention facility in Maiduguri, Borno state, security forces allegedly killed more than 600 detainees who fled during the attack. No member of the security forces has been brought to justice for these and previous violations of human rights, despite repeated pledges by the military to investigate them.

Local vigilante groups assisting Nigerian security forces to apprehend the militants and repel attacks were allegedly implicated in the recruitment and use of child soldiers, and ill-treatment and unlawful killing of Boko Haram suspects.

Nigerian authorities were at time of writing investigating video footage that appeared to show the execution of unarmed men by soldiers, including some in uniform, and members of the vigilante groups who can be identified by uniforms supplied by the Borno state government.

Inter-Communal and Political Violence

Inter-communal violence, which has plagued the Middle Belt states of Plateau and Kaduna for years, extended to other states in northern Nigeria, including Benue, Nasarawa, Taraba, Katsina, and Zamfara.

Recurring violence in these states since 2010 has resulted in the death of more than 4,000 people and the displacement of more than 120,000 residents. The failure of federal and state authorities to investigate and prosecute crimes committed by all sides, including ethnic and economic groups in these five states, exacerbated the struggle for political power between ethnic groups and failed to resolve contested access to grazing land by both sedentary farmers and nomadic herdsmen.

Political violence between supporters of two major political parties in the build-up to the February 2015 general elections led to bloody clashes in Rivers State in early 2014. In September, the president of the Nigerian Senate said that 2015 elections could be postponed because the nation "was at war with Boko Haram." The Independent National Electoral Commission, which supervises elections, had also suggested that it might be difficult to hold elections in the three states currently under emergency rule.

Government Corruption

Endemic public sector corruption continued to undermine the enjoyment of social and economic rights in Nigeria. In February 2014, the government suspended then-Governor of the Central Bank of Nigeria Sanusi Lamido Sanusi, on allegations of financial impropriety. Sanusi had alleged large-scale corruption by the Nigeria National Petroleum Corporation, which the government has yet to investigate.

In May, President Goodluck Jonathan told journalists that allegations of corruption against members of his cabinet were politically motivated and that most acts were no more than "common stealing."

The Economic and Financial Crimes Commission and its public sector counterpart, the Independent Corrupt Practices and Other Related Offences Commission, failed to effectively tackle high-level corruption and financial crimes in the country. Many of the arrests and prosecutions were against low-level officials, while allegations against highly placed politicians and the elite were not investigated.

Sexual Orientation and Gender Identity

In southern states, under the criminal code, consensual homosexual conduct can result in a 14-year prison term. In northern states, under Sharia law, punishments include caning, imprisonment, or death by stoning.

The Same-Sex Marriage (Prohibition) Bill, which President Jonathan ratified in January 2014, took things to what an observer described as "absurd levels" as the new law criminalizes public displays of affection between same-sex couples and penalizes organizations advocating for the rights of LGBT people. The law could inhibit the right to health by criminalizing outreach to LGBT groups. The vaguely worded law contradicts Nigeria's Constitution, as well as its obligations under regional and international human rights treaties. It has been roundly condemned by local and international human rights groups.

Freedom of Expression, Media, and Association

The Nigerian media is independent, strong, and free. However, it is not immune to intimidation and harassment for publishing materials that authorities deem to be uncomplimentary.

In June, security forces reacted to critical media reports about the military carrying out a campaign against several media houses, destroying newspapers and arresting at least two journalists. In July, a member of the federal House of Representatives introduced a bill to parliament designed to regulate foreign funding of civil society organizations. The bill mandates that voluntary organizations register with the Independent Corrupt Practices and Other Related Offences Commission and seek its approval within 60 days of accepting funds from international organizations. If passed into law, the bill would violate the right to freedom of association and assembly, guaranteed by the Nigerian Constitution and the African Charter on Human and Peoples' Rights.

Key International Actors

Under both domestic and international pressure in the wake of the massive media attention that followed the April Boko Haram abduction of hundreds of teenage schoolgirls, the Nigerian government requested assistance to combat the insurgency. The plea led to increased involvement by international actors and created an opportunity to exert pressure on the Nigerian government over its dismal human rights record.

At the London ministerial meeting on security in Nigeria in June, the United Kingdom outlined a substantial package of defense and development support to strengthen the capacity of the Nigerian military. The assistance includes provision of surveillance aircraft and the training of units to be deployed in counterinsurgency operations in the northeast.

At the August 2014 US-Africa Leaders' Summit, US President Barak Obama announced the launch of the Security Governance Initiative, of which Nigeria will be an inaugural recipient. This initiative is geared to help improve the transparency, governance, and effectiveness of the security sector.

In September, the US government also announced plans to launch a major border-security program for Nigeria, Cameroon, Chad, and Niger under the Global Security Contingency Fund launched by President Obama during the US-Africa Leaders' Summit. President Obama said that the US was committed to helping Nigeria address Boko Haram and urged Nigeria's government to adopt a comprehensive approach to protect its citizens.

In November, the US government confirmed allegations by Nigeria authorities that it denied the sale of military helicopters to Nigeria partly due to concerns about the failure of the Nigerian military to protect civilians during military operations.

In July, the European Parliament passed a resolution condemning Boko Haram abuses and urging the Nigerian government to ensure that efforts to tackle the insurgent violence are carried out in accordance with its obligations under international law. The violence in the north generated considerable attention from the United Nations: in May, the Security Council added Boko Haram to the UN's resolution 1267 [Al-Qaeda] sanctions list, which imposes an international asset freeze, travel ban, and arms embargo against the group. In May, the secretary-general's report on children and armed conflict included Boko Haram for the first time on its "list of shame" as a party to conflict that "kills and maims children," and "attacks schools and hospitals."

Navi Pillay, then-UN high commissioner for human rights, during a visit to Nigeria in March, emphasized the importance of transparent investigations into alleged violations by security forces in the northeast.

The prosecutor of the International Criminal Court (ICC) visited Nigeria in February, during which she reiterated her office's findings that Boko Haram is an armed group and the situation in northeast Nigeria is a non-international armed conflict. The situation in Nigeria has been under preliminary examination by the ICC since 2010.

Foreign Policy

Nigeria plays an important role in African and international affairs, and showed its commitment to the international human rights regime by ratifying all the major international and regional human rights treaties.

In Africa, which is the center of its foreign policy, Nigeria is a member of the African Union Peace and Security Council. President Jonathan is a co-mediator of the ECOWAS efforts to resolve the conflict in Mali, and the country currently contributes troops to the UN Multidimensional Integrated Stabilization Mission in Mali.

Nigeria has engaged with the UN and its organs, especially in the maintenance of international peace and security. It has regularly participated in UN and African Union peacekeeping operations across the world. In February, Nigeria was re-elected as chair of the UN Special Committee on Peacekeeping Operations and currently holds the chair of the Security Council Committee concerning Guinea-Bissau and the Ad Hoc Working Group on Conflict Prevention and Resolution in Africa. In October, Nigeria was elected to serve as a member of the UN Human Rights Council from 2015-2017.

Nigeria supports efforts to combat the illicit trade in small arms and light weapons and currently serves as one of the three vice-chairs of the Security Council's 1540 Committee on the non-proliferation of weapons of mass destruction. It is also one of the two vice-chairs of the Security Council Committee concerning Sudan.

The country has been at the forefront of demands for expanding the UN Security Council and is a leading African contender for permanent membership in a reformed version of the council.

North Korea

The human rights situation in the Democratic People's Republic of Korea (DPRK or North Korea) has remained dire under the control of Kim Jong-Un. The government is controlled by a one-party monopoly and dynastic leadership that do not tolerate pluralism and systematically denies basic freedoms. Tight controls on North Korea's border with China continued in 2014, further reducing the number of North Koreans able to flee and seek refuge in third countries.

A Commission of Inquiry (COI) established by the United Nations Human Rights Council (HRC), chaired by retired Australian judge Michael Kirby, published a devastating report in February 2014 that concluded that the North Korea government has committed systematic human right abuses at a scale without parallel in the contemporary world—including extermination, murder, enslavement, torture, imprisonment, rape, forced abortions, and other sexual violence.

On March 28, the HRC adopted a resolution supporting the COI's findings and calling for accountability. In October, heavy pressure on North Korea at the UN General Assembly in New York and North Korea's concern over the possibility of a referral to the International Criminal Court (ICC) prompted a first-ever meeting between North Korean diplomats and Marzuki Darusman, the HRC special rapporteur on human rights in North Korea.

On November 18, the third committee of the UN General Assembly, rejecting an amendment by Cuba that would have stripped accountability from the text, adopted the resolution by a 111 to 19 vote, with 55 states abstaining. The resolution endorsed the COI's conclusions and called on the UN Security Council to consider referring North Korea's leadership to the ICC for crimes against humanity committed against the people of North Korea.

Surprisingly, North Korea has ratified four key international human rights treaties and signed, but not yet ratified, another, and has a constitution that provides a number of rights protections on paper. But in practice, the government is among the most rights-repressing in the world. Political and civil rights are nonexistent since the government quashes all forms of disfavored expression and opinion and totally prohibits any organized political opposition, independent media, free trade unions, or civil society organizations. Religious freedom is systematically repressed.

North Koreans who seek to assert their rights are perceived to show insufficient reverence for supreme leader Kim Jong-Un or the ruling Korean Workers' Party. Those who act in ways viewed as contrary to state interests face arbitrary arrest, torture, and ill-treatment, detention without trial, or trial by state-controlled courts. North Koreans also face severe penalties for possessing unauthorized videos of foreign TV programs and movies or communicating with persons outside the country.

The government also practices collective punishment for supposed anti-state offenses, effectively enslaving hundreds of thousands of citizens, including children, in prison camps and other detention facilities where they face deplorable conditions and forced labor.

Torture and Inhumane Treatment

People arrested in North Korea are routinely tortured by officials in the course of interrogations. Common forms of torture include kicking and slapping, beatings with iron rods or sticks, being forced to remain in stress positions for hours, sleep deprivation, and, for female detainees, sexual abuse and rape. For less serious crimes, suspects endure abuse until they can pay bribes for better treatment or release, while for more serious offenses, torture is used to extract confessions.

Executions

North Korea's criminal code stipulates that the death penalty can be applied for vaguely defined offenses such as "crimes against the state" and "crimes against the people." In 2007, North Korea amended its penal code to extend the death penalty to additional crimes, including non-violent offenses such as fraud and smuggling, as long as authorities determine the crime is "extremely serious."

Political Prisoner Camps

Persons accused of serious political offenses are usually sent to brutal forced labor camps, known as *kwan-li-so*, operated by North Korea's National Security Agency. The government not only punishes the offender, but also the person's entire extended family.

These camps are characterized by systematic abuses and often deadly conditions, including meager rations that lead to near-starvation, virtually no medical care, lack of proper housing and clothes, regular mistreatment including sexual assault and torture by guards, and executions. People held in the *kwan-li-so* face backbreaking forced labor at logging, mining, agricultural, and other worksites. These are characterized by exposure to harsh weather, rudimentary tools, and lack of safety equipment, all of which create a significant risk of accident. Death rates in these camps are reportedly extremely high.

While a North Korean UN diplomat publicly acknowledged for the first time in October 2014 that "reform through labor" centers exist in North Korea where "people are improved through their mentality and look on their wrongdoings," Pyongyang still refuses to admit that *kwan-li-so* camps operate in the country.

United States and South Korean officials estimate that between 80,000 and 120,000 people are imprisoned in the four remaining *kwan-li-so:* camp No. 14 in Kaechun, No. 15 in Yodok, No. 16 in Hwasung, and No. 25 in Chungjin.

Freedom of Information

All media and publications are state-controlled, and unauthorized access to non-state radio or TV broadcasts is punished. Internet and phone calls are limited within the country and are heavily censored. North Koreans are punished if found with mobile media such as computer flash drives or DVDs containing unauthorized videos of foreign films or TV dramas. Authorities also actively track, and seek to catch and punish, persons using Chinese mobile phones to make unauthorized calls to people outside North Korea.

Freedom of Movement, Refugees, and Asylum Seekers

The government uses threats of detention, forced labor, and public executions to generate fearful obedience, and imposes harsh restrictions on freedom of information and movement, both within the country and across its borders.

North Korea criminalizes leaving the country without state permission, and in some instances, state security services actively pursue North Koreans and seek to detain and forcibly return those who have fled the country. The ascent to power of Kim Jong-Un saw significantly expanded efforts to stop irregular crossings of North Koreans into China across the northern border.

The government has increased rotations of North Korean border guards and cracked down on guards who permit crossings in exchange for bribes. Increased patrols, fences, and use of security cameras on the Chinese side of the border have also made crossings more difficult. Consequently, fewer North Koreans have been able to make the arduous journey from the North Korean border through China to Laos and then into Thailand, from where most are sent to South Korea.

China continues to categorically label all North Koreans in China as "illegal" economic migrants and routinely repatriates them, despite its obligation to offer protection to refugees under the Refugee Convention of 1951 and its 1967 protocol, to which China is a state party.

The certainty of harsh punishment upon repatriation has led many in the international community to argue that all North Koreans fleeing into China should be considered refugees sur place. Beijing regularly restricts access of staff of the UN Refugee Agency (UNHCR) to North Koreans in China.

Former North Korean security officials who have defected told Human Rights Watch that North Koreans handed back by China face interrogation, torture, and consignment to political prisoner or forced labor camps. The severity of punishments depends on North Korean authorities' assessments of what the returnee did while in China.

Those suspected of simple trading schemes involving non-controversial goods are usually sent to work in forced labor brigades (known as ro-dong-dan-ryeon-dae, literally labor training centers) or jip-kyul-so (collection centers), which are criminal penitentiaries where forced labor is required. Harsh and dangerous working conditions in those facilities purportedly result in significant numbers of people being injured or killed.

Those whom authorities suspect of religious or political activities abroad, or having contact with South Koreans, are often given lengthier terms in detention facilities known as *kyo-hwa-so* (correctional, reeducation centers) where detainees face forced labor, food and medicine shortages, and regular mistreatment by guards.

North Korean women fleeing their country are frequently trafficked into forced de facto marriages with Chinese men. Even if they have lived in China for years, these women are not entitled to legal residence and face possible arrest and repatriation. Many children of such unrecognized marriages lack legal identity or access to elementary education.

Labor Rights

North Korea is one of the few nations in the world that still refuses to join the International Labor Organization. Workers are systematically denied freedom of association and the right to organize and collectively bargain. The only authorized trade union organization, the General Federation of Trade Unions of Korea, is controlled by the government.

In 2003, a special administrative industrial zone at the southern border, the Kaesung Industrial Complex (KIC), was developed in cooperation with South Korea. According to data from June 2014, the KIC hosts 125 South Korean companies employing 52,742 North Korean workers, supervised by 780 South Korean managers. A joint North-South Korea committee oversees the KIC, but the law governing working conditions there falls far short of international standards.

Key International Actors

Pyongyang's record of cooperation with UN human rights mechanisms remains among the worst in the world.

In its report released in February, the UN Commission of Inquiry (COI) found that "systematic, widespread, and gross human rights violations have been and are being committed by the Democratic People's Republic of Korea, its institutions and officials. In many instances, the violations of human rights found by the commission constitute crimes against humanity. These are not mere excesses of the State; they are essential components of a political system that has moved far from the ideals on which it claims to be founded. The gravity, scale and nature of these violations reveal a State that does not have any parallel in the contemporary world."

The COI recommended that the international community pursue accountability for those responsible, either through a UN Security Council referral of the situation to the ICC or UN establishment of an ad hoc tribunal.

The COI visited South Korea, Japan, Thailand, the United States, and the United Kingdom, but China declined to let the three COI commissioners visit to conduct investigations. North Korea also declined to participate in the inquiry, but in September released its own human rights report that declared that North Koreans "feel proud of the world's most advantageous human rights system" and blamed the US, European Union, South Korea, and Japan for singling out North Korea for international condemnation.

In February 2014, the two Koreas organized reunions of more than 100 families separated during the Korean War, the first such reunions since 2010. An October 2014 visit to Seoul by Hwang Pyong So, vice-marshal of the Korean People's Army, marked the highest-level talks between the two sides since 2007. Following the release of the COI report, however, North Korea conducted a series of missile launches and threatened to hold another nuclear test.

Japan continues to demand the return of 12 Japanese citizens whom North Korea abducted in the 1970s and 1980s. Some Japanese civil society groups insist the number of abductees is much higher. South Korea's government has also stepped up its demands for the return of its abducted citizens, hundreds of whom were reportedly abducted during the decades after the Korean War.

Oman

During 2014, the government of Oman continued to restrict rights to freedom of expression, association, and assembly. Authorities detained and harassed critics and pro-reform activists, and withheld security clearance from some due to their peaceful political activities preventing their employment in state services.

On August 20, Oman became the eighth Arab state, and the 162nd country worldwide, to ratify the international Mine Ban treaty.

Freedom of Expression and Pro-Reform Activists

The authorities continued to target peaceful pro-reform activists using short term arrests and detentions and other forms of harassment. Since mass protests in 2011, authorities have engaged in a cycle of prosecutions of activists and critics on charges such as "insulting the Sultan" that criminalize free speech, leading to prison sentences followed by release under pardons granted by Sultan Qaboos. According to local activists, the arrests and prosecutions have had a chilling effect on free speech and the expression of dissent in Oman.

Articles 29, 30, and 31 of Oman's Basic Law protect freedom of expression and the press, but other laws undercut these safeguards. Authorities in practice did not respect these rights, continuing to restrict online criticism and other content using the 2002 Telecommunications Act, article 26, which penalizes "any person who sends, by means of telecommunications system, a message that violates public order or public morals."

Authorities arrested pro-reform activists and held them without access to lawyers and their families using a 2011 amendment; the criminal procedure code that empowers security forces to hold detainees without charge for up to 30 days. Some detainees arrested since 2011 have allegedly reported that security forces tortured or otherwise ill-treated them.

Khalfan al-Badwawi, a pro-reform activist, left Oman in December 2013 soon after police released him from several days of incommunicado detention for comments criticizing the government. Authorities refused to disclose his whereabouts to his family during his detention.

Authorities arrested Noah al-Saadi, a blogger and rights activist, on July 13, 2014, and detained him until August 7, before releasing him apparently without charge. Officials had previously detained al-Saadi in September 2013 after he used his blog to criticize the arrest by the authorities of Dr. Talib al-Maamari, a Shura Council member involved in anti-pollution protests at Sohar port and the 2011 mass protests in Sohar by Omanis demanding jobs and an end to official corruption.

Police arrested Mohammed al-Fazari, a prominent blogger and government critic, on August 30, 2014, when he obeyed a summons to appear at the Royal Oman Police headquarters in Muscat concerning "a personal matter." They detained him incommunicado, allowing him only one phone call, until September 4, when they released him without charge.

On October 31, authorities prevented Saeed al-Jaddad, a human rights activist and pro-reform blogger, from boarding a flight out of the country. They did not provide al-Jaddad with a reason for the travel ban. In 2013, he was arrested and held for eight days in solitary confinement on charges including calling for demonstrations and heaping discredit on state officials before releasing him on bail. In July of that year, the public prosecution summoned al-Jaddad on a new charges: "Undermining the status and prestige of the state." Authorities re-leased him on bail but threatened that he may again be interrogated and brought to trial on these charges.

Freedom of Assembly and Association

All public gatherings require advance official approval and the authorities arrest and prosecute participants in unapproved gatherings. Some private gatherings are also prohibited under article 137 of the penal code, which prescribes a pun-ishment of up to three years in prison and a fine for anyone who "participates in a private gathering including at least ten individuals with a view to commit a riot or a breach of public order." Authorities sharply increased the penalties under article 137 after the pro-reform demonstrations of 2011.

On August 6, 2014, an appeal court in Muscat imposed a one year prison term and a fine on Dr. Talib al-Maamari, a former Shura Council member from Liwa, on a charge of "illegal gathering," and a three-year prison term and a fine for calling for demonstrations against the authorities. The court also sentenced Saqr al-Baloushi, a former Liwa municipal councilor.

The case stemmed from an incident on August 22, 2013, when activists gathered in Liwa to protest industrial pollution at the nearby port of Sohar, which they consider a public health risk. Police used tear gas to disperse demonstrators who had blocked the port's entrance and, on August 24, arrested Dr. Talib al-Maamari, a local Shura Council member who had attended the demonstration. Authorities denied al-Maamari access to a lawyer for more than 17 days during his detention until the public prosecution had charged him with inciting a crowd and wrongful assembly at a public place. The lower court that tried al-Maamari and al-Baloushi sentenced them to seven and four year prison terms respectively and fines after convicting them of "illegal gathering" and "blocking traffic."

The authorities closed down the Elixir Cultural Saloon, run by a group of young men and women in Sohar, in September 2014. Oman's Law on Associations restricts the formation of independent associations, makes official registration mandatory, gives the Ministry of Social Development powers to deny registration without stating reasons and bans political parties.

Women's Rights

Article 17 of the Basic Law states that all citizens are equal and bans gender-based discrimination. In practice, however, women continue to face discrimination in law under the Personal Status Law that governs matters such as divorce, inheritance, child custody, and legal guardianship, and in practice.

Key International Actors

Oman ratified the international Mine Ban treaty—the Convention on the Prohibition of the Use, Stockpiling, Production and Transfer of Anti-Personnel Mines and on their Destruction—on August 20. The treaty bans the use, production, transfer, and stockpiling of antipersonnel landmines and requires clearance of mined areas within 10 years and assistance to landmine victims. The treaty takes effects for Oman in February 2015, six months after ratification.

During a visit to Oman in September the UN special rapporteur on the rights to freedom of peaceful assembly and of association noted "a pervasive culture of silence and fear affecting anyone who wants to speak and work for reforms in Oman," and said some activists had "reported reprisals, before and during my visit, following their attempts to contact or meet with me."

In late 2012, the Gulf Cooperation Council (GCC), of which Oman is a member, re-vised and re-signed its security cooperation agreement enabling each state party to take legal action against its own or other GCC citizens when they are judged to have interfered in the internal affairs of any GCC state.

Both the United States and the United Kingdom provide significant economic and military aid to the sultanate. Neither country publicly criticized Oman's human rights abuses in 2013, except in annual reports.

Pakistan

Pakistan had a tumultuous year in 2014. Sectarian attacks continued with impunity, military operations in North Waziristan displaced more than one million people, and massive floods wrought devastation in Sindh and Punjab provinces. Political instability reached a crisis point in August and September, as prolonged and violent opposition protests threatened to undermine gains achieved by the country's first civilian transfer of power following the May 2013 election of Nawaz Sharif as prime minister.

The protests in Islamabad—led by opposition politicians Imran Khan and Dr. Tahir-ul-Qadri, who demanded Sharif's resignation and the formation of a new government—prompted violence by both protesters and the security forces that resulted in at least three deaths and hundreds of injuries. The government responded to the protests by imposing a state of emergency in Islamabad and suspending fundamental rights such as the right to petition the courts to enforce constitutional guarantees. During the height of the crisis, the military intervened at the government's request, allowing it to dangerously reinsert itself into democratic political decision-making.

Violent attacks on religious minorities, fostered in part by the institutionalized discrimination of the "blasphemy laws," continued. Ongoing rights concerns in Balochistan province related to enforced disappearances, extrajudicial killings, and torture remained unaddressed. Lack of government response to continuing abuses by the security forces in Balochistan fostered a long-standing culture of impunity.

In July, the government passed the Protection of Pakistan Act (PPA), an overly broad counterterrorism legislation that violates international human rights standards and creates a legal pretext for abuses by the security forces without accountability. The PPA violates the right to fair trial by shifting the onus of proof on the accused in certain circumstances, and granting powers of arbitrary arrest and preventive detention to the security forces.

Fighting in Waziristan

Following a June 8 attack by militants at Jinnah International Airport in Karachi that killed more than 18 people, the military on June 30 launched an offensive in North Waziristan involving more than 30,000 troops. Severe military restrictions on independent media access to the conflict zone made it difficult to assess civilian casualty figures.

The conflict has displaced an estimated one million people in squalid displacement camps. The government has not adequately responded to their health needs. According to the United Nations High Commissioner for Refugees (UNHCR) Pakistan country representative in July, lack of potable water, sanitation facilities, and health care in the main internally displaced persons camp in the city of Bannu in Khyber Pakhtunkhwa province has led to the spread of communicable disease outbreaks.

The military offensive prompted the Punjabi faction of the Threek-i-Taliban Pakistan (TTP) in September to surrender and renounce terrorist attacks inside Pakistan. However, the TTP has said it will focus future violent attacks on military and government targets in Afghanistan.

Sectarian Violence

Sectarian violence, particularly attacks against the already beleaguered Shia community, continued to claim a high toll in 2014.

The militant group Lashkar-e-Jhangvi (LeJ) continued attacks on Shia Hazaras in Balochistan. The government failed to successfully prosecute and imprison suspects, in part due to sympathy for the group within the security forces. In June, twin suicide attacks in Taftan near Pakistan's border with Iran killed 24 Shia pilgrims and injured 18. The Sunni militant group Jaish-ul-Islam claimed responsibility, but authorities had not made any related arrests at time of writing.

The port city of Karachi remains a hotbed of sectarian violence, with at least 750 sectarian targeted killings in Karachi from September 2013 to September 2014. On September 6, 2014, unidentified gunmen killed Shia cleric Ali Abbas. Four days later, unidentified gunmen killed Sunni cleric Maulana Masood in an apparent revenge attack.

HUMAN
RIGHTS
WATCH

"We Are The Walking Dead"
Killings of Shia Hazaras in Balochistan, Pakistan

Religious Minorities

Section 295-C of Pakistan's penal code makes the death penalty mandatory for blasphemy, although no one has yet been executed for the crime. The Pakistani government failed to amend or repeal the blasphemy law provisions that provide a pretext for impunity and violence against religious minorities. Since 1990, at least 60 people have been murdered after being accused of blasphemy. At present, 17 people convicted of blasphemy are on death row; 19 others are serving life sentences.

In March 2014, a Lahore court sentenced Sawan Masih to death for blasphemy after he was accused of making derogatory statements regarding the Prophet Muhammad. In April, those allegations prompted a 3,000-strong mob to attack a Christian residential community in Lahore and torch hundreds of houses. Police arrested Masih, but failed to otherwise intervene.

On May 7, unidentified gunmen killed Rashid Rehman, a renowned human rights lawyer, in apparent retaliation for representing people accused of blasphemy. At the time of his murder, Rehman was representing Junaid Hafeez, a university lecturer accused of blasphemy, and had received death threats. Hafeez's trial was ongoing at time of writing.

In April, a court in Toba Tek Singh sentenced to death a Christian couple, Shafqat Emmanuel and Shagufta Kausar, for allegedly sending "blasphemous" text messages. In November, a mob beat to death a Christian couple after they allegedly committed blasphemy by burning pages of a Quran. Their bodies were later burned in the kiln of the factory in which they worked.

In July, a mob in Gujranwala burned down houses of the Ahmadi community killing three people and injuring eight others over alleged blasphemy. The provisions of Pakistan's penal code, which perpetuate discrimination against the Ahmadis, remain unchanged: the code explicitly prohibits Ahmadis from "indirectly or directly posing as a Muslim"; declaring or propagating their faith publicly; building mosques or referring to them as such; or making public calls to prayer.

Women's and Girls' Rights

In September, the government announced that police had arrested the attackers of 17-year-old Malala Yousafzai, a student and outspoken advocate for children's right to education, who was shot in an attack claimed by Tehreek-e-Taliban Pakistan on October 9, 2012. She subsequently recovered from her serious injuries and, in October, became the youngest person to ever receive the Nobel Peace Prize.

Violence against women and girls—including rape, murder through so-called honor killings, acid attacks, domestic violence, and forced marriage—remained routine. Pakistani human rights nongovernmental organizations (NGOs) estimate that there are about 1,000 "honor killings" every year.

In a notorious case, 25-year-old Farzana Parveen, who was three-months pregnant, was stoned to death in May in front of a Lahore courthouse by family members angry that she had married without their permission. Perpetrators of these killings often enjoy impunity because law enforcement officials routinely drop the case if the victim's family has offered "forgiveness." Intimidation and threats against women and girls who venture out in public places or take public roles continued in 2014.

Women who are members of religious minorities are particularly vulnerable. A report by the Movement for Solidarity and Peace in Pakistan found that at least 1,000 girls belonging to Christian and Hindu communities are forced to marry male Muslims every year. The coercion often originates from the prospective bridegrooms' families, and failure to comply can prompt serious violence against the girls and their families. The government has failed to act to stop such forced marriages.

Balochistan

The human rights situation in Balochistan remained abysmal. Despite the May 2013 election of a civilian government, the military has retained all key decision-making functions in the southwestern province and blocked efforts by civil society organizations and media to cover ongoing violence there.

Enforced disappearances linked to the security forces continued with impunity. On March 18, plainclothes gunmen later identified as belonging to Pakistan's paramilitary Frontier Corps allegedly abducted Zahid Baloch, chairperson of the Baloch Student Organization-Azad in the provincial capital, Quetta. Baloch's whereabouts and safety remained unknown at time of writing. Despite rulings from the Pakistan Supreme Court in 2013 demanding justice for victims of enforced disappearances, as well as recommendations from the UN Working Group on Enforced or Involuntary Disappearances in 2012, Pakistan's government has failed to meet its obligations under the constitution and international law prohibiting enforced disappearances.

Counterterrorism and Law Enforcement Abuses

Accountability of law enforcement agencies showed no signs of improving in 2014. In June, one of the most egregious incidents of excessive use of force against political protesters occurred in Model Town, a Lahore suburb. Police fired without warning on supporters of the Pakistan Awami Tehreek (PAT), an opposition political party, whose workers had tried to stop police demolition of security barriers erected in front of PAT headquarters. Authorities confirmed the deaths of at least eight PAT members. Another 80 PAT members were injured.

In July, the government enacted new repressive counterterrorism legislation. The Protection of Pakistan Act (PPA) is an extremely broad and ambiguously worded document that grants the security forces broad powers to implement preventive detention and carry out arrests without warrants. Such provisions can easily provide legal cover for abuses by law enforcement agencies and open the door for the violation of fundamental rights to freedom of speech, privacy, peaceful assembly, and a fair trial.

Freedom of Expression

Freedom of expression and media came under severe pressure from both state and non-state actors in 2014.

In April, unidentified gunmen attacked Hamid Mir, one of Pakistan's most famous television presenters, in Karachi. Mir survived the attack and Jang/Geo—his employer and the country's largest media conglomerate— accused the director general of the military's powerful Inter Service Intelligence (ISI) of involvement in the incident. The ISI denied the allegation and the central government punished Jang/Geo for the accusation by suspending its broadcast license and taking its channels off the air for 15 days.

Unidentified assailants also attacked the offices and employees of the media group. Other attacks on journalists in 2014 included the March shooting by unidentified gunmen of Raza Rumi, a prominent columnist and television anchor in Lahore. Rumi was injured in the attack, which killed his driver. At time of writing the police had yet to arrest any of the gunmen, who are suspected of belonging to the LeJ.

In August, journalist Omar Quraishi and columnist Kamran Shafi both received death threats from unidentified sources after the two men criticized the August protests in Islamabad led by opposition politicians Imran Khan and Dr. Tahir-ul-Qadri.

Key International Actors

Relations with the United States, Pakistan's largest donor of development and military aid, showed signs of improvement after years of disagreement and mistrust. While Prime Minister Sharif's US visit in October 2013 did not achieve any notable short-term diplomatic objectives, it did serve as a confidence-building measure between the two countries.

Pakistan's alleged persistent support for the Haqqani network, a militant group that US officials accuse of targeting US troops in Afghanistan, continued to undermine bilateral relations. Nonetheless, the US voiced public support for Sharif's government during the protests and sit-ins in Islamabad by issuing statements in favor of the democratic process.

Historically tense relations between Pakistan and India continued despite Sharif's visit to India in August to attend the inauguration of Indian Prime Minister Narendra Modi. Persistant tensions include security issues and longstanding disputes over the distribution of water from rivers that run through both countries.

Pakistan and China continued to deepen already extensive economic and political ties, although the relationship suffered a setback when Chinese President Xi Jinping postponed a scheduled visit in August due to the protests in Islamabad.

Papua New Guinea

Despite Papua New Guinea's (PNG) current extractives-led economic boom, an estimated 40 percent of the country lives in poverty. Pressing human rights issues include gender inequality, violence, corruption, and excessive use of force by police. Rates of family and sexual violence are among the highest in the world and perpetrators are rarely prosecuted.

In 2014, in a blow to rule of law and accountability, Prime Minister Peter O'Neill sacked key officials and disbanded the country's main anti-corruption body in response to efforts to arrest him for his alleged involvement in a multi-million dollar corruption case.

Torture and Other Police Abuse

Physical and sexual abuse of detainees—including children—by police and paramilitary police units continues to be widespread. In March, a videotape surfaced of police officers surrounding and unleashing three dogs on a defenseless man. Police officials later condemned the abuse and said the incident was being investigated.

Members of PNG's notorious paramilitary police units (Mobile Squads), detention center staff, and local residents were implicated in excessive use of force in quelling protests in February 2014 at the Manus Island detention center, which holds asylum seekers transferred by Australia for refugee status determination and resettlement. During the incident, many detainees sustained injuries and one detainee was beaten to death. Police allegedly entered firing their guns when violence broke out inside the facility. One detainee was reportedly shot in the buttocks. In May, then PNG Deputy Police Commissioner Simon Kauba denied any involvement of PNG police in the violence. At time of writing, authorities had arrested two local men working in the detention center in connection with the murder.

UN Special Rapporteur on Extrajudicial, Summary or Arbitrary Executions Christof Heyns visited PNG in March and expressed concerns about police use of excessive force during arrest, interrogation, and pretrial detention, sometimes resulting in death.

In October, Prime Minister O'Neill highlighted the problem of police brutality, admitting that the PNG police force lacks discipline and is not sufficiently serving the interests of the people of PNG. O'Neill announced that a hotline will be established for members of the public to report instances of police abuse.

Violence and Discrimination against Women and Girls

PNG is one of the most dangerous places in the world to be a woman, with an estimated 70 percent of women experiencing rape or assault in their lifetime. While such acts have long been criminalized and domestic violence was specifically proscribed under the 2013 Family Protection Act, few perpetrators are brought to justice. Lack of access to courts and police, as well as failure by many justice officials to take violence against women seriously, contribute to the extremely low arrest and conviction rates. The 2013 law presents an important opportunity to improve the situation, but the government must fully commit to its full enforcement and allocate the resources necessary to do so.

Reports of violent mobs attacking individuals accused of "sorcery," the victims mostly women and girls, continue to be reported. The instigators of such attacks rarely face justice, with few witnesses coming forward. In April, six people, including two children, were hacked to death when 500 men went on a sorcery hunt in Madang Province. Police arrested at least 180 suspects but police say they lack funds to complete investigations.

Disability Rights

People with disabilities in PNG are often unable to participate in community life, go to school, or work because of stigma and other barriers associated with disability. In many cases, people with disabilities are not able or allowed to leave their homes. Access to mental health care is limited, and traditional healers are the only option for many people with psychosocial disabilities.

Children with disabilities in PNG face abuse, discrimination, exclusion, lack of accessibility, and a wide range of barriers to education.

Death Penalty

Following PNG's 2013 expansion of the scope of crimes eligible for the death penalty and signaling its intention to resume executions, 14 prisoners were on death row at time of writing, but no executions had taken place. In March, UN expert Heyns urged PNG not to use the death penalty and pursue instead other measures including more effective policing of violent crimes.

Corruption

In April, PNG's Taskforce Sweep, a government anti-corruption initiative, successfully prosecuted prominent politician Paul Tiensten for misappropriating US$3.6 million in public funds. Tiensten was sentenced to nine years in jail.

In June, following investigations by Taskforce Sweep, the PNG police fraud squad filed a warrant for the arrest of Prime Minister O'Neill for his alleged role in approving fraudulent payments from the PNG Finance Department to a Port Moresby law firm. O'Neill then sacked the attorney general and deputy police commissioner and ordered the disbandment of the taskforce. The Police Commissioner was arrested and convicted on contempt of court charges and subsequently retired. O'Neill's lawyers won a stay of the warrant for his arrest and Sam Koim, the head of Taskforce Sweep, obtained a National Court order preventing the government from disbanding it. At time of writing, the Justice Ministry was withholding Koim's pay in an apparent attempt to induce him to resign.

Extractive industries

Extractive industries are an important engine of PNG's economic growth, but continue to give rise to serious human rights problems and environmental harm. Controversy raged around the alleged environmental impacts of the long-troubled Ok Tedi mine in 2014, and violent clashes erupted around the controversial Ramu Nickel project.

In 2011, Human Rights Watch documented gang rape and other violent abuses by private security personnel at PNG's Porgera gold mine, operated by Canadian company Barrick Gold. Along with other steps, Barrick responded by rolling out a compensation scheme that paid out claims to more than 100 women in 2014. Barrick's efforts on this front have been dogged by controversy, but could mark an important global precedent, particularly if they result in lasting positive out-comes for the women involved.

The government deployed security forces to Porgera and other restive areas of the highlands in 2014 as part of a state of emergency. This led to allegations of violent abuses including the destruction of homes around Porgera—allegations that mirror abuses linked to similar deployments in the past.

PNG's massive US$19 billion Liquefied Natural Gas (LNG) project, led by Exxon-Mobil, began production in 2014. The project could ultimately double the size of PNG's economy. The project has transformative potential but there are serious concerns as to whether ordinary citizens will derive any benefit from it. Key government institutions remain plagued by corruption and a questionable capacity to deploy the additional resources effectively.

Key International Actors

Australia remains the country's most important international partner, providing an estimated US$460 million in development assistance for 2013-2014. Australia provided an additional $556.7 million this financial year to support the Manus Island detention center.

Since 2013, Australia has transferred asylum seekers arriving irregularly by boat in Australian waters to PNG for refugee status determination. Those recognized as refugees are to be resettled in PNG or in a third country other than Australia. At time of writing, 1,084 men were detained on Manus Island and PNG immigration officials had completed 104 interim refugee determinations, 56 of which were positive. In November, PNG's immigration minister announced the first 10 final positive refugee determinations. At this writing, the 10 refugees were to be released on temporary visas issued initially for a period of 12 months. The PNG government has yet to formulate a policy to permanently integrate refugees and Australia has not yet found third countries willing to admit refugees transferred from PNG.

The facilities on Manus Island are overcrowded and dirty, and asylum claims are not processed in a fair, transparent, or expedient manner, contributing to de-tainee physical and mental health problems. Safety is also a concern. In Febru-ary 2014, an Iranian asylum seeker, Reza Berati, was killed during a riot at the

Manus Island facility. Two former detention center staff have been charged with his murder, and in March 2014, an inquiry into the incident was referred to the Australian Senate Legal and Constitutional Affairs Committee.

In a senate inquiry submission in May, the UN Refugee Agency (UNHCR) told the senate committee that PNG and Australia are failing to provide safe and humane conditions for asylum seekers in detention and that the lengthy delays in refugee status determinations and lack of timeframes for durable resettlement amount to punishment for affected asylum seekers.

In March, UN expert Heyns expressed regret that representatives of the private security firm G4S, which runs the detention center, were not available to meet him, and that he was refused access to the center and was unable to meet with asylum seekers.

At time of writing, the Australian government had deployed 73 Australian federal police officers to act as unarmed advisers to the Royal PNG Constabulary in Port Moresby and Lae to help combat high levels of violence in the country.

Peru

Public protests against large-scale mining projects and other private sector and government initiatives in Peru often lead to confrontations between protesters and police in which civilians are killed or wounded by police or army gunfire. While these confrontations resulted in fewer fatalities in 2013 and 2014 than in 2012, there has been little progress in investigating deaths and injuries, and recent legislation has further weakened police and army accountability.

Judicial investigations into grave human rights abuses committed during Peru's armed conflict continue, but progress in trials has been slow and limited.

Deaths in Protests

As of September 2014, 34 civilians had been killed during protests since President Ollanta Humala took office in July 2011. During the first nine months of 2014, four civilians died from gunshot wounds when police reportedly used live ammunition against protesters in three separate incidents. In September 2014, 16-year-old Jhapet Huilca was shot by police during a protest against a gas pipeline in Quillabamba, Cusco. The minister of the interior announced the suspension of the police chief responsible for the operation pending an investigation.

There has been little progress in determining the circumstances in which these deaths occurred or holding to account police or military personnel who used force unlawfully. In January 2014, a prosecutor closed without any charges an investigation into the alleged shooting by soldiers of four civilians during a protest in Celendín, Cajamarca, in July 2012, even though he concluded that those responsible had committed intentional homicide. His report revealed that the fatal shots were probably fired from army-issued Galil combat weapons, and that there was no evidence that any of the victims had been armed. His report stated, however, that the army had failed to provide a copy of the operational plan, the names of the participating soldiers, or details of the firearms issued to them, despite being requested to do so, and that it was impossible to identify the perpetrators.

Shielding Security Forces from Accountability

In January 2014, Law 30151 entered into force, providing immunity from prosecution to "armed forces and police personnel who in fulfillment of their duty and using their weapons or other means of defense, cause injury or death." This amendment to the criminal code eliminated language that made immunity conditional on police using lethal force in compliance with regulations and departs from international standards that require law enforcement officers use force in accordance with the principles of necessity and proportionality, and that they be held accountable for its misuse.

The jurisdiction of military courts in human rights cases involving members of the military remains an issue. Legislative Decree 1095, adopted in 2010 by the administration of President Alan García, could allow military courts to try members of the military accused of abuses against civilians in public security operations. International human rights bodies have consistently rejected the use of military prosecutors and courts in cases involving human rights violations. As of November 2014, the Constitutional Court had yet to rule on the decree's constitutionality, which Peruvian human rights advocates have challenged.

Confronting Past Abuses

Peru's Truth and Reconciliation Commission has estimated that almost 70,000 people died or were subject to enforced disappearance during the country's armed conflict between 1980 and 2000. Many were victims of atrocities by the Shining Path and other insurgent groups; others were victims of human rights violations by state agents.

In a landmark trial, former President Alberto Fujimori was sentenced in 2009 to 25 years in prison for killings and "disappearances" in 1991 and 1992. His intelligence advisor, Vladimiro Montesinos, three former army generals, and members of the Colina group, a government death squad, are also serving sentences ranging from 15 to 25 years for the assassination in 1991 of 15 people in the Lima district of Barrios Altos, and for 6 "disappearances."

Courts have made much less progress in addressing violations that occurred under the earlier administrations of Fernando Belaúnde (1980-1985) and Alan García (1985-1990). In a report issued in August 2013 to mark the 10th anniversary of the Truth and Reconciliation Commission's report, the human rights ombudsman found that, despite initial efforts, Peru had failed to consolidate a specialized judicial system with sufficient staff and resources to bring most cases to court.

As of 2013, 48 percent of 2,880 cases of human rights violations during the armed conflict reported to prosecutors had been dismissed, largely because prosecutors were unable to identify perpetrators and the Ministry of Defense was unwilling to provide documents to facilitate investigations. Only about 2 percent of the cases had been brought to trial, according to Human Rights Trials in Peru, a project based at George Mason University that monitors human rights prosecutions. In 2014, court hearings continued in their fourth year in two emblematic cases: torture and disappearances at the Los Cabitos military base in Ayacucho in 1983 and a massacre at Accomarca in 1985 in which an army unit killed 62 peasants.

In a recent trend, the Supreme Court has overturned an increasing number of convictions on appeal. While the court has sometimes based its decisions on contradictions in witness testimony, it ruled in a January 2014 verdict that the disappearance in 1983 of 6 people whose bodies were found and identified more than 20 years later was subject to a statute of limitations, contravening Peru's obligations to hold accountable those reponsible for enforced disappearances.

In June 2014, President Ollanta Humala appointed as minister of the interior a former army intelligence officer who was facing charges for his alleged role in the 1988 murder of Hugo Bustíos, the Ayacucho correspondent for *Caretas* magazine. Two soldiers were convicted in 2007 for Bustíos' murder, one of whom testified that the minister, Daniel Urresti, had commanded the soldiers who ambushed and shot Bustíos before blowing up his body with a grenade.

Urresti's appointment was highly questionable considering the gravity of the charge and that his public position as minister could influence the judicial outcome of his case and undercut the right to justice of Bustíos' relatives. In addition, President Humala's public statements in advance of the trial supporting Urresti's claims of innocence were an inappropriate interference in ongoing judicial proceedings.

Torture

Congress took a significant step in 2014 to combat torture, which continues to be a chronic problem in Peru. In June, it approved a bill mandating the human rights ombudsman to implement the National Preventive Mechanism against Torture (NPM), in fulfillment of Peru's obligations under the Optional Protocol to the Convention against Torture and Other Cruel, Inhuman or Degrading Treatment (OPCAT), which it ratified in 2006. The bill requires the ombudsman, inter alia, to visit and monitor conditions in prisons and detention centers without prior announcement, make proactive and preventive recommendations, and publish an annual report, but it did not state how these additional activities would be funded. As of November 2014, the bill was delayed in Congress pending clarification from the plenary on points that the president of the congressional committee that debated the draft had raised.

Freedom of Expression

Journalists investigating corruption by regional government officials, mayors, and business people are frequent targets of physical attack, threats, and criminal defamation suits, and the number of criminal defamation prosecutions increased in 2014.

In March 2014, journalist César Quino was given a six-month suspended prison sentence for defaming the then-governor of Ancash, César Alvarez, in an article published in *El Observador*, a paper Quino edits that is critical of the regional government. In recent years, Alvarez—now facing charges for the murder of a political opponent— has won several other defamation suits in efforts to silence his press critics.

In April 2014, a bomb exploded at the home of journalist Yofré López Sifuentes in Barranca, a port city north of Lima. López, who edits a weekly newspaper and presents a radio program called "Curfew" (Toque de Queda), was not hurt, but his mother and stepfather were injured. According to press reports, he had been a prominent critic of air pollution caused by local agrobusinesses.

Reproductive Rights

Women and girls in Peru have the right to seek abortions only in cases of risk to their health or life. In June 2014, the Ministry of Health published guidelines detailing the administrative procedures hospitals must follow in assessing individual cases. Addressing a previous regulatory vacuum that had been criticized by international human rights bodies, the rules allow health staff to perform abortions under 10 medical conditions, and to consider the rights and needs of women and girls not covered by those conditions on a case by case basis. Access to services in situations that fall outside the prescribed conditions—such as when a woman's or girl's mental health could be dangerously affected by an unwanted pregnancy—is left to the discretion of facility staff, with a facility-based appeals process.

Key International Actors

In its concluding observations on Peru's combined seventh and eighth periodic reports, the Committee on the Elimination of all Forms of Discrimination against Women urged Peru to adopt a comprehensive law to combat violence against women and implement a strategy to fight discriminatory gender-based stereotypes. It also recommended that Peru extend the grounds of legalized abortion to cases of rape and incest.

In August 2014, the Committee on the Elimination of Racial Discrimination (CERD) recommended that Peru take measures to avoid the propagation of material stigmatizing its indigenous and Afro-Peruvian population. The committee referred specifically to "The Peasant Jacinta" (La Paisana Jacinta), a popular television comedy show featuring a male actor dressed up as a grossly caricatured indigenous peasant woman. Following CERD's recommendations, Frecuencia Latina, the television channel which has broadcast the show since 1999, removed it from its prime-time slot.

As a member of the UN Human Rights Council, Peru supported United Nations action to put human rights violations in North Korea, Sri Lanka, Belarus, Iran, the Occupied Palestinian Territories, and Syria under close scrutiny.

Philippines

With less than two years left in office, the administration of President Benigno Aquino III continues to send mixed signals about its commitment to improve human rights in the Philippines. Although the number of cases of extrajudicial killings, torture, and enforced disappearances by state security forces has declined in the last four years, such abuses regularly occur. They are fueled by the government's lack of political will to end the longstanding impunity enjoyed by the police and armed forces, a dysfunctional criminal justice system, and military resistance to accountability.

While human rights was a key agenda for Aquino when he took office in 2010, he has failed to make good on many of his commitments, chiefly his expressed intent to end killings of activists and journalists and bring those responsible to justice. Aquino risked losing political capital by suggesting a term extension for the president, and he found himself at odds with the Supreme Court by calling it an impediment to his proposed reforms.

There has been some progress in tackling certain human rights problems. On August 12, the National Bureau of Investigation arrested retired army general, Jovito Palparan, who is implicated in the alleged enforced disappearance and torture of two activists and others in 2006. The Supreme Court has taken steps to improve the rule of law in the Philippines, for instance launching its "Justice Zone" program in which the investigation, prosecution, and trial of cases are expedited through such electronic or digital methods as issuances of "e-warrants" and "e-subpoenas."

The Philippine government and the rebel Moro Islamic Liberation Front signed a peace agreement on March 27, 2014, which would extend autonomy to Muslims in Mindanao and end the decades-long conflict there that has engendered serious human rights abuses by all sides.

Arrest of Retired General

The arrest of retired army general, Jovito Palparan, in August 2014 by a combined unit of the civilian National Bureau of Investigation and naval intelligence could prove to be a watershed moment in overcoming the military's historic unwilling-

**HUMAN
RIGHTS
WATCH**

"One Shot to the Head"
Death Squad Killings in Tagum City, Philippines

ness to prosecute personnel for serious human rights abuses. Palparan is implicated in extrajudicial killings, torture, and enforced disappearances by forces under his command in several regions between 2001 and 2005. He has been charged with the kidnapping and torture in 2006 of two women, Sherlyn Cadapan and Karen Empeno. Palparan has said that his actions during this period were to implement the counterinsurgency program of then-President Gloria Macapagal-Arroyo. Under the Macapagal-Arroyo administration from 2001 to 2010, hundreds of leftist activists were tortured, "disappeared," and killed.

Palparan was put in the custody of the provincial police in Bulacan, north of Manila, where the Cadapan-Empeno case is being tried. However, on September 15 the court allowed Palparan's transfer to military custody, prompting protests from families of victims and human rights advocates.

Killings

While killings appeared to decrease in 2014 compared to recent years, activists, journalists, environmentalists, and tribal leaders continued to be targets of attack. Among those killed was Fausto Orasan, a 64-year-old tribal group leader in the southern Philippines, who was shot by unidentified gunmen on September 13, 2014, while riding his motorcycle in a village in Cagayan de Oro City. Authorities said Orasan had been a leader of anti-mining efforts in the area. During one week in August, three other tribal leaders were gunned down in different parts of the country, according to the nongovernmental organization Karapatan. Human Rights Watch has long documented attacks on tribal leaders who opposed mining and other extractive business interests in their communities.

On August 24, 2014, unidentified gunmen shot dead human rights lawyer Rodolfo Felicio in Taytay, a city in Rizal province, east of Manila. Felicio was the fifth member of the activist group National Union of People's Lawyers to have been killed in the past 10 years.

Killings of journalists continued in late 2013 and early 2014: local media reported at least 26 such killings since Aquino took office in 2010. The trial of the Maguindanao Massacre case, in which 58 people—mostly journalists and media workers—were killed in 2009 allegedly by the militia of the powerful Ampatuan clan in the southern Philippines, was set back by the murder on November 18 of Dennis Sakal, a potential witness for the prosecution.

Although the Aquino administration vowed in 2012 to expedite investigations into killings of journalists by creating a "superbody," little progress appears to have been made. The superbody had only processed four cases at time of writing, resulting in the conviction of five people. However, the alleged masterminds who planned and financed these killings remained at large.

Urban Death Squads

A "death squad" in the southern city of Tagum that killed hundreds of suspected criminals, including children, was the subject of a Human Rights Watch report in May. The so-called Tagum Death Squad also branched out into contract killing, targeting a range of victims for as little as US$110 per hit, including journalists, village officials, business rivals, alleged drug dealers, tribal leaders, and a judge. The death squad was allegedly formed and financed by then-mayor Rey Uy with the cooperation of city hall officials and members of the local police force.

Despite evidence directly implicating Uy in the death squad operation, the authorities have not arrested him or others implicated in the Tagum City killings.

Death squad killings have been reported in cities across the country, with unidentified gunmen on motorcycles targeting people in public in broad daylight in so-called "riding in tandem" killings. Official responses in 2014 to stem such killings included police roadblocks specifically for motorcycles, banning motorcyclists from riding in pairs, and a proposed law that would ban the use of motorcycle helmets, so cyclists could not hide their identities.

Police Use of Torture

Rampant police corruption seriously undermines the country's criminal justice system and exacerbates the problem of impunity.

In January, an investigation by the Commission on Human Rights implicated members of the Laguna provincial police in the systematic torture of at least 22 inmates that began in February 2013. The police dealt out torture in a secret location using a spinning wheel like in the "Wheel of Fortune" game show in the United States. At time of writing, 10 police officers implicated in the torture had been dismissed from duty and faced prosecution, while several others were being investigated.

A November report by the Department of Justice detailed allegations of torture by members of the police in Zamboanga City against several suspects arrested in connection with the September 2013 attack on the city by Islamist militants. Human Rights Watch documented several instances of mistreatment of the detainees, several of them children, as well as the militants' use of civilians as human shields. The government has not investigated the alleged abuses.

Displaced People in Zamboanga

In September 2013, Islamist militants attacked Zamboanga, a predominantly Christian city in the south. Ensuing fighting between the militants and government armed forces, including the use of artillery and airstrikes, destroyed neighborhoods, resulted in dozens of deaths and injuries to civilians, and caused 120,000 people—mostly Muslims—to be displaced from their homes.

A year later, a third of the displaced residents remain in evacuation camps, and more than 160 had died from illnesses mainly linked to poor sanitation.

Key International Actors

President Aquino made trips to Europe and the US in 2014 in which Philippine activists protested against the government's human rights record, particularly the lack of accountability for abuses. The United States and European Union governments have sought to address the problem of impunity, such as by funding programs to improve the performance of police, prosecutors, and the courts.

The US government was more vocal in 2014 than in previous years in communicating its concerns about impunity to the Aquino administration. The US had conditioned a small part ($3 million) of its $20 million annual military aid to the Philippines on improvement in the human rights situation. In 2014, the US increased the military financial assistance to $50 million but most of it was allotted for the Philippine Navy, which has a better human rights record than the army.

The EU-Philippines Justice Support Program, now in its second phase, aims to improve the Philippine criminal justice system by, among other things, training police officers and investigators.

Qatar

Qatar has experienced a low level of domestic dissent compared to its neighbors, but since its successful bid to host the 2022 FIFA World Cup, it has become a focus of international criticism of the mistreatment of low-paid migrant workers. Despite this, Qatar has failed to enact meaningful reforms to its labor system, which continues to facilitate the trafficking and forced labor of workers. Qatar has enjoyed a reputation as a center for media freedom in the region, but a new cybercrime law poses a serious threat to freedom of expression.

Migrant Worker Rights

Qatar has a population of about 2 million, of whom only 10 percent are Qatari nationals. Low-paid migrant workers, mostly from countries in Asia and to a lesser extent Africa, continue to experience abuse and exploitation. Qatari authorities announced labor reforms in May 2014, in response to widespread condemnation of human rights abuses of construction workers as the country builds stadia and other facilities to host the 2022 World Cup.

However, the announced reforms will not adequately protect migrant workers from human trafficking, forced labor, and other rights violations. It is unclear whether they will provide some protection for migrant domestic workers, mostly women, who are especially vulnerable to exploitation and abuse.

Qatar's Law 14 of 2004, regulating labor in the private sector, limits workers' hours, requires that foreign workers receive paid annual leave, sets requirements on health and safety, and requires on-time payment of wages each month. In practice, employers continue to flout these requirements with impunity due to the failure of the authorities to enforce this and other laws intended to protect workers' rights.

Workers typically pay exorbitant recruitment fees and employers regularly take control of their passports when they arrive in Qatar. Many migrant workers complain that their employers fail to pay their wages on time, if at all. Migrant workers are prohibited from unionizing or engaging in strikes, although they make up 99 percent of the private sector workforce. Many migrant workers are obliged to live in cramped, unsanitary conditions, especially those working without documentation.

The *kafala* (sponsorship) system ties a migrant worker's legal residence to his or her employer or sponsor. In Qatar, it is codified into law under the terms of Law No. 4 of 2009, which regulates the sponsorship, employment, and residence of expatriate workers. The law provides for the transfer of workers to other sponsors under certain conditions, but in practice workers are rarely able to secure the No Objection Certificates that they require from their existing sponsor to transfer legally to another sponsor. It also requires that foreign workers obtain exit permits from their sponsors when they wish to leave Qatar; in practice, this enables employers to arbitrarily prevent their employees from leaving Qatar and returning to their home country. Workers can become undocumented when employers report them to the authorities as having absconded, or when they fail to pay to renew workers' annual ID cards. A lack of proper documentation leaves workers at risk of arrest and detention or deportation. It also leaves them at risk of further labor exploitation.

The exit visa requirement and the authorities' use of arbitrary travel bans means that Qatari employers can prevent their foreign employees from leaving Qatar indefinitely, a power they may use unfairly to secure concessions from foreign employees with whom they are in dispute. Formerly highly-paid expatriates trapped in Qatar in 2014 include former employees of the Al Jazeera Children's Channel.

In May 2014, Qatar announced a series of labor reforms via a Ministry of Interior press release. It announced that "the current *kafala* system will be replaced by a system based on employment contracts" but the details it provided indicated that workers would still be bound to their employers. The statement announced that workers would be able to secure No Objection Certificates, but only after 5 years of employment with one employer, and that an automated e-government system would issue exit visas after a 72-hour grace period prior to a foreign worker's departure.

The press release also said that Qatar would increase the number of labor inspectors, introduce an electronic wage payment system, increase the penalty for passport confiscation, and build suitable housing for 200,000 workers. The statement gave no details on how or when the government would implement the reforms. Nor did the authorities respond to a Human Rights Watch letter questioning the validity of the government's assertion that the changes amount to replacement of the *kafala* system. On June 5, the minister of labor added to the confusion when he announced that the model contract being developed by his ministry will determine whether or not a worker will require an exit visa to leave Qatar and whether or not they will receive a No Objection Certificate at the end of their contract.

In July 2014, the Qatar Foundation, a quasi-governmental organization heavily engaged in property development, issued a report on recruitment practices. Among its recommendations were that the government of Qatar should seek to ensure standardized ethical recruitment practices in labor-sending countries by developing bilateral agreements on recruitment, and that it should consider setting up its own recruitment agencies in major labor sending countries.

It is not clear how the proposed reforms will affect migrant domestic workers, a predominately female subset of the migrant worker population, who are especially vulnerable. In addition to the problems the general migrant worker population face, domestic workers suffer verbal, physical, and in some cases, sexual abuse at their places of work. Some are not allowed by their employers to speak to strangers or are locked into the homes in which they are employed. Many are required to work without receiving a day off.

Qatari labor law affords no protection to migrant domestic workers, and does not require employers to allow them rest days or rest periods when at work, or to limit their working hours. The Gulf Cooperation Council (GCC), of which Qatar is a member, is discussing a unified regional contract for domestic workers. However, the contract fails to provide key protections such as a limit on hours of work, and has weak enforcement mechanisms. It also falls short of the minimum standards outlined in the recently adopted International Labour Organization's Domestic Workers' Convention, which Qatar has yet to ratify. Even a strong contract, however, would be no substitute for labor law reforms.

Freedom of Expression

In September, Qatar issued a law "on the suppression of electronic crimes," which poses a clear threat to freedom of expression. Vaguely worded provisions provide for the prosecution of individuals who publish "false news with the intent of endangering the public order" and information that "infringes social prin-ciples or values."

Qatar's emir has not yet given final approval to a draft media law that would ex-pose journalists in Qatar to prohibitive financial sanctions if they publish infor-mation that damages relations with other Arab states.

Qatar's penal code contains provisions that are inconsistent with free speech standards under international law. Article 134, for example, prescribes a penalty of up to five years' imprisonment for anyone who is convicted of criticizing the emir or vice-emir.

In August 2014, authorities detained two British citizens who were in Qatar to re-search and document living and working conditions for migrant workers, and held them in incommunicado detention for 11 days before releasing them with-out charge.

Women's Rights

Provisions of Law No. 22 of 2006, Qatar's first codified law to address issues of family and personal status, discriminates against women. Under Article 36, a marriage contract is valid when a woman's male guardian concludes the contract and two male witnesses are present. Article 57 forbids husbands from hurting their wives physically or morally, but article 58 states that it is a wife's responsi-bility to look after the household and to obey her husband. Marital rape is not a crime.

Key International Actors

Saudi Arabia, Bahrain, and the United Arab Emirates withdrew their ambassa-dors from Qatar in March, in response to its support for Islamist groups, notably the Muslim Brotherhood. Normal diplomatic relations resumed in November. Qatar provided assistance in US-led air-strikes on militant Islamist forces in Iraq and Syria.

Russia

The Kremlin took another leap backward in 2014 by intensifying its crackdown on civil society, media, and the Internet, as it sought to control the narrative about developments in Ukraine, including Russia's occupation of Crimea and its support to insurgents in eastern Ukraine.

Parliament adopted laws, and authorities engaged in practices, that increasingly isolated the country and inflamed a level of anti-Western hysteria unseen since the Soviet era.

Freedom of Association

In June, parliament amended Russia's 2012 "Foreign Agent" law, which demonizes advocacy groups that accept foreign funding, by authorizing the Justice Ministry to register groups as foreign agents without their consent. By November, the ministry had forcibly registered 17 independent groups as such.

On December 17, the Supreme Court was due to review a Justice Ministry complaint against the Memorial umbrella organization requesting its closure under the pretext of technical breach of Russia's nongovernmental organization (NGO) legislation.

In September, a court vacated a previous ruling against Golos, an election monitoring group, for failing to register as a "foreign agent" due to lack of evidence that the group accepted foreign funding. However, at time of writing Golos remained on the "foreign agents" registry.

Freedom of Expression

Russian authorities blocked several independent media websites, adopted new laws, and proposed yet more measures that would further stifle freedom of expression.

In January 2014, TV Rain, one of Russia's few independent television stations, lost access to cable and satellite television after it posted a viewers' poll about whether the USSR should have surrendered Leningrad during World War II to save lives.

HUMAN
RIGHTS
WATCH

LICENSE TO HARM

Violence and Harassment against LGBT People and Activists in Russia

In March, the state agency for media oversight blocked three independent web-sites and an opposition leader's blog under a new law authorizing the prosecu-tor general to request that the agency block websites without a court order. Also in March, the editor and executive director of Lenta.ru, an independent current affairs portal, were dismissed and replaced by pro-Kremlin media executives.

In April, the founder and CEO of VKontakte, the most popular Russian-language social network, announced he had left Russia because of persistent demands by the Federal Security Service to block opposition users and communities. In Sep-tember, an Internet company controlled by an oligarch close to the Kremlin took full control of VKontakte by acquiring its remaining shares.

As the crisis in Ukraine escalated, Russian policymakers adopted laws imposing further, severe restrictions on media and independent groups. In May, President Vladimir Putin signed a law requiring bloggers with more than 3,000 daily visi-tors to register as mass media. In June, Putin signed a law imposing custodial terms for extremist calls on the Internet, including re-posts on social media. In July, a new law banned commercial advertising on cable and satellite television channels, effectively stripping hundreds of privately owned channels of a crucial income. Also in July, the president signed laws criminalizing "separatist" calls and prohibiting storing Russian Internet users' personal data on foreign servers. The latter will enter into force in 2016. A law adopted in October severely re-stricts foreign ownership of Russian media.

Several outspoken academics and public figures who work for government-funded cultural institutions were either fired or "rotated out" of their positionsfor example, historian Andrei Zubov, who lost his job after he publicly criticized Rus-sia's occupation of Crimea in a newspaper commentary.

Sexual Orientation and Gender Identity

Russian authorities fined four people during the year for violating the 2013 law banning distribution among children of positive information about "non-tradi-tional sexual relationships," which are known to signify lesbian, gay, bisexual, and transgender (LGBT) relationships.

Anti-LGBT vigilante groups continued attacking gay people across Russia. The authorities have conducted a few isolated investigations but largely failed to prosecute homophobic and transphobic violence.

Attacks on LGBT activists also persist. In April, a group of nationalists interrupted a Moscow screening of a documentary about LGBT discrimination. In September, groups of nationalists disrupted the opening night of an annual LGBT event in Saint Petersburg, QueerFest, throwing smoke bombs. Other QueerFest events were canceled due to threats and to venue operators breaking rental agreements.

Smear campaigns have targeted LGBT people working in the public education system. In at least six cases, employers did not renew their contracts, pressured them to resign, or simply fired them. Some LGBT people decided to leave Russia due to homophobia and fear of violations of their rights because of their sexual orientation.

Freedom of Assembly

Police interference in peaceful public gatherings continued in 2014. Authorities detained hundreds of peaceful protesters during the 2014 Winter Olympic Games and after the occupation of Crimea, in most cases arbitrarily and in some cases with unnecessary force. Between February 21 and March 4, police detained at least 1,300 peaceful protesters in Moscow alone. In March and September, two peaceful marches protesting Russia's interference in Ukraine took place without incident in Moscow.

The government toughened penalties for unauthorized public gatherings. A new law increased to up to 15 years prison terms for "mass rioting," the offense used to prosecute dozens of people who had protested at Moscow's Bolotnaya Square on the eve of Putin's 2012 inauguration.The law also introduced a new offense—"mass riots training"— punishable by up to 10 years in prison. New amendments significantly increased fines for unauthorized public gatherings and introduced criminal punishment of up to three years in prison for repeat offenders.

Human Rights Defenders and Political Opponents

In a March speech, Putin called independent groups and government critics "national traitors" and a "fifth column" working to destabilize the country.

Russia's biggest political trial, against the Bolotnaya Square protestors, continued. In December 2013, four of the accused were released under a federal amnesty. Between February and August 2014, 13 were sentenced to up to four-and-a-half years in prison for, variously, mass rioting, violence against police, and organizing mass riots.

In June, a court released Mikhail Kosenko, a Bolotnaya protester sentenced in 2013 to forced psychiatric treatment.

In February, unknown perpetrators attempted to set fire to the home of Igor Sazhin, a prominent human rights defender in the Komi region. Authorities failed to investigate. Also in February, police in Voronezh arrested Roman Khabarov, a former police officer and human rights defender, on trumped-up charges of membership in an organized criminal group that operated a network of unlawful gambling spots in the region. His trial was set to begin in late 2014.

On April 2, a Krasnodar court convicted Mikhail Savva, a civic activist and academic, of fraud and gave him a suspended prison sentence and a fine of 70,000 rubles (US$1,945). Savva had spent over seven months in pretrial custody.

On June 9, five men were sentenced for participating in the killing of one of Russia's most outspoken investigative journalists, Anna Politkovskaya, in 2006. Two received a life sentence; the others received prison terms ranging from 12 to 20 years. Others believed to have ordered the killing remained unpunished. The perpetrators of the 2009 killing of leading Chechen human rights defender Natalia Estemirova had still not been brought to justice at time of writing.

North Caucasus

The confrontation between the Islamist insurgency and law enforcement agencies continued in Russia's North Caucasus, particularly in Dagestan. According to Caucasian Knot, an independent online media portal, in the first nine months of 2014, 239 people were killed in the North Caucasus region, including 31 civilians, and 117 people were wounded, including 15 civilians. More than two-thirds of these casualties occurred in Dagestan.

Security forces raided Salafi mosques across Dagestan detaining, interrogating, photographing, and finger-printing hundreds of people. Police also subjected many Salafis to forced DNA testing. Abusive special operations in the mountain villages of Gimry and Vremennyi went on for months and involved destruction of property and enforced disappearances.

Abduction-style detentions, torture, and enforced disappearances persisted in the North Caucasus, as did attacks against government critics. In August, Timur Kuashev, a freelance journalist and rights activist, was found dead near Nalchik, in Kabardino-Balkaria. The official investigation had not yielded tangible results at time of writing. Several Dagestani activists and lawyers told Human Rights Watch that they frequently received threats aimed at silencing them. In July, a court in Chechnya convicted Ruslan Kutaev, a prominent local activist, on trumped-up drug charges and sentenced him to four years' imprisonment. The court disregarded torture allegations he made during his trial. On October 31, an appeals court decreased Kutaev's prison sentence by three months. Two days before his arrest, Kutaev publicly criticized an order handed down by Chechnya's leader, Ramzan Kadyrov.

Chechen authorities require women to wear headscarves in public places. In September, Kadyrov made a televised statement warning that as part of their fight against "non-traditional Islam," authorities would detain women who wear "Wahabi"-style headscarves, covering the forehead and the chin.

Abuses Linked to Preparations for the 2014 Olympic Games

Authorities harassed and intimidated organizations, individuals, and journalists in Sochi in advance of the 2014 Winter Olympic Games. In February, an appeals court upheld a politically motivated prison sentence for Evgenii Vitishko, an environmental activist and critic of Russia's Olympic preparations.

In January, the authorities announced that an inspection of more than 500 companies involved in Olympic construction exposed 277 million rubles (US$8.34 million) in unpaid wages to workers. However local activists report hundreds of migrant workers still did not receive full wages owed them.

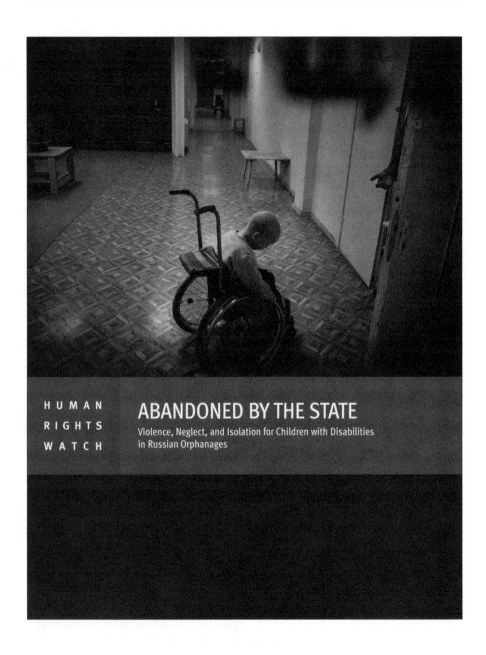

HUMAN
RIGHTS
WATCH

ABANDONED BY THE STATE

Violence, Neglect, and Isolation for Children with Disabilities
in Russian Orphanages

The authorities failed to resettle or fairly compensate some families evicted for Olympic development or whose homes or property suffered damage from it.

Palliative Care

2014 saw several positive developments in palliative care, including the introduction of clinical guidelines on pain treatment for children. The lack of access to quality pain treatment and palliative care remains a systemic problem. Access to morphine remains overly restricted for the vast majority of patients.

A doctor in Krasnoyarsk and another woman who had helped a man in final stages of cancer access pain medication were finally acquitted during a re-trial in October after they had initially been convicted and fined on charges of illegal drug trafficking of controlled substances.

Disability Rights

Adults and children living with various disabilities face many barriers to participating in their communities. These include physical barriers, such as the lack of ramps and elevators and inadequate accommodations in transportation systems; policy barriers, such as lack of inclusive education; and social barriers, such as employers' unwillingness to hire people with disabilities.

In positive steps in 2014, the Ministry of Labor and Social Protection introduced amendments to legislation to expand mandatory accommodations for people with sensory and physical disabilities and to prohibit disability-based discrimination. Russia successfully hosted the Sochi 2014 Winter Paralympic Games. However, Sochi residents and tourists with disabilities continued to face barriers to using public services and facilities due to lack of accessibility.

Hundreds of thousands of adults and children with disabilities currently live in closed institutions. Approximately 45 percent of children in orphanages have disabilities. Many children with disabilities in orphanages face physical and psychological violence and neglect and are denied adequate healthcare, education, and play. Russia has committed to addressing the high rates of children in state institutions, but current policies lack concrete implementation and monitoring.

Russia and Ukraine

Moscow has made clear its political support for armed insurgents in eastern Ukraine and clearly exerts influence over them. There is also evidence that they provide material support to the insurgents in terms of weapons and training. Mounting evidence, including images of military manouvers and the capture of Russian soldiers in Ukraine, showed that Russian forces are taking part in hostilities there. Yet Russia has taken no public steps to rein in abuses by insurgents (see Ukraine chapter).

Key International Actors

Russia's interference in Ukraine largely contributed to the drastic deterioration of relations between Russia and its international partners, including the European Union and the United States, both of which imposed sanctions over Russia's actions in Ukraine. Although the conflict in Ukraine eclipsed concerns about the crackdown in Russia, various actors sharpened their public criticism of Russia's domestic record, decrying new, restrictive legislation and the hostile climate for civil society activists and human rights defenders.

In February 2014, the International Olympic Committee (IOC) pressed Russian authorities to investigate arrears wages owed to migrant workers involved in the preparations for the 2014 Sochi Winter Olympics, but it failed to condemn the 2013 anti-LGBT law, despite the Olympic Charter's prohibition of discrimination.

In May, the Council of Europe's human rights commissioner noted that pressure on independent journalists in Russia had increased.

On June 3, the Parliamentary Assembly of the Council of Europe rapporteur on human rights defenders expressed regret over the continued repression of civil society and human rights defenders and the fact that Russia had not met its promises to revise the "foreign agents" law.

The International Criminal Court prosecutor continued to monitor Russian and Georgian investigations into crimes committed during the 2008 Georgia-Russian conflict over South Ossetia.

Rwanda

The 20th anniversary of the 1994 genocide was commemorated in ceremonies and other events across Rwanda, and in many other countries.

Progress in economic and social development remain impressive, but the government continues to impose severe restrictions on freedom of expression and association and does not tolerate dissent. Political space is extremely limited and independent civil society and media remain weak. Real or suspected opponents inside and outside the country continue to be targeted.

Detainees were held unlawfully for several weeks or months in police or military custody, in unrecognized detention centers. Dozens of people were reported disappeared. Some reappeared in prison after prolonged incommunicado detention, but others remain unaccounted for.

Political Opposition

The ruling Rwandan Patriotic Front (RPF) dominates all aspects of political and public life. Opposition parties cannot operate in a meaningful way.

In December 2013, the Supreme Court increased from eight to fifteen years the prison sentence of Victoire Ingabire, president of the FDU-Inkingi opposition party, who had been convicted of conspiracy to undermine the government and genocide denial in 2012. Several other FDU-Inkingi members, including the party's secretary general, Sylvain Sibomana, also remained in prison.

Bernard Ntaganda, leader of the PS-Imberakuri opposition party, was released in June after serving a four-year sentence for endangering national security and divisionism.

The Democratic Green Party of Rwanda, which was granted registration in 2013, joined the National Consultative Forum of Political Organizations in April. There were no arrests in connection with the murder of the party's Vice President André Kagwa Rwisereka in July 2010.

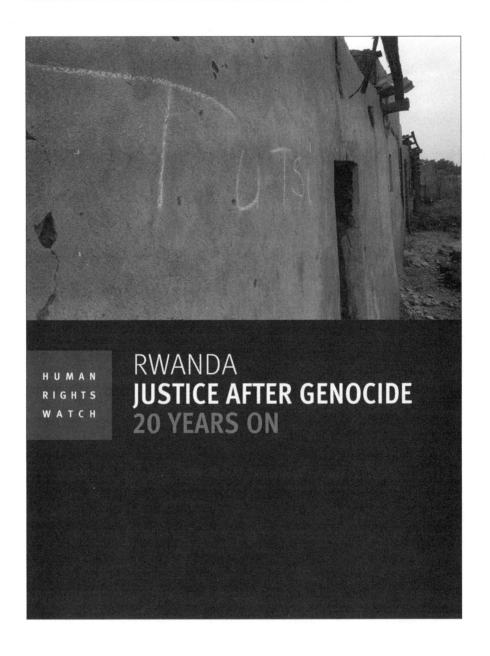

Attacks on Opponents Abroad

On January 1, Patrick Karegeya, former head of Rwanda's external intelligence services and a prominent government opponent exiled in South Africa, was found murdered in a hotel room in Johannesburg. South African authorities launched an investigation, which was ongoing at time of writing. Karegeya was a leading member of the Rwanda National Congress (RNC), an opposition group in exile. Other RNC members have also been attacked and threatened outside Rwanda. The Rwandan government denied any involvement in these attacks, but President Paul Kagame came close to publicly condoning Karegeya's murder on January 12, 2014, when he said, among other things, "whoever betrays the country will pay the price."

In August, a South African court convicted two Rwandans and two Tanzanians of the attempted murder of General Kayumba Nyamwasa—a former senior military official and leading RNC member—in South Africa in 2010, and sentenced them in September to eight years' imprisonment. It acquitted two other Rwandan defendants. The judge stated that the attack was politically motivated and emanated from a group of people in Rwanda.

Civil Society Organizations

Independent civil society organizations remain extremely weak as a result of years of state intimidation and infiltration. The only remaining effective Rwandan human rights group, the Rwandan League for the Promotion and Defence of Human Rights (LIPRODHOR), took legal action in protest at a takeover of its leadership by members sympathetic to the government in 2013. The Rwanda Governance Board, the state body with oversight of national nongovernmental organizations, recognized the new leadership in 2013. After numerous adjournments, a court in Kigali ruled on procedural grounds in August 2014 that the case was unfounded. The ousted LIPRODHOR leaders have filed an appeal.

In September, two police officers were arrested in connection with the murder of anti-corruption activist Gustave Makonene. After initially denying the murder charges, both suspects pleaded guilty in pretrial hearings in October. The trial had not started at time of writing. Makonene, coordinator of Transparency International Rwanda's Advice and Legal Advice Center in Rubavu, was found dead in July 2013.

In June the pro-government *New Times* newspaper published an "assessment" of Human Rights Watch's work in Rwanda by the Ministry of Justice, which grossly misrepresented the organization's work. Among other allegations, it accused Human Rights Watch of supporting the Democratic Forces for the Liberation of Rwanda (FDLR), a predominantly Rwandan armed group operating in eastern Congo, some of whose leaders participated in the 1994 genocide in Rwanda.

Freedom of Media

Media remained heavily dominated by pro- government views. Most journalists were unable or unwilling to engage in reporting on sensitive issues due to threats, intimidation, and prosecution in previous years. However, some radio stations occasionally broadcast call-in programs in which listeners can raise a broader range of issues and put questions to political leaders.

Agnès Uwimana, editor of *Umurabyo* newspaper, was released in June after serving four years in prison for endangering national security and defamation, in connection with articles published in the newspaper.

On October 24, the Rwanda Utilities Regulatory Authority (RURA) suspended the British Broadcasting Corporation's (BBC) Kinyarwanda service's broadcasts in Rwanda. RURA said it had received complaints of incitement, hatred, divisionism, genocide denial and revision from members of the public after the October 1 BBC television documentary, "Rwanda's Untold Story" was broadcast. On November 19 a commission of inquiry, established by RURA and headed by former Prosecutor General Martin Ngoga, began investigations into these allegations against the BBC. It was expected to produce its report in three months.

Unlawful Detention and Enforced Disappearances

Dozens of people were held unlawfully, incommunicado in the military Camp Kami and other detention centers, some for several weeks or months. Some were tortured and pressured to confess to alleged crimes or to incriminate others. Some of these detainees were later tried on security-related charges.

From March to time of writing, at least 30 people were reported missing, many in northwestern Rwanda. Some were arrested by state agents and taken to unknown destinations. After several weeks, some of the disappeared reappeared in police detention and were transferred to civilian prisons. Some were among a group of 16 people who appeared before a court in Rubavu in June, accused of endangering state security and collaborating with the FDLR. Government authorities did not acknowledge their unlawful detention or account for their whereabouts during the preceding period, failings which render their detentions enforced disappearances. In a speech on June 5, President Kagame said authorities would continue to arrest suspects and, if necessary, shoot in broad daylight those intending to destabilize the country.

Throughout the year, hundreds of men, women, and children—many of them street children, commercial sex workers, or street hawkers—were detained unlawfully, without charge or trial, in very poor conditions in an unrecognized detention center commonly known as Kwa Kabuga, in the Gikondo area of Kigali. Many were beaten by police, or by other detainees in the presence of police.

Security-Related Trials

The trial of Joel Mutabazi, a former presidential bodyguard forcibly returned from Uganda to Rwanda in October 2013, and 15 co-accused began before a military court in Kigali in January. The defendants were charged with terrorism, murder, forming an armed group, and other offenses, linked to alleged collaboration with the RNC and the FDLR. Mutabazi and several co-defendants stated in court that they had been tortured and forced to sign statements. Mutabazi was found guilty of all charges and sentenced in October to life in prison. Thirteen defendants received sentences ranging from 3 months to 25 years. Two were acquitted.

Well-known singer Kizito Mihigo, journalist Cassien Ntamuhanga, and co-defendants Agnès Niyibizi and Jean-Paul Dukuzumuremyi were arrested in April and charged, among other things, with offenses against the state and complicity in terrorist acts for allegedly collaborating with the RNC and FDLR. Mihigo's whereabouts were unknown for several days before he appeared in police custody. In November, he confessed to all the charges. Two of his co-defendants, Ntamuhanga and Dukuzumuremyi, pleaded not guilty. The trial was ongoing at time of writing and Niyibizi had not entered a plea.

In August, two senior military officers, retired Brig. Gen. Frank Rusagara and Col.Tom Byabagamba, were arrested and charged with, among other offenses, inciting insurrection and public disorder, and tarnishing the country's image. The accusations are believed to be related to their alleged contacts with the RNC. They appeared in a military court alongside a third co-defendant, demobilized Sgt. François Kabayiza. They were awaiting trial at time of writing.

Justice for the Genocide

The International Criminal Tribunal for Rwanda was expected to conclude all proceedings by the end of 2014, with the exception of one appeal due to conclude in 2015. Nine suspects wanted by the ICTR continue to evade justice. The ICTR and the United Nations mechanism for international criminal tribunals launched a new initiative in July to track and arrest these remaining fugitives.

Genocide trials took place in the domestic courts of several countries under the principle of universal jurisdiction, and further cases were pending. In the first such prosecution in France, conducted by a newly established war crimes unit, a court in Paris tried former intelligence chief, Pascal Simbikangwa, and sentenced him in March to 25 years in prison for genocide and complicity in crimes against humanity. In February, a court in Germany sentenced former Rwandan mayor, Onesphore Rwabukombe, to 14 years in prison for aiding and abetting genocide.

Key International Actors

The UN special rapporteur on freedom of association and assembly, Maina Kiai, visited Rwanda in January and expressed concern about restrictions on nongovernmental organizations and political parties, among other issues. In his report to the UN Human Rights Council in June, he raised a number of concerns, including the prevailing opposition to vigorous debate and free expression of opinions, the government's hostility toward peaceful initiatives by its critics and the existence of a legal framework that silences dissent. The Rwandan government refuted several of his findings.

In January, the United States Department of State publicly condemned the murder of Patrick Karegeya. It expressed concern about what appeared to be politically motivated murders of prominent Rwandan exiles and President Kagame's statements about the "consequences" for those who betrayed Rwanda. In June, a US government press statement expressed concern about the arrest and disappearance of dozens of people and incommunicado detention for periods of up to two months.

Saudi Arabia

Saudi Arabia continued in 2014 to try, convict, and imprison political dissidents and human rights activists solely on account of their peaceful activities. Systematic discrimination against women and religious minorities continued. Authorities failed to enact systematic measures to protect the rights of 9 million foreign workers. As in past years, authorities subjected hundreds of people to unfair trials and arbitrary detention. New anti-terrorism regulations that took effect in 2014 can be used to criminalize almost any form of peaceful criticism of the authorities as terrorism.

Freedom of Expression, Association, and Belief

The Specialized Criminal Court, Saudi Arabia's terrorism tribunal, sentenced prominent Eastern Province activist Fadhil al-Manasif to 15 years in prison, a 15-year ban on travel abroad, and a large fine on April 17 after it convicted him on charges that included "breaking allegiance with the ruler," "contact with foreign news organizations to exaggerate the news," and "circulating his phone number to [foreign] news agencies to allow them to call him." The charges arose from al-Manasif's assistance to international media covering the 2011 protests in Eastern Province.

A Specialized Criminal Court judge ordered the detention of prominent human rights lawyer Waleed Abu al-Khair on April 15. In July, the court convicted him on vague charges arising solely from his peaceful activism, sentencing him to 15 years in prison, a 15-year travel ban, and a fine of 200,000 Saudi Riyals (US$53,000). On August 11, the day after Abu al-Khair refused to cooperate in his transfer to another prison, Jeddah prison authorities beat him and dragged him from the prison with chains, injuring his ankles, then dispatched him to another prison almost 1,000 kilometers away from his family home.

Authorities continued to persecute activists associated with the Saudi Civil and Political Rights Association (ACPRA). In June, a court sentenced Fowzan al-Harbi to seven years in prison but suspended six years of the sentence on condition that he does not return to his activism. Issa al-Hamid, the brother of imprisoned activist Abdullah al-Hamid, was on trial in September on charges that included "inciting [people] to violate public order and spreading discord" and "insulting the judiciary." Others were under investigation.

An appeals tribunal inside the Specialized Criminal Court in July upheld a sentence of five years in prison and a 10-year travel ban for human rights advocate Mikhlif al-Shammari, based on his writings and exposure of human rights abuses.

Saudi officials continue to refuse to register political or human rights groups, leaving members subject to prosecution for "setting up an unregistered organization." Saudi officials did not pass a long-awaited associations law in 2014, leaving Saudi citizens with no legal avenue to set up non-charity nongovernmental organizations.

Saudi Arabia does not tolerate public worship by adherents of religions other than Islam and systematically discriminates against Muslim religious minorities, notably Twelver Shia and Ismailis.

In May, a Jeddah court convicted activist Raif Badawi and sentenced him to 10 years in prison and 1,000 lashes for "insulting Islam" by founding a critical liberal website, and for his comments during television interviews. An appeals court upheld the sentence in September.

Criminal Justice

Detainees, including children, commonly face systematic violations of due process and fair trial rights, including arbitrary arrest and torture and ill-treatment in detention. Saudi judges routinely sentence defendants to floggings of hundreds of lashes.

Judges can order arrest and detention, including of children, at their discretion. Children can be tried for capital crimes and sentenced as adults if physical signs of puberty exist.

Saudi Arabia applies Sharia (Islamic law) as the law of the land. Judges decide many matters relating to criminal offenses pursuant to Sharia in accordance with established rules of jurisprudence and precedent.

While there is no formal penal code, the government has passed some laws and regulations that subject certain broadly-defined offenses to criminal penalties.

In the absence of a written penal code or narrowly-worded regulations, however, judges and prosecutors can criminalize a wide range of offenses under broad, catch-all charges such as "breaking allegiance with the ruler" or "trying to distort the reputation of the kingdom."

Authorities do not always inform suspects of the crime with which they are charged, or allow them access to supporting evidence, even after trial sessions have begun in some cases. Authorities generally do not allow lawyers to assist suspects during interrogation and often impede them from examining witnesses and presenting evidence at trial.

Authorities continued to arrest and hold suspects for months and sometimes years without judicial review or prosecution. On May 15, an Interior Ministry database showed that criminal justice officials were holding 293 individuals whose pretrial detention exceeded six months without having referred their cases to the judiciary. At least 31 people had been detained "under investigation" for more than six months.

Saudi Arabia permitted representatives of certain foreign diplomatic missions to monitor trials of Saudi dissidents and activists in 2014 for the first time.

Saudi authorities promulgated a new anti-terrorism law on January 31 that contains serious flaws. Its vague and overly broad provisions allow authorities to criminalize free expression and it gives the authorities excessive police powers that are not subject to judicial oversight. On March 7, the Interior Ministry issued further regulations designating a list of groups the government considers terrorist organizations, as well as other provisions that proscribe acts such as "calling for atheist thought," throw[ing] away loyalty to the country's rulers," "contact or correspondence with any groups, currents [of thought], or individuals hostile to the kingdom," and participating in or calling for protests or demonstrations.

In June, the Ministry of Justice announced that prosecutors had filed 191 cases of alleged sorcery—a crime punishable by death—between November 2013 and May 2014, including some against foreign domestic workers.

According to media reports, Saudi Arabia executed at least 68 persons between January and mid-November 2014, mostly for murder, drug offenses, and armed robbery, including 31 between August 4 and September 4. Thirty-one of those executed were convicted for non-violent crimes, including one man sentenced for sorcery.

On October 15, Specialized Criminal Court sentenced prominent Shia cleric Nimr al-Nimr to death on a host of vague charges, based largely on his peaceful criticism of Saudi officials.

Women's and Girls' Rights

Saudi Arabia's discriminatory male guardianship system remains intact despite government pledges to abolish it. Under this system, ministerial policies and practices forbid women from obtaining a passport, marrying, traveling, or accessing higher education without the approval of a male guardian, usually a husband, father, brother, or son.

Authorities also fail to prevent some employers from requiring male guardians to approve the hiring of adult female relatives or some hospitals from requiring male guardian approval for certain medical procedures for women. In February, a member of the Senior Council of Scholars, the highest state body for the interpretation of Islamic law, issued a fatwa stating that women are not allowed to visit a male doctor without their male guardians. They are not allowed to expose parts of the body with the exception of a medical emergency. All women remain banned from driving in Saudi Arabia.

Likewise, under un-codified rules on personal status, women are not allowed to marry without the permission of their guardian; unlike men, they do not have a unilateral right to divorce and often face discrimination in relation to child custody. In September, the Supreme Judicial Council issued a decision to allow women granted custody of their children to handle all affairs related to their children including obtaining official documents. To travel outside the country with theirchildren, however, women still require the permission of the children's father .

In a welcome move in April, the Shura Council, Saudi Arabia's highest consultative body, directed the Education Ministry to study the possibility of introducing physical education for girls in Saudi public schools, which, if enacted, would end the longstanding ban on sports for girls.

Migrant Workers' Rights

Over 9 million migrant workers fill manual, clerical, and service jobs, constituting more than half the workforce. Many suffer abuses and exploitation, sometimes amounting to conditions of forced labor.

The *kafala* (sponsorship) system ties migrant workers' residency permits to "sponsoring" employers, whose written consent is required for workers to change employers or exit the country under normal circumstances. Some employers illegally confiscate passports, withhold wages, and force migrants to work against their will.

Saudi officials, wary that the domestic unemployment rate of 12 percent may grow as the domestic population increases, have issued a set of labor reforms since 2011 that create a tiered quota system for the employment of Saudi citizens in the private labor sector that differs according to the nature of the business. As part of these reforms, Saudi labor authorities in 2014 began allowing foreigners working in firms that do not employ the required percentage of Saudis to change jobs without employer approval.

Police and labor authorities in 2014 continued a vigorous campaign to arrest and deport foreign workers found in violation of existing labor laws, targeting workers who did not have valid residency or work permits, or those found working for an employer other than his or her legal sponsor. According to the International Organization on Migration (IOM), Saudi Arabia deported 163,018 Ethiopians between November 2013 and March 2014, and 458,911 Yemenis between June 2013 and June 2014. There were reports that prior to deportation some deportees were placed inovercrowded detention conditions, denied adequate food and water, and physically abused by guards. Between December and March 2014, Saudi Arabia deported 38,164 Somalis to Mogadishu, including hundreds of women and children, without allowing any to make refugee claims.

Domestic workers, most of them women, frequently endure a range of abuses including overwork, forced confinement, non-payment of wages, food deprivation, and psychological, physical, and sexual abuse without the authorities holding their employers to account. Workers who attempted to report employer abuses sometimes faced prosecution based on counterclaims of theft or "sorcery."

Key International Actors

During a visit to Saudi Arabia in March, US President Barack Obama did not discuss human rights issues with Saudi officials. State Department spokespeople stated that the US was "troubled" over the conviction of Waleed Abu al-Khair and "concerned" over Raif Badawi's harsh sentence. Otherwise the United States did not criticize Saudi human rights violations beyond Congressionally-mandated annual reports. In 2014, Saudi Arabia was classified as a Country of Particular Concern under the US International Religious Freedom Act for having engaged in or tolerated particularly severe violations of religious freedom.

On December 27, 2013, a Gulf Cooperation Council (GCC) joint security agreement came into force. The agreement's 20 provisions include a vaguely worded article that would suppress "interference in the domestic affairs" of other GCC countries, which could be used to criminalize criticism of Gulf countries or rulers. Another provision provides for sharing citizens' and residents' personal data at the discretion of Interior Ministry officials, apparently without judicial oversight.

Serbia

There was limited progress in human rights protection in Serbia in 2014. War crimes prosecutions are slow and lack political support. The Roma minority continue to face attacks and harassment. The situation for journalists remains precarious, including attacks, threats, and lawsuits for reporting on sensitive issues. Hostility towards members of the lesbian, gay, bisexual, and transgender (LGBT) community continued and included threats and attacks.

Accountability for War Crimes

War crimes prosecutions progressed slowly in 2014 due to a lack of political support, resources, and staff at the Office of the War Crimes Prosecutor. Few high-ranking former military and civilian personnel have been prosecuted for war crimes. During the year, the War Crimes Chamber reached judgments in six cases, including two appeals. The Office of War Crimes Prosecutor indicted five people for crimes against civilians, including former Yugoslav Army General Dragan Zivanovic for war crimes in Kosovo in 1999. At time of writing, 6 trials were ongoing, indictments had been issues in 16 cases awaiting trial, and 20 cases were under investigation.

In February, the chamber sentenced nine former members of the Yugoslav Army to a total of 106 years of imprisonment for the killing of over 120 Albanian civilians in Kosovo in 1999. Also in February, the chamber sentenced Djuro Tadic to 10 years for participating in the killings by Bosnian Serb forces of 18 people, including a 13-year-old girl, in northwestern Bosnia and Herzegovina (BiH) in September 1992. Two co-defendants were sentenced to 11 and 10 years respectively.

At time of writing, the February 2013 war crimes protocol signed between BiH, Serbia, Croatia and Montenegro that details information sharing and cooperation, had not led to new prosecutions or convictions derived from case transfers.

In February 2014, a first instance court in Belgrade dismissed 12 Croatian ex-prisoners' civil lawsuits against Serbia for torture in detention in 1991 on the grounds the claim was time-barred and there were no criminal convictions for the alleged abuse on which to base the civil claims.

In January, the International Criminal Tribunal for the Former Yugoslavia (ICTY) appeals chamber upheld the crimes against humanity conviction of former Serbian Assistant Minister of Interior Vlastimir Djordjevic for the murder, persecution, and forced deportation of Kosovo Albanians in 1999, but reduced his sentence from 27 to 18 years.

Also in January, the ICTY appeals chamber upheld its guilty verdict against former Yugoslav Deputy Minister Nikola Sainovic, former Yugoslav Army Generals Nebojsa Pavkovic and Vladimir Lazarevic, and former Serbian Police General Sreten Lukic for murder, deportation, and inhumane treatment of Kosovo Albanians in 1999. In doing so, a majority of the judges rejected the reasoning in the 2014 ICTY appeals chamber judgment in the Perisic case that an accused must have "specifically directed" assistance to commit crimes to be guilty of aiding and abetting.

Freedom of Media

Journalists continued to face threats, harassment, intimidation, and political and other interference. Between January and August, the International Journalist Association in Serbia reported five assaults on journalists, three direct threats, and 12 cases of political and other pressure.

In early July, FoNet News Agency Editor Davor Pasalic was severely beaten by three unknown assailants who demanded money and called him a Croatian fascist. Police were investigating at time of writing.

In May, online news sites Druga Strana and Teleprompter suffered cyber-attacks that temporarily shut down their websites, which had reported on the mismanagement and inefficiency of Serbian state institutions during severe flooding that the country experienced earlier the same month. The perpetrators of the cyber-attacks remain unknown. Srdjan Skoro, a former editor at the daily *Vecernje Novosti*, was dismissed from his post in May after speaking critically about the government's handling of the floods in a Radio Television Serbia broadcast.

The government commission established in 2013 to investigate the murders of three prominent journalists more than a decade earlier made progress in only one case, resulting in four people being charged. The seven-member commission is tasked with analyzing all prior investigations, ascertaining why they failed, and gathering evidence to assist future criminal investigations.

Treatment of Minorities

Attacks and harassment against the Roma minority continued.

In February, a group of non-Roma attacked members of a Romani nongovernmental organization (NGO) in Novi Sad, northern Serbia. The Roma managed to escape into their office and called police for help, who refused to assist, according to the European Roma Rights Centre (ERRC). In March, four members of the NGO were brutally beaten by two non-Roma carrying sticks. One Roma man received serious head injuries and two others suffered lighter head injuries. Police were investigating at time of writing.

In April, around 15 men threw Molotov cocktails at a Romani Protestant church in the village of Bosnajce in southern Serbia, setting fire to the room where church ceremonies are held. Nobody was injured. According to the ERRC, three people were convicted in April in connection with the attack and sentenced to 30 days in prison.

Sexual Orientation and Gender Identity

LGBT people continue to face intolerance, harassment, and in at least one case, physical violence.

In September, a 27-year-old German LGBT activist was brutally beaten by a group of men and suffered serious injuries that required hospitalization. Police arrested three suspects. In April, the Gay-Straight Alliance received repeated emails calling for the murder of LGBT people and cleansing of LGBT organizations in Serbia. Three weeks prior, Gay-Straight Alliance members received death threats over the phone. A local LGBT group reported that the police had failed to identify the perpetrators.

In February, the Commissioner for Equality Nevena Petrusic issued an opinion that held that the Belgrade Bosko Buha theatre discriminated against a gay magazine by refusing to allow it to have information about one of its shows for publication.

The May Belgrade Pride March, which had been cancelled for three consecutive years due to alleged security reasons, was held in late September amid heavy police security and was attended by 1,000-1,500 people, including three Serbian ministers, the European Union representative in Serbia, and several foreign diplomats. No violence against LGBT supporters was reported.

Asylum Seekers and Displaced Persons

In the first eight months of 2014, Serbia registered 6,974 asylum seekers, a significant increase from 2,567 during the same period in 2013. Syrians comprised the largest national group (3,696 people).

In 2014, three new reception centers opened in Serbia, adding to the existing two. For the first time since it assumed responsibility for the asylum procedure in 2008, the Asylum Office granted refugee status to one asylum seeker and subsidiary protection to three others. But its asylum procedures remain inadequate with thousands of pending claims.

By September, there were 96 unaccompanied migrant children registered in Serbia. According to the United Nations High Commissioner for Refugees (UNHCR), there are no formal age assessment procedures for unaccompanied migrant children, putting them at risk of being treated as adults and not receiving special protection. Guardians appointed to represent the interest of unaccompanied children are not sufficiently trained to accommodate their needs and rarely visit them after first contact.

Serbian authorities made little progress towards finding a durable solution for refugees and internally displaced persons (IDPs) from the Balkan wars living in Serbia. According to data from UNHCR, as of July there were 44,251 refugees in Serbia, most from Croatia, and as of September 204,049 IDPs, a majority of whom are from Kosovo.

Key International Actors

In April, Catherine Ashton, EU high representative for foreign and security policy, commended the new Serbian government's commitment to fight corruption and establish law and order, but failed to emphasize Serbia's human rights obligations.

EU Enlargement Commissioner Stefan Fule in May praised Serbia's progress towards EU membership and emphasized the need to strengthen rule of law, but did not mention Serbia's human rights record.

The European Commission's October progress report on Serbia stressed the need to enhance the constitutional and legal framework to ensure an effective independent judiciary, and expressed concerns about freedom of expression, including continued threats and violence against journalists. The report also noted the limited number of war crimes investigations by Serbian authorities against high-level officers in domestic war crimes and lenient sentences handed down by Serbian courts in such cases.

The United States State Department 2013 human rights report on Serbia highlighted discrimination and attacks against minorities, especially Roma, and harassment of journalists as the most serious human rights issues during the year.

In May, Organization for Security and Co-operation in Europe (OSCE) representative on media freedom, Dunja Mijatovic, expressed concern about online censorship in Serbia, citing cyber attacks on websites that report critically on the government's response to the flooding crisis.

Kosovo

The European Union and Kosovo government reached a landmark agreement in 2014 to establish a special court outside Kosovo to try crimes committed by former members of the Kosovo Liberation Army (KLA) during and after the 1998-1999 Kosovo war.

The continued failure to form a government after April elections and the crisis over the role of the Constitutional Court further weakened human rights protection. The justice system continued to be overburdened and international judges in Kosovo claimed widespread corruption among judges and prosecutors. Journalists and members of the lesbian, gay, bisexual and transsexual (LGBT) community continued to face threats and harassment. Inter-ethnic tensions flared mid-year and Roma, Ashkali, and Egyptian communities remained vulnerable to discrimination and social exclusion. Parliament changed an existing law to offer support to wartime rape victims.

Impunity, Accountability, Access to Justice

In April, the Kosovo parliament approved the establishment of a special court located outside Kosovo and presided over by international judges to adjudicate criminal prosecutions arising from the work of the European Union Special Task Force established in 2011 to investigate serious abuses during and after the Kosovo war. The Special Task Force based its work on findings of a 2010 Council of Europe report. The court will be based in the Netherlands and is expected to become operational once the Kosovo Assembly adopts necessary legislative changes.

Based on the decisions of European Union member states, the EU Rule of Law Mission (EULEX) mandate, although extended in April until June 2016, was significantly scaled back in June as a result of the transfer of some responsibilities to the local judiciary and prosecutorial branch. International EULEX judges, in a January letter to the head of the EULEX Executive Division, outlined their concerns with the downsizing of the mission, stating that the local judiciary was not fully equipped to handle sensitive and complex cases and that EULEX prosecutors should continue to prosecute war crimes, organized crime, and serious corruption cases.

Despite progress in recent years, the justice system in Kosovo remains weak, with inadequate security for judges, court staff, prosecutors, plaintiffs, and witnesses. This results in few prosecutions for serious crimes, such as organized crime and corruption.

In July, the EU Special Task Force published its findings and stated former senior KLA officials will face charges for crimes against humanity and other abuses committed after the 1998-1999 war.

As a result of an EULEX appeal to the 2013 November acquittal, the Kosovo Appeal's Court in September reopened the case against former KLA commander, Fatmir Limaj, and nine co-defendants suspected of abusing prisoners at the Klecka detention center in 1998-1999. Two EULEX judges and one Kosovar judge will oversee the proceedings. The case illustrates weakness in Kosovo's witness protection program: in the initial proceedings in 2012, testimony by the key witness, who was found dead in a park in Germany in December 2012 in what police called a suicide, was first ruled inadmissible, and on retrial, contradictory and unreliable.

In May, a first instance court in Mitrovica acquitted former KLA Commander Sylejman Selimi and three co-defendants of war crimes committed during the 1998-1999 conflict in a case concerning repeated assaults of two ethnic Albanian women held at the KLA detention center in Likovac. The court said the evidence was too weak and too much time had elapsed since the alleged abuse took place.

The trial of Kosovo Serb politician Oliver Ivanovic and other former Serb paramilitaries officials started in August. Ivanovic is suspected of war crimes by ordering the murder of four ethnic Albanians in Mitrovica in 1999 during the NATO bombing. He and three co-defendants are further charged with inciting others to commit murder during the February 2000 violence in Mitrovica where 10 ethnic Albanians were killed, 25 wounded, and more than 11,000 forced from their homes after being attacked by ethnic Serbs several months after the end of the war.

Between January and August, EULEX reported that two war crimes judgments had been issued by mixed panels of judges, one at the Basic Court and one at the Court of Appeals. A panel of EULEX judges also issued one judgment during

2014. At time of writing, there were 160 pending war crimes cases, of which 128 cases are with EULEX Special Prosecution Office prosecutors and 32 with Kosovo Special Prosecution Office prosecutors.

In November, the High Representative of the European Union for Foreign Affairs and Security Policy Federica Mogherini appointed an independent expert to review a EULEX internal investigation into alleged corruption in the mission. A EULEX prosecutor has alleged the mission failed to investigate her complaints about the matter and instead targeted her. The same month, EU Ombudsman Emily O'Reilly opened an inquiry into the EU's handling of the corruption allegations.

The Human Rights Review Panel, an independent body set up in 2009 to review allegations of human rights violations by EULEX staff, handed down three decisions between January and September, including that EULEX had violated a complainant's right to effective remedy in a case where a EULEX police officer attacked the complainant, who then could not work for several months.

The Human Rights Advisory Panel, an independent body set up in 2006 to examine complaints committed by or attributable to the United Nations Interim Administration in Kosovo (UNMIK), found violations in 59 out of 60 cases addressed between January and August.

In March, the Kosovo Assembly adopted legislation that recognized survivors of conflict-related sexual violence and abuse as veterans.

Treatment of Minorities

Roma, Ashkali, and Egyptian communities continued to face problems obtaining personal documents, which hamper their access to health care, social assistance, and education.

The continued failure to implement the 2010 Strategy and Action Plan for the Integration of Roma, Ashkali, and Egyptian communities stems from a lack of political will, funds, and cooperation between central and municipal authorities and between government and civil society.

A new strategy for reintegrating repatriated persons—including Roma, Ashkali and Egyptians—for 2014-2018 replaced the old 2010 strategy, improving the situation slightly for returnees in 2014.

Municipal Committees for Return were established dealing with assistance to returnees, mainly food and accommodation. Repatriated persons still face difficulties accessing employment, education, and health services and, as a result, more than 1,200 Roma, Ashkali, and Egyptians left Kosovo in 2014, according to Balkan Sunflowers, a local nongovernmental organization.

Inter-ethnic tensions in the north flared up in June, when a protest organized by Albanians from south Mitrovica sparked violence. Protesters clashed with Kosovo police and several people were injured and vehicles burned. In January, the Serb municipal councilor for north Mitrovica, Dimitrije Janicijevic, was shot dead outside his home. Police were investigating his murder at time of writing.

Between January and August, Kosovo Police Services reported three inter-ethnic incidents, without specifying their nature.

Asylum Seekers and Displaced Persons

During the first 10 months of the year, the United Nations High Commissioner for Refugees (UNHCR) registered 440 voluntary returns, including people from outside Kosovo and internally displaced persons, compared to 465 during the same period in 2013.

Deportations from Western Europe to Kosovo continued, with improved but limited assistance upon return. Between January and August, the Ministry of Interior registered 2,109 forced returns to Kosovo, including 261 Roma, 95 Ashkali, and 19 Egyptians. Most were returned were from Germany (341) and Switzerland (258).

Freedom of Media

Journalists continued to face attacks and threats during 2014, particularly those reporting on radical Muslim groups. In September, Visar Duriqi, a journalist at the *GazetaExpress* newspaper who had reported on political Islam, received death threats, including of beheading, when a radical Islamist group accused him of apostasy. Artan Haraqija, a journalist at Indeksonline news site, who worked on a joint report with Duriqi about radical Muslim groups operating in Kosovo, received death threats after he appeared on the KTV show "Rubikon" in September. Police were investigating both incidents at time of writing.

In September, the ombudsperson condemned threats against journalists and called on media, prosecutors, and police to act within the full scope of their mandates and not use methods that violate people's privacy and dignity.

Sexual Orientation and Gender Identity

According to QESh, the only public LGBT organization in Kosovo, the LGBT community faced physical attacks and threats during the year, particularly via social and online media and on radio. According to QESh, in August, three men assaulted a gay man in Prizren. In June, a transsexual 17 year old in Pristina was verbally abused and threatened by three other boys his age, and in April, an 18-year-old gay man was verbally abused by his school teacher.

Key International Actors

In January, the Organization for Security and Co-operation in Europe (OSCE) called on Kosovo authorities to establish exactly how many forcibly returned asylum seekers were still in Kosovo and, in particular, identify members of communities UNHCR considers to be "at risk" and in need of international protection, including Serbs, Roma, Ashkali, and Egyptian communities.

EU High Representative Catherine Ashton in April welcomed the extension of EULEX's mandate and the establishment of a specialist court to adjudicate abuses during and after the 1998-1999 Kosovo war.

The EU progress report on Kosovo highlighted shortcomings with rule of law, including judicial independence, stressed that witness intimidation remains a serious concern, and noted limited results in the fight against corruption and organized crime. The report called for the strengthening of the ombudsperson's institution, the adoption of anti-discrimination legislation, and for human rights issues to be put higher on the political agenda, such as the implementation of the action plan for integrating Roma, Ashkali, and Egyptian communities.

UN Secretary-General Ban Ki-Moon in a May report stated that strengthening rule of law institutions remains a long-term challenge and called on authorities to improve their performance in this area.

In September, OSCE Representative on Freedom of Media Dunja Mijatovic condemned death threats and attacks against journalists in Kosovo and called on authorities to bring perpetrators to justice.

The Council of Europe Venice Commission in March published its opinion on an amendment of the Law on Freedom of Religion in Kosovo, outlining the need for a number of improvements, including expanding the list of religious communities that "constitute the historical, cultural and social heritage of the country" from five groups to include all other established religious groups.

Singapore

Singapore's government limits political and civil rights—especially freedom of expression, peaceful assembly, and association—using overly broad legal provisions on security, public order, morality, and racial and religious harmony. Since the 2011 parliamentary election, however, in which the opposition made gains, Singaporean citizens have been increasingly asserting their rights through social media and rallies in designated areas.

Freedom of Expression, Peaceful Assembly, and Association

On September 10, Singapore's Media Development Authority (MDA) banned the film "To Singapore, With Love " on grounds that it undermined national security. The film features interviews with activists who fled Singapore rather than face political persecution and possible detention under the country's abusive Internal Security Act (ISA). Film director Tan Pin Pin filed an appeal, stating that people should be able to air "differing views about our past, even views that the government disapproves." On November 12, the Film Appeals Committee rejected her appeal by a 9-3 vote.

The MDA also continues to compel online news websites discussing domestic political issues to register under the Broadcasting Act. Registration requires posting a monetary bond, paying fees, undergoing annual registration, and, on notification, immediately removing anything the MDA deems to be against "public interest, public order or national harmony" or to offend "good taste or decency." Registered websites are also prohibited from receiving any foreign funding. In late March, the MDA ordered the news website Mothership.sg to register and, in late September, made the same demand of The Online Citizen (TOC).

The Newspaper and Printing Presses Act requires local newspapers to renew their registration every year and empowers the government to limit circulation of foreign newspapers.

The government maintains restrictions on freedom of assembly through provisions of the 2009 Public Order Act, which require a police permit for any cause-related assembly in a public place or to which members of the general public are invited. Grounds for denial are broad. On November 5, 2013, police arrested 10 people for planning a march without a permit in Singapore as part of a global "Million Mask March." A court convicted Jacob Lau Jian Ron of organizing the event and fined him S$1000 (US$800).

Protests and rallies conducted at the Speakers' Corner in Hong Lim Park do not need a police permit so long as the topic does not touch on religious or racial issues and the organizer and speakers are Singaporean citizens. Foreigners who are not permanent residents are not permitted to participate without a police permit. Despite these restrictions, there has been an increase in the size of crowds and the number of applications submitted to use the Speakers' Corner.

On September 25, 2014, the police notified activists Han Hui Hui and Roy Ngerng Yi Ling that permission had been withdrawn for their planned September 27 event at Speakers' Corner featuring speeches and a demonstration related to management of Singapore's Central Provident Fund (CPF), the state pension fund.

Hui and Ngerng refused to comply, and the demonstration went ahead. Police investigated at least 15 persons connected with the protest before charging Ngerng and Hui with unlawful assembly for demonstrating without a permit, and with causing a public nuisance. Four others (Janet Low Wai Choo, Chua Siew Leng, Goh Aik Huat, and Ivan Koh Yew Beng) were charged only with causing a public nuisance. The cases against the six were ongoing at time of writing.

Associations of more than 10 individuals are required to register with the government, and the Registrar of Societies has broad authority to deny registration if the registrar determines that the group could be "prejudicial to public peace, welfare or good order." The registrar approved a new political party, Singaporeans First, in May 2014.

Government officials continue to use criminal and civil defamation as a means to silence critics. In May 2014, Prime Minister Lee Hsien Loong filed a lawsuit in his personal capacity against activist and blogger Roy Ngerng Yi Ling who, Lee alleged, defamed him when he compared Lee's actions in managing the CPF to a criminal case involving misappropriation of funds. Ngerng agreed to apologize, removed the posts, and made an offer of compensation—but Lee refused and sought summary judgment in the case. In June, soon after being sued by Lee, the private hospital employing Ngerng fired him, an action that the Ministry of Health publicly applauded. As widely expected, on November 7, the Singapore High Court ruled in favor of Lee and determined that damages would be assessed at a later date.

Criminal Justice System

Singapore continues to use the Internal Security Act (ISA) and Criminal Law (Temporary Provisions) to arrest and administratively detain persons for virtually unlimited periods without charge or judicial review. Government authorities publicly maintain that such laws are necessary to protect Singapore from international terrorist threats. Authorities did not report any new arrests under the ISA in 2014.

While Singapore retains the death penalty, which is mandated for many drug offenses and certain other crimes, judges in 2014 continued to apply legal provisions that give them discretion to bypass the mandatory penalty and sentence low-level offenders to life in prison and caning where prosecutors attest that offenders have been cooperative. In July, convicted drug traffickers Tang Hai Liang and Foong Chee Peng declined consideration for re-sentencing and opted to be executed rather than to spend life in prison. In accepting the men's preferences, Singapore ended a de facto moratorium on executions in place since July 2011.

Use of corporal punishment is common in Singapore. For medically fit males ages 16 to 50, caning is mandatory as an additional punishment for a range of crimes, including drug trafficking, violent crimes (like armed robbery), and even immigration offenses. Sentencing officials may also order caning for some 30 additional violent and non-violent crimes.

Yong Vui Kong, who had his death sentence for drug-running commuted to life imprisonment and now faces a 15-stroke caning, has mounted a constitutional challenge to caning, asserting it violates Singapore's constitution and customary international law that prohibits torture and other cruel, inhuman, or degrading treatment or punishment. The challenge was pending before the Supreme Court at time of writing.

Sexual Orientation and Gender Identity

In 2014, top government leaders reiterated that Singapore society is not yet ready to accept LGBT rights. In October, the Supreme Court rejected a claim that the ban on gay sex is unconstitutional. The court said the legislature, not the judiciary, needs to address this issue. A constitutional challenge that would have prohibited employment discrimination against LGBT individuals also failed.

In July, the National Library Board removed three children's books with alleged LGBT themes from library shelves, including "And Tango Makes Three," a true story of two male penguins in New York City's Central Park Zoo who raised a penguin chick. One book ("Who's in Our Family?") was pulped, but after pushback from civil society groups, the board's decision to destroy "And Tango Makes Three" and "The White Swan Express: A Story About Adoption" was overruled, and the books were shifted to the adult section of the library. Comic books, including Archie and X-Men, also ran afoul of authorities when they included LGBT content.

The pro-LGBT Pink Dot festival was held for the sixth consecutive year, with an estimated 26,000 people attending in June 2014. For the first time, there was a protest mounted against the event. In August, police forced the cancellation of a running event connected to the 10th annual Indignation LGBT Pride celebration by refusing a permit in the "interest of public order."

Human Rights Defenders

M. Ravi, a lawyer who has played a central role in key human rights cases in Singapore, faced increasing government pressure in 2014. Ravi has mounted constitutional challenges to the death penalty, caning, and several laws that discriminate against LGBT individuals; has defended the right to counsel; and represents blogger Roy Ngerng Yi Ling.

In March, Singapore's attorney general issued a complaint against Ravi for releasing court documents to media before they were fully reviewed by government prosecutors. Ravi immediately apologized. Ravi also has been subject to several investigations by the Law Society of Singapore and faced disciplinary action related to his public campaign on behalf of death row inmate Cheong Chun Yin, whose case was subsequently accepted for re-sentencing.

Migrant Workers and Labor Exploitation

Migrant workers rioted in December 2013 in the Little India area, torching stores, houses, and vehicles after a migrant was hit and killed by a bus. The violence was the worst Singapore had faced in decades. Twenty-five Indians were charged in connection with the riots. Fifty-two were deported, others were fined, and at least eight were jailed.

Foreign migrant workers are subject to labor abuse and exploitation through debts owed to recruitment agents, non-payment of wages, restrictions on movement, confiscation of passports, and sometimes physical and sexual abuse. Foreign domestic workers are still excluded from the Employment Act and many key labor protections, such as limits on daily work hours. Labor laws also discriminate against foreign workers by barring them from organizing and registering a union or serving as union leaders without explicit government permission.

Key International Actors

Singapore maintains good relations with both the United States and China, and plays an important role in the Association of Southeast Asian Nations (ASEAN). It is an important military ally of the US, as the latter implements its security "pivot" to Asia; serves as a regional hub for international business; and maintains close trade relations with China, its largest trading partner.

In part because of these geopolitical and economic considerations, there has been little serious external pressure on Singapore to improve its poor human rights record.

Somalia

The warring parties in Somalia's long-running armed conflict continue to displace, kill, and wound civilians. Restrictions on humanitarian access exacerbate the human rights and humanitarian crises.

The Islamist armed group Al-Shabaab abandoned several towns after a joint military offensive by the African Union Mission to Somalia (AMISOM) and the Somali National Armed Forces in 2014. However, Al-Shabaab maintains control of large areas of south-central Somalia, where it administers public executions and beatings and restricts basic rights. Al-Shabaab carried out deadly attacks in government-controlled areas such as Mogadishu, targeting civilians, including lawmakers and other officials.

Somali government security forces, African Union (AU) troops, and allied militias were responsible for indiscriminate attacks, sexual violence, and arbitrary arrests and detention.

The Somali government largely failed to provide security and protect rights in areas under its control. Ongoing insecurity in government-controlled areas, including Mogadishu, and political infighting and reshuffles detracted from progress on justice and security sector reform. Political efforts to establish federal states fuelled inter-clan fighting in some areas.

Abuses by Government Forces

Civilians have been caught up in fighting between government forces and Al-Shabaab, skirmishes between government forces over control of checkpoints, and in inter-clan fighting over land and over the haphazard and politicized creation of federal states. They have become casualties of indiscriminate attacks by government forces in their heavy-handed responses to public protests and rebel attacks. On December 13, 2013, government soldiers shot dead Duduble clan elder Suldan Abdinaser Hussein Hassan at a checkpoint in Lower Shabelle; the country's military court issued warrants for the soldiers, but they were never apprehended, reportedly due to their commanders' protection.

Somalia's national intelligence agency, NISA, routinely carried out mass security sweeps, despite having no legal mandate to arrest and detain suspects. NISA has occassionally held detainees for prolonged periods without judicial review and mistreated suspects during interrogations.

Government forces and clan militia regularly clashed, causing civilian deaths, injuries, and destruction of property. In December 2013, government forces attacked KM-50 village, where they fought a local militia, beat residents, and looted and burned homes and shops. Several civilians were reportedly killed and many civilians fled the area.

The Somali government continued to rely on its military court to administer justice for a broad range of crimes not within its jurisdiction in proceedings that fall short of international fair trial standards. The court in 2014 sentenced to death and executed 15 people, 13 of whom were not members of the Somali armed forces.

Abuses by Al-Shabaab

Credible reports indicate that Al-Shabaab continues to carry out targeted killings, including beheadings and civilian executions. On June 2, the group publicly executed three men accused of spying for the federal government and foreign governments in the port-town of Barawe. Al-Shabaab also administers arbitrary justice and severely restricts basic rights.

Al-Shabaab regularly targeted for attack civilians and civilian objects, particularly in Mogadishu with a significant increase during the Ramadan holiday. On February 13, a suicide car bomb attack on a United Nations convoy near Mogadishu International Airport killed at least six civilian bystanders. Al-Shabaab claimed responsibility for the killings of three lawmakers in July and August.

Sexual Violence

While the full scope of sexual violence in Somalia remains unknown due to underreporting and absence of data, it is clear that internally displaced women and girls are particularly vulnerable to rape by armed men, including Somali government soldiers and militia members. Government forces and allied militia have also taken advantage of insecurity in newly recovered towns to rape local women and girls. The government endorsed an action plan to address sexual violence, but implementation was slow.

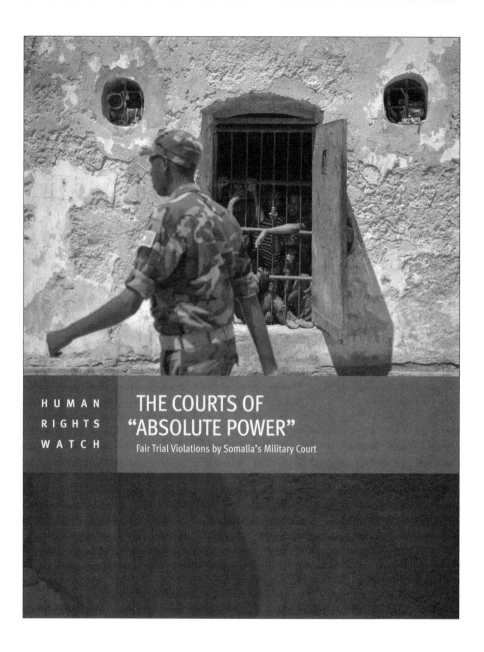

HUMAN
RIGHTS
WATCH

THE COURTS OF "ABSOLUTE POWER"
Fair Trial Violations by Somalia's Military Court

HUMAN
RIGHTS
WATCH

"The Power These Men
Have Over Us"

Sexual Exploitation and Abuse by African Union Forces in Somalia

Some soldiers from Uganda and Burundi deployed as part of the African Union Mission in Somalia sexually exploited and assaulted women and girls on their bases in Mogadishu. In some cases women and girls were offered humanitarian assistance, medicine, and food in exchange for sex. Few women filed complaints due to a fear of reprisals and an absence of effective and safe complaints mechanisms. At time of writing, the AU and troop contributing countries were investigating allegations of sexual abuse and exploitation by AMISOM forces. Thus far, accountability for these abuses has been limited despite AMISOM commitments.

Recruitment of Children and Other Abuses

Al-Shabaab in particular targets children for recruitment and forced marriage, and attacks schools. The UN documented recruitment and use of children by government forces and allied militia.

In August, the UN expert on children in armed conflict raised concerns about the unlawful detention of 55 children, reportedly formerly associated with armed groups, in the Serendi rehabilitation camp in Mogadishu.

Government authorities committed to implement action plans signed in 2012 to end the use of child soldiers, as well as the killing and maiming of children, but progress has been slow.

Access to Humanitarian Assistance

According to the UN, over 1 million people, many of them displaced persons, face acute food insecurity and 120,000 Somalis have been newly displaced since the beginning of 2014, as a result of ongoing military operations.

Tens of thousands of displaced people remain in dire conditions in Mogadishu and are subjected to evictions, sexual violence, and clan-based discrimination at the hands of government forces, allied militia, and private individuals including camp managers. Government plans to relocate displaced communities to the outskirts of Mogadishu stalled, but forced evictions by private individuals and the authorities increased in July and August.

Ongoing attacks on humanitarian workers, insecurity, local power struggles, and restrictions imposed by the warring parties posed challenges for humanitarian agencies trying to address basic needs. For example, on December 18, 2013, unidentified gunmen killed three Syrian doctors and one Somali doctor while traveling to a health post outside Mogadishu.

Al-Shabaab used its control of supply routes to impose blockades around Hudur, Bulo-Burte, Elbur and Qoryoley and other towns taken over by AMISOM and Somali government forces, severely restricting the movement of goods, assistance, and people—including by attacking civilian vehicles.

Attacks on Media

Somalia remains one of the most dangerous countries in the world to be a journalist; three media professionals, including two journalists, were killed in 2014. On June 21, Yusuf Ahmed Abukar—a reporter working with Mustaqbal, a privately owned radio station, and Ergo radio, which covers humanitarian affairs—was killed when a bomb exploded in his car. Impunity for these types of killings prevails.

Government harassment and intimidation of journalists in Mogadishu, particularly by NISA, and threats against media outlets increased. On February 11, NISA detained Mohamed Haji Bare from Radio Danan and Ibrahim Mohamed from Radio Haatuf, for three days, beating them severely and threatening them, reportedly for taking photos of a deputy governor previously injured in a car bomb.

On August 15, following two controversial broadcasts, including one criticizing the president's claims of widespread support for Al-Shabaab in the independent media, NISA raided Radio Shabelle and Sky FM and arrested 19 journalists and media workers. Sixteen were subsequently released, but the stations' leadership were reportedly charged with inciting violence. Several journalists complained of mistreatment during interrogations.

In Somaliland, the authorities harassed popular newspapers. On June 25, a regional court in Hargeisa charged and sentenced Yusuf Abdi Gabobe, chairman of the Haatuf Media Network, and Ahmed Ali, chief editor of the network, to three years and fours years in prison respectively for libel, false publication, and anti-state propaganda. They were later released following a presidential pardon. The Hatuuf license was revoked reportedly as a result of a series of reports on corruption in the Ministry of Energy.

Key International and Regional Actors

Foreign and regional partners prioritized financial assistance to AMISOM for the military offensives against Al-Shabaab and to mentor and train the Somali armed forces. On January 22, 4,395 Ethiopian troops formally merged with AMISOM, joining troops from Burundi, Uganda, Sierra Leone, Djibouti, and Kenya to bring the force's strength to 22,126 troops. Support to the Somali government has focused on building the security apparatus, resulting in a proliferation of new security entities, and integration of militias.

In January, the United States said it had deployed a number of military advisors to assist AMISOM and Somali security forces. The US Defense Department claimed responsibility for a September 1 airstrike that killed Al-Shabaab's leader, Ahmed Abdi Godane.

Much of the international and regional community focus, including that of the UN and European Union, has centered on the implementation of a federalist form of government. At time of writing, international support for the country's development agenda was strained by infighting between the Somali president and prime minister.

In addition to their large military presence in Somalia, Kenya and Ethiopia trained and provided military support to government-affiliated militia. Both focused on the status of border areas and have been involved in negotiations over the creation of new federal states in these areas.

Host countries of Somali refugees, including Kenya and several European countries, used alleged improvements in security in Mogadishu as grounds for returning Somalis, including asylum seekers and refugees, to Somalia, despite volatility on the ground and continued risk of persecution and serious harm from generalized violence.

Between April and mid-May, Kenya deported 359 Somalis, including registered refugees, to Mogadishu without access to the UN refugee agency, in violation of its international obligations. Saudi Arabia also deported 33,605 Somalis between December 2013 and May 2014 without giving them the opportunity to file protection claims.

South Africa

The government's inability to address critical socio-economic and political rights issues such as unemployment, corruption, and threats to freedom of expression remains a concern for many South Africans. In May 2014, President Jacob Zuma and the African National Congress (ANC) won a second term in office, but the majority victory was marred by the report of the public protector, Thuli Madonsela, accusing the president of misusing state funds for a security upgrade to his private residence in Nkandla, Kwa Zulu Natal.

South Africa also largely failed to utilize its membership at the United Nations Human Rights Council to support resolutions that would have helped the promotion and protection of human rights in various countries, most notably in North Korea, Syria, Sri Lanka, and Iran.

Police Conduct

Serious concerns remain about the conduct and capacity of the South African Police Services (SAPS), both in terms of the use of force in general, as well as the ability to deal with riots in a rights-respecting manner. The police lack proper equipment and training to quell riots which often leads to the use of excessive and disproportionate force.

In 2014, incidents of police violence were reported in Mothutlung in Brits, North West province, Relela in Kgapane, Limpopo province and Bekkersdal in Gauteng province. In January 2014, police killed three people during a protest over lack of water in Mothutlung.

In March 2014, the Independent Police Investigation Department launched an investigation into a video that showed an incident of police officers assaulting, stripping, and humiliating a man before dragging him on the sidewalk into a police van during an apparent arrest in Kensington, Cape Town. The officers were later arrested and charged with assault with intent to do grievous bodily harm.

Inquiry into Killing of Marikana Miners

Hearings by the Farlam Commission into the deaths of 44 people, including the police killing of 34 miners between August 11 and 16, 2012, continued throughout the year. Those called to testify before the commission included Deputy President Cyril Ramaphosa and the National Police Commissioner Riah Phiyega. The commission has faced significant delays due to loss of vital documents (including video evidence), the death of witnesses, and a legal battle over state funding for lawyers representing the families of the miners killed, injured, and arrested. In September, the president extended the term of the commission to March 2015.

Refugees, Asylum Seekers, and Migrants

In August 2014, the Department of Home Affairs announced the creation of the new Zimbabwean Special Dispensation Permit of 2014 (ZSP), to replace the 2009 Dispensation of Zimbabweans Project. In a move that grants further protection to Zimbabwean nationals who received permits under the previous dispensation, the ZSP will allow permit-holders to live, work, conduct business and study in South Africa, for the duration of the permit, which is valid until December 31, 2017.

However, concerns remain about the treatment of migrants, refugees, and asylum seekers by government officials from various departments. The right to access health care services is constitutionally guaranteed for everyone living in South Africa, and by the National Health Care Act and the Refugee Act. But local nongovernmental organizations expressed concern that many asylum seekers were denied access to health care services as officials were not aware that asylum seekers were entitled to health care.

On June 19, 2014 security officials and police used excessive force to control a crowd of foreign nationals who were attempting to renew their permits at Marabastad reception office in Pretoria. Security officials and police attacked the unarmed crowd with whips and pepper spray.

On August 28 2014, the Gauteng High Court ruled in favor of the the South African Human Rights Commission, People Against Suffering, Suppression, Oppression and Poverty (PASSOP), and 39 individuals who were detained in Lindela Repatriation Centre. The court found that the actions of the Department of Home Affairs and the minister in detaining migrants for over 120 days at Lindela were unlawful and unconstitutional. The High Court declared that individuals detained there had been inhumanely treated, and that officials had failed to follow fair and legal procedure by detaining individuals for longer than 30 days without the necessary warrant of a magistrate permitting extended detention.

In September 2014, the South African Human Rights Commission found that the government had violated the right to health of detainees at the Lindela Repatriation Centre. The commission's investigation found that there was a lack of provision for tuberculosis testing and isolation of infected persons, and psychological care; lack of tetanus vaccines; and overcrowding in rooms, among other concerns, in violation of South Africa's Regulations to the Immigration Act and the right to health care under the South African constitution.

Xenophobic Attacks on Foreign Nationals

Continued incidents of violence against foreign nationals and looting of foreign-owned shops in 2014 highlighted the government's inability to address the root causes of xenophobia. In June 2014, bands of local youths attacked Somali shopkeepers in Mamelodi East, Pretoria. Two Somalis were killed and around 100 men, women, and children fled their shops and homes. No one was held accountable for the attacks.

Sexual Orientation and Gender Identity

South Africa continues to play an important but inconsistent role in advancing the human rights of lesbian, gay, bisexual, and transgender (LGBT) people internationally. For example, South Africa was reluctant to publicly condemn the introduction of anti-LGBT laws in Uganda, Nigeria, and the Gambia. At the June 2014 session of the United Nations Human Rights Council, South Africa inexplicably supported a regressive resolution called "Protection of the Family" that brought into question its commitment to gender equality and the rights of lesbian, gay, bisexual and transgender people. Not only did South Africa vote in favor, but it also supported an aggressive move by Russia to shut down discussion of more inclusive "family" language.

Despite taking the initiative at the UN Human Rights Council in 2011 by tabling a precedent-setting resolution on human rights, sexual orientation, and gender identity, South Africa stalled in supporting a follow up resolution that called for bi-annual reporting on human rights abuses against LGBT people. South Africa eventually voted in favor of the resolution in September 2014.

On the domestic front, South Africa has taken positive steps in responding to widespread violence (including rape and murder) against lesbians and transgender men in the country. In an important move in April 2014, the Department of Justice and Constitutional Development launched a public campaign which includes a national intervention strategy to address anti-LGBT violence and strengthen institutional responses to LGBT hate crimes, violence, and discrimination.

Foreign Policy

South Africa's inconsistent foreign policy once again came to the fore in 2014. While the country regularly supports and mediates an end to conflicts on the continent, it has proved reluctant to protect the rights of victims at the UN Human Rights Council, and at times has taken decisions that contradict its human rights principles.

In February 2014, Zuma appointed Deputy President Cyril Ramaphosa as special envoy to South Sudan in a bid to help resolve the conflict in the country. Ramaphosa was also appointed special envoy to Sri Lanka. South Africa was also quick to try and mediate the political crisis in Lesotho following an aborted coup there. In August, at the annual summit of heads of state of the Southern African Development Community, South Africa was appointed to sit on the Organ on Politics, Defense and Security, a crucial role in ensuring stability in the region.

In an example of its contradictory stance, in September 2014, the South African government denied the Dalai Lama a visa to the country for the third time in five years and presented no valid reasons for doing so. The Dalai Lama had been due to attend the 14th World Summit of Nobel Peace Laureates in Cape Town.

At the UN Human Rights Council, South Africa is a strong supporter of the council's engagement on issues like racism and the council's action on the Occupied Palestinian Territories. It has also participated actively in the Universal Periodic Review process, a review of the rights records of all UN member states. However, its voting record on country specific situations and some rights issues has been considerably disappointing. For example, at the March 2014 session, South Africa sought to weaken a resolution on the right to peacefully protest jointly with Russia, Ethiopia, Saudi Arabia, Egypt, and China. It also took negative stances on other rights issues.

Contrary to its stance in repeatedly supporting resolutions on Palestine, it abstained on the votes of all other country situations, including on North Korea, Syria, Sri Lanka, and Iran. Despite country resolutions playing a key role in shedding light on abuses and giving a stronger voice to victims, South Africa has justified its actions by arguing that it does not support the council's work on country-specific situations because such measures and resolutions are perceived as highly politicized and divisive.

South Africa has firmly supported the establishment of the International Criminal Court and has been a key supporter of international justice. But in recent years it has often failed to use its influence to stand against impunity for human rights violations. In June 2014, South Africa supported an amendment to a protocol creating an African Court that provides for immunity from prosecution for serving heads of state and senior government officials, including war crimes, crimes against humanity and genocide.

In a landmark judgement, judges of the South African Constitutional Court unanimously ruled that the South African Police Service must investigate crimes against humanity perpetrated in Zimbabwe in 2007. The case was brought by the Southern Africa Litigation Centre and the Zimbabwean Exiles Forum to compel South Africa to abide by its domestic and international legal obligations to investigate and if appropriate prosecute Zimbabwean officials accused of crimes against humanity.

South Sudan

Horrific attacks on civilians began within 24 hours of the start of South Sudan's new war in mid-December 2013. Thousands of civilians have been killed and large parts of key towns, including civilian infrastructure such as clinics, hospitals, and schools, have been looted, destroyed, and abandoned. An estimated 1.5 million people were forced to flee their homes; 100,000 people still shelter in United Nations compounds, too afraid to return home. Three years after South Sudan's independence famine looms on the horizon, and the conflict continues, despite peace negotiations in Ethiopia.

The conflict, triggered by fighting in Juba, the capital city, between soldiers loyal to President Salva Kiir, a Dinka, and those loyal to his former deputy, Riek Machar, a Nuer, followed growing political tensions. Kiir maintains the violence was a coup attempt by Machar, a charge the now-leader of the Sudan People's Liberation Movement/Army-in Opposition forces has denied.

Lack of accountability for decades of violence during Sudan's long civil war helped fuel the conflict. Military and political leaders have failed to make any serious attempt to reduce abuses committed by their forces, or to hold them to account.

Attacks on Civilians and Civilian Property

In the period between mid-December and mid-April, armed forces on both sides targeted and killed hundreds of civilians, often because of their ethnicity, and pillaged and destroyed civilian property. These crimes amount to war crimes and in some cases may be crimes against humanity.

Following fighting between government and defecting Nuer soldiers in Juba on December 15, government forces conducted a brutal crackdown on Juba's Nuer population that included targeted killings, house-to-house searches, mass arrests, unlawful detention of hundreds of men in poor conditions, ill-treatment, and torture. Human Rights Watch documented more than 60 separate cases of targeted, extrajudicial killings of one or more individuals. In one of the worst incidents, government forces rounded up between 200 and 400 Nuer men on the

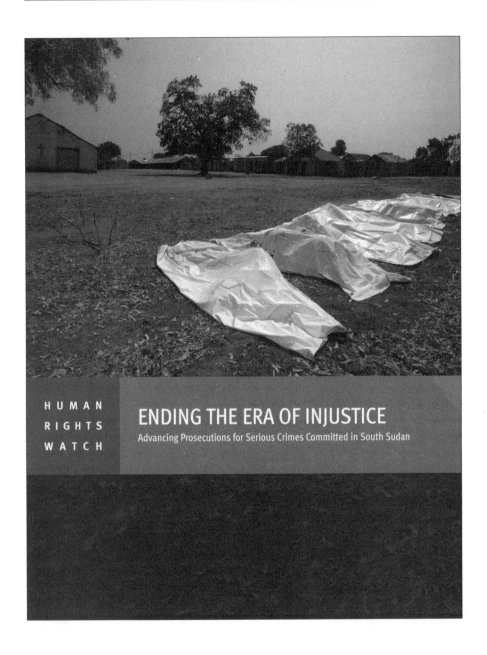

HUMAN
RIGHTS
WATCH

ENDING THE ERA OF INJUSTICE
Advancing Prosecutions for Serious Crimes Committed in South Sudan

night of December 15 and the following day, detained them in a building in the Gudele neighborhood and then massacred all but 13.

The conflict quickly spread to Jonglei, Upper Nile and Unity states. The largely ethnic Dinka town of Bor, Jonglei state, changed hands four times during the first two months of the war. Widespread targeting and killing of civilians took place in Bor in the first two weeks of January by opposition forces under the control of Gen. Peter Gadet. In one incident 14 women were killed by opposition fighters in a church compound.

Malakal, Upper Nile state, changed hands six times between December and April. Forces on both sides conducted house-to-house searches, arbitrary arrests, and killed many civilians, often based on their ethnicity. In a brutal attack in February, opposition forces killed civilians inside the Malakal hospital and attacked churches. In Bentiu, Unity state, government forces killed civilians during their recapture of the town in January, and in April, opposition forces attacking Bentiu slaughtered hundreds of civilians, including in appalling attacks on a mosque and hospital.

Civilians have also been attacked and killed while sheltering in bases of the United Nations Mission in South Sudan (UNMISS). On December 19, 2013, in Akobo town, Jonglei state, a group of armed Nuer civilians and security forces attacked the UN base and killed more than 20 Dinka men, as well as two peacekeepers. On April 17, a large group of Dinka youth and armed men, including some in government police and military uniforms, attacked the UN base in Bor town, killing at least 53 people, mostly Nuer, and injuring scores of others. The government has failed to investigate these killings or stop other harassment and attacks on Nuer civilians sheltering in UN bases.

Forces from both sides were responsible for widespread destruction of civilian property and mass looting. In Juba, during the first days of the conflict, government forces looted many neighborhoods, especially Nuer homes. Opposition forces in Bor looted and then destroyed the town's market in January, as well as numerous homes and other buildings, including clinics. Both government and opposition forces pillaged offices of aid agencies, markets and banks in Bentiu and Malakal, leaving behind emptied, destitute towns. In Unity state, government forces, together with the Sudanese rebel group, the Justice and Equality Movement, looted and burned many villages and much of Leer town, during an

HUMAN
RIGHTS
WATCH

SOUTH SUDAN'S NEW WAR
Abuses by Government and Opposition Forces

offensive in January and February, contributing to severe food insecurity there. By the end of February, some 4,700 tons of World Food Programme food had been pillaged, hampering relief efforts.

Attacks on numerous health facilities further reduced already very limited access to services for survivors of sexual violence and services for people with psychosocial disabilities, many of whom languish in prisons.

Recruitment and Use of Child Soldiers

Both government and opposition forces have used child soldiers in the conflict. Children were forcibly recruited by opposition forces in Bentiu in January and in other parts of Unity state later in the year. The latest UN secretary-general's report on children and armed conflict stated that thousands of children were reportedly mobilized by Nuer efighters alligned with the opposition, known as "White Army."

The government also deployed children on the front lines to defend Bentiu during an August opposition attack. The government and opposition have made little progress beyond signing agreements with the UN to end this abusive practice. According to the UN Office for the Coordination of Humanitarian Affairs (OCHA), armed forces were occupying more than 35 schools in South Sudan at time of writing.

Freedom of Expression

Abusive practices by South Sudan's government authorities, especially the National Security Service (NSS), have eroded freedom of expression since South Sudan's independence, but these intensified withthe conflict. Security forces have harassed, intimidated, and arbitrarily detained journalists; shut down one newspaper; taken a radio station off the air; and seized or held entire print runs of newspapers several times. South Sudan's Information Minister Michael Makuei has repeatedly verbally banned journalists from interviewing opposition figures, threating that such "agitators" will be punished.

Legislative Developments

In September, President Kiir signed the Convention against Torture and the African Charter on Human and Peoples' Rights after they were passed by South Sudan's Legislative Assembly (SSLA). South Sudan also ratified the Convention on the Elimination of all Forms of Discrimination Against Women and the Convention of the Rights of the Child, although at time of writing they had yet to deposit all the instruments of ratification to finalize the process of South Sudan being a party to these human rights treaties. Kiir also signed into law three media bills, including a right to information law, after they languished for years in the SLA.

A bill to define and limit NSS powers, passed by the SSLA amid controversy in October but not signed into law by the president at time of writing, gives NSS officers the same powers to arrest and detain as police, but does not specify permissible detention sites or guarantee basic due process rights, such as the right to counsel or to be tried within a reasonable period of time. It grants NSS officers powers to surveille and to search and seize property without clear judicial oversight. A pending bill to oversee nongovernmental organizations (NGOs) would restrict such groups to a government-approved list of activities.

Accountability and Justice

South Sudan's government has not provided accountability for abuses committed by its forces, nor demonstrated the will to hold them to account. The opposition has not, to Human Rights Watch's knowledge, investigated or punished any abusive forces. A presidential committee formed in January to investigate killings and abuses has made no public update on its findings. Many victims are reluctant to provide information to the committee because of its lack of independence, and because there are no clear mechanisms for victim and witness protection.

South Sudan's army and police investigated some killings by security forces in Juba in December 2013 but reports, which according to officials include names of alleged perpetrators, have not been made public. At least 11 alleged perpetrators were arrested but escaped from military detention in March during a gun battle. A military tribunal in Juba heard some looting cases, but no cases of killings were prosecuted.

The South Sudan Human Rights Commission released an interim report in March that described some abuses and called on the government to speed up investigations into alleged perpetrators.

Key International Actors

The Intergovernmental Authority on Development (IGAD) took on the role of peacemaker in December 2013, establishing envoys to mediate talks in Addis Ababa, Ethiopia. In January, the parties to the conflict signed a cessation of hostilities agreement prohibiting attacks on civilians or civilian property, which was quickly violated. IGAD has deployed teams to monitor compliance with the agreement.

Uganda, an IGAD member, sent forces to shore up the government in December 2013, putting IGAD's impartiality in question. Evidence of fresh cluster bombs used either by the government or Ugandan forces, was found near Bor town in February.

The United States, United Kingdom, Norway, China, and the European Union, have sent delegates or helped fund the peace process. In May, the US imposed sanctions on opposition commander Peter Gadet and the head of the government's presidential guard, Marial Chanuong, and have since sanctioned two other commanders. On July 10 the European Union imposed travel bans and asset freezes on on Gadet and a government SPLA commander, Santino Deng. The African Union (AU) Peace and Security Council said in December 2013 it intended "to take appropriate measures including targeted sanctions" against South Sudanese leaders who commit human rights abuses or incite violence.

UNMISS opened its gates to civilians fleeing the fighting and has sheltered over 100,000 civilians in its bases. The UN peacekeepers have not, however, been able to prevent many of attacks on civilians around their bases. A swifter military response by peacekeepers during an attack on their base in Bor in April may have prevented some casualties.

A report by the AU Commission of Inquiry in South Sudan (AUCISS)—headed by former Nigerian President Olusegun Obasanjo and mandated to investigate seri-

ous crimes committed in violation of law and make recommendations on accountability— anticipated issuing its report before the end of 2014. The UN secretary-general also stressed the need to exclude amnesty for serious crimes in
any peace agreement at a September high-level ministerial event on South
Sudan.

On December 24, 2013, the UN Security Council authorized the deployment of
5,500 more peacekeeping forces, bringing the total authorized to 12,500. In May,
it changed the mission's mandate, prioritizing protection of civilians, human
rights monitoring, investigations and public and regular reporting. By October
2014, there were close to 10,500 soldiers under UNMISS in South Sudan.

The UNMISS Human Rights Division released a May report concluding that there
are "reasonable grounds" to believe crimes against humanity had occurred. The
report recommended that any national justice process "be complemented by international assistance through a special or hybrid court" to ensure accountability and help build the capacity of national institutions.

Sri Lanka

The Sri Lankan government has made little progress in providing accountability for wartime abuses. The government's failure to comply with a March 2013 United Nations Human Rights Council resolution led to a new resolution in 2014. The resolution calls on the UN Office of the High Commissioner for Human Rights (OHCHR) to investigate serious violations of international human rights and humanitarian law and related crimes by both sides during Sri Lanka's civil war, which ended in 2009.

The government has also continued its crackdown on critics. In March 2014, it detained two prominent human rights defenders who were looking into the arrest of an ethnic Tamil activist. Although the two were subsequently freed, the government arrested scores of other Tamils under the draconian Prevention of Terrorism Act. It also labelled 16 overseas Tamil organizations as financers of terrorism without providing evidence of unlawful activity by the groups.

A rally by the ultra-nationalist Buddhist Bodhu Bala Sena (BBS) escalated into violence in June, resulting in the death of four Muslims, injuries to at least 80 people, and the destruction of numerous Muslim homes and businesses.

The government's treatment of Tamils forcibly returned to Sri Lanka after being denied asylum overseas continues to be a significant concern. In 2014, the government also started forcibly returning foreign nationals seeking asylum in Sri Lanka, many of them from communities at risk in Pakistan and Afghanistan.

The government is continuing its rehabilitation and reconstruction efforts in the war-affected northern areas. In 2014, a long-promised victim and witness protection bill was enacted into law.

Accountability and International Investigations

The Mahinda Rajapaksa government resisted taking meaningful steps to investigate and prosecute alleged war crimes by government forces and the Liberation Tigers of Tamil Eelam (LTTE), as recommended by Human Rights Council resolutions in 2012 and 2013. Instead, the government continued its longtime practice of refusing to investigate or prosecute credible allegations of torture, including sexual violence, against suspected LTTE members or supporters in custody.

As a result, the Human Rights Council approved a stronger resolution in March 2014, calling on the OHCHR to undertake a "comprehensive investigation into alleged serious violations and abuses of human rights and related crimes." The report is due in March 2015.

The resolution also calls upon OHCHR to investigate ongoing violations by the government, including the targeting of activists and attacks on Muslims. It reiterates past calls to the government to deliver justice and accountability in parallel with the OHCHR investigation.

In response, the Sri Lankan government has publicly stated that it will not cooperate with the international investigation and will deny visas to members of the investigative team seeking to enter the country. Members of the government also warned that Sri Lankan nationals who provide information to the UN investigation will be regarded as traitors. One cabinet member threatened that the government would "take appropriate action based on the evidence the detractors give."

In July, the government announced the appointment of an international expert team to assist its own "disappearances" commission, and authorized the commission to investigate allegations of laws-of-war violations and enforced disappearances.

Crackdown on Civil Society and Critics

Arbitrary arrests of Sri Lankan activists who advocate for accountability continued in 2014. The government also widened its crackdown against independent media and human rights defenders.

In March, prominent human rights activists Ruki Fernando, of the Colombo-based INFORM, and Father Praveen Mahesan, a Catholic priest, were detained for three days and questioned. They had been seeking to ensure the welfare of 13-year-old Balendran Vithushaini, who had been ordered into probationary care following the arrest of her mother, Balendran Jeyakumari, an activist working on behalf of the forcibly disappeared. Human rights lawyers Namal Rajapakshe, Manjula Pathiraja, and Lakshan Dais received threats from unidentified men.

Media, particularly in the northern Tamil-majority areas, continue to face restrictions on reporting. In 2014, security forces forcibly shut workshops organized in the south to train journalists from the north, and ordered participants home.

While various development, resettlement, and reconstruction projects have been undertaken in former war zones in the north and east, government pledges to address the rights concerns of the ethnic Tamil population remain largely unfulfilled. The government has blocked simple gestures, such as allowing Tamil communities to hold commemorative services for their dead or sing the national anthem in Tamil.

The government passed an order freezing the assets and financial resources of entities ranging from the LTTE to nonviolent Tamil organizations around the world. The government provided no factual evidentiary basis for this order. The chief military spokesman said that legal action would be taken against anyone with links with the listed groups, potentially placing local activists and alleged group members visiting the country at risk of arbitrary detention.

Attacks on Religious Minorities

Previous altercations in Aluthgama, about 60 kilometers south of Colombo, reached a violent apex in June. The incident was sparked by a minor traffic incident between Muslim youths and the driver of a van carrying a Buddhist monk. The BBS held a protest rally led by leader Galagodaaththe Gnanasara Thera the next day, purportedly to express concerns for the safety of Buddhists in the area. Soon after, mobs carrying poles and other objects went on a rampage, attacking Muslims. Even after the government ordered a curfew, Muslim homes and properties were targeted in nearby areas leaving at least four Muslims dead, 80 injured, and numerous homes and businesses destroyed in the town and surrounding areas.

Senior government officials, including President Rajapaksa, made public statements denouncing the violence. The government announced some arrests but had not filed charges against any suspects at time of writing.

Refugees

Serious concerns remain about the forced return of Sri Lankans who seek asylum abroad. Many of the forced returns took place in the midst of intensified government security operations since March 2014, which saw scores of arrests and several deaths due to hazardous conditions at sea. Human Rights Watch and others have documented the authorities' use of torture against people suspected of links to the LTTE, including those returned as failed asylum seekers from the United Kingdom and other countries.

In recent years and particularly since early 2014, the government also began forcibly returning individuals from other countries seeking asylum in Sri Lanka, including some persons registered with the United Nations High Commissioner for Refugees (UNHCR). Most of those forcibly returned are members of minority religions persecuted back home in Pakistan and Afghanistan. UNHCR has not been allowed access to detained asylum seekers prior to their deportation, some of whom it has previously recognized as refugees.

Migrant Workers

More than 1 million Sri Lankans are employed overseas, and many remain at risk of abuse at every stage of the migration cycle from recruitment and transit to employment, repatriation, and reintegration. Recruiters and unregulated subagents charge exorbitant fees leaving migrants indebted and often with inaccurate information about their promised employment overseas.

Over 90 percent of Sri Lanka migrants now work in the Middle East where they are subject to the restrictive *kafala* system that ties their visa to their employer. More than a third of Sri Lanka's migrants are domestic workers, almost exclusively female. The government has taken some steps to protect their rights abroad, but many continue to face long working hours with little rest, delayed or unpaid wages, confinement in the workplace, and verbal, physical, and sexual abuse.

Key International Actors

The UN Human Rights Council (HRC) adopted the recommendation of then-UN High Commissioner for Human Rights Navi Pillay to create an independent international inquiry into war crimes and other serious abuses committed during Sri Lanka's civil war.

The United States and the United Kingdom called upon Sri Lanka to ensure accountability for war crimes.

India, an important regional partner, continued to press for reconciliation and protection of Tamils, but it abstained from the HRC vote. Japan, a key donor, also abstained and in other public statements commended Sri Lanka on postwartime developments. The Chinese premiere visited Sri Lanka in an ongoing show of financial and political support for the government absent any human rights concerns.

Australia and Sri Lanka colluded to ensure that asylum seekers leaving Sri Lanka were either returned or else not allowed onto Australian territory. Australia sent back many asylum seekers to Sri Lanka after cursory interviews at sea; those found to have legitimate claims were processed in other countries. In an apparent bid to secure Sri Lanka's assistance in stopping migrants and asylum seekers, Australia failed to call for better human rights protections and advocated against the HRC resolution.

Sudan

Sudan saw no progress in its abysmal rights record in 2014. Instead, new episodes of conflict in Darfur, South Kordofan, and Blue Nile states resulted in large numbers of civilian deaths and displaced; security forces repeatedly suppressed protesters demonstrating against government policies; and authorities continued to stifle civil society and independent media.

The ruling National Congress Party and opposition parties, two of which signed an alliance in August, remained deadlocked over a national dialogue process that was to pave the way for elections and a new constitution. Sudan has yet to adopt a constitution after the Comprehensive Peace Agreement's six-year interim period ended in 2011 and South Sudan became independent.

Conflict and Abuses in Darfur

Fighting between government forces and rebel groups, and between other armed groups, often using government equipment and weapons, continues in several parts of Darfur. Conflict between the Rizeigat and Ma'aliya groups in South Darfur killed hundreds. More than 450,000 people have fled violence in Darfur since the beginning of 2014, according to the United Nations Office for the Coordination of Humanitarian Affairs.

Starting in February, the Rapid Support Forces, a Sudanese government force consisting largely of former militias, moved into Darfur from the Kordofan region, where they had been deployed to fight rebels in Southern Kordofan. The forces, led by the Darfuri former militia leader, Brig. Gen. Mohammed Hamdan Dagolo ("Hemmeti") carried out massive ground attacks on dozens of villages in South and North Darfur, targeting areas where they accused the population of sympathizing with rebels. They burned homes and shops, looted livestock, killed and robbed civilians, and forced tens of thousands of residents to flee to towns and camps for displaced people.

Government forces carried out raids in camps for internally displaced people, resulting in four deaths of residents at Kalma camp. The raids were ostensibly to search for weapons, alcohol, and other contraband as part of the governor's emergency response to rising criminality.

Starting in October 31, large numbers of Sudanese forces entered the North Darfur town of Tabit, beating men and raping women and girls over a two-day period. Sudan initially refused to allow the African Union (AU)/United Nations Hybrid Operations in Dafur (UNAMID) to access the town. When the peacekeepers did gain access, Sudanese security forces were present during their visit, undermining the credibility of their investigation

In its sixth year, UNAMID has been largely ineffective in protecting civilians from violence and has all but ceased public reporting on human rights issues. Sudanese government restrictions have seriously hampered access to conflict areas, including the rebel stronghold, Jebel Mara. Chronic security threats have also undermined its effectiveness: attacks on the peacekeepers have killed at least 207 since 2008.

Conflict and Abuses in Southern Kordofan and Blue Nile

In April 2014, the government intensified ground and aerial attacks in rebel-held areas of the Nuba Mountains, Southern Kordofan, deploying the Rapid Support Forces and other security forces to several areas. In May and June, government bombing damaged schools, mosques, churches, water sources and health centers, including a Médecins sans Frontières clinic. Dozens of civilians were killed or injured.

The attacks, which continued throughout the year, forced tens of thousands of people, some already displaced, to abandon their homes and fields. In government-controlled areas, government forces detained dozens of displaced civilians for their perceived political views.

Ground attacks and government bombing also persisted in Blue Nile, though many people have fled to refugee camps in South Sudan. In September, government forces attacked villages, carrying out numerous cases of sexual violence in Bau locality.

In August, the conflict in South Sudan spilled into the refugee camps when a local militia group, following clashes between government soldiers and ethnic Nuer opposition forces, targeted ethnic Nuer aid workers, killing five in the area of Bunj town. More than 220,000 refugees from Southern Kordofan and Blue Nile remain in camps in Unity and Upper Nile states in South Sudan.

HUMAN
RIGHTS
WATCH

"We Stood, They Opened Fire"
Killings and Arrests by Sudan's Security Forces
During the September Protests

Freedom of Peaceful Assembly, Association, Expression

Sudanese law enforcement officers continued to violently disperse protests and to arbitrarily arrest and detain protesters and activists. In September 2013, government forces used excessive force, including live ammunition, to disperse a wave of protests over austerity measures. The forces were implicated in over 170 deaths, and hundreds of injuries and arrests. Many people were held for weeks or months without charge or access to family or lawyers, and were beaten, verbally abused, deprived of sleep, and held for long periods in solitary confinement.

The government has failed to investigate or prosecute those responsible for the 2013 killings and related abuses. In September 2014, the UN's independent expert on sudan reported to the Human Rights Council (HRC) that the government had not conducted thorough and independent investigations. Of scores of complaints lodged, only one proceeded to trial, unsuccessfully.

On March 11, government security forces and pro-government student militia used live ammunition again to disperse a student demonstration protesting the escalating violence in South Darfur. The violence led to the death of a Darfuri student, Ali Abakar Musa Idris.

In September, government forces broke up memorial services for the one-year anniversary of the killing of protesters, and arrested more than 80 political opposition members, activists, and their family members.

In June, authorities shut down the Salmmah Women's Resource Center, a women's rights organization in Khartoum. The closure was the latest of several in recent years, provoking renewed fears the government would clamp down further on civil society and specifically women's rights activists. In August, security forces carried out searches of another civil society organization in Khartoum, but did not shut it down.

Authorities continued to censor media and blacklist journalists. Although the Sudanese Constitutional Court in March voided an order to suspend a newspaper, *al-Tayyar*, post-publication censorship continued. Security agents seized print runs of newspapers on dozens of occasions. In June, September and October, NISS detained at least three journalists for unknown reasons.

Arbitrary Detentions, Ill-treatment, and Torture

Sudan's National Intelligence and Security Service (NISS) and other security forces arrested opposition party members and activists throughout the year, despite promises by President Omar al-Bashir to release all "political detainees."

On May 12, NISS officials arrested Mohammed Salah, 25, Taj Elsir Jaafar, 26, and Moammer Musa Mohammed, 27, near the University of Khartoum. Authorities detained them without charge at a NISS facility in the suburb of Bahri. The activists, who participated in campaigns protesting the killing of a Darfuri student, Ali Abaker Musa Idris, by government security forces at Khartoum University on March 11, were subjected to ill-treatment and possibly torture; they were released in July.

Sadiq al-Mahdi, head of the National Umma Party, was arrested on May 17 after publicly criticizing the Rapid Support Forces' abuses in Darfur. He was released after a month in detention. Ibrahim al-Sheikh, head of the Sudan Congress Party, was arrested in al-Nuhood, North Kordofan, and detained from June 8 until mid-September without access to family or lawyers, or needed medical care, along with several other party members.

Sudanese military courts exercised their new power to try civilians, contrary to international standards. The courts acquitted one journalist but convicted at least eight Darfuri civilians whom they accused of being members of opposition forces. In July 2013, Sudan's parliament amended the Sudan Armed Forces Act of 2007 to allow military courts to exercise jurisdiction over civilians for a range of broadly defined offences such as undermining the constitution and publication of "false news."

Law Reform

The National Security Act of 2010, which gives security forces broad powers of arrest and detention, and many other laws contravene basic human rights norms. The government has also failed to implement various criminal justice reforms, including law reforms recommended by the AU's mediation body, the High-Level Panel on Darfur, in 2009.

Authorities continued to apply Shari'a law sanctions that violate international prohibitions on cruel, inhuman or degrading punishment. The penalties are applied disproportionately to women and girls, typically for "crimes" that include private beliefs and decisions about marriage, sexuality, or dress code.

In May, a judge in Khartoum sentenced a pregnant 27 year old, Mariam Yahya Ibrahim, to death for the crime of "apostasy," and to 100 lashings for "adultery." Ibrahim, detained for months, was initially accused of adultery because she is married to a non-Muslim of South Sudanese origin—a marriage the court did not recognize. The court added the apostasy charge after Mariam said she is Christian. Following intense international pressure, Ibrahim was released in June.

Key International Actors

Relations with South Sudan deteriorated with the outbreak of war there in December 2013 and renewed accusations of Sudan's support to armed opposition in South Sudan. The two governments made no progress on other outstanding issues, such as border demarcation, security, and status of the contested area of Abyei, as required in the 2012 cooperation agreement.

The AU's High-level Implementation Panel for Sudan and South Sudan, headed by former South African President Thabo Mbeki, continued to mediate peace talks for the Two Areas, Southern Kordofan and Blue Nile, and began simultaneous mediation on Darfur, as well as talks on a National Dialog process.

In August, the UN Security Council extended UNAMID's mandate for 10 months, at which time it is expected to alter the mandate. The Security Council also extended the UN Interim Security Force for Abyei to February 2015, and in September, the HRC extended the mandate of the independent expert for one year. The HRC resolution condemned violations of international humanitarian law in Darfur, South Kordofan, and Blue Nile; criticized Sudan for the shooting of protesters; and called for an independent public inquiry into the killing of protesters and release of political prisoners. However, the HRC postponed the appointment of a new independent expert for several months.

The International Criminal Court (ICC) has charges pending against five individuals, including Sudan's President Omar al-Bashir, for war crimes, crimes against humanity, and genocide in connection with atrocities in Darfur. Khartoum refuses to cooperate with the ICC and has obstructed its work. In September, the ICC issued an arrest warrant and vacated the November trial start for Abdallah Banda, a Darfur rebel commander accused of attacking a UN base in 2007.

HUMAN
RIGHTS
WATCH

RAZED TO THE GROUND
Syria's Unlawful Neighborhood Demolitions in 2012-2013

Damascus; February 4, 2013

Damascus; July 14, 2013

Syria

In 2014, Syria's armed conflict grew increasingly bloody with government and pro-government militias intensifying their attacks on civilian areas and continuing use of indiscriminate weapons. Government forces also continued to arbitrarily arrest, disappear, and torture detainees, many of whom died in detention. Non-state armed groups opposing the government also carried out serious abuses including deliberate and indiscriminate attacks on civilians, use of child soldiers, kidnapping, and torture in detention.

The extremist group Islamic State, also known as ISIS, and al-Qaeda's affiliate in Syria, Jabhat al-Nusra, were responsible for systematic and widespread violations including targeting civilians, kidnappings, and executions.

According to then-United Nations High Commissioner for Human Rights Navi Pillay, as of August 2014, the death toll in the conflict reached more than 191,000 people. The spread and intensification of fighting have led to a dire humanitarian crisis with millions internally displaced or seeking refuge in neighboring countries.

Government Attacks on Civilians, Indiscriminate Use of Weapons

Following the August 2013 chemical weapons attack on Ghouta, near Damascus, international pressure resulted in Syria acceding to the Chemical Weapons Convention and agreeing to eliminate its declared chemical weapons. All of the declared chemical weapons were removed from Syria for destruction in 2014. But, justice remains elusive for the victims of the attack and evidence strongly suggests that Syrian government helicopters dropped barrel bombs embedded with cylinders of chlorine gas on three towns in Northern Syria in mid-April. These attacks used a common industrial chemical as a weapon, an act banned by the Chemical Weapons Convention.

The Syrian government's extensive use of cluster munitions has caused numerous casualties and left a deadly legacy of explosive remnants of war. Human Rights Watch has identified at least 249 attacks in 10 of Syria's 14 governates where cluster munitions were used between July 2012 and July 2014. At least seven types of cluster munitions were used, including air-dropped bombs, dispensers fixed to aircraft, and ground-launched rockets, and at least ten types of explosive submunitions. Evidence indicates that government forces used a powerful type of cluster munition rocket not seen before in the conflict in attacks on Keferzita, a town in northern Syria, in February. Cluster munitions appear to have been used again on August 21 by Syrian government forces in the town of Manbij in Aleppo governorate, reportedly killing at least six civilians and wounding another 40.

The government also persisted in dropping large numbers of high explosive barrel bombs on civilians in defiance of UN Security Council resolution 2139 passed on February 22. These unguided high explosive bombs are cheaply made, locally produced, and typically constructed from large oil drums, gas cylinders, and water tanks, filled with high explosives and scrap metal to enhance fragmentation, and then dropped from helicopters. Between February and July, there were over 650 new major impact strikes in Aleppo neighborhoods held by armed opposition groups. Most of the strikes had damage consistent with barrel bomb detonations. One local group estimated that aerial attacks had killed 3,557 civilians in Aleppo governorate in 2014.

The Syrian government also continues to impose sieges, which are estimated to affect over 200,000 civilians. The sieges are in violation of Security Council resolution 2139, which demands that all parties "immediately lift the sieges of populated areas," including in Homs, Moadamiya and Daraya in Western Ghouta, Eastern Ghouta, and the Palestinian refugee camp in Yarmouk in south Damascus. The government has used siege strategies to effectively starve civilian populations into submission and force negotiations that would allow the government to retake territory.

Arbitrary Arrests, Enforced Disappearances, Torture, and Deaths in Custody

Syrian security forces continue to detain people arbitrarily, regularly subjecting them to ill-treatment and torture, and often disappearing them using an extensive network of detention facilities throughout Syria. Many detainees were young men in their 20s or 30s; but children, women, and elderly people were also detained. In some instances, individuals reported that security forces detained their family members, including children, to pressure them to turn themselves in. On August 30, the Syrian Network for Human Rights, a local monitoring group, estimated that 85,000 people were currently being held by the government in conditions that amount to enforced disappearance.

Despite a general amnesty declared by the government in June, scores of civil society activists, human rights defenders, media, and humanitarian workers remain in arbitrary detention, some of whom are on trial, including before military and Anti-Terrorism courts, for exercising their rights. Some of the activists who remain in detention include freedom of expression advocate Bassil Khartabil, and human rights defender Mazen Darwish and his colleagues Hani Al-Zitani and Hussein Ghareer, from the Syrian Center for Media and Freedom of Expression. Some activists, like the lawyer and human rights defender Khalil Maatouk, whom former detainees report to have seen in government detention, continue to be held in conditions amounting to enforced disappearance.

Security Council resolution 2139 demands an end to the practices of arbitrary detention, disappearance, and abductions, and the release of everyone who has been arbitrarily detained.

Released detainees consistently report ill-treatment and torture in detention facilities and prison conditions that lead to many cases of deaths in custody. Four former detainees released from the Sednaya military prison in 2014 described deaths in custody and harsh prison conditions that closely match the allegations of mass deaths in custody by a military defector made in January, who photographed thousands of dead bodies in military hospitals in Damascus. At least 2,197 detainees died in custody in 2014, according to local activists.

Jabhat al-Nusra and ISIS Abuses

Extremist Islamist groups Jabhat al-Nusra and ISIS committed systematic rights abuses, including the intentional targeting and abduction of civilians, such as the abduction by ISIS forces in May of 153 Kurdish children. The children were later released.

Based on reports of local Kurdish officials and photographic evidence, ISIS forces used cluster munitions on July 12 and August 14 during fighting between ISIS and Kurdish forces of the People's Protection Units (YPG) around the Syrian

HUMAN
RIGHTS
WATCH

"Maybe We Live
and Maybe We Die"

Recruitment and Use of Children by Armed Groups in Syria

town of ˋAyn al-ˋArab, also known by its Kurdish name of Kobani, in Aleppo governorate near Syria's northern border with Turkey.

On May 29, according to local accounts, ISIS forces executed at least 15 civilians, including seven children, after they entered the village of al-Taliliya near Ras al-ˋAyn in northern Syria. After it took over the town of Bukamal in Deir al-Zour governorate in July, a resident reported that ISIS forces summarily executed an Alawite and Christian resident in the main square during the month of Ramadan. Summary executions of residents by ISIS forces were also reported in Raqqa and Tabka cities in Raqqa governorate in 2014. ISIS forces have also summarily executed some of its hostages including American journalists James Foley and Steven Sotloff in August and September, British aid workers David Haines and Alan Henning in September and October, and American aid worker Peter Kassig in November.

Jabhat al-Nusra has made repeated claims of responsibility for lethal car bombing attacks that have targeted civilians in Syria.

ISIS and Jabhat al-Nusra have imposed strict and discriminatory rules on women and girls and they have both actively recruited child soldiers. In Bukamal, during Ramadan 2014, ISIS forces also reportedly whipped anyone that was eating or drinking in public and during and after Ramadan whipped anyone seen walking in the streets during prayer times. Using the Internet, listening to music, and smoking were also forcibly banned.

Abuses by Other Non-State Armed Groups

Non-state armed groups have launched indiscriminate mortar and other artillery strikes from areas under their control that killed civilians in neighborhoods under government control. These attacks repeatedly hit known civilian objectives, including schools, mosques, and markets.

On April 29, two mortar shells struck the Badr el-Din Hussaini educational complex in the al-Shaghour neighborhood of Damascus, an area under government control, reportedly killing 17 children, at least two parents who came to pick up their children from the school, and injured approximately 50 people. The mortars came from an area under the control of armed groups in the Yarmouk camp.

HUMAN
RIGHTS
WATCH

UNDER KURDISH RULE
Abuses in PYD-Run Enclaves of Syria

Non-state armed groups including the Free Syrian Army and the Islamic Front are also using children for combat and other military purposes. They have also put students at risk by using schools as military bases, barracks, detention centers, and sniper posts.

Non-state armed groups have also been responsible for abductions. At least 54 Alawite women and children that were taken hostage during a military offensive in Latakia countryside in August 2013 continue to be held by "the Mujahadeen room in Latakia countryside."

The prominent human rights defender, Razan Zeitouneh, and three of her colleagues, Wael Hamada, Samira Khalil, and Nazem Hammadi were abducted on December 9, 2013, in Douma, a city outside Damascus under the control of a number of armed opposition groups, including the Army of Islam. They continue to be held.

Despite the systematic nature of abuses by ISIS and Jabhat al-Nusra many other non-state armed groups in Syria have not ceased coordination and cooperation with these groups.

Areas under Kurdish Rule

In January 2014, the Democratic Union Party and allied parties established a transitional administration in the three northern regions: `Afrin, `Ain al-`Arab, and Jazira. They have formed councils akin to ministries and introduced a new constitutional law. Authorities there have committed arbitrary arrests, due process violations, and failed to address unsolved killings and disappearances. The local police and military forces, the YPG also used child soldiers, although they made commitments in June to demobilize and stop the use of child soldiers.

Displacement Crisis

The UN estimates that 7.6 million Syrians are internally displaced and that 12.2 million need humanitarian assistance. In 2014, humanitarian aid agencies experienced significant challenges in getting assistance to the displaced civilian population and others badly affected by the conflict because of sieges imposed by both government and non-state armed groups, the government's continuing refusal to allow assistance to come in across the border, and a general failure to guarantee security for humanitarian workers.

In July, a Security Council Resolution authorized deliveries of cross border humanitarian aid even without government permission.

As of September 3, 2014, over 3 million Syrians had registered or were pending registration as refugees with the UN Refugee Agency (UNHCR) in Lebanon, Jordan, Turkey, Iraq, and Egypt. In 2014, Iraq, Jordan, Turkey, and Lebanon all implemented measures to restrict the numbers of refugees entering their countries.

All four neighboring countries accepting Syrian refugees have denied Syrians secure legal status.

Palestinians from Syria have faced additional obstacles. They have been refused entry or forcibly deported from Jordan and some Palestinian-Jordanians who had been living in Syria had their Jordanian citizenship withdrawn. Palestinian refugees coming from Syria have also faced additional restrictions in Lebanon following new regulations by the Minister of Interior in May that limited Palestinians ability to enter the country or renew their residencies if they already were in the country.

In 2014, the number of refugees from Syria attempting to reach Europe, including through dangerous smuggling routes, has increased. While some European Union countries offer them safety, others such as Bulgaria and Greece have pushed back asylum seekers, sometimes violently, at their borders or from their territorial waters without allowing them to lodge asylum claims. Countries that do not neighbor Syria, including in the west have continued to only accept for resettlement small numbers of refugees.

At time of writing, only 51 percent of UNHCR's appeal for the regional refugee response was funded, leaving a budget shortfall of more than US$1.8 billion. As a result, UNHCR, the World Food Program, and others have cut assistance to refugees, including the provision of basic goods and health care subsidies.

Key International Actors

While parties to the conflict and their international backers met in Switzerland for a second round of political negotiations known as Geneva II in January, the meetings did not result in any tangible outcomes and negotiations have not since resumed.

International efforts to ensure credible justice for serious crimes under international law on all sides in Syria have also proved elusive. On May 22, Russia and China blocked a Security Council resolution that would have referred the situation in Syria to the International Criminal Court (ICC). Over 100 nongovernmental organizations urged the Council to approve the resolution, more than 60 countries co-sponsored it, and 13 of the Council's 15 members voted for it.

More than 140 nations have condemned Syria's cluster munition use in statements and resolutions, including dozens of states not party to the Convention on Cluster Munitions. The UN General Assembly adopted Resolution 68/182 on 18 December 2013, expressing "outrage" at the "continued widespread and systematic gross violations of human rights" in Syria "including those involving the use of … cluster munitions."

The Security Council did however pass a resolution on February 22 demanding safe and unhindered humanitarian access—including across conflict lines and across borders; that all parties cease "indiscriminate employment of weapons in populated areas, including shelling and aerial bombardment, such as the use of barrel bombs;" and an end to the practices of arbitrary detention, disappearance, and abductions, and the release of everyone who has been arbitrarily detained.

In light of the Syrian government's continued non-compliance with the resolution, on July 14, the council passed a second resolution directly authorizing UN agencies and their implementing partners to deliver aid across Syria's borders and conflict lines. No such follow up resolutions have been passed on detainees or indiscriminate attacks despite continued non-compliance with the resolution by all-parties to the conflict.

In addition to persistently blocking Security Council action to curb violations by the Syrian government, Russia, along with the Iranian government, continued to provide the Syrian government with military assistance in 2014, according to media reports .

On August 15, the Security Council passed resolution 2170 calling on all member states to take national measures to stop the flow of foreign fighters, financing, and arms to ISIS, Jabhat al-Nusra, and any other individual or group associate with al-Qaeda, and placed six individuals from these groups on the Al-Qaeda Sanctions List.

The Human Rights Council renewed the mandate of its independent International Commission of Inquiry on Syria in March 2014 for one year.

Countries neighboring Syria, and principally the Turkish government, have stepped up their border control policies to limit the flow of material and fighters to these groups but these measures were implemented after significant delay. Western states who fear their nationals are attempting to enter Syria to fight have also stepped up screening and other measures in an attempt to stem the flow of foreign fighters.

On September 24, the Security Council adopted resolution 2178, urging states to take a number of steps to counter terrorism including, that states should establish screening measures, effective border controls, and other measures to prevent the recruitment, organization, and movement of terrorists including those affiliated with ISIS and al-Qaeda affiliates. The resolution also urged that they improve cooperation, pursue prosecutions, improve assistance in pursuing prosecutions, and help build the capacity of other states to fight terror.

Individuals from Kuwait, Qatar, Saudi Arabia, and the United Arab Emirates have also financed and supported military operations led by ISIS or Jabhat al-Nusra. At the beginning of August, Kuwait announced new measures to curb funding for extremists. This included banning all fundraising in mosques, requiring greater transparency from charities regarding the source and destination of their donations, and obtainment of official receipts. Saudi Arabia has also taken new measures in the past year, announcing a royal decree to imprison Saudi nationals who fight abroad with terrorist groups in February, warning against donations to unauthorized groups in April, and pledging $100 million to establish a UN counterterrorism center in August.

Tajikistan

Tajikistan's human rights record deteriorated in 2014, as authorities continued to crack down on freedom of expression, imprisoned opposition leaders, pressured a leading independent news agency, and arrested an academic researcher on trumped up espionage charges. Authorities' use of torture to obtain confessions remained a serious concern. The government blocked various websites, considered introducing a new law that would require NGOs to register all sources of funding from foreign sources, subjected human rights groups to harassment, restricted media freedoms, and continued to enforce serious restrictions on religious practice, as it had in previous years.

In May, at least three people, including a police officer, were killed and at least seven, including three police officers, were injured during three-day clashes in Khorog, the capital of the autonomous republic of Gorno-Badakhshan in southeastern Tajikistan. The fatal clashes occurred during a police operation against suspected drug traffickers and protests by local residents upset with the police action. Some protesters used violence, attacking a security forces' building in Khorog using a grenade and firearms.

In a positive development, representatives of several nongovernmental organizations (NGOs) and Tajikistan's human rights ombudsman created a detention monitoring group to investigate human rights issues, including the prevention and documention of torture and conditions in prisons and detention facilities. It was too early at time of writing to evaluate whether the group, which includes government representatives, will be a genuinely independent body.

Crackdown on Political Opposition

In December 2013, a Dushanbe court sentenced businessman and former Minister of Industry Zaid Saidov to 26 years in prison on charges including embezzlement, corruption, polygamy, and rape, following a flawed investigation and trial during which Saidov was held incommunicado and denied access to counsel. Authorities arrested Saidov in April 2013, weeks after he announced plans to run for president and the creation of an opposition political party, New Tajikistan, to focus on economic reforms. During the investigation and trial, authorities ha-

HUMAN
RIGHTS
WATCH

"We Suffered When We Came Here"

Rights Violations Linked to Resettlements for Tajikistan's Rogun Dam

rassed and threatened Saidov's relatives, fellow party members, his legal team, and their families with prosecution.

In March, Tajikistan's Agency for State Financial Control and Combating Corruption arrested one of Saidov's lawyers, Fahriddin Zokirov, on fraud charges. Authorities released Zokirov under an amnesty on November 3.

In July, authorities arrested Shuhrat Kudratov, a well-known human rights lawyer also working on Saidov's case, for bribery. Kudratov had previously represented prominent public figures and the popular independent news agency "Asia Plus." On July 15, days before his arrest, Kudratov sent an appeal to NGOs, the news media, and diplomatic missions in Tajikistan highlighting what he called the ongoing persecution of Zaid Saidov's legal team. In a joint statement, 18 Tajik civil society groups called Kudratov's and Zokirov's arrests politically motivated.

In October, authorities responded to plans by the opposition party "Group 24" for a public demonstration in Dushanbe by blocking Internet and cell phone service throughout the country in the days leading up to the event. Authorities also denied visas to a number of representatives of international organizations throughout the end of the year, raising concerns that the government was seeking to block access to the country for independent observers.

In November, the Justice Ministry introduced a bill that, if adopted, would require NGOs to register grants from foreign donors in a state registry prior to being able to access them. The move raised concerns in Tajik civil society that the government planned to adopt measures to restrict the activities of independent NGOs similar to the "Foreign Agents" law adopted in Russia and currently under consideration in Kyrgyzstan.

Social and Economic Rights of Rogun Dam Resettlers

Tajikistan's Rogun Dam and Hydropower Plant stand to displace over 42,000 people before they become operational. Since 2009, the government has resettled 1,500 families to other regions around Tajikistan. Despite government commitments to comply with international standards on resettlement that protect the rights of those displaced, it has not provided the necessary compensation to displaced families to replace their homes or restore their livelihoods. Many families have suffered serious disruptions in access to housing, food, water, and education.

Criminal Justice and Torture

Torture is often used to coerce confessions and police and investigators routinely deny detainees access to counsel in pretrial custody.

On January 19, 34-year-old Umedjon Tojiev, a member of the opposition Islamic Renaissance Party of Tajikistan, died in a prison hospital in Khujand in northern Tajikistan. His death followed serious injuries he sustained on November 2, 2013, after allegedly jumping from the third floor window of a police station in the northern city of Isfara. According to his lawyer and relatives, Tojiev only leapt as he had been subject to three days of torture by police, including electric shock, asphyxiation with a plastic bag, severe beatings, and sleep deprivation. Authorities had arrested him on suspicion of belonging to a banned Islamist organization.

The authorities opened an investigation following calls by Tajikistan's NGO Coalition against Torture, but had yet to present any findings at time of writing. The coalition reported that authorities have undertaken investigations regarding at least three out of seven cases of suspicious deaths in custody over the past four years, but that none have produced meaningful results.

Freedom of Expression

Authorities' attempts to restrict media freedoms and access to critical or independent information, including on the Internet, and the intimidation or detention of journalists, NGO representatives, and academics in 2014 harmed freedom of expression.

Authorities periodically blocked access to independent websites. According to Internet service providers, the state telecommunications agency continued periodically to order that several websites be blocked, including Gmail, Facebook, and Radio Ozodi, the Radio Free Europe Tajik service.

In February, a court decision against Tajikistan's leading independent news outlet, Asia Plus, hampered freedom of expression in the country. On May 30, 2013, the site's editor Olga Tutubalina published an article, "Unintelligent about the

Intelligentsia." The piece criticized Tajikistan's intellectuals, and voiced skepticism over public praise for President Emomali Rahmon by Bozor Sobir, a poet and former government critic, including his call to Tajikistan's artists and intellectuals to "unite" around the president.

Three Tajik intellectuals not named in the article and five state-funded bodies sued Tutubalina, accusing her of attacking their "honor, dignity and reputation." A Dushanbe court ordered Asia Plus and Tutubalina to publish a retraction and pay the plaintiffs approximately US$6,100 (30,000 somoni), a decision upheld on appeal in April. The average monthly salary in Tajikistan is approximately $200.

In June, State Committee for National Security officers arrested scholar and well-known blogger Alexander Sodiqov in Khorog during an interview he was conducting with a leader of the May anti-government protests. For several days, authorities refused to confirm he was in their custody. They later confirmed that they were holding him in a Dushanbe detention facility where he was detained for two months without charge on suspicion of espionage. Following a robust international campaign that included public statements by numerous academic associations in support of academic freedom, Tajik authorities allowed Sodiqov and his family to leave the country and resume his PhD studies abroad. Human Rights Watch received credible reports that Tajikistan's security services intimated or harassed other foreign and Tajik scholars during 2014.

Despite 2012 amendments removing libel as an offense from the criminal code, Tajikistan retains criminal sanctions for "insulting the president" or any government officials, creating a chilling effect on freedom of speech.

Freedom of Religion

Tajik authorities maintained tight restrictions on religious freedoms, including on religious education and worship. Authorities suppress unregistered Muslim education throughout the country, bring administrative charges against religious instructors, control the content of sermons, and have closed many unregistered mosques. Regulations also restrict religious dress; headscarves are banned in educational institutions and beards are prohibited in public buildings.

Rights groups, religious communities, and international bodies continued to criticize the highly controversial Parental Responsibility law, passed in 2011, which stipulates that parents must prevent their children from participating in religious activity, except for state-sanctioned religious education, until they turn 18.

Under the pretext of combating extremism, Tajikistan continues to ban several peaceful minority Muslim groups. Some Christian minority denominations, such as Jehovah's Witnesses, are similarly banned.

Sexual Orientation and Gender-Based Abuses

Although Tajikistan decriminalized same-sex sexual activity in 1998, LGBT (lesbian, gay, bisexual, and transgender) people are subjected to wide-ranging discrimination and homophobia. In 2014, the State Committee for Religious Affairs instructed imams across the country to preach against "nontraditional sexual relations." Tajik NGOs continued to document cases of police violence against LGBT people. LGBT people are especially vulnerable to extortion, fearing that their sexual orientation could be revealed to their family or employers.

After long-time advocacy by local and international women's rights groups or NGOs, Tajikistan took the positive step of enacting a domestic violence law in March 2013. However, local women's rights activists indicate that little has been done to implement or enforce the law and that victims of domestic violence continue to suffer inadequate protection.

Key International Actors

After a follow-up visit in February to assess implementation of his 2012 recommendations, UN Special Rapporteur on Torture Juan Méndez stated that the punishment for torture needs to be increased in accordance with the severity of the crime, and that amnesty for torture should be prohibited. Mendez also expressed concern that there had been only four prosecutions involving cases of torture since 2012, despite persistent allegations that it takes place in prison and other places of detention.

In June, the European Union held its annual human rights dialogue with Tajik authorities , in which it highlighted its concerns shortcomings in the 2013 presidential elections and restrictions in press freedom, including the blocking of websites. The EU delegation in Tajikistan also publicly criticized Alexander Sodiqov's detention.

The United States Commission on International Religious Freedom recommended that Tajikistan be designated a "country of particular concern" for "systematic, ongoing, [and] egregious violations of religious freedom," but the administration elected not to do so.

In June, while stating it has no plans to finance the Rogun Dam, the World Bank released an assessment, including about the impact of the project on those who have been or could be resettled as a result, but did not consider relevant international human rights instruments that should guide resettlement.

HUMAN
RIGHTS
WATCH

TOXIC WATER, TAINTED JUSTICE
Thailand's Delays in Cleaning Up Klity Creek

Thailand

The military staged a coup on May 22, 2014, establishing the National Council for Peace and Order (NCPO) junta and sending Thailand's human rights situation into free fall. The NCPO has severely repressed the rights to freedom of expression, association and peaceful assembly, detained hundreds mostly without charge, and tried civilians in military courts with no right to appeal.

Political Upheavals and Coup

Attempts in November 2013 by then-Prime Minister Yingluck Shinawatra's government to pass a blanket amnesty for all those responsible for political violence and corruption since 2004 sparked mass protests in Bangkok and other provinces. Suthep Thaugsuban, former secretary-general of the Democrat Party, mobilized the People's Democratic Reform Committee (PDRC) to occupy major government buildings and business districts in Bangkok for months.

PDRC and its allies obstructed the general election in February, occasionally with violence, leading to political impasse. Street battles between PDRC's supporters, pro-government groups, and the police, as well as militia attacks on PDRC's protest sites, resulted in at least 28 dead and more than 800 wounded.

On May 20, army chief Gen. Prayuth Chan-ocha announced that the Martial Law Act of 1914 would be enforced throughout Thailand to prevent imminent riots arising from what he claimed were increasingly violent political confrontations. On May 22, General Prayuth staged a coup and arrested representatives of opposing political factions attending military-brokered negotiations at the Army Club in Bangkok after the caretaker government of Niwatthamrong Bunsongpaisal refused to resign.

On August 21, the junta-appointed National Legislative Assembly approved General Prayuth as Thailand's 29th prime minister while permitting him to retain his chairmanship of the NCPO.

Under a junta-promulgated interim constitution, the NCPO has broad authority to limit or suppress fundamental human rights, and is granted immunity for its actions.

Freedom of Expression and Association

Prior to the coup, PDRC supporters targeted journalists considered to back the Yingluck government. On May 7, PDRC security guards assaulted Nick Nostitz, a German freelance photojournalist. Two days later, thousands of people protesting the Yingluck government aligned with the PDRC to besiege major TV stations in Bangkok, harass reporters and prominent news presenters, and demand that the stations cease broadcasting information from government sources.

Using broad martial law powers, the NCPO forced satellite TV channels and community radio stations from all political factions off the air. Some were later allowed to resume broadcasting provided they excluded political issues.

The NCPO ordered print media not to publicize commentaries critical of the military. TV and radio programs were instructed not to invite guests who might comment negatively on the situation in Thailand. On July 26, the NCPO threatened to prosecute the weekly magazine *Phu Jad Karn Sud Sapda* if it continued to publish stories alleging military cronyism and corruption.

The junta has blocked more than 200 websites—including the Thailand page on the Human Rights Watch website—as threats to national security.

The NCPO has banned public gatherings of more than five people and prohibits alleged anti-coup activities. Protesters who have expressed disagreement with the junta through public acts of defiance—such as by showing a three-finger salute used in the movie "The Hunger Games," putting duct tape over their mouths, reading George Orwell's novel *1984* in public, or playing the French national anthem, "La Marseillaise"—have been arrested and sent to military courts, where they could face up to two years in prison.

The junta also perceives political discussions and debates to be a threat to stability and national security. On September 18, the NCPO ordered shut down a "Democracy Classroom" seminar at Thammasat University, and police detained the speakers for several hours. On September 2, the NCPO ordered the cancellation of a discussion on human rights at the Foreign Correspondents Club of Thailand.

Criticizing the monarchy is a serious criminal offense in Thailand. Persons charged with *lese majeste* (insulting the monarchy) are routinely denied bail and held in prison for many months awaiting trial. In most cases, convictions result in harsh sentences. In September 2014, Prime Minister Prayuth publicly stated that a top NCPO priority is to prosecute critics of the monarchy. Since the coup, at least 14 new *lese majeste* cases have been brought to the Bangkok Military Court and criminal courts around Thailand.

On July 31, the Ubon Ratchathani Court sentenced a 27-year-old man to 15 years in prison for posting messages on Facebook deemed insulting to members of the royal family. On September 19, the Appeals Court upheld the Bangkok Criminal Court's sentence against Somyot Prueksakasemsuk of 11 years in prison for publishing two articles in his magazine that made negative references to the monarchy.

Arbitrary and Secret Detention

Since the coup, the junta has detained more than 300 politicians, activists, journalists, and people that it accused of supporting the deposed government, disrespecting the monarchy, or being involved in anti-coup protests and activities.

The NCPO held people in incommunicado lockup in military camps. Some have been held longer than the seven-day limit for administrative detention provided for under martial law. Kritsuda Khunasen, a United Front for Democracy against Dictatorship (UDD) activist, was arrested by soldiers on May 27, in Chonburi province and held incommunicado until June 24.

Kritsuda alleged that soldiers beat her during interrogation and suffocated her with a plastic bag until she lost consciousness. Thai authorities quickly blocked access to an interview she gave on YouTube and to an English language online article about her case. There has been no official inquiry into Kritsuda's allegations or other reports of mistreatment in military custody.

The NCPO has refused to provide details about the release of detainees, many who were held without charge, and continues to arrest and detain others. Persons released from military detention are forced to sign an agreement that they will not make political comments, become involved in political activities, or travel overseas without the junta's permission. Failure to comply could result in a new detention, a sentence of two years in prison, or a fine of 40,000 baht (US$1,250). The junta canceled passports of at least 10 dissidents—including

Japan-based academic Pavin Chachavalpongpun—and issued arrest warrants after they failed to report to the NCPO when summoned.

Accountability for 2010 Political Violence

At least 90 people died and more than 2,000 were injured in the 2010 political violence. The large majority of casualties resulted from unnecessary or excessive use of lethal force by soldiers. Elements of the UDD, popularly known as the Red Shirts, were also responsible for deadly armed attacks against soldiers, police, and civilians.

Court inquests found that soldiers fatally shot 15 of the victims. The soldiers were acting under orders of then-Prime Minister Abhisit Vejjajiva and Deputy Prime Minister Suthep Thaugsuban. On August 28, 2014, the Bangkok Criminal Court ruled that it had no jurisdiction to try Abhisit and Suthep for premeditated murder on the basis of command responsibility because they were political officeholders at the time. No military personnel have been charged for the killings.

The NCPO has expedited the investigations into 2010 violence by the UDD-linked "Black Shirt" militants, leading to many arrests. However, despite clear photographic and other evidence, only a handful of violent crimes committed by supporters of the PDRC and its allies in 2013 and 2014 have been investigated. At time of writing, the April 23, 2014 murder of Kamol Duangphasuk, a prominent poet and Red Shirt political activist, remained unresolved.

The NCPO halted payment of financial reparations—initiated by the Yingluck government as part of political reconciliation measures—to all those harmed by the 2010 violence.

Violence and Abuses in Southern Border Provinces

Since January 2004, more than 6,000 ethnic Thai Buddhists and ethnic Malay Muslims have been killed in the armed conflict between separatist groups and the government in Thailand's southern border provinces. In the past year, the peace dialogue between the Thai government and the Barisan Revolusi Nasional (BRN) movement made no headway.

Thai security forces have not been prosecuted for illegal killings and other abuses against ethnic Malay Muslims, leading to further radicalization of separatists and their supporters. The Fatoni Fighters (also known as Pejuang Ke-merdekaan Fatoni), insurgents in the loose BRN network, regularly targeted civilians in bomb attacks, roadside ambushes, drive-by shootings, and assassinations. Separatists have killed at least 175 teachers during 10 years of insurgency.

Enforced Disappearances

Prominent ethnic Karen activist Por Cha Lee Rakchongcharoen, known as "Billy," was forcibly disappeared after officials at Kaengkrachan National Park arrested him on April 17, 2014 in Petchaburi province. At time of writing, there was no progress in police investigation to locate Billy and bring those responsible for his disappearance to justice.

Thailand signed the International Convention for the Protection of All Persons from Enforced Disappearance in January 2012, but has taken no steps to ratify the treaty. The penal code does not recognize enforced disappearance as a criminal offense. Thai authorities have failed to make a priority of solving any of the 64 known cases of enforced disappearance, including that of prominent human rights lawyer Somchai Neelapaijit, who was disappeared 10 years ago.

Human Rights Defenders

The Thai military and private companies used defamation lawsuits to try to silence human rights defenders and make it more difficult for victims to voice their complaints.

On August 8, 2014, the army's 41st Task Force in Yala province filed defamation suits against the Cross Cultural Foundation and its head, Pornpen Khongka-chonkiet, for allegedly damaging the army's reputation by publishing in May 2014 an open letter exposing torture of an ethnic Malay Muslim man by a paramilitary unit.

Chutima Sidasathian and Alan Morison, journalists from the online newspaper *Phuketwan*, were put on trial on May 26 for defamation and breach of the Computer Crimes Act for publishing a paragraph from a Reuters special report on Rohingya boatpeople. The Thai navy publicly said it initiated the complaint

HUMAN
RIGHTS
WATCH

TWO YEARS WITH NO MOON
Immigration Detention of Children in Thailand

because the article contained a passage implicating navy personnel in human trafficking.

On October 29, 2014, the Prakhanong Court in Bangkok dismissed criminal defamation charges filed by Natural Fruit Co. Ltd., one of Thailand's biggest pineapple processors, against labor activist Andy Hall regarding a report he co-wrote alleging serious labor rights abuses at one of its factories. Hall still faces more serious charges under the Computer Crime Act, which carries prison terms of up to seven years on each count.

Refugees, Asylum Seekers, and Migrant Workers

Prime Minister Prayuth announced in July 2014 that the 140,000 Burmese refugees living in camps in Thailand near the Burmese border would not be forced to return home against their will. However, Thai authorities imposed tighter restrictions on all camp residents and intensified scrutiny on unregistered camp residents, who comprise around 40 percent of the population and whom successive Thai governments have effectively blocked from being considered for refugee status, sparking fears in the camps of possible mass expulsions.

Thailand is not a party to the Refugee Convention and has no law that recognizes refugee status. Asylum seekers, including ethnic Rohingya from Burma and ethnic Uighurs from China, who are arrested often face long periods of detention until they are accepted for resettlement or agree to be repatriated at their own expense. Child migrants, asylum seekers, and other migrants are regularly held indefinitely in squalid immigration facilities and police lock-ups.

In June, several hundred thousand migrant workers from Cambodia, Burma, and Laos fled Thailand, fearing a crackdown by the junta. Thailand's labor laws provide little protection to migrant workers. A migrant worker registration scheme failed to effectively counter the impunity with which employers violate workers' rights. Migrant workers remain extremely vulnerable to exploitation, with female migrants enduring sexual violence and trafficking, and male migrants facing extreme labor exploitation, including being trafficked onto Thai fishing boats.

Anti-Narcotics Policy

The NCPO has shown no interest in launching criminal investigations of extrajudicial killings related to anti-drug operations, especially the more than 2,800 killings that accompanied then-Prime Minister Thaksin Shinawatra's 2003 "war on drugs."

Drug users are sent to "rehabilitation" centers, mostly run by the military and the Interior Ministry, where "treatment" consists mainly of military-style physical exercise, but little or no medical assistance for drug withdrawal symptoms.

Key International Actors

The May coup drew condemnation from the United Nations and Thailand's major allies, including the United States, Europea Union, and Australia, which downgraded their relationship with Thailand in 2014.

Following the coup, the US blocked US$4.7 million in military aid and in June uninvited Thailand from participating in its largest international maritime military exercise that took place in Hawaii. In October, the US announced plans to scale back its annual "Cobra Gold" military exercise in 2015 but did not cancel it. In contrast, China did not criticize the coup, earning it public praise from the NCPO, which also benefited from Beijing's continued unconditional political, military, and economic support.

In June, the US State Department downgraded Thailand to a Tier 3 ranking on its 2014 Trafficking in Persons Report for failing to combat human trafficking.

Thailand lost its bid for election to a seat on the United Nations Human Rights Council for 2015-2017.

The UN Thailand country team has yet to establish a monitoring and reporting mechanism for grave violations against children, as is the norm in conflict situations where violations such as attacks on schools and teachers and recruitment of children, occur.

Tunisia

Tunisia achieved significant progress in strengthening human rights protections following the adoption of a new constitution on January 26, 2014, three years after the uprising that toppled President Zine el Abidine Ben Ali. The first national parliamentary elections since the 2011 uprising, held in October, resulted in victory for the modernist party Nidaa Tounes, with 86 out of the 217 seats of the Assembly of the Peoples' Representatives. The new authorities will need to undertake a thorough overhaul of existing laws, reform public institutions, and implement constitutional guarantees to address deficiencies in the current protection of human rights.

The year 2014 saw important reforms, including the adoption of new laws to combat torture and the establishment of a truth commission into past human rights abuses. In contrast, the lenient sentences that the military appeals court passed on former officials and police responsible for killings of protesters during Tunisia's 2011 uprising sent the wrong message about accountability.

New Constitution

The 2014 constitution guarantees key civil and political, as well as social, economic, and cultural rights. These include the rights to citizenship; to freedom of expression and association, including the right to form political parties; to freedom of assembly and movement; and to bodily integrity and fair trial and freedom from arbitrary detention and torture. The right to political asylum is also guaranteed, as are rights to health, education, and work. The Tunisian authorities still need to amend existing laws or adopt new ones and institute other reforms to realize these rights.

The new constitution contains several weaknesses and ambiguities that could be used to suppress rights. For example, it contains a provision prohibiting "attacks on the sacred," which could be used to prosecute statements that the authorities consider "defamatory" of religion or religious beliefs, contrary to the freedom of expression guarantee contained in article 31.

The constitution fails to abolish the death penalty, although Tunisia has maintained a moratorium on executions since the early 1990s.

Several provisions of the penal code and the code of criminal procedure appear to contradict rights guarantees contained in the new constitution, such as that affording detainees the right, following arrest, to have access to legal representation. The code of criminal procedure continues to permit a detainee to have legal representation only when they are taken before an investigative judge.

Freedom of Expression

In 2014, there were fewer incidents of prosecutions for alleged defamation or "insult" of state officials and on charges of "harming public order" or "public morals."

In July, the head of government temporarily suspended two radio stations, accusing them of having links to terrorism and propagating hate speech, the day after an attack by armed men on July 16 killed 15 Tunisian soldiers near the border with Algeria. The government's action ignored the 2011 decree-law 116 on audiovisual media, which gives the High Independent Authority for Audiovisual Communications sole authority to suspend or otherwise sanction a media outlet.

Women's Rights

The new constitution provides improved protection for women's rights and obligates Tunisia to work towards achieving gender parity in elected assemblies.

In April, the government withdrew the reservations that Tunisia entered when it ratified the Convention on the Elimination of All Forms of Discrimination against Women (CEDAW). These reservations had enabled Tunisia to opt out of certain CEDAW provisions, including provisions on women's rights within the family, even though it had ratified the treaty.

Tunisia maintained, however, a general declaration that it had made in relation to CEDAW, indicating that it would not take "any organizational or legislative decision in conformity with the requirements" of the convention if that should conflict with chapter 1 of the Tunisian Constitution, which declares Islam the state religion of Tunisia.

Tunisia has a personal status code that gives women greater rights within the family than those allowed by other states in the region, but the code retains some discriminatory provisions. These deny women an equal share with men of any inheritance and prohibit a mother who has remarried, unlike remarried fathers, from having her children reside with her.

Accountability

Since 2011, Tunisian authorities have taken some steps to prosecute perpetrators of human rights violations, notably those committed during the uprising that began on December 17, 2010, and ended in February 2011. An official investigation concluded that the authorities' attempt to crush the uprising using excessive force caused the deaths of 132 protesters and injuries to hundreds more.

The trials of those accused of responsibility for these killings began in late 2011 before military courts, which have sole jurisdiction over cases involving members of the military and security forces. First instance military courts that began investigations in July 2011 determined that the accused should stand trial in groups, organized geographically, and trials opened in the military tribunals of Tunis and Le Kef in November and December 2011.

Defendants included the former president, charged in absentia, two former interior ministers, five general directors of the Interior Ministry, and several high-level and mid-level security force commanders. When the tribunals delivered their verdicts in June and July 2012, they convicted President Ben Ali, his interior minister at the time, and five directors of the Interior Ministry and imposed prison sentences ranging from 15 years to life. On April 12, 2014, the military court of appeals confirmed the life imprisonment sentence in absentia of former president Ben Ali but significantly reduced the sentences of all other former senior officials.

After reviewing the trials and the proceedings of the military court of appeals, Human Rights Watch concluded that the military courts had largely respected the rights of the defendants but had faced serious obstacles that prevented their ensuring full accountability for unlawful killings and other serious rights abuses committed during the 2011 uprising.

These included the failure of prosecuting authorities to obtain sufficient evidence to identify the individual perpetrators of unlawful killings and other crimes, and the lack of a provision in the penal code or other legislation making senior officers liable for crimes committed by forces under their command. The government's failure to press effectively for Ben Ali's extradition from Saudi Arabia to stand trial in Tunisia also undermined accountability.

On December 24, 2013, the National Constituent Assembly (NCA) adopted the Law on Establishing and Organizing Transitional Justice. The law sets out a comprehensive approach to addressing past human rights abuses. It provides criminal accountability via the creation of specialized chambers within the civil court system to adjudicate cases arising from past human rights violations, including abuses committed by military and security forces.

The law also provides for the establishment of a Truth and Dignity Commission tasked with uncovering the truth about abuses committed in the period since Tunisia's independence in July 1955 through to 2013. The NCA elected 15 of the commission's members on May 15, 2014. The December 2013 law also establishes mechanisms for victim reparation, institutional reform, vetting of civil servants, and national reconciliation.

Counterterrorism and Security

On June 24, Minister of Interior Lotfi Ben Jeddou told a press conference that a total of at least 2400 Tunisian armed militants had joined the conflict in Syria, mostly as fighters for the Al Nusra Front and the extremist group Islamic State, also known as ISIS. He made the announcement following the publication on Facebook of a video and photographs in which a man who identified himself as Tunisian appeared to participate in the summary killing of five captured Iraqi border guards.

In July, the government ordered 157 associations to suspend their operations, accusing them of having links to terrorism following an attack by armed men that killed 15 Tunisian soldiers near the country's border with Algeria. The government's action breached decree-law 2011-88, which the transitional government had adopted in September 2011 to replace a restrictive law that criminalized participation in officially unrecognized associations, bringing Tunisia's national law into conformity with its international law obligation to uphold freedom of association.

Decree-law 2011-88 gives the judiciary sole authority to order the suspension or dissolution of an association under a three-stage process of warning, then initial suspension for 30 days, followed by dissolution if the association fails to take corrective action. The government's suspension of 157 organizations in July 2014 ignored this process and took the form of a unilateral administrative decision. The associations appealed the government decision before the administrative tribunal.

Judicial Independence

The constitution guarantees the independence of the judiciary. It makes judges accountable solely to the constitution and to the law in the performance of their duties. Article 109 of the constitution prohibits outside interference in the judiciary.

In practice, the judiciary lacks independence from the executive branch and still labors under the legacy of the Ben Ali era, when the authorities used the judicial system as an instrument to suppress dissent. The new authorities have yet to reform law 67-29 of July 14, 1967, which places judges under the effective control of the minister of justice, who used his powers in 2012 to summarily dismiss 75 judges for alleged corruption or links to the Ben Ali regime. The Ministry of Justice has since rejected an administrative tribunal order to reinstate the dismissed judges.

Torture and Ill-Treatment

Torture and other ill-treatment reportedly remained common in detention facilities and prisons, despite the NCA's adoption on October 9, 2013, of a law to create a National Authority for the Prevention of Torture and Other Cruel, Inhuman or Degrading Treatment or Punishment. A year later, however, the NCA had yet to vote on the appointment of the National Authority's members.

Following his second visit to Tunisia since the revolution, in June the special rapporteur on torture, Juan Mendez, said that the eradication of torture in Tunisia required both political will and institutional, legal, and cultural reforms to strengthen safeguards against torture and to rebuild citizens' trust in the judicial and security apparatus.

Key International Actors

Since the January 2011 revolution, several United Nations agencies and foreign governments have committed to support Tunisia's transition, focusing on technical and financial assistance to Tunisia's economy and private sector, security sector support, and support for civil society and democratic practices. In 2014, the United States approved a sovereign loan guarantee to Tunisia of US$500 million. The International Committee of the Red Cross, the UN Development Program, and the European Union provided support in 2014 for security sector and judicial reform programs.

Turkey

The Justice and Development Party (AKP) and Recep Tayyip Erdoğan—elected president in August 2014—are undermining the gains of the past decade with steps that erode human rights and the rule of law in Turkey. In the wake of the mass protests in the summer of 2013 that began in Istanbul and spread to other cities, the government continued a policy of controlling media and the Internet and clamping down on critics.

Corruption allegations in December 2013 implicating the government, with Istanbul prosecutors ordering scores of arrests in December, were followed by circulation on social media of politically damaging leaked telephone calls supporting the allegations. In response, the government intensified its interference in the criminal justice system, reassigning judges, prosecutors, and police, attempted to exert greater executive control over Turkey's already politicized judiciary, and clamped down on Internet freedom.

The corruption allegations emerged in the context of a political contest between Erdoğan's circle within the AKP and their former long-term ally, the Gülen (or Hizmet) movement, led by the US-based cleric Fethullah Gülen, which the government accuses of exerting an undue influence in state institutions, the police, and the judiciary, and of attempting a "coup" against it.

More positively, negotiations with imprisoned Kurdistan Workers' Party (PKK) leader Abdullah Öcalan to end the decades-long armed conflict with the PKK announced at the beginning of 2013 continued in 2014. Bolder steps to address the rights deficit for Turkey's Kurds could address the root causes of the conflict and help further human rights for all ethnic and religious minority groups in Turkey. While the military and the PKK broadly maintained a ceasefire through 2014, around 50 civilians died in violent protests in early October in cities throughout the southeast. The circumstances of most of these deaths had not been fully investigated at time of writing, but the protests themselves followed the Kurdish political movement's strong criticism of the Turkish government's approach to the siege of the Syrian Kurdish city of Kobani (Ayn al-Arab) by the extremist group Islamic State, also known as ISIS.

HUMAN
RIGHTS
WATCH

TURKEY'S
HUMAN RIGHTS ROLLBACK

Recommendations for Reform

Freedom of Expression, Association, and Assembly

The government's erosion of media freedom continued. Readiness to limit freedom of expression, restrictive approach to freedom of assembly, and readiness to prosecute demonstrators while tolerating police violence against them, were among features most damaging to Turkey's democratic credentials and international reputation during the year.

The government responded to the use of social media to disseminate leaked phone calls implicating ministers and family members in corruption by tightening the already restrictive Internet law and blocking Twitter and YouTube in Turkey for several weeks, prompting a joint statement in March from three United Nations special rapporteurs. Both sites were reopened in April and May respectively after the Constitutional Court ruled against the blocking orders.

The clampdown included a rise in broadcasting watchdog disciplinary fines applied selectively to anti-government media, criminal defamation cases against journalists, the firing of some prominent journalists, and blocking orders on particular accounts and content on social media. Through these measures, the government is impeding the ability or likelihood of media to hold government authorities to account or to scrutinize their activities.

In the year after the Taksim Gezi Park protests in Istanbul and anti-government protests in other cities across Turkey, thousands of demonstrators faced legal proceedings. In some cases the courts acquitted defendants at the first hearing, but other trials continued at time of writing. Some defendants charged with terrorism offenses and still on trial spent up to 10 months in pretrial detention before being bailed.

In June, the trial began of five organizers of Taksim Solidarity, a platform of 128 nongovernmental organizations supporting the Gezi Park campaign and sit-in. They were charged with forming a criminal gang, inciting and participating in unlawful demonstrations, and refusing orders to disperse. Their trial with 21 code-fendants continued at time of writing. In September, an Istanbul prosecutor indicted 35 people associated with the Beşiktaş football club fan group Çarşı for their participation in the Gezi protests on a range of charges including an alleged coup attempt against the government.

Trials continued of Kurdish political activists, journalists, students, and lawyers on widely used terrorism charges such as "membership of an armed organization." The evidence against them in most cases concerned nonviolent political association and protest.

However, in March the government took the welcome steps of abolishing the Special Heavy Penal courts whose remit was terrorism offenses, and cutting the maximum period for pretrial detention to 5 years (from 10), resulting in the release on bail of many defendants. Among those bailed were hundreds of defendants tried for alleged links to the outlawed Union of Kurdistan Communities (KCK), including human rights defender Muharrem Erbey, bailed in April after spending over four years in pretrial detention on terrorism charges. The abusive application of terrorism charges remains a serious problem.

Judicial Independence

Turkey has long-standing defects in its justice sytem including concerns over judicial independence, inadequate investigations into abuses by state actors, excessive length of proceedings, and politically motivated prosecutions.

Developments in 2014 highlighted the politicization of Turkey's judiciary. In responding to the corruption investigations, the government asserted that followers of the Gülen movement were strongly represented in the judiciary and police.

In the name of reducing the alleged influence of the Gülen movement in the justice system, the government took steps to bring the police, prosecutors, and judges under greater executive control. The government oversaw the mass reassignment or demotion of judges, prosecutors, and police, including all those involved in the corruption investigations. It adopted a law in February to restructure the Higher Board of Judges and Prosecutors (Hâkimler ve Savcılar Yüksek Kurulu, HSYK) responsible for the administration of the judiciary, to tie it closer to the executive, and created in July a new category of criminal judges of the peace responsible for key decisions at the criminal investigation stage.

In April, the Constitutional Court partially quashed key provisions of the HSYK law concerning enhanced powers for the Minister of Justice on the grounds that they violated the separation of powers in important respects, threatened judicial independence, and opened the way to political pressure on the judiciary.

In June, 237 military personnel serving sentences after convictions for coup-plotting in the Sledgehammer case were released from prison after the the Constitutional Court ruled that they had not had a fair trial and ordered retrials. Defendants in the Ergenekon trial whose convictions were under appeal were bailed in March when pretrial detention was cut from 10 to 5 years.

Combating Impunity

Great obstacles remain in securing justice for victims of abuses by police, military, and state officials. In April 2014, the government introduced a law giving immunity from prosecution to personnel of the National Intelligence Agency (Milli İstihbarat Teşkilatı, MİT), unless the agency itself expressly authorizes prosecution. This measure, which is incompatible with Turkey's human rights obligations, creates a risk that intelligence personnel might be immune from accountability for serious human rights violations committed during their duties, including torture. At time of writing, the law was under appeal before the Constitutional Court.

Despite thousands of killings and disappearances of Kurds by state officials in the 1990s, only a handful of trials of officials have taken place. The 20-year statute of limitations on the prosecution of unlawful killings remains a major obstacle to justice and many cases risk being timed out without urgent action to address it. Stronger efforts to combat impunity are vital to support the Kurdish peace process.

In June, a military court upheld a decision of non-prosecution in the case of the attack by the Turkish Air Force in December 2011 that killed 34 Kurdish villagers near the village of Roboski (Ortasu) close to the Iraqi Kurdistan border. An appeal by the families of the victims to the Constitutional Court was pending at time of writing.

Few investigations were concluded into police violence and disproportionate use of force against demonstrators during the May-June 2013 Gezi protests around the country. In a July 2014 communication to the Committee of Ministers of the Council of Europe on the right to freedom of assembly (regarding the Oya Atman group of cases), the Turkish government claimed that after the countrywide Gezi protests, 329 criminal investigations into the police had been launched in 13 provinces, of which 59 had resulted in decisions of nonprosecution, 6 in prosecutions, and the remainder were still pending.

A police officer who shot dead Ethem Sarısülük in June 2013 during an Ankara protest received an eight-year sentence for "probable intent to kill." There were delays in the trials of police and civilians charged with killing demonstrators Ali İsmail Korkmaz and Abdullah Cömert. Decisions in these cases to transfer the trials to locations at significant distance from the place of the crime disadvantages the families of the victims and their lawyers. At time of writing there was an ongoing investigation into police for the shooting with a tear gas canister of 14-year-old Berkin Elvan who died in March after nine months in a coma.

The retrial of a group of young men for the January 2007 murder of journalist Hrant Dink continued. In July, the Constitutional Court ruled that the murder investigation had not been conducted in an effective manner.

Refugees

As of October 2014, according to official estimates, Turkey was hosting 1.6 million refugees from Syria, 220,000 in camps and the remainder in urban areas, as well as around 80,000 mostly Afghan asylum seekers and refugees from other nationalities.

A new asylum law, which went into effect in April 2014, maintains Turkey's geographical limitation to its accession to the Refugee Convention but, for the first time, enshrines asylum and subsidiary protection as a matter of law, including provisions for legal aid, on unaccompanied children and on nonrefoulement. It limits administrative detention of migrants pending deportation to six months (extended for another six months for noncooperation) with the stipulation that detention ordinarily should not be used for asylum seekers.

Key International Actors

The European Union, EU member states, and the United States expressed concerns about Turkey's record on Internet freedom, judicial independence, and moves to undermine the rule of law, while commending Turkey for hosting over one million refugees from the war in Syria.

The European Commission in its annual progress report released in October commended the Turkish government's moves to put the Kurdish peace process on a legal footing, advised that full revision of the 1982 constitution constitutes "the most credible avenue for advancing further democratization of Turkey," and raised "serious concerns" about government interference in the judiciary following corruption allegations and blanket bans on Twitter and YouTube.

There was no progress in the EU accession process. An EU readmission agreement with Turkey came into force in October, allowing EU governments to return Turkish citizens residing in the EU without authorization to Turkey, and after a three-year transition period permitting the EU to return irregular migrants from other countries to Turkey in cases where it is established that they entered the EU via Turkey.

Among the European Court of Human Rights rulings against Turkey in 2014, a September decision on religious education classes (*Mansur Yalçın and Others v. Turkey*) found that when it comes to compulsory religious instruction, the Turkish education system is still inadequately equipped to ensure respect for parents' convictions because of the overwhelming emphasis on Sunni Islam. The court ruled that, without delay, Turkish authorities had to permit pupils the right to be exempt from religion and ethics classes without requiring a reason.

In September, the Turkish government announced that it would sign two International Labour Organization (ILO) conventions (nos. 167 and 176) on safety and health in mining and construction. The May 13 mining accident at the Soma mine in western Turkey in which 301 miners died highlighted that Turkey has one of the world's worst records on fatal accidents in the mining and construction industries, lacks effective oversight and inspection to ensure safety and work conditions, and has a poor record of holding companies accountable for accidents.

Foreign Policy

The conflicts in Syria and Iraq had a growing impact on Turkey, particularly in the wake of the June 2014 consolidation of power by ISIS when it occupied large swathes of Syria and Iraq and took hostage Turkey's Mosul consul general and 48 consular staff and their family members. Turkey managed to secure their release in September. The Turkish parliament voted in October to grant the Turkish government wide-ranging powers to intervene militarily in Syria and Iraq.

Turkey's approach to Syria primarily advocated the overthrow of the Assad government, viewing the US coalition focus on combating ISIS as inseparable from that aim.

As prime minister, and now president, Erdoğan has consistently and publicly criticized the Egyptian government of Abdel Fattah al-Sisi since it deposed President Mohamed Morsy in 2013. Turkey's stance on Egypt has reduced its ability to influence powers in the Middle East supportive of the Sisi government.

Turkey was a strong critic of Israel's military operations in the Gaza Strip in July-August and diplomatic relations between the two countries remain limited. There was no normalization in relations with Armenia and their shared border remained closed.

Turkmenistan

The Turkmen government's abysmal human rights record saw no real improvements in 2014. The president, his relatives, and their associates maintain unlimited control over all aspects of public life. The government thoroughly denies
freedoms of association, expression, and religion, and the country is closed to
independent scrutiny. Relatives of dozens of people imprisoned during the massive waves of arrests in the late 1990s and early 2000s have had no official information about their fate. Proposed "reform" of the constitution promises no
actual expansion of fundamental rights and freedoms.

Cult of Personality, No Pluralism

According to the Turkmen Initiative for Human Rights (TIHR), a Vienna-based
group, several books written by and about President Gurbanguly Berdymukhamedov, who uses the title "Arkadag" (Protector), were added to the secondary school curriculum in January, replacing the study of writings by former
President Saparmurat Niyazov.

TIHR also reported that in May, parents of schoolchildren in Ashgabat were
obliged to sign a pledge to raise their children in accordance with Turkmen tradi-
tions. In one school, the pledge obliged students to "become faithful sons and
daughters" of the president.

In August, a commission led by Berdymukhamedov convened to discuss constitutional reform and the creation of a human rights ombudsman to bring legislation in line with international standards. It was unclear at time of writing which
articles and laws would be considered for amendment.

Civil Society

Repressive government policies make it extremely difficult for independent nongovernmental organizations (NGOs) to operate. Civil society activists and journalists, including those living in exile and their families in Turkmenistan, face
constant threat of government reprisal.

In May, Berdymukhamedov signed a new Law on Public Associations. The law
states that only a court, not the Ministry of Justice, can cancel registration or sus-

pend the activities of an NGO. However, the Ministry of Justice reserves a long list of reasons to deny registration to new NGOs, and unregistered NGOs are deemed unlawful. Non-state funding is subjected to extensive government controls.

Housing and Property Rights

In January 2014, a new housing law entered into force allowing citizens who have resided in public housing under rental agreements for more than 10 years to privatize their rented properties. It was unclear at time of writing whether the new law will be fully implemented.

In June, during peak high temperatures of over 100 degrees Farenheit (around 40 degrees Celsius), some residents in Ashgabat clashed with authorities after local officials prohibited air conditioning units in multi-story apartment buildings because of their alleged unsightly appearance. Following the protests, officials relented.

Arbitrary evictions continue in Ashgabat, where house demolitions make way for monuments, hotels, and office buildings. Residents, many of whom own their properties, are often not given adequate notice of imminent demolitions and must accept compensation from authorities of government-subsidized apartments of lesser value on the outskirts of the city. In April, the minister of construction and architecture was dismissed, though this has not resulted in any evident improvements.

Freedom of Media and Information

The total absence of media freedom in Turkmenistan remains unchanged. The state controls virtually all print and electronic media; Internet access remains limited and heavily state-controlled; and social media and many websites are blocked, including those of foreign news organizations. The government is known to monitor electronic and telephone communications.

According to TIHR, in June, secret service officials mobilized efforts to cover up news of a Turkmen air force plane that crashed in a residential area near Mary, killing the pilot and a trainee. Residents of neighboring houses were reportedly obliged to sign statements acknowledging their liability for "disclosure of state secrets."

The Russian mobile operator MTS, the only competitor to the state-run Altyn Asyr operator, has faced licensing problems launching a 3GB network that would offer better Internet access to users. In October, MTS was able to launch the network, but at time of writing it was unclear how reliable the network would be due to limited channel capacity.

Freedom of Movement

Turkmenistan's government continues to restrict the right of its citizens to travel freely outside the country by means of an informal and arbitrary system of travel bans commonly imposed on civil society activists and relatives of exiled dissidents.

For example, in April, Turkmen authorities barred Ruslan Tukhbatullin from flying to Istanbul to visit his brother, Farid, the head of TIHR. Border police informed him that he is on a list of people banned from foreign travel. In November, Tukhbatullin received official notification from the Federal Migration Service that he was no longer on the list.

Geldy Kyarizov, former director of the state-run organization "Turkmen Atlary" (Turkmen Horses) who was imprisoned in 2002 for alleged abuse of office and later granted a presidential pardon in 2007, is subject to constant surveillance by authorities.He has been denied permission to travel abroad for medical treatment.

A new law granting citizenship to stateless persons, many of whom hold expired USSR passports from former republics, entered into force in June. Since October 2013, stateless persons had faced problems leaving the country after the authorities stopped issuing them passports.

In June 2013, the migration service announced it would issue new biometric passports to all Turkmen citizens, including those who also have had Russian passports since June 2003. However, according to TIHR, in April 2014 the Turkmen State Migration office suspended issuing biometric passports to dual citizens, though some were reportedly able to get new passports by paying bribes.

Since July 2013, travel outside of the country is prohibited without a biometric passport.

According to Radio Azatlyk, in recent years Turkmen authorities have restricted travel to Turkey, Iran, and Russia for medical treatment by requiring complicated paperwork to obtain exit visas.

Forced Labor

Amendments to the Law on Guarantees of the Rights of the Child introduced in May 2014 prohibit child labor in the agricultural and other sectors in cases where children have to be taken out of school. However, an in situ RFE/RL report found that the past year saw record numbers of children, some under the legal working age of 16, supervised by teachers and local officials being taken into the fields to harvest cotton, and a report by Alternative News of Turkmenistan, a Netherlands-based group, also found forced labor in the cotton and other sectors.

Freedom of Religion

Unregistered religious groups or communities are forbidden to operate by law, and several religious communities have been unable to register for years. In 2014, a new administrative offenses code entered into force, which establishes harsher fines for involvement in unregistered religious activity.

According to Forum 18, an independent international religious freedom group, in August, Jehovah's Witness Bibi Rahmanova was sentenced to four years' imprisonment for allegedly resisting police. Police had detained her a month earlier when she was picking up religious literature from Ashgabat that had been sent to her. In September, her sentence was suspended on appeal, and she was serving her conditional four-year sentence under house arrest at time of writing. According to Forum 18, she allegedly suffered "severe physical abuse" while in detention.

In January, Murat Sapargeldyyev, a conscientious objector to Turkmenistan's compulsory military service, was charged with refusal to serve in the armed forces during peacetime and given a suspended sentence of two years' corrective labor. In February, another conscientious objector and Jehovah's Witness, Pavel Paymov, was sentenced to one year in prison. In October, Paymov, along with five other conscientious objectors and two other Jevovah's Witnesses, all imprisioned in the Seydi Labor Colony, were released under presidential amnesty.

Ruslan Narkuliev, sentenced to two years' imprisonment in September, also for refusal to serve in the armed forces during peacetime, remained imprisoned at the Seydi Labor Colony.

Muslims who want to take the haj pilgrimage to Mecca must do so through a state-organized trip. In one region, Muslims have to wait up to 11 years to make the annual pilgrimage.

Political Prisoners, Enforced Disappearances, and Torture

More than a decade after their arrest and show trials during several waves of repression under former President Niyazov, several dozen people remain victims of enforced disappearances. They include former Foreign Minister Boris Shikhmuradov, his brother Konstantin, and Turkmenistan's former ambassador to the Organization for Security and Co-operation in Europe (OSCE), Batyr Berdiev. In 2014, Human Rights Watch received unverified information that several of the disappeared had died in custody.

The government continues to use imprisonment as a tool for political retaliation. It is impossible to determine the actual number of those jailed on political grounds because the justice system lacks transparency and there is no independent monitoring of these cases. Dissident Gulgeldy Annaniazov and former troop commander Tirkish Tyrmyev both remained in prison on politically motivated charges.

In May, Mansur Mingelov, who is serving a 22-year sentence on several bogus charges, began a three-week hunger strike to demand a retrial. Mingelov had been arrested in 2012 after sending video evidence of police torture against Turkmenistan's Baloch ethnic community to diplomats and the Prosecutor's Office.

Torture remains a grave problem. A 2014 report by a coalition of independent human rights groups, Prove They Are Alive!, described the torture of inmates in the Ovadan Tepe prison, a facility shrouded in secrecy that houses many people believed to have been sentenced on politically motivated charges. The government has persistently denied access to independent human rights monitors, including the Red Cross and 10 United Nations special procedures.

Sexual Orientation and Gender Identity

Consensual sex between men is criminalized with a maximum prison sentence of two years. Turkmenistan rejected recommendations made during the April 2013 UN Universal Periodic Review to decriminalize consensual sex between adults of the same sex.

Key International Actors

At time of writing, the World Bank Group was in the process of developing a new short-term strategy with the government of Turkmenistan, building on its 2013 re-engagement with the government.

In May, the European Bank for Reconstruction and Development (EBRD) adopted a new country strategy for Turkmenistan, reaffirming its prior stance of linking its level of investment to the government's progress in meeting benchmarks on pluralism and accountability, media freedoms, and improving the country's overall human rights record. Because of the govermnent's lack of progress in these areas, the EBRD's engagement in Turkmenistan remains limited.

In July, the United States State Department designated Turkmenistan as a "country of particular concern for religious freedom" following the US Commission for International Religious Freedom's recommendation.

Also in July, the OSCE's Parliamentary Assembly adopted a declaration expressing concern about the disappeared and their families in Turkmenistan and asking the government to provide information about them, including Boris Shikhmurdov and Batyr Berdiev. US Ambassador to the OSCE Daniel Baer raised specific cases of the forcibly disappeared in his February 2014 meeting with Turkmen Foreign Minister Rashid Meredov.

In September, the European Union held its annual human rights dialogue with Turkmenistan, raising concerns about torture and ill-treatment, enforced disappearances, and restrictions on the rights of expression, association, and religion. The outcomes of the dialogue, if any, were not publicly disclosed.

Uganda

President Yoweri Museveni, in power for 28 years, and his ruling National Resistance Movement party continue to curtail freedom of expression, assembly, and association, among other basic rights. In February and July respectively, Museveni signed the Anti-Homosexuality Act and the HIV Prevention and Control Act into law, after five years of parliamentary debates. Although the Anti-Homosexuality Act was overturned by a constitutional challenge in August, the government continues to voice outspoken support for its discriminatory provisions. In some parts of the country, police prevented opposition members from holding public meetings, relying on the sweeping police powers under the 2013 Public Order Management Act. Impunity for abuses by the security forces, particularly during protests, remains a serious problem.

Donors reduced or redirected some assistance in the wake of the Anti-Homosexuality Act, but aid has largely continued to flow despite large-scale corruption scandals in recent years.

Freedom of Assembly and Expression

The Public Order Management Law, passed in August 2013, grants police wide discretionary powers to permit or disallow public meetings. It has generally been implemented to undermine or obstruct Ugandans' assembly rights when protesting against government.

In March, police in eastern Uganda blocked two demonstrations organized by the opposition pushing for electoral reforms. Police claimed the politicians had not sought permission from the inspector general of police, as required under the new law. Eventually the rallies were permitted, but those seeking to protest against the current electoral laws often face unclear procedures and prolonged delays when seeking permissions.

In June, two men were arrested for smuggling two pigs into parliament as a protest against high youth unemployment rates. The two were charged with criminal trespass and conspiracy, and were awaiting trial at time of writing. In August, police arrested 20 members of the Uganda National Students Association for holding a protest at the Ministry of Education, which police deemed to be an

HUMAN
RIGHTS
WATCH

"How Can We Survive Here?"
The Impact of Mining on Human Rights in Karamoja, Uganda

unlawful assembly. The same month, police arrested seven young men in Kampala who were peacefully demonstrating against unemployment.

Media and Civil Society

The closure of two newspapers and a radio station in 2013 and new ad-hoc policies introduced by the minister of information negatively impacted media's operating environment. Station managers and journalists report fear of reprisals if programs are highly critical of the government. In June, the government regulatory body, the Uganda Communications Commission, informed all radio stations that they are required to reserve one hour of prime time air to promote government programs.

In March, a regional police commander stormed the studios of Guide Radio in Kasese, western Uganda, and stopped a program in which the leader of the opposition Forum for Democratic Change was participating. The police commander claimed to be under orders to stop the program because it was "inciting violence." In August, the executive director of the Uganda Communications Commission wrote to a radio manger in Fort Portal warning him of running programs that "cause disharmony" in the community and requested recordings of all programs.

The minister of internal affairs proposed amending the current nongovernmental organization (NGO) law to further constrict civil society operating space. The government has accused organizations of engaging in "political activism," and in one case suspended an NGO working on sexual rights, arguing that it was "promoting homosexuality." Four NGO offices in Kampala were burgled and computers and servers stolen, raising concerns among civil society that the incidents were an orchestrated attempt to curtail NGO operations. The incidents were reported to the police, though only limited investigations occurred, no one was arrested and no stolen items were recovered.

Sexual Orientation and Gender Identity

In December 2013, parliament passed the Anti-Homosexuality Act, increasing prison sentences for same-sex conduct and criminalizing "promotion of homosexuality." President Museveni signed the bill into law on February 24 and a diverse group of individuals and NGOs subsequently challenged the law's constitutionality.

On August 1, the Constitutional Court declared the Anti-Homosexuality Act null and void on procedural grounds because of lack of parliamentary quorum during the vote. The court did not take the opportunity to affirm the rights to freedom of expression, association, and privacy. There are signals that the government may appeal the ruling, and a new draft legislation entitled the Prohibition of Promotion of Unnatural Sexual Practices Bill was pending with an ad-hoc committee of parliamentarians, but had yet to be formally introduced to parliament at time of writing. The new draft bill retains the criminalization of "promotion," which would effectively criminalize the activities of groups that advocate for the rights of LGBT people and render it illegal for such organizations to receive funds or advertise their work and activities in any form. Same-sex conduct remains a crime under Uganda's colonial-era sodomy law.

On April 3, police raided a US-funded health clinic and medical research facility, the Makerere University Walter Reed Project, accusing the clinic of conducting "unethical research" and "recruiting homosexuals." On July 9, the Ugandan High Court upheld the government's forced closure of a 2012 LGBT rights workshop, ruling that its participants were "promoting" or "inciting" same-sex acts.

With the passage of the Anti-Homosexuality Act, some LGBT people reported increased arbitrary arrests, police abuse and extortion, loss of employment, and evictions.

Health and HIV/AIDS

In August, President Museveni signed the HIV Prevention and Control Act into law. The law allows medical providers to require mandatory HIV testing for pregnant women and their partners, and to disclose a patient's HIV status to others, violating human rights related to consent, privacy, and bodily autonomy. Contrary to international guidelines, the new law criminalizes intentional HIV transmission, attempted transmission, and behavior that might result in transmission by those who know their HIV status. The act has been widely condemned by health care providers as counterproductive to national HIV goals, discouraging people from seeking testing and treatment.

Corruption and Investment

Major corruption scandals have surfaced repeatedly in the last few years, but no high-ranking officials have served prison sentences for corruption-related offences. Scandals have rocked health services, particularly regarding the misuse of funds intended for the provision of immunizations and essential medicines to fight HIV, tuberculosis, and malaria.

Uganda's government promotes private investment in mining in northeastern Karamoja, which could provide jobs and improve security, access to water, roads, and other basic infrastructure. But the extent to which local populations will benefit, if at all, remains unclear. As companies have begun to explore and mine the area, communities have voiced serious fears of land grabs, environmental damage, and lack of information as to how and when they may prevent, or receive compensation for, encroachment on their land.

Lack of Accountability

The government failed to credibly investigate violence in which at least 100 people were killed in the western Rwenzori region. Numerous reports suggest that after a July 5 attack on a military barracks and some police posts, civilians were mutilated, tortured, and killed, some buried in mass and unmarked graves, and that government forces may have been involved in reprisals against members of the ethnic group believed to be responsible for the initial attacks.

Despite numerous promises to investigate, no police or military personnel have been held accountable and there have been no credible investigations into killings during protests in 2009 and 2011. In December 2011, police disbanded the Rapid Response Unit but there have been no investigations into the killings or torture by the unit, and one case involving a suspect tortured to death during an interrogation did not advance in the courts. Similarly, no inquiries have been made into cases of people who were tortured or died in the custody of the Joint Anti-Terrorism Task Force.

The government has also failed to protect street children and investigate abuses against them. Despite a strong legal child protection framework, homeless children face violence, beatings, unlawful detention, and forced labor at the hands of police, including cleaning detention cells and police quarters. Government of-

HUMAN
RIGHTS
WATCH

"Where Do You Want Us to Go?"
Abuses against Street Children in Uganda

ficials and police also carry out targeted mass roundups of homeless children. On the streets, homeless adults and older children harass, beat, sexually abuse, force drugs upon, and exploit street children, often with impunity as police neglect to investigate crimes against them.

The Lord's Resistance Army

The Ugandan rebel group the Lord's Resistance Army (LRA) remains active across Central African Republic, South Sudan, and northern Democratic Republic of Congo, with ongoing allegations of killings and abductions, though on a much lesser scale than in previous years.

Warrants issued in 2005 by the International Criminal Court for LRA leaders remain outstanding. Former LRA fighter Thomas Kwoyelo, charged before Uganda's International Crimes Division with willful killing, taking hostages, and extensive destruction of property, has been imprisoned since March 2009 but his trial had yet to begin at time of writing. The Supreme Court has not yet heard the state's 2012 appeal of the High Court order that Kwoyelo be granted amnesty and released.

Key International Actors

In a significant departure from the past, several key donors moved beyond condemnatory statements when President Museveni signed the Anti-Homosexuality Bill into law. This pressure may have contributed to the Constitutional Court's swift hearing of the challenge to the law. The World Bank delayed a US$90 million loan to cover a funding shortfall for the renovation of health care facilities, according to bank President Jim Kim, because the bank could not be sure that the "loan would not lead to discrimination or endangerment of the LGBT community." It remained unclear at time of writing if the loan would be released.

The United States and Dutch governments, among others, cut or diverted assistance, including to the police and justice sector. The US issued visa sanctions against individual human rights abusers, including those who violate the rights of LGBTI people. US support to Uganda's army for the counter-LRA mission and the African Union peacekeeping mission in Somalia continued, though a military conference to be held in Kampala was cancelled.

Ukraine

The "Maidan" uprising in Kiev led to the ouster of President Viktor Yanukovich in February and a complete overhaul of Ukraine's political system. The uprising that began in November 2013 was marked by clashes between police, street fighters, and protesters, which killed over 100 people.

Yanukovich's overthrow, and a law that would have disfavored the Russian language, which the interim president vetoed, prompted violent clashes in southeastern Ukraine between pro and anti-Kiev protesters. May clashes in Odessa alone left 46 people dead. After Russia's occupation of Crimea in March, Russia-backed armed insurgents seized control of many cities and towns in the Donetsk and Luhansk regions, resulting in armed conflict with Ukrainian forces. Both sides violated laws of war in the conflict that by October had claimed the lives of over 4,000 combatants and civilians and wounded over 9,000.

Mounting evidence, including the capture of Russian soldiers in Ukraine, exposed Russian forces' direct involvement in military operations, constituting an international armed conflict between Russia and Ukraine.

Between April and October, hostilities resulted in over 450,000 displaced persons, including 16,000 from Crimea, having to flee their homes to other parts of Ukraine.

Russian officials and state media grossly distorted, manipulated, and at times invented information about the conflict. In response, the Ukraine government imposed excessive restrictions on freedom of media, including by banning Russian channels and barring foreign journalists from entering the country.

Following a September cease-fire agreement between the Kiev government and pro-Russian rebels, parliament passed a law granting three years of semi-autonomy to rebel-controlled areas and amnesty to rebels who have not committed grave abuses. In November, after insurgents organized elections in the Donetsk and Luhansk regions, which Kiev deemed illegal, President Petro Poroshenko requested that parliament repeal the law. Also in November, Poroshenko issued decrees shutting down all governmental institutions and banking services, as well as cutting all state funding to rebel-held areas.

In September, the Ukrainian government stated the need for a new defense doctrine defining Russia as an "aggressor state" and to move towards joining the North Atlantic Treaty Organization (NATO), and introduced into parliament a draft law abolishing Ukraine's non-bloc status.

Maidan Violence

On November 30 and December 1, 2013, riot police violently dispersed and severely beat numerous peaceful demonstrators in Kiev protesting Yanukovich's rejection of a political and trade agreement with the European Union. Police detained some of the protesters and beat them in custody.

Violent clashes between police and street fighters, who intermingled with protesters, killed over 100 people between January 19-21 and February 18-20, including some police, and injured many more. Police used rubber bullets, tear gas, and live munitions against protesters and street fighters armed with bats, firearms, and improvised explosives. At least 98 people were killed between February 18-20, including dozens by sniper fire presumably from Ukrainian security forces, although several former officials later claimed that Maidan organizers orchestrated the shooting. An investigation was pending at time of writing.

Riot police trying to disperse street fighters and protesters assaulted dozens of journalists. Police beat journalists who were covering the protests and sometimes deliberately shot them with rubber bullets or injured them with stun grenades.

Ukraine is not party to the treaty of the International Criminal Court (ICC), but in April 2014, the acting government lodged a declaration accepting the court's jurisdiction over alleged crimes committed in the country between November 17, 2013, and February 22, 2014. The ICC prosecutor's examination into whether criteria for opening a full investigation, as set out in the ICC's treaty, are met was ongoing at time of writing.

Crimea

In February, extra-legal, so-called self-defense units, aided by Russian security forces, seized administrative buildings and military bases across Crimea and installed a pro-Russian leadership. Following an unrecognized referendum on

HUMAN
RIGHTS
WATCH

RIGHTS IN RETREAT
Abuses in Crimea

Crimea's status, Russian President Vladimir Putin and Crimea's leadership signed agreements claiming to make Crimea and the city of Sevastopol part of the Russian Federation. Ukraine's authorities and most international actors declared the referendum unlawful, and there was no lawful transfer of sovereignty to Russia. At time of writing, Russia remains an occupying power of Crimea under international law.

Between February and April, "self-defense" units committed serious abuses, including abductions, attacks, torture and harassment of activists, journalists, and others they suspected of being pro-Kiev.

Crimean Tatars, the predominantly Muslim ethnic minority of the Crimean peninsula, faced increased harassment and persecution. Since March, local authorities issued several warnings to Mejlis, the Crimean Tatar highest representative body, for "extremist" activities and threatened it with closure.

In April and July, respectively, authorities banned Tatar elders Mustafa Jemilev and Refat Chubarov from entering Crimea for five years. In September, they seized all property and bank accounts of the charitable fund that administered Mejlis, claiming it violated the law by having Jemilev, a Ukrainian citizen banned from Russia, on the board of directors.

Police searched the homes of dozens of Crimean Tatars, as well as Islamic schools and mosques, for "prohibited literature." In May, the authorities banned all mass gatherings before the 70th anniversary of the community's deportation.

Over 16,000 people have fled Crimea since March, primarily for mainland Ukraine.

Abuses in Eastern Ukraine

Between May and September, mortar, rocket, and artillery attacks killed hundreds of civilians in the Donetsk and Luhansk regions. Both armed insurgents and government forces violated laws of war by using weaponry indiscriminately, including unguided rockets in civilian areas. Both sides fired salvos of Grad rockets into heavily populated civilian areas.

The use of ground-launched Smerch and Uragan cluster munition rockets with explosive submunitions was recorded in several parts of eastern Ukraine after June. While evidence suggests all parties may have used cluster munitions, it was not possible to determine which forces were responsible for each attack, although the evidence indicates Ukrainian government forces were responsible for some attacks on Donetsk in October. Neither Ukraine nor Russia are parties to the 2008 Convention on Cluster Munitions that comprehensively bans the weapons.

Between April and September, intense fighting led to the complete collapse of law and order in several rebel-controlled areas. Rebels attacked, beat, and threatened hundreds of people whom they suspected of supporting Kiev, including journalists, local officials, and political and religious activists, and carried out several summary executions. They also subjected detainees to forced labor and kidnapped civilians for ransom, using them as hostages. In May, militants kidnapped eight military observers with the Organization for Security and Co-operation in Europe (OSCE) and held them for several weeks.

Also in May, Ukrainian authorities captured the "defense minister" of the self-proclaimed Donetsk Republic. The next day, the leader of Ukraine's Radical Party posted on his social media page photos of the detained man, naked, scratched, and with hands bound, stating that he planned to exchange him for the ousted President Yanukovich. Ukrainian authorities held the man in custody until September, when he was released in exchange for a Ukrainian serviceman during prisoner exchanges between insurgents and government forces.

As counterinsurgency operations continued, Ukrainian security services and pro-Kiev volunteer battalions detained over 1,000 persons suspected of involvement in the insurgency, sometimes holding them for over 14 days and subjecting them to ill-treatment. In September, Kiev authorities opened a criminal investigation into alleged crimes by the pro-Kiev Aydar battalion, which have reportedly included arbitrary detention, enforced disappearances, and torture.

Armed militants obstructed work of journalists covering the conflict. In some cases, rebels physically assaulted journalists they accused of "biased" reporting. In July, insurgent leaders prohibited journalists from filming in combat zones and public places, threatening them with prosecution before a military tribunal if they did so. Rebels harassed, threatened, beat, and abducted domestic and international journalists. At time of writing, most abducted journalists had been released, although the whereabouts of at least three remained unknown.

Kiev's forces disappeared and arbitrarily detained 13 journalists, often accusing them of assisting insurgents. For example, in May, security services detained two Russian reporters and held them for a week in incommunicado detention for suspected assistance to insurgents. The reporters later alleged they were beaten and threatened with execution.

At least seven media workers have been killed since the fighting began.

Internally Displaced Persons

According to the United Nations High Commissioner for Refugees (UNHCR), at least 450,000 people have been displaced from the armed conflict in Ukraine and Crimea; approximately 814,000 went to Russia, according to the Russian government. Ukrainian authorities have struggled to provide adequate protection and assistance for internally displaced people, and the bodies that the government tasked with coordinating efforts in various regions to provide housing and social assistance to IDPs lacked resources to carry out those tasks.

In October, parliament passed a law extending a specific set of rights to IDPs, including protection against discrimination and forcible return, and simplifying access to social and economic services, including residence registration and unemployment benefits.

Freedom of Media

Throughout the year, as political rhetoric grew more heated and polarized, central authorities imposed excessive restrictions on freedom of media. By September, the authorities, seeking to control slanted reporting and to counter Russian propaganda, banned 15 Russian channels from broadcasting in Ukraine, arbitrarily denied entry to at least 20, and barred 35 Russian journalists from entering Ukraine for between three and five years. During the year, authorities expelled at least nine Russian journalists covering the armed conflict.

In March, members of a Ukrainian nationalist party stormed the office of a major Ukrainian television station and attacked its acting president, hitting him several times and forcing him to resign over its Crimea coverage. Authorities opened a criminal investigation into the incident but closed the case in September due to "lack of evidence." The same month, security services raided the Kiev office of a major news outlet that is considered to be pro-Russian, claiming authorities suspected it of attempting to "undermine Ukraine's territorial integrity."

After Russia's occupation of Crimea, local media outlets in Crimea identified as pro-Ukrainian increasingly came under threat. Authorities issued warnings to critical journalists and bloggers, searched their homes, and detained several of them.

In July, Russian security services questioned the editor of a major Crimean Tatar newspaper in connection with the newspaper's suspected "extremist" publications. In September, security services raided the newspaper's office, seized some recent publications, and threatened it with closure.

Sexual Orientation and Gender Identity

Unlike last year, the Kiev 2014 March for Equality was canceled because authorities in the city were afraid they could not protect lesbian, gay, bisexual, and transgender (LGBT) participants and their allies.

Russia's state-sanctioned intolerance of the LGBT community crept into Ukraine. There was an attempt to pass Ukrainian legislation mimicking Russia's so-called "anti-gay propaganda bill," which aims to outlaw "pro-homosexual propaganda," any "positive depiction" of gay people, gay pride marches, or the screening of films with an LGBT theme, like *Milk*.

Key International Actors

Throughout the year, the European Union, United States, NATO, and other key actors showed overwhelming support for the Ukrainian government without adequately pressing human rights issues. The actors condemned Russia's occupation of Crimea and it's backing of the armed insurgency in the east.

In June, President Petro Poroshenko stated that Russia and Ukraine were at war, and in August accused Russia of invading Ukrainian territory. More than a dozen nations have condemned the reported use of cluster munitions in Ukraine.

In March, the United Nations General Assembly passed a resolution, supported by 100 members states but with 58 abstentions, on the territorial integrity of Ukraine, which underscored that the referendum held in Crimea in March had "no validity" and could not "form the basis for any alteration of the status of the Autonomous Republic of Crimea or of the city of Sevastopol."

Since the beginning of the conflict in the east, the UN Office of the High Commissioner for Human Rights and the OSCE have set up on-the-ground monitoring missions and deployed teams of human rights monitors to Ukraine, providing regular reports and updates on human rights abuses. In June, the UN Human Rights Council adopted a resolution on cooperation and assistance to Ukraine in the field of human rights, calling upon the government of Ukraine to investigate all allegations of rights violations and upon all concerned parties to provide access to human rights monitors in Ukraine, including Crimea.

Throughout the year, the OSCE's representative on media freedom issued numerous statements expressing concern over deteriorating media freedom in Ukraine. In September, the representative called for an immediate stop to "hostile behavior" against media in Crimea, citing in particular the fate of the weekly newspaper of the Mejlis of the Crimean Tatar People, which had faced intimidation by the de facto authorities since early September.

In April, the secretary general of the Council of Europe (CoE) set up an international advisory panel to oversee investigations into violence during the Maidan protests and in Odessa in May. The Council's Parliamentary Assembly held three urgent debates on the situation in Ukraine, suspending the Russian delegation's voting rights in April.

The CoE commissioner for human rights visited Ukraine three times. Following his trip to Crimea in September, he called for an effective investigation into abuses by the "self-defense" units in March. In February, the Committee for the Prevention of Torture visited Kiev to look into treatment of people held during the Maidan protests.

In September, the European Parliament and Ukrainian authorities ratified the Association Agreement on deeper political association and free trade between the EU and Ukraine. In response to Russia's threat to impose harsher trade conditions on Ukraine if the agreement went into effect immediately, Ukraine and the European Union agreed to postpone implementation of the agreement until December 2015.

United Arab Emirates

The United Arab Emirates (UAE) continued in 2014 to arbitrarily detain individuals it perceives as posing a threat to national security, and its security forces continued to face allegations that they torture detainees in pretrial detention. UAE courts invoked repressive laws to prosecute government critics, and a new counterterrorism law poses a further threat to government critics and rights activists. Migrant construction workers on one of the country's most high-profile projects continued to face serious exploitation, and female domestic workers were still excluded from regulations that apply to workers in other sectors.

Arbitrary Detention, Torture, and Fair Trial

In January 2014, 20 Egyptians and 10 Emiratis received five-year jail sentences on charges that they set up a branch of the Muslim Brotherhood in the country. They alleged that UAE authorities subjected them to torture in detention and denied them access to legal assistance for many months.

In August, authorities detained 10 Libyan businessmen, at least 2 of whom forcibly disappeared. In September, UAE authorities detained six Emiratis with suspected links to local Islamist groups. At time of writing, authorities have not charged any of the men, and their whereabouts remain unknown.

Two British nationals alleged that they endured torture in pretrial detention. Hasnan Ali, whom a court acquitted of drug charges in April 2014, alleged that police in Dubai beat and threatened to shoot and sexually assault him. Ahmed Zeidan, who received a nine-year sentence for drug possession in May 2014, alleged that police in Dubai held him in solitary confinement for eight days and threatened him with sexual assault. Both men claim they signed legal statements in Arabic, a language neither can read.

In February 2014, the UN special rapporteur on the independence of judges and lawyers criticized the lack of judicial independence in the UAE, arguing that the executive branch exerts *de facto* control over the judiciary. She also expressed concern over reports of the use of secret detention facilities and the ill-treatment and torture of individuals held in incommunicado detention.

Freedom of Expression, Association, and Assembly

In August, the UAE issued a counter-terrorism law that will give UAE authorities the power to prosecute peaceful critics, political dissidents and human rights activists as terrorists. The law classifies a broad range of peaceful and legitimate conduct as terrorism offenses and provides for the death penalty for, among other things, undermining national unity.

The UAE continued to use a repressive 2012 cybercrime law to prosecute critics of the government. On March 10, 2014, a court found Emirati nationals Khalifa Rabia and Othman al-Shehhi guilty of criticizing state security on Twitter, sentencing them to five years in prison and fining them 500,000 AED (US$98,378). The day after Rabia's arrest, the government-linked Emirati television channel 24.ae aired a piece analyzing in detail his Twitter account, accusing him of "affiliation with secret cells," and referring to his use of Twitter hashtags such as #UAE_freemen as evidence.

On November 25, the Federal Supreme Court sentenced Osama al-Najer to three years in jail for charges that included "damaging the reputation of UAE institutions" and "communicating with external organisations to provide misleading information." Al-Najer had criticized the June 2013 conviction of 69 Emiratis with ties to an Islamist group and was quoted in a Human Rights Watch press release that contained credible allegations that the detainees had been tortured during interrogations.

In January 2014, authorities denied entry to a Human Rights Watch staff member and placed two others on the blacklist as they left the country in the immediate aftermath of the release of Human Rights Watch's 2014 World Report. According to UAE immigration law, the blacklist includes the names of individuals prohibited to enter the country "for being dangerous to public security."

Migrant Workers

Foreigners account for more than 88.5 percent of UAE residents, according to 2011 government statistics, but despite labour reforms, low-paid migrant workers continue to be subjected to abuses that amount to forced labor. Domestic workers are particularly vulnerable to abuse, since they do not enjoy even the minimal protection afforded by UAE labor law. The *kafala* sponsorship system,

which operates in all Gulf Cooperation Council states, ties migrant workers to individual employers who act as their visa sponsors. In practice, the system severely restricts workers' ability to change employers. The system gives employers inordinate power over workers by entitling them to revoke migrant workers' sponsorship at will, thereby removing their right to remain in the UAE and making them liable to deportation.

Under new regulations from 2010, workers covered under the labor law can switch employers in certain cases. However, domestic workers—who are excluded from this reach—cannot transfer employers before their contract ends or they receive their employer's consent.

Nearly five years after Human Rights Watch first revealed systematic human rights violations of migrant workers on Abu Dhabi's Saadiyat Island, a development project which will host branches of the Louvre and Guggenheim museums and New York University, some employers continued to withhold wages and benefits from workers, failed to reimburse recruiting fees, confiscated worker passports, and housed workers in substandard accommodation. The government summarily deported Saadiyat workers who went on strike to protest low pay after their employers contacted the police. Despite significant and laudable labor law reforms and policies implemented by the development companies involved in the project, the lack of rigorous investigation, enforcement and sanction resulted in ongoing abuses of workers.

Domestic workers, a predominately female subset of the migrant worker population, continued to experience a range of abuses. Some accused their employers of having physically abused them, confined them to the homes in which they worked, and confiscated their passports. Many said their employers failed to pay the full wages due to them; forced them to work excessively long hours without breaks or days off; or denied them adequate food, living conditions or medical treatment. Some workers continued to be employed in circumstances that amount to forced labor, slavery, or trafficking.

Domestic workers are excluded from Ministry of Labor regulations that apply to other migrant labor sectors, such as one that imposes fines on employers who make the workers they contract pay recruitment fees. In March 2014, the Federal National Council passed a motion to curb the increasingly high recruitment agency fees for domestic workers. In June 2014, the authorities issued a revised standard contract for domestic workers that now provides them with weekly days off and 8 hours of rest in any 24-hour period. The contract, however, is no substitute for labor law protections.

Women's Rights

Federal law No. 28 of 2005 regulates matters of personal status in the UAE and some of its provisions discriminate against women. For example, it requires that a male guardian conclude a woman's marriage contract; likewise,*talaq* (unilateral divorce) occurs when the husband makes a declaration before a judge.

Domestic violence is permitted under UAE law. Article 53 of the UAE's penal code allows the imposition of "chastisement by a husband to his wife and the chastisement of minor children" so long as the assault does not exceed the limits prescribed by Sharia, or Islamic law. Article 56 of the UAE's personal status code obligates women to "obey" their husbands. In 2010, the UAE's Federal Supreme Court issued a ruling—citing the UAE penal code—that sanctions beating and other forms of punishment or coercion by husbands on their wives, provided they do not leave physical marks.

Key International Actors

The UAE participated in United States-led airstrikes on militant Islamist forces in Iraq and Syria during the year, and along with Egypt bombed Islamist militia forces in Libya.

The European Union holds human rights working group sessions with the UAE, where it discusses women's rights and migrant worker issues, but more contentious topics such as freedom of expression and torture are not on the agenda.

United States

The United States has a vibrant civil society and strong constitutional protections for many basic rights. Yet, particularly in the areas of criminal justice, immigration, and national security, US laws and practices routinely violate rights. Often, those least able to defend their rights in court or through the political process—racial and ethnic minorities, immigrants, children, the poor, and prisoners—are the people most likely to suffer abuses.

The August 2014 police killing of an unarmed teenager, Michael Brown, in Ferguson, Missouri, and the subsequent police crackdown on protesters, underscored the gulf between respect for equal rights and law enforcement's treatment of racial minorities. The repressive US response to a surge in unauthorized migrants crossing the border from Mexico and Central America highlights the urgent need for US immigration policy reform.

US national security policies, including mass surveillance programs, are eroding freedoms of the press, expression, and association. Discriminatory and unfair investigations and prosecutions of American Muslims are alienating the communities the US claims it wants as partners in combatting terrorism.

A redacted summary of an extensive Senate report on CIA torture released in December is a first step toward addressing serious abuses committed in the years after the attacks of September 11, 2001, but the Obama administration has failed to bring those responsible for torture to justice.

Harsh Sentencing

Reversing 3 years of slightly declining prison populations, at the end of 2013, the state and federal prison population had grown by 0.3 percent to an estimated 1,574,700 people. At mid-2013, there were also 731,200 people in jails, resulting in a total estimated 2.3 million people behind bars, the largest reported incarcerated population in the world.

Although crime continues to decline, punitive sentencing policies continue to propel high rates of incarceration. Among state prisoners, over 46 percent were incarcerated for nonviolent drug, property, and public order offenses. In the federal system, 50 percent of federal prisoners are serving time for drug offenses.

Between 90 and 95 percent of all state and federal criminal cases are resolved by plea bargains. Prosecutors threaten defendants with far higher sentences if they do not plead and instead choose to assert their right to a trial. Among federal drug defendants, for example, those who refuse to plead receive sentences that are on average three times higher than those received by people who plead guilty. Not surprisingly, only three percent of federal drug defendants risk going to trial.

The US Sentencing Commission took a step towards fairer drug sentencing when it amended its guidelines to reduce sentences for most federal drug offenders, including over 46,000 federal prisoners currently serving unnecessarily long sentences who now will be eligible to seek a reduction.

For the first time in 3 years, no states changed their laws to abolish the death penalty; 18 states and the District of Columbia do not impose death sentences. Washington State Governor Jay Inslee announced in February that he would grant reprieves to any death penalty case that came before him, instituting, in effect, a moratorium.

At time of writing, 33 people had been executed in the US in 2014, by lethal injection. Due to European drug manufacturers' ban on the use of their products for executions, many US states are using experimental drug combinations, while refusing to disclose their composition. At least four of the men executed in 2014 showed visible signs of distress before they died.

Racial Disparities in Criminal Justice

Racial disparities have long plagued the US criminal justice system. African American men are incarcerated at six times the rate of white men, and three percent of all black males are currently incarcerated in a state or federal prison. There are many causes of racial disparities in incarceration, including drug law enforcement practices. For example, whites and African Americans engage in drug offenses at comparable rates, but are arrested, prosecuted, and incarcerated for drug offenses at vastly different rates.

Although African Americans are only 13 percent of the US population, they represent 31 percent of all drug arrests and 41 percent of state and 42 percent of fed-

HUMAN
RIGHTS
WATCH

IN HARM'S WAY
State Response to Sex Workers, Drug Users, and HIV in New Orleans

eral prisoners serving time for drug offenses. African Americans are nearly four times more likely than whites to be arrested for marijuana possession.

Racial disparities in criminal justice contributed to the outrage that erupted in Ferguson, Missouri, following the August police killing of Michael Brown, an unarmed 18-year-old African American. While Ferguson protests began in response to that shooting, they revealed longstanding problems between the predominantly black Ferguson community and the almost entirely white police force. In response to the protests, law enforcement agencies in a number of instances used teargas, rubber bullets, and other intimidating tactics in apparent violation of the right to peaceful assembly and freedom of expression, and engaged in possible excessive use of force.

Drug Policy Reform

Since the 1980s, the US has spent hundreds of billions of dollars to arrest and incarcerate drug offenders in the US. Its heavy reliance on criminal laws for drug control has had serious human rights costs, including infringement of the autonomy and privacy rights of those who simply possess or use drugs.

In 2014, voters in Oregon and Alaska approved measures to legalize the production, sale, distribution, and use of marijuana for recreational purposes, joining Colorado and Washington State. The District of Columbia also decriminalized possession of small amounts of marijuana for personal use. New York, Maryland, and Minnesota joined 20 states and the District of Columbia in legalizing marijuana for medical purposes.

Prison Conditions

Pressed by litigation and public advocacy, some US states and local governments are reconsidering their solitary confinement policies. Ohio agreed to lessen and eventually end the use of solitary confinement in its juvenile facilities. New York corrections officials agreed to develop strict new guidelines, limiting the use of solitary as a punishment except for the most severe infractions and eliminating the use of solitary confinement for inmates younger than 18. In California, a federal court ordered prisons to change policies on the use of solitary as punishment for prisoners with mental illness. Nonetheless, many prisoners and jail inmates—including children—are still held in harsh conditions of nearly round-the-clock isolation and idleness, often for months or even years on end.

Poverty and Criminal Justice

Many poor defendants across the country languish in pretrial detention in large part because they cannot afford to post rising bail costs. Extremely high court and monitoring fees are also increasingly common, as cash-strapped counties and municipalities often expect their courts to pay for themselves or even tap them as sources of public revenue. The impact on poor defendants is particularly harsh.

In 2014, Human Rights Watch reported on widespread abuses linked to the privatization of misdemeanor probation services in several US states. Operating under an "offender-funded" model, probation companies charge offenders directly for their services and may secure the arrest of those who fail to pay. Fees are structured in ways that penalize the poor, and there is a general lack of proper government oversight or accountability.

In April, Georgia Governor Nathan Deal vetoed a bill that would have helped shield probation companies from public scrutiny. Georgia's legislature is likely to take the issue up again in 2015, and will have an opportunity to introduce badly-needed oversight and accountability mechanisms that could be a model for other states.

Youth in the Criminal Justice System

Every US jurisdiction allows children under the age of 18 to be prosecuted as adults and sentenced to adult prison terms in certain circumstances. At the end of 2013, 1,200 children were being held in adult state prison facilities. Florida held a greater number of children in adult facilities than any other state, partly as a result of its policy of granting prosecutors sole discretion over the prosecution of children in adult court. Fourteen other states also permit prosecutors to send children to adult courts for prosecution without judicial review in at least some cases.

BRANDED FOR LIFE

Florida's Prosecution of Children as Adults under its
"Direct File" Statute

HUMAN RIGHTS WATCH

"You Don't Have Rights Here"

US Border Screening and Returns of Central Americans to Risk of Serious Harm

States continue to grapple with a US Supreme Court decision banning mandatory life without parole sentences for youth offenders convicted of homicides. While a majority of US states have found the Supreme Court ruling to be retroactive, in July, the Michigan Supreme Court found that the decision did not apply to youth already serving mandatory life without parole sentences.

Rights of Non-Citizens

From October 2013 through September 2014, US Customs and Border Protection apprehended 68,541 unaccompanied children from Central America and Mexico and 68,445 non-citizens in family units near the US-Mexico border. These figures represent 77 percent and 361 percent increases from the previous year, respectively. In response, the Obama administration dramatically expanded detention of unauthorized families and expedited deportations. In October, Human Rights Watch documented how Central American migrants who had fled to the US fearing for their lives were deported without sufficient opportunity to seek protection.

In June, the administration opened the first of three new family detention centers dedicated primarily to holding and facilitating the deportation of mothers and children from Central America. Many detained families are seeking asylum; yet, even when the US finds them to have a credible fear of returning to their countries, it denies them release on bond, categorically arguing that they are "national security" threats without conducting individualized risk assessments.

Legislative efforts toward legal status for millions of unauthorized migrants in the US foundered in 2014. In November, the Obama administration announced executive branch policy changes to provide temporary legal status to over four million unauthorized immigrants without certain criminal convictions who have lived in the United States for five years or more and have US citizen or legal permanent resident children. These policies will likely protect millions of families from the threat of arbitrary separation. However, they do not alter border policies that result in the summary deportation and criminal punishment of people with deep ties to the US.

In 2014, over 166 local jurisdictions instructed police not to fulfill some requests from federal authorities to further detain apprehended non-citizens for immigration reasons under a program known as "Secure Communities." President

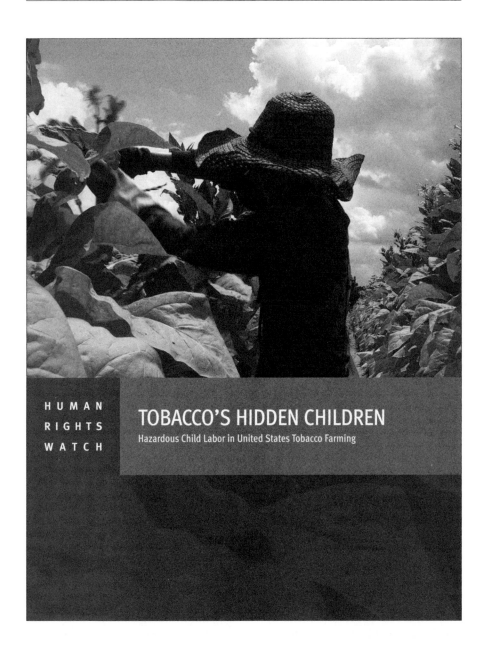

TOBACCO'S HIDDEN CHILDREN
Hazardous Child Labor in United States Tobacco Farming

Barack Obama's November executive action limited such federal-local collaboration on immigration matters, recognizing it had exacerbated mistrust of law enforcement.

Labor Rights

Hundreds of thousands of children work on US farms. The 1938 Fair Labor Standards Act exempts child farmworkers from the minimum age and maximum hour requirements that protect other working children. Child farmworkers often work 10 or more hours a day and risk pesticide exposure, heat illness, and injuries.

Child labor is common on tobacco farms in the US, the world's fourth largest tobacco producer. Child tobacco workers suffer vomiting, headaches, and other symptoms consistent with acute nicotine poisoning.

Congress has not closed a legal loophole allowing children to do hazardous work in agriculture at 16; hazardous work is prohibited in all other jobs until 18. US laws and regulations include no special provisions to protect child tobacco workers from nicotine exposure.

Health Policy

US military veterans face systemic barriers in accessing health care, including long delays in obtaining adequate care at Department of Veteran Affairs (VA) health centers.

Tens of thousands of veterans are unable to get effective help to prevent overdose, treat opioid dependence, and end chronic homelessness. The US Congress passed the Veterans' Access to Care through Choice, Accountability and Transparency Act of 2014 in August, to improve and expand veterans' access to medical services.

Thirty-four states have criminal laws that punish HIV-positive people for exposing others to the virus. In June, Iowa became the first to amend (but not fully repeal) its criminalization statute.

HUMAN
RIGHTS
WATCH

NO TIME TO WASTE
Evidence-Based Treatment for Drug Dependence at the
United States Department of Veterans Affairs

Women's and Girls' Rights

In June, the US Supreme Court ruled in *Burwell v. Hobby Lobby Stores, Inc.* that certain for-profit corporations can refuse to cover contraception in employee health insurance plans based on the corporate owner's religious views that life begins at conception. Over two-thirds of employed US adults under 65 get their health insurance through an employer.

While state legislatures enacted fewer regulations targeting abortion providers in 2014, the impact of the surge in restrictions from 2011 to 2013 became more visible. In Texas, the number of abortion clinics has declined by almost half since 2011, with more closures possible depending on the outcome of litigation over onerous abortion provider and facility requirements passed in 2013.

One in five women is sexually assaulted in college, according to a 2010 report by the US Centers for Disease Control and Prevention. In January, the Obama administration established the White House Task Force to Protect Students from Sexual Assault, which published its first set of recommendations in April. Meanwhile, survivors from colleges across the country continued to expose how schools and local police mishandled their cases.

Police in Memphis, Detroit, and Cleveland analyzed forensic exams (rape kits) that had been left in storage for years. The test results led to the discovery of dozens of serial rapists and scores of indictments. The backlogs underscored a broader problem of police not properly investigating sexual assaults.

Following Human Rights Watch's exposure of the Metropolitan Police Department's mishandling of sexual assault cases, the District of Columbia Council passed a law establishing independent oversight of police and allowing victims to have an advocate present during police interviews.

Sexual Orientation and Gender Identity

At time of writing, same-sex couples can marry in 35 states, the District of Columbia, and the city of St. Louis. The US Supreme Court decided in October 2014 to let stand three federal appeals court rulings that overturned same-sex marriage bans in five states, and since then has declined to intervene in similar cases.

WITH LIBERTY TO MONITOR ALL

How Large-Scale US Surveillance is Harming Journalism, Law, and American Democracy

HUMAN
RIGHTS
WATCH

President Obama signed an executive order in June 2014 that prohibits workplace discrimination on grounds of sexual orientation or gender identity by companies awarded federal contracts and outlaws discrimination based on gender identity for federal employees. In August 2014, in response to a 2012 Equal Employment Opportunity Commission decision, the US Department of Labor announced plans to issue new guidance making clear that discrimination on the basis of transgender status is prohibited under the existing definition of discrimination based on sex in Title VII of the Civil Rights Act of 1964.

However, the US Supreme Court's broad interpretation of religious exemption in the *Hobby Lobby* case could set a precedent undermining protections for lesbian, gay, bisexual, and transgender (LGBT) people on religious grounds.

Twelve US states retain sodomy laws. Since April 2013, legislatures in Montana and Virginia have repealed their states' sodomy laws. Louisiana's legislature voted to uphold the state's law in April 2014.

National Security

For the 13th year, the US detained men at Guantanamo Bay without charge or trial; at time of writing, 143 detainees remained at the facility. The Obama administration resumed transfers from Guantanamo in August 2013 after a long lull, sending 11 detainees to their home or third countries by the end of that year. In late 2013, Congress added new provisions to the National Defense Authorization Act (NDAA) that gave the administration more flexibility to make transfers. Yet, since the change, the pace of transfers out of Guantanamo has not changed significantly; at time of writing, only 12 detainees had been transferred out of Guantanamo in 2014.

The Defense Department continued to force-feed Guantanamo detainees on hunger strike using methods that remain classified and has stopped reporting on the number of ongoing hunger strikes. The few details disclosed raise serious concerns that the forced-feedings violate medical ethics and care standards, and amount to ill-treatment under international law. A federal court ordered the release of videos of the forced-feeding of one detainee but refused to issue an injunction to change the forced-feeding procedures. The US, at time of writing, was considering appealing the decision regarding the release of the videos.

The Obama administration continued to pursue cases before the military commissions at Guantanamo Bay. This system fails to protect attorney-client communications, allows the introduction of coerced evidence, and uses rules that block defense counsel from access to information essential to the case—such as their clients' treatment while in secret CIA custody.

The US brought one new case in the commissions against a detainee accused of crimes connected to attacks on US troops in Afghanistan, among other allegations. Two other pending cases, including the one against five men accused of plotting the September 11, 2001 attacks, languished in pretrial hearings, with a trial date likely years away.

In July, Human Rights Watch released a report documenting abusive counterterrorism investigations against often vulnerable American Muslims, including indigent people or those with intellectual and mental disabilities, who were unlikely to ever have been involved in terrorist activities were it not for the government's involvement. The government also makes use of overly broad material support charges, prosecutorial tactics that may violate fair trial rights, and harsh conditions of confinement.

The US continued to conduct targeted killing operations in Afghanistan, Pakistan, Yemen, and Somalia, purporting to follow administration policy guidelines announced in 2013 that the targets of strikes pose a continuing, imminent threat to the US and that there be near certainty that no civilians will be harmed.

A Human Rights Watch investigation of a December 2013 strike on a wedding procession in Yemen that killed 12 people and wounded at least 15 more found that many, if not all, of those killed were civilians, contrary to the policy guidelines and in apparent violation of the laws of war. The Yemeni government reportedly paid more than US$1 million in total to the families of those killed or injured in the strike. Payments were also reportedly made to the relatives of an anti-Al-Qaeda cleric killed in a US drone strike in 2013.

US policy and practice of targeted killings remained shrouded in secrecy. In response to a court case, the administration was forced to disclose a Justice Department memo, substantially redacted, providing the legal rationale for a strike that killed a US citizen in Yemen in 2011. However, the administration has not provided the legal memoranda justifying targeted killings in other contexts.

The US Senate Intelligence Committee released in December a 499-page redacted executive summary of a 6,700-page report on the Central Intelligence Agency's (CIA) detention and interrogation program. The report shows that the interrogation techniques used by the CIA were far more brutal and widespread than previously reported, including previously unreported forms of torture and sexual assault such as "rectal rehydration." The report also found that the interrogation techniques used by the CIA were ineffective at gathering useful or valuable intelligence, and that the CIA repeatedly lied about the program and for years sought to cover up its crimes. The US has failed to prosecute the US officials responsible for authorizing and carrying out torture and other ill-treatment of detainees in US custody since 9/11.

Documents leaked to journalists by former National Security Agency (NSA) contractor Edward Snowden continued to reveal new details about US surveillance programs. In the last year, reports based on the Snowden documents show that the US may be collecting millions of text messages worldwide each day and intercepting all phone calls and metadata in the Bahamas and Afghanistan, and gathering all phone metadata in Mexico, Kenya, and the Philippines. A July news story said several prominent American Muslim leaders, including the head of a Muslim civil liberties group, were targeted with electronic surveillance.

On January 17, 2014, President Obama announced additional measures to restrict the use, retention, and dissemination of personal data gathered by intelligence services in Presidential Policy Directive 28. However, these measures fell short of ensuring that interference with privacy was limited to what was necessary and proportionate, and they left open the possibility of large-scale collection. Also, while the measures purported to bring rules on surveillance of non-US persons (foreigners abroad) closer to those governing data collected on US persons, the rules are vague and create no justiciable rights.

In March, the UN Human Rights Committee called on the US to ensure that its surveillance activities respect privacy rights under the International Covenant on Civil and Political Rights, regardless of the nationality or location of individuals being monitored. It also expressed concern over the lack of transparency in US laws and court rulings governing surveillance.

In July, Human Rights Watch released a report documenting how large-scale US surveillance is hampering journalists and lawyers in their work, making it more difficult to protect sources, and leading journalists to go to extreme lengths to avoid detection: from using encryption to burner phones, to ceasing all electronic communication. As a result, far less information about matters of public concern may be seeing the light of day.

Also in July, Senator Patrick Leahy introduced a new version of the USA Freedom Act that would have limited some forms of domestic surveillance, while doing almost nothing to safeguard the privacy of foreigners abroad. However, it failed to move forward in the Senate.

Foreign Policy

In August, the US launched air strikes against the extremist group Islamic State (also known as ISIS) forces in Iraq as part of a US-led coalition that includes five Arab countries; in September, the US expanded the air strikes to Syria against ISIS and another extremist group, Jabhat al-Nusra. President Obama also announced he was deploying additional US military personnel to Iraq and was increasing military assistance to armed groups opposed to the Assad government in Syria.

Following the disputed presidential election results in Afghanistan in April and August, US Secretary of State John Kerry helped broker a power-sharing agreement in Afghanistan. US troops prepared to withdraw from Afghanistan by the end of the year, leaving about 10,000 to train, advise, and assist Afghan security forces. The US signed a Bilateral Security Agreement with the new Afghan government in October.

Following the ouster of Ukrainian President Viktor Yanukovich in February and ensuing violence, the US placed sanctions on Russia's financial, energy, and defense sectors.

In June and September, the Obama administration announced a US ban on the production and acquisition of antipersonnel landmines as well as on their use outside of the Korean peninsula, measures that bring it in closer alignment with the Mine Ban Treaty.

In August, the US hosted 45 African heads of state at the first US-Africa Summit, with discussions focusing on economic development, governance, and security.

Uzbekistan

Uzbekistan's atrocious rights record did not discernibly improve in 2014. Authoritarian President Islam Karimov, who entered his 25th year in power, continued to employ a widespread security apparatus to monitor and crack down on activities of real and perceived opponents.

Authorities repress all forms of freedom of expression and do not allow any organized political opposition, independent media, free trade unions, independent civil society organizations, or religious freedom. Those who attempt to assert rights, or act in ways deemed contrary to state interests, face arbitrary detention, lack of due process, and torture. Forced labor of adults and children continues.

A much-publicized feud between Gulnara Karimova, the president's daughter, and her sister and mother, as well as with the country's repressive National Security Services (SNB) that unfolded on Twitter and in the press revealed a level of infighting within the political elite in unprecedented fashion. Karimova's accusations about corruption within the political elite and SNB officials' use of torture brought to the fore many politically sensitive topics. But there were no signs that the feud led to more space for free expression inside the country.

Imprisonment and Harassment of Critics

The Uzbek government has imprisoned thousands of people on politically motivated charges to enforce its repressive rule, targeting human rights and opposition activists, journalists, religious believers, artists, and other perceived critics.

Among those imprisoned for no other reason than peacefully exercising their right to freedom of expression were 14 human rights activists: Azam Farmonov, Mehriniso Hamdamova, Zulhumor Hamdamova, Isroiljon Kholdorov, Gaybullo Jalilov, Nuriddin Jumaniyazov, Matluba Kamilova, Ganikhon Mamatkhanov, Chuyan Mamatkulov, Zafarjon Rahimov, Yuldash Rasulov, Bobomurod Razzokov, Fahriddin Tillaev, and Akzam Turgunov. Five more are journalists: Solijon Abdurakhmanov, Muhammad Bekjanov, Gayrat Mikhliboev, Yusuf Ruzimuradov, and Dilmurod Saidov. Four others are opposition activists: Murod Juraev, Samandar Kukanov, Kudratbek Rasulov, and Rustam Usmanov. Three are independent religious figures: Ruhiddin Fahriddinov, Hayrullo Hamidov, and Akram Yuldashev.

"Until the Very End"
Politically Motivated Imprisonment in Uzbekistan

Seven others are perceived to be government critics or witnesses to the May 13, 2005 Andijan massacre, when Uzbek government forces shot and killed hundreds of mainly peaceful protesters. Those imprisoned include Dilorom Abdukodirova, Botirbek Eshkuziev, Bahrom Ibragimov, Davron Kabilov, Erkin Musaev, Davron Tojiev, and Ravshanbek Vafoev. Many were in serious ill-health, had been tortured, and had their sentences arbitrarily extended in prison.

In January, police detained and fined independent photographer Umida Akhmedova, her son, and five others for holding a peaceful demonstration near the Ukrainian embassy in Tashkent in support of Ukraine's "Euromaidan," a pro-democracy movement. Akhmedova and her son were released one day later; at least 3 others were sentenced to 15 days' administrative detention.

In March, after investigations that lacked due process, a Tashkent court sentenced Fahriddin Tillaev and Nuriddin Jumaniyazov, labor rights advocates, to more than eight years in prison on fabricated human trafficking charges.

The same month, authorities arbitrarily extended for an unspecified number of years the sentence of imprisoned rights activist Ganikhon Mamatkhanov, who had been serving a five-year sentence on politically motivated fraud charges.

In June, rights activist Abdurasul Khudoynazarov died just 26 days after his release from prison, having served more than eight years of a nine-year sentence on trumped up charges. Officials released him the same day that prison doctors diagnosed him with advanced liver cancer. He told rights groups that officials had consistently denied his requests for medical treatment since his imprisonment in 2006.

Also in June, a Tashkent court convicted journalist Said Abdurakhimov, who writes under the pseudonym "Sid Yanyshev" for FerganaNews, a site banned in Uzbekistan, on charges of "threaten[ing] public security," among others. The court fined Abdurakhimov 100 times the minimum wage (approximately US$3,200) and confiscated his video camera.

In September, authorities introduced amendments that imposed new restrictions on bloggers, including a ban on "untrue posts and re-posts." Dunja Mijatovic, the Organization for Security and Cooperation in Europe (OSCE) representative on freedom of the media, warned the measures would further undermine free expression in Uzbekistan.

Also in September, airport authorities prevented Feruza Khurramova, wife of exiled opposition activist Bahodir Choriev, and her son, both Uzbek citizens, from entering the country after they flew to Tashkent from the United States, where they reside. After being detained for several hours, authorities notified Khurramova that she and her son had been "stripped of their citizenship" and deported them to Turkey. Uzbek officials later informed other relatives of Choriev living outside Uzbekistan that they had also been stripped of their citizenship, citing an order of President Karimov.

Criminal Justice and Torture

In November 2013, the United Nations Committee against Torture stated that torture is "systematic," "unpunished," and "encouraged" by law enforcement officers in Uzbekistan's police stations, prisons, and detention facilities run by the SNB. Methods include beating with batons and plastic bottles, hanging by wrists and ankles, rape, and sexual humiliation.

Although authorities introduced habeas corpus in 2008, there has been no perceptible reduction in the use of torture in pretrial custody or enhanced due process for detainees. Authorities routinely deny detainees and prisoners access to counsel, and the state-controlled bar association has disbarred lawyers that take on politically sensitive cases.

A lawyer for imprisoned activists Nuriddin Jumaniyazov and Fahriddin Tillaev told Human Rights Watch that, in January 2014, authorities stuck needles between Tillaev's fingers and toes during an interrogation to force a false confession related to trumped-up charges.

In July, the wife of imprisoned rights activist Chuyan Mamatkulov told Human Rights Watch that on April 20, a prison captain named Sherali had repeatedly struck Mamatkulov on the head with a rubber truncheon in his office after Mamatkulov had asked to see a dentist. He was then put in solitary confinement for 24 hours.

The Andijan Massacre

For nearly a decade, the Uzbek government has refused an independent investigation into the 2005 government massacre in Andijan. Authorities persecute anyone suspected of having witnessed the atrocities or who attempts to speak about them publicly.

In 2014, Human Rights Watch confirmed that authorities in 2012 arbitrarily extended by 8 years the 10-year prison sentence of Dilorom Abdukodirova, an eyewitness to the massacre. After fleeing to Kyrgyzstan in 2005, she settled in Australia. She was immediately arrested and imprisoned on her return in 2010, despite assurances she would not face prosecution.

Forced Sterilization

In 2014, Human Rights Watch interviewed gynecologists from Uzbekistan who reported that the Ministry of Health orders some doctors to perform a certain number of forced sterilizations each month. Some women who have given birth to two or more children have been targeted for involuntary sterilization, especially in rural areas. Gynecologists confirmed that surgical sterilizations are performed without women's informed consent and in unsafe medical facilities.

Freedom of Religion

Authorities imprison religious believers who practice their faith outside state controls. In July, the Initiative Group of Independent Human Rights Defenders (IGIHRD) estimated that more than 12,000 persons are currently imprisoned on vague charges related to "extremism" or "anti-constitutional" activity, with several hundred convicted in the past 12 months. Authorities also harass and fine Christians who conduct religious activities for administrative offenses, such as illegal religious teaching.

In October, Forum 18 reported the death in custody at a women's prison outside Tashkent of Nilufar Rahimjonova. Rahimjonova, 37, had been serving a 10-year sentence on "terrorism" charges—apparent retaliation for her links to her father, theologian Domullo Istaravshani and husband, both based in Iran and critics of the Uzbek government. After her arrest in 2011, Rahimjonova was forced to give an incriminating TV interview against her family and was sentenced following a flawed trial and allegations of ill-treatment. She was not known to have suffered any chronic illnesses prior to her death on September 13, 2014, the cause of which remains unknown. Authorities ordered her brother to bury her body quickly without an autopsy. Human rights activists fear Rahimjonova may have died of torture.

Sexual Orientation and Gender Identity

Consensual sexual relations between men are criminalized with a maximum prison sentence of three years. Activists report that police use blackmail and extortion against gay men due to their sexual orientation, threatening to out or imprison them. LGBT community members face deep-rooted homophobia and discrimination.

Forced Labor

State-organized forced labor of children and adults in the cotton sector remains widespread. Authorities force over two million adults and schoolchildren, mainly ages 15-17 but some even younger, to harvest cotton for up to two months each autumn.

Following international pressure, the government reduced the numbers of young children sent to harvest cotton in 2014, as it had done in 2013, but increased the use of older children and adults. The forced labor of adults disrupts the delivery of essential services nationwide, as authorities mobilize public sector workers— including doctors, nurses, and teachers—to fill quotas.

In February, the International Labour Organization (ILO) reported the findings of its mission to monitor child labor during the 2013 cotton harvest. While finding that the practice was not "systematic," the report noted the use of child labor, and emphasized concerns about the use of forced labor, which it recommended the government take steps to eliminate. Uzbek civil society reported that the ILO mission did not undertake a comprehensive assessment of the harvest since it did not include forced adult labor or ensure Uzbek civil society's participation, and was not independent because monitoring teams included Uzbek government representatives.

Key International Actors

Uzbekistan's record of cooperation with UN human rights mechanisms is arguably among the worst in the world. For the past 12 years, it has ignored requests for access by all 11 UN human rights experts, and has rejected virtually all recommendations that international bodies have made for human rights improvements.

The United States government resisted imposing any serious policy consequences for Uzbekistan's dismal rights record, viewing Tashkent as a key ally along the Northern Distribution Network (NDN) that it is using to withdraw supplies from the war in Afghanistan.

In 2014, for the second year in a row, the State Department's human trafficking report placed Uzbekistan in the lowest category—"Tier III"—based on Tashkent's systematic use of forced labor. For the sixth consecutive year, the State Department also designated Uzbekistan as a "country of particular concern" due to its serial violations of religious freedom, but the White House waived the sanctions envisaged under both statutes citing national security grounds.

The European Union did not publicly express concern about Uzbekistan's deteriorating record, nor did it follow through with any known consequences for Tashkent's failure to meet the reform expectations that EU foreign ministers set out in 2010. President Karimov was invited for state visits to European capitals, including Riga and Prague, although the latter was canceled in February after an outcry by rights groups.

In 2014, the Asian Development Bank and World Bank approved investments in Uzbekistan's irrigation sector, despite concerns raised by civil society activists that doing so before the Uzbek government has acted meaningfully to end forced labor and allow monitoring by independent civil society could support ongoing abuses during the cotton harvest.

Venezuela

In 2014, security forces used excessive force against largely peaceful demonstrators, many of whom were arbitrarily arrested, subject to severe beatings and other abuses during their detention, and denied basic due process rights. These human rights violations, which occurred over a period of several weeks in different locations, were practiced systematically by Venezuelan security forces.

Under the leadership of President Hugo Chávez and now President Nicolás Maduro, the accumulation of power in the executive branch and the erosion of human rights guarantees have enabled the government to intimidate, censor, and prosecute its critics. While some Venezuelans continue to criticize the government, the prospect of reprisals—in the form of arbitrary or abusive state action—has undercut judicial independence, and forced journalists and rights defenders to weigh the consequences of publicizing information and opinions that are critical of the government.

Police abuse, poor prison conditions, and impunity for abuses by security forces remain serious problems.

Excessive Use of Force against Unarmed Protesters

Beginning in February 2014, state security forces—including the Bolivarian National Guard, the Bolivarian National Police, and state police forces—routinely used unlawful force against unarmed protesters and bystanders. The violations included severe beatings; the indiscriminate firing of live ammunition, rubber bullets, and teargas into crowds; and, in some cases, the deliberate firing of pellets at point blank range at unarmed individuals already in custody. Security forces also tolerated and sometimes collaborated directly with armed pro-government gangs that attacked protesters with impunity. According to the Attorney General's Office, 3,306 people, including 400 adolescents, were detained during the demonstrations.

Detainees were often held incommunicado on military bases for 48 hours or more before being presented to a judge. During their detention, they suffered a range of abuses that included severe beatings, electric shocks or burns, and

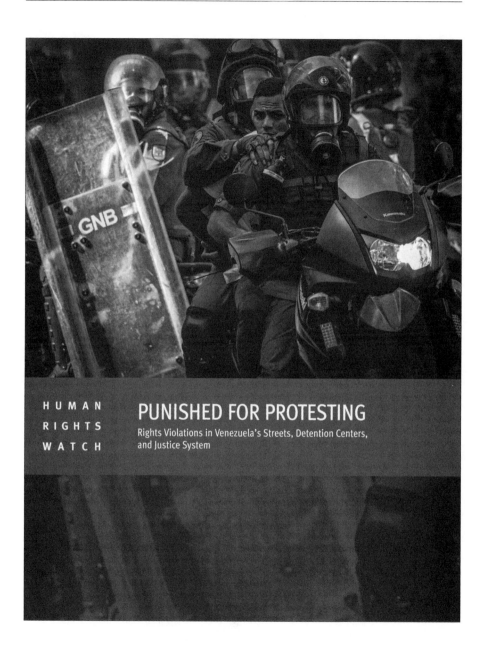

PUNISHED FOR PROTESTING

Rights Violations in Venezuela's Streets, Detention Centers, and Justice System

being forced to squat or kneel, without moving, for hours at a time. In some cases, the ill-treatment constituted torture.

Judicial Independence

Since former President Chávez and his supporters in the National Assembly conducted a political takeover of the Supreme Court in 2004, the judiciary has largely ceased to function as an independent branch of government. Members of the Supreme Court have openly rejected the principle of separation of powers, publicly pledged their commitment to advancing the government's political agenda, and repeatedly ruled in favor of the government, validating the government's disregard for human rights.

Judge María Lourdes Afiuni remains under criminal prosecution as a result of a 2009 ruling in which she authorized the conditional release of a government critic. Although Afiuni's ruling complied with a recommendation by international human rights monitors—and was consistent with Venezuelan law— a provisional judge who had publicly pledged his loyalty to Chávez ordered her to stand trial on charges of corruption, abuse of authority, and "favoring the evasion of justice." She continues to be forbidden from making any public statements about her case.

During the 2014 protests, justice officials failed to fulfil their role as a safeguard against abuse of power and instead were party to serious due process violations. Scores of victims were denied access to a lawyer until minutes before judicial hearings, which were often scheduled in the middle of the night. Prosecutors and judges routinely turned a blind eye to evidence suggesting that detainees had been physically abused, or that security forces had planted evidence against them.

Justice officials also acted on the government's unsupported claim that its political opponents were responsible for the violence that erupted during the demonstrations. The government accused Leopoldo López, an opposition leader, of being the "intellectual author" of the protest-related deaths and attacks against public offices and vehicles on February 12. The Attorney General's Office promptly sought his arrest for several alleged crimes. López has been in detention in a military prison since he turned himself in on February 18. During his trial, which began in July, the presiding judge has not allowed his lawyers to present evidence in his defense.

In April, the Supreme Court summarily tried and sentenced two opposition mayors to 10 and 12 months in prison, respectively, in proceedings that violated basic due process guarantees, including their right to appeal their convictions.

Freedom of Expression

Over the past decade, the government has expanded and abused its powers to regulate media. While criticism of the government is available in some newspapers and radio stations, fear of government reprisals has made self-censorship a serious problem.

In 2010, the National Assembly amended the telecommunications law to grant the government power to suspend or revoke concessions to private outlets if it is "convenient for the interests of the nation." It also expanded the scope of a restrictive broadcasting statute to cover the Internet, allowing the arbitrary suspension of websites for the vaguely defined offense of "incitement." Previous amendments to the criminal code had expanded the scope and severity of defamation laws that criminalize disrespect of high government officials.

The government has taken aggressive steps to reduce the availability of media outlets that engage in critical programming. Venezuela's oldest private television channel, RCTV, which was arbitrarily removed from public airwaves in 2007, was driven off cable TV in 2010. In 2013, Globovisión, which was for years the only major channel that remained critical of Chávez, was sold to government supporters because, according to its owner, it had become politically, economically, and legally unviable. Since then, Globovisión has significantly reduced its critical programming.

In January, the president of the National Assembly, Diosdado Cabello, filed a criminal defamation suit against a citizen who published an opinion piece in the newspaper *Tal Cual*, and four directors of the company that owns the paper, including its editor. The article cited unofficial sources for the number of people killed in Venezuela in 2013, and quoted Cabello saying: "If you don't like insecurity, leave." Cabello argued that he had never said that, and that the article undermined his reputation. A criminal court admitted the case in March, ordered the five men to present themselves before the courts once a week, and forbade them from leaving the country without prior judicial authorization.

During the 2014 protests, the government blocked transmission of NTN 24, a cable news channel, and threatened to prosecute news outlets over their coverage of the violence. In many instances, victims of security force abuses were professional journalists and people who had been taking photos or filming security force confrontations with protesters.

Human Rights Defenders

The Venezuelan government has sought to marginalize the country's human rights defenders through repeated unsubstantiated allegations that they are seeking to undermine Venezuelan democracy with the support of the US government. In March, President Maduro stated that Rocío San Miguel, director of a nongovernmental organization (NGO) that promotes accountability of security forces, was "fully involved in an attempted coup" in Venezuela. In May, the minister of justice said that Humberto Prado, director of an NGO that monitors prison conditions in Venezuela, was involved in a conspiracy plot to undermine the Venezuelan government. In November, the president of the National Assembly, Diosdado Cabello, citing information provided by "patriotic informants," said that 12 NGOs that submitted reports on torture during the United Nations Committee Against Torture's review of Venezuela had "dark interests."

In 2010, the Supreme Court ruled that individuals or organizations that receive foreign funding could be prosecuted for "treason." In addition, the National Assembly enacted legislation blocking organizations that "defend political rights" or "monitor the performance of public bodies" from receiving international assistance.

Impunity of Abuses of Security Forces

As of November, prosecutors had received 242 complaints of alleged human rights violations committed during the 2014 protests, including only two cases of torture. According to the Attorney General's Office, prosecutors had concluded 125 investigations, bringing charges against 15 members of public security forces. Official sources reported that two police officials were convicted for "events occurred in Anzoátegui" but provided no additional information on the case nor the convictions.

Killings by security forces are a chronic problem in Venezuela. In October, members of the Scientific, Penal, and Criminal Investigative Police killed five civilians during a search in the building of a pro-government group in Caracas. The Attorney General's Office issued arrest warrants against seven officers, who, according to official news accounts, remained at large at time of writing.

According to the most recent official statistics, law enforcement agents allegedly killed 7,998 people between January 2000 and March 2009. Impunity for these crimes remains the norm.

Prison Conditions

Venezuelan prisons are among the most violent in Latin America. Weak security, deteriorating infrastructure, overcrowding, insufficient and poorly trained guards, and corruption allow armed gangs to effectively control prisons. Children deprived of liberty are routinely held with adults, particularly during pretrial detention. According to the Venezuelan Observatory of Prisons, as of August there were approximately 55,000 inmates—most of them in pretrial detention—in prisons with a capacity for 19,000. Since the Ministry of Penitentiary Matters was created in June 2011, at least 1,463 people have died in prisons, including at least 150 in 2014, according to unofficial sources.

Labor Rights

Labor legislation adopted in April 2012 includes provisions that limit the freedom of unions to draft their statutes and elect their representatives. In practice, the National Electoral Council (CNE), a public authority, continues to play a role in union elections, violating international standards.

In July, President Maduro denounced protesting workers at the state-owned steel corporation Sidor, accusing them of being "mafias" that had "kidnapped" the company. Clashes between workers and members of the National Guard dispersing the demonstrations left some injured protesters, according to press reports. In August, the communications minister tweeted that the government had reached an agreement with the "true workers" of Sidor. Protests and strikes by workers who argued that the agreement was not signed by competent union representatives continued during that month.

Key International Actors

Several international human rights monitors have expressed concern regarding abuses during the 2014 protests. In February, the Inter-American Commission on Human Rights urged Venezuela to investigate unlawful actions and guarantee public security. In March, six UN rapporteurs called on the Venezuelan government to ensure "prompt clarification of allegations of arbitrary detention, excessive use of force and violence against protesters, journalists and media workers during protests."

In September, the UN Working Group on Arbitrary detention stated that Leopoldo López and one of the mayors convicted in April had been arbitrarily detained. In October, the UN high commissioner for human rights urged Venezuela to release arbitrarily detained protestors and politicians. For years, Venezuela's government has refused to authorize these human rights experts to conduct fact-finding visits in the country.

The regional organization Unasur engaged with the government of Venezuela and opposition leaders in early 2014 to promote dialogue. The Unasur representatives, however, failed to call on Venezuela to address abuses, even though Unasur's constitutive treaty states that "fully effective democratic institutions and the unrestricted respect for human rights are essential conditions for building a common future of peace, economic and social prosperity and for the development of integration processes among the Member States." The dialogue was stalled at time of writing.

In July, the US Department of State revoked the visas of 24 Venezuelan officials in response to allegations of excessive use of force and arbitrary detentions against protesters.

Since 2013, as a consequence of the government's decision to withdraw from the American Convention on Human Rights, Venezuelan citizens and residents are unable to request the intervention of the Inter-American Court of Human Rights when local remedies for abuses are ineffective or unavailable for any abuses committed since that date. The Inter-American Commission has continued to monitor the situation in Venezuela applying the American Declaration of Rights and Duties of Man.

The Venezuelan government continued to support a campaign by Ecuador to undermine the independence of the commission and limit the funding and effectiveness of its special rapporteurship on freedom of expression.

In light of local groups' claims that patients with cancer, HIV/AIDS, and hemophilia, among other illnesses, had limited access to medicines and basic medical supplies, the UN special rapporteur on the right to health urged the Venezuelan government in April 2014 to "adopt all the necessary measures to guarantee the protection and full enjoyment of the highest attainable standard of physical and mental health for all the population."

As a member of the UN Human Rights Council, Venezuela regularly voted to prevent scrutiny of serious human rights situations around the world. Venezuela voted down resolutions spotlighting abuses in North Korea, Syria, Iran, Sri Lanka, Belarus, and Ukraine. In October, Venezuela was elected to a two-year term on the UN Security Council.

Vietnam

The human rights situation in Vietnam remained critical in 2014. The Communist Party of Vietnam (CPV) continued its one-party rule, in place since 1975. Maintaining its monopoly on state power, it faced growing public discontent with the lack of basic freedoms. While fewer bloggers and activists were arrested than in 2013, the security forces increased various forms of harassment and intimidation of critics.

Denial of rights and endemic official corruption are widely seen as stifling Vietnam's political and economic progress. The growth of critical discourse on blogs, Facebook, and other forms of social media has challenged the government's ability to dominate public opinion. Anti-China sentiment has continued to grow as the maritime dispute between Vietnam and China has intensified. In May 2014, violent protests against China erupted in Binh Duong and Ha Tinh provinces, causing the death of four Chinese nationals and the destruction of facilities of many foreign-owned companies, including Chinese, Taiwanese, South Korean, and Japanese businesses.

Vietnam accepted 182 of the 227 recommendations made by the United Nations Human Rights Council (HRC) at its June 2014 periodic review of Vietnam's human rights record, but rejected crucial recommendations such as release of political prisoners and people detained without charge or trial, legal reform to end politically motivated imprisonment of people for their peaceful exercise of fundamental human rights, the creation of an independent national human rights institution, and other steps to promote public political participation. In November, the National Assembly ratified the UN Convention against Torture and the Convention on the Rights of Persons with Disabilities (CRPD).

Political Prisoners and Misuse of the Criminal Justice System

Vietnamese courts lack independence and continue to be used as political tools of the CPV against critics. Trials are often marred by procedural and other irregularities to achieve a politically pre-determined outcome. For example, during the September 2014 trial of land rights activists from Duong Noi ward (Hanoi) charged with "fighting against those on public duty," the court refused to summon witnesses who might have provided statements in favor of the accused and prevented defense lawyer Tran Thu Nam from presenting his defense.

Authorities use penal code provisions on "undermining national unity" and "abusing the rights to democracy and freedom to infringe upon the interests of the state" to crack down on dissent, though other laws such as disrupting public order are also used.

Independent writers, bloggers, and rights activists face police intimidation, harassment, arbitrary arrest, and prolonged detention without access to legal counsel or family visits.

In February 2014, activists Bui Thi Minh Hang, Nguyen Thi Thuy Quynh, and Nguyen Van Minh were arrested on their way to visit fellow activist Nguyen Bac Truyen on trumped up charges of causing traffic jams. The three were convicted in August 2014 for causing public disorder under article 245 of the penal code and received sentences of between two and three years in prison.

The continued persecution of bloggers was highlighted in 2014 by the March trials of Truong Duy Nhat and Pham Viet Dao for allegedly "abusing rights to democracy and freedom" under article 258 of the penal code. Truong Duy Nhat was sentenced to two years and Pham Viet Dao to 15 months.

In May, the authorities arrested prominent blogger Nguyen Huu Vinh (often known as Anh Ba Sam) and his colleague Nguyen Thi Minh Thuy, also for allegedly violating article 258. In total, at least 10 people were convicted under article 258 in 2014.

Physical assaults against rights campaigners are common. In February 2014, anonymous thugs assaulted and beat Huynh Ngoc Tuan and his son, Huynh Trong Hieu, both of whom write blogs, in Quang Nam province. Two months earlier, Huynh Ngoc Tuan had suffered broken bones in another assault that occurred while he was campaigning for former political prisoners.

In May thugs assaulted rights activist Tran Thi Thuy Nga, breaking her leg and arm. In August, blogger Nguyen Bac Truyen was hit by a motorbike driven by two anonymous men who had been keeping intrusive surveillance on him and his family for months prior to the accident. In November, thugs assaulted and injured former political prisoner and blogger Truong Minh Duc. Other bloggers and activists who were assaulted by anonymous thugs include Le Quoc Quyet, Le Thi

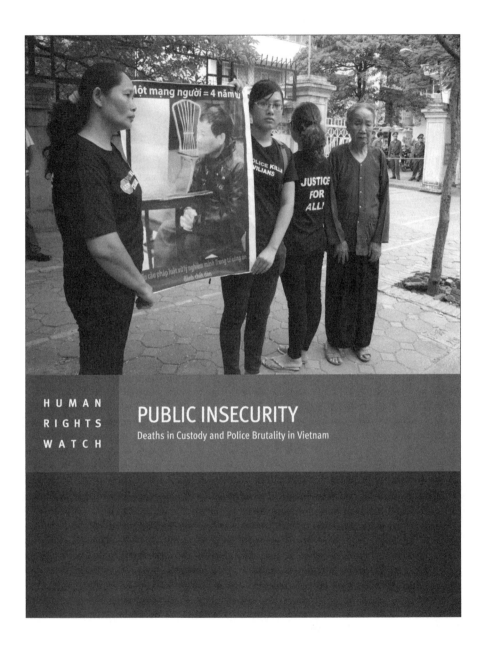

HUMAN
RIGHTS
WATCH

PUBLIC INSECURITY
Deaths in Custody and Police Brutality in Vietnam

Phuong Anh, Nguyen Van Thanh, Trinh Anh Tuan, Truong Van Dung, Tran Ngoc Anh, Bui Tuan Lam, Pham Ba Hai, and Le Van Soc. No one was charged in any of these cases.

Freedom of Assembly, Association, and Movement

Vietnam bans all independent political parties, labor unions, and human rights organizations. Authorities require official approval for public gatherings and refuse to grant permission for meetings, marches, or protests they deem politically or otherwise unacceptable.

In April 2014, the police of Nha Trang city forcibly dispersed a human rights meeting organized by prominent blogger Nguyen Ngoc Nhu Quynh (also known as Mother Mushroom) and other activists. In July 2014, the Independent Journalists Association of Vietnam (IJAVN) was established. In August and September, police summoned members of the IJAVN— including founder Pham Chi Dung and freelance journalist Nguyen Thien Nhan—for questioning about their writing.

Domestic restriction of movement is used to prevent bloggers and activists from participating in public events, such as anti-China protests, human rights discussions, or attending trials of fellow activists. For example, writer Pham Dinh Trong was detained briefly twice in 2014 so he could not participate in an anti-China protest in Ho Chi Minh City in May or attend blogger Bui Thi Minh Hang's trial in August.

The government has also prevented many critics from making trips outside Vietnam, citing "national security." In February 2014, freelance journalist Pham Chi Dung was prohibited from leaving Vietnam to attend Vietnam's Universal Periodic Review session in Geneva. Other bloggers and activists who have been stopped from leaving Vietnam include Nguyen Thi Huyen Trang and Nguyen Thanh Thuy (in April), and Pham Dac Dat (in July).

Freedom of Religion

The government monitors, harasses, and sometimes violently cracks down on religious groups that operate outside official, government-registered, and government-controlled religious institutions. Targets in 2014 included unrecognized branches of the Cao Dai church, the Hoa Hao Buddhist church, independent

Protestant and Catholic house churches in the central highlands and elsewhere, Khmer Krom Buddhist temples, and the Unified Buddhist Church of Vietnam. At least 20 people were convicted in the first nine months of 2014 for participating in independent religious groups not approved by the government.

In July, while Professor Heiner Bielefeldt, UN special rapporteur on freedom of religion or belief, was visiting Vietnam on an official mission, police intimidated and put many dissidents and religious activists under house arrest so they could not meet him. Fearing for the safety of activists, Bielefeldt cut short his planned visits to An Giang, Gia Lai, and Kon Tum provinces.

Abuses in Detention and Prison

Police brutality, including deaths in police custody, are an increasing source of public concern in Vietnam. In 2014, even the heavily controlled state media frequently published reports about police abuse. In many cases, those killed in police custody were being held for minor infractions. Police frequently engaged in cover-ups, including by alleging the detainee's suicide. Many detainees said they were beaten to extract confessions, sometimes for crimes they say they did not commit. Others said they were beaten for criticizing police officers or trying to reason with them. Victims of beatings included children.

In July, the Ministry of Public Security issued Circular 28 in attempt to curb police abuse and misconduct during investigations. In September, the National Assembly Judicial Committee held its first public hearing on forced confessions, torture, and other misconduct by police during investigations.

Abuses in Drug Detention Centers

People dependent on drugs, including children, continue to be held in government detention centers where they are forced to perform menial work in the name of "labor therapy." Violations of center rules and failure to meet work quotas are punished by beatings and confinement to disciplinary rooms where detainees claim they are deprived of food and water. In 2014, the government developed a plan to "reform" the system that would not do away with forced labor and, despite promises to close some centers and reduce the overall number of detainees, would still leave more than 10,000 detainees in the system in 2020.

Key International Actors

Vietnam's most important foreign relations are with China and the United States, but ties to Japan, the European Union, the Association of Southeast Asian Nations, and Australia are also significant.

Vietnam's relationship with China was complicated in 2014 by maritime territorial disputes, which led to large street protests and violent riots in Vietnam.

In the context of its "Asia pivot" aimed at containing China, the US pursued improved military and economic relations with Vietnam while making efforts to press Vietnam to improve its human rights record, delivering mixed messages. Japan, the EU, and Australia, focusing on commercial relations, made inadequate efforts to support detained activists or otherwise advocate for improved respect for basic rights in Vietnam.

Yemen

The fragile transition government that succeeded President Ali Abdullah Saleh in 2012 following mass protests failed to address multiple human rights challenges in 2014. Violations in the context of several different armed conflicts, legally sanctioned discrimination against women, child offenders facing the death penalty, child marriage, child soldiers, attacks against journalists, unlawful detention, human trafficking of migrants, and lack of accountability for the previous government's human rights violations all persisted.

All sides committed laws of war violations in fighting that broke out repeatedly in different parts of the country in 2014, involving multiple actors including the Yemeni armed forces, Houthi rebels, Islamist fighters, and the Islamist armed group Al-Qaeda in the Arabian Peninsula (AQAP).

In September, following instances of security forces using excessive force against Houthi protesters, a four-day armed conflict rocked Sanaa as Houthi armed forces took the capital. The fighting in Sanaa ended on September 21 with the signing of a peace agreement, the resignation of the prime minister, and the formation of a new government in November.

By September 2014, 334,512 people across Yemen were officially registered as internally displaced due to fighting.

Accountability

Yemen's parliament voted in January 2012 to give former President Ali Abdullah Saleh and his aides immunity from prosecution. In September 2012, however, Saleh's successor, President Abdrabuh Mansour Hadi, decreed the creation of an independent commission of inquiry to investigate alleged rights abuses committed during the 2011 uprising, and recommend measures to hold perpetrators accountable and afford redress to victims. By November 2014, Hadi had still to nominate the inquiry's commissioners and no progress had been achieved.

The government failed to implement human rights reforms recommended at the 10-month-long national dialogue conference (NDC) that concluded in January 2014. The NDC made hundreds of human rights and other recommendations for legal reforms and relating to the drafting of a new constitution. However, the government took no significant steps to address the issue of accountability for past human rights crimes by establishing a national human rights institution or passing a transitional justice law, as the NDC had recommended.

In response to NDC recommendations, in June the minister of social affairs and labor and the minister of legal affairs jointly submitted a draft transitional justice law for cabinet review. In November, both it and another bill on looted funds had yet to be transmitted to parliament by the cabinet.

Attacks on Health Workers

According to media reports, AQAP militants seized a hospital and two medical centers in Shabwa governorate in southern Yemen on April 20, following a series of government airstrikes that targeted AQAP training camps in the region. After forcibly evacuating the hospital's medical staff, AQAP militants reportedly brought in a number of their own doctors to treat their wounded. In addition, according to Yemeni media, suspected AQAP militants opened fire on a minibus carrying staff members from a military hospital in Aden, southern Yemen, on June 15, killing at least six people and wounding at least nine others. Human Rights Watch was not able to independently verify these reports.

Women's and Girls' Rights

Women in Yemen face severe discrimination in law and in practice. Women cannot marry without the permission of their male guardian; they do not have equal rights to divorce, inheritance, or child custody; and a lack of legal protection leaves them exposed to domestic and sexual violence. The NDC produced many recommendations to bolster women's and girls' rights.

In response, in April, the minister of social affairs and labor, and the minister of legal affairs, submitted a draft Child Rights Law to the cabinet. The draft law sets the minimum age for marriage at 18, and provides criminal penalties of between two months and one year in prison and a fine of up to 400,000 Yemeni Riyal (US$1,860) for any authorized person who draws up a marriage contract knowing that at least one party is under 18. Any witnesses or signatories to the marriage contract, including the parents or other guardians, who know that at least

HUMAN
RIGHTS
WATCH

A WEDDING
THAT BECAME A FUNERAL
US Drone Attack on Marriage Procession in Yemen

one party is under 18 face a prison sentence of between one and three months and a fine of between 100,000 YER ($460) and 250,000 YER ($1,160).

The draft law also addresses other important rights for girls and women, including criminalizing the practice of female genital mutilation, with penalties of between one and three years in prison and a fine of up to 1,000,000 YER ($4,644) for those who carry out the cutting. The law remained pending in the cabinet at time of writing.

Children and Armed Conflict

The Child Rights Bill also addresses the recruitment of child soldiers and child labor. Articles 162 and 250(b) prohibit the use or recruitment of child soldiers, imposing a fine of up to 300,000 YER ($1,393).

In May, Yemen signed an action plan with the United Nations to end and prevent the recruitment of children by the armed forces. The plan includes reforming national laws, issuing military orders prohibiting the recruitment and use of children, investigating allegations of recruitment, and providing for the reintegration of child soldiers into their communities. According to the United Nations Children's Fund, UNICEF, the government has already taken concrete steps to implement the plan.

According to the Ministry of Education and Teaching, armed conflicts in Amran, Sanaa, and Shabwa led to the damage or destruction of at least 41 schools and the occupation by armed forces of at least 6 schools in 2014. In addition, 31 schools were being used to house internally displaced persons. In November alone, fighting in Ibb pushed authorities to temporarily close 169 schools serving 92,000 students, reopening them a week later. In Al Bayda, 11 schools in Rada' remained closed as of October 31, leaving 6,000 students without classes to attend.

US Drone Strikes

The United States continued its drone campaign against alleged AQAP members. Independent research groups reported 23 US drone strikes in Yemen from January through November. The US remained unwilling to publish basic information on the attacks, including how many people the strikes killed or wounded, how many of those were civilians, and which, if any, strikes it found to be unlawful.

Previously, a US drone strike in December 2013 struck a wedding procession, killing 12 people and wounding at least 15 others. A Human Rights Watch investigation concluded that some, if not all, of the dead were civilians. In August 2014, evidence surfaced that the families of those killed in the wedding strike altogether received more than $1 million in compensation from the Yemeni government. Previously, compensation has only been provided by the Yemeni government when those killed were civilians.

Unlawful Use of Landmines

In November 2013, the government admitted, in response to reports by Human Rights Watch and others, that a "violation" of the Mine Ban Treaty had occurred in 2011 during the uprising that eventually ousted the Saleh government. Republican Guard forces loyal to the Saleh government laid thousands of antipersonnel mines in 2011 at Bani Jarmooz, northeast of Sanaa, causing numerous civilian casualties.

As a party to the Mine Ban Treaty, Yemen has committed to never use antipersonnel mines under any circumstances, and to prevent and suppress any prohibited activities. At least 15 governments expressed concern at the use of landmines in Yemen. In June at the Treaty's Third Review Conference, Yemen stated that the Military Prosecutor's Office had begun an investigation to identify those responsible.

In March 2014, Yemen provided the Mine Ban Treaty's president with an interim report that outlined plans for clearance, marking, risk education, and victim assistance in relation to the Bani Jarmooz mines. In October, Human Rights Watch was informed by locals that soldiers carried out mine clearance in one of the contaminated areas. The soldiers also erected warning signs in the area. However, in a neighboring contaminated area there has been no mine clearance or marking. Locals said that they had not received any risk education or victim assistance.

Since April 2013, Human Rights Watch has recorded at least seven new incidents of civilian casualties cause by landmines, including one death. Since late 2011, landmines in the area have killed at least two civilians and wounded twenty others.

In September 2014, the UN Office for the Coordination of Humanitarian Affairs reported that the Yemeni Mine Action Center suspended 30 percent of its high-priority survey and mine clearance activities due to a lack of funds.

Human Trafficking

Since 2006, and particularly since a weakening of government control in some areas following the 2011 uprising, human trafficking has thrived in Yemen. Traffickers hold African migrants in detention camps, torturing them to extort payment from their families, often with the complicity of local officials. Following the release of a report by Human Rights Watch documenting the trafficking industry, the government stated that it embarked on a number of raids against the smugglers.

It also requested the assistance of international organizations in addressing the rescued migrants' immediate needs, and to facilitate the voluntary return of those wishing to return home. According to residents in the area where traffickers operate their detention camps, by July 2014, government forces had ceased their raids and the camps continued to function and held large numbers of refugees from Syria as well as African migrants.

Attacks on Journalists

In the first half of 2014, the Freedom Foundation, a Yemeni organization that monitors press freedom, recorded 148 attacks affecting members of the media, ranging from verbal harassment and threats, confiscations, looting, destruction of property, and politicized prosecutions, to unlawful detention, and one killing. In 47 percent of the cases reported, the abuses were attributed to the government and its agents. In most other cases, the government had not condemned the attacks, investigated them, or held those responsible to account. Nor did the government take broader measures to protect journalists.

Death Penalty

Yemen retains the death penalty for murder and a range of other crimes but the authorities

do not publish data on its use or publicize executions, which are normally carried out by firing squad. In the past, Yemen has executed juvenile offenders—those sentenced for crimes committed when they were under age 18—but following international pressure, no juvenile offenders were sentenced to death or executed in 2014, as far as Human Rights Watch is aware.

Key International Actors

At their seventh ministerial level meeting in February, the 39 countries and 8 international organizations that comprise the Friends of Yemen agreed a new structure to realign support for Yemen with the priorities established by the NDC. This saw the creation of working groups to support economic, political, and security reforms needed to complete Yemen's democratic transition and agreement on the allocation of most of approximately $7.9 billion previously pledged funding assistance.

The US, the largest non-Arab donor, allocated $142.6 million in bilateral aid to Yemen for 2014.

Since May 2012, US President Barack Obama has in place an executive order allowing the Treasury Department to freeze the US-based assets of anyone who "obstructs" implementation of Yemen's political transition. The implementation of this executive order was scheduled to end with Yemeni presidential elections in 2014.

In October 2014, for the sixth consecutive year, Obama issued a full waiver allowing Yemen to receive military assistance, despite documented use of child soldiers by various forces, including government troops and progovernment militias.

On February 26, the UN Security Council adopted Resolution 2140, which established a sanctions regime that includes asset freezes and travel bans for those undermining the political transition, impeding the implementation of the final report of the NDC through violence or attacks on essential infrastructure, or having responsibility for international humanitarian law violations, and international human rights law violations or abuses in Yemen. In November, the Yemen Sanctions Committee imposed sanctions on former president Saleh and two Houthi commanders that include a global travel ban and asset freezes.

In September, the UN Human Rights Council adopted a resolution on Yemen that highlighted the need for investigations into past abuses, the passage of a transitional justice law, and the creation of an independent national human rights institution. In its report presented to the Human Rights Council and released in August 2014, the Office of the High Commissioner for Human Rights encouraged the international community to establish an independent, international mechanism to investigate violations of human rights that took place in 2011.

Zimbabwe

The government of President Robert Mugabe continued to violate human rights in 2014 without regard to protections in the country's new constitution. An expected legislative framework and new or amended laws to improve human rights in line with the constitution never materialized.

Some 20,000 people, displaced by flooding from the Tokwe-Mukorsi dam in Masvingo province in February, were evicted and resettled with little government protection. They have not received adequate compensation, including land for resettlement, and were pressured to relocate to land with disputed titles. When displaced people protested in August, over 200 anti-riot police used excessive force and beat and arrested about 300 people; 29 were charged with public violence. At time of writing, the case was still being heard in court.

In the capital, Harare, many people have little access to potable water and sanitation. Police violated basic rights, such as freedom of expression and assembly,using old laws that are inconsistent with the new constitution. Activists and human rights defenders, including lesbian, gay, bisexual, and transgender (LGBT) people, faced police harassment. There has been no progress toward securing justice for human rights abuses and past political violence, including violence after the 2008 election.

New Constitution

The new constitution, which parliament approved in May 2013, enshrines respect for the rule of law, and commits the government to fully implement and realize the right to freedom of association, assembly, expression, and information.

In a landmark ruling on July 22, 2014, the Constitutional Court declared criminal defamation laws unconstitutional based on an interpretation of the old constitution. However, the government has yet to repeal or amend as appropriate other laws, including the Access to Information and Protection of Privacy Act (AIPPA) and the Public Order and Security Act (POSA), the provisions of which severely restrict basic rights. Failure to amend or repeal these laws, and to address the partisan conduct of police, severely limits the rights to freedom of expression, association, and assembly guaranteed in the new constitution and international law.

The Zimbabwe Human Rights Commission (ZHRC), which was established as an independent body under the constitution, is not fully operational due to lack of adequate financial and human resources. The government has failed to strengthen this institution. Its mandate remains narrow and limited to investigating alleged human rights abuses since February 2009. This prevents the commission from investigating previous serious crimes, including election-related violence in 2002, 2005, and 2008; the massacre of an estimated 20,000 people in the Matebeleland and Midlands provinces in the 1980s; and mass demolitions of homes and the evictions of 2005.

Internally Displaced Persons

In February, the government removed an estimated 20,000 people from the flooding of Tokwe-Mukorsi dam in Masvingo province, through a process fraught with human rights problems. Many activists believe that the displacement could have been done in a manner that minimized suffering, as those displaced lost much moveable property for which they had not been compensated at time of writing.

The government failed to respect and protect the basic rights of those displaced under domestic laws and the African Union Convention for the Protection and Assistance of Internally Displaced Persons in Africa, which Zimbabwe has ratified. Instead of receiving fair compensation for the land they lost and allowed freedom of movement, families were given the choice of tiny plots and becoming farmworkers on a sugar cane plantation, or losing the inadequate aid offered by the government. Should they accept the government's deal, it is unclear whether they could derive a sustainable living from, or steady tenure over, the plots, whose titles appear to be in dispute.

LGBT Rights

The government of Zimbabwe continues to violate rights of LGBT people guaranteed in the new constitution and international law, including the rights to non-discrimination; liberty and security of the person and privacy; freedom of expression and thought; association; and peaceful assembly. For instance, it was only after a lengthy court trial that the Harare Magistrates Court in February cleared Martha Tholanah, chairperson of the Gays and Lesbians of Zimbabwe (GALZ), a nongovernmental organization (NGO). She was charged with running an "unregistered" organization in contravention of article 6 of the Private Voluntary Organization (PVO) Act, which requires that all private voluntary organizations register with the PVO board.

In March, police arrested two GALZ officials on charges of organizing a media training workshop without police clearance, in violation of POSA. These attacks on LGBT people, arbitrary arrests of LGBT activists by police, and the harassment by state agents of GALZ in previous years, continue to drive many LGBT people underground.

Economic and Social Rights

Presenting the 2014 National Budget in December 2013, Finance and Economic Development Minister Patrick Chinamasa noted that Zimbabwe faced severe socio-economic challenges, which he partly attributed to lack of transparency and accountability in the exploitation of mineral resources, including diamonds.

According to figures released by the International Monetary Fund in June, Zimbabwe's external debt obligations at the end of 2013 were estimated be US$10.6 billion (over 80 percent of the country's gross domestic product). The government is failing to achieve greater transparency in diamond production and revenue collection, affecting its ability to invest in desperately needed public services, including essential services such as water, education, health, and sanitation.

Public sector corruption and the deteriorating economy have severely impacted the enjoyment of social and economic rights. By not addressing corruption and other misuse of resources, the government has violated basic rights, such as the right to water and sanitation, of millions of people in Harare, adversely impacting their right to health.

Accountability for Past Abuses

Lack of accountability for past abuses remains a serious problem in Zimbabwe. The government has failed to ensure justice for victims more than five years after the 2008 politically motivated violence in which the ruling Zimbabwe African National Union- Patriotic Front (ZANU-PF), backed by state security forces, committed widespread and systematic abuses that led to the killing of up to 200 people, the beating and torture of 5,000 more, and the displacement of about 36,000 people.

Human Rights Defenders and Opposition Political Parties

Police frequently misused provisions of POSA to ban lawful public meetings and gatherings. Opposition and civil society activists were wrongly prosecuted and charged under these laws. For instance, when hundreds of Women of Zimbabwe (WOZA) members marched to petition parliament over the national economic situation on February 13, police violently broke up the march and dispersed the demonstrators.

In January, police arrested five activists from four NGOs—Chitungwiza Residents Trust, Combined Harare Residents Association, Centre for Community Development in Zimbabwe Trust, and Zimbabwe Human Rights Association—for participating in a demonstration in Chitungwiza. They were later released without charge. Also in January, police arrested 12 leaders of the Zimbabwe National Students Union. The students, who were beaten in police custody, were arrested during a demonstration against poor education standards at Harare Polytechnic College.

On June 28, police in Victoria Falls arrested and detained for two days four members of the Bulawayo Agenda organization on charges of contravening POSA by allegedly failing to notify police of their public meeting. The court acquitted the four.

In July, authorities in Nyanga and Gweru separately charged the leader of the opposition political party Transform Zimbabwe, Jacob Chengedzeni Satiya Ngarivhume, with violating POSA for allegedly holding political meetings without police clearance. Ngarivhume was later acquitted in the courts.

Key International Actors

In August, Zimbabwe took over the leadership of the Southern Africa Development Community (SADC), the 15-nation regional economic institution, for a year. Zimbabwe's poor human rights record could weaken the regional body's ability to press for human rights improvements across southern Africa.

The European Union and other international donors in 2014 continued their policy of re-engagement with the government of Zimbabwe. This policy may have contributed to the failure of donors to publicly confront the government over its poor human rights record and to press it to respect and protect everyone's rights.

HUMAN
RIGHTS
WATCH

NOT SAFE AT HOME
Violence and Discrimination against LGBT people in Jamaica

WORLD REPORT
2015

2014
HUMAN RIGHTS WATCH
PUBLICATIONS

The following is a list of Human Rights Watch reports published from December 2013 to mid-December 2014. This list does not include press releases or other Human Rights Watch material released during the year.

DECEMBER 2013

Cracks in the System: Conditions of Pre-Charge Detainees in Tunisia, 65pp.

An Offer You Can't Refuse: How US Federal Prosecutors Force Drug Defendants to Plead Guilty, 132pp.

"They Treat Us Like Animals": Mistreatment of Drug Users and "Undesirables," 65pp.

In Harm's Way: State Response to Sex Workers, Drug Users, and HIV in New Orleans, 74pp.

"Leave Everything to God": Accountability for Inter-Communal Violence in Plateau and Kaduna States, Nigeria, 152pp.

Challenging the Red Lines: Stories of Rights Activists in Saudi Arabia, 54pp.

"They Came to Kill": Escalating Atrocities in the Central African Republic, 48pp.

JANUARY 2014

Priorities for Legislative Reform: A Human Rights Roadmap for a New Libya, 69pp.

"They Said We Deserved This": Police Violence against Gay and Bisexual Men in Kyrgyzstan, 71pp.

Razed to the Ground: Syria's Unlawful Neighborhood Demolitions in 2012-2013, 53pp.

FEBRUARY 2014

"How Can We Survive Here?": The Impact of Mining on Human Rights n Karamoja, Uganda, 147pp.

Profiting from Probation: America's "Offender-Funded" Probation Industry, 78pp.

"No One is Safe": The Abuse of Women in Iraq's Criminal Justice System, 111pp.

Abused and Expelled: Ill-Treatment of Sub-Saharan African Migrants in Morocco, 87pp.

HUMAN
RIGHTS
WATCH

PROFITING FROM PROBATION
America's "Offender-Funded" Probation Industry

HUMAN
RIGHTS
WATCH

WHOSE DEVELOPMENT?

Human Rights Abuses in Sierra Leone's Mining Boom

"I Wanted to Lie Down and Die": Trafficking and Torture of Eritreans in Sudan and Egypt, 87pp.

"There Are No Investigations Here": Impunity for Killings and Other Abuses in Bajo Aguán, Honduras, 80pp.

"Here, Rape is Normal": A Five-Point Plan to Curtail Sexual Violence in Somalia, 80pp.

A Wedding That Became a Funeral: US Drone Attack on Marriage Procession in Yemen, 36pp.

Whose Development?: Human Rights Abuses in Sierra Leone's Mining Boom, 126pp.

MARCH 2014

The Role of Communities in Protecting Education from Attack: Lessons Learned, 58pp.

"I've Never Experienced Happiness": Child Marriage in Malawi, 76pp.

Exploitation in the Name of Education: Uneven Progress in Ending Forced Child Begging in Senegal, 51pp.

The Crisis in Buenaventura: Disappearances, Dismemberment, and Displacement n Colombia's Main Pacific Port, 40pp.

Central African Republic: Materials Published Since the Seleka Coup, 141pp.

"They Know Everything We Do": Telecom and Internet Surveillance in Ethiopia, 145pp.

APRIL 2014

Under China's Shadow: Mistreatment of Tibetans in Nepal, 105pp.

"No Answers, No Apology": Police Abuses and Accountability in Malaysia, 129pp.

Hidden Away: Abuses against Migrant Domestic Workers in the UK, 64pp.

Branded for Life: Florida's Prosecution of Children as Adults under its "Direct File" Statute, 108pp.

"We Stood, They Opened Fire": Killings and Arrests by Sudan's Security Forces during the September Protests, 40pp.

"They Say We're Dirty": Denying an Education to India's Marginalized, 85pp.

"We Were Sent to Kill You": Gang Attacks in Western Kenya and the Government's Failed Response 41pp.

"Containment Plan": Syrian and Other Asylum Seekers and Migrants, 82pp.

Democracy in the Crossfire: Election Period in Bangladesh, 74pp.

MAY 2014

Without Dreams: Children in Alternative Care in Japan, 129pp.

Collapse, Conflict and Atrocity in Mali: Human Rights Watch Reporting on the 2012-13 Armed Conflict and Its Aftermath, 152pp.

Punished for Protesting: Rights Violations in Venezuela's Streets, Detention Centers, 107pp.

Shaking the Foundations: The Human Rights Implications of Killer Robots, 33pp.

Tobacco's Hidden Children: Hazardous Child Labor in US Tobacco Farming, 147pp.

"One Shot to the Head": Death Squad Killings in Tagum City, Philippines, 79pp.

The Courts of "Absolute Power": Fair Trial Violations by Somalia's Military Court, 39pp.

Torture Camps in Yemen: Abuse of Migrants by Human Traffickers in a Climate of Impunity, 88pp.

Shattered Dreams: Impact of Spain's Housing Crisis on Vulnerable Groups, 92pp.

Criminalizing Dissent, Entrenching Impunity: Persistent Failures of the Bahraini Justice System Since the BICI Report, 74pp.

JUNE 2014

Protecting Education Personnel from Targeted Attack in Conflict-Affected Countries, 58pp.

Under Kurdish Rule: Abuses in PYD-run Enclaves of Syria, 112pp.

"Maybe We Live and Maybe We Die": Recruitment and Use of Children by Armed Groups in Syria, 37pp.

"We Suffered When We Came Here": Resettlements for Tajikistan's Rogun Dam, 139pp.

"We are the Walking Dead": Killings of Shia Hazaras in Balochistan, Pakistan, 72pp.

JULY 2014

No Time to Waste: Evidence-Based Treatment for Drug Dependence at the United States Veterans Administration, 45pp.

"We Are Still Here": Women on the Front Lines of Syria's Conflict, 52pp.

"We Are Also Dying of AIDS": Barriers to HIV Services and Treatment for Persons with Disabilities in Zambia, 79pp.

"Where Do You Want Us to Go?": Abuses against Street Children in Uganda, 76pp.

Illusion of Justice: Human Rights Abuses in US Terrorism Prosecutions, 220pp.

With Liberty to Monitor All: How Large-Scale US Surveillance is Harming Journalism, Law, and American Democracy, 126pp.

AUGUST 2014

Human Rights in Africa, 116pp.

Not Welcome: Jordan's Treatment of Palestinians Escaping Syria, 50pp.

South Sudan's New War: Abuses by Government and Opposition Forces, 108pp.

All According to Plan: The Rab'a Massacre and Mass Killings of Protesters in Egypt, 196pp.

Locked Up in Karaj: Spotlight on Political Prisoners in One Iranian City, 67pp.

Cleaning Human Waste: "Manual Scavenging," Caste, and Discrimination in India, 104pp.

SEPTEMBER 2014

Two Years with No Moon: Immigration Detention of Children in Thailand, 67pp.

Staying Strong: Key Components and Positive Precedent for Convention on Cluster Munitions Legislation, 79pp.

"The Power These Men Have Over Us": Sexual Exploitation and Abuse by African Union Forces in Somalia, 98pp.

"Make Their Lives Miserable": Israel's Coercion of Eritrean and Sudanese Asylum Seekers to Leave Israel, 91pp.

Abandoned to the State: Violence, Neglect, and Isolation for Children with Disabilities in Russian Orphanages, 168pp.

Public Insecurity: Deaths in Custody and Police Brutality in Vietnam, 108pp.

The Long Arm of Justice: Lessons from Specialized War Crimes Units in France, Germany, and the Netherlands, 118pp.

Silenced and Forgotten: Survivors of Nepal's Conflict-Era Sexual Violence, 86pp.

"Until the Very End": Politically Motivated Imprisonment in Uzbekistan, 131pp.

"I'm Scared to Be a Woman": Human Rights Abuses Against Transgender People in Malaysia, 100pp.

Turkey's Human Rights Rollback: Recommendations for Reform, 44pp.

OCTOBER 2014

"You Don't Have Rights Here": US Border Screening and Returns of Central Americans to Risk, 50pp.

Off the Radar: Human Rights in the Tindouf Refugee Camps, 102pp.

Not Safe at Home: Violence and Discrimination against LGBT people in Jamaica, 96pp.

"I Already Bought You": Abuse and Exploitation of Female Migrant Domestic Workers in the United Arab Emirates, 85pp.

Care When There Is No Cure: Ensuring the Right to Palliative Care in Mexico, 128pp.

No Way Out: Child Marriage and Human Rights Abuses in Tanzania, 101pp.

"Those Terrible Weeks in their Camp": Boko Haram Violence against Women and Girls in Northeast Nigeria, 69pp.

NOVEMBER 2014

Rights in Retreat: Abuses in Crimea, 45pp.

Operation Likofi: Police Killings and Enforced Disappearances in Kinshasa, Democratic Republic of Congo, 65pp.

DECEMBER 2014

"Treated Worse than Animals": Abuses against Women and Girls with Psychosocial or Abuses against Women and Girls with Psychosocial or Intellectual Disabilities in Institutions in India, 112pp.

Ending the Era of Injustice: Advancing Prosecutions for Serious Crimes Committed in South Sudan's New War, 44pp.

License to Harm: Violence and Harassment against LGBT People and Activists in Russia, 108pp.

All reports can be accessed online and ordered at www.hrw.org/en/publications.